EGYPTIAN ART IN THE AGE OF THE PYRAMIDS

EGYPTIAN ART
IN THE AGE OF
THE PYRAMIDS

THE METROPOLITAN MUSEUM OF ART, NEW YORK
DISTRIBUTED BY HARRY N. ABRAMS, INC., NEW YORK

This volume has been published in conjunction with the exhibition "Egyptian Art in the Age of the Pyramids," organized by The Metropolitan Museum of Art, New York; the Réunion des musées nationaux, Paris; and the Royal Ontario Museum, Toronto, and held at the Galeries nationales du Grand Palais, Paris, from April 6 to July 12, 1999; The Metropolitan Museum of Art, New York, from September 16, 1999, to January 9, 2000; and the Royal Ontario Museum, Toronto, from February 13 to May 22, 2000.

The exhibition is made possible by Lewis B. and Dorothy Cullman.

Additonal support has been provided by The Starr Foundation.

An indemnity has been granted by the Federal Council on the Arts and the Humanities.

Educational programs have been supported by the Malcolm Hewitt Wiener Foundation.

The publication is made possible by The Adelaide Milton de Groot Fund, in memory of the de Groot and Hawley families.

Published by The Metropolitan Museum of Art, New York

John P. O'Neill, Editor in Chief
Carol Fuerstein, Editor, with the assistance of Ellyn Childs Allison, Margaret Donovan, and Kathleen Howard
Patrick Seymour, Designer, after an original concept by Bruce Campbell
Gwen Roginsky and Hsiao-ning Tu, Production
Robert Weisberg, Computer Specialist

Site and new object photography by Bruce White; additional new object photography at the Metropolitan Museum by Anna-Marie Kellen and Oi-Cheong Lee, the Photograph Studio, The Metropolitan Museum of Art, New York. For a more complete listing of photograph credits, see p. 536.

Set in Sabon and Adobe Weiss by Professional Graphics, Rockford, Illinois

Separations by Professional Graphics, Rockford, Illinois

Printed and bound by Arnoldo Mondadori, S.p.A., Verona, Italy

Translations from the French by James P. Allen of essays by Nadine Cherpion and Jean-Philippe Lauer; by John McDonald of essays by Nicolas Grimal, Audran Labrousse, Jean Leclant, and Christiane Ziegler; by Jane Marie Todd and Catharine H. Roehrig of entries

Maps adapted by Emsworth Design, Inc., from Ziegler 1997a, pp. 18, 19

Jacket/cover illustration: Detail, cat. no. 67, King Menkaure and a Queen
Frontispiece: Detail, cat. no. 67, King Menkaure and a Queen

Hieroglyphic dedication on page v from *Teachings of Ptah-hotep*, 509–10.

Library of Congress Cataloging-in-Publication Data
Egyptian art in the age of the pyramids
    p. cm.
   Catalogue of an exhibition held at the Metropolitan Museum of Art, Sept. 16, 1999–Jan. 9, 2000.
   Includes bibliographical references and index.
   ISBN 0-87099-906-0 (HC). — ISBN 0-87099-907-9 (pbk.) — ISBN 0-8109-6543-7 (Abrams)
   1. Art, Egyptian Exhibitions. 2. Art, Ancient—Egypt Exhibitions. 3. Egypt—Antiquities Exhibitions. 4. Egypt—Architecture Exhibitions. I. Metropolitan Museum of Art (New York, N.Y.)
   N5350.E37 1999
   709'.32'0747471—dc21   99-22246
                                         CIP

To Henry George Fischer
Curator Emeritus of Egyptian Art

in admiration and appreciation
for all he has done
to further understanding of the
Old Kingdom

CONTENTS

INTRODUCTORY ESSAYS

CATALOGUE

LENDERS TO THE EXHIBITION

The numbers in the following list refer to works in the catalogue.

AUSTRIA
Vienna, Kunsthistorisches Museum, Ägyptisch-Orientalische Sammlung 49, 80, 87, 93, 133, 135, 159, 166, 168, 169, 178c, 198, 213, 214

BELGIUM
Brussels, Musées Royaux d'Art et d'Histoire 69, 150a, 177b

CANADA
Toronto, Royal Ontario Museum 2, 39, 106, 151, 156

DENMARK
Copenhagen, Ny Carlsberg Glyptotek 24ab, 59, 189

EGYPT
Cairo, Egyptian Museum 3, 5, 17, 19a–c, 22ab, 31, 56, 68, 85, 86, 88, 89, 90, 91, 92, 100, 102, 132, 134, 144, 150b, 185, 186

FRANCE
Paris, Musée du Louvre, Département des Antiquités Égyptiennes 9, 11, 12, 13, 14, 18, 51, 54, 55, 78, 117, 122, 123, 124, 157, 177d, 179, 180, 181, 183, 187, 191, 192

GERMANY
Berlin, Ägyptisches Museum und Papyrussammlung, Staatliche Museen zu Berlin 28, 29a–k, 111, 112, 113, 115ab, 118, 119, 120, 146a, 152

Heidelberg, Sammlung des Ägyptologischen Instituts der Universität Heidelberg 114
Hildesheim, Roemer- und Pelizaeus-Museum 44
Leipzig, Ägyptisches Museum, Universität Leipzig 61, 62, 64, 77, 83, 142, 143, 162, 163, 164, 212
Munich, Staatliche Sammlung Ägyptischer Kunst 6, 24c, 34, 50, 121

GREAT BRITAIN
Cambridge, The Syndics of the Fitzwilliam Museum 98, 177c, 200, 201
Edinburgh, Trustees of the National Museums of Scotland 171
London, The Trustees of the British Museum 8, 20a–c, 26, 35, 36, 37, 82, 95, 96, 97, 165, 188, 190, 204
London, Petrie Museum of Egyptian Archaeology, University College London 101, 116, 150cd, 176, 177a, 205, 206
Manchester, The Manchester Museum, University of Manchester 25c
Oxford, The Visitors of the Ashmolean Museum 207, 208, 210ab, 211

ITALY
Turin, Soprintendenza al Museo delle Antichità Egizie 7a–c, 16, 158, 199

NETHERLANDS
Leiden, Rijksmuseum van Oudheden 15, 149

SWITZERLAND
Lausanne, Fondation Jacques-Edouard Berger 202, 203

DIRECTORS' FOREWORD

Ancient Egypt continues to exert a real fascination for the public, as attested by the unfailing success of the major exhibitions devoted to the subject. Remarkably, however, these exhibitions have usually featured a specific theme or a particular pharaoh—Amenhotep III, Tutankhamun, Ramesses II—and have often given precedence to the New Kingdom. Thus we sometimes fail to remember that pharaonic history extends over several millennia and that the pyramids of Giza and the Sphinx were created more than a thousand years before the well-known achievements of the Eighteenth Dynasty.

One of the notable qualities of the exhibition "Egyptian Art in the Age of the Pyramids," the first to be devoted entirely to the approximately five centuries of the Old Kingdom, is that it restores our temporal perspective. In doing so, it demonstrates the extraordinary flowering of the arts at the time the pyramids were built, when not only architecture but also sculpture, painting, and the decorative arts were at their peak. The exhibition also allows us to reunite works of the same provenance that have been dispersed throughout the world by the vicissitudes of acquisition. In addition to offering enormous aesthetic pleasure, the reassembling of these works has great art-historical value: for a brief period of time, it gives us the opportunity to evaluate, on the basis of the objects themselves, the attribution of certain dates and the pertinence of certain hypotheses.

We would like to express our warm gratitude to all those who conceived and organized the exhibition, especially the curators of Egyptian art at our own museums: Christiane Ziegler in Paris; Dorothea Arnold in New York; and Krzysztof Grzymski in Toronto. We also wish to thank all the lenders in charge of public and private collections who made the exhibition possible and, in particular, the Egyptian authorities who generously agreed to lend the masterpieces without which our presentation of this first golden age of Egyptian art would have been much the poorer.

The Metropolitan Museum is extremely grateful to Lewis B. and Dorothy Cullman for their outstanding generosity toward the exhibition and their ongoing friendship and dedication to the Museum's endeavors. We also wish to express special thanks to The Starr Foundation for its important financial commitment to all aspects of the project. The support provided by the Malcolm Hewitt Wiener Foundation is noteworthy as well, since it has helped to make our splendid educational programs a reality. Junko Koshino has also kindly furnished support for the project, and we extend our sincere thanks for her gesture. In addition, we are thankful for the assistance given by the Federal Council on the Arts and the Humanities. The realization of the accompanying publication was made possible with the assistance of The Adelaide Milton de Groot Fund, in memory of the de Groot and Hawley families.

Françoise Cachin
Directeur, Musées de France
Président, Réunion des Musées Nationaux

Philippe de Montebello
Director, The Metropolitan Museum of Art

Lindsay Sharp
Director and President, Royal Ontario Museum

ACKNOWLEDGMENTS

All exhibitions are collaborations, and none more so than a large enterprise such as this one, which inevitably involves a great number of people. The authors and organizers of this exhibition and catalogue extend their heartfelt gratitude to all the museum directors and administrators, department heads, curators, conservators, and registrars who have lent objects from their collections, facilitated the photography of these pieces, and answered numerous queries. Thanks are also offered to the support staffs of all these institutions, which provided essential assistance in innumerable ways.

The first of our specific thanks go to the directors of our three institutions, without whom this enterprise could not have been realized: Françoise Cachin, Directeur des Musées de France, Président de la Réunion des Musées Nationaux, Paris; Philippe de Montebello, Director of The Metropolitan Museum of Art, New York; and Lindsay Sharp, Director and President of the Royal Ontario Museum, Toronto. Of special importance to this endeavor was Mahrukh Tarapor, Associate Director for Exhibitions at The Metropolitan Museum of Art.

Loans from Egypt could not have been secured without the generous support of His Excellency Farouk Hosny, Minister of Culture of the Arab Republic of Egypt, and Professor Gaballa Ali Gaballa, Secretary General, Supreme Council of Antiquities in Egypt. Zahi Hawass, Director of the Monuments of Giza and Saqqara, provided resolute support to the project from its inception, in addition to contributing to the catalogue. Mohamed Saleh, former Director of the Egyptian Museum, Cairo, played a crucial role in selecting the pieces from that museum. Heartfelt thanks are also due to Mohamed Ghoneim, First Undersecretary, Ministry of Culture; His

Excellency Aly Maher el-Sayed, Egyptian Ambassador to France; His Excellency Ahmed Maher el-Sayed, Egyptian Ambassador to the United States; Ahmed Nawar, Director General of Egyptian Museums; Mohamed Abdel Hamid Shimy, Director of the Egyptian Museum, Cairo; Ibrahim Abdel Galel Ibrahim, Director of Exhibitions at the Egyptian Museum; Mahmoud el Helwagy, Curator of Old Kingdom Art at the Egyptian Museum; Amal Samuel, Chief Inspector of the Giza Pyramids; Mohammed Hagrass, Director of Antiquities for Saqqara; and Magdy el Ghandour, Chief Inspector of South Saqqara and Dahshur. Our appreciation is extended to the members of the Permanent Committee of the Supreme Council of Antiquities. Gratitude is also due to the staff of the Egyptian Museum and the antiquities inspectors of Giza and Saqqara. Assistance was furnished as well by Mark Easton and Amira Khattab of the American Research Center in Egypt, Cairo; the Honorable Daniel C. Kurtzer, United States Ambassador to Egypt; and the staff of the Cultural Affairs Office, United States Embassy, Cairo. Among those in New York, we extend our special thanks to His Excellency Ahmed Aboul-Gheit, Egyptian Ambassador to the United Nations.

Among our French partners at the Réunion des Musées Nationaux we would like to acknowledge: Irène Bizot, Administrateur Général; Ute Collinet, Secrétaire Général; Bénédicte Boissonnas, Chef du Département des Expositions; Vincent David, Coordinateur d'Expositions; Francine Robinson, Coordinateur d'Expositions; Anne de Margerie, Chef du Département du Livre et de l'Image; and Bernadette Caille, Éditeur. Our gratitude particularly goes to our colleagues at the Musée du Louvre: Pierre Rosenberg, Président-Directeur, and in le Département des Antiquités Égyptiennes: Laurence Berlandier, Dominique Brancart, Catherine Bridonneau,

Laurence Cotelle-Michel, Élisabeth David, Isabelle Franco, Sylvie Guichard, Sophie Labbé-Toutée, Nadine Palayret, Patricia Rigault, and Marie-Françoise de Rozières. Also most helpful were Jean-Marc Rochereau de La Sablière, French Ambassador to Egypt; Fabyène Mansencal, French Cultural Attaché to Canada; and Pierre-Jean Vandoorne, French Consul General to Canada.

Warmest appreciation is extended to our colleagues at the Royal Ontario Museum, Toronto—Harriet Walker, N. B. Millet, Roberta Shaw, Julie Anderson, Nur Bahal, Tricia Walker, Bill Pratt, Margo Welch, Lory Drusian, Laura Matthews, and Meg Beckel—and to the ROM Foundation.

Heartfelt gratitude is expressed to our colleagues at the following European institutions: Ägyptisches Museum und Papyrussammlung, Staatliche Museen zu Berlin: Dietrich Wildung, Karl-Heinz Priese, Hannelore Kischkewitz, Anja Bernhardt, Dunja Rütt; Musées Royaux d'Art et d'Histoire, Brussels: Francis Van Noten, Luc Limme, Viviane Xhignesse; Fitzwilliam Museum, Cambridge: Duncan Robinson, Eleni Vassilika, Penny Wilson, Thyrza Smith, Liz Woods; Ny Carlsberg Glyptotek, Copenhagen: Flemming Johansen, Mogens Jørgensen; National Museums of Scotland, Edinburgh: Mark Jones, Rosalyn Clancey, Lesley-Ann Liddiard, Lyn Stevens; Sammlung des Ägyptologischen Instituts der Universität Heidelberg: Erika Feucht; Roemer- und Pelizaeus-Museum, Hildesheim: Arne Eggebrecht, Annamaria Geiger, Konrad Deufel, Gabriele Pieke, Bettina Schmitz; Fondation Jacques-Edouard Berger, Lausanne: René Berger; Rijksmuseum van Oudheden, Leiden: Maarten J. Raven; Ägyptisches Museum, Universität Leipzig: Elke Blumenthal, Renate Krauspe, Frank Steinmann; British Museum, London: Robert Anderson, W. Vivian Davies, Morris L. Bierbrier, Jeffrey Spencer, Claire Messenger, H. J. Morgan; Petrie Museum of Egyptian Archaeology, University College London: Barbara Adams, Sally MacDonald, Stephen Quirke; The Manchester Museum, University of Manchester: Tristram Besterman, Rosalie David; Staatliche Sammlung Ägyptischer Kunst, Munich: Sylvia Schoske, Alfred Grimm; Ashmolean Museum, University of Oxford: Christopher Brown, P. R. S. Moorey, Helen Whitehouse, Mark Norman; Museo delle Antichità Egizie, Turin: Anna Maria Donadoni Roveri, Enrichetta Leospo, Elisabetta Valtz; and Kunsthistorishes Museum: Wilfried Seipel, Helmut Satzinger.

Thanks are also extended to Wolf-Dieter Dube, Generaldirektor, Staatliche Museen zu Berlin; Mario Serio, Direttore Generale per i Beni Culturali, Rome; Giuseppe Perrone, Cultural Affairs Officer, Italian Embassy, Washington, D.C.; and Madame Arigotti, Cultural Affairs Section, Italian Embassy, Paris.

Our sincerest thanks are offered to our colleagues at these museums in the United States: Phoebe Apperson Hearst Museum of Anthropology, University of California at Berkeley: Rosemary A. Joyce, Joan Knudsen, Madeleine Fang, Cathleen Keller; Museum of Fine Arts, Boston: Malcolm Rogers, Rita E. Freed, Peter Der Manuelian, Kim Pashko, Nancy S. Allen; Brooklyn Museum of Art: Arnold L. Lehman, Richard Fazzini, James Romano, Ken Moser, Christina Dufresne; Harvard University Semitic Museum, Cambridge, Massachusetts: Lawrence E. Stager, Joseph A. Greene; The Field Museum, Chicago: Janice B. Klein; The Oriental Institute of The University of Chicago: Karen L. Wilson, Emily Teeter, Raymond D. Tindel; The Cleveland Museum of Art: the late Robert P. Bergman, Lawrence Berman, Mary E. Suzor; The Detroit Institute of Arts: Maurice D. Parrish, William H. Peck, Michelle S. Peplin; The Nelson-Atkins Museum of Art, Kansas City: Marc. F. Wilson, Robert Cohon, Cindy Cart; The University of Pennsylvania Museum of Archaeology and Anthropology, Philadelphia: Jeremy Sabloff, David Silverman, Jennifer Houser Wegner, Sylvia S. Duggan, Charles S. Kline; The Art Museum, Princeton University: Peter Bunnel, Michael Padgett, Maureen McCormick; Worcester Art Museum, Massachusetts: James A. Welu, Lawrence Becker, Christine Kodoleon, Nancy L. Swallow; and special thanks to Nanette B. Kelekian, New York. Assistance was also provided by Katharine C. Lee and Richard Woodward, Virginia Museum of Fine Arts, Richmond, and David Restad, Phoenix Art Museum.

Most of the excellent photographs of the objects were taken by Bruce White, who must be considered a full partner in the project. Many of the photographs of Egyptian sites are the work of the late Artur Brack. Additional photographs were taken by Anna-Marie Kellen and Oi-Cheong Lee of the Photograph Studio of the Metropolitan Museum; John Woolf of the Museum of Fine Arts, Boston; Jürgen Liepe; John Ross; Peter Der Manuelian; Dieter Johannes; and Adela Oppenheim. Photographs were supplied by Zahi Hawass; the Museum of Fine Arts, Boston; Rijksmuseum van Oudheden, Leiden; and the Soprintendenza al Museo delle Antichità Egizie, Turin. The drawings and plans are by Liza Majerus, Peter Der Manuelian, Dieter Arnold, Thomas Scalise, and JoAnn Wood. The computer reconstruction of the sun temple of Niuserre at

Abu Ghurab is by David S. Johnson of The Museum of Reconstructions, Inc.

Last but certainly not least we acknowledge our colleagues at The Metropolitan Museum of Art. In the Director's Office our appreciation goes to Doralynn Pines, Martha Deese, and Sian Wetherill.

In the Editorial Department John P. O'Neill provided invaluable assistance with the catalogue. Carol Fuerstein expertly edited the book and coordinated the work of the many authors with patience, grace, and good humor. Ellyn Childs Allison, Margaret Donovan, and Kathleen Howard ably assisted with the editing. Indispensable were Gwen Roginsky, who oversaw production, and Hsiao-ning Tu, who carried out the myriad tasks of production. Jean Wagner served as the editor of the bibliography. Patrick Seymour designed the volume after an original concept by Bruce Campbell. Robert Weisberg served as computer specialist. The essays were translated by James P. Allen and John McDonald with Catharine H. Roehrig, all of the Department of Egyptian Art; the entries were translated by Catharine H. Roehrig and Jane Marie Todd.

Our great thanks go to Richard R. Morsches and Linda M. Sylling of the Operations Department; Emily K. Rafferty of the Development Office; James H. Frantz, Ann Heywood, Deborah Schorsch, Jean-François de Lapérouse, Jeffrey W. Perhacs, Nancy S. Reynolds, Frederick J. Sager, and Alexandra Walcott in the Objects Conservation Department; Herbert Moskowitz of the Registrar's Office; Franz J. Schmidt, William Brautigam and the riggers, and the staff of the workshops in the Buildings Department; Jeffrey L. Daly, Michael C. Batista, Jill Hammarberg, and Zack Zanolli of the Design Department; Marceline McKee and Suzanne L. Shenton of the Loans Office; Sharon H. Cott and Stephanie Oratz Basta of the Secretary and General Counsel's Office; and Ronald E. Street and Wayne Moseley of the Three-Dimensional Reproductions Department.

The entire Department of Egyptian Art—James P. Allen, Susan Allen, Dieter Arnold, Sherine Badawi, William Barrette, Miriam Blieka, Laurel Flentye, Donald Fortenberry, Marsha Hill, Dennis Kelly, John McDonald, Adela Oppenheim, Diana Craig Patch, Elena Pischikova, Catharine H. Roehrig, Isidoro Salerno, and Thomas Scalise—contributed to the exhibition and the catalogue. Their many months of thoughtful scholarship, utmost attention to detail, and just plain hard work are deeply appreciated.

Dorothea Arnold, Lila Acheson Wallace Curator in Charge, Department of Egyptian Art, The Metropolitan Museum of Art, New York

Krzysztof Grzymski, Senior Curator, Egyptian Section, Royal Ontario Museum, Toronto

Christiane Ziegler, Conservateur Général Chargé du Département des Antiquités Égyptiennes, Musée du Louvre, Paris

CONTRIBUTORS TO THE CATALOGUE AND KEY TO THE AUTHORS OF THE ENTRIES

JPA James P. Allen
Curator, Department of Egyptian Art,
The Metropolitan Museum of Art, New York

SA Susan Allen
Research Associate, Department of Egyptian
Art, The Metropolitan Museum of Art,
New York

JA Julie Anderson
Research Associate, Egyptian Section, Royal
Ontario Museum, Toronto

DA Dieter Arnold
Curator, Department of Egyptian Art,
The Metropolitan Museum of Art, New York

DoA Dorothea Arnold
Lila Acheson Wallace Curator in Charge,
Department of Egyptian Art, The Metropolitan
Museum of Art, New York

Nadine Cherpion
Professor, University of Louvain

Élisabeth David
Docteur en Égyptologie, Attachée au
Département des Antiquités Égyptiennes,
Musée du Louvre, Paris

Nicolas Grimal
Directeur de l'Institut Français d'Archéologie
Orientale, Cairo; Professeur, Université de
Paris IV–Sorbonne, Paris

KG Krzysztof Grzymski
Senior Curator, Egyptian Section, Royal
Ontario Museum, Toronto

ZH Zahi Hawass
Director of the Monuments of Giza and
Saqqara

MH Marsha Hill
Associate Curator, Department of Egyptian
Art, The Metropolitan Museum of Art,
New York

Peter Jánosi
Research Associate, Institut für Ägyptologie,
Universität Vienna

SL-T Sophie Labbé-Toutée
Attachée au Département des Antiquités
Égyptiennes, Musée du Louvre, Paris

Audran Labrousse
Directeur de Recherche au Centre National de la Recherche Scientifique; Directeur de la Mission Archéologique Français de Saqqara

Jean-Philippe Lauer
Directeur de Recherche Honoraire au Centre National de la Recherche Scientifique

Jean Leclant
Secrétaire Perpétuel de l'Académie des Inscriptions et Belles-Lettres, Paris

PDM   Peter Der Manuelian
Research Fellow, Department of Ancient Egyptian, Nubian and Near Eastern Art, Museum of Fine Arts, Boston

NBM   N. B. Millet
Senior Curator, Egyptian Section, Royal Ontario Museum, Toronto

AO   Adela Oppenheim
Research Associate, Department of Egyptian Art, The Metropolitan Museum of Art, New York

DCP   Diana Craig Patch
Egyptologist, Department of Egyptian Art, The Metropolitan Museum of Art, New York

Elena Pischikova
Researcher, Department of Egyptian Art, The Metropolitan Museum of Art, New York

PR   Patricia Rigault
Chargée d'Études Documentaires, Département des Antiquités Égyptiennes, Musée du Louvre, Paris

CHR   Catharine H. Roehrig
Associate Curator, Department of Egyptian Art, The Metropolitan Museum of Art, New York

DW   Dietrich Wildung
Director, Ägyptisches Museum und Papyrussammlung, Staatliche Museen zu Berlin; Professor, Freie Universität, Berlin

CZ   Christiane Ziegler
Conservateur Général Chargé du Département des Antiquités Égyptiennes, Musée du Louvre, Paris

EGYPT

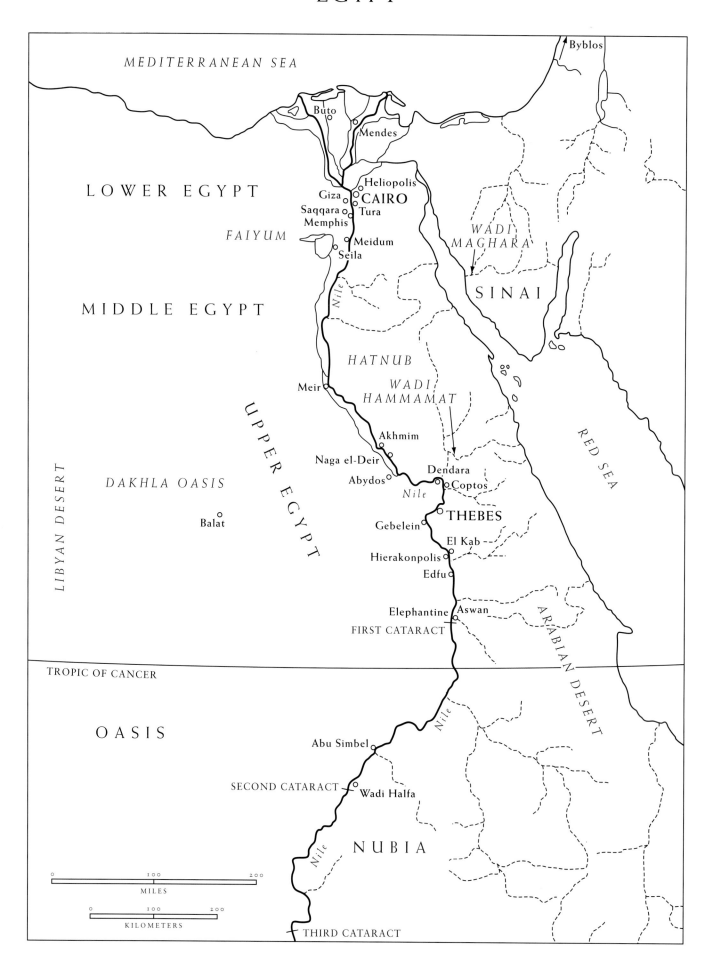

MEDITERRANEAN SEA

Byblos

Buto

Mendes

LOWER EGYPT

Heliopolis

Giza

CAIRO

Saqqara Tura

Memphis

Meidum

FAIYUM

Seila

WADI MAGHARA

SINAI

MIDDLE EGYPT

HATNUB

Meir

WADI HAMMAMAT

UPPER EGYPT

Akhmim

RED SEA

Naga el-Deir

Dendara

DAKHLA OASIS

Abydos

Coptos

Nile

LIBYAN DESERT

Balat

THEBES

Gebelein

El Kab

Hierakonpolis

Edfu

Elephantine

Aswan

FIRST CATARACT

ARABIAN DESERT

TROPIC OF CANCER

OASIS

Abu Simbel

Nile

SECOND CATARACT

Wadi Halfa

Nile

NUBIA

0   100   200
MILES

0   100   200
KILOMETERS

THIRD CATARACT

THE MEMPHITE REGION

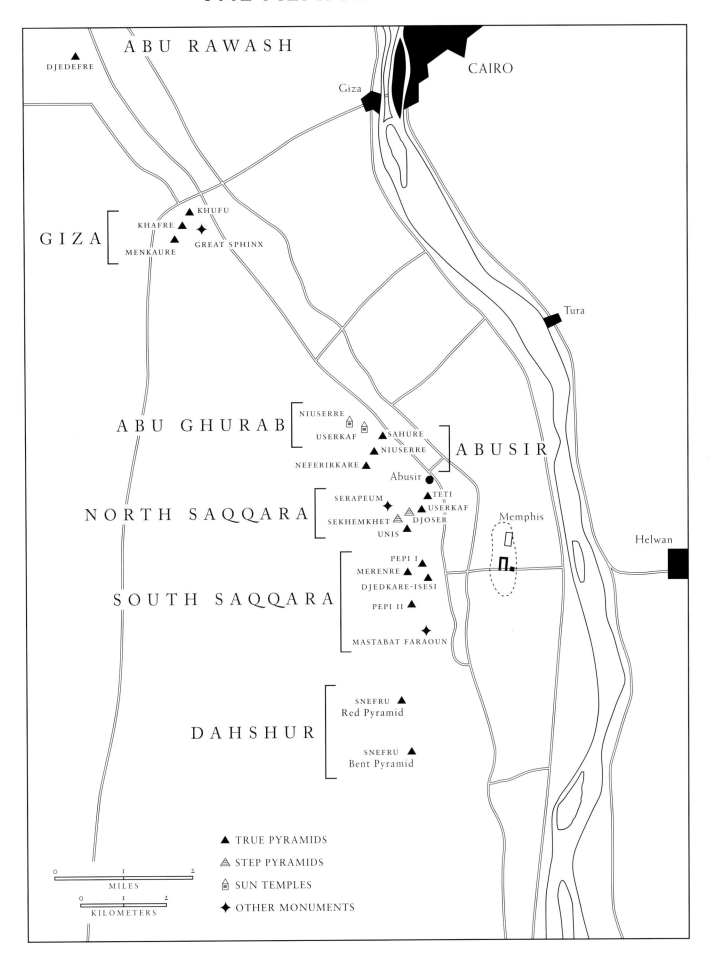

ABU RAWASH

DJEDEFRE

CAIRO

Giza

GIZA

KHUFU

KHAFRE

MENKAURE

GREAT SPHINX

Tura

ABU GHURAB

NIUSERRE

USERKAF

SAHURE

NIUSERRE

NEFERIRKARE

ABUSIR

Abusir

NORTH SAQQARA

SERAPEUM

SEKHEMKHET

UNIS

TETI
II

USERKAF
II

DJOSER

Memphis

SOUTH SAQQARA

PEPI I

MERENRE

DJEDKARE-ISESI

PEPI II

MASTABAT FARAOUN

Helwan

DAHSHUR

SNEFRU
Red Pyramid

SNEFRU
Bent Pyramid

▲ TRUE PYRAMIDS

⌂ STEP PYRAMIDS

⌂ SUN TEMPLES

◆ OTHER MONUMENTS

0   1   2
MILES

0   1   2
KILOMETERS

XVII

NOTES TO THE READER

The works in the catalogue section are arranged chronologically according to dynasty. Within each dynasty they are ordered by the reigns of individual kings. Works of uncertain date are placed in the period in which they are most likely to have originated. Royal commissions generally precede works that belonged to nonroyal individuals.

The spelling of ancient Egyptian names and terms is based on the transliteration of their hieroglyphic forms. Royal names are given in their transliterated hieroglyphic forms rather than in the often better known Greek versions. James P. Allen translated or made consistent the inscriptions in essays and entries by authors from the Metropolitan Museum. In translations of ancient Egyptian texts,

brackets indicate material that is missing from the original but can be restored. Parentheses enclose interpolations made for clarity.

The chronology on page xx is employed throughout for consistency but does not necessarily reflect the opinions of all contributors to the catalogue. The abbreviations B.C.E. (Before the Common Era) and C.E. (Common Era) have been used for dating.

In the headings of the catalogue entries, dimensions are abbreviated as follows: h., height; w., width; d., depth; l., length; diam., diameter.

Citations are abbreviated throughout the catalogue; full references are provided in the bibliography, which also includes material not cited in the text.

CHRONOLOGY

A NOTE ON EGYPTIAN CHRONOLOGY

Any chronology of Old Kingdom Egypt must be imprecise because historians do not agree about how to interpret the existing contemporary and later sources. Although there are Old Kingdom king lists, none that is both complete and contemporary is known. The Palermo Stone, which records the royal annals from the beginning of Egyptian history until the mid-Fifth Dynasty, is fragmentary. A similar text, recently assigned to the Sixth Dynasty, is very worn. All the other king lists postdate the period by one or two millennia: the Chapel of the Ancestors of Thutmose III, the Royal Canon of Turin, the lists from Saqqara and Abydos, and the various transcriptions of Manetho.

Further clouding the issue, Egyptian kings had several names (there were five in the titulary that was standardized beginning in the Fifth Dynasty: the Horus name, the Two Ladies name, the Horus of Gold name, a throne name, and a birth name). We do not always know all the names of Old Kingdom monarchs, and the monuments do not enumerate them systematically. Thus two distinct names inscribed on two monuments may be attributed to two different pharaohs, although in reality they belong to a single king, designated alternatively by one or the other name. As a result, the number of Old Kingdom rulers, the duration of their respective reigns, and even the order of succession are not always secure and vary according to the opinions of historians.

We are accustomed to absolute dates, given in relation to events that are considered starting points from which time unfolds in a linear fashion (for example, the Romans designated dates *before* or *after* the founding of Rome, and Christians record them *before* or *after* the birth of Jesus Christ). Our manner of understanding time seems to have been foreign to the Egyptians, who oriented themselves according to the reigns in which they lived and described dates in like fashion: such and such year of king so and so. This system notwithstanding, we could at least assign a length to the Old Kingdom by simply adding up the years and months of the reigns of its kings—if we knew with certainty the number and durations of those reigns. But, as we have seen, this is impossible. Moreover, since we do not have a single undisputed fixed reference point supplied by the objective date of an occurrence (such as an astronomical phenomenon or a concordance with a securely dated event that took place outside Egypt), it is very difficult to even propose a definitive date for the beginning of the period. Depending on the sources consulted, we may therefore find dates for any given event varying by as much as one hundred or two hundred years. Thus, all dates given here should be understood as approximations.

Élisabeth David

DYNASTIC AND REGNAL DATES

The following chronology is currently used by The Metropolitan Museum of Art; the dates do not necessarily reflect the opinions of all the scholars who have contributed to this catalogue. The names in parentheses preceded by equal signs are the more commonly used Greek equivalents of the ancient Egyptian names, which were first recorded by the traveler and historian Herodotus in the fifth century B.C.E. A name in parentheses preceded by the word "or" is an alternative form; Egyptologists are not certain which form of the name is correct.

ca. 5450–2960 B.C.E.   PREDYNASTIC
PERIOD

ca. 2960–2649 B.C.E.   ARCHAIC PERIOD
(*First and Second Dynasties*)

ca. 2649–2150 B.C.E.   OLD KINGDOM
(*Third to Sixth Dynasty*)

ca. 2150–2040 B.C.E.   FIRST INTERMEDIATE
PERIOD (*Seventh to Early
Eleventh Dynasty*)

ca. 2040–1640 B.C.E.   MIDDLE KINGDOM
(*Later Eleventh to
Thirteenth Dynasty*)
ca. 1991–1962 B.C.E.   Amenemhat I
(*Twelfth Dynasty*)

ca. 1640–1550 B.C.E.   SECOND INTERMEDIATE
PERIOD (*Fourteenth to
Seventeenth Dynasty*)

ca. 1550–1070 B.C.E.   NEW KINGDOM
(*Eighteenth to Twentieth
Dynasty*)

ca. 1070–743 B.C.E.   THIRD INTERMEDIATE
PERIOD (*Twenty-first to
Early Twenty-fifth Dynasty*)

743–332 B.C.E.   LATE PERIOD
(*Later Twenty-fifth
to Thirty-first Dynasty*)

332–30 B.C.E.   PTOLEMAIC PERIOD

30 B.C.E.–476 C.E.   ROMAN PERIOD

OLD KINGDOM, ca. 2649–2150 B.C.E.

Third Dynasty, ca. 2649–2575 B.C.E.
ca. 2649–2630 B.C.E.   Zanakht
ca. 2630–2611 B.C.E.   Djoser
ca. 2611–2605 B.C.E.   Sekhemkhet
ca. 2605–2599 B.C.E.   Khaba
ca. 2599–2575 B.C.E.   Huni

Fourth Dynasty, ca. 2575–2465 B.C.E.
ca. 2575–2551 B.C.E.   Snefru
ca. 2551–2528 B.C.E.   Khufu (= Cheops)
ca. 2528–2520 B.C.E.   Djedefre (or Radjedef)
ca. 2520–2494 B.C.E.   Khafre (= Chephren)
ca. 2494–2490 B.C.E.   Nebka II
ca. 2490–2472 B.C.E.   Menkaure (= Mykerinos,
Latinized: Mycerinus)
ca. 2472–2467 B.C.E.   Shepseskaf
ca. 2467–2465 B.C.E.   Djedefptah
(=Thamphthis)

Fifth Dynasty, ca. 2465–2323 B.C.E.
ca. 2465–2458 B.C.E.   Userkaf
ca. 2458–2446 B.C.E.   Sahure
ca. 2446–2438 B.C.E.   Neferirkare
ca. 2438–2431 B.C.E.   Shepseskare
ca. 2431–2420 B.C.E.   Neferefre (or Raneferef)
ca. 2420–2389 B.C.E.   Niuserre
ca. 2389–2381 B.C.E.   Menkauhor
ca. 2381–2353 B.C.E.   Djedkare-Isesi
ca. 2353–2323 B.C.E.   Unis

Sixth Dynasty, ca. 2323–2150 B.C.E.
ca. 2323–2291 B.C.E.   Teti
ca. 2291–2289 B.C.E.   Userkare
ca. 2289–2255 B.C.E.   Pepi I
ca. 2255–2246 B.C.E.   Merenre I
ca. 2246–2152 B.C.E.   Pepi II
ca. 2152 B.C.E. Merenre II
ca. 2152–2150 B.C.E.   Netjerkare Siptah
(= Nitocris)

James P. Allen

INTRODUCTION

gyptian Art in the Age of the Pyramids," shown in Paris, New York, and Toronto in 1999 and 2000, is the first major, comprehensive presentation that offers a view of the fruits of ancient Egypt's greatest period of artistic achievement, the Old Kingdom. The exhibition also acquaints the general public with the results of an exciting scholarly reevaluation of this formative phase of Egyptian art that has taken place internationally during the last ten years.

Over the course of the roughly five-hundred-year duration of the Old Kingdom, Egyptians not only created the pyramids, the world's most abstract building form; on the basis of initiatives originating in the Archaic Period, they also once and for all defined the essence of their art. Centering their attention on the human image but depicting animals, plants, landscapes, and inanimate objects as well, Old Kingdom artists used stone as their primary medium. This was a material whose durability best served the culture's all-encompassing goal of defeating death, by preserving life in the form of statues and reliefs destined for tombs. Distilling the multiplicity of existence, artists created a limited number of standard types and a canon of circumscribed formal concepts that was flexible enough to allow the depiction of life's diversity through subtle variation and an infusion of innumerable realistic details. Keen observation of nature and a thorough understanding of the functioning of both human and animal bodies led to the invention of images of an organic truthfulness unparalleled at the time. As Heinrich Schäfer wrote, "Egyptians were probably the first to be aware of the nobility inherent in the human form and express it in art." That more than a sense of form is expressed in Egyptian statues becomes clear, however, when we encounter Old Kingdom art, where so much emotion is conveyed by spare, tender gestures. Compared with other periods of Egyptian history, the Old Kingdom, as reflected in its artistic legacy, emerges as a time of utter confidence in human achievement. Its images are sometimes stark and always straightforward, graced by what Eberhard Otto termed the irresistible "charm of the first time."

The concept of "Egyptian Art in the Age of the Pyramids" originated with Christiane Ziegler, Conservateur Général Chargé du Département des Antiquités Égyptiennes at the Louvre, who has herself contributed to the recent renaissance of Old Kingdom art studies with her publication of the Louvre's vast collection of Old Kingdom reliefs, paintings, and statues. In the midst of this undertaking, five years ago, she proposed to the Réunion des Musées Nationaux that Old Kingdom art from museums throughout the world should be united in a major exhibition. Her idea met with a favorable response; the project was, however, too ambitious to be accomplished by a single institution and by a single curator, let alone one who had to supervise the complete reinstallation of the Louvre's entire Egyptian collection at the same time the exhibition was taking shape. Dr. Ziegler therefore invited other curators and institutions to participate in the venture, and the Royal Ontario Museum in Toronto and The Metropolitan Museum of Art in New York joined the project. Thus Krzysztof Grzymski, Senior Curator, Egyptian Section, at the Royal Ontario Museum, and Dorothea Arnold, Lila Acheson Wallace Curator in Charge of the Department of Egyptian Art at the Metropolitan Museum, became Dr. Ziegler's partners in the planning and preparation of the exhibition and its French and English catalogues. Nadine Cherpion, of the University of Louvain, played a vital role by taking part in many discussions with Christiane Ziegler and Dorothea Arnold and writing a major essay for the catalogue. Bruce White, who photographed the bulk of the exhibited works, was an important collaborator in the making of the catalogue.

The idea of mounting an exhibition of Pyramid Age art arose at an exciting time in the history of Old Kingdom studies. Old Kingdom works of art were first brought to light beginning in the middle of the nineteenth century, thanks to the excavations of the French Egyptologist Auguste Mariette and his countrymen Gaston Maspero, Émile Chassinat, and Jacques de Morgan. From the turn of the century until World War II more material was uncovered through the efforts of George Reisner, Georg Steindorff, Hermann Junker, and Selim Hassan, to name only a few of the Egyptologists active during this period. Soon after the war excavations resumed, providing new and unexpected finds and insights: in 1952 Ahmed Fakhry found the statue-cult temple at the Bent Pyramid, and in the 1960s Jean Leclant and his associates began explorations at the pyramids in South Saqqara. However, the pace of Old Kingdom research both in the field and at scholars' desks accelerated notably during the 1980s and 1990s. Recent accomplishments in the field are due to the very effective activity of the Supreme Council of Antiquities, most recently represented by the excavations of Zahi Hawass; the work of Mark Lehner of the Harvard University Semitic Museum and the University of Chicago, carried out in the Old Kingdom industrial quarters at Giza; the French Archaeological Mission's continuing excavations at South Saqqara; and the efforts of the French Institute of Near Eastern Archaeology in the Dakhla Oasis, of the Czech Mission at Abusir, and of the German Archaeological Institute at Dahshur. Also notable have been the collaboration of the University of Geneva and the Supreme Council of Antiquities at Abu Rawash and the Louvre's excavations around the tomb of Akhet-hotep at Saqqara under Christiane Ziegler. At the same time, the excavation and publication of tombs of Old Kingdom officials have proceeded apace, vastly enriching the documented corpus of relief decoration available for study. Key in this context are the *Giza Mastabas* series of the Museum of Fine Arts, Boston, edited and written in part by William Kelly Simpson, with volumes by Ann Macy Roth and Kent Weeks and forthcoming installments by Edward Brovarski and Peter Der Manuelian; the many publications of Naguib Kanawati of Macquarie University, Sydney, and his colleagues, which include tombs at provincial

sites; and the German Archaeological Institute's volumes by Hartwig Altenmüller, Ahmed Moussa, and others. No wonder that all this newly discovered and documented material has inspired scholars to rethink hitherto unquestioned concepts.

William Stevenson Smith's *History of Egyptian Sculpture and Painting in the Old Kingdom* of 1946 so authoritatively presented the finds and researches of the archaeologists who worked during the first century of modern Egyptological exploration that more than a generation passed before scholars challenged some of the views set forward in the book. After some years, however, reevaluation did begin in the realm of intensive iconographical studies, such as Henry George Fischer's many works and Yvonne Harpur's study of decoration in Old Kingdom tombs, and, above all, in the field of dating. Here Marianne Eaton-Krauss, Edna R. Russmann, Biri Fay, and Hourig Sourouzian have made significant contributions, and Cherpion's work has been decisive. The state of Old Kingdom research that resulted from these reassessments was aptly summarized by Rainer Stadelmann in his foreword to the published papers read at the first international conference on the art and culture of the Old Kingdom, held at the German Archaeological Institute in Cairo in 1991: "Several recently published studies with revolutionary proposals of new dates for outstanding works of both royal and nonroyal art have created a lively discussion among scholars concerned with the art history of the Old Kingdom." As Stadelmann noted, a symposium concerning the dating of Old Kingdom works seemed desirable to the participants. Thus the first conference was followed by a second in 1994, sponsored by the French Institute of Near Eastern Archaeology in Cairo, and this meeting was suceeded by a third, at the Louvre in 1998. The papers read at all three conferences have now been published, adding immensely to the general knowledge of the subject.

The curators of "Egyptian Art in the Age of the Pyramids" are presenting to a wider public some of the results of this recent scholarly work. The wider audience may well ask why changes in the dating of Old Kingdom works of art are important. The answer is that these changes affect a fundamental aspect of Old Kingdom culture and art: the relationship between the royal and the nonroyal spheres. To be sure, few works created for the pyramid precincts and solar temples of Old Kingdom rulers have been touched by the recent changes in dating, for royal statuary, reliefs, and minor arts either were found inside the pharaonic building complexes or are inscribed with the names of rulers, so that their attributions are fairly secure. The new datings primarily involve material from the tombs of Old Kingdom officials and their families, and each transfer of an official's statue, relief, or painting from one dynasty or reign to another changes the relationship of that work to the royal art that is now seen to be contemporary with it. For example, Renate Krauspe's redating to the Fourth Dynasty of the statue of Iai-ib and his wife, Khuaut (cat. no. 83), which Junker, its excavator, placed in the Sixth Dynasty, brings this astonishingly lively piece into close connection with the dyad of King Menkaure and a queen (cat. no. 67), thus opening up new insights into the manner in whichOld Kingdom artists were influenced by royal works. In the nonroyal pair the representational character of the Menkaure dyad evidently was transformed into an intimate depiction of the relationship between a man and his wife.

Redating has had other important ramifications. Thus, when reattributions placed many nonroyal sculptures in the Fourth Dynasty, this period emerged as a time characterized by much greater artistic diversity than previously thought. Smith's *History* acquainted us with a handful of nonroyal statues (and a number of very fragmentary pieces) from the Fourth Dynasty, while the reader of this catalogue and visitor to the exhibition is presented with eleven works of widely varied styles and types now dated to this dynasty. It is true that not all of the new placements will necessarily withstand intense scrutiny. Some viewers may, for instance, find it difficult to reconcile the differences between the pair statue of Iai-ib and Khuaut and that of Memi and Sabu (cat. no. 84). And, indeed, one of the aims of this exhibition is to allow judgments to be made in such instances by juxtaposing problematic works in one gallery. However individual cases may be resolved, the fact remains that the great Fourth Dynasty, the period that produced the most imposing of all pyramids, as well as the statuary of Khafre and Menkaure, can no longer be regarded as the monolithic artistic phase once envisaged.

While reattributions remove some important works from the orbits of the Fifth and Sixth Dynasties, the new dating scheme makes the artistic language of these periods more closely definable. Significant recent studies by Russmann and James F. Romano have defined a late Old Kingdom style, predominantly of the Sixth Dynasty, as the Second Style. The exhibition does not deal with this style in detail, but the works of this type that are included demonstrate the existence of an artistic language whose hallmarks are expressiveness and otherworldliness.

Ultimately, reading this catalogue and viewing the exhibition it accompanies should be a rewarding voyage through still widely uncharted lands.

Dorothea Arnold
Christiane Ziegler

EGYPTIAN ART IN THE AGE OF THE PYRAMIDS

A BRIEF HISTORY
OF THE OLD KINGDOM

JEAN LECLANT

The Age of the Pyramids—Egypt during the Old Kingdom—is surely one of the most glorious periods in human history. Its monuments are among the most celebrated, and what remains of their decoration provides valuable information not only about the magnificent life-styles of the pharaohs but also about the daily lives and occupations of the humble fellahs, or peasants. Despite all this evidence, however, it remains especially difficult to present a "historical" overview of the Old Kingdom.

For one thing, the ancient Egyptians' cosmos is the product of conceptions very different from our own; for another, their notion of the passage of time was radically different from ours. The chroniclers of each reign felt no need to establish a temporal succession of events, but rather saw it as their duty to simply mark the individual years. Thus, one typically finds mentions only of day X of season Y of sovereign Z ("day 4 of the *shemu* season of King Pepi," for example). The woefully incomplete Palermo Stone (cat. no. 115) is the sole record from the earliest years that attempts to cover a broad period, providing the annals of rulers from Aha, the first king of the First Dynasty, to Neferirkare, the third ruler of the Fifth Dynasty; fragmentary details have recently been added to this information by the so-called Stone of South Saqqara. After these two documents in stone, the next record we have dates to Ramesside times: a fragmentary papyrus written during the reign of Ramesses II (1279–1212 B.C.E.), which was acquired by the Museo Egizio in Turin, where Jean-François Champollion was the first to reconstruct its Canon of Kings. Similar lists have been retrieved from the Chamber of Ancestors at Karnak, now at the Louvre, and from the temple of Seti I at Abydos. Much later, when the Ptolemies needed to secure their claim to the throne, they revived the cult of the rulers, and about 280 B.C.E. an Egyptian priest, Manetho, undertook to translate into Greek the list of kings preserved in the archives of the temple at Sebennytos. Excerpts from Manetho's manuscript have survived in the texts of various chroniclers, including Sextus Julius Africanus and Syncellus.

While Manetho's text classifies the sequence of pharaohs into "dynasties," these were determined more by the geographical center of power or by affinities of other sorts than by family lineage. It was not until the 1840s that the great Prussian scholar Karl Richard Lepsius grouped the chief dynasties into the Old Kingdom (Third to Sixth Dynasty), Middle Kingdom (Eleventh to Twelfth Dynasty), and New Kingdom (Eighteenth to Twentieth Dynasty). In this terminology, inspired by Baron von Bunsen, we can detect the influence of the tradition of the Holy Roman Empire. The French school of Egyptologists, led by Auguste Mariette, did not at first adopt this terminology, but eventually, for the sake of convenience, the entire community of Egyptologists came to accept the classification of pharaonic history into thirty-one dynasties, further divided into the Old, Middle, and New Kingdoms, which are separated by "intermediate" periods. Nonetheless, differences—even important ones—still exist among experts.

To contemporary minds, chronology implies, at the very least, the establishing of dates.[1] Yet in the study of early periods, much uncertainty persists concerning dating, despite data obtained from carbon 14 and thermoluminescence tests. The determination of relatively discrete time frames, which these methods implicitly strive for, itself rests on the trustworthiness of their results and on parameters that are fairly broad. Given the fragmentary and ambiguous nature of such evidence, the syntheses that periodically flow from the pens of Egyptologists, including those who are otherwise extremely competent, are really only tentative, even in the realm of economic and social history.

Fig. 1. Papyrus columns, North House court, funerary complex of Djoser, Saqqara

Nowadays we agree that the Old Kingdom covers approximately five centuries (about 2700–2200 B.C.E.), although there is some question concerning whether the Third Dynasty should be included in that period, with five kings (or even eight or nine, following the various versions of Manetho). Its first king, Zanakht, who bore the Horus name Nebka, was probably descended from Khasekhemui, the last pharaoh of the Second Dynasty, who had established himself in Upper Egypt. But the kings of the new dynasty settled at the boundary between Upper and Lower Egypt, at a place later known as Memphis. This city remained the major center for subsequent dynasties, and the Old Kingdom can in fact be called the Memphite Kingdom.

The decisive reign of the Third Dynasty was that of Nebka's successor, Djoser, whose name is written in red ink in the Turin Canon. Contemporary sources give him the Horus name Netjeri-khet (Divine of Body), which perhaps should rather be read as Netjeri-er-khet (More Divine than the Body), "the Body" referring to the assembly of other gods. The name Djoser (Holy One or Magnificent), by which he is known to history, is his *nebti* name, the one that identifies him as the king of Upper and Lower Egypt, and is not found before the

Middle Kingdom. Djoser's renown was immense, as was that of his architect and prime minister, Imhotep (He Who Comes in Peace). During his reign, large-scale stone architecture was perfected: his funerary complex of fifteen hectares (fig. 1) included the Step Pyramid, which was more than sixty meters high, hewn-limestone walls, and a series of superb reliefs. With Djoser, Egyptian civilization underwent an evolutionary leap, as pharaonic Egypt broke free of the cultural stops and starts of earlier periods: for the next three millennia, the art of the Nile Valley would continue to be as powerful and elegant as that developed in Djoser's time. The Egyptians themselves were very much aware of the importance of this turning point and, in the Ptolemaic period, made a god of Imhotep, whom the Greeks called Imouthes and equated with Asclepius, their god of medicine. No definitive historical evidence remains from Djoser's glorious reign. The famous Famine Stela, carved on a boulder on Sehel Island, purportedly of this time, is a late forgery devised by the priests of the god Khnum to buttress their claims to the lands of Lower Nubia.

The name of Djoser's successor remained unknown until 1951, when vestiges of a huge rectangular enclosure with the leveled foundation of an unfinished step pyramid similar to Djoser's were found on the Saqqara plateau. Jar sealings discovered at the site were inscribed for a king called the Horus Sekhemkhet, to whom a relief cut on a cliff near the Wadi Maghara in Sinai should also be assigned.

After Sekhemkhet's brief reign (seven years according to the Manethonian tradition), next to nothing is known of the remainder of the Third Dynasty. However, there must have been some progress in the development of Egyptian philosophy, some enrichment of its pantheon and religious rites. Clearly, the foundations of monarchy were firmly established during this time, and the pharaoh, a god-king, ultimately took his place at the peak of a pyramidal structure; below him were the royal court and the administrative officials of a highly stratified society. Thus were worked out the mechanics of a cosmic institution whose balanced structure bound Egypt to the rest of the universe under the aegis of Maat, goddess of world order and justice.

The period from about 2600 B.C.E. until about 2200 B.C.E.—the Fourth through the Sixth Dynasty—witnessed a succession of universally known and recognized accomplishments. Giza and Saqqara, their royal pyramids, nobles' mastabas filled with stunning reliefs, and famous statues of rulers and scribes are the cultural legacy of all humankind. While the daily lives of both the nobles and the peasants of the period remain astonishingly alive through such works, the history of Egypt during these centuries continues to be obscure. The number of sovereigns is very much a matter for discussion, and the exact length of their respective reigns—the one element that would make it possible to write a continuous chronology in the modern sense—is quite often unclear. For instance, was Snefru, the first king of the Fourth Dynasty, a son of Huni, the last of the Third? Did he reign for four decades, as graffiti in a mortuary temple at Meidum would have us believe, even though the Turin Canon accords him twenty-four years and one version of Manetho gives twenty-nine?

From the Middle Kingdom onward, tradition has considered He of the Two Ladies Snefru, also called the Horus Neb-maat, an excellent pharaoh. Recent studies indicate that he reconfigured the step pyramid of Huni at Meidum by adding a revetment, transforming it into a true pyramid, the first of its kind. Reflecting the influence of the solar religion, the pyramid at Meidum—and henceforth all such structures—was considered, in some sense, a petrification of the sun's rays. Snefru next turned his attention fifty kilometers north, to Dahshur, where he built two pyramids. The first is called the Bent Pyramid,

by reason of its unusual shape. Its lower portion has a slope of 54 degrees 27 minutes, while its upper portion is inclined 43 degrees 21 minutes. It attains a height of 105 meters instead of the 138 meters that was originally intended. The reason for this change in the angle of inclination is not known, but it is so beautifully executed that the line separating the two slopes is almost perfectly horizontal. The interior had two burial chambers, another inexplicable feature of this enigmatic monument. The second of Snefru's pyramids at Dahshur, north of the first, has a base measuring a little more than 220 meters on each side. This dimension is comparable to that of the baseline of his son Khufu's Great Pyramid at Giza, but Snefru's second pyramid is not as high (104 meters instead of 146). Although it looks squatter than Khufu's monument, it easily dominates the vast desert at the southern limit of the Memphite necropolis. The use of corbeling in its funerary apartments, which consist of two antechambers and a main room, created a vaulted ceiling that was more than twelve meters high.

Snefru's monuments dominate by their sheer mass and by the technical perfection of their construction, yet, again, scarcely anything is known of his reign. He built boats for the transport of goods and for military expeditions to Nubia, Sinai, and Libya. The brilliant court life is evoked in the celebrated Westcar Papyrus, written at a later period, and reflected in the furniture and jewelry of Queen Hetep-heres I (cat. nos. 31–33), which were buried at the bottom of a very deep shaft located east of her son Khufu's pyramid at Giza.

Snefru's successor, Khufu, is mentioned in Herodotus as Cheops, the Greek form of his name. In hieroglyphs he is called Khufu, an abbreviation of Khnum-khuef-wi (May the God Khnum Protect Me); the reading of his Horus name, transcribed as Medjedu, is only conjectural. Modern historians think the prince must have been about forty when he assumed power. The Turin Canon gives twenty-three years as the length of his reign, but Herodotus gives fifty and Manetho sixty-three. Among the scant details known concerning his reign is the fact that expeditions were conducted outside the Nile Valley—to Sinai in quest of turquoise and copper; to the deserts of Nubia, northwest of Abu Simbel; to the Wadi Hammamat to exploit sources of green breccia; and to Lebanon for cedar logs. Vases bearing Khufu's cartouche have been found at Byblos. The Palermo Stone records information about events from a mere four years of his reign, including the height of one inundation and an uncertain reference to the making of statues of the king, only one of which has unquestionably come down to us—a modest example in ivory

Fig. 2. The Great Pyramid of Khufu, Giza

His second son, Djedefhor or Har-djedef, was remembered as a sage author of moral precepts; his name was associated with that of Imhotep, and he was the object of a similar type of deification. Although he never ruled, his name is written within a cartouche in the Wadi Hammamat together with that of Baufre, his brother.

When Khufu died, the royal succession was so hotly contested that work was abruptly interrupted on the mastabas of many royal princes. Out of these palace intrigues, Djedefre emerged the victor, but he was considered a usurper according to some traditions and thus his name was excluded from the royal lists. Djedefre or Radjedef, the Horus Kheper (He Who Evolves), was the husband of Khufu's eldest daughter, Princess Hetep-heres. He reigned for only a short period—eight years is the span given in the Turin Canon—just long enough to decide to build a pyramid outside Giza, on a superb site overlooking the apex of the Delta near the present-day village of Abu Rawash. His funerary complex remains unfinished, and the pyramid itself seems not to have been completed; only a superb cutting, intended to serve as the burial chamber, remains. Excavations at the beginning of the twentieth century also uncovered a head of the king in red quartzite (cat. no. 54). One of the masterpieces of Egyptian art, it is now in the Louvre, along with numerous statue fragments. Excavation at the site has recently resumed under a Franco-Swiss team.

The return to the plateau at Giza was to be made by Khafre, another son of Khufu. Perhaps his claim to the throne was through his wife Mer-si-ankh, but many princesses bore that name, including a younger daughter of Khufu and a daughter of Queen Hetep-heres II, the widow, it seems, of both Kawab and Djedefre. Known as Chephren in Herodotus, the ruler was also identified as Ra-khaef or He of the Two Ladies Khafre, the Horus User-ib (Powerful of Heart). It was during his reign that the cartouche bearing the king's actual birth name, or Son of Re name, preceded by the epithet "Netjer nefer" (Perfect God), first appeared in the royal titulary. Although renowned for his pyramid and for the Great Sphinx, cut from the living rock near his valley temple, Khafre is actually little known: nothing concerning his period of kingship is preserved on the Palermo Stone, no length of reign is given in the Turin Canon, and Manetho's information concerning him is not credible.

Khafre's pyramid is only slightly less important than Khufu's. While its base is smaller by fifteen meters and its height by four, its steeper slope makes it appear somewhat higher than Khufu's. In the valley temple, built of enormous blocks of granite and alabaster, Mariette

nine centimeters high, now in the Egyptian Museum, Cairo (JE 36143). On the other hand, the perfection of artistic production during the period is attested by many statues of dignitaries and the decorated walls of their mastabas, such as the depictions of Snefru's son and daughter-in-law, Ra-hotep and Nofret (fig. 31), and the famous painting of geese from Meidum, all now in the Egyptian Museum, Cairo (CG 1742).

The crowning achievement of Khufu's reign is the celebrated pyramid at Giza, called the Great Pyramid, 146 meters in height on a base 230 meters per side and with an amazing ascending corridor (fig. 2). Admired throughout the centuries, it remains the focus of endless speculation and mystical-fantastical interpretations by those dedicated to the study of pyramids.

Khufu himself has been detested as harsh and cruel in Egyptian folk memory ever since the First Intermediate Period, when the authority of the central power came into question. He had a large family, with many wives and more than twelve children. Prince Kawab, the eldest son of his first wife, Meret-ites, died before his father.

found a magnificent diorite statue of the seated Khafre, the back of his neck protected by the wings of Horus, the dynastic falcon. This symbol of the Old Kingdom monarchy is now in the collection of the Egyptian Museum, Cairo (fig. 28).

Khafre's chief wife, Kha-merer-nebti, was buried near her husband's pyramid. Her daughter bore the same name and became the first wife of Menkaure, who did not directly follow his father, Khafre. The Turin Canon notes an intermediate reign of four years by a king with an indecipherable name, sometimes read as Nebka (II). This could also be the Bicheris of Manetho, who in turn may be identical to the Baufre in the Wadi Hammamat. Whatever the case, this ruler has not left a single monument.

By contrast, Menkaure shares the glory of Khufu and Khafre and of the Giza plateau. His name appears as Mycerinus in Herodotus and as Mencheres in Manetho. These grecized forms clearly derive from the hieroglyphic Menkaure (Stable Are the Kas of Re), but the reading of his Horus name is still unclear. The Turin Canon indicates a reign of eighteen years, much of which is lacking in historical documentation, but Menkaure's artistic legacy survives through numerous monuments. His pyramid at Giza, cased on its lower courses with red granite from Aswan, once held a basalt sarcophagus, a mummiform coffin, and some of the royal remains, but all of these were lost in a shipwreck during transportation to England. Menkaure's valley temple has furnished some fine statues of the king, his wife, and several female deities (cat. nos. 67–70).

The last king of the Fourth Dynasty mentioned in contemporary records was Menkaure's son Shepseskaf, whose name does not contain the syllable "re," which represents the divine solar element. In fact Shepseskaf was buried not beneath a pyramid—the solar monument par excellence—but under a masonry mastaba in South Saqqara that is shaped like a gigantic sarcophagus and called in Arabic Mastabat Faraoun. The only extant story regarding the transition from the Fourth Dynasty to the Fifth is found in the Westcar Papyrus. It relates that the magician Djedi had predicted to Khufu that his descendants would be removed from power by a new dynasty of divine origin and that the mother of this dynasty's first three kings would be the wife of a priest of Re.

The titulary of the first king of the Fifth Dynasty gives his name as the Horus Ir-maat (He Who Makes Order) and the King of Upper and Lower Egypt Userkaf (Powerful Is His Ka). Although the name "Re" is not given, this ruler did use the epithet "Son of Re." His greatest achievement was the building of a new type of structure called a sun temple. Located near the present-day village of Abusir, this included a massive obelisk constructed of masonry blocks and capped with a pyramidion that stood on a broad base in the form of a truncated pyramid. Userkaf, whose funerary complex is located at Saqqara near the pyramid of Djoser, also completed temples in Upper Egypt and helped to promote the cult of the goddess Hathor. Seal impressions with his cartouche have been discovered in Nubia.

Czech excavations at Abusir over the last twenty years have produced new archaeological evidence that emphasizes the importance of a queen called Khent-kawes, who bears the title "mother of two kings of Upper and Lower Egypt." A queen of this name had an important funerary edifice at Giza, not far from the pyramid of Menkaure. Although Menkaure fathered his successors Shepseskaf and Userkaf with his first wife, he also had two other sons, named Sahure and Neferirkare, who both became kings and whose mother was this very Khent-kawes. Khent-kawes' strong personal character ensured that there was continuity as well as change during the transition from the Fourth to the Fifth Dynasty. Her sons chose Abusir (fig. 3) and not Giza as the location for the royal cemetery. The decision to build sun temples during this period brings to mind the story of Khufu and Djedi in the Westcar Papyrus; Manetho considered it of such significance that he introduced a new dynasty of kings for this era in his list.

Some important historical information exists concerning the reign of Sahure, which is estimated at approximately fifteen years. While his solar temple has not been excavated, his funerary complex at Abusir (cat. no. 110) has yielded several beautiful limestone reliefs (cat. nos. 111–114), testifying to his victories in Libya and Asia, as well as splendid basalt pavings and granite palmiform columns. Sahure's involvement in the Sinai and the Eastern Desert led him to send an expedition to the Land of Incense, the fabled country of Punt, now thought to have been situated on the African coast, near the southern limit of the Red Sea.

A collection of papyri revealing the organization of the pharaonic funerary cult has been found at Abusir among the ruins of the funerary temple of the next king, Neferirkare (cat. no. 117). These sources relate, for instance, that the solar temple provided for the daily funerary offerings to the pyramid complex (reduced to its foundations). The Palermo Stone (cat. no. 115) dates to the reign of Neferirkare, who seems to have been the first king to think it useful to record the royal annals from the start of the historical period, noting major religious,

Fig. 3. The pyramids of Abusir, from a canal

political, and economic events. During this period, the form of the royal titulary was also regularized as five elements, two of which were enclosed in cartouches, one giving the name of the king of Upper and Lower Egypt and the other the Son of Re name—in this case, Neferirkare-Kakai.

The name of his successor, Shepseskare (Distinguished Is the Ka of Re), occurs on only one small item from his reign. The Czech excavations conducted at Abusir have given us a rich harvest of material for the next king, Neferefre, or Raneferef, including papyrus archives, statues, and statuettes.

With regard to historical events, much more has long been known about Niuserre, the Horus Iset-ib-tawi (Darling of the Two Lands), thanks to his funerary complex at Abusir and his sun temple at Abu Ghurab. His rule lasted approximately thirty years, and one of his daughters married a vizier named Ptah-shepses, whose fine mastaba (fig. 4) near the royal pyramid has been restored. One room in Niuserre's sun temple is famous: the Weltkammer, or Room of the Seasons (cat. nos. 119, 120), which was decorated with reliefs depicting personifications of the seasons of the Egyptian year. Behind the representation of each season there is a scene showing, in sequence, the major activities of a day during the

season, including depictions of animals mating and giving birth. These paeans to nature also represent the nomes, or provinces, bringing their gifts to the creator god Re. Niuserre's funerary complex has yielded statues of the king and important reliefs that, along with other material, attest to the king's activities outside the Nile Valley in Syria-Palestine, Libya, and Sinai. The temple at Byblos contained objects with his name, and his cartouche appears with those of Userkaf, Sahure, and Neferirkare on jar sealings at Buhen in Nubia, at the downstream limit of the second cataract.

The reign of Menkauhor seems to have been brief. While it is known that the priests of his funerary cult were active as late as the New Kingdom, neither the sun temple of this ruler nor his pyramid has been definitively located. Would it be productive to search for the latter at North Saqqara?

The eighth king of the Fifth Dynasty was Isesi, the Horus Djed-khau (Permanent of Appearances), whose Son of Re name was Djedkare (Permanent Is the Ka of Re) and whose reign is said to have exceeded forty years. In a rupture with previous reigns, he located his funerary complex (which has still not been fully excavated or published) at South Saqqara. Isesi's active foreign policy is indicated by the fact that his name appears in Sinai, at

Byblos, and at Buhen, ancient gateway to Upper Nubia, in present-day Sudan.

The Turin Canon and Manetho suggest that the Fifth Dynasty closed with the Horus Wadj-tawy (He Who Makes the Two Lands Flourish), the Son of Re Unis—a suggestion confirmed by the newly interpreted Stone of South Saqqara. His reign must have lasted about thirty years. That a dynastic break occurred after he ruled should, however, be questioned, since it is by no means supported by archaeological evidence (which instead underscores continuities in art and architecture) nor by any interruption in the administrative life of the country. The official Ka-gemni, for instance, initiated his career under Isesi, continued it under Unis, and finished it, loaded with honors, under Teti. Even more decisive in terms of continuity is the possibility that Unis, who may have been the son of Isesi, may also have been the grandfather of Pepi I.

That Unis enjoyed considerable prestige is attested by the fact that his cult lasted into the Middle Kingdom.

Fig. 4. Entrance with lotus-bundle columns, mastaba of Ptah-shepses, Abusir

The layout of his funerary complex (figs. 11, 12) is generally similar to that of his predecessor and to those of the Sixth Dynasty kings (although his pyramid itself is smaller), but it is marked by one major innovation. The walls of Unis's burial chamber are inscribed with a series of texts designed to guarantee his resurrection and immortality. Known as Pyramid Texts, inscriptions of this kind would be augmented under subsequent kings (cat. no. 177), but even from the outset they affirmed the wish of the deceased sovereign to triumph over every obstacle that might jeopardize his survival in the afterlife. Furthermore, that survival is envisioned in numerous ways that may appear contradictory to us but did not seem so to the ancient Egyptians. In the dark world of the dead, in the West, the sovereign is master of Osiris's kingdom. But each morning he is reborn, as he sails alongside his father, Re, in the solar bark; each night he rejoins the imperishable stars that endlessly circle the globe. Unis's name is linked not only with this spiritual revolution—which recorded on the walls of the pharaoh's tomb humankind's oldest funerary ritual—but also with actions undertaken beyond the frontiers of Egypt, in Libya, on the shores of Lebanon, and in Nubia.

Manetho assigned a length of 203 years to the Sixth Dynasty, in which he included six kings originally from Memphis. Other sources are more tentative, particularly regarding the end of the dynasty and the transition into the years that modern historians refer to as the First Intermediate Period. Critical examination of extant texts and consideration of the dates of the Sothic cycle (the cycle of the star Sirius), carbon 14 results, and data derived from other laboratory tests have led the most recent textbooks to suggest dates between about 2350 and 2200 B.C.E. for the Sixth Dynasty. While many impediments to our historical understanding of this era still remain, advances in archaeological methods may one day provide some help. At South Saqqara, for instance, the necropolis of the dignitaries associated with Pepi I and Merenre I has still not been excavated; without such basic documentation, the diversity of views offered on the period should not be surprising. Over the course of a ten-year excavation, the funerary complex of Pepi I and his queens has revealed vestiges of the burials and the names of five additional—and until now totally unknown—queens. The clearance of the Sixth Dynasty governors' mastabas at Balat in the Dakhla Oasis has provided new information on the extent of the Egyptian kingdom at that time. While certainly welcome, such new discoveries also often create a host of new problems for historians.

The first king of the Sixth Dynasty—Teti, the Horus Sehetep-tawi (He Who Pacifies the Two Lands)—came to the throne in uncertain circumstances, but at least his accession does not seem to have been violent. Indeed continuity is attested by the king's funerary complex at North Saqqara, which is in perfect harmony with those of his predecessors. The burial chambers are still inscribed with the Pyramid Texts; at most, the only significant changes are that images of the god Seth (but not his name) are prohibited and that certain signs, such as *desher*, "the red one" (an epithet of Seth), are avoided. The nobles associated with Unis are known to have continued to serve under Teti. Although the Manethonian tradition attributes at least thirty years to Teti's reign, the Palermo Stone assigns him only six biennial cattle censuses, or a total of twelve or thirteen years.

The Turin Canon and the Stone of South Saqqara both indicate that there was a pharaoh between Teti and Pepi I. This could be the king of Upper and Lower Egypt Userkare (Powerful Is the Ka of Re) from the List of Seti I from Abydos. Might he be the Son of Re Ity mentioned in two inscriptions at the Wadi Hammamat? Was he perhaps responsible for the murder of Teti, reported in Manetho? Only a few documents bore his name, his pyramid remains unknown, and biographical texts of the period pass directly from Teti to Pepi I.

The Horus Mery-tawi (Beloved of the Two Lands), the Son of Re Pepi, King of Upper and Lower Egypt Meryre (Beloved of Re), originally named Neferzahor (Excellent Is the Protection of Horus), had a long reign. His twenty-fifth biennial cattle census is known, and the Manethonian sources assign him a rule of fifty-three years. The apogee of the Old Kingdom may have been reached under Pepi I, judging by the number of temples built throughout the country during the administrative reorganization that took place and by his activities outside Egypt, which are reported in the great biographical inscription from the mastaba chapel of Weni at Abydos. (The same inscription also mentions, with appropriate discretion, a conspiracy hatched in the royal harem.) Pepi I sent forth major expeditions to the quarries of Wadi Hammamat and the copper mines of Sinai, and his presence is attested from Byblos to present-day Tumas, deep in Nubia. The Heb Sed, or royal jubilee, celebrated in the thirty-sixth year of Pepi's reign, is mentioned in many sources, including an inscription on a beautiful alabaster vase (cat. no. 179).

The funerary temple of Pepi I, which the French team excavated at South Saqqara, is still well preserved in some sections, but many statues of kneeling prisoners with their arms tied behind them have been reduced to fragments. The expressive countenances of these statues make for an astonishing ethnographic gallery of the peoples of Africa and Asia with whom the Egyptians were in contact. Pepi's pyramid, which was fifty meters high and therefore easily visible from the Nile Valley, was called Men-nefer-pepi (Pepi Is Stable and Perfect). The first part of this name came to be applied to the nearby capital and was later transcribed by the Greeks as Memphis. Only twelve meters of the pyramid's height remain, but it has been possible to clear its entire perimeter, the sides of which measure a little more than seventy-five meters. During the excavation of the burial chamber, more than three thousand fragments of various sizes were collected, and these were used to reconstruct the walls at the site. The magnificently carved, finely chiseled hieroglyphs often preserve, in its first freshness, their original green paint—an eternally fertile green, the color of the young shoots that ceaselessly revitalize the Nile Valley. The sarcophagus itself had been broken into, but at its head a granite chest contained the canopic vases holding the remains of the viscera, which were carefully swathed in fine linen bandages.

The cemetery of the queens, just south of the pyramid of Pepi I, was found by means of electromagnetic detectors supplied by Électricité de France. This site has yielded the remains of funerary temples and sculpted images of several queens whose names were unknown until now: Nubunet, whose charming profile is found on a pair of doorjambs; Inenek-Inti, who bears the title of vizier; Nedjeftet; and Mehaa, mother of a Prince Hornetjeri-khet. The results of excavations now underway relating to Queen Meret-ites should clarify the relationship of this queen with the Sixth Dynasty sovereigns. Also of note is the very recent find of the extensive funerary structure of Queen Ankh-nes-pepi (also known as Ankh-nes-meryre), wife and mother of kings. The queen's name has been well known since the discovery of the Abydene inscription of Djau—a noble who was a son of the nomarch Khui and who was promoted to vizier under Pepi I—mentioning that his two sisters had married the king. The inscription goes on to say that both sisters were named Ankh-nes-pepi, which certainly seems odd. Modern historians consider them to be the respective mothers of the two pharaohs Merenre I and Pepi II. It is to be hoped that archaeologists will soon shed some light on a matter that has long been anything but clear.

There is much controversy concerning the length of the reign of Pepi I's successor, the Horus Ankh-khau (The Living Apparition), Son of Re Antiemsaf (Anti [a funerary god] Is His Protection), King of Upper and Lower Egypt Merenre (He Whom Re Loves). Manetho assigns him seven years, the Turin Canon more than forty; in any case, a fifth counting of cattle, signifying a year ten or eleven, is known. Monuments bearing Merenre's name are fairly numerous, and one in particular, a gold object associating his cartouche with that of Pepi I, may suggest a coregency. The partial excavation of Merenre's funerary temple reveals that it remained unfinished. The Pyramid Texts were first discovered there in 1880 by Gaston Maspero, who also found the king's mummy, which has since deteriorated so badly that it cannot furnish any indication of Merenre's age. The walls of the burial chamber, which were also very damaged, were decorated with long columns of inscriptions. When restored from collected fragments, these inscriptions revealed an epigraphy that is less elegant than that found in the texts of Pepi I.

The last, relatively well known pharaoh of the Sixth Dynasty is the Horus Netjer-khau (Divine of Appearances), Son of Re Neferkare, King of Upper and Lower Egypt Pepi, called Pepi II by Egyptologists to distinguish him from his father. At the death of his half brother Merenre, Pepi II was exceedingly young—only six according to Manetho—but he ruled until his hundredth year, thus achieving the longest reign in history. While some new readings of fragmentary texts limit his reign to seventy years, only a single date is clearly attested to, "year thirty-three of the counting," perhaps the sixty-sixth year of his rule.

Many celebrated inscriptions date to the reign of Pepi II. One, in the rock-cut tomb of the official Har-khuf in Aswan, tells of the expeditions that Har-khuf directed southward as far as the country of Yam, to bring back "all sorts of rare and excellent products." On his return from his third journey, he brought with him three hundred donkeys loaded with incense, ebony, oil, panther skins, and elephant tusks, as well as a Pygmy for the pharaoh's amusement. Among the less successful expeditions was the one in which the prince and seal bearer Mehu lost his life (his remains were carried back by his son Sabni in the course of yet another campaign). It would appear that the relations between Egypt and the lands to the south were difficult: inscriptions often speak of the necessity to "pacify" (*sehetep*) the regions traversed, although the exact meaning of the verb is uncertain.

The Swiss archaeologist Gustave Jéquier excavated the funerary complex of Pepi II in the 1930s and later published his findings, including the excellent bas-reliefs decorating the funerary temple. Near Pepi's pyramid were found the remains of the pyramids of three of his queens, Neith, Iput II, and Wedjebten, which were also embellished with Pyramid Texts.

How did the Sixth Dynasty come to an end? How did Egypt enter the dark age of the First Intermediate Period? For a long while it has been sufficient to invoke Pepi II's advanced age to support the conclusion that the entire country weakened and was thereafter delivered into the hands of the supposedly rivalrous nomarchs. Following Manetho, some point to the ephemeral one-year reign of a King Antiemsaf-Merenre, recorded as Merenre II, and then a Queen Menkare-Nitocris. But for now nothing further is known of these two sovereigns.

The Turin Canon cites the names of six additional rulers, whose reigns are all exceedingly short and for whom no archaeological evidence is attested. Of the seventeen royal cartouches given for this period in the List of Seti I from Abydos, only three can be confirmed by contemporary monuments. Manethonian sources end the Sixth Dynasty with Nitocris, who is followed by "seventy kings of Memphis reigning for seventy days" and then by the First Intermediate Period. Specialists will no doubt debate for many years to come the circumstances surrounding the collapse of Old Kingdom Egypt.

For more than two millennia, generations of Egyptians have drawn inspiration from the great example of the Old Kingdom and its astonishing achievements—the superb pyramids; the system of rules governing art, technology, and thought; and the religious beliefs. Despite our ignorance of so many events that transpired during these glorious five centuries, we people of modern times cannot help but marvel as well.

1. In the absence of a verified chronology, the early period of Egyptian history must be treated in relative terms and there still remains a high degree of uncertainty about dates among scholars.

THE STEP PYRAMID PRECINCT OF KING DJOSER

JEAN-PHILIPPE LAUER

The funerary complex of King Djoser at Saqqara, with its Step Pyramid, is the most extraordinary architectural complex of the Old Kingdom (fig. 5). Its architect was Imhotep, deified after the New Kingdom by the people of Memphis, who ascribed medical skills to him. The Greeks in turn saw in him their healing god Asclepius. In the third century B.C.E. the Egyptian historian Manetho repeated the traditional belief that Imhotep had invented the art of building in stone during Djoser's reign. In 1926, in a dump south of the entrance colonnade at the complex, the Antiquities Service found a statue base and fragments of a statue of King Djoser on which is engraved, next to the king's Horus name, that of Imhotep with the following titles: "Seal Bearer of the king of Lower Egypt, first after the king of Upper Egypt, Administrator of the Grand Palace, hereditary noble, high priest of Heliopolis, Imhotep, builder and sculptor. . . ." The dedication allows this godlike man to step out of legend and assume his place in history.

The last royal monument of the Second Dynasty had been erected at Abydos, near the necropolis known as the Umm el-Qaab. Long considered the tomb of the Horus-Seth Khasekhemui, it consists of a significant aboveground mud-brick structure measuring about 70 meters long (north to south) and 13.4 meters wide (east to west) and containing one principal room, which has walls faced with fine limestone, the first stone lining known in Egypt. Nothing, however, marks this as the burial chamber, which in this period was always below ground and sealed by one or more stone blocks. Despite its great number of rooms—nearly fifty, some of which were perhaps subsidiary tombs—this structure cannot be interpreted as a royal tomb. At most it may be a cenotaph, like the neighboring and far smaller monument of the Seth Peribsen, one of Khasekhemui's predecessors.

We do not know whether Djoser was the direct successor of Khasekhemui or whether the Horus Zanakht reigned between them (Zanakht seems to have been Djoser's brother, since they were both apparently sons of Queen Neith-hotep). Even if Zanakht was king, however, his reign must have been very short.

The superb site of Saqqara overlooked the ancient capital of Memphis and its palm groves as well as the pleasant valley to the south and the beginnings of the Delta to the north. Here Imhotep erected numerous markers and stelae with the names of the king and his two daughters, delineating a rectangular site of 544 by 277 meters, about forty times larger than that of the famous mud-brick structure at Naqada. Imhotep may have been trying to replicate the traditional Naqada Palace Facade recessed paneling with the immense bastioned enclosure of this site. In terms of scale, however, the architecture of the White Walls of Menes (as Memphis was first called) was a more likely model. Imhotep brilliantly translated architecture employing mud-brick panels into stone, using fine white limestone from the quarries at Tura, on the east bank of the Nile. Like an indestructible counterpart of mud bricks, the stone was shaped into blocks and arranged in regular rows that were 26 to 40 centimeters high. Fourteen dummy gates were placed at different intervals all along the exterior. The only real entrance to the precinct was through a fifteenth gate, whose open double-leaf door was imitated in stone. The location of the gates seems to indicate that the enclosure wall was a replica of one in which the position of each gate was determined by its function.

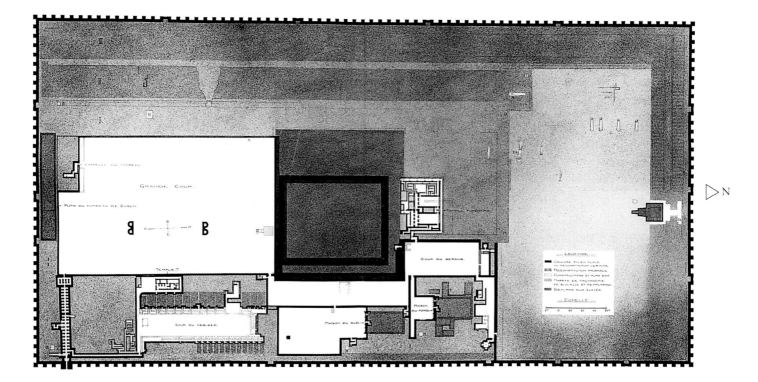

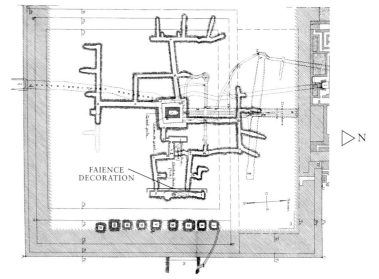

Near the center of the vast rectangular site was found a shaft more than 7 meters square and 28 meters deep. At its bottom a burial chamber was built of limestone blocks (its ceiling, decorated with large five-pointed stars, was later disassembled and replaced with one of Aswan granite). A cylindrical opening, cut in the ceiling at the north, must have allowed the introduction of the mummy. This hole was sealed after the funeral by an enormous granite plug 2 meters thick and 1 meter in diameter, weighing about 3.5 tons. A descent, cut initially as a trench and later as a tunnel, gave access to the shaft and the tomb.[1] The tomb had various subterranean galleries (fig. 6), which were filled with funerary furnishings, especially vessels of alabaster and hard stone. A subterranean suite of rooms decorated in blue faience tiles (cat. no. 1) was reserved for the king's ka. One of its rooms, the east wall of which duplicates the wattle-and-daub facade of the Ka Palace, replete with doors and windows, has three magnificent reliefs of the king set in imitation doorways between the tiles. In the adjoining room, panels of faience tiles (Egyptian Museum, Cairo) crowned with an arch of *djed* pillars represent lofts.

Over the burial shaft, Imhotep first built a flat core 63 meters square and about 8 meters high (some 2 meters lower than the enclosure wall). This core, made of rubble cemented with clay mortar, had a revetment of carefully hewn white limestone covered, doubtless as a precautionary measure, by a second revetment, 3 meters thick. A series of shafts 32 meters deep were dug along the east face of the building, each terminating in a long horizontal

Fig. 5. Map of funerary complex of Djoser, Saqqara. From Firth and Quibell 1935 (pl. 1)

Fig. 6. Subterranean galleries beneath Step Pyramid of Djoser. From Firth and Quibell 1935 (pl. 22)

gallery about 30 meters in length and running from east to west (fig. 6). These shafts and galleries were meant to be used as tombs and as repositories for the funerary furnishings of various members of the royal family: princesses, royal children who had died young, and probably the queen as well. To accommodate them, the mastaba was expanded eastward, becoming, contrary to custom, slightly longer from east to west than from north to south.

This modified mastaba remained entirely hidden behind the enclosure wall; only the latter was visible to the inhabitants of Memphis, on the desert crest to the west of the city. Imhotep then conceived the innovative idea of a step monument, a gigantic stairway to the sky that would help the king's soul ascend after death to sojourn among the gods, with the "Imperishable [polar] Stars" and with Re (the sun), whose chief priest he had been at Heliopolis. The edifice first had four steps, which completely encompassed the three stages of the original mastaba (fig. 7). Its imposing vertical mass, visible at a great distance, became the new focal point of the funerary complex, at once breaking and emphasizing the regularity of the enclosure wall. A final modification, which increased the number of steps to six, made the structure even more dominant by raising its height to nearly 60 meters.

The construction of the Step Pyramid allows us to glimpse the transition from the royal tombs of Saqqara—large mud-brick rectangular cores with broad faces oriented north-south and ornamented with recessed paneling—to the true pyramid in cut stone.

Another equally important innovation of Imhotep was the incorporation of ritual buildings within the funerary monument. Adjacent to the north side of the pyramid (at the head of the descending passage) he erected a cult temple, with its own access (colonnaded entry and various courts). To the east he constructed a group of dummy buildings, intended as a symbolic representation of the realm in which the king's ka would evolve after death. For that reason the complex contained a Heb Sed temple and two additional buildings, which we call the South House and the North House. After Djoser, from the reign of Snefru onward, the environment necessary for the deceased king to live in the otherworld was achieved more economically by means of painted relief representations on the funerary temple walls.

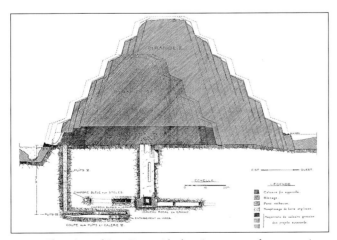

Fig. 7. Elevation of Step Pyramid, showing stages of construction

Fig. 8. Entrance and enclosure wall

THE ENTRANCE TO THE ENCLOSURE

A single passageway only 1 meter wide leads into this immense enclosure (fig. 8), reflecting the fact that the complex was a private domain, reserved for the king's ka and the rites performed within. The entrance is an imposing gateway in the east face of the enclosure wall, 24 meters from the southeast corner; nearly 10.5 meters high, it was destroyed in antiquity but has been reconstructed on the basis of its surviving blocks. A corridor about 5 meters long leads from the entrance to a small court with walls carved in imitation of the gate's two huge door leaves, shown open. Since this single entryway could not be closed, it must have been under constant guard.

A second passage, a little wider than the first, leads from the court and ends at a second open door, with a single imitation door leaf. This opens into a magnificent colonnade, a long narrow hall bordered on either side by two rows of twenty engaged limestone columns. The style of these columns is unique in Egyptian art. Still bearing traces of red paint, they look like petrified wood columns, themselves imitations of the bundled reed stalks or palm ribs that must have been quite common in domestic buildings. In Imhotep's initial plan the entrance corridor was open to the sky, with columns about 5 meters high. When it was later roofed, the column height had to be increased to about 6.6 meters to allow the gallery to be illuminated by clerestory windows.

The colonnade ends at a wide rectangular hall with four linked pairs of columns, originally nearly 5 meters high, supporting the roof. The passage leading out of this hall contains a remarkable imitation of a partly open door: even the ends of its reinforcing battens are rendered in stone.

THE GREAT SOUTHERN COURT

The entrance opens onto a huge court, bordered on the north by the pyramid and on the south by the bulk of the enclosure wall. Projecting from the latter is the wall of Djoser's cenotaph, ornamented with a frieze of cobras. At the north end of the courtyard are the bases of two small D-shaped structures and about 45 meters to the south the remains of a second pair. In the coronation ritual and the Heb Sed (thirty-year jubilee), the king ran a circuit between these two groups while holding the insignia of his power. Such a scene is represented on stelae in the pyramid itself and on the walls of the Southern Tomb (fig. 9). Within the funerary enclosure these structures would have been at the service of the king's ka, as were the majority of structures that Imhotep rendered for eternity in stone.

Near the pyramid is an almost square altar with a short approach ramp. In front of this is a hollow in which a bull's head with lyre-shaped horns had been buried.

THE KING'S PAVILION (TEMPLE T)

From the paneled east wall of the Great Southern Court a passage leads to a small rectangular court with a building at its north end. Known as Temple T, this structure is dominated by three elegant fluted columns, engaged like those of the entrance colonnade. The building very likely represents the pavilion in which the king waited before the rites of the Heb Sed, which took place in the larger court to its east. Its central niche, surmounted by a lintel decorated with openwork *djed* pillars, undoubtedly held a statue of the king.

THE HEB SED COURT

Djoser's Heb Sed was not celebrated in the funerary enclosure during his lifetime. By representing the monumental setting required by the festival, the structures in the Heb Sed Court allowed the king's ka to confirm its functions and royal powers periodically in the afterlife and so preserve them for all time. The jubilee evoked in this manner remains purely symbolic. In the same way, the quarter-circle wall at the southeast end of the King's Pavilion was intended to attract and direct the cortege of spirits that would solemnly escort the king's ka from the pavilion into the Heb Sed Court.

The focus of the court is the platform at its southern end. There, two stairways led to a double dais facing east (toward the capital), which would have sheltered statues of Djoser enthroned as king of Upper and Lower Egypt during the Heb Sed. The court is lined on either side with chapels. Those on the west side were of two kinds. The first, of which there were at least three examples (one at either end of the row and one in the middle), had corner torus moldings and a flat roof with a slight overhang—the transposition into stone of wickerwork structures with reinforced corners. The second type, of which there were probably ten, rested on a foundation about 2 meters high and supported an arched cornice. Its facade was embellished with three thin fluted columns, re-creations in stone of the trunks of tall coniferous trees. Their capitals, unique in Egyptian art, are formed of two elongated fluted leaves, which lie along the shaft and frame a small cubic abacus. The abacus may represent the end of a rafter, while the two fluted leaves may signify a clump of tied plant matter, used in rustic constructions to reinforce the junction of the rafter and the post; the banded cornice resembles reeds bent inward to increase the strength of primitive roofs. A cylindrical hole through the abacus was meant to hold the ensign of the god to whom the chapel was dedicated. Each of the southernmost two chapels of this type had a large niche in the south end of the facade, reached by a stairway with shallow, sloping steps.

Each chapel was fronted by a baffle wall and had only one small room—a sanctuary with a vaulted niche; otherwise the structure was entirely solid. Simulated wood barriers were carved in high relief on the walls separating the access corridors from each of the fluted-column chapels, and doors with hinges and pivots, likewise simulated in stone, marked the entrances to these corridors and the chapels.

On the east side of the court were twelve chapels of a third type, with an arched roof like that of the second type but narrower and without columns. Beyond this row of chapels, to the south, three caryatid statues of King Djoser, which were found lying on the ground, have been re-erected against the enclosure wall (their original position is unknown). Two of them are unfinished, roughed out at different stages of completion; the third, though more finished, is only partly preserved.

In a small room of the last eastern chapel are the feet of four otherwise-vanished statues, representing two adults and two children. These feet probably belonged

Fig. 9. Relief of Djoser from subterranean gallery beneath Southern Tomb, east wall

Fig. 10. Facade, South House

to statues of Djoser, as king of Upper and Lower Egypt, and two very young royal princesses.

THE SOUTH HOUSE AND NORTH HOUSE

A narrow passage at the north end of the Heb Sed Court leads to the east side of the pyramid and two long courts running parallel to it. These were originally separated by a north-south wall; an imitation open door allowed movement between the two. The eastern court is bordered on the north by a structure called the South House (fig. 10), which appears to have been some 12 meters high, with a banded cornice like those of the chapels in the Heb Sed Court. Its facade is decorated with four engaged fluted columns with sharp ridges, recalling a Greek Doric column, and two banded pilasters at the ends.

Curiously off-center, the entrance to the building leads via a narrow passage, which makes two ninety-degree turns, to a small cruciform sanctuary with three niches, for offerings or statuettes. On the west and north walls of the corridor are two beautiful hieratic graffiti left by visitors during the New Kingdom in admiration of the beauty of Djoser's monument, which at this time was already fifteen to sixteen hundred years old. It is in these graffiti that the name "Djoser" first appears at Saqqara; during his reign the king was always designated by his Horus name, Netjeri-khet.

From the northeast corner of the pyramid a corridor led eastward to a small court, north of the South House, that had a second building, called the North House, at its northern end. The facade of this structure was decorated with four fluted columns similar to those of the South House. An off-center doorway opened onto a curving corridor that led to a small sanctuary—with five niches instead of three as in the South House.

In the east wall of the court in front of the North House there were three narrow engaged columns with triangular shafts representing the papyrus, the emblem of northern Egypt (fig. 1). The remains of a small column with a cylindrical shaft were found against the corresponding wall in the court of the South House, no doubt representing the liliform plant symbolic of southern Egypt. Together, the South House and North House probably represent structures in which the king's ka received the homage of his subjects after his enthronement in the Heb Sed as king of Upper and Lower Egypt.

THE SERDAB

At the north side of the pyramid is the serdab, a small, sealed room that backs against the casing. It contained a singular statue of Djoser that is now in the Egyptian Museum, Cairo (JE 49158). On the north face of the serdab are two cylindrical holes through which one can now see a plaster cast of the original statue. Like the slits found in important tombs, these allowed the statue to communicate with the outside and, in this case, to see the long lines of offering bearers entering the temple. In front of the serdab, at the right and left, are two open door leaves carved in stone.

THE FUNERARY TEMPLE

The actual funerary temple abuts the pyramid's north face west of the serdab. A dummy open door with a single leaf led, by way of a curving passage, to two symmetrical interior courts, where fluted columns formed part of the facades. The western court gives access to subterranean areas of the pyramid, a huge maze of deep galleries on two levels.

THE CENOTAPH OF THE GREAT SOUTHERN COURT

In the southwest corner of the Great Southern Court is Djoser's second tomb, or cenotaph. It is marked by a prominent oblong superstructure measuring 84 by 12 meters and having a transverse arched roof. It had a revetment of fine limestone, several courses of which remain on the south side.

At the top of the cenotaph is a fine frieze of uraei evoking Wadjet, goddess of Buto and protectress of Lower Egypt. Immediately to the left of the cobra-frieze wall is the cenotaph's deep shaft; this has the same dimensions as the one in the pyramid (7 by 28 meters), but its granite burial crypt is smaller and square (1.6 meters on a side) instead of oblong. The bottom of the shaft communicated on the east with a suite of rooms for the ka, which included, as under the pyramid, rooms decorated with blue faience tiles and three false-door stelae showing Djoser in relief with his titulary and Horus name in a *serekh*.

Stairs in the enclosure wall left of the cobra-frieze wall lead to an upper terrace. There, several meters to the west, is a stairway cut into the wall's thickness and situated parallel to the enclosure wall, between two finely built retaining walls dating to the Third Dynasty; this stairway rejoins the large shaft by means of a tunnel to the east.

Why was there a second tomb for the same king in the same complex? Could this be a symbolic tomb connected with a ritual of the king's imaginary death in the course of the Heb Sed? Or was it meant to evoke the tombs, or rather the cenotaphs, that the two previous royal dynasties had erected at Abydos, where the necropolis of the canine god Khenti-amentiu had been the site of interment for the Predynastic kings of Upper Egypt? Djoser, for whom no monument has been found at Abydos, would thus have broken with tradition, having only a symbolic representation of the tomb-cenotaph of Upper Egypt at the southern edge of his vast funerary enclosure, the location perhaps of his canopic jars.

With its references to the funerary architecture of his predecessors and its innovative step mastaba and stone masonry, Djoser's monument at Saqqara represents both the culmination of the funerary architecture of the First and Second Dynasties and the beginning of Egypt's glorious Age of the Pyramids.

1. See Lauer 1938, pp. 551–65.

PYRAMIDS AND THEIR TEMPLES

AUDRAN LABROUSSE

For more than four centuries, from the Fourth through the Sixth Dynasty, most Egyptian kings and many queens were interred in pyramid tombs. Beginning in the Predynastic Period, Egyptian tombs evolved from a simple mound marked with stones, to a mastaba constructed of brick or stone, and finally, at the dawn of the Third Dynasty, to the monumental stairway of Djoser's Step Pyramid. Interpretation of the symbolism of this progression is difficult but the following theories can be proposed.

THE TOMB AS AN IMAGE OF THE TERRESTRIAL WORLD

The landscape changes profoundly as one moves from Memphis, the ancient Egyptian capital, to its necropolises, Saqqara and Giza, toward the setting sun to the west. The Nile Valley, its rich vegetation humming with life, must be left behind to reach the realm of the dead, which lies in desertlike solitude on a silent plateau. This separation between the world of the dead and that of the living is expressed in the funerary architecture: a subterranean chamber is reserved for the mortal remains, while a superstructure with a clearly visible chapel or funerary temple evokes the house or palace frequented by the living.

The pyramid is the most spectacular element in a vast ensemble including, on the level of the Nile Valley (the domain of the living), a funerary port on a branch of the great Memphis canal. A valley temple, which lies at the port's center, provides ramps for landing and for access to the necropolis (fig. 11). A long covered causeway rises to the world of the dead on the plateau's summit, where the cult temple is located adjacent to the pyramid's east side (fig. 12). Some ancillary installations complete the royal funerary complex. The function of a small pyramid to the southeast, enclosed within its own

precinct, remains uncertain, but it may have had some connection with Upper Egypt. Sacred boats for the use of the deceased were buried in long pits.

The monuments of officials and royal relatives were grouped around the pharaoh's tomb. The well-ordered layout of the royal necropolis, with its different sectors, organized into street grids, expressed the social organization of the court. During the reign of the Fourth Dynasty king Khufu the more modest queens' pyramids came to be located near that of the king. The queen's tomb, which included a small cult temple, was a simplified version of the king's monument. The mastabas of privileged functionaries, some associated with the royal family, were organized as groups of funerary houses. These had the two components essential to a tomb: an underground burial chamber (with an access shaft) and an above-ground ensemble, which included a cult chamber for offerings, a serdab containing the statue of the deceased, and a suite of decorated rooms, which increased in number into the Sixth Dynasty (see "The Tombs of Officials" by Peter Jánosi in this catalogue).

The social hierarchy of the court that persisted beyond death is revealed clearly only in Fourth Dynasty cemeteries at Dahshur and Giza and to a lesser extent in the Sixth Dynasty cemetery at Saqqara near the pyramid of King Teti. The exceptional honor of having a tomb in the royal necropolis offered nonroyal persons the hope of achieving individual survival as well as retaining their courtly offices in the beyond. Over time, distinctions became obscured by later burials whose sites were chosen to secure the protection of still-prestigious monuments.

THE TOMB AS A LOCUS OF REMEMBRANCE

The essential activity of the funerary cult, the presentation of offerings for the dead, testifies not only to the obligation of the living to remember but also to the hope of survival in the beyond. Only the deceased are immortal, since they have been called to eternal life and cannot die again. Remembrance, however, must still be sustained. Thus each of the majestic pyramids commemorates the earthly past of a dead king, while glorifying his mummy's resting place.

The tomb is a monument where the eternal past looks toward the future through a continuous present. The transition from mud brick to hewed stone exemplifies this movement toward immortality, also evident in the increasing size of the monuments.

Pyramid construction was not without risk, and in the Fourth Dynasty, particularly during the erection of the three large pyramids of King Snefru, many schemes were devised to keep the burial chamber from collapsing under the pyramid's weight. Numerous spanning systems were employed in the extraordinary tomb of Khufu: juxtaposed lintels in chamber three (King's Chamber); a corbeled ceiling in the area where the closing blocks were stored (Grand Gallery); and the chevron, or pointed saddle, vault, an innovation that was used above the entrance and in chamber two (the so-called Queen's Chamber). The last, which shows a growing understanding of the dynamics of load bearing, came to be widely used.

The plan of the subterranean royal funerary apartment was standardized by the Fifth Dynasty. The essential elements, which henceforth did not vary, were a descending access, a horizontal corridor, a funerary chamber situated beneath the pyramid's center, and elaborate protective mechanisms.

THE TOMB AS A FRAMER OF ETERNITY

Beginning in the reign of Unis, the final sovereign of the Fifth Dynasty, Pyramid Texts were inscribed on the walls of the royal funerary apartments. These texts, which include statements of religious beliefs, magical spells, and incantations, helped the pharaoh in his passage through the underworld to eternal bliss. The Egyptians believed that rebirth could be achieved through three primary avenues (they were not disturbed by the inherent contradictions among these, as the heirs of Aristotelian logic would be). In Osirian eschatology the deceased reaches the world of the dead, a mysterious kingdom, ruled by Osiris as the Lord of the Westerners, from which no one ever returns. In the solar cosmology the pharaoh is reborn each morning and accompanies the sun in his bark across the sky, disappearing with the sun but reemerging

Fig. 11. Port and valley temple, funerary complex of Unis, Saqqara. Axonometric reconstruction by Audran Labrousse, 1997

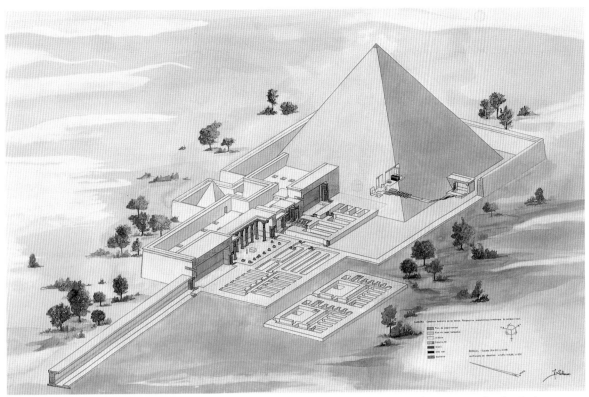

Fig. 12. Pyramid temple and pyramid, funerary complex of Unis, Saqqara. Axonometric reconstruction by Audran Labrousse, 1997

with it at dawn. Alternatively, the pharaoh rises northward at night to rejoin the abiding stars that endlessly circle the pole, giving undying light.

Architecture evolved to support these strivings for resurrection. Beginning with Djedefre, Khufu's successor, after the priests chose the pyramid's location, a huge T-shaped trench was cut into the rock of the plateau. The leg of the T became the access corridor to the funerary chambers, while the crossbar, with its east-west orientation, held the antechamber and burial chamber. Construction of this funerary apartment was accomplished while the trench was open to the sky. Thick stone slabs were placed on a layer of packed sand to form a pavement; then the stone walls of the chambers and corridors were built; finally, a vault of huge stone chevrons was put in place, supported by two opposite sides of the trench. From the reign of Unis onward, the roof's interior was decorated with stars, conjoining death and the cosmos. The sarcophagus was put in place before the vault was completed. These chambers were then buried under the pyramid's mass. After the burial of the king, the participants made the long ascent from the funerary apartment; they returned to the land of the living through a ground-level chapel at the center of the pyramid's north face. This journey paralleled the ascent of the soul of the deceased to the polar stars. Once the king was interred, no one ever again entered the pyramid, and the rituals due the sovereign were held only in the temple and its precincts.

From the Fourth Dynasty forward, architects chose an east-west axis for the cult, or pyramid, temple, paralleling the sun's path through the sky. After passing through the entry gate, the priests who celebrated offering rites moved through the hall, the great court, and a number of other chambers before reaching the innermost temple with the statue room and the sanctuary. In the holy of holies was a granite stela, placed to allow the spirit of the deceased in the pyramid to enjoy the offerings made for it. Over time, magazines for cultic goods multiplied, contributing to the isolation of the hallowed spaces from the exterior world.

Set apart on a plateau bordering the Nile Valley, the world of the pyramids escaped to some extent the vicissitudes of the passing centuries. The excellence of their architecture allowed the Egyptians, who were bent on a quest for immortality, to realize their obsessive goal: the conquest of time, the triumph over forgetfulness, and the attainment of eternity in the memory of future generations.

DYNASTY	NUMBER OF PYRAMIDS	KING	LOCATION
Third	3	Djoser	North Saqqara
		Sekhemkhet	North Saqqara
		Khaba	Zawiyet el-Aryan
Fourth	9	Snefru (?)	Meidum
		Snefru	Seila
		Snefru	Dahshur (Bent Pyramid)
		Snefru	Dahshur (Red Pyramid)
		Khufu	Giza
		Djedefre	Abu Rawash
		Khafre	Giza
		Nebka	Zawiyet el-Aryan
		Menkaure	Giza
Fifth	8	Userkaf	North Saqqara
		Sahure	Abusir
		Neferirkare	Abusir
		Neferefre	Abusir
		Niuserre	Abusir
		X (or queen of Djedkare-Isesi?)	South Saqqara
		Djedkare-Isesi	South Saqqara
		Unis	North Saqqara
Sixth	4	Teti	North Saqqara
		Pepi I	South Saqqara
		Merenre	South Saqqara
		Pepi II	South Saqqara

DYNASTY	NUMBER OF PYRAMIDS	QUEEN	LOCATION
Fourth	7	Meret-ites I (?)	Giza
		X (G I b)	Giza
		Henutsen (?)	Giza
		X (G III a)	Giza
		X (G III b)	Giza
		X (G III c)	Giza
		Khent-kawes I	Giza (mastaba-pyramid)
Fifth	4	Nefer-hetepes	North Saqqara
		Khent-kawes II	Abusir
		X (L 24)	Abusir
		X (L 25)	Abusir
Sixth	8	Khuit II	North Saqqara
		Iput I	North Saqqara
		Inenek-Inti	South Saqqara
		Nubunet	South Saqqara
		Ankhes-en-pepi	South Saqqara
		Neith	South Saqqara
		Iput II	South Saqqara
		Wedjebten	South Saqqara

THE TOMBS OF OFFICIALS
Houses of Eternity

PETER JÁNOSI

Make good your dwelling in the graveyard,
Make worthy your station in the West.

The house of death is for life.

From the "Instruction of Prince Har-djedef"

While our attitude toward the transitoriness of life often is primarily negative and tends to avoid contemplating death, ancient Egyptians regarded the preparation for their welfare after death as a major task to be undertaken during life. Providing for the afterlife meant not only building a tomb and equipping it with the necessities but also establishing a mortuary cult maintained by individuals who would provide for the requisite offerings and perform the essential rituals after the tomb owner was buried. Certainly, preparing for life after death involved one of the largest investments Egyptians had to make.

Only the elite of Egyptian society had enough means to create and support an eternal abode. The tombs and burial customs of ordinary men and women for the most part remain unknown, for throughout pharaonic history the majority of Egyptians were interred simply, in shallow pits with a few necessary items. This must be stressed to make clear that in studying Egyptian tombs and their extraordinary reliefs, statues, and burial equipment, we are concerned with the art, architecture, and funerary practices and beliefs of only a small portion of the society, the upper class.

Inscriptional as well as archaeological evidence seems to support the idea that the Egyptians regarded their tombs as houses or dwelling places for eternity. A survey of the development of funerary architecture during the

Pyramid Age does not contradict this idea; yet it also demonstrates that this concept represents an oversimplification that leaves unexplored a number of crucial features or phenomena that are vital to the understanding of Egyptian concerns about the afterlife.

In general, Old Kingdom tombs, regardless of their size and the status of the owner, consist of two parts: a substructure situated below ground level containing the interment, and a superstructure, the mastaba,[1] erected above the burial place, which is the monument of the deceased. The parts form a unit but developed separately and in different ways in the course of history.

It was in the Second and Third Dynasties that the idea of the dead living in their tombs was most evidently manifested in funerary architecture. A number of mastabas of the period surmount complex substructures comprising a multiplicity of chambers, some of which duplicated installations the deceased would have used in earthly life.[2] The superstructure, built of mud bricks and adorned with elaborate Palace Facade paneling since the First Dynasty, gradually became simplified in this period, until the paneling was relegated to a single side.[3] The tomb of Hesi-re (Saqqara 2405), from the later part of the Third Dynasty,[4] shows a substructure that retains a complex of rooms (even disposed on a number of different floor levels) as well as a superstructure that has become more complicated, with corridors, an offering chamber, a serdab, or statue chamber, delicately carved wood panels

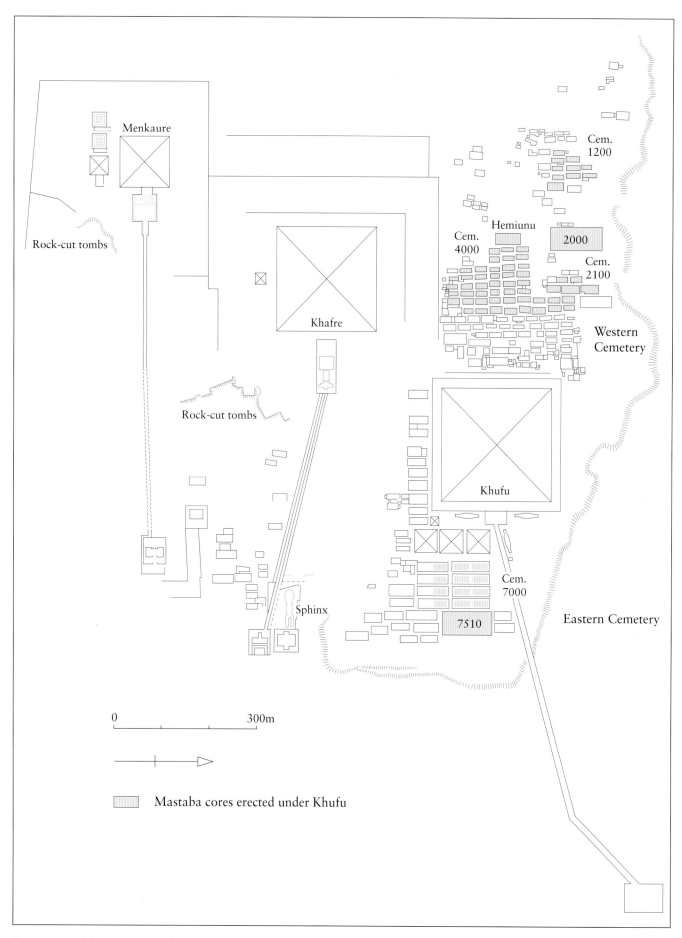

Menkaure

Rock-cut tombs

Khafre

Rock-cut tombs

Sphinx

Cem.
1200

Hemiunu

Cem.
4000

2000

Cem.
2100

Western
Cemetery

Khufu

Cem.
7000

Eastern Cemetery

7510

0   300m

Mastaba cores erected under Khufu

Fig 13. Map of the Giza necropolis. Drawing by Liza Majerus after Reisner 1942, general plan of the Giza necropolis

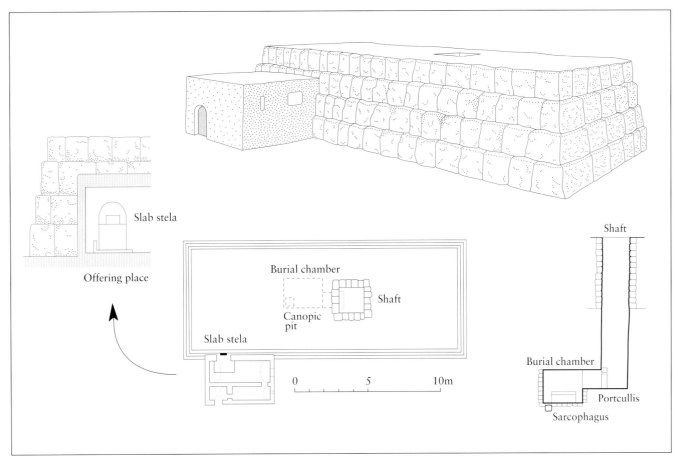

Fig. 14. Core mastaba with mud-brick chapel, from the reign of Khufu. Drawing by Liza Majerus after Junker 1929, figs. 3, 3a, 4, 6

set into the false doors (cat. no. 17),[5] and wall decorations, all features demonstrating that the accessible part of the tomb has gained importance.[6]

With the Fourth Dynasty the classic type of Old Kingdom tomb, the stone mastaba, emerged,[7] as limestone gradually replaced the mud bricks that were still the primary building material at the beginning of the period.[8] In Meidum, offering chapels (of Nefer-maat and Itet, Rahotep and Nofret) and burial chambers (such as the example in the anonymous mastaba M 17)[9] were erected in limestone during the reign of Snefru. Some tombs of the same period to the southeast of the Red Pyramid at Dahshur were built with superstructures of rubble cased with limestone (M II/1).[10] The east facade of each Dahshur monument contains two false doors, the southern being larger and decorated, and a small mud-brick chapel that is the main offering place of the tomb has been added.[11]

When Khufu, one of Snefru's many sons, ascended the throne early in the Fourth Dynasty, he chose a new place for his pyramid complex, a location commonly referred to as the necropolis or plateau of Giza (fig. 13).[12] There Khufu not only constructed the largest pyramid ever built in Egypt but also ordered the erection of rows of tombs to the east and west of his own funerary monument. The tombs to the east were given to his wives (who were buried in small pyramids) and close relatives, while the mastabas to the west were built for his officials and more distant relatives. The tombs of these initial, or nucleus, cemeteries, the oldest in the necropolis,[13] display a number of features that seem to set them apart from the funerary architecture of the previous reign and from later monuments as well. The mastabas in the various sections are set in rows equidistant from one another and separated by streets and avenues[14] with a degree of symmetry unparalleled in both previous and later necropolises. The cores of the tombs either are solid, consisting of well-laid stone blocks, or have a rubble filling cased with stone blocks.[15] Massive rectangular structures with stepped courses (fig. 14), the mastabas for the most part are not cased or decorated on their exteriors with palace facade paneling, nor were they given false doors.[16] There are no entrances into rooms inside the core superstructures like those in the tombs at Meidum or Saqqara, where a cruciform chapel within the mastaba became the standard offering room.[17] The serdab, present in earlier tombs and a common feature from the end of the Fourth Dynasty onward,[18] is absent from the mastabas of these nucleus cemeteries, whose only decoration is a small limestone tablet, or slab stela, with delicate painted low relief (cat. nos. 51–53) set into the southern part of the east facade. A small mud-brick chapel with whitewashed walls usually encloses the place of worship and protects the slab stela, which in these unfinished structures must be regarded as a substitute for the false door that was a standard element of funerary architecture before the time of Khufu and in later tombs. A shaft penetrates the northern half of the superstructure as well as the rock below and leads to a short horizontal passage that ends in the burial chamber to the south. Except for its roof, this chamber is cased with fine limestone painted to imitate granite.[19] From the middle of the Fourth Dynasty onward, cased burial chambers gradually disappear, and in the Fifth and Sixth Dynasties only in very large tombs are such chambers occasionally cased with white limestone.[20] The only sculpture associated with these tombs was the reserve head, which was set up in the substructure (see "Reserve Heads" by Catharine H. Roehrig in this catalogue).[21]

The high quality of the relief carving and painting of the slab stelae has led to the supposition that these objects, issued from royal workshops, were distributed by the king as marks of ownership or assignment during the lifetimes of the recipients.[22] It seems more probable, however, that the stelae were made at various times during Khufu's reign, most likely once the owners died, in order to provide for the basic requirements of the mortuary cult when the tomb remained unfinished (without a casing, a stone chapel, and a false door). This theory accounts for the many epigraphic and iconographic variations the stelae display despite their uniformity in other respects.[23] It also accords with the fact that most tombs were furnished with only mud-brick chapels that could not have survived long and certainly did not fulfill the initial aims of the builders. When the owner was buried, building activities usually ceased or were reduced to a minimum,[24] the relatives contented themselves with preparing a place of worship simpler than originally intended, and the royal workshops contributed the slab stela as a gift. (For a somewhat different interpretation, see "Excavating the Old Kingdom" by Peter Der Manuelian in this catalogue.)

Archaeological evidence shows that in several instances either the tomb owner's family or the king's office of works completed a core mastaba that had a mud-brick chapel by replacing the latter with a stone chapel with a false door and adding a stone casing. These alterations clearly indicate that the tomb as it was previously constituted did not embody the form of the funerary monument the owner desired.[25] In some mastabas the remains of the old mud-brick chapel were preserved underneath the additional stone construction,[26] and in four of them slab stelae have been found behind the stone wall, apparently having been left in place and hidden when the new chapel was built.[27]

Reconstructions of this kind, which probably took place during the reign of Khufu or shortly thereafter, did not much alter the form of the mastabas. However, other alterations pursued at the same time and later had considerable impact on the size and layout of the tombs. Three methods of changing the original design can be distinguished in the monuments of the Western Cemetery. The first left the core of the mastaba intact and added new structures to the existing one. The second broke a hole in the existing core or removed part of the existing mastaba and built a chapel in the new space created (fig. 15f). Although this procedure seriously interfered with the original structure, it was undertaken in a considerable number of tombs,[28] the earliest of which are the huge twin mastabas in G 7000.[29] The third method, which seems to have developed from the second, did not modify an existing structure but rather created a new design in which the chapel was built within a space left inside the core. This last procedure was used in the tombs surrounding the nucleus cemeteries and can be dated to the reigns of Khafre and Menkaure.[30]

The first method allowed different kinds of alteration to the form of the tomb, which can be observed in the archaeological remains (fig. 15). The simplest variation, visible in the tomb of Nefer (G 2110) (fig. 15c), involved setting up two false doors in the east facade and adding a stone chapel around the main false door.[31] A more complicated alteration, undertaken in the tomb of Kani-nisut I, from the end of the Fourth Dynasty (G 2155) (fig. 15d), not only introduced a casing but also extended the mastaba core to the south by building a new structure that contained the offering chamber and a serdab behind the south false door.[32] A third variation incorporated a chapel or offering place in the mass by constructing it within masonry that was added to the entire east side of the original core (fig. 15e).[33] An impressive example of such an enlargement is the monumental mastaba of Hemiunu (G 4000) (fig. 15a).[34] In the east facade of the original core of this tomb two holes were broken out and reconstructed as serdabs, the north one containing the owner's splendid statue (fig. 15b; cat. no. 44). A long, narrow corridor with two false doors in its west wall and

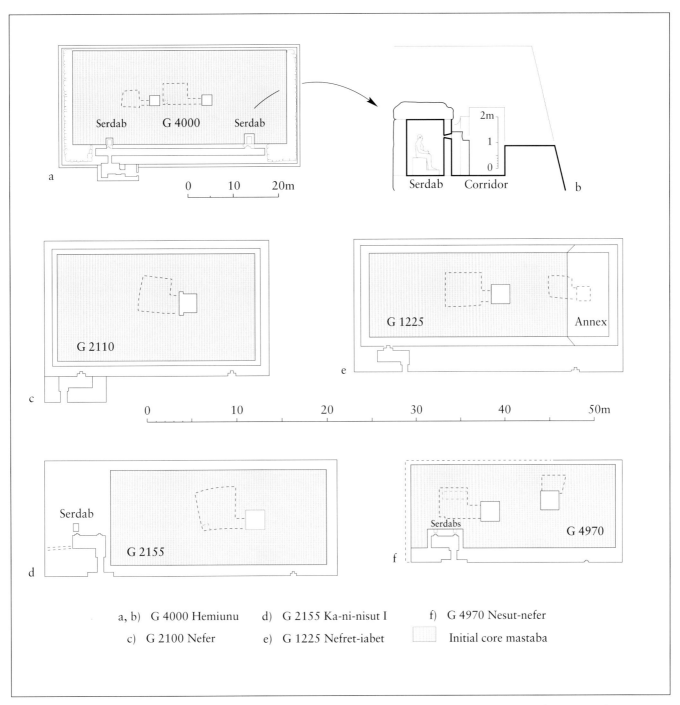

Fig. 15. Types of mastabas in the Western Cemetery, Giza. Drawing by Liza Majerus, (a, b) after Junker 1929, figs. 18, 20, pl. 21a; (c) after Reisner 1942, plan of cemetery G 2100; (d) after Junker 1934, fig. 12; (e) after Reisner 1942, plan of cemetery G 1200; (f) after Junker 1938, fig. 26

an entrance at its south end was erected in the new masonry. A small mud-brick structure was placed in front of the entrance to the corridor.

These procedures all increased the size of the tomb and added a chapel inside the new structure. A fourth not only accomplished these same alterations but also changed the original purpose of the tomb. All tombs of the nucleus cemeteries were built as one-shaft mastabas that served as resting places for one person.[35] However, in the Western Cemetery six mastaba cores[36] were enlarged

by the addition of masonry that includes a shaft for a second burial (fig. 15e). Because these tombs were destined to be cased, nothing in their final forms would have revealed that in each, two substructures are incorporated under one superstructure. Each single tomb had become a two-shaft mastaba.

All of these alterations clearly served to accomplish one intention of the tomb owners: to move the offering room, in one way or another, into the core of the superstructure. Another goal, the creation of a second burial place in the substructure, probably for the owner's wife or a near relative, was less frequently attempted, but its realization had major consequences for the development of tomb building.

The few epigraphic remains from slab stelae in the core cemeteries show that most tombs were owned by men and only a small percentage can safely be assigned to women.[37] The sex of tomb owners is sometimes deduced not from the epigraphic traces but from the reserve heads found in the substructures (cat. nos. 46–49).[38] However, identifications made in this manner are controversial: for example, although the owner of G 1203 is beyond doubt a man named Ka-nefer, the head found in his tomb is considered by some scholars to represent his wife.[39] The identification of a head as female in a tomb owned by a male might seem to be merely a case of confusion caused by subjective misjudgment regarding the sex of the person represented if archaeological evidence did not point in another direction: two reserve heads, one male and one female, have been found in the substructures of each of two mastabas (G 4140 and G 4440),[40] indicating that both a man and a woman may have been buried in each (but see "Reserve Heads" by Catharine H. Roehrig in this catalogue)—and by extension that the head in Ka-nefer's tomb, if female, is a representation of a woman who was interred with him. This evidence suggests that perhaps women were occasionally, but not necessarily as a rule, buried with their husbands in the husband's mastaba.[41] If this was indeed the case, it would account for the small number of women's tombs found in the nucleus cemeteries.

Yet two mastabas in the Western Cemetery, G 1225 and G 4140, belonging to the titular princesses Nefret-iabet and Meret-ites,[42] demonstrate that generalizations should not be too strictly applied regarding the gender and relative importance of tomb owners and those who were buried with them. Each mastaba was augmented by an annex containing a second shaft (fig. 15e), raising questions about the ownership of these additional burial places.[43] Since women were laid to rest in the original substructures, the secondary shafts must certainly have been intended for their husbands or offspring and clearly, then, it would be rash to argue that women's burials were less important than or subordinate to those of their male counterparts.[44]

A somewhat different picture of tomb building, although quite enlightening in this matter, is offered in cemetery G 7000, to the east of Khufu's pyramid, where the royal children were buried (fig. 13).[45] In this part of the necropolis twelve mastaba cores that are larger than those in the Western Cemetery were originally erected and arranged in three rows, each of which contains four tombs.[46] Nothing is known about the initial intentions regarding the finishing of these structures or the forms of their offering places. It is obvious, however, that the cores were planned as one-shaft mastabas and had not been assigned to specific owners.[47] During the later part of Khufu's reign these twelve cores were converted into long twin mastabas (fig. 13).[48] The cores of the mastabas in the two northern rows were joined in four pairs, while each of the southern cores received an extension. In each core a recess was broken and a chapel with a false door and relief decoration was built.[49] Most of the structures were cased and received additional buildings of mud bricks.[50] These changes created more burial places, for the original twelve tombs for twelve individuals were converted into eight tombs, which, however, served as resting places for eight couples, that is, sixteen people.[51]

In the second half of the Fourth Dynasty, probably by the later part of Khafre's reign, a new type of tomb appeared at Giza. This was the rock-cut tomb,[52] which became especially popular during the second half of the Old Kingdom.[53] As the name implies, these funerary monuments are set apart by one main feature: their cult chambers are hewed vertically into the walls of abandoned quarries. From one of the upper cult chambers the burial shaft is driven down into the burial chamber below, and although both parts are completely cut into the rock, they are distinguished as superstructure and substructure. The upper section, then, is not a real superstructure like a mastaba, and, indeed, in numerous examples in the necropolis at Giza the tomb owner had a dummy mastaba (lacking the shaft leading into the burial chamber) erected atop the cliff, directly above the rock chapel.[54]

The oldest rock-cut tombs belonged to Khafre's queens and their offspring; their rock-cut chapels are considerably larger than earlier stone chapels of mastabas, for they contain at least two rooms, and these are bigger than the chambers in the mastabas that preceded them. They show a concomitant increase in wall space available for decoration[55] and were adorned in their interiors with a new type of statuary: nearly lifesize figures of the tomb owner, sometimes accompanied by smaller representations of relatives, cut into the nummulitic limestone walls of the rock chapels.[56] These figures did not replace the other statues commonly found in mastabas, either free-standing, in serdabs, or in niches closed with wood doors (see "Old Kingdom Statues in Their Architectural Setting" by Dieter Arnold in this catalogue). Rather they appeared exclusively in rock-cut monuments, representing an

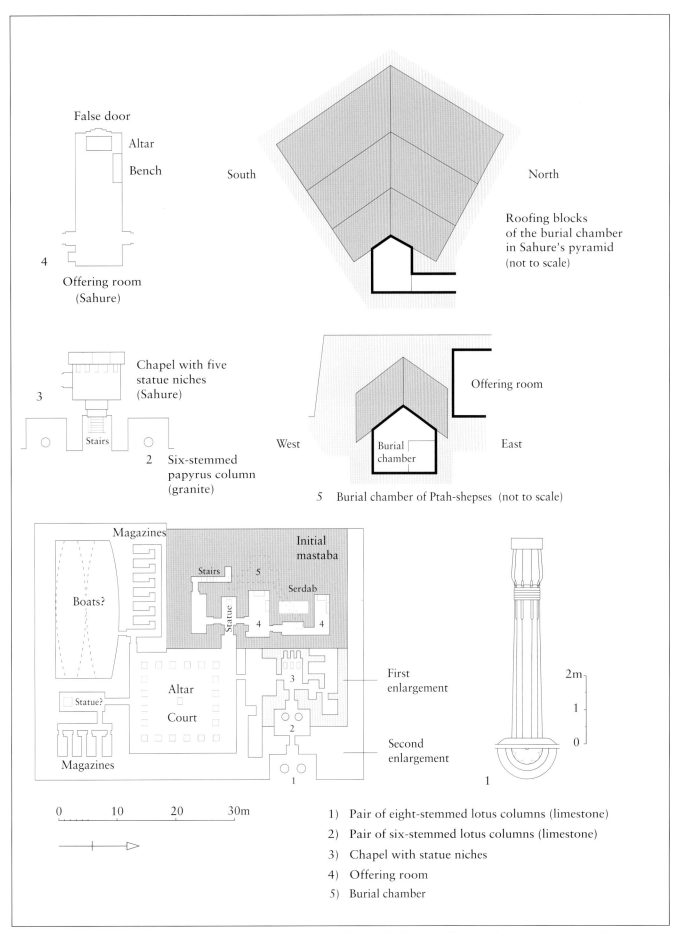

False door

Altar

Bench

South

North

4

Offering room
(Sahure)

Roofing blocks
of the burial chamber
in Sahure's pyramid
(not to scale)

Chapel with five
statue niches
(Sahure)

3

Stairs

2 Six-stemmed
papyrus column
(granite)

Offering room

West

East

Burial
chamber

5 Burial chamber of Ptah-shepses (not to scale)

Magazines

Initial
mastaba

Stairs

5

Boats?

Serdab

Statue

4

4

Statue?

Altar

Court

3

First
enlargement

2

Magazines

Second
enlargement

1

0   10   20   30m

2m

1

0

1

1) Pair of eight-stemmed lotus columns (limestone)
2) Pair of six-stemmed lotus columns (limestone)
3) Chapel with statue niches
4) Offering room
5) Burial chamber

Fig. 16. Mastaba of Ptah-shepses, Abusir. Drawing by Liza Majerus after Borchardt 1910, pl. 12; *Preliminary Report* 1976, fig. 2; Korecky 1983, figs. 285, 291, 293–95; and Verner 1994b, figs. on pp. 175, 177

addition to the repertory of sculptural depictions of the tomb owner,[57] and remained in use until the end of the Old Kingdom.[58]

In the middle of the Fifth Dynasty, during the reigns of Neferirkare and Niuserre, major changes took place in the building of private tombs. Wealthy Egyptians did not content themselves with the simple mastabas considered adequate in the previous dynasty but started to erect funerary monuments of impressive size that featured multiroomed superstructures.[59] Among the most outstanding tombs of this kind, and one that certainly marks a turning point in tomb building, is the funerary complex of Ptah-shepses at Abusir (fig. 16). His tomb is the largest private funerary monument built in the Old Kingdom and also a nonroyal structure that displays architectonic features derived from royal pyramid complexes. As Overseer of All Construction Projects and married to a daughter of King Niuserre, Ptah-shepses had a remarkable career, to which the growth of his tomb attests. His monument was originally the usual mastaba consisting of the few rooms necessary for the mortuary cult and a burial chamber (fig. 16).[60] However, in the course of the second and third building stages the initial mastaba was enhanced with a structure to the east containing a chapel with three niches for statues and additional rooms. Access to this complex was provided by a portico with two six-stemmed lotus columns made of high-quality limestone. This entrance soon fell into disuse, when the second enlargement was executed and a new and larger one was constructed farther to the east. The new portico was equipped with a pair of eight-stemmed lotus columns, also of fine limestone, reaching a height of 6 meters. A courtyard with twenty pillars and a complex of rooms were built to the south, and added to the southwest were a set of magazine rooms as well as a unique large boat-shaped room that probably housed two large wood boats.[61] In its final form the vast monument attained a size of 80 by 107 meters (whereas the grand tomb complex of Mereruka from the Sixth Dynasty [fig. 17] measures a mere 48 by 81 meters). The rooms were adorned with numerous colored reliefs depicting a variety of scenes, only a small portion of which remain in place,[62] and numerous statues of different sizes and materials were set up throughout the structure.[63]

Ptah-shepses' complex without doubt inspired other tomb owners to build similar elaborate monuments, none of which, however, succeeded in surpassing his impressive example. Thus the architectural features of Ptah-shepses' tomb are significant and merit discussion both because many reflect royal prototypes and because

a number were adopted by various private tomb owners for generations to come. Even the initial mastaba shows details that imitate or at least paraphrase features of royal buildings. The room to the south with a staircase leading to the roof of the monument, for example, follows models from the valley and pyramid temples and, moreover, inspired copies in numerous private tombs of later times, such as those of Nebet, Idut, Mereruka, Ka-gemni (fig. 17), Ankh-ma-hor, and Nefer-seshem-re.[64] The function of this staircase is by no means clear. One argument holds that the coffin with the mummy was dragged up the staircase to the roof, from which it was lowered into the burial chamber.[65] Since the entrance corridor or shaft into the substructure in some tombs with staircases—including those of Ptah-shepses himself and Mereruka—is situated in a special room within the superstructure, this explanation is not completely convincing and the issue remains open.

Also in Ptah-shepses' original mastaba are two large offering rooms, one to the south belonging to Ptah-shepses himself and one to the north belonging to his wife; both are oriented east-west, and each was once equipped with an altar placed in front of a huge false door in the west wall and a stone bench set up along the north wall. This kind of chamber is first observed in the pyramid temple of Sahure, the second king of the Fifth Dynasty, and prevailed in royal architecture until the Twelfth Dynasty, where it is relatively well preserved in the pyramid temple of Senwosret I at Lisht.[66] The earliest nonroyal example discovered may be the offering room in the mastaba of Persen at Saqqara (D 45), dating to the time of Sahure.[67] The type continues to appear in most of the large multiroomed mastabas of the latter part of the Fifth Dynasty and of the Sixth Dynasty and displays a standard form of decoration.[68] While the west wall is almost entirely occupied by the false door, the east wall shows scenes of butchering of meat in the lower registers and offering bearers and piles of food offerings in its upper portions. The north and south walls depict offering bearers marching toward the tomb owner, who is shown seated in front of a table and receiving their goods.[69]

The most impressive architectural feature in Ptah-shepses' tomb is without doubt the roof of the sarcophagus chamber, which, however, was certainly not visible once the mastaba was finished and is of a type that was not adopted in any of the later private tombs. A saddle roof consisting of four pairs of huge monolithic limestone blocks like those used in the royal pyramids of the Fifth and Sixth Dynasties, this element presents clear

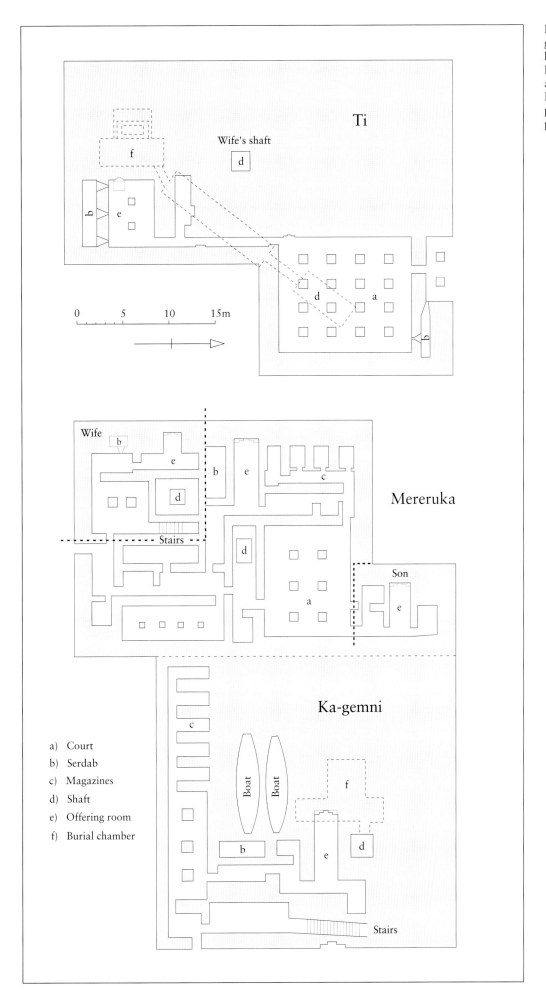

Ti

Wife's shaft

d

f

b

e

d

a

b

0   5   10   15m

Wife

b

e

b

e

c

d

Mereruka

d

Stairs

d

Son

a

e

Ka-gemni

c

a) Court
b) Serdab
c) Magazines
d) Shaft
e) Offering room
f) Burial chamber

Boat   Boat

f

b   e   d

Stairs

Fig. 17. Tombs of Ti, Ka-
gemni, and Mereruka with
his wife and son, Saqqara.
Drawing by Liza Majerus
after Bissing 1905, pl. 1;
Firth and Gunn 1926,
pl. 51; and Duell 1938,
plan opp. pl. 2

evidence that Ptah-shepses was familiar with the building techniques used in the pyramids of his era.[70]

With their pairs of limestone lotus columns, the entrance porticoes of the second and third building stages of Ptah-shepses' complex are even more exceptional than the roof of his sarcophagus chamber. Indeed the columns are a unique invention, unparalleled in both earlier and later monuments. Although kings employed columns made of granite in their pyramid temples during the Fifth Dynasty, they were either papyriform (those of Niuserre) or, more often, palmiform (those of Sahure, Djedkare-Isesi, and Unis), whereas any lotus examples that appeared in their buildings were wood.[71] Only sporadically were stone columns used in porticoes of later mastabas,[72] and these never display a specific type of plant[73] but rather show the simple and undecorated stem column that was introduced in the side entrances to Sahure's pyramid complex.[74]

A chapel with three niches, which is placed on a level higher than other chambers in the superstructure and reached by small staircases, was one of the most important places of worship in Ptah-shepses' tomb.[75] Lifesize statues representing Ptah-shepses must have been put in these niches, hidden behind the narrow two-leaved wood doors that fronted them.[76] Ptah-shepses found royal precedents for this type of chapel. In royal precincts five niches became the norm for kings, at the very beginning of the Fifth Dynasty, in the pyramid temple of Userkaf, marking the west end of the outer temple (see "Pyramids and Their Temples" by Audran Labrousse in this catalogue).[77] Such chapels with three niches seem to have been the standard in the pyramid temples of queens in the Sixth Dynasty[78] but only very rarely were incorporated in mastabas.[79]

Ptah-shepses' pillared courtyard, which measures 18.4 by 17.6 meters, must be regarded as a copy of earlier royal examples, which date from the Fourth Dynasty through the time of Userkaf. At Abusir the kings adorned their pyramid courts with columns. Pillared courts are also a typical feature of pyramid temples belonging to queens of the Fifth and Sixth Dynasties.[80] They remain important—although in much smaller form—in large private tombs, such as those of Ti, Ptah-hotep I, Akhti-hotep, Ka-gemni, Mereruka, and Khentika-Ikhekhi (fig. 17), until the middle of the Sixth Dynasty; they reappear, moreover, at the beginning of the Twelfth Dynasty in the small tombs of Ihy and Hetep at Saqqara.[81]

We know that the walls of Ptah-shepses' court were once decorated with reliefs but not whether statues of him were set up there as well. The existence of a huge altar[82] in this impressive place indicates its function as the area in which offerings were presented and ritually cleaned before they were used in the mortuary cult.[83]

The many magazine rooms and their arrangement, set symmetrically along one side of a narrow corridor, are also clearly inspired by the model of royal pyramid temples, for such complexes did not exist in earlier private tombs, where only one or two chambers, if any, served as storerooms. Multiroomed magazine complexes are found in numerous mastabas of the second half of the Fifth Dynasty and of the entire Sixth Dynasty, some of which—for example, the tombs of Mereruka and Khentika-Ikhekhi and the queens Nebet and Khenut—contained rooms with two floor levels.[84]

Multiroomed mastabas following the model of Ptah-shepses' monument—albeit in much smaller versions—became the prevalent form of funerary architecture for the upper class, while simpler tombs continued to serve individuals with fewer economic resources. None of the large mastabas are precisely alike, but all display more or less similar elements: entrance porticoes, pillared halls, complexes of magazines, serdabs, niches for statues, the east-west–oriented offering room with a huge false door. All share an increase in the number of rooms and, consequently, an increase in the wall space available for decoration, one of the main features that distinguish them from the tombs of previous periods. The massive mastaba above the substructure of earlier days was transformed into a superstructure that is a multiroomed cult complex in which hardly any solid masonry remains, as exemplified, for instance, in the tombs of Mereruka and Ka-gemni.

These architectural changes are reflections of a gradual development of funerary practices and the concept of the afterworld. The tomb in its new form was no longer regarded as a house of the dead but had instead become a monument or temple for the veneration of the deceased. The inclusion in the superstructure of an increasing number of reliefs and inscriptions—the latter stressing the tomb owner's deeds and personal achievements[85]—and the growing use of statues set up to confront the visitor (fig. 16) indicate that the offering room with the false door was now a secondary feature. How strong was the shift of meaning and priorities within the tomb complex is also revealed by a significant invention: the decorated burial chamber, which appeared at the very end of the Fifth Dynasty or, more likely, at the beginning of the Sixth.[86] Indeed, the subjects treated in these decorations are lists and depictions of offerings, demonstrating that the deceased's welfare in the afterlife had become a concern centered in the burial chamber rather than in the superstructure. Thus, two threads are discernible in the development of the multiroomed tombs of the later Old Kingdom: the first, and probably the more important, being the transformation of the superstructure into the locus of worship of the deceased as a venerable person, and the second the confinement to the offering room and the sarcophagus chamber of the mortuary cult and provisioning for the dead in the afterlife.

1. The Arabic term *mastaba*, or "bench," was applied by Egyptians to the rectangular benchlike form of the superstructure of these Old Kingdom tombs. In modern Egyptological usage the word commonly denotes the entire tomb, that is, both the substructure and the superstructure, although it correctly refers only to the upper part. That the narrower meaning is appropriate is borne out by the existence of numerous tombs that consist of a rock-cut chapel, a subterranean burial place, and a mastaba added as a superstructure on top of the rock-cut chapel (see p. 32 of this essay), indicating that it was considered a distinct, separate entity.

2. The tomb of Ruabu (QS 2302), for example, consists of twenty-seven rooms, among which a bedroom, a bathroom, and a lavatory can clearly be distinguished (Quibell 1923, pp. 11f., pl. 30). On the idea of living in the tomb, see Scharff 1947; and Bolshakov 1997, pp. 28ff.

3. Kaiser 1982, pp. 256ff., fig. 13; Kaiser 1985, pp. 25–38.

4. Quibell 1913.

5. Wood 1978, pp. 9–24.

6. The building stages of this tomb are still insufficiently investigated and documented. Because Hesi-re's monument is unique in the context of the few other known mastabas of the late Third Dynasty, it is difficult to make a clear presentation of tomb development in this epoch based on its example.

7. Reisner 1942, pp. 5f.

8. See Reisner 1936, pp. 184ff., 219ff.; Saad 1947; Saad 1951; Wood 1987, pp. 59–77; and D. Arnold 1994, pp. 246f.

9. Petrie 1892, pp. 11–20, pls. 1, 6, 7; Petrie, Mackay, and Wainwright, 1910, pp. 3–5, pls. 10, 12, 20/4–6; Reisner 1936, pp. 206ff., 234f.

10. Stadelmann et al. 1993, pp. 268–90; Alexanian 1995, pp. 1–18.

11. Alexanian in Stadelmann et al. 1993, pp. 278–81, fig. 12; Alexanian 1995, pp. 3ff., fig. 1.

12. The name derives from a suburb of Cairo located about eight miles to the east of the pyramids. For the area enclosing the pyramids and tombs, see Zivie 1974, pp. 53ff.; and Zivie 1976, pp. 1f., 15 n. 2.

13. Reisner (1942, pp. 13f., 66ff.) numbered these initial cemeteries G 1200, G 2100, G 4000, and G 7000 and called them "nucleus cemeteries," since they form the oldest parts of the necropolis.

14. Junker 1929, pp. 82ff.; Reisner 1942, pp. 56ff., 61ff.

15. Reisner and Fisher 1914, pp. 232ff.; Junker 1929, pp. 14ff., 75ff., 82ff.; Reisner 1942, pp. 39ff., 177f.

16. Only seventeen of the sixty-three mastabas in the Western Cemetery had casings, and many of these were left unfinished. Six of the eight huge twin mastabas in the Eastern Cemetery were cased. In many instances the casing was added after the original core of the mastaba had undergone considerable alteration and enlargement (see text below); thus, it is necessary to distinguish between the time the casing was executed and the time the core was erected.

17. Reisner 1936, pp. 262–78.

18. Bárta 1998, pp. 65–75.

19. Junker 1929, pp. 47f., 96 (tombs G 4150, G 4160, G 4360, G 4450, G 4560).

20. See the tomb of Ra-wer in the Central Field at Giza (no number) from the Fifth Dynasty (Hassan 1932, p. 30).

21. Although most reserve heads have been found in burial chambers and shafts, the original position of these superb works of art is still a matter of debate. Lacovara (1997, pp. 28–36) correctly questions Junker's theory (1929, pp. 57–61, pl. 10) that they were placed in the horizontal passage between the bottom of the shaft and the burial chamber.

22. Junker 1929, pp. 17, 36f.; Reisner 1942, pp. 64, 79. Smith (1949, p. 159) remarks that they were "given to certain persons for the decoration of their mastabas by the king as a mark of royal favour."

23. Barta 1963, pp. 41ff., 56; Der Manuelian 1998a, pp. 115–34.

24. A similar situation existed in the royal pyramid complexes: as soon as the king was buried, the parts of the monument needed for establishing the royal mortuary cult and guaranteeing the sovereign's afterlife were constructed, often with poor materials (wood and mud bricks), while the rest remained unfinished. No pyramid of the Old Kingdom is known to have been completed by a ruler's successor as initially intended.

25. Although Junker (1928, pp. 9ff.; 1929, pp. 14, 35, 75ff.; 1955, pp. 31ff.) always understood that these tombs should have been given casings and false doors, he explained that their seemingly unfinished state was the form of the private funerary monument intended during the reign of Khufu. He designated this type of mastaba the "normal mastaba" (*Normalmastaba*) and regarded every change and addition in the architecture of the prototype as a deviation from the original concept. Haeny (1971, pp. 153–59) has shown, however, that Junker's reconstruction of the *Normalmastaba* is not sustained by the archaeological evidence. For the most recent treatment of this question in connection with the slab stelae, see Der Manuelian 1998a.

26. Reisner and Fisher 1914, pp. 234f.; Reisner 1942, p. 427, fig. 243.

27. G 4150 (Iunu): Junker 1929, p. 173, pl. 26; Junker 1955, p. 53; G 1201 (Wep-em-nefret), G 1223 (Ka-em-ah), and G 1225 (Nefret-iabet): Reisner and Fisher 1914, pp. 234f.; Reisner 1942, pp. 64, 385f., 399, 403, pl. 11b–d. Some Egyptologists believe that the slab stelae were hidden in response to an order by the king that curtailed or forbade the practice of any funerary cult by private individuals (Shoukry 1951, pp. 31ff.; Helck 1981, p. 54; Helck 1986, p. 20). That a number of private tombs had casings, false doors, and stone chapels added to them clearly shows that this explanation is incorrect and that there could not have been any such royal order. Concerning private sculpture under Khufu, see Russmann 1995b, p. 118.

28. G 2130, G 2140, G 2150, G 4710, G 5010, G II S, G III S, G VI S.

29. Reisner 1942, p. 72. In some tombs, such as that of Seshemnefer III (G 5170), sufficient superstructure was removed to allow the erection not only of an offering place but also of other cult chambers. See Junker 1938, p. 193, fig. 36.

30. Reisner 1942, pp. 69f., 81f.

31. Ibid., pp. 422f., fig. 109. Similar reconstructions can be found in the tombs of Akhi (G 4750; Junker 1929, pp. 234ff., fig. 55)

and of Snefru-seneb (G 4240; Reisner 1942, p. 465, fig. 110, map of cemetery 4000).

32. Tomb G 2155 = G 4780; see Junker 1934, pp. 138ff., fig. 12; and Reisner 1942, pp. 446f.

33. See G 1201 and G 2210, both left unfinished, and G 1201, completed in mud bricks (Reisner 1942, pp. 385f., 433).

34. Junker 1929, pp. 132ff., figs. 18–20, pls. 15, 16, 18.

35. One of the few early exceptions is the mastaba of Hemiunu (G 4000), with two substructures, the southern one of which was excavated later and left unfinished (ibid., pp. 141–45, fig. 18).

36. G 1223, G 1225, G 1227, G 1233, G 4140, G 4150. In all cases the addition was built on the north side of the mastaba.

37. Of the sixty-three mastabas in the nucleus cemeteries only eight can be assigned to women, while twenty-six clearly belonged to men. The inequality is obvious even though the considerable number of remaining tombs cannot be taken into account, as they are anonymous (either because they were never occupied or because the names of their owners are lost). Moreover, only about 15 percent of false doors executed throughout the entire Old Kingdom are known to have belonged exclusively to women. See Wiebach 1981, pp. 227, 255, n. 200.

38. Tefnin 1991, pp. 41–52, 97–129.

39. Smith 1949, p. 26 (21), pl. 9b. There is also uncertainty regarding the sex of the individuals represented in heads from G 4340, G 4350, G 4540, and G 4560; see Junker 1929, pp. 64f.; Tefnin 1991, pp. 64ff., 104, 114, 122, 127; and Junge 1995, pp. 105ff.

40. Reisner 1915, pp. 30f., figs. 5–7, 10; Reisner 1942, p. 462, pls. 46c,d, 52a,b, p. 477, pls. 49c, 54a,b.

41. Reisner and Fisher 1914, p. 240; Junker 1929, p. 38. It is possible, of course, that at least the second reserve heads in tombs G 4140 and G 4440 were placed there randomly, after they had been stolen from their original sites in other burial chambers, in which case serious doubts would be raised about the original locations of all the other heads found in burial chambers; if, however, they were left there deliberately, the only reasonable explanation for their pairing would be that they represent men and women who were buried together. Yet in no burial chamber have the fragments of more than one limestone sarcophagus been found, which indicates that second burials must have been carried out in wood coffins. Fragments of both wood and stone have been discovered in a number of burial chambers—the usual explanation for this being that the wood coffins were put inside the stone sarcophagi (Junker 1929, pp. 45, 54, 190, 233f., 247).

42. Reisner 1942, pp. 460ff., 403ff. The simple forms of the women's titles do not give any clue as to whether or not they were descendants of the king. Since no direct offspring of Khufu were buried in the Western Cemetery, it has been deduced that Nefret-iabet and Meret-ites are merely honorary princesses. See Schmitz 1976, pp. 123, 127f., 133; and Ziegler 1990b, p. 188.

43. Shaft G 1225–annex A has been completely plundered (Reisner 1942b, p. 405, fig. 230).

44. See ibid., p. 285; this assumption is refuted not only by these two tombs but also by a number of others.

45. Ibid., pp. 72ff., 80f.

46. Ibid., pp. 59, 72.

47. Ibid., pp. 52, 72. No complete slab stelae or fragments thereof were found in this part of the necropolis.

48. Ibid., pp. 72f., 80f., 296.

49. These were of the so-called L-shaped chapel type, which became standard at Giza during the Fourth Dynasty (ibid.,

pp. 183, 187–211), whereas the so-called cruciform chapels were prevalent at Saqqara into the Fifth Dynasty (ibid., pp. 302ff.).

50. The casing was not executed or was left unfinished on the three eastern mastabas in the southern row (ibid., pp. 72f.).

51. The two shafts of the mastabas in the southern row are both in the original cores rather than in the extensions. Thus the original cores are of the two-shaft type but in their finished form are twin mastabas, for example, G 7130/40 (ibid., pp. 54, 298). The twin mastaba was not an invention of the Fourth Dynasty but was introduced in the Third Dynasty with the clear intention of joining the burial places of a man and a woman under one superstructure. Third Dynasty tombs of this type are found mainly at Saqqara and also in Nag el-Deir and Beit Khallaf (Reisner 1936, pp. 285ff.). The tombs of Kha-bau-sokar and Hathor-nefer-hotep (FS 3073) at Saqqara and of Nefer-maat and Itet (M 16) at Meidum, in which the relationship between husband and wife is corroborated by inscriptions, are the most famous (the other known examples are anonymous).

52. Reisner (1942, p. 219) and Smith (1949, p. 166) dated the first appearance of the earliest rock-cut tombs to the reign of Menkaure; however, their findings must be corrected in view of the fact that certain Khafre's queens and sons owned some of these monuments.

53. Reisner 1942, pp. 219–47, 300f. The most important sites with large rock-cut tombs are located in the provinces and date to the later part of the Old Kingdom: see Brunner 1936; Steckeweh 1936; Vandier 1954, pp. 293ff.; Kanawati 1980–92; El-Khouli and Kanawati 1989; El-Khouli and Kanawati 1990; Kanawati 1993; and Kanawati and McFarlane 1993.

54. See Reisner 1942, p. 219, for the tombs of Khuen-re in the Menkaure quarry (MQ 1), Mer-si-ankh III in cemetery 7000 (G 7530/40), and Rekhetre in the Central Field (no number).

55. Ibid., pp. 247, 300f., 346–70; Harpur 1987, pp. 104–6.

56. See the tomb of Queen Mer-si-ankh III, from the time of Shepseskaf (Dunham and Simpson 1974, pls. 6, 8, 9a,b, 11b–d) and the late Fifth Dynasty tomb of Ka-kher-ptah (Kendall 1981).

57. Brunner 1936, pp. 16f.; Hassan 1944, pp. 45–50; Shoukry 1951, pp. 238–55; Rzepka 1995, pp. 227–36.

58. Shoukry 1951, pp. 248–55.

59. Harpur 1987, pp. 106f.

60. For similar types of mastabas at Abusir, see Borchardt 1907, pp. 25–32, 109–34.

61. Verner 1992a, pp. 58ff.; Verner 1992b, pp. 599f. A similar although smaller installation for boats is encountered in the tomb of Ka-gemni at Saqqara (fig. 17; Firth and Gunn 1926, p. 21, pl. 51).

62. Verner 1986a. The number of fragments no longer in situ is estimated at about ten thousand (Rochholz 1994b, p. 261, n. 10). Concerning some of the scenes depicted, see Vachala 1992, pp. 109–11; Vachala 1995, pp. 105–8; and Vachala and Faltings 1995, pp. 281–86.

63. It is estimated that about forty sculptures made of limestone, calcite (Egyptian alabaster), quartzite, granite, gneiss, and basalt were once present; see Rochholz 1994b, pp. 259–73; Verner 1994a, p. 187; and Patocková 1998, pp. 227–33. The number may seem high but it is not entirely unprecedented, for as early as the Fourth Dynasty some tombs were equipped with large quantities of sculpture: see, for instance, the tomb of Kawab in cemetery 7000 (G 7110/20, time of Khufu), which probably housed ten to twenty statues (Simpson 1978, p. 7) and the tomb complex of Ba-baef in the Western Cemetery

(G 5230, end of Fourth Dynasty), where between thirty and fifty sculptures are estimated to have been installed (see cat. no. 87; Smith 1949, pp. 46, 50). In the large late Fourth or Fifth Dynasty mortuary complex of Ra-wer at Giza twenty-five serdabs and twenty statue niches were built (Hassan 1932, pp. 1, 4–38; Porter and Moss 1974, pp. 267ff.).

64. See, for instance, Munro 1993, pp. 43f., 82f., foldout 2; Macramallah 1935, pls. 2, 3.

65. Badawy 1978, p. 12.

66. D. Arnold 1988, pp. 48f., pls. 75, 105, foldouts 1, 2; Jánosi 1994, pp. 143–63.

67. H. Petrie and Murray 1952, p. 9, pl. 19 (4); Strudwick 1985, p. 30; Harpur 1987, p. 107, fig. 99.

68. Harpur 1987, pp. 107f.

69. See, for example, James 1953, pls. 18–22.

70. Fiala in *Preliminary Report* 1976, p. 53, figs. 16, 17; Verner 1994a, p. 177, ill. For the royal examples, see D. Arnold 1991, pp. 191ff.; and Labrousse 1996, pp. 94ff., figs. 56, 57, 71, 78, pls. 8, 9.

71. Lotus columns made of wood were set up in the court of Neferirkare's mortuary precinct to finish the complex quickly after the king died, and it can perhaps be surmised that stone lotus columns were originally intended (Borchardt 1909, p. 21, figs. 16–18). Six-stemmed lotus columns of wood were also employed in the pyramid temple of Neferefre (Verner et al. 1990, p. 36).

72. Only stone pillars were used in the courts of mastabas.

73. See the tombs of Senedjem-ib Inti (Reisner 1942, fig. 162) and Seshem-nefer IV (Junker 1953, p. 101, figs. 49, 50, pl. 11).

74. The royal type shows the titles and names of Sahure (Borchardt 1910, pp. 9f., 24f., 35, figs. 5, 20, 28, 79, 81, pls. 3, 8).

75. Verner in *Preliminary Report* 1976, pp. 64ff., fig. 28; Verner 1986a, pls. 29, 76.

76. Verner 1994a, pp. 181f. According to the Abusir papyri, statues representing the seated king were set up in the five chapels in pyramid temples (Rochholz 1994b, p. 262).

77. Borchardt 1910, pp. 12, 20f.; Ricke 1950, pp. 35f., 70; Leclant 1979b, p. 359; D. Arnold 1997, pp. 63–72, figs. 21–24.

78. Jánosi 1996, pp. 145–49. An exceptional shrine with four chapels was built in the mastaba tomb of Queen Nebet (wife of Unis); see Munro 1993, pp. 31, 34, pls. 4, 6, foldout 2.

79. They appear, for example, in the mastaba of Ankh-ma-re (D 40) at Saqqara (end of Fifth Dynasty; Mariette and Maspero 1885, pp. 280ff.), the tomb of Ra-shepses (LS 16/S 902) at Saqqara (time of Djedkare-Isesi; Naville 1897–1913, vol. 1 [1897], p. 166), and the rock-cut tomb of Tjauti (No. 2) at Qasr el-Said (late Sixth Dynasty; Brunner 1936, p. 46, fig. 24).

80. Jánosi 1996, pp. 150–53.

81. Firth and Gunn 1926, pp. 61–65, fig. 72.

82. Verner 1994a, p. 187.

83. The royal courtyards also feature an altar of the king that served similar purposes; see D. Arnold 1977, pp. 7f.; D. Arnold 1988, p. 44; and Málek 1988, pp. 23–34.

84. Munro 1993, p. 31, pl. 4, foldout 2; James 1953, pp. 27, 29, pl. 3.

85. Assmann 1991, pp. 169–99.

86. Concerning the dates of the tombs with decorated burial chambers, see Junker 1940, pp. 2, 4; and Lapp 1993, pp. 10ff., § 25 (Saqqara), pp. 29ff., § 89–91 (Giza), p. 36, § 104. A list of decorated burial chambers is offered by Bolshakov (1997, pp. 116f.).

OLD KINGDOM STATUES IN THEIR ARCHITECTURAL SETTING

DIETER ARNOLD

Rarely conceived as an integral part of architecture, Old Kingdom statuary had a powerful but secluded existence. Statues were considered to be repositories for the living ka, the actual life force of gods, kings, and human beings. The ka of these entities could inhabit any number of statues at one time.[1] The statues were powerful and dangerous but also vulnerable and dependent on ritual treatment for survival. They needed, first of all, protection from climatic and human damage and were therefore sheltered, with the degree of seclusion and the kind of housing varying considerably. But statues—especially those representing the king—were also the recipients of complex rituals[2] and for that reason needed to be accessible to the officiating priests. The standard emplacement of such images was a wood or stone naos with wood doors. Early examples of images receiving a daily cult are known from the statue-cult temple of Snefru at Dahshur (fig. 48).[3] This temple housed a row of six chapels built against its rear wall; each contained a statue of the ruler, expressing an aspect of Egyptian kingship. A more advanced version of such multiple statue-shrines appeared later in the pyramid temples of the Fifth and Sixth Dynasties, where five shrines were set up at the entrance to the rear part of the temple to accommodate royal cult figures (fig. 57). These statue shrines sat on a flat platform and had wood doors.

The Fourth Dynasty pyramid temple of King Khafre had a different arrangement of chapels. A row of five chapels, each of which measured 10.5 meters deep and 1.5 meters wide, was placed behind the temple court. The narrow elongated shape of the chapels suggests that they housed wood boats that carried royal images and were

similar to the divine ships in New Kingdom and Late Period temples.[4]

Some nonroyal statue-cult shrines in Old Kingdom tombs were apparently imitations of the royal prototypes. A statue-cult temple was added to the original structure of the mastaba of Ptah-shepses at Abusir (time of Niuserre) (fig. 16).[5] It contained a row of three shrines raised on a platform. This private statue-cult temple clearly reflected the multiple-shrine disposition of a divine or royal temple.[6]

An example of a statue niche is found in the north wall of the pillared hall of Mereruka's mastaba at Saqqara (time of Teti) (fig. 17). Four steps lead to an altar behind which the statue niche opens 1.20 meters aboveground (fig. 18). The majestic lifesize statue of Mereruka steps forward from the niche, ready to reenter life.[7]

In addition to the cult images in chapels, Old Kingdom royal temples housed large numbers of freestanding statues and statue groups. The valley temple of Khafre contains a monumental pillared hall on a T-shaped ground plan.[8] There twenty-three lifesize seated figures of the king were arranged along the interior walls in groups of three, seven, three, seven, and three (fig. 19). Many smaller figures of the king were placed among them. It is not known whether the valley temple was built to accommodate these statues or whether it was a multipurpose structure, which housed the statues but also had other functions. The use of the valley temple as the royal embalming place has been disputed.[9]

The valley temple of Menkaure at Giza would also have contained a great number of statues, but it remained unfinished (figs. 85, 86). Some of the statues (cat. nos. 67, 68) were delivered and stored in the

Fig. 18. Statue niche, mastaba of Mereruka, Saqqara

Fig. 19. Reconstruction of interior, valley temple of Khafre, Giza. From Hölscher 1912 (pl. 5)

unfinished building.[10] These works included many types of royal statues, six or more being triads (cat. no. 68), which showed the king with the goddess Hathor and a representative deity of Upper Egyptian nomes.[11] Nothing is known about the intended emplacement of these statues.[12]

The statues of the king in the valley temple of Khafre might have been participants in specific royal rituals.[13] The Menkaure triads appear to have evoked a primordial historic-religious situation. The figure of Hathor accompanying the king in these groups probably plays the part of the royal mother guaranteeing the rebirth of the king. The nome deities recall the Archaic Period idea of gatherings of all Egyptian divinities around the king as their foremost god and leader. In general, the royal-statue assemblies in the Old Kingdom temples seem to express a kind of petrified cultic action or play. Similar actors in ritual performances were later depicted in the kneeling statues of Queen Hatshepsut at Deir el-Bahri,[14] the deity statues in the Kom el-Hetan temple of Amenhotep III,[15]

and the Ramesside action groups representing, among other activities, the purification of the king.[16]

The statues of kneeling foreign captives, which were probably placed in long lines along the causeway and entrance hall walls of Old Kingdom royal pyramid temples (cat nos. 173, 174), apparently were also action figures of a similar kind. Evoking the king's power, they appear to have undergone an enemy-destruction ritual.[17]

Further interesting examples of Old Kingdom royal statuary emplacements are provided by remains in the pyramid temple and the valley temple of Khafre, the nearby Harmakhis temple, and the Great Sphinx of Giza, towering over the Harmakhis temple. It has been suggested that groups of seated over-lifesize statues of King Khafre lined the courts of the king's pyramid temple and his Harmakhis temple at Giza (figs. 20, 21).[18] These figures—twelve in the pyramid temple and ten in the Harmakhis temple—had their backs against the court walls. Entrances between the statues created the impression of pillared porticoes (fig. 20). The existence

Fig. 20. Reconstruction of court, pyramid temple of Khafre, Giza. From Ricke 1950 (pl. 2)

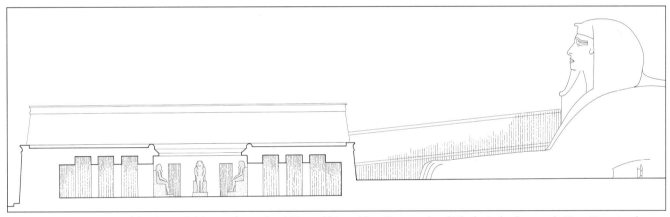

Fig. 21. Reconstruction of the Great Sphinx and temple of Harmakhis, with valley temple of Khafre in background, Giza. Drawing by Dieter Arnold after Ricke 1970, plan 4

of such statues has been deduced from the rectangular pits found in front of the wall pillars, for no fragments of them were found. In the pyramid temple court they would have been half-sheltered by recesses in the rear wall, while in the Harmakhis temple they would have been completely exposed. Although these statues may have received a special cult,[19] they were mainly monuments of divine kingship. In contrast to all the other statuary considered here, such pillar statues would have formed an integral part of the temple architecture, their intense presence enhancing the centralized organization of the courts.

Like these royal statues in open courts, statues of sphinxes were also exposed to the sky. Of course, the Great Sphinx, which could be seen easily from a distance,

had nothing to fear from weather or people (fig. 21). Visibility of the upper part of this sphinx may have been essential for the priests who officiated in the small open court of the Harmakhis temple in front of it. The Great Sphinx and the Harmakhis temple were architecturally separate but seem to have formed a functional unit, emphasizing the solar aspects of the divine king.

Remains suggest that two pairs of sphinxes, each eight meters long, were positioned in front of Khafre's valley temple. Their threatening presence and visibility may have been intended to deter intruders. The sphinxes certainly fulfilled a symbolic purpose, but they may also have been meant as visual enhancements of the two gates in the temple's huge plain facade. Striding royal sphinxes were depicted in relief on the walls of the causeway of

Fig. 22. Reconstruction of facade, mastaba of Seshem-nefer IV, Giza. From Junker 1953 (pl. 1)

King Sahure, suggesting an association between sculpture and relief.

In the New Kingdom, colossal statues of kings and queens were frequently erected in front of pylons. The closest Old Kingdom parallel is the arrangement of the four seated alabaster figures of Menkaure in pairs at both sides of the entrance from the court into the sanctuary of this king's valley temple.[20] The existence of other royal or divine prototypes for such emplacements is suggested by the two lifesize seated statues that flanked the sides of the entrance porch of the mastaba of Seshem-nefer IV at Giza (fig. 22).[21] The association with a temple facade is underlined by the six small obelisks found in the area around the entrance to this tomb. These obelisks may have been aligned in two rows of three along the approach through the court of the tomb. In addition, the two famous statues of Ra-nefer from Saqqara[22] appear to have stood opposite the entrance of a cult chamber.[23] Such remains clearly indicate that publicly accessible statues of kings and officials were not entirely unknown during the Old Kingdom.

Only rare examples of statues of private persons from Old Kingdom temples of deities are preserved.[24] The vast majority of nonroyal statues were found in tombs. After death the ka of the individual was released to live in the tomb or to inhabit the tomb statue. The ka was summoned to receive the invigorating funerary repast either at the tomb's false door or in front of a statue.[25] Most often, the statue of the deceased was enclosed in an inaccessible room, the serdab (from an Arabic word meaning a closed, cellarlike hiding place).[26] Ideally the serdab's location would have been kept secret to ensure the statue's safety. In such a hidden place the statue could not enjoy actual contact with the priest and could not directly receive the kind of daily offerings that were presented to the statues of gods and kings. As a compromise, small window slots often connected the serdab with the cult chamber; if the serdab was situated behind the false door, a horizontal window slot beneath the door frequently allowed better contact. In the Third Dynasty, however, mastabas were still built without serdabs, and only during the reigns of the early Fourth Dynasty kings Snefru and Khufu were existing mastabas modified to include statue chambers. Prince Hemiunu's monumental mastaba at Giza (fig. 15a), for example, was originally built without a serdab, but two limestone chambers were

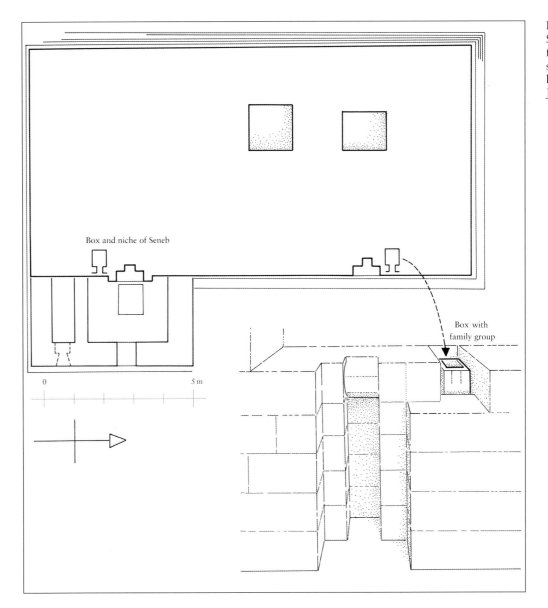

Fig. 23. Plan of mastaba of
Seneb and view of northern
false door of Senet-ites, with
serdab niche, Giza. Drawing
by Dieter Arnold after
Junker 1941, fig. 2

Box and niche of Seneb

0   5 m

Box with
family group

later inserted into the front of the monument to accommodate his statues. The famous seated figure of Hemiunu (cat. no. 44) was found in the northern niche (fig. 15b); the southern niche was empty at the time of excavation.[27]

The well-known seated limestone figures of Prince Rahotep and his wife, Nofret (fig. 31), of the early Fourth Dynasty were situated in a cult chamber in the mastaba core.[28] The emplacement of these statues must have occurred before the mastaba received a second brick facing, which disguised the chamber. One may assume, therefore, that during the Third Dynasty, before the addition of special statue chambers, statues were placed in the cult chamber. Even after the introduction of separate serdabs, in a few tombs statues were still positioned in cult chambers.[29]

The most common situation, however, is represented by mastabas like that of the dwarf Seneb at Giza, which probably dates from the Fourth Dynasty (fig. 23).[30] Secluded cavities that housed small limestone chests were located beside the two cult niches of the mastaba front. The southern chest contained a wood statuette of Seneb, the northern one the well-known family group of the dwarf and his wife, Senet-ites, and their children.[31]

During the later Fourth Dynasty and the Fifth Dynasty, growth of prosperity and concern that single statues might not survive led to an increase in the number of images produced, and thus a need for larger serdabs. Spacious serdabs in the interior of the mastaba were used to house lifesize statues such as that of Ti (fig. 38).[32]

The Fifth Dynasty mastaba of Seshem-nefer II at Giza had special installations for the statue cult.[33] Here eight chambers, each holding three or more statues, were arranged behind the south, west, and north walls of a central corridor. The corridor's south wall displays three-dimensional representations of five false doors, with all the details of wood doors depicted in stone (fig. 24). The facade of the chambers on the opposite side replicated

Fig. 24. Reconstruction of front of serdab, mastaba of Seshem-nefer II, Giza. From Junker 1938 (fig. 34)

the paneled facade of the royal palace, symbolically transforming the serdab into a small but magnificent statue temple.

Since it was difficult to integrate larger and more numerous statue chambers into the mastaba core, separate statue houses also began to be added to the exterior of the mastaba. The most striking example of this type of structure is associated with the mastaba of Ba-baef (or Khnum-baef, time of Shepseskaf).[34] Here two square statue houses of stone were erected in front of the mastaba (fig. 25). Each statue house had four parallel elongated statue chambers, communicating with a common transverse cult chamber through windows. Since the chambers had been robbed before they were excavated, the original number of statues is not known.

The insecure conditions at the end of the Old Kingdom probably encouraged tomb builders to reduce aboveground display of riches and to hide essential wall

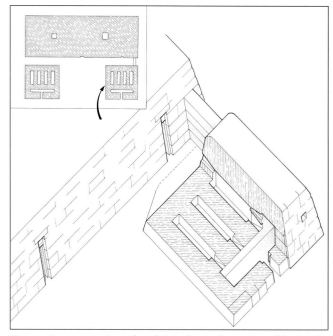

Fig. 25. Reconstruction of serdab in front of mastaba of Ba-baef, Giza. Drawing by Dieter Arnold from D. Arnold 1994 (p. 235)

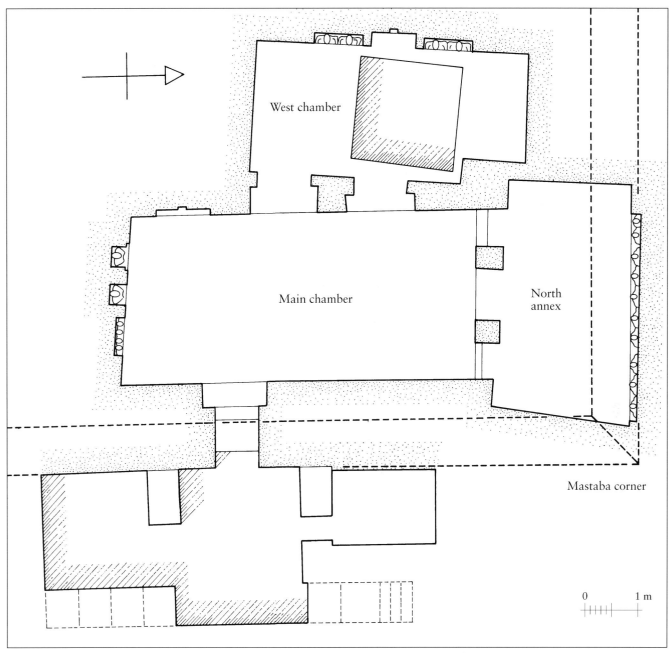

West chamber

Main chamber

North annex

Mastaba corner

0   1 m

Fig. 26. Plan of underground cult chambers of Queen Mer-si-ankh III, Giza (structures within dotted lines are above ground). Drawing by Dieter Arnold after Dunham and Simpson 1974, plans B, C

decoration and statuary underground. There are indeed numerous examples of statue niches inside or at the bottom of the shaft. In some tombs, a statue was even placed in the burial chamber.[35] This practice has an interesting antecedent in the so-called reserve heads of the Fourth Dynasty (cat. nos. 46–49): none of these heads was discovered in situ, but the large number of them found in shafts or burial chambers makes an original underground location very probable (see "Reserve Heads" by Catharine H. Roehrig in this catalogue, pp. 74–75).[36]

Thus nonroyal tomb statues of the Old Kingdom were usually, although not exclusively, hidden behind walls or placed in the tomb shaft. In some cases images of the tomb owner appeared in the cult chamber or cult corridor, where they were accessible to family members and priests. Such statues in cult chambers were not completely free-standing: they protruded in three-quarter relief from the masonry of a wall or, more frequently, from the bedrock from which they were chiseled. Not hidden in a serdab, this eye-catching statuary was certainly part of the architectural design of the tomb, serving to intensify the magical life of the surrounding relief decoration.

The most extensive examples of this type of statue are found at Giza in the mastaba of the granddaughter

Fig. 27. Wall of funerary chapel, with engaged statues, tomb of Iru-ka-ptah, Saqqara

of King Khufu, Mer-si-ankh III (time of Shepseskaf) (fig. 26).[37] On the southern wall of the mastaba's main chamber two male scribes, each squatting in a flat niche, and four scribes in a group have been chiseled from the bedrock. To the north a portico opens into a smaller haremlike annex that houses a group of ten standing female figures. This gathering of female members of the royal household and their officials is a unique and as yet unexplained feature. The attached rock-cut west chamber displays, in two separate groups, two figures of Mer-si-ankh III and two of her mother, Hetep-heres II, standing at both sides of a central false door. Similar rows of standing figures of the tomb owner appear along the walls of the cult chambers of the Sixth Dynasty tombs of Idu (G 7102) at Giza and Iru-ka-ptah at Saqqara (fig. 27). A false door niche was cut in the center of the opposite west wall of Idu's offering chamber. In the bottom half of the false door his upper body appears; seeming to rise from the ground, he extends his arms and hands to receive the offering deposited on the altar slab in front of him.[38]

Another impressive design is displayed in the small cult chamber of Khui-wer at Giza from the end of the Fifth Dynasty.[39] A strongly articulated torus-and-cavetto frame in this chamber is derived from a chapel front. The standing figure of Khui-wer appears in three-quarter relief at both sides of the central false door. And in the tomb of Iteti the deceased appears in the false door slot of a tomb wall.[40]

The emplacement of the Old Kingdom statues helps illuminate their meaning. Egyptian statues were never considered pure art, and during the Old Kingdom they were not displayed as monuments or memorials. Filled with magic life, they were participants in cultic performances, either as passive recipients of cultic ceremonies or as active sharers in cultic plays. In these capacities statues were simultaneously subordinate to the architectural framework needed for cultic performances and a main reason for the existence of the vast Old Kingdom temples and tombs, which were meant to house them.

1. Junker 1938, pp. 118–22.
2. Fairman 1954, pp. 165–203; Barta 1980, cols. 840–44.
3. That this building, which is located at the side of the causeway, was the actual valley temple is rather improbable.

4. See Landström 1970, pp. 116–21.
5. *Preliminary Report* 1976, pp. 64–68, fig. 28.
6. There are numerous examples in the pyramid temples of the Fifth and Sixth Dynasties.
7. Duell 1938, vol. 2, pls. 123, 147–48.
8. Hölscher 1912, pp. 89–104; Krauspe 1997b, pp. 13–40, 118–21, 126–27.
9. Compare the old interpretation by Ricke (1950, pp. 86–102) with that of Stadelmann (1985b, cols. 189–93).
10. See Reisner 1931, pp. 108–29.
11. Upper Egypt had twenty-two nomes. Each nome would ideally have been represented by its main deity.
12. Seidel (1996, pp. 25–49) convincingly refutes the reconstruction by Wood (1974, pp. 82–93), which includes only eight triads in the front rooms of the temple.
13. Ricke (1950, pp. 96–99, 178–80) developed the fascinating theory that the two groups of three statues in the transverse section of the T-shaped arrangement took part in a ritualistic mummification, while those in the longitudinal hall played a role in the Opening of the Mouth ceremonies. Seidel's more recent interpretation (1996, p. 24)—that the pillared hall was dedicated to the deified king, guaranteeing him command over the two countries in the other world—remains rather ambiguous.
14. See Hayes 1959, pp. 89–101, fig. 53.
15. See Haeny 1981, pp. 56–61.
16. See the list in Altenmüller 1980b, cols. 575–77.
17. Lauer and Leclant 1970, pp. 55–62, figs. 1–6, pls. 8–10.
18. Hölscher 1912, pp. 27–28, fig. 16; Ricke 1950, p. 52, pl. 2; Ricke 1970, pp. 12, 25, plans 3, 4.
19. Schott (1970, p. 70) assumes that the solar cult in the Harmakhis temple required twelve statues representing the months of the year.
20. Reisner 1931, pp. 108–15, pls. 36–64.
21. Junker 1953, p. 110 (51a), pl. 1. There are similar remains at a mastaba east of this tomb in Reisner's cemetery 7000.
22. Egyptian Museum, Cairo (CG 18, 19); Saleh and Sourouzian 1987, nos. 45, 46.
23. Lange and Hirmer 1961, pls. 61–65; see also Mariette and Maspero 1889, p. 122.

24. The kneeling attitude of the figure of a priest or king of the Third Dynasty from Mitrahina (Egyptian Museum, Cairo, CG 1) may lead us to expect that this statue was dedicated to a temple (Saleh and Sourouzian 1987, no. 22).
25. From the beginning of the Fifth Dynasty forward, kings received a mortuary offering that required architectural installations similar to those of private tombs—for example, a false door.
26. Junker 1938, pp. 118–22.
27. Junker 1929, pp. 134–38, figs. 19, 20, pls. 16, 18.
28. It is impossible to reconstruct the exact position of the statues because the reports on the discovery by Mariette and Daninos in 1871 are superficial and no photographs were taken; see Daninos 1886, pp. 69–73.
29. Junker 1941, p. 146; Junker 1955, p. 54.
30. Junker 1941, pp. 3–124; Cherpion 1984.
31. Egyptian Museum, Cairo (JE 51280). A chamber with a second serdab was later added to the front of the southern cult niche.
32. Egyptian Museum, Cairo (JE 10065; Saleh and Sourouzian 1987, no. 49).
33. Junker 1938, pp. 189–91, figs. 33–35. Seshem-nefer III also added a huge serdab house to his mastaba; the new installation was accessible from the pillared antechamber of the main tomb; see ibid., 1938, p. 194, fig. 36, p. 199.
34. G 5230; see Lepsius 1849–58, vol. 1, p. 24; Reisner 1942, pp. 248–50; and Junker 1944, pp. 151–55.
35. Firth and Gunn 1926, vol. 1, pp. 41–42, fig. 47; Junker 1941, p. 180; Junker 1944, pp. 85, 125, pl. 17a; Junker 1947, p. 140; and Junker 1950, p. 24.
36. Junker 1929, pp. 57, 60, pls. 9, 10; Junker 1955, p. 55. Junker reconstructed a small niche in the blocking of the crypt, which he believed held the reserve heads. This theory has been refuted. (See "Reserve Heads" by Catharine H. Roehrig in this catalogue, n. 21.)
37. Dunham and Simpson 1974, plan C, pls. 6, 8, 9, 11.
38. Simpson 1976, pls. 6b, 11a. The statue in the tomb of Qar (G 7101) at Giza is similar. See ibid., pls. 21–23.
39. Lepsius 1849–58, vol. 1, pl. 44 (tomb LG 95).
40. Lange and Hirmer 1961, pl. 73.

ROYAL STATUARY

KRZYSZTOF GRZYMSKI

S tatues of Egyptian rulers form a unique category, separate from that of the members of the royal family, nobles, and ordinary human beings. When admiring the superior workmanship and artistry of Old Kingdom royal statuary, we must keep in mind that Egyptian art was not made for purely aesthetic purposes but was in fact primarily functional. The royal statues had a specific role: to make manifest the position of the ruler in Egyptian society. The king was the key element of the society, not because of the political power of his office but because of his centrality to Egyptian ideology and religion. Without a king there would be no society to speak of, no state, no order; there would be only chaos. Any Old Kingdom pharaoh could state "l'État, c'est moi" with far more justification than Louis XIV.

The exact nature of the king and kingship in Egypt is an often-discussed issue. While some scholars stress the divine character of Egyptian kingship, others emphasize its human aspect.[1] There are few literary sources that give an Egyptian account of the character of kingship. Thus, scholars attempt to define Egyptian kingship through study of royal iconography, whether in sculpture, painting, or relief, with literary and religious texts providing some elucidation of symbolism and conventions. At the very least the king had a semidivine, superhuman status and acted as an intermediary between the gods and humankind. One is tempted to see the royal statue serving the same cultic function as did any other statue of a divinity. However, among the preserved Old Kingdom sculptures royal statues outnumber statues of gods by a wide margin. Moreover, most of the known royal statuary comes from mortuary temples and is therefore an expression of the cult of the deceased king and not of the living ruler. In this context it is often not clear whether a royal statue depicts a divine king, the embodiment of Osiris, ruler of the netherworld, or whether it simply represents the king's ka.[2]

Whatever the relationship between the divine and human aspects of the king, it is almost certain that the office itself, rather than the individual, was considered divine.[3] An Egyptian royal sculpture was not an exact representation of a particular human being but a depiction of the divine aspects of an individual who held the highest office. Such sculptures did, however, often display elements unique to a particular king, distinguishing him from his predecessors and successors. The ruling pharaoh was the image of a god on earth; the statue embodied this fact and therefore legitimized the ruler's exalted status. Certain conventions and symbols were used when depicting the king. The workmanship had to be of superior quality, and the pose, regalia, and choice of material and color all had symbolic meaning. Interestingly, the Egyptian royal sculptures seem to appeal to the modern viewer more than any other sort of Egyptian art. These three-dimensional figures, despite such peculiarities as the use of so-called negative space and back pillars, are highly realistic to our eyes. The inimitably Egyptian depiction of the body in two-dimensional relief, which strikes some modern viewers as awkward, is not a factor here.

Depictions of statues on First Dynasty seal impressions and stone vessels indicate that the Egyptians produced royal statuary from the beginning of their civilization.[4] Early textual evidence confirms that royal statues, particularly of copper or gold, were manufactured in the Archaic and Old Kingdom Periods. Interestingly, almost all of the statues referred to in the texts were made for the temples of various gods and not for the mortuary complexes that are the source of most of the known examples. Royal funerary statues are, however, mentioned in at least one Old Kingdom text, from the famous Abusir papyri (cat. no. 117), which refers to a festival honoring royal statues of the deceased pharaoh.

None of the Old Kingdom royal statues bears the signature of a sculptor, except perhaps for one from the time of Djoser.[5] It is generally, albeit incorrectly, assumed that Egyptian artists worked anonymously. In fact, the names of several artists, including sculptors, were preserved in

Fig. 28. Detail, Khafre Seated with the Horus Falcon behind His Head. Egyptian Museum, Cairo, CG 14

Fig. 29. Detail, Djoser Seated. Egyptian Museum, Cairo, JE 6008

the paintings and reliefs that served as tomb decorations. Some of these scenes depict the actual making of sculptures, thus allowing art historians to reconstruct the production process and techniques used by the Egyptians.[6] George Reisner's discovery of a group of unfinished stone statuettes of King Menkaure prompted him to posit eight stages of production, beginning with the pounding of the block with a stone to create the figure's general shape, followed by stages involving rubbing, sawing, and drilling, and ending with the final polishing. Although the canon of proportions certainly existed during the Old Kingdom, there is no evidence of the use of a square grid at that time.[7] The chief artist simply indicated the guiding lines and points in red paint for his assistants and apprentices. These lines from the early stages of production are preserved on the Menkaure figures (cat. no. 73).

The Old Kingdom royal statues were made in a variety of materials: ivory, wood, limestone, quartzite, Egyptian alabaster, graywacke, anorthosite gneiss, gabbro gneiss, and granite. The choice of material may have had

symbolic and religious significance, although this remains an open question. The examples most often cited to establish such meaning were the royal statues of Djedefre. The magnificent head of this king (cat. no. 54) and almost all the other sculptures of him were made of red quartzite quarried at Gebel Ahmar, not far from Heliopolis, the principal sanctuary of the sun god Re. The growing importance of the cult of the sun god, evident in the name of the king himself, makes this association between the solar cult and the choice of material plausible. The same material was also frequently used to depict another Egyptian sun king, the New Kingdom pharaoh Amenhotep III.[8] Red granite, popular with the Fifth Dynasty pharaoh Niuserre, may also be connected with the solar cult. Problems arise, however, in identifying the symbolic and religious significance of other stones whose use was not limited to royal or even private statuary but extended to stone vessels and palettes. Perhaps the ease of crafting the statues from limestone and graywacke was a primary consideration when selecting these materials.

52

The Cairo Khafre (fig. 28) is the best-known anorthosite gneiss sculpture, but many others were made for this pharaoh (cat. no. 61) and for Sahure (cat. no. 109). The choice of anorthosite gneiss, often incorrectly called "Chephren's [that is, Khafre's] diorite," is puzzling. Found in a distant Nubian quarry, it is hard to work and only moderately attractive. However, it has a rare optical property—it glows in sunlight. Its deep blue glow, caused by the presence of the iridescent mineral bytownite, was noticed by geologists visiting the quarry. This quality is not evident in the artificial light of a museum and therefore went unremarked by scholars until recently. Now, however, it has been suggested that this blue glow, visible in the desert sunlight, attracted Egyptians to the material.[9] Interestingly, art historians frequently mentioned the "radiant" facial expression of Khafre's statues, a term that now seems to refer to the physical properties of the stone itself. One could speculate that this blue radiance signifies the celestial connection and association with the cult of Horus. It must be remembered, however, that many statues, and almost certainly all the limestone sculptures, were either partially or completely covered by paint, thus veiling the material's possible symbolic and religious content.

Whatever the material, a number of attributes separated the image of a king from that of a mere mortal. Among these are formal headdresses such as the white crown of Upper Egypt (cat. no. 63), the red crown of Lower Egypt (cat. no. 62), and the *nemes*, the traditional royal head cover (cat. no. 170). These may be enhanced by the attachment of the uraeus, the royal cobra, to the front of the headdress (the earliest sculptural examples of the uraeus date to the reign of Djedefre). In the few instances in which the king wears a simple wig, the uraeus distinguishes him from private individuals. Often the king is depicted with cosmetic lines at the outer corners of his eyes, a feature also found on nonroyal sculptures. Sometimes a royal false beard is shown attached to the chin by a strap. The king may hold one or more of the symbols of his earthly power, among them a flail, a crook, and a mace. It was technically difficult to represent such long, thin objects, and the artists used short, round forms variously interpreted as either symbolic representations of a staff or simply as handkerchiefs. The dress of an Old Kingdom pharaoh was simple. Sculpted images show the king wearing either the knee-length robe associated with the Heb Sed or the characteristic tripartite kilt known as a *shendyt*. The king is shown naked in only two Sixth Dynasty representations, in which he appears as a child.

The repertoire of kingly postures was limited. Seven different poses can be identified:[10]

1. Standing with feet together (Djoser's Osiris-like figure at Saqqara)
2. Striding with left foot advanced and usually with both arms hanging and fists clenched (cat. no. 67)
3. Sitting on a throne or a block and wearing either the kilt, with the left hand placed on the knee and the right hand in a fist vertically on the thigh (cat. no. 109), or the Heb Sed robe, with one or both arms crossed over the chest and usually holding the regalia
4. Appearing as a sphinx (cat. no. 171)
5. Appearing as part of a group sculpture, accompanied either by a deity or by the principal queen (cat. no. 67), or as a pseudogroup, that is, a double statue of the king (Staatliche Sammlung Ägyptischer Kunst, Munich, ÄS 6794)
6. Kneeling and presenting a pair of *nu* pots (cat. no. 170)
7. Squatting with one hand held to the mouth.

The first five attitudes date from the early phases of the Old Kingdom; the last two are known only from Sixth Dynasty examples.

Identification of materials, attributes, and attitudes deepens our understanding of iconography, stylistic changes, and dating. More than four decades have passed since the publication of the last great syntheses of Old Kingdom art.[11] During this period previously unknown royal statues have come to light either through museum acquisitions from private collections or through archaeological excavations. This new material revived interest in the art of the Pyramid Age, and recent years have seen the publication of several monographs discussing the royal sculpture of the First to the Third Dynasty, the Fourth Dynasty, and the Sixth Dynasty.[12] The discovery of Fifth Dynasty statues of King Neferefre in 1984[13] and the 1997 publication of Old Kingdom sculpture at the Louvre[14] added yet more works to the corpus of royal statuary. Since most of these royal representations are well provenanced and therefore attributable to individual rulers, their study has increased knowledge of the stylistic and iconographic elements typical of a given period or dynasty. The dating and attribution of unprovenanced objects have been facilitated to a degree, but differences of opinion about individual pieces will continue, given our reliance on personal experience and instinct in assessing works.

Only four royal statues are presently known from the Archaic Period, which includes the first two dynasties. One, a faience figurine of Djer, was found at Elephantine;[15] three others, an ivory figurine of an unidentified king and two stone statues of the Second Dynasty king Khasekhemui, were excavated at Abydos. The feet from a pair of wood statues excavated at Saqqara, possibly of King Qaa, should perhaps be added to this list.[16] Third Dynasty royal statuary, especially that of Djoser, is better represented in the corpus of pharaonic sculpture. The famous seated limestone statue from the serdab of the Step Pyramid at Saqqara (fig. 29) shows the king dressed in a Heb Sed robe; a large wig surmounted by a *nemes* frames his broad face, with its high cheekbones, large ears, wide mouth, and long beard. The sense of heavy, somber majesty is striking. The unfinished pillar-statue of the standing Djoser, still in the festival court at Saqqara, also has a broad face and a long beard, but because of the shape of its wig it is more reminiscent of the early divine images in Brooklyn (cat. no. 10) and Brussels[17] than of the serdab statue. Fragments of other statues of Djoser are also known, some identified only recently in the site magazine. Two magnificent early royal portraits—the oldest surviving colossal head of a king from the Brooklyn Museum (cat. no. 21) and a small limestone head from Munich (cat. no. 34)—can be dated to the end of the Third Dynasty or to the early Fourth Dynasty. In both, the round full face, the undefined eyebrows, and broad nose are similar to features of the ivory figurine of Khufu from Abydos that is now in the Egyptian Museum, Cairo (JE 36143), while the depth of the crown and the cupped ears are reminiscent of the Khasekhemui statues. Whether the Brooklyn and Munich heads depict Huni, Snefru, or even Khufu remains an open question. Together with the figurine of Khufu, they form a stylistic group that documents the transition from one dynasty to another.

The earliest undisputed examples of Fourth Dynasty royal sculpture are the two broken statues of Snefru discovered at Dahshur, one of which is now on display in the Egyptian Museum, Cairo.[18] They mark the birth of a new style in Egyptian sculpture, known by the German term *Strenger Stil* (severe style), which emphasizes sharpness, strength, and simplicity of form rather than expressiveness of subject. Except for the two images of Snefru, all other examples of this style fall into the class of nonroyal statuary.

The royal portraits of Snefru's successors vary in number. Ironically, the visage of Snefru's son Khufu, who built the Great Pyramid at Giza, is known from only one small statuette, while that of his little-known successor, Djedefre, whose pyramid at Abu Rawash lies in ruins, is represented by numerous statues. The portraits of Djedefre in red quartzite show a characteristically bony and angular face with prominent cheekbones and a strong jaw evincing strength and determination. In the Louvre head (cat. no. 54), among the greatest masterpieces of Egyptian art, this force is tempered by a certain resigned wisdom expressed in the pouches under the eyes and tensed muscles at the corners of the mouth.

Most surviving royal images of the Fourth Dynasty date to Djedefre's successors Khafre and Menkaure and were found during excavations of their temples at Giza. A statue of Khafre protected by Horus in the shape of a falcon and group statues of Menkaure (fig. 28; cat. nos. 67, 68) are among the greatest art objects ever created. The sculptors who made these royal images remain anonymous to us. However, differences in treatment of the physiognomies of the two pharaohs are easily recognizable, as are differences among images of the same ruler, suggesting that there were at least two and probably more sculpture schools or ateliers. Sorting out these styles is problematic; opinions differ and ultimately the decision rests with the viewer. The choice of material may have an important bearing on this matter. The limestone image of Khafre (cat. no. 62) is quite different from Khafre's graywacke head in Leipzig (1946). The latter has some resemblance, however superficial, to the head of Djedefre in the Egyptian Museum, Cairo (JE 35138-Suez S 10), but it also has the wide face, soft cheeks, and serene expression of the gneiss statues of Khafre (fig. 28; cat. no. 61). Likewise, the fleshy round nose, full cheeks, and faint smile appear in all depictions of Menkaure,[19] but the alabaster portraits of this king have such distinctively prominent eyeballs (cat. no. 70) that at least one has been thought to portray another pharaoh, Menkaure's successor, Shepseskaf.

The attribution of most Fourth Dynasty sculpture was based on inscriptions or archaeological context. This information is rarely available for Fifth Dynasty royal statuary, perhaps the least homogenous group of all the Old Kingdom assemblages. Userkaf, the first king of the Fifth Dynasty, is known from a colossal head found at his temple at Saqqara (cat. no. 100). The attribution to this ruler of other portraits, including an example in the Cleveland Museum of Art and one found at Abusir, is often based on their similarities to heads of Menkaure. Using this criterion, one could also assign two other statues (Louvre, Paris, AF 2573, and Egyptian Museum, Cairo, JE 39103) to Userkaf or another early Fifth

Dynasty ruler. The group statue of Sahure (cat. no. 109), whose identity is assured by its inscription, also continues the traditions of Fourth Dynasty artists, and it has even been redated, albeit unconvincingly, to the reign of Khafre.[20]

Statues of the later Fifth Dynasty pharaohs Neferefre and Niuserre form the bulk of the corpus of Fifth Dynasty royal portraits. A statuette of Neferefre showing the king wearing a wig and protected, like the Khafre mentioned above, by the falcon-headed Horus,[21] has a rare feature: the limbs were carved in the round. The six known statuettes of Neferefre were made in a variety of materials and show different attitudes and attributes but have common traits, such as the roundness of the face, the shape of the eyes, and the modeling of the nasolabial furrows. In three statuettes the king holds a mace, a royal symbol that rarely appears in sculpture. The head of a statuette in Brussels[22] may also be identified as that of Neferefre. Niuserre is known from five remarkably similar statues: all show the king wearing the *nemes*, and all but one are made of red granite, the exception being the calcite pseudogroup in Munich, the only Old Kingdom double statue of a king. Three other royal portraits of unidentified kings (Athens, L120; Ägyptisches Museum und Papyrussammlung, Berlin, 14396; Egyptian Museum, Cairo, JE 39103) may be attributed to the Fifth Dynasty, although different dates have also been proposed. The only attributable image of the later kings of this dynasty is a small and possibly unfinished statuette of Menkauhor (Egyptian Museum, Cairo, CG 40).

A recent study by Romano of the fourteen securely identified and eleven undated statues of the Sixth Dynasty found that many (for example, cat. no. 170) show an "exaggeration of details including wide, piercing eyes and thick everted lips, bodies with unnaturalistically attenuated torsos, and long thin arms with little trace of musculature."[23] These characteristics are typical of the so-called Second Style, first identified in private sculpture.[24] Romano has also noted that while many individual details appeared in earlier periods, the combination of them is new. An example of this innovative use of iconographic details is the placement of the Horus falcon on the back pillar of an alabaster statue of Pepi I, where it serves both as a sculpted hieroglyph of the royal name and as the protector of the pharaoh (Brooklyn Museum of Art, 39.120).

The representation of queens is beyond the scope of this essay, but it may be worthwhile to note the gradual elevation of the queen from a small and subservient figure on one of Djedefre's statues, to an equal partner of Menkaure, and finally to the embodiment of Isis protecting her son, Horus, in the statue of Ankh-nes-meryre II with her son Pepi II (cat. no. 172).[25]

Generally speaking, the royal statuary of the Old Kingdom shows the same characteristic elements known from the private statuary, such as cubic form emphasized by placing the subject on a base and using a back pillar to support the figure. Art historians have noted that the best Old Kingdom sculptures are slightly asymmetrical in such details as the placement of the ears and the execution of eyes or lips. In fact, one could posit that all the statues are asymmetrical because of the forward stride of the left foot and the different positions of hands or other body parts or attributes. Indeed, axiality and frontality rather than symmetry characterize Egyptian sculpture. This exhibition presents a unique opportunity to study these and other aspects of the historical and stylistic development of Egyptian royal sculpture, which was one of Egypt's most important contributions to our civilization.

1. Frankfort 1948; Posener 1960; Wildung 1980b; Baines 1995.
2. Helck 1966, p. 40.
3. Goedicke 1960, pp. 3–6.
4. Eaton-Krauss 1984, pp. 89–94.
5. Lauer 1996.
6. Smith 1946, pp. 350–60.
7. Robins 1994, p. 64.
8. Kozloff and Bryan 1992, p. 133.
9. Harrell and Brown 1994, pp. 54–55.
10. Reisner 1931, pp. 123–25; Romano 1998. I would like to express my gratitude to Dr. Romano for placing at my disposal the galley proofs of his article prior to its publication.
11. Smith 1946; Vandier 1958; see also Altenmüller 1980b, cols. 557–63.
12. Sourouzian 1995; Stadelmann 1995b; Romano 1998.
13. Verner 1994a; Verner 1995.
14. Ziegler 1997a.
15. Dreyer 1986, pp. 101–2.
16. Sourouzian 1995, pp. 133–40.
17. Wildung 1972.
18. Fakhry 1961b, pls. 33–37; Stadelmann 1995b, pp. 164–66.
19. In this respect the facial expression on the so-called Mycerinus (Menkaure) head at Brussels (cat. no. 69), with its upwardly turned mouth, differs from other graywacke portraits of that king; see Gilbert 1961; and Tefnin 1988, pp. 18–19.
20. Seidel 1996, pp. 51–53.
21. Verner 1985a; Verner 1994a, pp. 143–48.
22. No. E.7117; Tefnin 1988, pp. 20–21.
23. Romano 1998, p. 269.
24. Russmann 1995a.
25. A discussion of nine statues of Old Kingdom royal women was recently published by Fay (1998).

NONROYAL STATUARY

CHRISTIANE ZIEGLER

The nonroyal statuary of the Old Kingdom was not intended for public display. Destined for tombs, these "living images," as they were called by the ancient Egyptians, or images done "from life," were placed in offering chapels accessible to the priests who served there, shut away in a small concealed room called a serdab, or sometimes buried near the sarcophagus of the person for whom they were made. Texts in the cult chapels of the deceased explain that the statues were an integral part of the cult ceremony. Identified by the names and titles of the deceased, the statues received incense and nourishment. Before a funeral a priest performed a special rite called Opening of the Mouth[1] to bring the image magically to life. Their chief purpose was to receive offerings, in particular the nourishment[2] that would sustain the deceased in the afterlife.

They are thus not portraits in the modern sense of the term[3] but elevated and timeless images conforming to a canon, or set of rules, established in very ancient times. The limited range of poses, suppression of movement, and self-containment of the figures are doubtless attributable to their specific function.[4] Many reveal an attempt to convey the physical characteristics of the individual. These works can be described as realistic without anachronism, for, unlike neighboring peoples, the Egyptians firmly believed that they would not sink into a sea of anonymous souls after death but would keep their identities intact.[5]

Although Egyptian artists paid particular attention to recording facial features, achieving a faithful likeness was not always essential. Other details contribute to the identification of the statue. There were perhaps fifty poses[6] showing the deceased standing with left foot forward, sitting on the ground or on a seat, and—occasionally—kneeling; the person may be represented several times, in what is known as a pseudogroup, or in the company of various family members, or alone. This catalogue shows that individual statues of women are not numerous, and their tombs are few. Certain details of dress, such as the kilt, elaborate jewelry, and scepter, indicate the subject's prestige or—more rarely—his office, revealed, for example, by the wide sash of the ritual priest.[7] Inscriptions—carved in relief on the walls and the false door of the chapel and written on funerary furniture and on the statue itself—enrich the architectural and religious setting.

Inscribed texts from the Old Kingdom are not long, including merely the name and principal titles of the person shown. Occasionally a dedication indicates that the statue was offered by a relative; for example, one of the statues of Sekhem-ka[8] was dedicated by his son Ma-nefer. Less often the artist who sculpted the figure is alluded to (cat. no. 77). Texts might be placed on the base of the statue or on the subject's seat, generally on the front but sometimes on the sides. We do not know why the ample surface of the back pillar of nonroyal statues was not employed for this purpose during the period; at most, a short line of text may appear on its upper edge. It is almost unnecessary to say that the relationship between inscription and image is extremely close: the absence of any determinative at the end of a proper name suggests that the statue itself played that role.[9]

MATERIALS, TECHNIQUES, AND CRAFTSMEN

Only a limited number of royal statues survive from the Old Kingdom, whereas 948 statues of private persons have been recorded,[10] and this figure does not include the many extant serving statuettes, which are not covered in this essay (see introduction to cat. nos. 136–143). Certain tombs contained no fewer than a hundred images![11] Fashioned from a rich selection of materials—wood, hippopotamus ivory, and stone—nonroyal statuary offers examples of work in almost every medium used by Egyptian sculptors beginning in the earliest dynasties.[12] Only works in metal are absent, royal examples of which are known chiefly from written sources.[13] As for wood, recent analytic studies of the Louvre collections[14] show that acacia (*Acacia* sp., Mimosaceae family), a tree common in the Nile Valley, was the type most often used. The Egyptians also employed acacia, which was easy to carve and may have had symbolic importance in the cult of the goddess Hathor,[15] for bas-reliefs and the false doors of mastabas. Jujube (*Ziziphus* sp., Rhamnaceae family) and ficus (*Ficus* sp., Moraceae family)[16] were used for works whose style is characteristic of the Sixth Dynasty.[17] Nothing testifies to the use of such exotic woods as ebony, although imported wood is mentioned in the tomb reliefs of Ra-shepses and Ti.[18]

Most nonroyal statues are carved in stone.[19] Those dating from the inception of the Old Kingdom—from the Third Dynasty to the beginning of the Fourth—show a predilection for red granite from Aswan, as well as for the dark diorite that was also used sporadically throughout the Fifth Dynasty. No statue securely datable to the Sixth Dynasty seems to have been made of this material. Alabaster was also used (cat. nos. 26, 87) and, less frequently, anorthosite gneiss[20] and Bekhen stone (graywacke).[21] Crystalline sandstone (quartzite), whose dense texture is marvelously suited to the modeling of the human face, seems to have been reserved for works of exceptional quality.[22] Limestone overwhelmingly predominates as the medium for nonroyal statuary, from the monumental figures of Sepa and Nesa (cat. nos. 11–13) to the delicate pair statue of the governor of Balat and his wife (figs. 44, 45). Examination reveals that it was obtained from many locations: for the region around Cairo, from the Saqqara plateau, Helwan, and Tura; for the provinces, from oasis quarries, Middle Egypt, and Thebes. The richest tombs contained many statues; the number in the mastaba of Ptah-shepses, son-in-law of King Niuserre, has been estimated at almost twenty, and they were worked in stone of varying colors and textures, including alabaster, granite, and quartzite.[23] However attractive the luster and polish of the material, the surface of these statues was at least partially covered with bright paints, and the garish effect conveyed was sometimes heightened by inlaid eyes.

Although most nonroyal statues are sculpted from limestone, the Egyptian artist did not take advantage of the properties of this soft stone. There is no openwork or drilled or punched detail, and no voids or effects of light and shade appear.[24] Limestone was worked as if the sculptor had to obey the same constraints observed when granite was used. The Egyptian artist preserved the contours of the block of stone from which the human form emerged, delimiting the base of all statues, even those in wood, and the quadrangular seat on which the figure sat. The frontal view was primary, and the earliest statues indicate that a right-profile view that allowed both legs to be seen—the left extended in front of the right—was the most important (cat. nos. 11, 12). The artist of the Third Dynasty worked the back of a statue, but beginning in the Fourth Dynasty the back could be masked by a high slab (fig. 31),[25] so any attack on the block was essentially made from the front.[26] An essential feature of Egyptian stone statuary, the back pillar against which a statue rests is attested from the end of the Fourth Dynasty (cat. no. 91).

All the conventions of later Egyptian sculpture are present at the outset of the Old Kingdom. Glancing at the plates in this volume, the reader will sense the influence of the Egyptian canon, which manifests itself with seeming uniformity. There exists, in effect, an extraordinary degree of conceptual similarity between works made by different artists in highly diverse materials, owing to a shared system of rules applied in different contexts.[27]

The first principle in the canon is that of frontality,[28] which translates into axial, symmetric organization.[29] The articulated volumes of a subject's body represented in this way do not give a natural impression but rather the impression of a person completely still, with absolutely no tilting of shoulders or hips or overlapping of arms and legs. The stiffness that results is somewhat tempered by the advance of the left leg—hallmark of the characteristic pose of the standing male figure—and by asymmetries in the rendering of ears and eyes.[30] Recent studies have shown that some figures twist slightly to their left.[31] In groups represented according to the principle of frontality (cat. no. 83) the individuals are aligned in one plane and thereby isolated from one another. Only the gesture of an arm or clasped hands link the figures. At the close of the Old Kingdom, sculptors found a new solution, showing two persons at right angles to each other (cat. no. 172).[32]

Convention also determined the rendering of clothing. Beginning in the Third Dynasty the pleats of a man's kilt are represented by lines, and the decorative folds cover body parts without acknowledging their contours. With the exception of the clothing in one queen's statue,[33] women's robes cling like an imperceptible sheath, hiding nothing of the shape beneath yet obscuring anatomical details, and thus expressing the body, according to Roland Tefnin, "in its dual essence, natural and cultural."[34] Even the most fully realized sculptures, which can truly be called realistic, omit such details as skin folds, wrinkles, veins, and rippling tendons that convey the impression of real life and which the artists of the Archaic Period tended to overdo.[35]

Was this strict and invariable canon of conventions a characteristic expression of a principle of Egyptian thought,[36] or should we see it, rather, as the conscious effort of an elite to define and sustain a particular world-view?[37] Many interpretations have been advanced, but they all remain conjectural. Nevertheless, it is clear that at the very moment the Egyptians invented architecture in stone, they presented a coherent and perfected system for representing the human figure, executed with a flawless technique. This achievement especially elicits admiration in comparison to the accomplishments of contemporary cultures. The canon, whose formulas are probably the result of deliberate choice, would endure during the following millennia.

Nevertheless, in the sculpture of the Old Kingdom, which spans five centuries, a stylistic evolution is discernible, and it can be described—only provisionally, however, because dating the works is difficult. Although royal statuary defines the style of the period, comparing it with private statuary is not always useful. We must employ other dating criteria and begin with those statues whose owners can be assigned to a particular reign.[38]

The Birth of Monumental Statuary in Stone

During the reign of Djoser a departure in sculpture took place that was equal in importance to contemporary advances in architecture. An increase in scale, a relaxation in demeanor, the objective rendering of anatomical detail, and a heightened realism are innovations that separate the stiff statue of Khasekhemui, the last ruler of the Archaic Period (Egyptian Museum, Cairo, JE 32161), from the arresting portrait of Djoser (fig. 29).[39] These changes reflect skillful stoneworking that developed as a result of technical progress. They also indicate new ideas. In the private realm the break is less noticeable, since few nonroyal statues of the Archaic Period are preserved; however, the exceptional group of three statues of Sepa and Nesa from the early Third Dynasty illustrates the remarkable advance (cat. nos. 11–13). The provenance of these works is assumed to be Saqqara, and their dates can be further refined if Sepa can be identified with a person mentioned on a vase fragment discovered in the Step Pyramid of Djoser.[40] None of the nearly lifesize limestone

Fig. 30. Ankh-wa Seated. Trustees of the British Museum, London, 171

figures has a back pillar. Traces of paint are abundant: black on the wigs and eyes, green on bracelets and the cosmetic bands beneath the eyes. Despite their close-to-lifelike proportions—the body is seven times the height of the head—they have broad, flat faces and an air of solidity that is accentuated by such features as a short neck, stiff arms held close to the body or bent at a sharp right angle, thick legs and ankles, and incompletely disengaged legs. Special attention was given to the faces, whose finely detailed features reflect peace and contentment. Noteworthy is Nesa's unusual wig: in front, the parallel tresses end in narrow tiers, giving the impression

Fig. 31. Ra-hotep and
Nofret Seated. Egyptian
Museum, Cairo, CG 3,
CG 4

of triple thickness. Two smaller female statues are executed in the same vein: the Lady of Brussels[41] and the Princess Redjief Seated (cat. no. 16). The latter bears a relation to the statue of Djoser (fig. 29) in the careful treatment of the face with its perfect polish.

Carved, like the Princess Redjief Seated, of hard stone and featuring a similar seat that imitates bentwood furniture are four statues dating to the Third Dynasty: two of Ankh (cat. nos. 14, 15), who probably served Djoser; one of Ankh-wa,[42] who clutches an adze as a sign of his profession (he was a carpenter) (fig. 30); and one of Metjen (cat. no. 28), found in a chapel, with inscriptions dating to the reign of Snefru. Although these individuals

are all seated, there is great diversity in the position of the arms—with hands joined, holding an emblem on the shoulder, and placed on the chest or on the knee. Two types of wigs are worn: one with horizontal waves, the other with tight curls like the headdress seen in the reliefs of Hesi-re (cat. no. 17). The priest Hetep-dief,[43] who was probably a contemporary of Metjen since the statues of the two men have stylistic affinities, is shown kneeling, a pose rarely repeated.[44] This sculpture's features are entirely characteristic of nonroyal statuary of the early Old Kingdom: a disproportionately large head, a short neck, and stiff angular limbs held against the compact body, which the artist worked on all four sides.

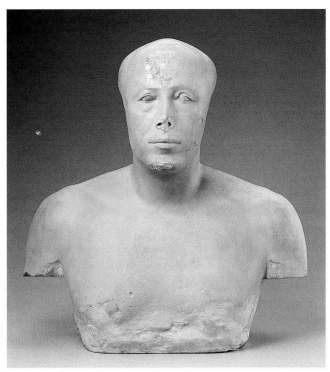

Fig. 32. Ankh-haf. Museum of Fine Arts, Boston, Harvard University–Museum of Fine Arts Expedition, 27.442

THE QUEST FOR INDIVIDUALITY

Found in a tomb at Meidum, the seated statues of Ra-hotep—presumably a son of King Snefru—and his wife, Nofret, mark a crucial step in the direction of realistic representation (fig. 31). Every feature of the works contributes to this impression. Both figures are nearly lifesize. The various planes of Ra-hotep's nude torso, although summarily modeled, emerge harmoniously articulated from the block of limestone (the back of the block was used to make a high back slab). The carefully sculpted facial features and details of dress give each figure individuality. A rich polychromy contrasts with the immaculate white of the clothing and thrones, and the impact of the eyes inlaid with rock crystal and quartz is extraordinary. The artist achieved his goal of creating living images, and we can appreciate the fright that gripped the workmen when they discovered the figures in 1871. The naturalism of these works is achieved with austere modeling and with a simplified rendering of surfaces.

The same effect and technical skill are evident in the statue of the vizier Hemiunu (cat. no. 44), a close associate of King Khufu. The flaccid pectoral muscles and the fleshy, distended abdomen are unflattering observations that suggest the corpulence of a mature man, whose aquiline nose and imperious mouth express an inflexible

character. An equally powerful individuality and severity are achieved through the elimination of minor details in the reserve heads deposited in the burial chambers of the Western Cemetery at Giza (cat. nos. 46–49).[45] This austere style contrasts with a contemporary trend that stressed sensitivity to modeling, softness, and a taste for detail here as in royal statuary. The bust of Ankh-haf (fig. 32) illustrates the tendency perfectly. To his keen observation of bone structure, the artist was able to bring to bear delicate modeling that conjures with precision and subtlety the weary visage of King Khafre's vizier, his tired gaze, and the quiver of sagging flesh. Few other nonroyal statues from the Fourth Dynasty are as securely dated.

Differing sharply from the royal model are statues of scribes. The series commences with the figure of Kawab, a son of Khufu, in the Museum of Fine Arts, Boston (13.3140), and includes other princes: Setka (cat. no. 55), son of King Djedefre, with paunchy belly and a face riddled with fat; and Khuen-re (cat. no. 72), son of King Menkaure, whose torso is re-created in ample volumes and whose otherwise conventional face is enlivened by the asymmetry of the mouth. In these examples the arms remain attached to the torso, although the technique of separating them from the body below the shoulder had already been mastered by the reign of Khufu.[46]

Fig. 33. Scribe. Musée du Louvre, Paris, N 2290 (=E 3023)

Fig. 34. Sheikh el-Beled. Egyptian Museum, Cairo, CG 34

recalling the identical pose of the wife of Menkaure in the monumental pair statue in the Museum of Fine Arts, Boston (cat. no. 67). Memi wraps his arm around his wife's neck (cat. no. 84), expressing his affection in exactly the same way Hetep-heres II reveals her feelings toward her daughter Mer-si-ankh III in a statue also in Boston (30.1456). This manner of showing familiarity vanishes at the start of the Fifth Dynasty and thus can be used as a criterion for dating.[48]

Among the rare family groups that are dated is that of the lady Khentet-ka and her son (cat. no. 80).[49] Seated on a throne with a high back slab, Khentet-ka is in many ways similar to the figure of Nofret from Meidum (fig. 31). Her radiant face is framed by a large wig that permits her own parted hair to show. With an ample body and stout ankles, she exudes the same "air of robust health" observable in the royal statuary of the period.[50] The nude little boy, shown standing at his mother's feet, wears the braided "sidelock of youth" and holds a finger to his mouth; he is as tall as his mother's seat, following a convention of scale peculiar to Old Kingdom statuary.[51]

Long of uncertain date, the statue group of Seneb the dwarf and his family (Egyptian Museum, Cairo, JE 51280) is today firmly assigned to the reign of Djedefre.[52] Seneb's wife, who embraces him affectionately, closely resembles Khentet-ka and displays the same coiffure. The two standing children, who balance the composition, are also no taller than the top of the bench shown behind them. The cross-legged pose of the dwarf somewhat obscures the difference in height of the principal figures without concealing his overlarge head and atrophied legs. The artist lightened the work by dispensing with a back slab and incorporating voids, or negative space, into the ensemble, achieving a masterpiece of equilibrium.

Other famous works of art can be dated to this period of experiment, during which artists tended in the direction of the realistic and the particular, scrupulously observing the marks of age or infirmity. The original forms they created were forgotten, however, in the Fifth Dynasty. One superb example is the Scribe in the Louvre (fig. 33),[53] in which the artist paid close attention to the gaunt face and the inlaid eyes. The restrained modeling of the torso and abdomen calls to mind the treatment of the statue of Hemiunu. The same technique characterizes another fine example, the Sheikh el-Beled (fig. 34).[54] This undisputed masterpiece of large-scale statuary in wood may be a transitional example between the Archaic Period, when the art of monumental wood carving is well attested, and the Fifth Dynasty, from which time we have better-known works. Dating from the close of the Fourth

Dated to the Fourth Dynasty are several statues of couples who demonstrate a special tenderness toward each other, with a restraint typical of Egyptian art. The lady Mer-si-ankh[47] lovingly embraces her husband, Ra-her-ka, and ventures to place a hand on his forearm,

Dynasty, the tomb of Queen Mer-si-ankh III yielded one of the oldest series of statuettes of servants going about their tasks. The popularity of these attractive so-called models grew throughout the Old Kingdom (see introduction to cat. nos. 136–143).

CONFORMITY AND GENERALIZATION

Beginning in the reign of Shepseskaf, at the end of the Fourth Dynasty, the locale of nonroyal cemeteries and royal tombs shifted from Giza to Saqqara, and most of the statuary of the Fifth Dynasty comes from the latter site. The "king's son and vizier" Ba-baef[55] chose to build his tomb at Giza, and it affords fine examples from the transitional phase when statuary of high quality was made for a small number of privileged individuals. The archaeologists who discovered the tomb recovered fragments of between thirty and fifty statues.[56] Types, sizes, and media are extremely varied. A small, perfectly preserved statue in granite of Ba-baef as a scribe[57] is notable for the slight inclination of the prince's head, suggestive of his concentration on the papyrus he is reading. A series of lifesize limestone standing statues shows Ba-baef with an athletic body and large shoulders. The modeling is excellent but simplified. The heads have, unfortunately, disappeared. There is little variation in his clothing, which consists of either a short kilt with pleated flap or a midlength kilt with hanging belt. In a series of alabaster statues, however, three styles of coiffure are displayed: curls clinging tightly to the subject's skull (cat. no. 87); a short, round wig; and a flaring wig that leaves the earlobes exposed. The face, which in one example once had inlaid eyes, is doll-like, and the fullness of the cheeks is accentuated by furrows at the edges of the mouth.[58] In the same tomb were fragments of two pseudogroups in granite. In each group, two images of Ba-baef appear side by side, one seated and one standing. These constitute the earliest evidence of this special type of statue, of which there exists only a single royal example—that of Niuserre[59]—although perhaps thirty such works showing nonroyal persons are known (see cat. no. 187).[60]

During the course of the Fifth Dynasty, as the administration of Egypt became more complex, an increasing number of private persons had access to a wide range of careers. Nonroyal tombs multiplied, and the statuary that filled them is abundant, although of less homogeneous quality and often smaller in size than the earlier examples. For these sculptures wood seems to have been the material of choice, but this impression may be the

Fig. 35. Ka-em-ked Kneeling. Egyptian Museum, Cairo, CG 119

result of the vagaries of preservation.[61] Even in the most finished examples the workmanship seems perfunctory, and the types are so generalized that they can be compared to hieroglyphs.[62] Countenances, suffused with a timeless youth, are less distinctive, and the repertoire of accessory elements diminishes. It is difficult to say whether this development is a consequence of mass production[63] or of a shift in funerary beliefs. That there are exceptions to the rule must be noted, and we can point to original poses and details. The kneeling figure of the funerary priest Ka-em-ked[64] (fig. 35) is remarkable for its pose and the superb treatment and brilliance of its eyes inlaid with black stone—a novel technique. The otherwise unremarkable statue of Ma-nefer[65] is noteworthy for the

Fig. 36. Nen-khefet-ka Seated. Egyptian Museum, Cairo, CG 30

Fig. 37. Nen-khefet-ka Seated. Egyptian Museum, Cairo, CG 31

scepter lying across the subject's breast; here the artist revived a theme dating back to the Third Dynasty. Unusual, too, is the procession of offering bearers that decorates the cubic seat of Sekhem-ka.[66] On one of the three statues of Akhet-hotep recently discovered at Saqqara, the emblem of the goddess Bat, suspended against a beaded sash, is picked out in sharp relief.[67]

This subdued and less expressive style of the Fifth Dynasty, often achieved with a sure technique, is found in two diorite statues from the tomb of Nen-khefet-ka, a courtier of King Sahure (figs. 36, 37).[68] A fragmentary sculpture shows the courtier beside his wife, who stands with her hand on his arm.[69] A second Nen-khefet-ka, who probably lived at the same time and was buried in the provincial cemetery of Deshashah, in the south of Faiyum, commissioned statues in all respects analogous

to those from the Memphite region.[70] Made some twenty years later, the monumental statue of Ti (fig. 38), a contemporary of Niuserre, is striking for the simplification of the musculature and the schematic modeling of the face. This statue is very different from the subtle bas-reliefs that adorn this official's famous funerary chapel at Saqqara.[71] We can detect a refined sensibility and a taste for detail in the series sculpted for Overseer of the Granary Ni-ka-re (see introduction to cat. nos. 127–130), a less important contemporary of Ti. Several family groups accompany individual statues of the deceased, who is rendered in a variety of poses and materials.

Some tombs at Saqqara that probably date to the end of the Fifth Dynasty have yielded clusters of stuccoed and painted wood statues of exceptional size and condition. Of eleven acacia-wood statues showing Mit-re and his

Fig. 38. Ti Standing. Egyptian Museum, Cairo, CG 20

Fig. 39. Detail, Senedjem-ib Mehi Standing. Museum of Fine Arts, Boston, Harvard University–Museum of Fine Arts Expedition, 13.3466

family—located in New York, Cairo, and Stockholm—many are lifesize. Despite the plasticity of the medium, the group is very rigid, the postures are stiff, and the modeling of the faces is rough. Special mention must be made of a female figure in the Egyptian Museum, Cairo, who wears a rare tripartite wig,[72] and the large figure of a scribe with inlaid eyes in the same museum.[73] It should also be noted that in the serdab of Mit-re was found a wood statuette of a hunchback (Egyptian Museum, Cairo, JE 52081). Hunchbacks are among the subjects depicted in a sequence of models from the end of the Fourth Dynasty; the material prefigures the statuettes of servants of the First Intermediate Period and Middle Kingdom.

Of quite a different quality is the splendid statue of Senedjem-ib Mehi, chief architect of King Unis, which was found at Giza (fig. 39). The entirely nude large-scale figure stands with one arm extended. The treatment of the slim body is extremely delicate, and the modeling of the face, with eyes that were once inlaid, is done with close attention to realistic details. The oblique lines between mouth and nose, and the mouth with its thick lips and truncated corners announce the advent of

Fig. 41. Nekhebu Seated. Museum of Fine Arts, Boston, Harvard University–Museum of Fine Arts Expedition, 13.3161

Fig. 40. Qar Seated. Egyptian Museum, Cairo, JE 43776

what Egyptologists call the "Second Style" of the Sixth Dynasty,[74] as do the subject's nakedness and his elongated silhouette.

Some of these features, as well as the long kilt with quilted front panel worn by Ti, are also found in two representations of Metjetji,[75] whose tomb is customarily dated to the reign of Unis (cat. nos. 151–157), while other statues of him are executed in the style of the earlier Fifth Dynasty.[76]

THE SECOND STYLE

The Second Style was probably created at Saqqara during the reign of Unis. It developed during the course of the Sixth Dynasty and was broadly disseminated at the moment that the emergence of provincial power centers offered artists new sources of patronage for their work. During this period statues in wood were made in great numbers. These are usually small in scale and show such

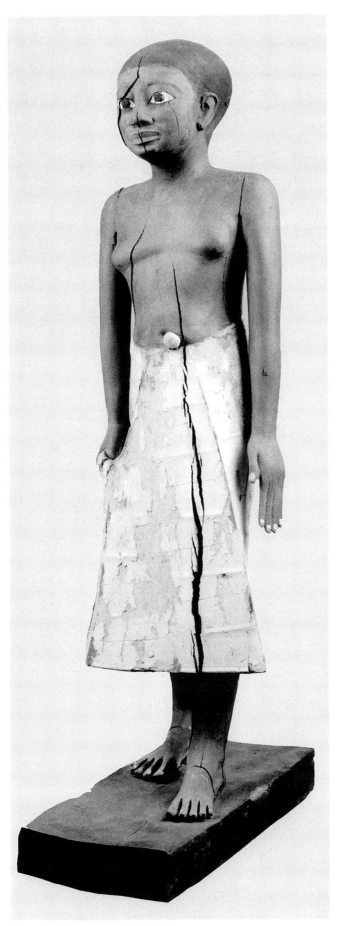

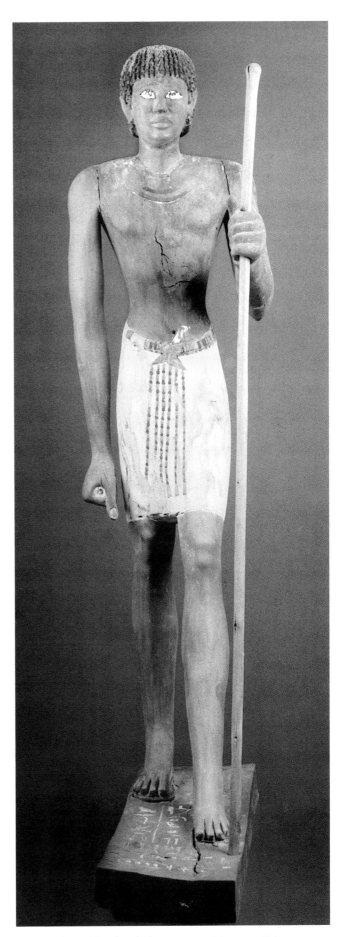

Fig. 42. Pepi-ankh "the Black." Egyptian Museum, Cairo, CG 60

Fig. 43. Pepi-ankh "the Black." Egyptian Museum, Cairo, CG 236

Fig. 44. Pair Statue of Ima-
Pepi and His Wife Seated

Fig. 45. Pair Statue of Ima-Pepi and His Wife Seated

an idiosyncratic view of the human form that it is possible to speak of mannerism[77] or exaggeration[78] in describing them. The head is disproportionately large; the body is elongated, with a pinched waist; and the musculature is only minimally delineated. The face is characterized by immense and often staring eyes, a short, stubby nose, and a strong mouth. The corners of the lips can be marked with a vertical stroke or left open. The vitality of the countenance is heightened by the emphatic use of grooves emanating from the nose and from the corners of the upper lip. Also characteristic of the statuary of this dynasty is the pairing of the slender and often nude figure of an adolescent with depictions of the same person when mature,[79] probably in an attempt to immortalize the individual at various stages of life. Examples of this practice have been found in the necropolises at Akhmim (figs. 42, 43) and Meir.

The stone and wood standing figures of Tjetji from Saqqara (Metropolitan Museum, 26.2.8, 26.2.9) illustrate the distinctive features of the style:[80] a flaring wig revealing the ears, hair either cut short against the skull or bristling, and a long kilt. The navel, which had long been shown as a semicircle, becomes a circular hollow; and the limbs are cut free of the body, creating negative space.[81] Unfortunately these works cannot be assigned to a particular reign.

The limestone statue of Nekhebu (fig. 41), interred at Giza during the kingship of Pepi I, has very pronounced features: huge almond-shaped eyes that convey a haggard look, a large nose, and a thick mouth.[82] The work can be compared with the seated statue of Qar (fig. 40), governor of the province of Edfu in the time of Merenre I.[83] Less distorted, however, than the statue of Nekhebu, the latter is done with care and simplicity. The various surfaces of the figure are sharply differentiated. The pinched waist and the elongated fingers and toes are also noteworthy. The flaring wig curves to frame a face with Second Style features.

A pose unusual for its asymmetry came into fashion during the Sixth Dynasty. The subject is shown seated on the ground with one knee drawn up and the other flat on the ground (cat. no. 186).[84] Numerous isolated instances of the type are known, and it occurs in a series of statues recently found at Saqqara that are inscribed with the name Ipi.[85]

In this era of innovation, themes abandoned after the Fourth Dynasty were rediscovered. Ima-pepi, governor of Balat in the time of Pepi I, chose to be shown seated with his wife, and the couple share an unusual chair with lion-footed legs (figs. 44, 45).[86] The slimness of his body, the thickness of his lips, slightly notched where they join, and the furrows accentuating the nostrils are all typical of the Sixth Dynasty style. But the provincial artist, who used a local limestone, returned in this work to a theme introduced at Giza in the rock-hewed statues of Queen Mer-si-ankh III—that of figures closely intertwined. Similarly, Izi of Edfu and Pepi-ankh the Middle of Meir, two local governors who served under Pepi I and Pepi II, respectively, are each shown seated on a chair with a very high back slab in the company of their wives, who make affectionate gestures.[87]

Do such stylistic changes reflect the determination of new patrons—more and more of whom were commoners living in the provinces—to impose their own values?[88]

The stylistic trend began at the start of the Sixth Dynasty, at a time when the power of the pharaoh was not threatened by provincial elites, and the contrary is likely: it is probable that royal statuary created in the Memphite region and the focus of cults in the Ka Houses helped to spread the new style throughout Egypt.[89] The reasons for this change, perhaps religious in origin, were in any case sufficiently profound that this late Old Kingdom style persisted in the workshops of the First Intermediate Period and at length inspired the early masterpieces of the Middle Kingdom.

1. Otto 1960, vol. 2, pp. 2–4.
2. Eaton-Krauss 1984, p. 4 § 103.
3. Assmann 1996, pp. 55–81.
4. Schäfer 1986, p. 317.
5. Assmann 1996, p. 80.
6. Vandier 1958, pp. 60–92.
7. Saqqara SA 96/74 (= OAE 41); Ziegler 1997c, pp. 232–37.
8. Louvre, Paris; Ziegler 1997a, pp. 131–34, no. 36 (N 111 = A 105 = E 3022).
9. Fischer 1986.
10. Nadine Palayret, corpus Djedefre, database described in Chappaz and Poggia 1996, p. 101.
11. Ra-wer, Egyptian Museum, Cairo, CG 29; Hassan 1932, p. 1; Smith 1946, p. 46.
12. Sourouzian 1995, p. 154.
13. See "Royal Statuary" by Krzysztof Grzymski in this catalogue.
14. Ziegler 1997a, pp. 8, 310.
15. Edel 1970a, pp. 19–21; Wood 1977, pp. 25–28; Eaton-Krauss 1984, p. 60, n. 297.
16. Ziegler 1997a, no. 52.
17. Ibid., no. 56 (Menascé collection).
18. Eaton-Krauss 1984, p. 56.
19. On the different types of stone, see Lucas and Harris 1962; Klemm and Klemm 1981; and De Putter and Karlshausen 1992.
20. See Wildung 1972, p. 150; and Priese 1991, p. 27, no. 16 (Berlin 1122).
21. For fragments from Ba-baef's tomb, see Smith 1946, p. 50.
22. Ny Carlsberg Glyptotek, Copenhagen, AEIN 660; Jørgensen 1996, pp. 56–57; Potočková 1998, pp. 227–33.
23. Potočková 1998, pp. 227–33.
24. Zuber 1956, p. 161.
25. Saleh and Sourouzian 1987, no. 27.
26. Wittkower 1995, p. 123.
27. Davis 1989.
28. "Geradvorstellung" in German. Baines in Schäfer 1986, p. xvii; Schäfer 1986, pp. 91–92. Some art historians call this principle "aspective"; see Brunner-Traut in ibid., pp. 420–46.
29. Nowadays we can see an interesting application of this principle in African art.
30. Fischer 1995, pl. 27b–d.
31. Wildung 1990; Fischer 1995, pp. 84–85, pl. 27a.
32. See also the statue of Pepi I (Brooklyn Museum, 39.120).
33. Khafre's queen, wearing a long coat and tunic, both pleated (Egyptian Museum, Cairo, JE 48828); compare with Oriental Institute, Chicago, 10618, and Metropolitan Museum, 62.201.2.
34. Tefnin 1987, pp. 165–66.

35. Ivory foot of a bed (Louvre, E 11019A) and the bull palette (Louvre, E 11255).
36. Schäfer 1986.
37. Davis 1989, pp. 4, 208–10.
38. On the criteria for dating tombs and on their decoration, see, most recently, Cherpion 1989. For an overview of the question and reports of colloquia on the history of Old Kingdom art, see *Sonderschrift des Deutschen Archäologischen Instituts, Abteilung Kairo* 28 (1995); *Bibliothèque d'étude* 120 (1998); and *L'art de l'Ancien Empire* 1999.
39. Vandersleyen 1975a, p. 26.
40. Helck 1987, pp. 242–44, no. 11 (the inscription mentions some unusual titles that recur on the two statues of Sepa in the Louvre [cat. nos. 11, 12]: "priest of Nezer[?] and of the ram deity Kherty"; the owner's name is lacking).
41. Musées Royaux d'Art et d'Histoire, Brussels, E 752; Seipel 1992, pp. 84–87, nos. 8, 9.
42. Otherwise known as Bedjmes, British Museum, 171.
43. Egyptian Museum, Cairo, JE 34557 (= CG 1).
44. Instances of the pose are, however, known up to the Sixth Dynasty: statues of Ka-em-ked (fig. 35) and Pepi I (cat. no. 170).
45. Tefnin 1991.
46. Statues of Tjenti (Louvre, E 10776) and Seneb (Egyptian Museum, Cairo, JE 51280).
47. Louvre, E 15592.
48. Cherpion 1995, pp. 33–47, pls. 2–8.
49. Porter and Moss 1974, pp. 143–44; Khentet-ka was the spouse of Nesut-nefer, who was, without doubt, a contemporary of Khafre (Cherpion 1989, pp. 114, 226).
50. Vandersleyen 1975a, p. 28.
51. Vandersleyen 1973, pp. 13–15.
52. Cherpion 1984, pp. 35–54, pls. 1–11; Cherpion 1989, p. 89.
53. Most recently, Ziegler 1997a, pp. 204–8.
54. Vandersleyen 1983, pp. 61–65.
55. LG 40 = G 5230; archives of the Museum of Fine Arts, Boston, unpublished.
56. Smith 1946, p. 50.
57. Ibid. (Reg. No. 14-12-7,82).
58. Compare also a head of a statue of Ba-baef (Kunsthistorisches Museum, Vienna, ÄS 7786).
59. Staatliche Sammlung Ägyptischer Kunst, Munich, ÄS 6794.
60. Eaton-Krauss 1995, pp. 57–74.
61. Eaton-Krauss 1984, p. 58; Harvey 1994.
62. Most recently, Assmann 1996, pp. 65–67.
63. Wildung 1982b, pp. 8–10.
64. Funerary priest of Wer-irni, whose titles mention Neferirkare.
65. Bibliothèque Nationale de France, Paris, 53, no. 11.
66. Central Museum and Art Gallery, Northampton, England; James 1963, pp. 5–12; see also Egyptian Museum, Cairo, CG 21.
67. SA 96/7 (= OAE 42); Ziegler 1997c, pp. 237–43.
68. Saqqara, mastaba D 47; this person figures in the reliefs of Sahure, and in his tomb the names of Userkaf and Sahure occur. The tomb yielded sixteen statues in various positions. Two represent scribes, and many, unfortunately, are headless.
69. Egyptian Museum, Cairo, CG 94, limestone.
70. British Museum, 1239.
71. Egyptian Museum, Cairo, JE 10065 (= CG 20; h. 1.98; Saqqara D 22); Smith 1946, p. 78; Cherpion 1989, p. 131.
72. Egyptian Museum, Cairo, JE 51738.
73. Egyptian Museum, Cairo, JE 93165; Russmann 1995a, p. 275, n. 66.
74. Ibid., p. 276.
75. Brooklyn Museum, 51.1; Nelson-Atkins Museum of Art, Kansas City, 51-1.
76. Russmann 1995a, p. 274.
77. Vandersleyen 1982, col. 1076.
78. Russmann 1995a, p. 271.
79. Pepi-ankh, "the Black," Egyptian Museum, Cairo, CG 60 and CG 236; the two royal statues of copper found at Hierakonopolis may express this duality.
80. Russmann 1995a, p. 269, n. 5.
81. This practice, known since the Fourth Dynasty, had already been adopted for some statue types, particularly scribes, dwarfs, and most model sculpture.
82. Smith 1946, pp. 84–85, pl. 26a–c.
83. Ibid., p. 88.
84. Also see the statue of Niankh-re, Egyptian Museum, Cairo, JE 53150, which probably dates to the Fifth Dynasty; Cherpion 1998, p. 105.
85. Russmann 1995a, p. 272.
86. Valloggia 1989, pp. 271–82.
87. Izi of Edfu, Louvre, Paris, E 14399; Pepi-ankh the Middle, Mallawi Antiquities Museum; see Hittah and Misihah 1979, p. 23, pl. 26; and Ziegler 1997a, pp. 96–99.
88. Donadoni 1993, p. 104.
89. Russmann 1995a, p. 277.

RESERVE HEADS
An Enigma of
Old Kingdom Sculpture

CATHARINE H. ROEHRIG

While excavating at Dahshur in 1894, Jacques de Morgan discovered the first reserve head ever encountered. It came from a tomb dated to the Fourth Dynasty, sometime between the late years of Snefru's reign and the middle of the reign of his son Khufu.[1] This head has close affinities with two others found later in the Western Cemetery at Giza and is probably among the earliest of the entire series. It is also one of only four found outside the Giza necropolis,[2] which has yielded twenty-seven examples,[3] most from the reigns of Khufu and Khafre, who was Khufu's son and second successor in the Fourth Dynasty.[4]

Reserve heads are unique in Egyptian art because each one was made to be complete in itself, not as part of a statue. Every head is cut off flat at the base of the neck, allowing it to stand upright. All are represented with short-cropped hair or perhaps shaven heads. A large proportion also show evidence of intentional damage to the ears and the back of the head. Many reserve heads were carved from fine white limestone with the features well formed and the surface carefully smoothed. Some, however, were quite crudely carved and appear to have been finished with substantial amounts of plaster,[5] and two were made from finely ground Nile mud.[6]

RESERVE HEADS AS PORTRAITS

Although there are many affinities among the heads, each has particular characteristics that distinguish it from the others, as can be seen in a photograph of a group from Giza (fig. 46).[7] This individuality has led many scholars to describe reserve heads as portraits. George Reisner,

who discovered more than half of the excavated examples, went a step further, perceiving family relationships among the heads he uncovered.[8] For example, on the basis of similarities between heads from mastabas G 4240 (Cairo JE 46215; fig. 46d) and G 4440 (Boston 14.718; fig. 46g) he identified the tomb owners as brothers. At approximately 30 centimeters in height, these heads are two of the largest.[9] The chief feature they share is the long, narrow shape of the face, apparent when they are seen from the front; however, when viewed from any other angle, the resemblance dissipates.[10] Reisner also believed he could determine the ethnic background of individuals represented by the heads. For example, he identified Cairo JE 46218 (G 4340; fig. 46c) and Cairo JE 46216 (G 4640; fig. 46a) as west Asiatic,[11] although both have characteristics in common with others he thought represented native Egyptians. While individual reserve heads may have been made to resemble the people in whose tombs they were placed, it is equally possible that the similarities among these works are the result of conventions used by an individual artist or group of artists.

Any study of the reserve heads must involve grouping them according to type, a highly subjective exercise in which each viewer will find different affinities. The chief obstacle to any definitive comparison or analysis of the heads is a lack of good, comprehensive photographs. No photographs exist of certain examples, and only one view has been published of others. In many cases photographs have been taken from different angles: some from above, some from below, some with the head turned slightly to the right or left but almost never rotated to the same degree. And views of the backs of the heads are largely unavailable. There are, however, excellent scaled photographs of most of the examples excavated by Reisner,

A   B   C   D

Fig. 46. Eight reserve heads excavated in 1913 at Giza by the Harvard University–Museum of Fine Arts Expedition, displayed at the Harvard Camp, Giza, December 17, 1913. The heads were divided between the Egyptian Museum, Cairo, and the Museum of Fine Arts, Boston. From left to right, they are: a. Cairo JE 46216 (G 4640); b. Boston 21.328 (G 4540; cat. no. 47); c. Cairo JE 46218 (G 4340); d. Cairo JE 46215 (G 4240); e. Cairo JE 46217 (G 4140); f. Boston 14.717 (G 4140); g. Boston 14.718 (G 4440); h. Boston 14.719 (G 4440; cat. no. 48)

and Roland Tefnin has provided multiple views of many pieces.[12] Using these resources, it is possible to discern numerous stylistic parallels among the sculptures. For example, it is apparent that Cairo JE 46218 (G 4340; fig. 46c), one of Reisner's west Asiatics, has a number of features in common with Boston 14.717 (G 4140; fig. 46f) and Boston 21.328 (G 4540; fig. 46b; cat. no. 47), two heads Reisner considered to represent native Egyptians.[13]

Most of the reserve heads found at Giza probably were created by one or two generations of sculptors whose careers spanned the reigns of Khufu, Djedefre, and Khafre, and it is not surprising that these examples can be divided into other stylistic groupings.[14] More unexpected are the affinities that seem to connect the head unearthed by Morgan at Dahshur, Cairo CG 519, with two excavated at Giza, Berkeley 6-19767 (G 1203; cat. no. 46) and Cairo JE 46217 (G 4140; fig. 46e).[15] The proportions of the three faces, with their full cheeks and soft chins, are very similar, and the mouths, eyes, and sculpted eyebrows have much in common as well. These parallels appear to bind the two Giza heads very closely in date, and perhaps

even in site of manufacture, with the head from Dahshur, a royal necropolis approximately fourteen miles to the south that was diminishing in importance while Giza was becoming the preeminent royal burial ground.[16] Further attempts to link heads stylistically using firsthand examination and up-to-date, comprehensive photographs might produce very interesting results.

ARCHAEOLOGICAL CONTEXT

The archaeological context of the thirty-one excavated reserve heads is somewhat ambiguous. The majority were found in the substructures of their respective tombs, in either the shaft or the burial chamber,[17] and not one was associated with an aboveground offering chapel. This distinguishes them from other types of Old Kingdom funerary statues, which played a role in the offering cult and usually were either located in full view somewhere in the offering chapel[18] or hidden in a statue chamber, or serdab.

With one exception the mastabas in which reserve heads were discovered had been ransacked by thieves in ancient

74

E   F   G   H

times. Some may also have been entered later by ancient
Egyptians searching for reusable building materials. The
only head discovered in a context resembling its original
location was excavated by Selim Hassan at Giza in a
tomb that had been penetrated by water and mud but
not plundered by thieves. This head was found in the
burial chamber in front of the sarcophagus, lying on its
side near floor level in the mud that had filled the room.[19]
Although it was no longer in its original position, it
seems most likely that the head was intended to stand
upright on the floor. This find suggests that reserve heads
were originally placed in the burial chamber of the tomb[20]
rather than in the blocking of the entrance corridor[21] or
in the shaft, where most were found, presumably having been thrown there when a tomb was robbed.[22]

DISTRIBUTION IN GIZA CEMETERY 4000

The majority of reserve heads were distributed among
the three earliest cemeteries constructed to the west of
Khufu's pyramid at Giza (collectively called the Western

Cemetery). Cemeteries 1200 and 2100 yielded only one
head each, but eighteen were found in cemetery 4000,
nearly all of them in the group of twenty-one mastabas
that belong to the first three building phases identified by
Reisner.[23] These structures form three rows of seven tombs
to the east of the huge mastaba of Hemiunu (G 4000;
fig. 47).

The mastabas in this section of cemetery 4000 and in
cemetery 1200 yielded a number of slab stelae (see cat.
nos. 51–53). Although most of the stelae were found in
cemetery 1200, where only one reserve head was discovered, it seems that these two types of funerary equipment appeared together more often than the numbers
imply. While only four complete or fragmentary slab stelae seem to have been found in the tomb chapels in cemetery 4000, nine other mastabas in the earliest tombs of
this cemetery contain emplacements for stelae. Only nine
reserve heads were unearthed in these thirteen tombs (see
fig. 47), but it is quite possible that they all once housed
such heads.[24]

Two of the mastabas that Reisner excavated contained
two reserve heads each. One of these tombs, G 4140,

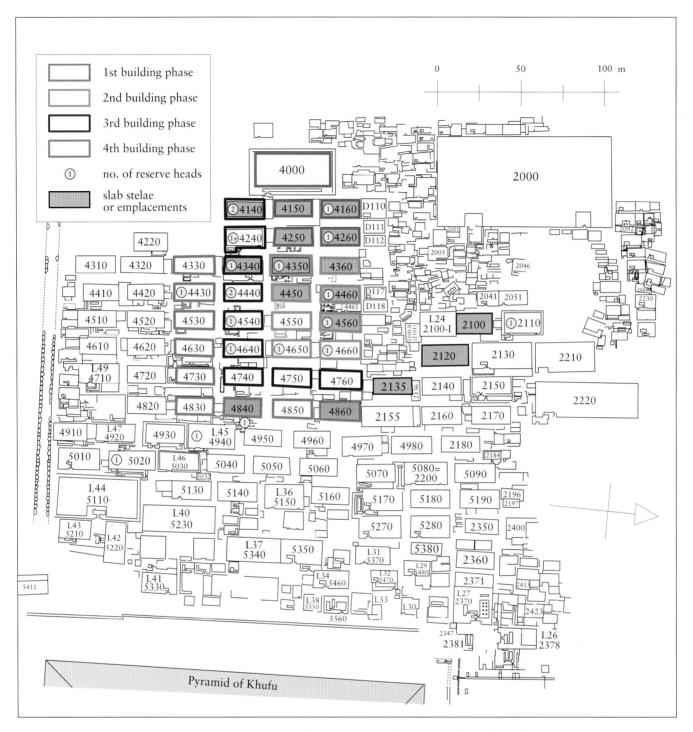

Fig. 47. Map of cemeteries 2100, 4000, and 5000 at Giza, showing locations of reserve heads and slab stelae emplacements. Drawing by Peter Der Manuelian

belonged to the king's daughter Meret-ites, whose name was recorded on a slab stela in her offering chapel. One head was found lying in the burial chamber, and the other had been uncovered near the bottom of the shaft. Reisner identified them as representing, respectively, Meret-ites (fig. 46e) and her husband (fig. 46f). The two heads in the second mastaba, G 4440, were located together near the bottom of the shaft, and these Reisner identified as a prince (fig. 46g) and his Nubian wife (fig. 46h; cat. no. 48). Reisner believed that a third mastaba in the same area had also once housed two reserve heads. In 1913 he had found a head (fig. 46d) and a neck fragment from a second one in mastaba G 4240, which contained a slab stela inscribed for the king's son Snefru-seneb. During a later excavation season, while clearing mastaba G 5020 some distance to the southeast, he discovered a reserve head with a large chip broken out of its neck. The archaeological context of this head, which lay in shaft debris above the burial chamber door, convinced Reisner that it was intrusive, and he suggested that it portrayed the wife of Snefru-seneb and had originally been deposited in G 4240.[25]

The presence in each of these mastabas of two reserve heads belonging to a husband and wife poses a problem that Reisner failed to address. The large core mastabas in the great Western Cemetery were designed with only one shaft leading to a single, relatively small burial chamber, and the archaeological evidence suggests that they were used for only one burial. Neither mastaba G 4240 nor G 4440 has any contemporary subsidiary shafts for family members, and, since both men and women owned mastabas, a husband and wife might well have had separate, neighboring tombs. In the case of G 4140, the mastaba of Meret-ites, an annex was added to the north end of the superstructure and excavation of a shaft was begun, presumably for the burial of a close family member. However, there is no chamber at the bottom of this shaft, nor was the shaft itself used for a burial.[26] Since each reserve head seems to be an integral part of the burial equipment for a specific individual, one must ask why there would be two heads in tombs intended for only one person. The simplest answer is that one of the heads in each tomb is intrusive. Several of the earliest mastabas of cemetery 4000 that were designed to have slab stelae contained no reserve head when excavated. Three of these, G 4150, G 4250, and G 4450, are immediately north of the three mastabas in which Reisner found a pair of heads. This pattern of distribution leads to the obvious suggestion that one of the heads in G 4140, one in G 4440, and the neck fragment in G 4240 (together

with the head from G 5020, if it fits with that fragment)[27] came from the neighboring mastabas to the north, having been displaced by robbers.

Another reserve head, found in G 4940 but considered to be intrusive by Reisner, may also have come from one of the twenty-one earliest mastabas in cemetery 4000.[28] In addition, it should be noted that two heads of unfired clay were uncovered in cemetery 4000, suggesting that some of the mastabas that contained no heads may have been equipped with examples of this more fragile variety, which either did not survive or were so badly damaged that they were not recognized by the excavators.[29]

PURPOSE

Since the heads clearly did not play a part in the offering cult, which was carried out aboveground, scholars have long attempted to formulate another explanation for their existence. The earliest theory concerning their purpose was put forward by Ludwig Borchardt, who in 1903 discovered a head at Abusir that was only the second to have been found.[30] He suggested that they were intended to protect or replace the head of the deceased,[31] an idea with which both Reisner and Hermann Junker generally agreed. Junker went on to suggest that the heads served a purpose similar to that of the plaster face masks (cat. no. 197) uncovered in a number of Old Kingdom tombs. William Stevenson Smith carried this thought a step further, hypothesizing that the heads and masks were precursors of the cartonnage mummy masks that began to appear in the First Intermediate Period.[32]

Theories connecting the reserve heads to the evolution of mummy masks, and perhaps even to anthropoid coffins, are supported by the fact that the heads do not seem to correspond to any other type of funeral equipment documented for later periods. Although there is no evidence that they were used outside the Memphite area during the Old Kingdom, one possible distant parallel, documented at Thebes, appeared some twelve centuries later in the tomb of Tutankhamun. This is the wood sculpture of a lifesize head emerging from a lotus blossom.

The Tutankhamun piece was made in several sections, with the head as a separate element. Although entirely different in style and medium from the Old Kingdom reserve heads, the Tutankhamun head has various features in common with them: it was not made as part of a statue; the neck is cut off flat at the bottom, which would allow it to stand on its own; and the hair, represented by small dots that cover the top of the skull, is close shaven. This sculpture, whose precise find spot unfortunately is in question,[33] is generally understood to represent the infant sun god being born—a powerful symbol of the pharaoh's anticipated rebirth. Its connection to Old Kingdom reserve heads, although extremely tenuous, suggests a magical function for the earlier works that is consistent with the generally accepted theories associating them with the development of the mummy mask and anthropoid coffin. It is quite possible that reserve heads served as symbols of the sun god or the god Atum appearing at the moment of creation on the primeval mound, which itself may even have been imitated by a mound of earth or sand on the floor of the burial chamber.

INTENTIONAL DAMAGE

Although existing theories concerning the function of reserve heads explain why they were placed in the substructure of the tomb, none successfully accounts for the widespread mutilation of the heads.

Since all reserve heads were discovered in disturbed archaeological contexts, it is not surprising that even the best-preserved examples have suffered abrasions and chips to the surface and even occasionally have lost part of the nose. However, two types of damage typically found among reserve heads are notable because they occur rarely in other types of Egyptian sculpture. For this reason they are presumed to represent intentional mutilation rather than accidental damage. Only twenty-six of the thirty-one excavated reserve heads are well enough preserved to be used in a discussion of intentional mutilation and accidental damage.[34]

The most universal form of mutilation is removal of the ears. Among fifteen heads that probably had sculpted ears, only Boston 14.719 (cat. no. 48) has its ears intact. Removal of the ears takes several forms. On some heads, such as Vienna 7787 (cat. no. 49), they have been chiseled off close to the surface in a relatively careful and even manner. On others, for example Berkeley 6-19767 (cat. no. 46), the prominent parts have been chipped away, leaving a distinct outline, or hacked off in a more haphazard fashion, as on Boston 21.328 (cat. no. 47).

Most members of a small group of heads whose ears were made as separate elements and attached with plaster or tenons were found with one or both ears missing.[35] One might assume that these ears broke off due to rough handling by tomb robbers if it were not for the fourteen examples missing their sculpted ears. A third group,

which includes the Dahshur head, was created without any provision for ears. This omission may represent a stylistic preference of a particular artist or patron or may be connected in some way to the intentional removal of ears from at least fourteen heads.

Another type of mutilation suffered by a significant number of reserve heads is the single or double line that was scratched or more often gouged into the finished surface from the crown to the nape of the neck. Because written descriptions of the heads are not always complete and the backs often have not been photographed, this form of damage is not as well documented as the removal of the ears. However, it is known that of the twenty-six examples under consideration fifteen, including cat. no. 49, exhibit these lines and five, including cat. nos. 46–48, do not, leaving six in question.

Junker and Reisner both mentioned that the ears were usually missing from the heads, but neither appears to have found this particularly significant. Both excavators also described the grooves that appear in many examples. While Junker made no attempt to account for this phenomenon, Reisner suggested that the gouges may have been made by thieves trying to determine if the heads were hollow.[36] This explanation is rather unsatisfactory, however, since such information could have been obtained more easily by simply smashing the objects.[37]

In more recent years scholars have put forward a number of other theories regarding the mutilation of reserve heads. Nicholas Millet has proposed that they served as sculptors' models (see introduction to cat. nos. 46–49).[38] In addition he suggests that molds were taken of the heads for the preparation of plaster mummy masks and speculates that the gouges down the backs of some were made when the molds were cut open and removed, a process that also caused the damage to the ears.

This interesting theory finds no support in the preserved record. No contemporary statuary has been found in tombs containing reserve heads,[39] and, in fact, the only type of sculpture that can be connected firmly with them is the slab stela, with its single representation of the deceased seated before an offering table.[40] Thus, there would seem to have been no need for sculptors' models, certainly not ones carved of fine limestone. Moreover, all of the extant plaster masks appear to have been modeled on the mummy itself, not cast (see entry for cat. no. 197).

Another, far more elaborate explanation for the mutilation has been set out by Tefnin.[41] In his detailed study Tefnin catalogues what he believes to be ritual mutilation carried out when the heads were placed in their tombs. He likens this practice to the mutilating of animal figurines and hieroglyphs of dangerous animals on objects deposited in tombs of the First Intermediate Period and Middle Kingdom. According to this theory, the heads had to be ritually "killed" in order to render them harmless to the deceased, because they were in the substructure of the tomb, in close proximity to the body.

Tefnin's suggestions are well presented and intriguing but somewhat problematic. In order to make his case, the author classifies four types of ritual mutilation,[42] which one would expect to see with some consistency in contemporary heads found in the same area if such acts had been performed to protect the deceased. Yet among the heads found in core mastabas of cemetery 4000 at Giza, all of which were probably carved and buried within a generation or two, not a single example exhibits all of Tefnin's forms of ritual damage; at least three show no evidence of a groove cut into the back of the head—the most unequivocal type of intentional damage; and one (cat. no. 48) shows no damage that cannot convincingly be explained as accidental.

A much simpler explanation of the damage found on reserve heads was recently presented by Peter Lacovara, who hypothesizes that the grooves and a number of other marks they display are sculptors' guidelines, comparable to the incised guidelines seen on the so-called trial pieces of the Ptolemaic Period.[43] However, the guidelines on the Ptolemaic objects are always finely and precisely carved on an unfinished flat surface, not gouged or hacked into a finished one like most of the grooves on reserve heads.

In fact, the gouging of lines and damage to ears are inflicted too inconsistently to constitute conclusive evidence of ritual mutilation performed to protect the dead. Yet these forms of mutilation occur far too frequently to allow them to be discounted as accidental, and the gouges are too haphazardly and/or violently executed to be sculptors' guidelines. It seems only marginally more likely that these types of damage were intentionally inflicted when the tombs were robbed or later when they were mined for reusable materials: why would a robber or other intruder who feared the magical powers of the objects take the time to carefully remove the ears and scratch the backs of the heads, when smashing them would have taken less effort? Indeed, plunderers do seem to have broken at least two heads, Vienna 9290 (G 4260) and New York 48.156 (G 7560B), and possibly a third discovered in fragmentary form by Junker in G 4460, about which almost nothing is known.[44] And in three other examples, Hildesheim 2158 (G 4160), Boston 36-12-6 (G 7560B), and Boston 27-4-1219 (G 7650C), the face was

separated from the skull by a few well-placed blows and shows much abrasion around the eyes, nose, and mouth.[45]

The question of why many reserve heads suffered unusual forms of mutilation must remain open for the present, since complete documentation of all the excavated examples is not available. One can only hope that new information derived from complete examinations of all the heads will help us to better understand the purpose of this unique group of objects.

Reserve heads are referred to in this chapter by their present city location and a museum accession or inventory number. The museums, which are not named, are as follows: Berkeley, California: Phoebe Apperson Hearst Museum of Anthropology; Berlin: Ägyptisches Museum und Papyrussammlung, Staatliche Museen zu Berlin; Boston: Museum of Fine Arts; Cairo: Egyptian Museum; Hildesheim, Roemer- und Pelizaeus-Museum; London: Petrie Museum of Egyptian Archaeology, University College; New York: The Metropolitan Museum of Art; Vienna: Kunsthistoriches Museum.

1. This is Cairo CG 519. See Morgan 1895, p. 9, and fig. 7, a drawing that oddly enough, appears to reconstruct the broken nose.
2. The other non-Giza heads are all later in date: Berlin 16455 from Abusir is probably Fifth Dynasty; the head found by Fakhry at Saqqara is no earlier than Sixth Dynasty; and a head discovered in 1989 at Lisht by Dieter and Dorothea Arnold is dated to the early Twelfth Dynasty. The Lisht head is only 10.25 centimeters in height and seems to have been part of the debris from a sculptor's workshop that was used as fill (personal communication from Dorothea Arnold).
3. Tefnin (1991) documents three unprovenanced reserve heads that do not enter into this discussion: Cairo JE 89611, London 15988, and one in a private collection. The ears found without heads in four mastabas in cemetery 4000 also have not been considered here.
4. Twenty-one reserve heads (including the one found in G 5020) can be associated with the early core mastabas in cemeteries 1200, 2100, and 4000, the construction of which Reisner dated to the reign of Khufu, although the tombs were not always used during this king's reign.
5. Boston 21.329, for example, has a thick glob of plaster that adheres to the left cheek near the nose and extends from the eye to the mouth. This plaster appears to have a finished surface just above the mouth. The eyes are imperfectly carved, the nose has been flattened, and no attempt has been made to smooth the sharp curves of the brow ridges. Berlin 16455 is almost completely modeled in plaster (see Wildung 1998), but it will not figure significantly in this discussion since it is from a different site and a later dynasty than the majority of the heads.
6. One nearly complete example, Cairo JE 44975, was found by Junker in an intrusive shaft east of G 4840; the other, a very fragmentary head, Obj. Reg. 13-12-1, probably in Boston, was discovered by Reisner in G 4430.
7. Reisner found eight reserve heads in cemetery 4000 between early November and mid-December of his 1913–14 excavation season. Several photographs of these, including this one, were taken in an expedition workroom on December 17.

8. Reisner 1915, pp. 32–35.

9. Most heads from the great Western Cemetery are between 25 and 27 centimeters high.

10. This is especially evident in the profile views of these two heads published in Reisner 1915, figs. 8, 12.

11. On the basis of his consideration of heads found by Reisner and himself, Junker came to somewhat different conclusions, identifying two broad groups, one of more noble and one of more peasant origin; see Junker 1929, pp. 63–65. For an extensive critique of both authors' conclusions, see Tefnin 1991, pp. 62–69.

12. See Reisner 1942, pls. 22a–e, 34c–f, 52–56, which usually give a frontal, two profile, and one or two other views of the heads; and Tefnin 1991, which usually offers more than one view of heads that were available for the author's examination.

13. See entry for cat. no. 47.

14. Boston 14.718 (G 4440) and Cairo JE 46215 (G 4240) have features in common with Hildesheim 2384 (G 4650); the shapes of Vienna 7877 (G 4350) and Vienna 9290 (G 4260) are very similar (unfortunately, the latter has none of the facial features preserved); Boston 21.239 (G 4940) shares many characteristics with Boston 06.1886 (G 2110). Similarities can also be found among the three heads found by Reisner in cemetery 7000: Boston 36-12-6 (G 7560B), New York 48.156 (G 7560B), and Boston 27.4.1219 (G 7660C).

15. See entry for cat. no. 46, esp. n. 5.

16. It is my belief that these three heads were the earliest made, but further study of the subject is necessary. Unfortunately, there seems to be only one published photograph of Cairo, CG 519, making comparison of it with other heads difficult. This photograph was first published in Smith 1946, pl. 6, and reprinted in later publications (Simpson 1949, p. 289, ill.; Tefnin 1991, pl. 13c).

17. Three heads were found in robbers' debris in the streets that separate the large core mastabas at Giza: Hildesheim 2158 was uncovered west of mastaba G 4160 and probably came from this tomb; Cairo temp. 19/11/24/5 was discovered in debris between G 4560 and G 4660 and was assigned by Junker to G 4660; Boston 27.4.1219 was found in the street separating G 7650 and G 7660, and Reisner thought it belonged to G 7660.

18. These statues could be either freestanding or carved into the walls of the offering chapel.

19. Hassan 1953, pp. 4–5, pls. 3–4a. The excavator proposed that the owner of this tomb was a daughter of Khafre. Whether or not this identification is correct, the tomb probably dates to the late Fourth or early Fifth Dynasty, and it is reasonable to assume that the head was deposited in the burial chamber following the same practice common a generation or so earlier in the great Western Cemetery, where the majority of the heads were found.

20. Reisner (n.d., p. 239) suggested that the heads might have been placed on the coffin, on the stone slab used to cover the canopic pit, or simply on the floor of the chamber. I am grateful to Rita E. Freed for allowing me to consult Reisner's unpublished manuscripts housed in the Department of Egyptian, Nubian, and Ancient Near Eastern Art at the Museum of Fine Arts, Boston.

21. Junker, one of the principal excavators of reserve heads at Giza, believed that they were originally placed in the corridor leading from the shaft to the burial chamber. After the burial, these corridors were blocked with stones and the entrance on the shaft side was then covered with a large portcullis. According to Junker, the heads were placed in a niche left in the stone blocking immediately behind the portcullis. He equated the holes found in many of the portcullis stones with the holes or slits that usually connect a serdab with its offering chamber and thus symbolically link the statues with the outside world. However, the archaeological evidence does not support this theory; see Kelley 1974, pp. 7–8; and Lacovara 1997.

22. The small head found by Fakhry at Saqqara reveals little, if anything, about the use of reserve heads. Fakhry (1959, p. 30) describes its archaeological context as follows: "In the shaft there was found a damaged small reserve limestone head (19.5 cms in height) re used and put in the filling of the shaft just above the entrance." No description of the head is given other than the information about its height, which tells us that it is small (the average height of the Giza heads is 26 centimeters), and no photographs were ever published. Although the thieves who plundered this tomb evidently did not enter through the shaft, it is not clear that the head was placed in the shaft as part of the burial. It is quite possible that the head is a sculptor's small trial piece that was discarded and became mingled with debris used to fill the shaft, like the even smaller example found at Lisht in 1989; see note 2 above.

23. Two others, found in G 4940 and G 5020, may also have come from the twenty-one earliest tombs.

24. G 4840 does not have a slab-stela emplacement and the fragment associated with this tomb may not be from a slab stela; see Der Manuelian 1998a. The head associated with this mastaba was not found in the principal shaft and may have come from another tomb. If it was from another tomb, this would mean that eight heads were found in twelve mastabas with slab stelae or slab-stelae emplacements.

25. Because of its position Reisner (n.d., p. 234) maintained that it could not have come from the burial chamber but had been thrown into the shaft with the debris.

26. Reisner (1942, p. 464) describes the shaft as completely plundered or unused.

27. I have been unable to find evidence that Reisner ever joined the neck fragment from G 4240 with the head from G 5020, and it seems possible that the chip is part of the fragmentary head that Junker found in G 4260 (Vienna 9290). It is also possible that it belongs to an incomplete head Junker discovered in G 4460. Unfortunately, the current location of the neck fragment is unrecorded.

28. According to Reisner (ibid., p. 234), this head was found in the shaft above the burial-chamber door, where it had obviously been thrown during recent illicit excavations. He suggested, parenthetically, that it had come from G 4740.

29. Reisner himself (ibid., p. 236) thought that there might have been other heads, particularly in cemetery 1200, where only one was found and where the burial chambers had been stripped of their fine limestone lining.

30. This is Berlin 16455.

31. Borchardt 1907, p. 133.

32. Smith 1946, pp 24–25.

33. Of course, the position of this piece when it was discovered by Howard Carter was not necessarily its location at the time of burial, but may have represented a secondary placement made after the tomb was robbed and restored.

34. Three examples from Giza mastabas G 4430 (Boston, unaccessioned), G 4460 (Cairo, unaccessioned), and G 4660 (Cairo temp 19/11/24/5) are too fragmentary or too little known to provide the necessary information. The head from Lisht, as has been noted, appears to have been a sculptor's trial piece found in fill and exhibits no mutilations; the one found at

Saqqara, as has been mentioned, is probably a similar type of object and was never fully described.

35. Occasionally one or both of the detached ears were found in tombs with the heads to which they belonged, and whole or fragmentary ears in three mastabas that contained no heads were discovered in cemetery 4000.

36. Reisner n.d., p. 238. Reisner also considered the possibility that the grooves were made to secure a layer of plaster over the heads, but he correctly discarded this idea.

37. As pointed out in Lacovara 1997, pp. 34–35.

38. Millet 1981.

39. But see entry for cat no. 46.

40. G 4650 (Iabtit) and G 4240 (Snefru-seneb) contained decorated false doors, and G 2110 (Nefer) had a decorated offering chapel, but these may well have been modifications made after the burials; see "The Tombs of Officials" by Peter Jánosi in this catalogue. It is next to impossible to make a comparison between a reserve head and a slab stela found in the same tomb, since the facial features of either one or the other are invariably damaged. For example, the reserve head believed to represent Princess Meret-ites (Cairo JE 46217) is missing its nose, and the figure on her slab stela has a damaged chin, thus eliminating the chance to compare the two most distinctive features of the profile.

41. Tefnin 1991.

42. Two are the removal of the ears and the gouging of the back of the head, the typical, widespread forms mentioned above. The other two, a line scratched around the neck near the base and a retracing of the hairline, are so sporadic, and often so difficult to discern, that their classification is questionable.

43. Lacovara 1997.

44. Mentioned in Junker 1929, p. 190. Breakage of the two heads of Nile mud is difficult to assess because of the inherent fragility of the material.

45. One of these three faces was not found; the other two are very badly damaged. Hildesheim 2158 and Boston 27-4-1219 were discovered in the street, which may account for some of the damage they have suffered. Another head, Cairo temp. 19/11/24/5 (G 4660), described by Junker as being very much abraded, was also found in the street between the mastabas.

ROYAL RELIEFS

DOROTHEA ARNOLD

By the beginning of the Middle Kingdom the royal temples of the Pyramid Age had already started to fall into decay.[1] What remained was often dismantled under the Ramesside kings of the Nineteenth and Twentieth Dynasties (about 1295–1070 B.C.E.), who sent demolition parties to obtain stone material for vast new building projects.[2] As a result, modern excavations have brought to light few standing Old Kingdom temple walls. Typically only the foundations and lower wall courses are extant, while thousands of larger and smaller fragments from the original relief decoration cover these remains and the surrounding area.[3] It is therefore not surprising that this publication and the exhibition it accompanies are in the main concerned with fragments from the once-large-scale royal reliefs of the Old Kingdom.

Examining fragments has special advantages: the viewer is induced to focus on details of iconography and artistic execution that may be overlooked in a scrutiny of full-scale, relatively undamaged compositions. However, true appreciation of details must be based on some knowledge of a fragment's original context. Since Egyptian artists repeated a rather circumscribed set of iconographic configurations from temple to temple and from wall to wall, Egyptologists have been able to reconstruct, at least on paper, the overall compositions of a fair number of Old Kingdom royal reliefs.[4]

BEGINNINGS

Much Old Kingdom relief iconography was codified by the start of the Third Dynasty. The system had been developed during later Predynastic times and the Archaic Period on objects of minor, or decorative, arts (vessels, combs, cosmetic palettes, and the like, often having ceremonial or funerary significance)[5] and possibly in paintings on now-vanished mud-plastered brick walls.[6] Rare remains of late Second Dynasty architectural relief decoration[7] testify to a pre–Third Dynasty emergence of large-scale stone reliefs, if only in specific parts of monuments otherwise built of mud brick. From the Third Dynasty onward many sacred buildings were erected entirely of stone and over time provided increasingly larger wall spaces on which established iconographic configurations could be developed and refined. The result was one of the world's most coherent illustrative systems, a complex pictorial language for the visual propagation of ideas on kingship and its religious connotations.

BASIC FIGURAL SCHEMES

The Old Kingdom relief language is based on a strikingly small number of fundamental figural schemes.[8] The possibilities of combination were, however, unlimited, allowing this vocabulary to meet an infinite variety of pictorial needs and to be adapted to various forms of architecture. The basic figural element of Egyptian pictorial art is the single human figure (male or female), either standing (the male almost always with legs apart as if walking), seated, or in action.[9] In royal reliefs the most conspicuous single figure in action is a man running or striding with legs wide apart and knees bent. Two nonactive standing figures of approximately equal rank often form a unit in which the figures face each other or embrace.[10] The classic group of two figures of unequal rank shows the powerful pharaoh in a striding position: his raised right arm swings a weapon, and an enemy cowers at his feet (cat. no. 8).

From early on, single and double figures appeared on relief slabs set into niches (cat. no. 9)[11] and on pillars in temple courtyards.[12] Occasionally two single figures might flank important architectural elements such as the statue niches in the temple of Snefru at Dahshur;[13] on the whole, however, single figures were not used in royal monuments to emphasize such architectural features as niches, false doors, or doorways.[14] Even the important

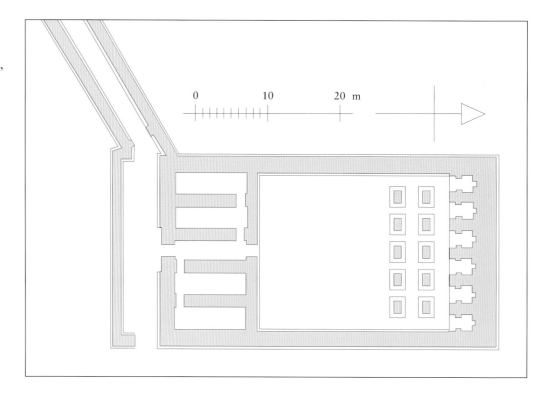

Fig. 48. Plan of statue-cult temple of Snefru, Dahshur. Drawing by Dieter Arnold from D. Arnold 1997, p. 45, fig. 11

central niched doorways in the valley and pyramid temples were not flanked by large single images of the king or a god but rather by groups of two or more large interacting figures (cat. no. 118). The most important role of the prominent single figure in Old Kingdom royal relief was to serve as the focal point and unifying element in large-scale relief compositions, and it was as part of such compositions that large figures of the king dominated walls and rooms.

Repetition of identical or similar single figures creates a row of figures that may be depicted along the walls of a room or a set of rooms, emphasizing the movement from one architectural space to the next. This scheme was employed to great advantage in the statue-cult temple of Snefru at Dahshur,[15] the earliest royal building from which a relief decoration is preserved to a substantial extent.[16] Situated roughly halfway between agricultural land and the king's Bent Pyramid, the temple was entered through an area containing five parallel rooms of elongated shape, the central one of which led into the temple courtyard (fig. 48).[17] On both long walls of this corridorlike central room, rows of exquisitely adorned women were represented in the bottom register, all facing toward the temple interior (figs. 49, 50).[18] The women (cat. no. 22) represented royal estates dedicated to providing sustenance in perpetuity for the ritual performances in the temple. Although the figures in Snefru's temple stand in the fashion customary for females—with feet side by side—their repeated appearance, one

behind the other, creates the image of a long cortege of offering bearers moving into the building. In later representations most female estate personifications and fertility figures are shown in striding poses like those of their male counterparts.[19]

In Snefru's Dahshur temple reliefs the registers above the estate personifications consisted mainly of large-figure compositions showing the king enacting rituals of the Heb Sed, the renewal festival of kingship, or conversing with gods and goddesses. One especially poignant scene depicted Snefru embraced by a lion goddess.[20] The combining of large compositions of two or three stationary figures in upper registers with rows of uniform smaller figures below was a major design achievement that was realized in the very first stages of Egyptian royal relief art.

In addition to the units of stationary single and double figures and the progressions of rows of figures, Egyptian relief art had another principal scheme: the group-action tableau.[21] Considerably more intricate in composition than single- and double-figure configurations, group-action tableaux show a multiplicity of figures in a wide range of poses, handling a variety of objects and interacting with one another in numerous ways. Although much has been written about the absence of truly narrative art in ancient Egypt (that is, art depicting specific historical events),[22] there can be no doubt that group-action tableaux are of a narrative character, because they all tell a story in one way or another.[23] Most nonroyal reliefs

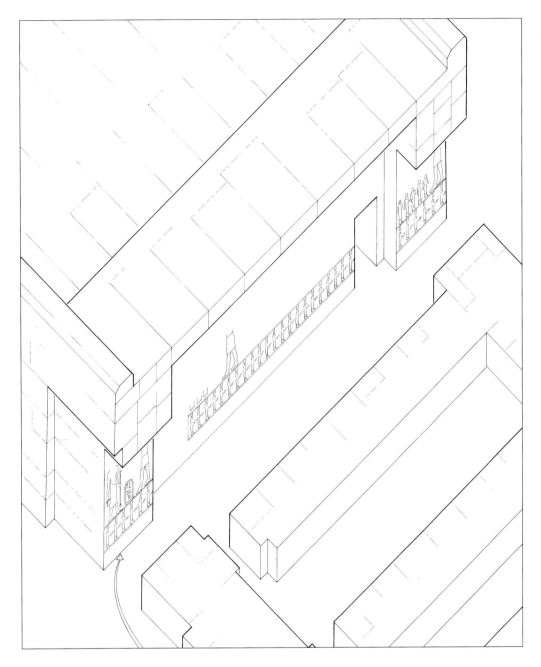

Fig. 49. Isometric recon-
struction of entrance corridor, statue-cult temple of
Snefru, Dahshur. Drawing
by Dieter Arnold after
Fakhry 1961b, p. 45, fig. 18

Fig. 50. Estate personifications, west wall of statue-cult temple of Snefru, Dahshur, shortly after excavation

decorating tombs of Old Kingdom high officials depict scenes in which objects and provisions are produced for the funeral cult in workshops and through agriculture, animal husbandry, and so on.[24] In royal reliefs, scenes that show the making of things are less important, while representations of ritual performances and of the king acting as guarantor of state and cosmic order predominate.[25]

The composition of group-action tableaux[26] relies largely on the requirements of the subject matter, but it is characteristic of Egyptian art that even multifaceted narrative scenes were structured to fit into a general compositional scheme. Important organizational means were the arrangement of figures on common baselines (the typical register of Egyptian art), the placing of figures in groups in which everyone performs the same action, and the juxtaposition and repetition of gestures and poses.

Informative examples of royal group-action tableaux are the ritual scenes from the king's Heb Sed, seen here in an example from the Fourth Dynasty (cat. no. 23) and in a version on two blocks from the Fifth Dynasty sun temple of King Niuserre (fig. 51; cat. no. 121). Both works show a high degree of structural organization. With the exception of the standard-bearer in the Fourth Dynasty piece (cat. no. 23), all figures act on common baselines and thus inside a firm system of registers. In the earlier relief the close-knit group of officials on the right

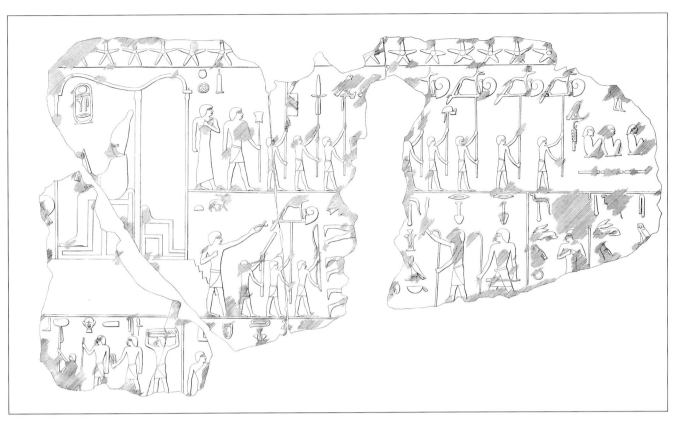

Fig. 51. Two blocks representing Heb Sed (thirty-year jubilee) rituals, sun temple of Niuserre, Abu Ghurab. From Bissing and Kees 1923 (pl. 11)

clarifies the compositional structure. In the Fifth Dynasty version the somewhat larger figure of the enthroned king, impressively isolated in his double pavilion, serves as a focus and resting point in the narrative. A similar figure of the pharaoh must have appeared to the right of the preserved scene, and it is toward this missing royal person that most activities in the extant section are directed.

Comparison of the two uppermost registers on the Niuserre blocks gives further insights into group-action tableaux. In the register at the very top an evenly spaced row of standard-bearers advances toward the king on the right. A highly charged encounter takes place in the register below: two groups of officials and priests confront each other across three prostrate figures identified in the inscription as "great ones" (that is, leaders) in the center, with the first priest on the right crying, "Back!" at the "great ones." The narrative burden is conveyed by the expressive gestures of the opposed figures, the detailed depiction of various religious objects, and the written words.[27]

Group-action tableaux often appear consecutively, with each scene depicting a separate episode of a single narrative. While rows of stationary figures achieve progression in space, sequences of group-action tableaux convey progression in time. Sequential group-action tableaux are often divided by vertical lines, such as those in the lower left corner of the Niuserre blocks and in the lower register of the blocks depicting the seasons (cat. nos. 119, 120). Such lines seem analogous to those used in the transcriptions of ritual instructions (or other texts) on papyrus rolls.[28] This correspondence is especially noticeable in the Niuserre Heb Sed scenes, which lacked the unifying elements of wall-high figures of the king or a god.

The Niuserre reliefs depicted the Heb Sed in more or less the same set of scenes at least five times, not only inside the chapel but also outside to the left and right of the doorway from the main courtyard.[29] Such repetition of a set of ritual images, reminiscent of litany incantations, reveals the intensity with which ancient Egyptian relief decoration attempted to magically evoke a meaningful other reality beyond everyday life.

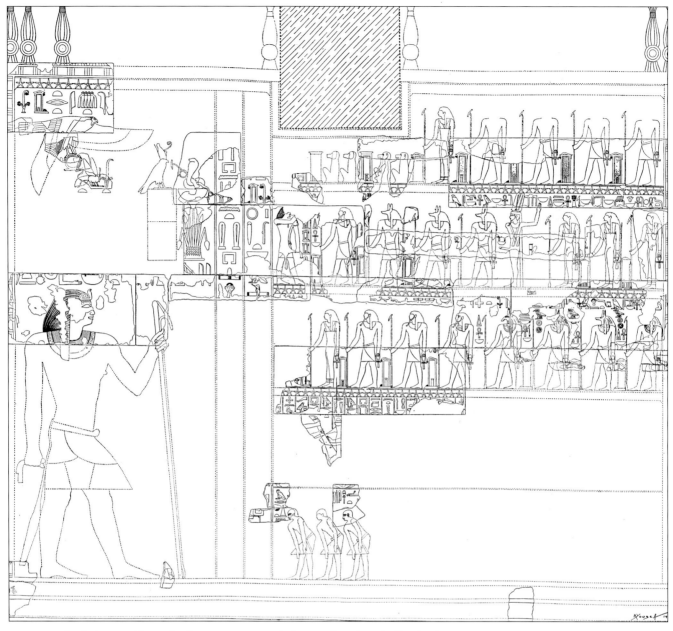

Fig. 52. Wall relief, pyramid temple of Pepi II, Saqqara: the king with gods and officials of Upper Egypt. From Jéquier 1938 (pl. 50). For position within the temple, see fig. 59.

The Combination of Figural Schemes and Organization of Large Wall Spaces

The rather uniform assemblage of register upon register of ritual group-action tableaux in the Heb Sed antechamber room of Niuserre is unusual (fig. 51). Generally, Egyptian royal reliefs are part of an overall compositional system whose primary structural element is a very large, often wall-high figure of the king, a deity, or both.[30] In the most common type of composition, a large figure of the pharaoh is combined with several registers of smaller, nonroyal personages, arranged in simple rows or participating in group actions. A classic example of such a composition, which comes from the pyramid temple of King Pepi II at Saqqara (fig. 52),[31] shows three rows of gods meeting the king in the upper registers, while in the bottom register state officials, likewise arranged in a neat row, bow before him. Between gods and officials the remains of another register present a group-action tableau of the butchering of offering animals.

It is possible to follow the evolution of the compositional principle of combining a large focal figure with rows of smaller ones from its rudimentary beginnings in

Fig 53. Relief on mace head of King Scorpion, late Predynastic (ca. 3100 B.C.E.). Ashmolean Museum, Oxford. Drawing by Richard Parkinson after Marion Cox after Spencer 1993

the late Predynastic and Archaic Periods to the end of the Old Kingdom. While the principle of arranging figures in horizontal registers was firmly in place by late Predynastic times,[32] that of combining a single large figure with several registers of smaller figures developed much more slowly. On the front of the famous Narmer palette from the beginning of the First Dynasty,[33] the king's figure is considerably larger than those of his followers, but only the beheaded enemies are shown in several rows, one above the other. On the reverse of the palette a falcon figure, leading an emblematically depicted enemy by the nose, appears in front of the shoulders and head of the king; however, there is no clear indication that this falcon-on-enemy group occupies a register of its own above the larger and fully human enemy who kneels before the king.[34] A much clearer juxtaposition between a

large royal figure and nonroyal images in registers is found on the King Scorpion mace head (fig. 53),[35] although even here a distinction is made between nonroyal figures of medium size, which interact with the king in a landscape of astonishingly free composition, and the rows of small figures that precede and follow the pharaoh on several register levels.

The combination of a large focal figure with several registers of smaller figures was not fully established at the end of the Archaic Period, as is demonstrated by a group of royal reliefs from the reign of Khasekhemui, the last king of the Second Dynasty.[36] On a granite door-frame found at the important Upper Egyptian town of Hierakonopolis, a number of small figures in four registers, one above the other, are inserted rather clumsily between two of the large principal figures, seemingly as

89

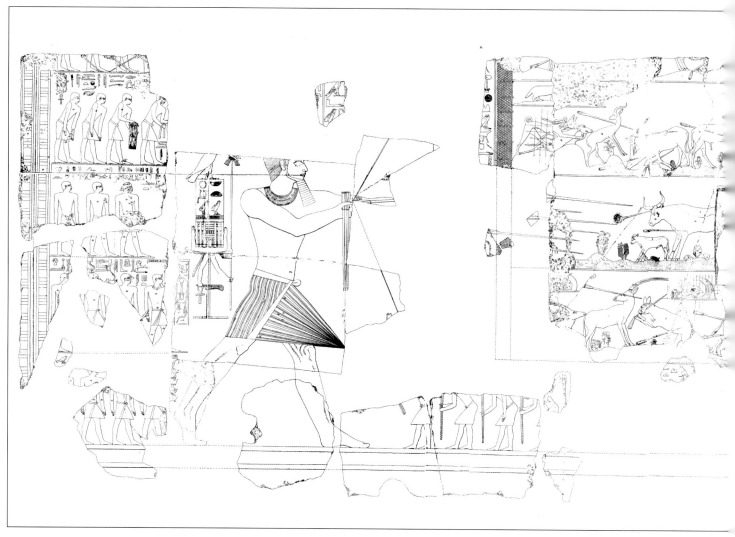

Fig. 54. Wall relief, pyramid temple of King Sahure, Abusir: the king hunting desert animals. Ägyptisches Museum und Papyrussammlung, Staatliche Museen zu Berlin, 21783. From Borchardt 1913 (pl. 17). For position in the corridor south of the central courtyard, see fig. 57. See also cat. no. 110.

an afterthought. None of the fragments from another architectural granite relief from the so-called fort at Hierakonopolis provides evidence for more advanced compositions. But on a piece that may date to the early Third Dynasty, a relief from the temple of Hathor at the Upper Egyptian site of Gebelein, the combination of registers of smaller individuals behind the large figure of the king is handled with a marked increase in assurance and structural clarity. This relief does, however, still show a follower's figure of intermediate size standing on the same baseline as the king, a type of arrangement seen on the earlier King Scorpion mace head.[37]

From at least the early Fourth Dynasty onward the combination of a large figure with several registers of smaller figures is handled by artists with ever greater proficiency. In the statue temple of Snefru at Dahshur only a few of the more than fifteen hundred preserved relief fragments employ this format.[38] The majority of

scenes above the rows of estates (fig. 50) in that temple consisted of large single figures or groups of two or three large figures. Large figures and rows of smaller ones were skillfully combined, however, in reliefs from the later years of Snefru's reign and the reign of Khufu, which followed. For instance, in the Heb Sed scene dating late in Snefru's reign (cat. no. 23) the large figure of the pharaoh, which originally followed the standard-bearer on the left, was surely at least as tall as two of the registers that are partially preserved on the fragments.[39] The presence of the same kind of arrangement can be deduced from the fan bearer's position in a relief fragment (cat. no. 39) from the pyramid temple of Khufu: the man's placement close to the top makes sense only if he was part of at least two registers of attending figures located behind or in front of a large figure of the pharaoh.[40]

During the early part of the Fifth Dynasty, under Kings Userkaf[41] and Sahure (cat. no. 113), the practice of linking

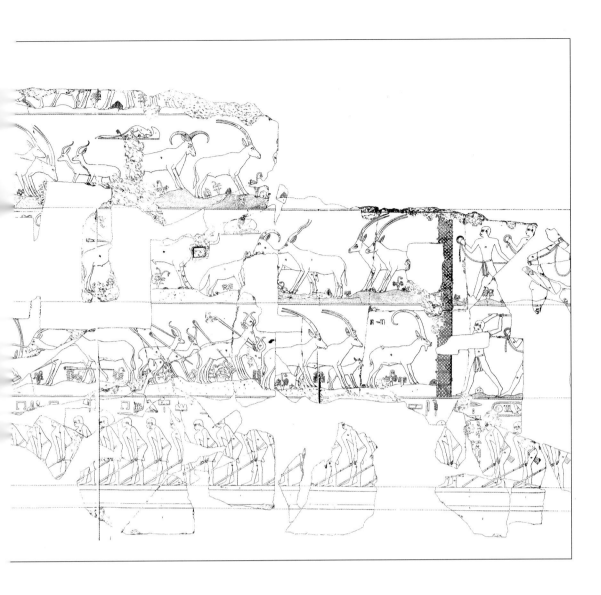

a large focal figure with rows of smaller figures reached its highest development, with artists achieving great variety and remarkable subtlety in the figure correlations. A magnificent example is the depiction of the desert hunt of King Sahure (cat. no. 112). This masterpiece of royal relief art (fig. 54)[42] had its original place in the corridor south of the pyramid temple's central courtyard (see cat. no. 110). The simple figural lineup in front of a large image of the king has been transformed in this relief into a densely packed mass of terribly wounded and frightened animals inside a netted stockade. The animals are shown in a multiplicity of postures and groupings with figures facing in diverse directions and overlapping

Fig. 55. Wall relief from pyramid temple of Niuserre, Abusir. Ägyptisches Museum und Papyrussammlung, Staatliche Museen zu Berlin, 16100. From Borchardt 1907, pl. 16

Fig. 56. Wall relief, pyramid temple of Pepi II, Saqqara: at left, the king slaying enemies, enemies supplicating, booty, and the goddess Seshat writing; at right, the king with the goddesses Buto and Nekhbet. From Jéquier 1938 (pl. 36). For position within the temple, see fig. 59.

in a variety of ways. The irregular assemblage contrasts with the dignified uniformity of the officials who march sedately behind Sahure and at the bottom of the scene. This is an example of the age-old Egyptian juxtaposition of order and chaos, but Sahure's artists have given unusual drama to the basic scheme and have depicted each of the animals with unequaled care and compassion.

The poor state of reliefs from the funeral monuments of the kings who followed Sahure makes it difficult to generalize about scene composition during their reigns. Fragments from the pyramid precinct of King Niuserre present many instances of rather uniform rows of officials and offering bearers.[43] Niuserre's designers appear to have lacked the compositional inventiveness of Sahure's relief artists, but this judgment may be unfair given the much smaller number of preserved blocks from this reign. It should also be noted that in Niuserre's sun temple artists used the traditional register system in a very innovative manner to describe the various natural events of the akhet (inundation) and shemu (harvest) seasons. The skill with which the register system was adapted to narrative requirements in these reliefs is evident in a block (cat. no. 119) where the height of the

right scene spans two registers and a bush is used to mask the transition between it and the smaller one at the left.[44]

The most impressive relief remains from Niuserre's pyramid precinct, however, are large-figure compositions, for example, the seven royal sphinxes with enemies' bodies under their paws, that adorned the causeway[45] and the magnificent throne scene (fig. 55). Such scenes appear to indicate that large-figure compositions gained renewed importance in the late Fifth Dynasty and the Sixth Dynasty, a hypothesis that is not contradicted by the few published blocks from the pyramid temples of Kings Djedkare-Isesi and Unis[46] and is supported by the reliefs in Pepi II's pyramid temple, the last monument of its kind built in the Old Kingdom. Enough relief fragments were preserved from Pepi II's important precinct to have allowed the excavator, Gustave Jéquier, to reconstruct a great number of scenes in their entirety. The reconstructions reveal that by the late Sixth Dynasty royal relief design had undergone a striking change. In the pyramid temple of Pepi II compositions such as that showing the king with gods and officials (fig. 52) are found only on the walls of the causeway,[47] in the square

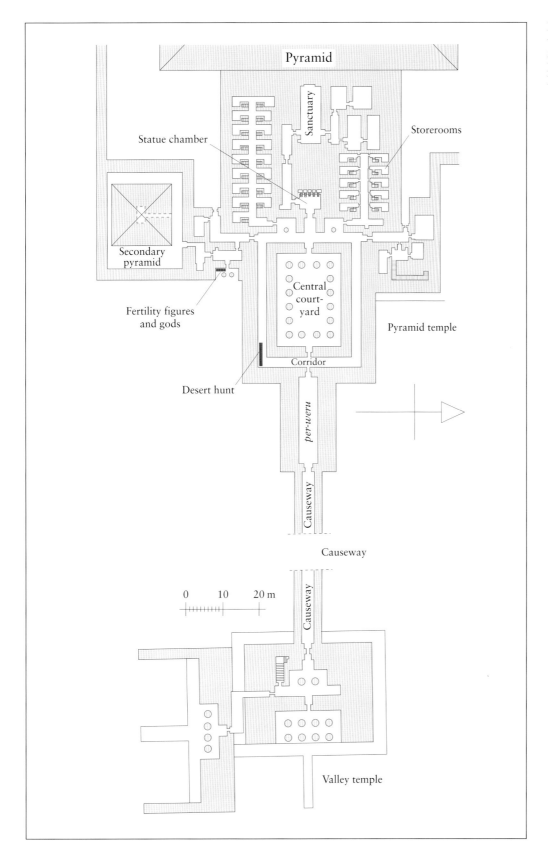

Pyramid

Sanctuary

Statue chamber

Storerooms

Secondary
pyramid

Central
court-
yard

Fertility figures
and gods

Pyramid temple

Desert hunt

Corridor

per-weru

Causeway

Causeway

0   10   20 m

Causeway

Valley temple

Fig. 57. Plan of pyramid
temple and valley temple of
Sahure, Abusir. Drawing by
Peter Der Manuelian after
Porter and Moss 1974, pl. 38

antechamber,[48] and in the mortuary cult sanctuary—the
last one with a figure of the king seated instead of standing.[49] None of these reliefs are very inspired compositions, and in all the other rooms of the temple a variant
scheme prevails. In this variant, large—often almost wall-
high—figures of the king and various deities take up the
greatest amount of space, while rows of small figures are
not present[50] or are reduced to rudimentary groups that
occupy little space in relation to that of the large figures
(fig. 56).[51]

93

The large-figure scenes in room after room of Pepi II's temple must have been awe-inspiring, and it is possible that a development toward large-figure temple reliefs that began here influenced much later relief decoration in temples of the Middle and New Kingdoms.[52] In the framework of the history of Old Kingdom relief composition, however, these large-figure scenes are strongly reminiscent of early Fourth Dynasty compositions (fig. 50) and appear to indicate archaistic tendencies in royal relief art at the end of the Old Kingdom.[53] The scheme of a large focal figure with rows of smaller ones having lost its appeal, artists must have looked back to the earlier type of composition, undoubtedly because it was more appropriate for changed views of the function of the pyramid temple and its reliefs.

ENSEMBLES OF ROYAL RELIEFS IN THEIR ARCHITECTURAL SETTINGS

Any speculation about the function and significance of pyramid temple reliefs is, of course, closely linked to general questions concerning the function of the temples and their various rooms. In the 1940s and 1950s Ricke and Schott maintained that the buildings of Old Kingdom pyramid complexes were predominantly stages and sets for royal funerals,[54] but wall reliefs of the buildings provide no support for such an interpretation. Beginning in the 1970s scholars therefore reconsidered the function of pyramid complexes, paying more attention to the content of the reliefs.[55] It is now argued that the royal funeral—a single event whose renewal in perpetuity would have little significance—had at best only an indirect impact on a temple's architecture and reliefs. Our present understanding is that most scenes either perpetuated the rituals and offerings that ensured the king's eternal life or evoked and magically strengthened the power of kingship and its victory over chaos.

It is important to note how differently designers treated these ideas in each complex. A brief description of a walk through a pyramid complex with relatively well-preserved reliefs will convey the general sense of one such design. Like most of its kind, the pyramid complex of King Sahure at Abusir (figs. 57, 58; cat. no. 110) consisted of a valley temple, causeway, pyramid temple, pyramid, and secondary (smaller) pyramid. At the valley temple, which could be understood as a quayside reception place, reliefs depicted marshlands (the environment of the valley temple and a traditional Egyptian symbol of rebirth)[56] and the arrival of a large royal ship accompanied

by running troops (cat. no. 114).[57] Other reliefs appear to have served as a preparation for what would be shown in greater detail in the pyramid temple itself. Among these preparatory representations are depictions of the king in the presence of major deities and scenes from the Heb Sed;[58] one impressive relief shows the young pharaoh suckled by a goddess.[59] (The last scene is documented in the exhibition by a similar block from the valley temple of King Niuserre [cat. no. 118].)

On the north wall of the valley temple's two-columned hall, in front of the niched doorway, large griffins, the mythical embodiments of kingship, trampled on enemies[60] while deities led bound prisoners toward them. The scenes of bound prisoners were repeated on the causeway walls just behind the valley temple,[61] emphasizing movement from valley temple to causeway and farther on to the pyramid temple.[62] Recently excavated reliefs from the upper part of Sahure's causeway depict men bearing offerings, butchers slaughtering animals, and a building crew bringing the gilded capstone to the pyramid amid festivities connected with the event. Also represented are emaciated desert people, a possible reference to the mountainous area from which the pyramid capstone came (for a later example, see cat. no. 122).[63] Scenes referring to the construction of the pyramid complex[64] may be regarded as elaborations of earlier reliefs in which the temple foundation was depicted in connection with the Heb Sed.[65]

From the causeway one entered the first room of the pyramid temple, a long vaulted hall, called the per-weru (House of the Great Ones) in ancient Egyptian. This room is thought to have been a copy of a hall in the living king's residence where he received notables and performed certain rituals.[66] The position and shape of the per-weru in Fifth and Sixth Dynasty pyramid temples are strikingly like those of the entrance corridor in the temple of Snefru in which rows of estate personifications appeared in the bottom registers of wall reliefs. Fragments of similar reliefs were found in Sahure's per-weru, but it is not known what ritual scenes, if any, made up the rest of the decoration.[67]

The per-weru opens into the columned courtyard that is the central feature of the outer part of the pyramid temple. Sahure's courtyard, surrounded by corridors on all four sides, is different from those of other pyramid temples. The courtyard, its porticoes, and its outer walls have the character of a closed architectural block. Representations of ships were carved on the west walls of the eastern corridor[68] and on the east walls of the western corridor,[69] indicating that the courtyard block

Fig. 58. View of pyramid temple of Sahure, from top of his pyramid, Abusir

should be understood as an island surrounded by water. In Egyptian mythology the creation of the world began with the emergence of an island from the primeval water, and thus the courtyard island of Sahure becomes analogous to the first created land. The palm capitals of the portico columns allude to the plants on the primeval island.[70]

Inside the corridors on the north and south faces of the courtyard block, ritual scenes were depicted; they showed dancing, music making, and the bringing of offering animals into the presence of large figures of the king and certain deities.[71] Scenes from the Heb Sed may also have been included.[72] All these ritualistic images underline the sacred nature of the island. The corridor walls opposite the island block were carved with magnificent relief compositions showing the king hunting in the desert (cat. no. 113) and in the marshes.[73] Such royal

occupations traditionally symbolized the king's struggle against the forces of chaos and the triumph of life over death.[74] Their depiction served to avert evil from the primeval island and all that happened there. The events that were believed to occur in a symbolic way on the island were shown in the portico reliefs facing the open court. On the southern and northern portico walls the king was depicted subjugating enemies on Egypt's western (Libyan)[75] and eastern (Asiatic)[76] borders and taking large numbers of their cattle and other domestic animals. On the western portico walls more scenes from the Heb Sed were depicted.[77] The paramount theme of Egyptian kingship was expressed in reliefs decorating the alabaster altar in the courtyard center, which depicted the unification of Upper and Lower Egypt accompanied by fertility figures.[78] Thus through its relief decoration the primeval

95

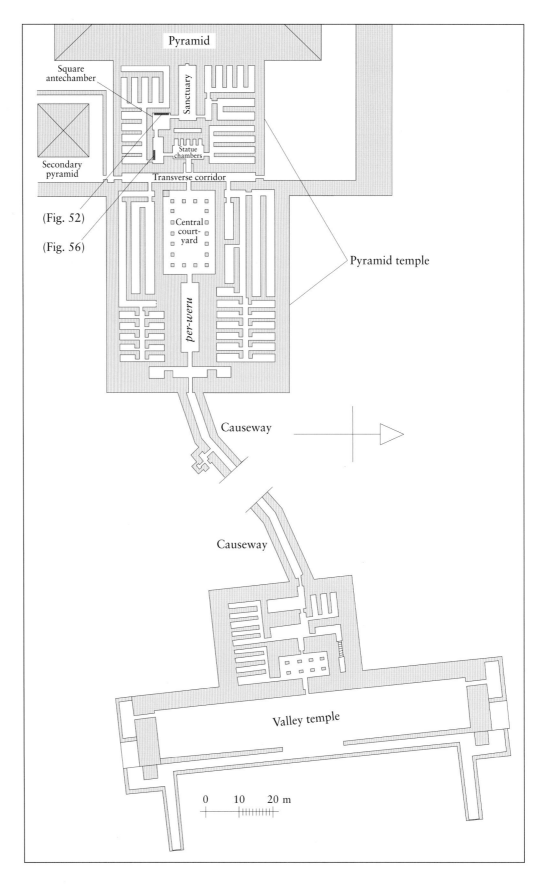

Fig. 59. Plan of pyramid temple and valley temple of Pepi II, Saqqara. Drawing by Peter Der Manuelian after Porter and Moss 1978, pl. 44

Pyramid

Square antechamber

Sanctuary

Secondary pyramid

Statue chambers

Transverse corridor

(Fig. 52)

(Fig. 56)

Central court-yard

Pyramid temple

per-weru

Causeway

Causeway

Valley temple

0   10   20 m

island at the center of Sahure's pyramid temple became a stage for the king's enactment of his quintessential role as guarantor of order and prosperity. Through repeated emphasis on this role's cosmic significance, the king's deeds were interpreted as the fulfillment of creation.[79]

At this point it may be telling to compare the court-yard of the temple of Pepi II (fig. 59) with that in the temple of Sahure. In Pepi's courtyard no reliefs adorned the portico walls, and scenes found in and around the courtyard block in Sahure's temple appear in other rooms of Pepi II's temple.[80] Without doubt these differences in relief position express a changed concept of kingship and the religious ideas surrounding it. Sahure was regarded as a hero who performed deeds to ensure stability and abundance, while in the large-figure reliefs of his pyramid temple Pepi II is primarily a performer of rituals and a companion of the gods. In Sahure's temple an impressive desert hunt is depicted, but in Pepi II's temple the triumph over evil is represented by a scene of the ritual killing of a single antelope.[81] Evidently the designers of the Pepi II complex no longer regarded the pyramid temple courtyard as a place where kingship triumphant was made manifest. They decorated the pillars of the courtyard porticoes with double-figure groups showing Pepi embraced by gods[82] and left the rest of the walls undecorated.

A central doorway in the corridor west of Sahure's courtyard led into a hall with five statue chambers. The statues of the king in these five chambers received a daily cult and were thus a primary ritual focus, as they were in all pyramid temples (see "Old Kingdom Statues in Their Architectural Setting" by Dieter Arnold in this catalogue). The hall of statue chambers and all rooms that opened from it—including the sanctuary for the mortuary cult—were situated at a higher level than the rest of the temple, a fact that emphasized their greater importance.[83] Two massive walls flanked the central entrance into the statue hall, creating a deep recess for the doorway and transforming it into the typical niched doorway that Ricke called the "door of [the goddess] Nut."[84] An important secondary entrance south of the center courtyard led directly from the open desert into rooms that connected with the secondary pyramid of the king to the south and with the western courtyard corridor to the north. An impressive relief that flanked this entrance (cat. no. 113) depicted deities and beneficial spirits endowing the king with prosperity, stability, and eternal rule.

Reliefs in the rooms behind the side entrance showed the king worshiping the lion-headed goddess Bastet.[85] Allusions to this goddess may also be found in a monumental statue of a lion or lioness that stood in the pyramid temple of King Niuserre in a small recess beside the niched central doorway, or "door of Nut."[86] Female deities (Nekhbet and Bastet or Sakhmet) played an important role in the relief decoration of all niched central doorways in Old Kingdom pyramid temples. In the temple of Sahure a large human-headed goddess suckling the young king must have been depicted on the walls flanking the doorway, as well as in the similarly shaped entrance from the valley temple into the causeway.[87] The parallel image from the valley temple of Niuserre (cat. no. 118) showed the goddess with a lion head.

The impressive images of the king being nurtured by a goddess can be regarded as a proclamation of the king's eternal rebirth. For the statues inside the five chambers behind the central courtyard, the niched doorway functioned as a kind of birth canal, through which the king—after being revived by the statue cult—stepped down into the courtyard to perform his heroic deeds.[88] Papyri tell us that in Neferirkare's pyramid temple the central statue of five represented the king as Osiris, the foremost Egyptian resurrection deity, while the two outermost ones depicted him as king of Upper and Lower Egypt.[89] The most important record of the appearance of statues in pyramid temple statue chambers is found in a relief from the temple of King Niuserre (fig. 55), which shows the enthroned king being presented with ankhs by Anubis, the necropolis god. Small disks at the bottom of the throne may depict rollers on which the statue was moved from its niche during ritual performances.[90] The presence of both Osiris and Anubis is a reminder that, despite the great emphasis on kingship in general, a pyramid temple is always dedicated to a deceased king.

Storerooms were located on both sides of the five-chambered hall. These contained the implements and provisions necessary for ritual performances. Reliefs in the corridors leading to these rooms depicted how such objects were packed and handled: "sealing a box containing incense" is written above one scene[91] and the "presentation of gold" to officials is shown in the corridor leading to storerooms in the north.[92] An area of solid stone separated[93] the mortuary cult sanctuary from these storerooms, the statue chambers, and the rest of the temple.[94] Although a mortuary cult chamber was not part of Fourth Dynasty pyramid temples, and may have been introduced into royal funerary architecture[95] only under influences from tombs of nonroyal persons,[96] by the time of King Sahure the room was certainly a place of important ritual performances that ensured the king's eternal life.[97] The reliefs in this room were more standardized than any others in the temple and did not differ essentially from reliefs in the mortuary cult chambers of nonroyal persons. A long list of offerings was usually shown in front of the seated king on both long walls of the chamber; rows of offering bearers moved toward the pharaoh, and there were depictions of a rich display of goods piled on tables (compare cat. no. 194). On the back wall a false door—the traditional place of communication between the living and the dead—was surrounded by fertility figures and deities.[98]

Sahure's pyramid temple had relief decoration on almost four hundred running meters of wall space, constituting the largest program of its kind. Calculations involving monuments from Snefru's statue-cult temple to the pyramid temple of Pepi II show that the amount of wall space suitable for relief decoration in pyramid temples gradually increased until it reached this peak and then decreased, as the following table indicates.[99]

King	Running meters of wall space suitable for relief in pyramid temples
Snefru	64
Khufu	100
Userkaf	120
Sahure	370
Pepi II	200

These necessarily very rough calculations not only underline the singular richness of the Sahure relief decoration[100] but also show the close link between the development of relief decoration and of architecture during the Pyramid Age. Each increase in available wall space must have spurred the relief designers to create yet more elaborate scenes, and each new pictorial elaboration must have been a challenge to the architects to provide more space.

1. This fact can be deduced (particularly for the valley temples) from the finds of Old Kingdom royal relief blocks in the pyramid of Amenemhat I, first king of the Twelfth Dynasty; see Goedicke 1971. The following royal names are attested on these blocks: Khufu, Khafre, Userkaf (see cat. nos. 38, 41, 65, 103), Unis, and Pepi II. See also Labrousse and Moussa 1996, p. 67, for Middle Kingdom repairs made on the valley temple of Unis.

2. Borchardt 1907, pp. 160–61. For the longer life of the pyramid temple of Sahure, see Borchardt 1910, pp. 106–7; contradicted by Baines 1973, pp. 9–14.

3. See, for instance, Borchardt 1907, pp. 51, 53, 58, figs. 32, 34, 38; and Borchardt 1910, pp. 6, 7, figs. 2, 3.

4. Especially Borchardt 1913; Jéquier 1938; and Jéquier 1940.

5. See Vandier 1952a, pp. 533–60, 570–605; Vandier 1952b pp. 724–30, 793–863; and Spencer 1993, pp. 52–71, 87–91, figs. 32–37, 42–46, 67.

6. Vandier 1952a, pp. 561–70; Spencer 1993, pp. 36–39, fig. 20.

7. Engelbach 1934, pp. 183–84, pl. 24; Alexanian 1998, pp. 5, 9–10, 11, 12, pl. 7b.

8. The following necessarily very cursory attempt at a grammar of Old Kingdom royal relief owes much to the thoughtful study by Yvonne Harpur (1987). See also Smith 1965, pp. 137–54.

9. Smith 1946, pp. 273–304; Harpur 1987, pp. 49–58.

10. Smith 1946, pp. 297–301.

11. The left margin of the Qahedjet slab (cat. no. 9) is considerably wider than the right, suggesting that the slab was set into the right side of a niche decorated on three sides with reliefs.

12. For slabs, see Firth and Quibell 1935, pls. 15–17, 40–42, 44. For pillars, see Jéquier 1940, pl. 45; and Fakhry 1961b, pp. 59–110, esp. figs. 35, 43, 48, 63, 84, 91.

13. Fakhry 1961b, pp. 111–23, figs. 119–27.

14. Compare multifigured relief compositions around doorways in royal temples—such as those shown in Jéquier 1938, pls. 36, 54; and Borchardt 1910, p. 62, fig. 79—with the large single figures frequently used to flank doorways of private tombs (fig. 18 in this catalogue; Harpur 1987, pp. 43–58). This fundamental difference in the way single figures were used in royal and private monuments is difficult to explain. It might be argued that in private tombs the mortuary cult is of primary importance, while in royal pyramid temples it is important only in the back of the building. Even in the royal mortuary cult rooms, however, no large single figures of the king appear to have flanked the false door: see Borchardt 1913, pp. 39–40, fig. 6, pl. 23. More common in royal monuments are large inscriptions with the king's name at the sides of doors; see Labrousse, Lauer, and Leclant 1977, pp. 16, 42, 44, figs. 5, 26, 29.

15. This building has usually been called a valley temple since Fakhry (1961b, passim) identified it as such. However, Stadelmann (1991, p. 98) has correctly described it as a structure combining elements of the later valley temples and the outer pyramid temples.

16. No relief decoration (beyond a king's figure and large inscriptions on stelae) is known from the buildings at the east side of Snefru's pyramid at Meidum and the Bent Pyramid at Dahshur. Stadelmann (1991, pp. 87, 98) holds that the simple form of the places designated for worship at these pyramids developed because these pyramids were cenotaphs and the structures in front were not funerary temples but royal cult installations. Relief fragments were found at the small pyramid temple east of the Red Pyramid at Dahshur, arguably Snefru's final burial place: Stadelmann 1983, pp. 233–34, fig. 5, pl. 73. The fragments show that scenes from the Heb Sed were depicted in the building.

17. Fakhry 1961b, pp. 2, 11, figs. 1, 4 B4.

18. Ibid., pp. 17–58; Jacquet-Gordon 1962.

19. Harpur 1987, p. 138. See, for instance, Borchardt 1913, pl. 27.

20. Fakhry 1961b, pp. 20–23, 35–45, 53, 57, figs. 9, 10, 16–18, 25, 31, 32. For the lion-goddess fragment, see ibid., frontis.

21. This pictorial configuration is called a "scene" or a "basic scene type" by Harpur (1987, pp. 175–221). Smith (1965, p. 140) writes of "rectangular units containing conceptually related subject matter."

22. The three classic studies are Groenewegen-Frankfort 1951 (1987 ed.), esp. pp. 23, 85–87; Kantor 1957, pp. 44–54; and Gaballa 1976, esp. pp. 21–25 (Old Kingdom royal reliefs). Gaballa points out the numerous New Kingdom depictions of specific historic events (ibid., pp. 6, 94–129).

23. David O'Connor, in a fall 1995 seminar for graduate students at the Institute of Fine Arts, New York University, argued strongly for a less restricted view of narration in Egyptian art. He bases this view on recent studies in the history of Greek and Roman art that have been collected in Holliday 1993. I thank Professor O'Connor for allowing me to read his introductory paper to the seminar.

24. For an overview of scenes in nonroyal Old Kingdom tombs, see Porter and Moss 1974, pp. 355–58; Porter and Moss 1981, pp. 903–7; and Harpur 1987, pp. 81–85, 110–15, 139–73, 176–220.

25. For an overview of scenes in royal temples, see Porter and Moss 1974, pp. 314–40; and Porter and Moss 1978, pp. 417–32. For the pyramid precinct of Unis, see Labrousse and Moussa 1996; and Labrousse, Lauer, and Leclant 1977. Representations depicting the making of things appear in the reliefs in pyramid causeways; see Hassan 1938, pp. 519–20, pls. 96, 97. Among the scenes depicted are metal workshops and fish markets; all the subjects and iconography derive from the tombs of nonroyal persons

26. Smith 1946, pp. 333–50; Harpur 1987, pp. 175–221.

27. See Fischer 1986, esp. pp. 24–46.

28. On the written tradition of ritual texts and their illustrations, see Altenmüller 1972; and Altenmüller 1975, cols. 1132–40.

29. Bissing and Kees 1923, pp. 8–15; Kaiser 1971, pp. 87–105, esp. p. 93.

30. Smith 1946, pp. 333–34.

31. Jéquier 1938, pls. 50 (west wall of the square antechamber), 51–53.

32. The most obvious examples are the ivories, palettes, and mace heads from the late Predynastic Period: Vandier 1952a, pp. 533–60, 579–605, figs. 358–74, and esp. figs. 388, 392–94. The close relation of the register system and writing is demonstrated in ivory plaques from Archaic times: ibid., pp. 827–55, esp. figs. 556, 560, 562, 565, 570.

33. For the most recent depiction, see Schulz and Seidel 1998, p. 29, figs. 38, 39.

34. Indeed, the falcon leading an enemy by the nose has the character of a rebus or an inscription.

35. Vandier 1952a, p. 601, fig. 393.

36. Alexanian 1998.

37. Donadoni Roveri 1988, p. 65, no. 75. See especially Smith 1946, pp. 137–38; and most recently Donadoni Roveri and Tiradritti 1998, p. 257, no. 236, with earlier bibliography. See also Seidelmayer 1998, p. 39, fig. 61. This relief and its companion in the Egyptian Museum, Cairo (Alexanian 1998, p. 13, n. 57) are not dated by inscription. Judging from the advanced clarity of design and the indications of musculature in the legs of the king, a date in the Third Dynasty seems most appropriate. The lengthened proportions of the main figure can be understood as regional style. For the style of Second Dynasty reliefs, see Alexanian 1998, pp. 17–21.

38. On one block (Fakhry 1961b, p. 20, fig. 9) the feet of a large figure (the king?) are confronted by a smaller foot. It is therefore possible that smaller figures in several rows were depicted marching toward the king. Relief fragments found in the temple of the northern pyramid, or Red Pyramid, of Snefru showed large figures of the king. But not enough is preserved to allow a definite statement about the compositions of the scenes.

39. In the nonroyal sphere the use of the scheme in its early Fourth Dynasty stage is well attested in the tomb of Metjen (Harpur 1987, plan 2) and the Meidum mastabas (Petrie 1892, pls. 9, 10, 19, 25, 27; Harpur 1987, plan 1); see cat. nos. 22, 23.

40. For another relevant example of the combination of a large figure and several registers of smaller ones conceivably of the time of Khufu, see Goedicke 1971, pp. 33–35, nos. 14, 15. For nonroyal tombs of the mid-Fourth Dynasty and their adept, if still somewhat stiff, use of the scheme, see especially Simpson 1978, pl. 33; see also Smith 1965, pp. 139–41.

41. See also Smith 1981, p. 129, fig. 122.

42. Borchardt 1913, pp. 30–35, pl. 17.

43. Borchardt 1907, pp. 70–96, figs. 48–75. See, however, the fine quality of fragments of a marsh scene from the valley temple (ibid., pp. 37–38, figs. 15, 16).

44. For other instances of skillful variations in the heights of adjoining registers, see Edel and Wenig 1974, pls. 10, 11.

45. Borchardt 1907, pp. 46–49, figs. 29, 31, pls. 8–12.

46. Large-figure compositions: Goyon 1969, pl. 39 (Djedkare-Isesi's pyramid precinct); Labrousse, Lauer, and Leclant 1977, pp. 78–83, figs. 44–46, 51–53, pp. 94–97, figs. 72, 73, pls. 28–30, 33, 34 (Unis).

47. For reconstructions, see Jéquier 1940, pls. 12, 19, 24, with disproportionately long rows of small figures.

48. For reconstructions, see Jéquier 1938, pls. 46, 50, 54, 58. For the mythological function of the square antechamber, see D. Arnold 1977, pp. 10–11; and D. Arnold 1997, pp. 35, 67–70.

49. For reconstructions, see Jéquier 1938, pls. 61, 62, 81, 82, 97.

50. For reconstructions, see ibid., pls. 18 (transverse corridor), 41 (vestibule before square antechamber), 30, 32 (niched central doorway).

51. For reconstructions, see Jéquier 1938, pls. 8, 12 (transverse corridor), 36 (vestibule to the square antechamber). These scenes are not well preserved, and it is impossible to say how much space was given to rows of small figures in the compositions of the king hunting the hippopotamus and carrying a bow and slaying the enemies in the hall known as the per-weru (Jéquier 1940, pls. 30, 32, 36).

52. Smith (1946, p. 203) writes of ties between the decorated pillars of Pepi II's temple (Jéquier 1940, pp. 22–24, pls. 44, 45) and later architecture. Smith (1946, p. 204) also mentions how strongly the reliefs in the mortuary cult chapel of Pepi II resemble those in the sanctuary of Queen Hatshepsut at Deir el-Bahri.

53. Here we cannot discuss the intricate question of archaism in the Sixth Dynasty, the extent of which Cherpion (1989, pp. 83–109) has minimized.

54. Ricke 1944; Ricke 1950, pp. 1–128; S. Schott 1950, pp. 135–224.

55. D. Arnold 1977, pp. 1–14; Brinks 1979; Stadelmann 1991, pp. 205–14; Rochholz 1994a, pp. 255–80. Most recently O'Connor has stressed the cosmic aspects of pyramid temples (O'Connor 1998, pp. 135–44). For cosmic aspects of the underground chambers of pyramids as revealed in the Pyramid Texts, see Allen 1994, pp. 5–28.

56. Borchardt 1913, pl. 15; Harpur 1987, pp. 185–86. For the interpretation of marsh scenes, see Martin 1986, cols. 1051–54.

57. Borchardt 1913, pl. 9 and p. 22, fig. 4 (the reconstruction).

58. Ibid., pl. 19.

59. Ibid., pl. 18; placed by Borchardt (ibid., p. 35, and 1910, pp. 20, 54) in the niched doorway of the pyramid temple. But considering that the Niuserre block showing the same scene was also found in the ruins of the valley temple, it seems more likely that this relief also would have been located in a niched doorway of the valley temple, anticipating similar scenes in the pyramid temple.

60. Borchardt 1913, pl. 8.

61. Ibid., pls. 5–7. The griffin is reconstructed as the focus of these rows of gods and prisoners by Borchardt (ibid., p. 18) on the basis of scenes in Niuserre's causeway (Borchardt 1907, pp. 46–49, pls. 8–12).

62. Similar scenes were depicted at the beginning of Unis's cause-way (Labrousse and Moussa 1996, pp. 95–97, 99, figs. 97, 98, 101). The appearance of booty animals in the Unis reliefs underlines the function of valley temple reliefs as a prepara-tion for what appears in the main temple. The animal group is very close to the Libyan booty shown in Sahure's courtyard relief (Borchardt 1913, pl. 1).

63. Hawass 1996c, pp. 177–86, pls. 54–56.

64. Portrayals of ships transporting columns and other building blocks in reliefs of the causeway of Unis belong to the same genre of scenes (Hassan 1955, pp. 137–38, fig. 1).

65. Bissing and Kees 1923, pls. 1, 2; Fakhry 1961b, pp. 94–98, figs. 91–95.

66. D. Arnold 1977, pp. 6–7.

67. In the entrance corridor of Snefru's temple, remains of the upper registers indicate that the king was shown visiting the gods in their chapels and running in the Heb Sed; see Fakhry 1961b, p. 41, fig. 17, p. 53, fig. 25.

68. Borchardt 1913, pl. 14.

69. Ibid., pls. 11–13.

70. Ricke (1950, pp. 22, 73) interpreted the palm capital columns as depictions of a mythical burial at Buto in the Delta. For O'Connor (1998) the central courtyard is the place of the ris-ing of the sun from the primeval ocean.

71. Borchardt 1913, pls. 32–34, 54, 56.

72. Ibid., pl. 65.

73. Ibid., pl. 16.

74. For the hunt in the desert, see Altenmüller 1980a, cols. 224–30. For the hunt in the marshes, see note 56 above.

75. Borchardt 1913, pls. 1, 2.

76. Ibid., pls. 3, 4. The theme of the subjugation of foreign lands was carried over into the ship representations on the east wall of the western corridor, where seagoing ships were depicted leaving Egypt for the Levant and returning with foreign peo-ples whom the Egyptian mariners teach to revere Pharaoh (ibid., pls. 11–13). These scenes were interpreted by Bietak (1988, pp. 35–40) as indicating the employment of foreign mariners by Egypt.

77. Borchardt 1913, p. 69, pl. 67 (the position of the reliefs).

78. Borchardt 1910, pp. 48–51, figs. 51–56. For the function of this altar, see "The Tombs of Officials" by Peter Jánosi in this catalogue, pp. 33, 39, n. 83.

79. It may be significant that in the pyramid temple of Khafre (Ricke 1950, pp. 48–52, figs. 16–19, pl. 2) statues of the king stood around the courtyard, and in the courtyard of the pyra-mid temple of Userkaf a monumental statue of the king was erected (Egyptian Museum, Cairo, JE 52501; Firth 1929, p. 65, pl. 1). See "Old Kingdom Statues in Their Architectural Setting" by Dieter Arnold in this catalogue.

80. The fowling scene, for instance, in Sahure's temple in the northern corridor of the courtyard, is probably depicted in the per-weru of Pepi II (Jéquier 1940, pls. 41, 43); the king slaying enemies (in Sahure's temple in the courtyard portico) appears in the temple of Pepi II in the transverse corridor (Jéquier 1938, pl. 8) and in the vestibule to the square ante-chamber (ibid., pl. 36).

81. Jéquier 1938, pls. 41–43.

82. Jéquier 1940, pl. 45.

83. According to Borchardt (1910, p. 54), steps or a small ramp must have connected the lower level of the outer temple around the courtyard with the level of the statue chamber, which was eighty to ninety centimeters higher. For steps pre-served in the temple of Teti, see Lauer and Leclant 1972, pp. 24, 27, pl. 13; and D. Arnold 1997, p. 68, fig. 28.

84. Ricke 1950, pp. 60–62.

85. Borchardt 1913, pls. 35, 36. See also Borchardt 1907, p. 94, fig. 72.

86. Borchardt 1907, pp. 16–17, 69–70, figs. 7, 47.

87. Borchardt 1913, pl. 18. See also Labrousse, Lauer, and Leclant 1977, p. 84, pl. 29.

88. Another reference to birth is represented by the alabaster statuette of Pepi II as a child that was found in the square antechamber of that king's pyramid temple and which, according to the excavator, may originally have been placed in the serdab behind the statue room (Jéquier 1940, pp. 30–31, pl. 49).

89. Posener-Kriéger 1976, vol. 2, pp. 502, 544–45; Rochholz 1994b, p. 262.

90. Borchardt 1907, pp. 88–90, pl. 16. The relief is now in the Ägyptisches Museum und Papyrussammlung, Berlin, 16100. Borchardt (1910, p. 54) mentions having found the fragment of a similar relief close to Sahure's recessed doorway, but the fragment is not identified in Borchardt 1913. A parallel scene was depicted in the pyramid temple of King Djedkare-Isesi (Goyon 1969, p. 156, n. 2, pl. 29). A standing statue appears to have been placed in the center chapel of Pepi II's pyramid temple (Jéquier 1938, p. 25). Papyri from the pyramid tem-ple of Neferirkare tell us something about the rituals (Open-ing of the Mouth, anointing, and presentation of cloth) performed with the statues; see Posener-Kriéger 1976, vol. 2, pp. 537–38.

91. Borchardt 1913, pl. 59, with pp. 66–67 (on the original place of the reliefs), pls. 60, 61.

92. Ibid., pls. 52–54.

93. Borchardt 1910, p. 57.

94. The presence of this solid stone mass is explained by Stadel-mann (1991, p. 207) as a way to simulate the situating of the statue chambers in caves, since one of the chapels was called "the cave" in the papyri (Posener-Kriéger 1976, vol. 2, p. 503, n. 1; Wörterbuch der Aegyptischen Sprache, vol. 5 [1931], pp. 364–66).

95. D. Arnold 1997, pp. 59–61, 71–72.

96. For the opposing theory—that false doors and offering places for the mortuary cult were already provided in Fourth Dynasty pyramid temples—see Stadelmann 1983, pp. 237–41, with earlier bibliography on the question.

97. Posener-Kriéger 1976, vol. 2, pp. 539–40. For the elaborate installations for the cleaning of cult vessels, see Borchardt 1910, pp. 76–83.

98. Borchardt 1913, pl. 23, with p. 40, fig. 6. For remains of the false door, see Borchardt 1910, pp. 57–58, fig. 68. The best-preserved offering chamber reliefs are in the temple of Pepi II; see Jéquier 1938, pls. 61–104. For the very similar reliefs in the chapels that were erected over the northern entrances into the pyramids, from Djedkare-Isesi onward, see Lauer and Leclant 1972, pp. 43–44; and D. Arnold 1988, pp. 78–83, pls. 49–56.

99. I want to thank Dieter Arnold for undertaking these calcula-tions. We confined ourselves to calculating running meters, because the heights of pyramid temple walls are uncertain. Storerooms and other spaces believed to have been without decoration were not included in our investigation. Nor did we

consider valley temples and causeways, which would have introduced further uncertainties.

100. The impressive body of surviving reliefs is in striking contrast to the almost total lack of preserved statuary in Sahure's temple (see, however, cat. no. 109 and Borchardt 1910, pp. 48, 51, fig. 57 [fragments from a base of an alabaster statue]), which may not be due to accidents of preservation alone. There are indications that pyramid precincts of the Fourth Dynasty achieved with a rich statuary program what in the Fifth and Sixth Dynasty precincts was expressed in reliefs. In this context Stadelmann (1991, pp. 210–11) writes of a "Verdichtung" (compression) of three-dimensional architectural elements into reliefs. It might also be appropriate to call Fifth and Sixth Dynasty reliefs an elaboration of Fourth Dynasty royal statuary.

THE HUMAN IMAGE IN OLD KINGDOM NONROYAL RELIEFS

NADINE CHERPION

When Van Eyck or Titian painted the portrait of a bourgeois or grandee of his day, several factors entered into the composition of the picture: the painter's own personality, the patron's desire to be depicted more or less realistically, and a third consideration of which neither was completely aware—the political, economic, and geographic conditions in which they lived. The influence of each of these factors is what makes the portraits of Van Eyck and Titian, as individual as they are, recognizably different from each other. When an Egyptian sculptor decorated the walls of a mastaba with the likeness of a dignitary—someone who had attained sufficient status and wealth to commission a tomb with relief decoration—the same three factors doubtless also entered into the equation and could involve in turn the artist's vision, the subject's expectations, or the atmosphere of their times.

After the pharaoh himself, the owners of mastabas embodied the human ideal in the Old Kingdom. It is possible to determine what the concept of the individual was in this era by examining several aspects of the human figure as it appears in relief.

The interest in facial features, or realistic portraiture. To the extent that portraiture, as we understand it today, existed at all in royal sculpture during the different periods of Egyptian history,[1] we may reasonably ask if it might not have existed in nonroyal images as well. The only way to assess the degree of realism that sculptors of the Old Kingdom achieved in the depiction of faces is to note whether a particular facial feature is limited to a single representation or is common to all those in the tomb.

Facial expressions. These are another index of individual personality or social groups.

Stature. This is clearly the feature that changes the least in Old Kingdom reliefs, in contrast to sculpture in the round, where there is a world of difference between a wood statue of Meryre-ha-ishetef (Sixth Dynasty)[2] and the Sheikh el-Beled (probably Fourth Dynasty; fig. 34),[3] the former with its fluid, almost feminine—in fact, mannerist—pose and the latter with its characteristic stoutness and nascent hyperrealism. Even in relief, however, subtle differences reflect the transition from one reign to the next.

The interest in anatomy, or modeling, in the outline of a human figure as well as its surface.[4] Since the face and legs almost always present a minimum of relief, it is appropriate to speak of an interest in anatomy only when the modeling extends to other parts of the body.

Only first-rate monuments for which we also have photographs of the same level of quality allow us to appreciate these numerous stylistic variations.[5] To complete the picture of the masculine and feminine ideals in the Old Kingdom, it is also a good idea to complement the study of style with a consideration of the variations that occur in the layout of portraits of couples.[6] These variations doubtless have more to do with the evolution of conventions for portraying the human figure than with the evolution of the society's mentality, but they help to re-create the image of a society, just as portraits of couples or groups do in Dutch painting of the seventeenth century.

Not all of the nonroyal monuments of the Old Kingdom have yet been precisely dated.[7] For that reason, the sketch that follows, done in rather broad strokes, should be considered incomplete and provisional. For the purpose of this discussion I have adopted a chronological approach, from the Third through the Sixth Dynasty.

Reliefs from the Third Dynasty are rare, but the fortuitous preservation of two monuments of exceptional quality allows us to see how the officials of that time chose to have themselves represented for eternity. These are the mastaba of Hesi-re, on the one hand,[8] and that of Kha-bau-sokar and his wife, Hathor-nefer-hotep, on the other.[9] The first of these two men was Greatest of the King's Scribes and Chief of Dentists; the second, Overseer of Works in the Necropolis (which put the best artisans at his disposal) and priest of Seshat and Anubis as well as other deities.[10] The mastaba of Hesi-re most likely dates to the reign of Djoser, since the last basket of earth excavated from its burial chamber, and therefore probably from the floor of the tomb, contained two jar stoppers with seal impressions in that king's name.[11] The mastaba of Kha-bau-sokar might be a little later than that of Hesi-re, although it is not certain that the observable differences between the two monuments should be attributed solely to the passage of time.[12] In this period the representation of couples did not yet exist: Hesi-re is always shown without a wife, while Kha-bau-sokar and Hathor-nefer-hotep have separate chapels.

In the case of Kha-bau-sokar, what first strikes the observer is the impression of physical force, of raw power exuded by the deceased's profile on the side walls of his limestone niche.[13] The torso is heavy, not with the puffy fat that would often be seen later, in the Sixth Dynasty, but with a heaviness more indicative of aged flesh. The legs are as massive as the rest of the profile.[14] The sculptor—perhaps at the behest of his patron—has rendered the details of the musculature and bones of this heavy body with such delight and care that he has made of it a veritable anatomical chart.[15] The most remarkable features are the indications of the back of the knee[16] and the ilium (hipbone).[17] I know of no other Old Kingdom relief that shows the first detail; the latter appears only rarely in mastaba reliefs but is visible here even "transparently," under the cloak that Kha-bau-sokar wears on the back wall of the niche.

No smile lights up the face of this official. Instead, the eyes are small—one might even say sly—with large bags beneath them. The nose is short and bent, with a marked bump on the bridge. The lips are thick, the lower one decidedly more advanced.[18] In a way, the harshness of this face reflects that of the body.

The whole is realized with a sense of meticulousness surprising for such a remote period—a quality that characterizes not only the anatomy but also the locks of the wig,[19] the pattern of the kilt, the minuscule folds of skin surrounding the nails,[20] and the hieroglyphic signs. Yet this is not really astonishing. The most realistic and detailed works are generally found at the birth of a civilization or the beginning of an artist's career; simplification and stylization come only later. Thus, the first tree drawn by Mondrian and the first bull rendered by Picasso are each absolutely realistic. The more Mondrian would draw trees and Picasso bulls, the less would these be easily identifiable as such. Eventually, the tree and the bull would become hardly recognizable, as the work of the two painters neared pure abstraction.

In contrast to her husband, Hathor-nefer-hotep is spectacularly slender. Her thinness is visible overall[21] and particularly in the arms and fingers, as well as in her dried-up face, where it is expressed by prominent cheekbones in a work in the Egyptian Museum, Cairo (CG 1386; fig. 60). It is also visible in the aged breast, whose nipple points downward and rests on the forearm in another relief in Cairo (CG 1387), exactly as that of Isis does centuries later on the first pylon at Philae,[22] there, however, reflecting the weight of the flesh. In any case, nothing here, in the Third Dynasty, anticipates the round, firm breasts that would be part of the feminine canon of the Old Kingdom,[23] for this is a woman who was meant to be shown as aged, or at least—following the example of her husband—as mature.

The face of Hathor-nefer-hotep is even less attractive than that of Kha-bau-sokar. It may seem more marked by time on CG 1386 than on CG 1387, because of the collapse of the flesh above the cheekbones, certain African traits, and a disagreeable disposition; yet on both walls we see the same turned-up nose, double chin, and jutting lower jaw. But the most extraordinary aspect of Hathor-nefer-hotep's reliefs is certainly that of their modeling. No other female body in the Old Kingdom is treated with such concern for anatomical realism,[24] although the male profile would always be the object of a certain anatomical interest, sometimes minor or minimal, sometimes more developed. Nothing has been omitted,[25] not even the iliac crest or the modeling of the abdomen,[26] two details exceptional in bas-reliefs.[27] The form of Hathor-nefer-hotep's belly—two ridges on either side of the navel, which are separated from the pubic region by a flat area—is especially significant: there are a number of conventions for representing the female abdomen, and this one is exactly paralleled by an example in the statue of Nesa (cat. no. 13), which dates precisely to the same period as the reliefs of Hathor-nefer-hotep.

On the five wood panels discovered in the niches of Hesi-re's tomb and now on display in the Egyptian

Fig. 60. Detail, Hathor-nefer-hotep. Third Dynasty. Egyptian Museum, Cairo, CG 1386

Fig. 62. Detail, Neferi. Fourth Dynasty. Western Cemetery, Giza

Fig. 61. Detail, Hesi-re. Third Dynasty. Egyptian Museum, Cairo, CG 1426

Fig. 63. Detail, Mer-ib. Fourth Dynasty. Ägyptisches Museum und Papyrussammlung, Staatliche Museen zu Berlin, 1107

Museum, Cairo, the face of the deceased is consistently that of a mature man, sour and sullen. This disagreeable expression even appears in panel CG 1430 (cat. no. 17), in which Hesi-re is shown as much younger. The narrow eyes, at times almost closed, seem to express cunning.

The turned-down corners of the lips—rimmed and delicate—are hardly appealing. The raised chin gives its owner an air of complete arrogance. The impression of age is best seen on panel CG 1426, where the face is most deeply furrowed and creased, with wrinkles extending

Fig. 64. Akhet-hotep.
Fourth Dynasty. The Metropolitan Museum of Art,
New York, Funds from
various donors, and by
exchange, 1958, 58.123

from the inner canthus of the eye and the base of the nose, framing and setting off the chin (fig. 61). The strong, aquiline nose, repeated systematically from one relief to the next, also serves clearly to make these true portraits.

There seems to be an undeniable parallelism between the facial treatment of Hesi-re, or of Kha-bau-sokar and his wife, and that of the royal portraits of the time. They display the same sternness—or in any case, the

same seriousness—of expression and the same realism: the strong, hooked nose and jutting jaw of Djoser, both in his reliefs and in his statue;[28] the thick nose and narrow eye of Horus Qahedjet (cat. no. 9); the beaked nose, slanted and barely open eye, and fully everted lips of Zanakht.[29]

Another remarkable feature displayed in Hesi-re's mastaba is the deceased's penchant, or that of his sculptor, for depictions of anatomy. The panel that best illustrates this is CG 1427, which Richer used in his study of the nude in art,[30] as much for the exhaustiveness of its anatomical description as for its great exactitude. As in the reliefs of Kha-bau-sokar, the hipbone is shown and can even be discerned under the cloak worn by the deceased.[31]

In comparison to Kha-bau-sokar, Hesi-re is quite slender, and this slimness is equally visible in the objects that surround him: the *medu* staff and *sekhem* scepter, the leg of the offering table, and the hieroglyphic signs. This is the artist's choice, one that can be compared with the treatment of the human figure in Dirck Bouts's *Trial of Otho*. In the figure of Hesi-re seated at the offering table, his legs may be characterized as more gaunt than slender.[32]

THE FOURTH DYNASTY

With the reign of Snefru, the style of the previous dynasty relaxes. In contrast with the wish of nobles in the Third Dynasty to have themselves represented at an advanced stage of their career and with pitiless realism, several contemporaries of the first king of the Fourth Dynasty appear in relief with a demeanor that is particularly youthful and pleasant, even sweet. This is especially the case with Metjen (cat. no. 29),[33] Netjer-aperef,[34] and Akhet-hotep (Saqqara A 1),[35] but it is true as well for Iy-nefer,[36] Ra-hotep,[37] and Akhet-aa (cat. no. 18).[38]

The smooth surface of the figures in the mastabas of these officials is intentional on the part of the artist; modeling was apparently of no interest at this time. Variations in the perfectly flat surface are rare and extremely subtle. In the relief of Akhet-hotep now in the Brooklyn Museum (57.178), they are limited to summary indications of the collarbone, left biceps, and right elbow and to even more superficial modeling on the lower limbs. But the thickness of the relief is rarely so spectacular in the Old Kingdom as it is here—so much so that Mariette described the decoration of Akhet-hotep's mastaba as sculpture in the round (fig. 64).[39] This is something extremely rare in Egyptian art, where relief is, by nature, rather thin.[40] The proportions of the figures of the deceased are often massive, particularly in the legs. The sole exception to this state of affairs is found in the tablet of Ra-hotep's false door (British Museum, London, 1242), in which the abnormal slenderness of the legs is exactly in the spirit of the Third Dynasty, as are two other details: the chair seat shown from above, which disappears completely after King Khufu;[41] and the sculptor's unusual interest in anatomy, expressed here in the neck muscle (the sternocleidomastoid), the collarbone,

the lower ribs, the deltoid shoulder muscle, the muscles of the forearm extended toward the offering table, the hipbone showing under the cloak (as rare as the two sharply differentiated knees), the fibula, and the ankle-bone. All this suggests that the tablet of Ra-hotep's false door, which looks quite isolated with respect to the rest of the tomb walls, was carved before the other walls or by an artist rooted in the past.

From Snefru to Khufu there is not much change in the depiction of the human figure, except in the thickness of the relief, which passes abruptly from exceptionally high to much lower raised relief. The latter, in fact, sometimes even comes close to the kind of low relief found on modern coins or medals, as in the slab stelae from Giza (cat. nos. 51–53) or the relief from the tomb of Irery.[42]

Despite longstanding opinion, nonroyal monuments of the Fourth Dynasty are quite numerous, enough so that they may be counted by the dozens; several of them have simply been attributed wrongly to the Sixth Dynasty.[43] A good example of relief in the Fourth Dynasty is found in the mastaba of Khufu-khaf (G 7140).[44] The tomb owner was probably a son of Khufu—perhaps even the same man as the future pharaoh Khafre,[45] for whom the mastaba had been prepared before his accession to the throne. In the reliefs of his imposing tomb, located in the Eastern Cemetery of Giza, the figures of Khufu-khaf strike the visitor both by their exceptional height and by their marvelous workmanship. The most representative scene shows the official and his wife with their arms entwined, turning to the left to receive offering bearers and scribes (fig. 65).[46] The key characteristics of the two figures here are their lack of expression and the nearly total absence of individuality in their faces[47]—qualities so marked that they almost call to mind the classicism of ancient Greece. Just as in Greek classicism, the man has an athletic physique, with a thin waist, well-proportioned shoulders, and strong legs. Another characteristic—this time in contrast to Greek classicism, which sought to emphasize anatomy—is the absence of modeling to animate Khufu-khaf's exemplary silhouette: he is a cartoon cutout, in which the muscles of the forward arm and forearm are barely perceptible.[48] This indifference to anatomy is certainly not due to a lack of means; instead, it reflects a particular vision of the human being, since in the same tomb the hieroglyphs are executed with precision and an incomparable refinement.

Although their faces show no sentiment, the figures of the couple themselves are arranged with a touching intimacy. The pose of Khufu-khaf's wife, Nefret-kau, has nothing conventional about it. In Old Kingdom reliefs the wife normally puts her arm around her husband's neck,[49] but here Nefret-kau holds on to her husband's arm, looping her own arm about that of Khufu-khaf and putting her other hand on his wrist, actually snuggling up against him.[50] There is no way of knowing whether the official himself or the artist who designed his chapel's reliefs was the one who took the initiative in showing conjugal tenderness with such daring. Be that as it may, the period itself doubtless also played a part: such freedom of expression could have existed only when the rules of composition had not yet been set into a fixed routine.[51]

The dominant features of Khufu-khaf's relief reappear in most Fourth Dynasty mastabas. Faces with little individuality but often rather youthful features (which is a means of idealizing the deceased), serene, smiling, or even blissful expressions, and a general lack of interest in anatomy all serve to make the figures of the officials depicted in these monuments representations that are timeless in character.[52] Noteworthy in this respect are the grace and striking youthfulness in the face of Neferi (fig. 62), even at the peak of his career, when he has a flabby chest and potbelly,[53] or the ravishing smile of Mer-ib (fig. 63), at the beginning of the Fourth Dynasty. It is hard not to see these images as comparable to the statue of Ra-her-ka and Mer-si-ankh as it appears on the cover of the recent catalogue devoted to Old Kingdom statuary in the Louvre, with its chief characteristic a kind of faith in the future illuminating the faces of the official and his wife.[54] Considering the harsh "facsimiles" of nobles of the Third Dynasty, we can only wonder what might explain this new direction in the Fourth Dynasty's concept of the individual. Is it the expression of political and social well-being, or simply a reaction against the art of the preceding period? Or are we to see in the use of the same mold for everyone the desire to leave no place for the individual?[55]

This overall picture of the Fourth Dynasty has to be amended somewhat, because not all the officials of that time are shown with angelic faces or innocuous features. Senenu-ka (G 2041), for example, has a big nose, fat lips, and a double chin and is neither smiling nor youthful.[56] Nefer (G 2110) is famous for his raptor's beak of a nose, which occurs both in his reliefs (cat. no. 79) and his "magic head" (usually called "reserve head"), and for his double chin.[57] As for the woman named Debet (British Museum, London, EA 157A)—an appellation meaning "female hippopotamus," which she can hardly have received by chance—her bovine neck, short and quite pointed nose, little eyes, and waistless body all give her a very individual appeal.[58]

There are also exceptions in the use of modeling. On the false-door jamb of Irery (British Museum, London, 1168)[59] and the false-door tablet of Huti (cat. no. 85),[60] the normal cookie-cutter aspect of the foreground is relieved by modeling atypical of the Fourth Dynasty—in the case of Irery, even despite the thinness of the relief. In Huti's relief the representation of the iliac bone, added to that of numerous other anatomical details, leads me to believe that this mastaba is nearer in time to the Third Dynasty than I have argued elsewhere: it could date to the beginning of Khufu's reign rather than to the time of Djedefre.[61]

THE FIFTH DYNASTY

On the whole, the faces of the Fifth Dynasty are much more mature and more austere than those of the Fourth Dynasty. Youth, smiles, and amiability have disappeared from most of them (fig. 66), notably because of a small fold that descends from the wing of the nose (beginning, apparently, in the reign of Userkaf)[62] or a very typical wrinkling of the nostril.[63] In addition to their greater maturity, these faces are often quite individual. The official Nefer-iretenef, in whose mastaba the name of King Neferirkare appears, has a very large nose that favors him not at all;[64] Ka-em-nefret, whose mastaba preserves the name of King Niuserre, has a puffy face, with bags under the eyes, thick, rimmed lips, and a double chin (fig. 67). In the Fifth Dynasty the philtrum—the furrow that joins the upper lip to the nose, also called for that reason the nasolabial furrow—is quite regularly indicated.[65] It can be found as early as the Third Dynasty, in the reliefs of Hesi-re, but it is virtually if not entirely absent in the Fourth Dynasty. The lips are generally rimmed;[66] at the end of the Fifth Dynasty this even includes the corners of the mouth, as would normally be the case later, in the Sixth Dynasty,[67] although this is entirely at odds with physical reality.

These diverse indications of folds in the skin (the rimmed lips, the philtrum, the fold extending from the wing of the nose) should probably be seen as part of the extraordinary feeling for modeling—and, therefore, the taste for realistic anatomical detail—that characterizes the rest of the depictions of the human figure in the Fifth Dynasty, despite the extreme thinness of the relief.[68] This is another area in which the Fifth Dynasty distances itself from the Fourth. Good examples of this interest in anatomy can be found in the mastabas of Ti (Saqqara D 22),[69] Ni-ankh-khnum and Khnum-hotep (King Unis causeway),[70] Hetep-herakhti (Rijksmuseum

Fig. 65. Khufu-khaf and His Wife, Nefret-khau. Fourth Dynasty. Giza G 7140

van Oudheden, Leiden, 1904/3.1),[71] Ma-nefer (Ägyptisches Museum und Papyrussammlung, Berlin, 1108),[72] Metjetji (cat. nos. 151–156), and the two Akhet-hoteps (Louvre, Paris, E 10958,[73] Saqqara D 64[74]). In some mastabas even secondary figures receive meticulously detailed anatomical rendering.[75] All these examples come from Saqqara; at Giza in the same period the reliefs are generally void of modeling, because the local limestone, of poor quality, does not permit the same surface treatment.

Among the mastabas of the Fifth Dynasty, the funerary complex D 64 at Saqqara seems to me to be the work of an exceptional artist, both for the stunning quality of its reliefs and for their style. This complex comprises three chapels—two in the name of Akhet-hotep and the third dedicated to his son, Ptah-hotep—on whose walls the latest royal name is that of Djedkare-Isesi, the next-to-last king of the Fifth Dynasty. A prime example of the artist's skill can be seen in the chapel of Ptah-hotep,

Fig. 66. Detail, Ti. Fifth Dynasty. Saqqara D 22

Fig. 68. Detail, Ni-ankh-nesut. Sixth Dynasty. Los Angeles County Museum of Art, 47.8.3

Fig. 67. Detail, Ka-em-nefret. Fifth Dynasty. Museum of Fine Arts, Boston, 04.1761

Fig. 69. Detail, Ipy. Sixth Dynasty. Egyptian Museum, Cairo, 1536

where the scene of hunting in the desert, with its pictorial sense and the finesse of its details, and the still life of the pile of offerings to the right of the deceased's table are both virtuoso performances. The last is a sheer visual delight, forming a kind of picture within a picture, since the sculptor has executed it on a level different from that of the rest of the scene. As depicted in the chapel, the figures of Ptah-hotep himself, handsome and tall in stature, are elegant and alluring.[76]

Mastaba D 64 has no parallel in any other Fifth Dynasty mastabas, and particularly not in those with the name of Djedkare-Isesi, such as the mastaba of Ma-nefer (Saqqara H 2). Ptah-hotep's relief is markedly thicker and rounder than that of Ma-nefer. The deceased's face contains no individual traits, no mark of age (neither wrinkling of the nostril nor fold along the nose), and no trace of severity: on the contrary, it breathes youthfulness and exudes great sweetness, essentially owing to the wide-open

Fig. 70. Detail, Ptah-hotep.
Sixth Dynasty. Saqqara
D 64

eyes and delicately rounded cheeks (fig. 70). To all appearances it is an idealized face, but one that differs from the
idealizations of the Fourth Dynasty in the full curves of
the relief. These characteristics of Ptah-hotep's reliefs pre-
figure aspects of Sixth Dynasty examples, as do the strongly
angular knees of the deceased when he is shown seated.[77]

I have suggested elsewhere that the two chapels of
Akhet-hotep date to the reign of Djedkare-Isesi, the last
king mentioned on its walls, because of the shape of the
chair cushions represented there.[78] It is more difficult to
date the chapel of Ptah-hotep exactly, because I do not
know of any iconographic criterion precise enough to
permit a distinction between the end of the Fifth Dynasty
and the beginning of the Sixth. Everything I have noted
above concerning the style of these reliefs leads one to
think of the time of Teti rather than the reign of Djedkare-
Isesi. Nonetheless, I believe that if Ptah-hotep, who
served in the cults of three successive rulers (Niuserre,
Menkauhor, and Djedkare-Isesi), had also been in service under Djedkare-Isesi's successor, Unis, he would not

have failed to note this on the walls of his tomb.[79]
Consequently, I am tempted to believe that the decoration of Ptah-hotep's chapel itself is contemporary with
Djedkare-Isesi, but that it is the work of an innovative
sculptor ahead of his time, which is to say an artist truly
out of the ordinary.

With regard to the arrangement of the portraits of
couples, a new convention was occasionally adopted in
the Fifth Dynasty: the wife is no longer shown on the
same scale as her husband, but at approximately half his
size. This technique, which had appeared as a short-lived
experiment in the mastabas of Ra-hotep and Nefer-maat
at Meidum (under Snefru),[80] recurs most notably in the
tombs of Ti,[81] Nefer-iretenef,[82] Nefer and Ka-hay,[83] and
Ptah-shepses.[84]

THE SIXTH DYNASTY

It is more difficult to determine the ideal vision of man
and woman for the nobles of the Sixth Dynasty, since

outside the reign of Teti there are fewer great mastabas and fewer large-scale representations of the deceased than in preceding dynasties. Nonroyal monuments from the exceptionally long reign of Pepi II (at least sixty-four years)[85] are limited primarily to false doors, whose representations of officials are often less than meticulously sculpted. Larger private monuments can be found outside the Memphite necropolis, but good photographs of these are rare.

In mastabas with the names of Teti or Pepi I we continue to see the stylistic features already attested in the chapel of Ptah-hotep but more marked than before: fairly thick and often full relief,[86] very angular knees when the deceased is seated,[87] quite large eyes,[88] round cheeks,[89] and rimmed lips with the rim extending around the corners of the mouth,[90] as well as an amiable, even smiling, expression (figs. 68, 69).[91] Some officials, such as Izi (Louvre, Paris, E 14329),[92] also have a large mouth and a stiff, almost mannered pose;[93] others have a nose that descends directly from the forehead.[94] The large eyes and mouth are expressionistic distortions that are also to be found in the statuary of the same period. Finally, what distinguishes the smiling faces of the Sixth Dynasty from those of the Fourth are essentially the fullness of the relief and the less youthful appearance of the faces.

The taste for modeling is a highly variable element in the Sixth Dynasty. The relief is generally quite far removed from the splendid mechanics of the Third and Fifth Dynasties, although quite detailed anatomical representations do appear occasionally.[95] The deceased is frequently represented on the pillars and door reveals of the tomb (as if preparing to leave it) with full belly and sagging breasts—that is, in the twilight of life.

In portraits of couples, the wife is sometimes shown at a realistic scale with respect to her husband, but occasionally she is miniaturized beside the deceased as a sort of hieroglyph or image for the record.[96] This technique had already appeared in statuary of the Fifth Dynasty,[97] but only rarely in relief of the same period.[98]

From this survey it would appear that changes in the concept of the individual, as evidenced by the walls of mastabas, were primarily a function of the spirit of the times, since each dynasty shows a new type of the male and the female figure. This does not, however, preclude the possibility that the taste of particular individuals—artists or patrons—could have overridden the current climate at any given moment during the Old Kingdom.

What seems most striking to me is how the faces of the mastaba owners fall into groups dynasty by dynasty, both in their expressions and in their realism (or lack of it). The severity of faces in the Third Dynasty contrasts clearly with the optimism of those in the Fourth Dynasty, just as the maturity and austerity of Fifth Dynasty faces contrast with the youthfulness of Fourth Dynasty portraits and the serene or smiling fullness of those in the Sixth Dynasty.

Style thus becomes a very concrete and reliable means of dating a relief, although it must remain a supplementary criterion. In matters of style we are always at the mercy of the sculptor's imagination, or that of his model. For that reason it is best to continue classifying the nonroyal monuments of the Old Kingdom first of all by criteria less dependent on subjectivity, such as the shape of a chair leg or the length of a necklace.[99] It is not impossible that one day a finer stylistic analysis will enable us to date mastaba reliefs reign by reign and not merely dynasty by dynasty—or even to identify particular artists, in the same way that we can easily recognize today the hand of Van Eyck or Titian.

1. Vandersleyen 1975b, pp. 5–27; Vandersleyen 1980, pp. 133–37; Vandersleyen 1982, cols. 1074–80; Vandersleyen 1997, pp. 285–90.
2. Egyptian Museum, Cairo, JE 46992; Petrie and Brunton 1924, pls. 7 (right), 10. See also cat. no. 188; ibid., pls. 7, 8.
3. Egyptian Museum, Cairo, CG 34; Porter and Moss 1978, p. 459; Vandersleyen 1983, pp. 61–65.
4. Maspero (1912, p. 72) has given a nice description of modeling: "Contrary to first impressions, the line with which they surrounded objects and bodies is neither stiff nor inflexible: it undulates, it sets, it swells, it thins, it breaks apart, according to the nature of the forms it defines and the movements that animate them. The flat surfaces do not just contain large planes of flesh with a summary indication of the bones: each muscle is marked in place by rises so subtle and depressions so slight that one can hardly imagine how the artist achieved them with the tools at his disposal. In the fine white limestone of Tura he was able to depict them in relief sometimes two millimeters high at most." Even if this description is a little florid, it shows well the distinction between modeling of the contour, rendered by the undulating line that surrounds the figures, and that of the surface, achieved by variations in depth in the upper surface of the relief.
5. In cases where I have not been able to refer to a publication, my observations were made directly from the originals or from private photographic archives.
6. Cherpion 1995, pp. 33–47.
7. Cherpion 1989; Cherpion 1995, pp. 39–42.
8. Saqqara A 3 = Egyptian Museum, Cairo, CG 1426–30; Porter and Moss 1978, p. 437.
9. Saqqara A 2 = Egyptian Museum, Cairo, CG 1385 (Kha-bau-sokar), 1386–87, 57129 (Hathor-nefer-hotep); ibid., p. 449.
10. For the other titles of these officials, see Kahl, Kloth, and Zimmermann 1995, pp. 104–11 (Hesi-re), 188–97 (Kha-bau-sokar).

11. Quibell 1913, p. 3. The occasional dating of the mastaba to the Fourth Dynasty (Borchardt 1937, p. 108; Helck 1968, p. 91) is unfounded.

12. Cherpion 1980, pp. 79–90. There is no reason to think, as Helck did (1968, pp. 90–91), that this mastaba dates to the reign of Khufu. The following differences have been noted between the mastabas of Hesi-re and Kha-bau-sokar: (a) the mastaba of Kha-bau-sokar has two cruciform chapels rather than the simple niches found in Hesi-re's; (b) Kha-bau-sokar's offering lists are more developed than those of Hesi-re (perhaps because there is more room for them in the former monument); (c) the legs of Kha-bau-sokar, but not those of Hesi-re, cover the front legs of his chair (this feature, however, can already be seen in monuments of the Second Dynasty; Saad 1957, pls. 6, 7, 12, 13, 16, 17); (d) Hesi-re's short, round wig shows small, pointed circles, while that of Kha-bau-sokar has ordinary locks of hair.

13. Cherpion 1980, pl. 1 (the folds of fat can be seen better on the left wall than on the right wall reproduced in this plate); see Terrace and Fischer 1970, p. 39.

14. Except on the back wall of the niche, where the legs are abnormally thin. See also the descriptions of Hesi-re and Ra-hotep, below.

15. Cherpion 1980, pp. 86–88, fig. 2.

16. Ibid., pl. 6.

17. For example, in the reliefs of Ra-hotep (British Museum, London, 1242; see below), Neferi (Porter and Moss 1974, p. 51 [1b], under Khufu; Cherpion 1989, pp. 97–98), and Metjetji (cat. nos. 151–156).

18. Cherpion 1980, pl. 5.

19. Ibid.

20. Ibid., pl. 6.

21. Ibid., pl. 2.

22. Sauneron and Stierlin 1975, p. 138.

23. Visible, for example, in the wives of Iy-ka (Egyptian Museum, Cairo, JE 72201, Fourth Dynasty; Cherpion 1989, p. 115) and Wer-bau (Fifth Dynasty; Moussa and Altenmüller 1971, p. 37), and in Louvre E 10971 (Sixth Dynasty; Ziegler 1990b, pp. 277–79).

24. On the contrary, there is a total lack of modeling, for example, in the figure of Nofret (wife of Ra-hotep: Egyptian Museum, Cairo, 19.11.24.3 F), even though she lived under Snefru and is therefore close in time to Hathor-nefer-hotep, and in that of the mother of Mer-ib (Ägyptisches Museum und Papyrussammlung, Staatliche Museen zu Berlin, 1107; photo Marburg 67520), under Khufu or a little later.

25. Cherpion 1980, pp. 88–90, fig. 3.

26. Ibid., pl. 4.

27. The iliac bone appears, exceptionally, in the figure of another woman, Nefret-khau, wife of Khufu-khaf (see fig. 65 in this essay; Porter and Moss 1974, p. 189 [9]; Cherpion 1989, pl. 16), but there it is treated with less naturalism and emphasis than in the depictions of Hathor-nefer-hotep.

28. Porter and Moss 1978, pp. 401, 409, 414.

29. Petrie 1906, fig. 48.

30. Richer 1925, pp. 28–30; see also Borchardt 1937, pl. 25.

31. This detail is also present in another Third Dynasty monument, the stela of Ibnub, now in the Rijksmuseum van Oudheden, Leiden (V 121; Boeser, Holwerda, and Holwerda et al. 1905, atlas, pl. 23).

32. This is also the case in the representation of Kha-bau-sokar seated (on the back wall of the niche), in contrast to the walls that show him standing, where the legs are quite massive.

33. Photos FERE 6807, 6810, 6812; Porter and Moss 1978, p. 493. On the back wall of the false door the deceased has quite full cheeks, which add to his youthful appearance. The mastaba of Metjen (cat. no. 29) has the cartouche of Snefru on its walls.

34. Porter and Moss 1981, p. 879 (with the cartouche of Snefru).

35. On reliefs in the Kofler-Truniger collection (A 85) and the Metropolitan Museum (58.44.2); Porter and Moss 1978, p. 453. Only the fragment in the Bible Lands Museum, Jerusalem (EG 1), shows the deceased somewhat morose. The reliefs in Akhet-hotep's mastaba have no royal names, but all their stylistic features resemble those of monuments from the time of Snefru.

36. On the left jamb of the false door Egyptian Museum, Cairo, CG 57121; Porter and Moss 1981, p. 894 (with the cartouche of Snefru).

37. On the relief Louvre, E 11.430 (Ziegler 1990b, p. 191) the deceased looks almost simple-minded. It should be noted that Ra-hotep has quite different features elsewhere in the tomb. On the British Museum fragment (see below) he has a much more mature face, with small eyes, thick lips, and a strong nose with a bump in profile. The same prominent nose appears on a fragment in the Egyptian Museum, Cairo (19.11.24.3 G), where only its profile is preserved, and on Ra-hotep's statue (fig. 31). No royal name occurs in the mastaba of Ra-hotep, but all its stylistic features associate it with the time of Snefru.

38. On the relief Louvre, B 2. Because of his round cheeks and very sweet expression, Akhet-aa appears younger in this relief than in Louvre, B 1 (cat. no. 18). Even when he seems older, however, he still has relaxed features. Akhet-aa's mastaba has occasionally been dated to the end of the Third Dynasty (Ziegler 1990b, p. 96, with earlier bibliography) because the statue found in the tomb is archaic in style. This is not a totally convincing argument, since the statue of Metjen (cat. no. 28) is of the same type, yet we know that Metjen ended his career under Snefru. Moreover, the relief style of Akhet-aa is immensely closer to that of Snefru's time than to that of Hesi-re and Kha-bau-sokar (for instance, in its texts with column dividers, which do not appear in the reliefs of Hesi-re and Kha-bau-sokar).

39. Mariette and Maspero 1889, p. 69.

40. Except in the reign of Senwosret I, during the Amarna Period, and under the Ptolemies.

41. Cherpion 1989, pp. 32 nn. 28, 29, p. 155.

42. British Museum, London, 1168–71. In other monuments, such as those of Khufu-khaf (G 7140) and Senenu-ka (G 2041), the relief is moderately thick.

43. There are in fact hundreds of square meters of relief and dozens of statues from the Fourth Dynasty; see Cherpion 1989, pp. 83–110; Cherpion 1995, pp. 39–41; and Cherpion 1998, pp. 108–10. The striking number of nonroyal monuments with the name of Khufu (at least fifty; see Cherpion n.d.) is enough in itself to make us reconsider the question.

44. Porter and Moss 1974, pp. 188–90.

45. Stadelmann 1984a, pp. 165–72.

46. Porter and Moss 1974, p. 189 (9).

47. Khufu-khaf, however, has a rather long nose, which rises from his face at a marked angle, and his wife has a small and fairly individual chin. But in PM 2 (ibid., p. 188), the deceased and his mother have practically interchangeable faces, with the same angle of the chin and the same pretty face; in PM 10 and 13 (ibid., p. 190) the portraits are frozen stereotypes.

48. The deceased's figure in PM 5 (ibid., p. 189) has not much more modeling. The deltoid and the muscles of the knee and legs are discernible; see Cherpion 1989, pl. 14.

49. Cherpion 1995, pp. 33–34.

50. I cannot help recalling here the following anecdote. In May 1998, when Hosni Mubarak visited France, *Paris-Match* wanted to publish a photograph of the Egyptian president and his wife. Mubarak agreed, even though the presidential couple had never appeared together in an official portrait in Egypt. The photograph that resulted, however, was quite different from that normally seen in European courts. Mme Mubarak spontaneously took the arm of her husband, thereby adopting the custom of ancient Egypt, in which it is the wife and not the husband who displays a gesture of affection. In doing so she duplicated, without realizing it, the precise pose of Khufu-khaf's wife (*Paris-Match*, May 28, 1998, p. 49).

51. The only royal names associated with monuments in which the gesture of Khufu-khaf's wife appears are those of Snefru, Khufu, Djedefre, and Khafre; see Cherpion 1995, p. 33.

52. Several such reliefs are dated by royal names appearing in the monuments: from the time of *Sened* and *Peribsen:* Sheri (Cherpion 1989, pp. 22–23); *Khufu:* Neferi (ibid., pp. 97–98, pls. 10, 11), Min-nefer (unpublished, excavations of Zahi Hawass), Akhet-hotep (G 7650; Barracco 3, Alinari photograph 34761), Nen-sedjer-kai (G 2101), and the wife of Ni-hetep-khnum (Cherpion 1989, pl. 3); *Djedefre:* Seneb (Cherpion 1984, pl. 10, which contrasts with the realism of his statue, ibid., pl. 11); *Khafre:* Nesut-nefer (G 4970; Porter and Moss 1974, p. 144 [4]; Junker's photographs do not allow for judgment); *Menkaure:* Ka-nefer (G 2150; Porter and Moss 1974, p. 78 [8]). Others, *without cartouches*, can be dated to the same general period on other grounds: Dedi (unpublished, excavations of Zahi Hawass); Hetep-her-en-ptah (Cherpion 1989, pl. 25b); Irery (British Museum, London, 1168–71; ibid., cover ill., pl. 27a); Ka-aper (Nelson-Atkins Museum of Art, Kansas City, 46.33; the wife, however, has an awful face, with little eyes and turned-down lips); Ka-em-heset (Egyptian Museum, Cairo, JE 47749; Forman, Forman, and Vilímková 1962, pl. 25); Mery (Carnegie Museum of Art, Pittsburgh, 73.11, with a rather inane expression); Setju (Ny Carlsberg Glyptotek, Copenhagen, AEIN 6–7, from Saqqara B 6; the dating to the end of the Fourth Dynasty or the beginning of the Fifth proposed by Jørgensen [1996, p. 54] is unlikely because of the wig, whose profile exhibits a single, sharp setback; see Cherpion 1989, p. 56, criterion 30).

53. Cherpion 1989, pp. 97–98 (time of Khufu).

54. Cherpion 1995, pp. 36–37; Ziegler 1997a.

55. Is it in this sense that we are to understand Herodotus's report of the tradition that Khufu was a tyrannical king because he leveled society during his reign? Probably not, since the artistic features described here apply not only in the reign of Khufu but throughout the Fourth Dynasty, including the reign of the "good king Snefru."

56. Museum of Fine Arts, Boston, 07.1000/1003–05 (with the cartouche of Khufu).

57. For the nose, see also Louvre, B 51, and Museum of Fine Arts, Boston, 06.1886; for the double chin, Louvre B 51, and Barracco 1. For the term "magic head," see Tefnin 1991.

58. Cherpion 1989, pp. 100–102. The other women represented on the same false door are not as heavy as Debet.

59. Ibid., pp. 129–30.

60. Ibid., pp. 111–12.

61. The time of Snefru seems unlikely because Huti's relief does not have the characteristic thickness of examples produced during that reign.

62. Examples are the representations of Ni-kau-hor (Metropolitan Museum, New York, 08.201.2, with Userkaf's cartouche), Ka-em-rehu (Ny Carlsberg Glyptotek, Copenhagen, AEIN 1271, with the cartouche of Niuserre), Nefer (G 4761, time of Niuserre; Cherpion 1989, pp. 137–38), Akhet-hotep (Saqqara D 64, with the cartouche of Djedkare-Isesi), Ma-nefer (Ägyptisches Museum und Papyrussammlung, Staatliche Museen zu Berlin, 1108, with the cartouche of Djedkare-Isesi; photograph FERE 7072), Ni-ankh-khnum and Khnum-hotep (Moussa and Altenmüller 1977, pl. 90, with the cartouche of Niuserre), and Akhet-hotep (Louvre, E 10958; photographs FERE 6921, 15.855; Cherpion 1989, pp. 133–34, time of Niuserre).

63. Examples can be seen in the reliefs of Tep-em-ankh (Egyptian Museum, Cairo, CG 1564, with the cartouche of Sahure), Ti (Steindorff 1913, pl. 130, with the cartouche of Niuserre), Nefer and Ka-hay (Moussa and Altenmüller 1971, pl. 37; Cherpion 1989, pp. 134–35, time of Neferirkare or Niuserre).

64. Photograph 7466b of the Institut Royal du Patrimoine Artistique, Brussels; Cherpion 1989, pl. 35. A strong nose seems to be the prerogative of several Fifth Dynasty officials: Nefer-bau-ptah (G 6010, with the cartouche of Niuserre), Ma-nefer (Ägyptisches Museum und Papyrussammlung, Staatliche Museen zu Berlin, 1108, with the cartouche of Djedkare-Isesi; photo FERE 7072), Tep-em-ankh (Egyptian Museum, Cairo, CG 1564, with the cartouche of Sahure), Hetep-herakhti (Rijksmuseum van Oudheden, Leiden, F. 1904/3.1, with the cartouche of Niuserre), Ti (Steindorff 1913, pl. 130, with the cartouche of Niuserre).

65. For instance, in the depictions of Nefer-iretenef (photograph 7466b of the Institut Royal du Patrimoine Artistique, Brussels; Van de Walle 1978, pl. 18; Cherpion 1989, pl. 35), Hetep-herakhti (Rijksmuseum van Oudheden, Leiden, F. 1904/3.1; Porter and Moss 1979, p. 594 [7]), Ka-em-rehu (Ny Carlsberg Glyptotek, Copenhagen, AEIN 1271), Ti (Steindorff 1913, pl. 130), Akhet-hotep (Louvre, Paris, E 10958; photographs FERE 6878, 6882), Akhet-hotep (Saqqara D 64), and Ni-ankh-khnum and Khnum-hotep (Moussa and Altenmüller 1977, pls. 61, 87).

66. For instance, in the faces of Hetep-herakhti (Rijksmuseum van Oudheden, Leiden, F. 1904/3.1; Porter and Moss 1979, p. 593 [1]), Ka-em-nefret (fig. 67), Nefer-iretenef (photograph 7466b of the Institut Royal du Patrimoine Artistique, Brussels; Van de Walle 1978, pl. 18; Cherpion 1989, pl. 35), Ka-em-rehu (Ny Carlsberg Glyptotek, Copenhagen, AEIN 1271), Metjetji (cat. no. 154), Unis-ankh (Field Museum, Chicago, A 24448), Akhet-hotep (Louvre, Paris, E 10958; photograph FERE 6878), Ptah-hotep (Saqqara D 64), Akhet-hotep (Saqqara D 64), Nefer-seshem-seshat (Egyptian Museum, Cairo, CG 1491), and Ni-ankh-khnum and Khnum-hotep (Moussa and Altenmüller 1977, pls. 61, 65, 73, 87).

67. For instance, Metjetji (cat. no. 154), Akhet-hotep (Louvre, Paris, E 10958; photograph FERE 6878), Ptah-hotep (Saqqara D 64), Akhet-hotep (Saqqara D 64), Nefer-seshem-seshat (Egyptian Museum, Cairo, CG 1491).

68. This feature distinguishes the modeling of the Fifth Dynasty from that of the Third Dynasty, which is executed on vigorous, thick relief (Cherpion 1980, pl. 3). If the tomb of Nefer and Ka-hay at Saqqara presents a decidedly thicker relief, it is probably because it is a rock tomb carved in the local limestone and not a mastaba with relief executed on a facing of Tura limestone.

69. Steindorff 1913, pls. 18, 19, 121, 130.

70. Moussa and Altenmüller 1977, pls. 4, 5, 16, 17, 87.

71. In the scene of hunting and fishing; Porter and Moss 1979, p. 594 (8).

72. Photograph FERE 6972 (Porter and Moss 1979, p. 576 [5]).

73. Photographs FERE 6882, 6921, 15.855.

74. Porter and Moss 1979, p. 599 (3, 4, 8, 9). This is the mastaba that shows the most complete rendering of anatomy.

75. Akhet-hotep (Louvre, Paris, E 10958; photograph FERE 6886); Ma-nefer (Ägyptisches Museum und Papyrussammlung, Staatliche Museen zu Berlin, 1108).

76. Cherpion 1989, pls. 42–45.

77. In Akhet-hotep's scenes both the relief and the deceased's cheeks are not as rounded as in those of Ptah-hotep. In addition, the small figures of Akhet-hotep at the base of the false door (Porter and Moss 1979, p. 600 [14]), with their large noses and wrinkled nostrils, recall those of the rest of the Fifth Dynasty.

78. Cherpion 1989, pp. 132–33.

79. This was already the opinion of Griffith (in Paget and Pirie 1898, p. 33).

80. Petrie 1892, pls. 9, 10, 19, 27.

81. Steindorff 1913, pls. 24, 58, 59, 88, 94, 121, 128, 130, 132.

82. Van de Walle 1978, pls. 1, 6 (no difference in scale, however, appears in ibid., pls. 2, 3, 12).

83. Moussa and Altenmüller 1971, pl. 24a.

84. Verner 1992a, nos. 16, 22.

85. Vercoutter 1992, p. 332.

86. This is especially true in the reign of Teti: Ka-gemni (Bissing 1911, pl. 5; Porter and Moss 1978, pp. 522 [12], 524 [28]), Sabu-Ibebi (Egyptian Museum, Cairo, CG 1418), Nefer-seshem-ptah (photograph Marburg 154981), Mereruka (Duell 1938, vol. 1, pls. 1–68, vol. 2, pls. 123, 125, 127, 138, 154), Ipy (fig. 69), Ni-ankh-nesut (fig. 68), Mehu (Altenmüller 1998, pls. 18, 30, 55). The relief seems thinner under Pepi I: compare Senedjem-ib (Nationalmuseet, Copenhagen, 15002), Khuen-khnum (Cherpion 1989, pl. 47), and Ankh-meryre (Altenmüller 1998, pls. 81, 86).

87. For instance, Ankh-ma-hor (Capart 1907, pl. 21 = facade), Sabu-Ibebi (Egyptian Museum, Cairo, CG 1418), Nefer-seshem-ptah (photograph Marburg 154981), Mereruka (Duell 1938, vol. 1, pl. 63, vol. 2, pls. 113, 120, 171), Ni-ankh-nesut (Cleveland Museum of Art, 30.735; photograph 7853 of the Institut Royal du Patrimoine Artistique, Brussels), Mehu and Ankh-meryre (Altenmüller 1998, pls. 15, 64, 81, 86).

88. For instance, Ankh-ma-hor (Capart 1907, pl. 21 = facade), Ka-gemni (Bissing 1905, pl. 15; Bissing 1911, pl. 5; Porter and Moss 1978, pp. 523 [20], 524 [28]), Izi (Louvre, Paris, E 14329; Ziegler 1990b, pp. 79, 81), Ipy (Egyptian Museum, Cairo, CG 1536), Senedjem-ib (Nationalmuseet, Copenhagen, 15002).

89. For instance, Ka-gemni (facade), Mereruka (Duell 1938, vol. 1, pl. 63, vol. 2, pls. 179, 183), Ni-ankh-nesut (fig. 68), Sabu-Ibebi (Egyptian Museum, Cairo, CG 1418).

90. For instance, Ka-gemni (Bissing 1905, pl. 15; Bissing 1911, pls. 5, 37; Porter and Moss 1978, pp. 523 [20], 524 [28], 525 [41]), Ankh-ma-hor (Capart 1907, pl. 21 = facade; the rim describes a very large circle around the corners; the lips here are also especially fleshy, and this, together with a flat nose, gives the deceased an African appearance), Ipy (fig. 69), Senedjem-ib (Nationalmuseet, Copenhagen, 15002), Mereruka (Duell 1938, vol. 1, pls. 16, 63, 96, vol. 2, pls. 151, 156).

91. For instance, Ni-ankh-nesut (fig. 68; the sweet smile has an almost feminine quality), Ankh-ma-hor (Capart 1907, pl. 21 = facade), Ka-gemni (Bissing 1905, pl. 15; Bissing 1911, pl. 5 and facade; Porter and Moss 1978, pp. 523 [20]; 524 [28]; the face is much less affable in Bissing 1911, pl. 37; Porter and Moss 1978, p. 525 [41]), Sabu-Ibebi (Egyptian Museum, Cairo, CG 1418), Idut (Porter and Moss 1979, p. 617), Mereruka (Duell 1938, vol. 1, pl. 63, vol. 2, pls. 151, 181, 184).

92. Ziegler 1990b, ill. pp. 79, 81.

93. The same kind of pose appears in the mastaba of Ankh-meryre (Altenmüller 1998, pl. 86).

94. Khuen-khnum (Ägyptisches Museum der Universität Leipzig, 48; Schäfer 1908, p. 14, fig. 14; Cherpion 1989, pl. 47), Tjetju (Firth and Gunn 1926, vol. 2, pl. 38), Ipy (Egyptian Museum, Cairo, CG 1536).

95. For instance, Ka-gemni (facade), Ankh-ma-hor (Capart 1907, pls. 21 [facade], 50), Ni-ankh-nesut (Cleveland Museum of Art, 30.735; photograph 7853 of the Institut Royal du Patrimoine Artistique, Brussels; modeling in the upper part of the body).

96. Duell 1938, vol. 1, pls. 9, 17, 26, 39, 46, 48a,d, 57, 63, 71. In contrast, the wife is shown at a more realistic scale in Duell 1938, vol. 1, pls. 14, 23b,c, 35b, 40b, 41, 48c, 91.

97. And perhaps also of the Fourth Dynasty, since there is as yet no manual for dating the private statuary of the Old Kingdom. For group statues, see Vandersleyen 1973, p. 14.

98. Moussa and Altenmüller 1971, pls. 26, 30.

99. Cherpion 1989, pp. 19–24.

FURNITURE OF
THE OLD KINGDOM

JULIE ANDERSON

Carpentry and furniture manufacture were among the earliest trades plied in ancient Egypt, and by the Old Kingdom woodworking had become a well-developed craft practiced by accomplished artisans. The elegant furniture found within the Fourth Dynasty tomb of Queen Hetep-heres I attests to the high level of craftsmanship that had been attained and to a skilled tradition of woodworking, which made it one of the most significant Egyptian minor arts. The discovery of this remarkable tomb not only provided tangible examples demonstrating the advanced technical prowess of Egyptian carpenters but also opened a unique window into the Old Kingdom through which we might better understand the domestic life-style and household goods of the ancient Egyptians. Depictions of furniture in statuary, tomb paintings, and reliefs expand and enhance our knowledge of the development of the craft and, as comparatively few examples of Old Kingdom furniture have survived to the present day, must be the source of much of our information on the subject. Most of this material, whether artifactual or pictorial, originated in royal or nobles' tombs.

THE MATERIALS AND TYPES OF OLD KINGDOM FURNITURE

Wood was the material most commonly employed for furniture construction, but ivory, stone, metal, and wicker were also utilized on occasion. The wood available in Egypt is poor in quality and limited in quantity—circumstances that make the development of a highly skilled carpentry trade striking. Although the identification of wood species has often been overlooked during artifact analyses, we know that some indigenous trees used by furniture makers from the Predynastic Period through the Old Kingdom included acacia, tamarisk, willow, sycamore, date palm, poplar, and sidder. It is possible that carob, fig, doom palm, and persea were also employed, because they are either mentioned in inscriptions or supplied fruits that have been found in early tombs. The lack of superior wood in Egypt made its importation imperative. Thus cedar, cypress, fir, pine, yew, and perhaps also birch were transported from the area of Syria and Lebanon, while ebony was brought in from regions to the south of Egypt, particularly the Sudan and Ethiopia.[1] Evidence that Egyptians imported wood appears on the Palermo Stone (cat. no. 115), which records that during the Fourth Dynasty King Snefru sent forty ships to acquire cedar from Lebanon. This inscription not only tells us that wood was imported but also suggests that good-quality timber, and particularly cedar, was an important and highly valued commodity in the culture of ancient Egypt.

Although there is a paucity of extant examples, the evolution of furniture can be traced from the Predynastic and Archaic Periods, which precede the Old Kingdom, on the basis of the sparse evidence that does survive. Preserved by the arid environment, the First Dynasty tombs at Abydos have yielded remains of wood furniture, often decorated with basketry motifs and ivory inlays. Hippopotamus and elephant ivories, finely carved in the shape of bulls' legs, that were used as furniture supports[2] have been unearthed, and similarly wrought wood examples have also been discovered. The base of each leg, beneath the carved bull's hoof, terminates in a ribbed cylinder designed to protect the foot of the support. Furniture legs continued to be finished with pedestal feet of this kind even after the Old Kingdom.

Many well-preserved pieces of early furniture were found by W. M. F. Petrie at the Upper Egyptian site of Tarkhan.[3] There, within the First Dynasty mastaba tombs, he discovered small, simple tables, trays, and four different types of bed frame—an assemblage that supplies valuable insight into the practices of daily life and the sort of furniture in common use in Predynastic and Archaic times. The bed frames vary in style from very simple objects, constructed from four fortuitously bent tree branches, to complex examples. The latter display a high degree of woodworking prowess, as the carved rails are often finished with papyrus-shaped terminals and the heavy bovine legs are attached to them by lashing and mortise-and-tenon joints. Most beds were inclined slightly from the head down toward the foot. Interestingly, no stools or chairs were discovered at Tarkhan; however, several examples are illustrated in Second Dynasty tomb stelae from Helwan.[4]

Finely detailed wall paintings uncovered by James Quibell in 1911 within the Third Dynasty mastaba of Hesi-re at Saqqara[5] depict a considerable quantity of household furniture and other furnishings for use by the tomb owner in the afterlife. Among the goods illustrated are numerous bed frames, stools, chairs, chests, tables, game boxes, and headrests, all items that would typically have equipped a noble's home. In comparison with the preceding Archaic Period furniture, these exhibit more refined design and carpentry techniques and a strikingly wider variety of styles and models. Particularly notable is the range of box and chest types, each of which may have served a different function. The Hesi-re paintings suggest not only an evolution of this kind but also that inlays, gilding, paint, and imported woods were being used by the Third Dynasty and that the basic conventions, traditions, and forms governing Egyptian furniture production had been established by this time. This development is corroborated by eleven beautifully carved wood panels discovered in Hesi-re's mastaba by Auguste Mariette during the mid-nineteenth century: these show Hesi-re in raised relief assuming a variety of poses with refined furnishings of various kinds; for example in one panel he is seated upon a bovine- or gazelle-legged stool in front of a table (cat. no. 17).

The funerary assemblage of Queen Hetep-heres I, wife of Snefru, the first ruler of the Fourth Dynasty, was discovered in 1925 by George Reisner.[6] This rare archaeological find lay in a small room at the bottom of a deep shaft near the pyramid of the queen's son Khufu at Giza. Among the grave goods was a collection of royal furniture including a bed, a portable canopy, several boxes, two chairs, and a carrying chair (cat. no. 33). Many objects were inlaid and covered with gold foil, but unfortunately much of the original wood had deteriorated,

leaving gilding and inlay fragments on the floor. Several pieces that were painstakingly reconstructed by the excavators are characterized by both an elegance and a simplicity of design and proportion. Like the earlier furniture known from artifacts and depictions, these objects incorporate animal and floral elements that display a high degree of realism. Hetep-heres I's gilded bed bears a striking similarity to the beds represented in the tomb of Hesi-re but differs from them in its addition of a footboard and use of leonine rather than bovine legs. Her chairs are also fitted with leonine legs, which from the Fourth Dynasty forward became common. Of the two chairs found only one could be reconstructed completely, but both appear to have had similar solid cubic forms with low, deep seats and decorated side panels. Carved in an openwork pattern beneath the armrests of the reconstructed chair are three gilded papyrus heads and stalks tied together in a cluster. Motifs based on natural forms appear as well in the ornamentation of other pieces from the tomb: for example, the ends of the carrying poles of the sedan chair are finished with gold palmiform capitals (cat. no. 33); a faience feather pattern decorates the bed's footboard; while rosettes alternate with a feather motif on the back of the second armchair, each of whose side panels bears a falcon sitting upon a palm column. Basketry and mat patterns long in use are also seen in Hetep-heres I's furniture, decorating uprights from her portable canopy and the reconstructed chair.

TOOLS AND METHODS OF PRODUCTION

At the beginning of the Archaic Period copper implements became widespread, largely replacing the flint tools of earlier times and making finely detailed woodworking feasible. Walter Emery discovered a large cache of copper carpenters' tools in the First Dynasty mastaba tomb 3471 at Saqqara,[7] which provides evidence that the implements of the ancient carpenters are in many respects similar to those of today's artisans. Axes and saws were employed initially to split and shape green wood. Larger pieces of timber were tied to an upright post and cut from the top downward with a short saw. However, unlike many modern saws that cut when pushed or pulled, ancient saws cut only when the tool was pulled; moreover, the teeth of the early saws face in the direction of the handle and do not necessarily extend over the entire length of the blade. (The use of this type of saw combined with the poor quality of indigenous timbers often resulted in the production of short planks of wood.) The freshly manufactured planks would have been left to dry before they were made into furniture in order to avoid problems created by the contraction of moist green wood. For curved elements timbers were heated and then bent, or naturally curved pieces of wood were adapted and integrated.[8] Carpenters relied upon copper adze blades lashed to wood handles to plane and trim wood surfaces, while bow drills and awls bored holes that were required—in joints for the insertion of lashing or in chair frames for attachments for woven seats, for example. Several types of copper chisels were used. Some were hit with heavy wood or stone mallets to cut joints, whereas others were employed for hand carving and detail work, with the required pressure being administered by hand. The final smoothing of the piece was accomplished with sandstone polishers. The sharpness of a tool edge was maintained by honing it on an oiled sharpening stone, usually a flat piece of slate.[9]

Butt joints and simple miter joints were the most commonly used type of joint; however, mortise-and-tenon joints, half-lap joints, scarf joints with butterfly clamps, dovetail joints, and many more complex varieties of miter joints, including shoulder, double shoulder, dovetailed miter-housing, and miter-housing corner joints, were also employed.[10] Throughout much of the Old Kingdom wet leather thongs drawn through holes were used to lash components together and to reinforce joints. As the leather dried it contracted, thus securing the connection. Holes drilled in the top of a bed leg, for example, allowed it to be tied to the bed's wood frame with a thong. The addition of a tenon on the leg top, fitted into a mortise on the frame, often provided additional support.[11] However, wood dowels, animal glues, and cleats gradually supplanted much thong lashing. Dowels appeared as early as the Second Dynasty,[12] and during the Fifth Dynasty the use of animal glues became widespread. These glues were manufactured from boiled animal hides and bone, much as they are today, and applied by brush. Gesso made from gypsum was also employed as an adhesive for inlays and gold leaf. Thicker gold sheeting was attached by small nails.[13] Occasionally the surface of poor-caliber wood was covered with a thin sheet of finer wood, often ebony. This veneer was affixed with a resin early in the Old Kingdom and with a glue later in the period, while larger fragments were attached by small dowels or nails. The use of veneer as early as the First Dynasty is documented by a box discovered by Emery in the tomb of Hemaka at Saqqara.[14]

A carpenters' workshop depicted in the Fifth Dynasty mastaba of Ti at Saqqara (fig. 71)[15] shows artisans

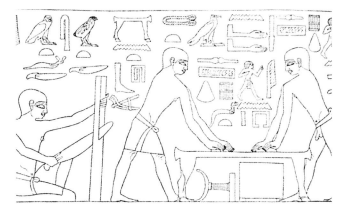

Fig. 71. Detail, wall relief from mastaba of Ti, Fifth Dynasty, Saqqara: a carpenter's workshop. From Wild 1966 (pl. 174)

engaged in the preparation of wood, which they are shaping, sawing, smoothing, bending, drilling, and polishing, and in furniture construction. A headrest sits on the floor, while craftsmen polish a chest, drill a hole in a box lid, and fashion boxes and a bed. In a similar scene from the Fifth Dynasty tomb of Mereruka at Saqqara, carpenters are making a bed, a door, and several other objects, notably chests and tables, many of which incorporate architectural elements—there are, for example, chests with gable lids.[16] Moreover, chests with cavetto cornices are depicted in the early Fifth Dynasty pyramid temple of Sahure at Abusir.[17] Such representations of furniture and everyday scenes of carpenters at work, as well as the frequent inclusion of furniture and models within tombs, underscore the importance of the role furniture played in the lives of the ancient Egyptians.

1. Lucas and Harris 1962, pp. 429–48; Killen 1980, pp. 1–7; and Killen 1994b, pp. 7–8.
2. Petrie 1901, pl. 34.
3. Petrie, Wainwright, and Gardiner 1913, pp. 1–31.
4. See Saad 1957.
5. Quibell 1913.
6. Reisner and Smith 1955.
7. Emery 1949, pp. 17–57; concerning carpenters' tools, see also Petrie 1917.
8. See Montet 1925, pp. 311–15.
9. Baker 1966, pp. 24–25, 296–301; Killen 1980, pp. 12–22; Der Manuelian 1982, pp. 63–64; Killen 1994b, pp. 12–13, 19–21, 33–34. See also Petrie 1917.
10. Aldred 1954, pp. 684–703; Baker 1966, pp. 297–301; Killen 1980, pp. 8–11; Killen 1994b, pp. 12–16.
11. Baker 1966, pp. 21–26.
12. Killen 1980, p. 10.
13. Baker 1966, pp. 301–3; Killen 1980, pp. 8–11; Killen 1994b, pp. 16–18.
14. Emery 1938, no. 432, pl. 23a.
15. Concerning carpenters, see Montet 1925, pp. 298–315.
16. Duell 1938, vol. 1, pls. 29–31.
17. Borchardt 1913, pl. 60.

STONE VESSELS
Luxury Items with Manifold Implications

DOROTHEA ARNOLD AND ELENA PISCHIKOVA

S tone vessels of the Old Kingdom are luxury items that owe their beauty to skilled craftsmanship and an exquisite sense of refinement in design and decoration. The art of stone-vessel making goes back almost to the beginning of Egyptian history, and consequently, in the Third Dynasty, when King Djoser's artisans were given the task of producing tens of thousands of stone vases for the subterranean storerooms of his Step Pyramid at Saqqara (cat. no. 5),[1] they were fully equipped to meet the demand. Since the fifth millennium B.C.E., long before stone was used for building and statuary, vessels had been fashioned from hard stones; indeed, the art had reached its peak just before the reign of Djoser, during the first two dynasties,[2] with the production of vessels that imitated in extremely hard and brittle stone, and with astonishing accuracy, such flimsy items as a basket made of reeds and the leaf of a lotus plant.[3]

STONE MATERIALS

By the Third Dynasty, stone-vessel making had become a somewhat more conventional craft than it had been during Archaic times. The materials used were less varied than in the earlier period, when they had encompassed practically every type of hard stone available in stone-rich Egypt.[4] Throughout the Old Kingdom most stone vessels were made of the white or yellowish white, sometimes even brownish, so-called Egyptian alabaster.[5] This semitranslucent, beautifully veined material is actually calcite, not a true alabaster.[6] Some scholars prefer to call it travertine,[7] although the typical travertine does not share the distinctive translucency of Egyptian alabaster.[8] True alabaster (a fine-grained granular aggregate

of gypsum) was occasionally used for stone vessels in the Archaic Period but not—as far as is known—during the Old Kingdom.[9] The ancient Egyptian word for Egyptian alabaster is *šst* (pronounced *sheset* by Egyptologists).[10] The material occurs at many places in the limestone region of the Egyptian deserts. Quarries known to have been exploited for it by the ancient Egyptians are predominantly located in the Eastern Desert, from south of Cairo (Wadi el-Garawi) to Asyut; best known among them is the quarry of Hatnub, near Amarna.[11] Although through trace-element analysis it is possible to determine from which location the material of specific stone vessels derived, such investigations have so far been undertaken on only a small number of objects.[12] In addition to Egyptian alabaster, stone-vessel makers of the Old Kingdom relied on diorite, gneiss (cat. no. 99), and, above all, limestone[13] with some frequency, but they rarely employed porphyry, granite, breccia, basalt, quartz crystal, and obsidian.[14] Some of these materials were available to the craftsmen as refuse from sculptors' workshops.[15]

THE SHAPES AND DECORATION OF STONE VESSELS

The stone-vessel makers of the Old Kingdom worked too much under the influence of their forebears to create a totally new set of shapes. Their contributions to the formal repertoire of Egyptian stone-vessel art were the refinement of preexisting shapes and the introduction of shapes imitating terracotta and metal prototypes (fig. 72). Since the beginning of the art form in Predynastic times, Egyptian stone-vessel shapes typically had been close to basic geometric solids.[16] In the Archaic Period

Fig. 72. The most important types of stone vessels found in Old Kingdom tombs and pyramid temples. * indicates a shape introduced in periods earlier than the Old Kingdom; ** indicate shapes that imitate vessels of clay or metal. Drawing by Peter Der Manuelian after Aston 1994, pp. 123, 137, figs. 9–14

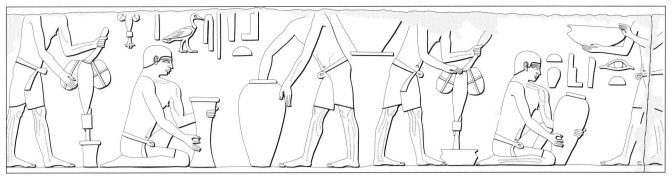

Fig. 73. The making of stone vessels as depicted in an Old Kingdom relief from an unknown tomb at Saqqara. Egyptian Museum, Cairo JE 39866. Drawing by Peter Der Manuelian after Maspero 1915b, pp. 25–27, pl. 22

and the Old Kingdom, however, subtle deviations from pure geometric form became characteristic. The traditional ointment jars, for instance, had been cylindrical with straight or slightly bulging sides from the Predynastic Naqada I Period (about 3850–3650 B.C.E.). During the Archaic Period these vases started to become conical, a tendency that continued during the Old Kingdom,[17] when, moreover, most of their walls were concave and they showed ever wider bases. In vessels of the Fifth and Sixth Dynasties (cat. nos. 179, 180) the splayed foot was beautifully counterpoised by a broad rim.[18]

During the Sixth Dynasty stone-vessel making entered a new phase of creativity. Vessel shapes of that period (cat. nos. 178–180, 184) are of a variety unparalleled since the end of the Archaic Period.[19] They also reveal traits that can only be called mannerist—for instance, the widely splayed bases of some cylindrical vessels (cat. nos. 179, 180)[20] and the exaggeratedly lengthened proportions of jars, among which an intricately shaped collared type is especially common (fig. 72, bottom right).[21]

Decoration on stone vessels of the Old Kingdom is mainly confined to rope patterns and designs that imitate the nets in which Egyptians daily carried large and small containers (cat. no. 5). Other decorative elements are incised hieroglyphic inscriptions and symbolic motifs (cat. nos. 179, 180, 184), which are discussed below. Some delightful examples are sculpted (cat. no. 178).[22] Like most high-quality stone vessels, these intriguing vases were doubtless the work of court artisans.[23]

THE TECHNIQUES OF STONE-VESSEL MAKING

The production of stone vessels is frequently depicted in Old Kingdom wall reliefs and paintings.[24] Because few workshops have been found,[25] much of what is said about methods of manufacture must rely on inference from these representations and other evidence.[26] The craftsman appears to have started by cutting a stone roughly into the desired shape of the vessel. This must have been done with the help of dolerite pounders (cat. no. 36) and copper chisels. Pieces discarded in an unfinished state show that the outside of the container was then fully finished and smoothed by rubbing with a hard stone. Only after the exterior shape was achieved did the craftsman start to hollow out the interior, a task accomplished, at least from the Archaic Period, with the so-called crank drill (fig. 73).[27] This instrument consisted basically of a long piece of wood with a handle on top. Below the handle two heavy stones were fastened with ropes. Recent investigations by the experimental archaeologist Stocks have revealed that these stones did not provide momentum during the work process but served solely to weigh down the drill.[28] The instrument often had a forked bottom that helped to fasten the drill bit. Both this fork and the handle on top of the drill were made of single naturally shaped tree branches. Some representations of the crank drill show a shaft composed of two parts that are lashed together (fig. 73). Stocks has convincingly explained that shafts of this kind must have been fashioned to facilitate replacement of the lower end of the drill when it wore down from use.[29]

Drill bits were made in various shapes and of many materials. There were triangular bits of flint whose points wore off through use—which accounts for the fact that discarded bits of flint found in excavations are usually crescent-shaped. There were also drill bits of diorite, quartzite, and limestone. Shapes included figure-eight forms and roughly rectangular cones with indentations in the center of both long sides into which the forked ends of the drill could be fitted.[30] Tubular bits of copper may sometimes have been employed as well, especially for the initial drilling of the cavity—indeed a small groove

around the bottom of the interior of a number of conical ointment vessels perhaps indicates their use.[31] The
drill shaft to which such copper tubes might have been
fitted would, of course, have had no fork at its lower end.

Stocks has demonstrated that the crank drill was
probably not turned continuously in one direction but
rather was twisted forward and backward, clockwise and
counterclockwise, either between the two hands that held
the shaft and handle of the instrument or by one hand
while the other steadied the instrument or the vessel.[32]
This procedure appears to assure a high degree of stability and a well-centered drilling process. Archaeological
evidence reveals that the ancient Egyptian drilling technique also involved placing the vessel in a hole in the
ground or other work area. Thus, in the Old Kingdom
stone-vessel workshop excavated at Hierakonopolis
sockets suitable for holding vessels were found in a work-
bench of beaten earth.[33] And a wood model of early
Middle Kingdom date represents in miniature a carpenter's workshop in which a stone-vessel maker has also
found a home. This artisan uses a large round white
object, probably a stone with a hole in its top, as a support for the vase he is drilling.[34]

A difficult stage in the hollowing process must have
been reached when the center cavity of a jar of broad
shape was bored and the craftsman had to enlarge the
interior space on all sides. Some archaeologists believe
that the drill was held obliquely to widen the cavity,
while others have followed Reisner, who maintained that
a succession of ever larger drill bits was used.[35] Certainly
a number of bits of different shapes were employed to
obtain the desired volume and shape of the interior.
Whenever possible the artisan probably effected the final
thinning of the walls by inserting his hand into the vessel and smoothing down the interior by rubbing with a
hard stone (fig. 73). Sand and other suitable powdery
substances were used as abrasives during all stages of the
work, including the final polishing of the outer surface.[36]

THE FUNCTION AND DISTRIBUTION OF STONE VESSELS

Stone vessels served various purposes in the life and afterlife of the ancient Egyptians. Three groups can be distinguished among the Old Kingdom vessels: cosmetic oil
and ointment vases, many inscribed with the names and
titles of kings (cat. nos. 178–180); imitations in stone of
terracotta utilitarian vessels (cat. nos. 160, 161); and
miniature vases (cat. no. 214). Imitation vases and minia-

Fig. 74. King Niuserre anointing the standard of the god
Wepwawet using his little fingers. From Bissing and Kees
1923 (pl. 13)

ture vessels will be dealt with exclusively in the relevant
entries, but some general remarks about the cosmetic oil
and ointment vases are called for here.

The storage of cosmetic oils and ointments was by far
the most important function of stone vessels in ancient
Egypt.[37] Their thick stone walls helped to keep the fatty
substances they held cool, and their exquisite workmanship and high quality underlined the precious nature of
the contents. Cosmetic ointments were used in everyday
life and also in important rituals in temples and tombs.
Cult statues and cult objects (fig. 74) in temples of gods
and in pyramid temples, for instance, were treated daily
with cosmetic materials and reviving ointments.[38] No
wonder temple storerooms were filled with precious vessels containing these ingredients[39] and that stone vases
were left as votives in sanctuaries[40] and were standard items
in foundation deposits.[41] Anointing and cosmetic treatment
also played a role in the preparation of mummies[42]—
which were treated with oils—and in the funerary cult[43]—

based on the belief in the reviving effect of the oils and ointments. Thus there was a double reason for these stone receptacles to accompany the deceased into the grave. Accordingly, they appear frequently in burial sites,[44] including royal ones, as evidenced by the numerous stone cosmetic vases discovered in the Eighteenth Dynasty tomb of Tutankhamun.[45]

Stone vessels were deposited not only in the tombs of later pharaohs but also in the pyramids and pyramid precincts of Old Kingdom rulers. Today, having escaped centuries of plunder by virtue of their durability, these receptacles are often the only surviving remains from the once-rich assortment of goods that accompanied a Pyramid Age king into his afterlife and served the cult of his statues in the pyramid temple. Their numbers are considerable, as demonstrated by the tens of thousands of Djoser's stone vessels mentioned above, which still rest in the underground chambers of the ruler's Step Pyramid at Saqqara, too numerous to ever be fully extracted.[46]

The custom of burying vast quantities of vessels inside the tombs of kings and other individuals of high status goes back to late Predynastic times and the Archaic Period.[47] However, after the Third Dynasty, as subterranean space in royal tombs diminished and the size of the pyramid temples increased, vessels were deposited in greater numbers in the storerooms of the aboveground temples. Testifying to this development, hundreds of stone vessels were found in the storerooms of the valley temple of Menkaure,[48] and considerable remains of vessels—mostly broken and incomplete—were excavated from the pyramid temples of Sahure, Neferirkare, and Niuserre.[49] Stone vessels were, nevertheless, also deposited in the interiors of pyramids; in the pyramid of King Pepi II, for instance, precious remains of inscribed stone jars were discovered inside the passage leading to the ruler's burial chamber (fig. 75).[50]

Many stone vessels found inside pyramid precincts were inscribed with the names of predecessors of the owner of the pyramid, while others can be dated on stylistic grounds to periods earlier than his own.[51] Evidently, then, such stone vessels were deposited in royal pyramid complexes to make use of items left over from previous royal burials or bygone festivities.[52] It is also possible that very old vessels were left in the pyramid precincts in the belief that their proven longevity ensured an eternal flow of provisions even more effectively than did contemporary objects.

Not all stone vessels of the Old Kingdom inscribed with royal names (cat. nos. 178–180, 184)[53] were part of the burial equipment of kings, for there have been finds of such vases in the pyramids of queens and the tombs of high officials and even in the burial sites of members of the middle class, especially in the provinces.[54] These finds indicate that stone vases were customary gifts from the pharaoh to members of his family, worthy officials, and other favored individuals, a good number of whom were women.[55] Such gifts may have been intended to serve as grave goods from the outset, as favored individuals were commonly recompensed with items for the tomb in the Old Kingdom.[56] Or they may have been granted during the recipient's lifetime, to find their way into the tomb later, when the proud owner died.

Stone vases were not only bestowed upon those favored by the king but also were given to him by appropriate persons. The latter especially seems to have been the custom during the Third Dynasty,[57] as is suggested by several vases found in the underground galleries of the Djoser pyramid. These vessels are inscribed with the names of contemporaries of Djoser, who Helck believed had been employed in preparing the king's funeral, an office that perhaps entitled them to make contributions to the royal burial equipment.[58]

Inscriptions on a number of stone vases testify to one important event during which a pharaoh might have given or received stone vessels: the Heb Sed or first Heb Sed, that is, the thirty-year jubilee of a king (fig. 51; cat. nos. 178–180).[59] As various authors indicate in this catalogue, this jubilee and successive ones marked at varying intervals thereafter were more than commemorations of a prosperous and happy rule over the course of many years; they were occasions for the performance of age-old rituals believed to grant the king physical, and probably also mental, rejuvenation. Anointing and cosmetic pigment application were included in several of these rituals, as various representations reveal.[60] One image (fig. 74), for instance, shows the king in the traditional Heb Sed garment applying ointment to the sacred standard of the god Wepwawet in his chapel. Does it go too far to suggest that the leftovers of the oils and cosmetics used at the Heb Sed were distributed in stone vessels to meritorious individuals and members of the royal family in order to let them partake of the beneficial effects of the rituals? And can it also be surmised that officials bestowed their gifts upon the pharaoh at the festival itself—just as a courtier of high status is shown in one tomb giving pectorals to Amenhotep III of the New Kingdom on the occasion of his third Heb Sed[61]—in the hope of benefiting from the magic power of the rituals enacted there?

The designs of the inscriptions incised on the stone vessels underline the significance of the gifts. The writing

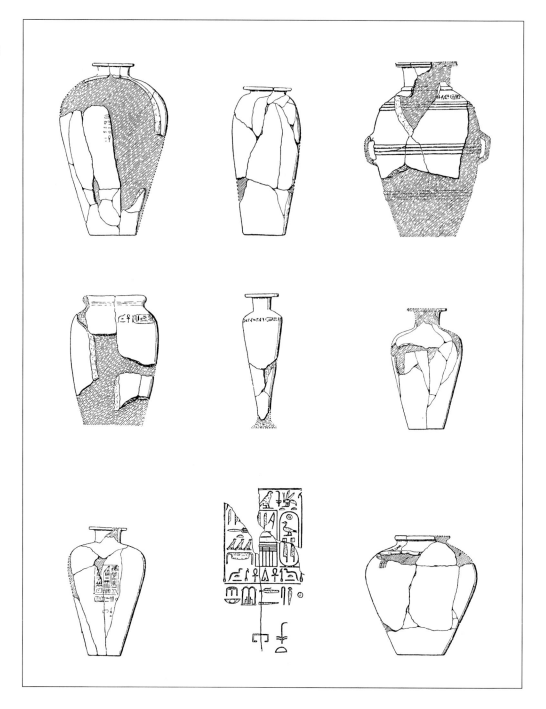

Fig. 75. Stone vessels found in the pyramid of Pepi II, Saqqara. From Jéquier 1936 (p. 7, fig. 6)

is invariably arranged inside a rectangular panel the top of which is formed by the hieroglyph for "sky" and whose sides are two *was* (dominion) scepters,[62] a well-known device depicting the world.[63] Royal names are inscribed within this kind of emblematic framework, albeit mostly without reference to a Heb Sed, on luxury objects, such as a box and an ivory headrest in the exhibition (cat. nos. 181, 183), on the sides of the thrones of royal statues beginning in the Fourth Dynasty,[64] and on architectural elements. In the pyramid temple of Sahure, for instance, the columns surrounding the central courtyard carry the image (fig. 76);[65] here one of the two heads of the earth god Aker flanks either end of the

baseline of the rectangle, identifying it unmistakably as a representation of the earth.[66]

In the rectangles on all these objects, statues, and architectural elements, the names and titles of the king are usually arranged vertically so that the hieroglyphic signs for "king of Upper and Lower Egypt" and "Horus" are located directly below the sky emblem. Parts of the inscription, moreover, often face each other (cat. no. 180), an arrangement made possible by the nature of hieroglyphic script, which can be written, and read, both right to left and left to right. As a result of this confrontation, the main images and signs tend to face toward the interior of the panel, thus transforming the inscription into

Fig. 76. The royal name and titles surrounded by the hieroglyphs for "sky," "earth," and *was* scepters, from a column on the north side of the central courtyard, pyramid temple of Sahure, Abusir. From Borchardt 1910 (p. 45)

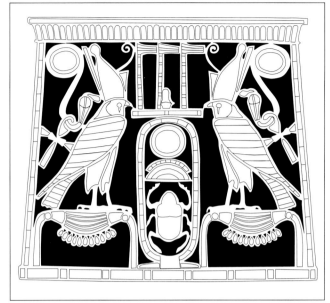

Fig. 77. Pectoral of Princess Sit-Hathor from her burial near the pyramid of Senwosret III at Dahshur, showing the name of Senwosret II flanked by figures of Horus on the hieroglyph for "gold" and topped by the king's Golden Horus name, "He who makes the gods content." Drawing by Peter Der Manuelian after Aldred 1971, pl. 33

a heraldic motto that proclaims the idea of kingship.[67] Good wishes for eternal life, stability, and health are incorporated at the bottom of the panels, and on many stone vessels a reference to the Heb Sed or first Heb Sed appears within, under, or to the side of them (cat. no. 179).

The carefully structured royal-name panels served to propagate the idea of the central position of kingship in a stable universe that is upheld by divine powers and protection. Even more explicit in terms of this function are the designs on a number of globular jars. On one inscribed for King Unis, for instance, a Horus falcon stretches its wings, while its claws clutch *shen* signs of universality. From each *shen* sign a royal cobra extends beneath each wing, and in front of each cobra's hood a symbol for life points toward a cartouche bearing the ruler's name (cat. no. 123).[68] As Ziegler has noted, this configuration is remarkably similar to Middle Kingdom royal jewelry designs;[69] yet there are also obvious parallels between the rectangular name panels and royal jewelry motifs, especially the beautiful pectorals of the Middle Kingdom (fig. 77), New Kingdom, and Third Intermediate Period. True, most of these pectorals are framed not by the sky hieroglyph, earth emblem, and *was* scepters but by the cornice roof of a shrine or temple supported either by simple borders of various colors or by plants, and in one case even by columns.[70] Nevertheless, the link exists, for the temples of ancient Egypt

were generally considered to symbolize the world, with the roof representing the sky (with stars), the columns the plants, and the floor the earth. Also clearly underscoring the connection between the shrine-enclosed pectoral designs and the sky plus *was* scepter image are a mid-Twelfth Dynasty pectoral in the Metropolitan Museum without sides or top frame but showing a baseline identified as the primeval water[71] (one of the earliest known of its type) and one of Tutankhamun's many pectorals that use the device of the sky with *was* scepter supports.[72]

It is well known that pectorals played an important role in the rituals of the Heb Sed.[73] Indeed, in the tomb of Kheruef, a high official of the Eighteenth Dynasty king Amenhotep III and the steward of Amenhotep's queen, Tiy, Kheruef is depicted offering elaborate pectorals to the pharaoh on the occasion of his third Heb Sed.[74] That pectorals and other jewelry of the Middle Kingdom also figured in the Heb Sed has been shown as well.[75] And during the Middle Kingdom female members of the royal family wore pectorals inscribed with the king's name and titles, which were buried with them when they died. In all these contexts strikingly close analogies can be drawn between the post–Old Kingdom pectorals and Pyramid Age stone vessels: both groups of objects served to propagate basic ideas about kingship, played parts in the Heb Sed, and involved not only male officials but also female members of the royal family, court ladies, and even women of not much more than middle-class station.[76]

We must assume that a king's gifts of pectorals in the Middle and New Kingdoms and of stone vessels in the Old Kingdom made during the recipient's lifetime were intended to strengthen the awareness of the royal ideology among the pharaoh's associates; and it should be assumed as well that the eventual burial of these objects secured benefits not only for the recipient of the gift but also for the king himself. The presence of hundreds of stone vessels carrying the royal motto in tombs in all areas of the country (including the outlying oases in the desert) certainly broadened the magical basis that ensured the king's eternal life and everlasting power and might even have served to procure a Heb Sed for him in the afterlife.[77] This kind of magical proliferation, it appears, was thought to have worked especially well when a female burial contained the object decorated with the royal name, since the king's rebirth was believed to be guaranteed in a particularly potent way through females (wife, mother, court lady, indeed any woman).[78]

The association of stone cosmetic vases with revivifying female forces is also apparent in the delightful group of stone vessels sculpted in the shape of mother monkeys with their young (cat. no. 178). Through the monkey forms these flasks evoke aspects of fertility and motherhood linked with the rejuvenating powers of the cosmetic oils they held, the exotic provenances of some of their ingredients, and associations with certain gods. Thus myrrh, a frequently used substance, was imported from Punt, an east African country bordering the Red Sea that according to the mythology of ancient Egypt was the country of the gods[79] and, in a more mundane sense, the home of monkeys.[80] And in an important ancient Egyptian myth it is the god Thoth in the shape of a monkey who cajoles the goddess Hathor to come back to Egypt after her flight to the faraway south.[81] Significantly, the monkey flasks also refer to kingship because the arms and bodies of most of the animals bear the names of Sixth Dynasty rulers, often accompanied by mentions of the Heb Sed (cat. no. 178a).[82]

Archaeological excavations have revealed additional important information about the uses of monkey vessels. Like other stone cosmetic vessels, vases in the shape of mother monkeys were found in the tombs of high officials, such as the governor of the Dakhla Oasis,[83] and were buried in graves of women.[84] But monkey flasks were also dedicated as votives in the sanctuaries of female deities—for instance, the sanctuary of the goddess Satet at Elephantine[85] and the temple of Hathor Baalat-Gabal

at Byblos, near present-day Beirut in Lebanon,[86] once again underlining the strong association of the ointment vessels, kingship, and female forces. The locations of the finds at the oasis in Dakhla, in the sanctuaries at the southern border of Egypt in Elephantine, and in the foreign port of Byblos add another dimension to the picture, for the desert and foreign lands were traditionally the realm of female deities, in particular Hathor. If the king saw to it that vessels with his name were distributed to these far-flung areas, he must have done so to procure for that name and his might the greatest possible range of magical proliferation and at the same time to enlist the support of the divine mistress of all outlying regions.[87]

The finds of monkey vases and other Egyptian stone vessels at Byblos, moreover, offer significant evidence that religion, mythology, and magic were intricately linked with politics and the economy in Old Kingdom Egypt. Byblos was a main trading partner of Egypt during the period and as such the most important port through which valuable cedarwood was supplied for the pharaohs' buildings and for fine carpentry work in the royal workshops—and thus a place to which Egyptians would have sent goods such as stone vessels.[88] In the pyramid temple of Sahure the departure and return of an entire fleet of seagoing ships is depicted in relief.[89] Although their destination is not named among the preserved fragments of the scene, that it was in Asia can be deduced from the fact that the returning ships bear Asiatics. Just such ships may well have transported stone vessels, presumably filled with precious oils and ointments, to Byblos.[90] We can perhaps assume that at least some of these vases were originally gifts from the pharaohs to dignitaries of the city with whom they wished to strengthen ties. Because a number of vessels appear to be inscribed with the names of nonroyal Egyptians, it is also possible that Egyptian officials brought the vessels with them on trading missions to Byblos. These officials may have presented the vases directly to the local goddess,[91] or they may have given them to their trading partners, who subsequently dedicated them to the deity.[92]

However the vases reached this foreign city, they were obviously cherished by the inhabitants in a special way and for considerable time. Archaeological evaluation has demonstrated that the stratum in the temple area in which the vessels were found was laid down well after the period of the Old Kingdom, during the Twelfth Dynasty (about 1991–1878 B.C.E.).[93] Several possible scenarios can be deduced from this fact. If the vessels were originally dedicated to the sanctuary at the time of the Old Kingdom, they may have been kept in the temple storerooms for hundreds of years and deposited in the ground during the Twelfth Dynasty, presumably when an old temple building was demolished to make way for a new one.[94] It is also possible that the vases were buried in the era of the Old Kingdom and that the debris in which they were deposited was relocated during the Twelfth Dynasty. However, if the monkey vases were initially gifts to inhabitants of Byblos, they may have remained in the families of the recipients as heirlooms until the Twelfth Dynasty, when they found their way into the temple. If that was the case, it is noteworthy that even the remote descendants of the first owners of the monkey vases were aware of a meaningful connection between the vessels and the female deity who was the temple's mistress.

This reminds us that Old Kingdom stone vessels not only are objects of impeccable design and refined craftsmanship but also had deep significance in the culture. While we enjoy their beauty, then, it is also well worth reflecting on their close relationship to two of the most important concepts held by the ancient Egyptians: the cosmic nature of kingship and belief in the god-given powers of rejuvenation and rebirth.

1. Quibell 1934, pp. 70–75, pls. 1–4. It is estimated that there were thirty thousand in one gallery alone (Lucas and Harris 1962, p. 422). Djoser's craftsmen produced the greatest number of these vessels, although many came from stores of earlier kings, on which see Lacau and Lauer 1959–61; Lacau and Lauer 1965; and Helck 1979, pp. 120–32.

2. For the history of stone-vessel making, see El-Khouli 1978; Jaroš-Deckert 1984b, cols. 1283–87, with earlier bibliography; and Aston 1994.

3. Emery 1961, pls. 38a, 39a; Fischer 1972a, p. 16, figs. 21–23; Saleh and Sourouzian 1986, no. 13; Aston 1994, p. 32.

4. Aston 1994, pp. 11–73.

5. The primary use of alabaster in the stone-vessel making of the Old Kingdom was stressed by Junker (1929, p. 109).

6. Klemm and Klemm 1993, pp. 199–223.

7. Aston 1994, pp. 42–47. Other names for the material used in the Egyptological literature are aragonite, calcite, calzit alabaster, and calcareous or calcium-based rock; see Lucas and Harris 1962, pp. 59–61, 406–7; Valloggia 1986, p. 106; and Lilyquist 1995, p. 13.

8. D. Klemm 1991, pp. 57–70.

9. Lucas and Harris 1962, p. 413; Aston 1994, pp. 47–51. For vessels of true alabaster, see ibid., p. 50.

10. *Wörterbuch der Aegyptischen Sprache*, vol. 4 (1957), pp. 540–41.

11. Klemm and Klemm 1993, pp. 200–221.

12. Ibid., pp. 221–23.

13. Aston 1994, pp. 13–15 (diorite), 62–64 (gneiss), 35–40 (limestone). For vessels of materials other than alabaster, see, for instance, Jéquier 1933, pp. 28–30, figs. 9–11, and Jéquier 1934, pp. 108–9, figs. 15, 16.

14. For a granite vase, see Firth and Gunn 1926, p. 26, fig. 20, which is probably of Second Dynasty date. See also Reisner 1931, p. 157, fig. 34, no. 9; and Aston 1994, pp. 15–18 (granite), 18–21 (basalt), 23–26 (obsidian in vessels for the Opening of the Mouth ceremony), 53–54 (breccia), 60–61 (porphyry), 64–65 (quartz crystal in vessels for the Opening of the Mouth ceremony). For a table of stone materials used in vessels, see ibid., p. 170.

15. Junker 1950, pp. 125–26.

16. For a survey of the stylistic development of these vessels from Predynastic and Archaic times to the period of the Old Kingdom, see Do. Arnold 1977, col. 492. The most comprehensive and recent treatment of the subject is Aston 1994, pp. 75–140. Aston (pp. 75–78) correctly points out the numerous problems that still exist in evaluating stone-vessel shapes. For the shapes of Old Kingdom stone vessels in particular, see Junker 1929, pp. 109–12, figs. 10, 11; Reisner 1931, pp. 174–78, figs. 43, 44; Reisner 1932, pp. 61–75; Reisner and Smith 1955, pp. 90–102, figs. 134–47; and Aston 1994, pp. 102–40. Marguerite Bernard's thesis of 1966–67 was not available to the author at this writing.

17. Aston 1994, p. 99.

18. Ibid., pp. 99–100, 104–5.

19. A typical group is the one found in the pyramid of Queen Neith, for which see Jéquier 1933, p. 11, fig. 4, pp. 28–33, figs. 9–15; and Jéquier 1934, pp. 105–13, figs. 14–19. The spouted vessel (ibid., p. 109, figs. 16, 17) is identifiable as a baby-feeding cup by analogy with a Middle Kingdom faience vessel of the same form that is decorated with child-protecting demons (Friedman 1998, p. 207, no. 67). The Old Kingdom stone version was identified as a cosmetic spoon by Vandier d'Abbadie (1972, pp. 104–5, nos. 399–403); see also Minault-Gout 1992, p. 111, no. 1804.

20. Aston 1994, p. 104, no. 35; Ziegler 1997b, pp. 461, 465–66, figs. 5–13.

21. See, for instance, Brunton 1927, p. 53, pls. 27–30, nos. 41–45, 53, 57–58, 70, 101–6. These examples possibly imitate metal vases that are depicted frequently in reliefs and paintings; see Wild 1953, pls. 53 (top register 3d item from right), 59 (top register right of center, 4th register 4th vessel from right, and in many other places); and Minault-Gout 1992, pp. 107–8, nos. 1810–12, 1876, 1880.

22. For examples with rich relief decoration among Djoser's stone vessels, see one in the Egyptian Museum, Cairo (JE 64872); Lauer 1934, pp. 58–59; Quibell 1934, p. 72, pl. 4; and Saleh and Sourouzian 1986, no. 19.

23. The find of an extensive Old Kingdom stone-vessel workshop at Elephantine, where vases of local stone apparently were produced in large quantities may, however, indicate that vessel making for the royal court was not confined to Memphis; see note 25 below.

24. El-Khouli 1978, vol. 2, p. 799, n. 3; Porter and Moss 1981, p. 905; Jaroš-Deckert 1984b, cols. 1285–87.

25. For exceptions, see Quibell 1902, pp. 17–18, 51, pl. 68, and pl. 62, nos. 3–6 (grinders). For the recently excavated workshop at Elephantine referred to in note 23 above, see *Mitteilungen des Deutschen Archäologischen Instituts, Abteilung Kairo*, forthcoming.

26. Lucas and Harris 1962, pp. 421–28, with earlier bibliography; El-Khouli 1978, pp. 789–801; Stocks 1986, pp. 14–18.

27. See Drenkhahn 1975, cols. 845–46; and note 26 above.

28. Stocks 1986, p. 16.

29. Ibid.

30. Quibell 1902, pl. 62, nos. 3–6; El-Khouli 1978, pl. 144.

31. Reisner 1931, p. 180. For a juxtaposition of vases thought to have been made with a tubular drill bit and those probably made with stone bits, see Reisner and Smith 1955, pp. 92–93, fig. 135.

32. Stocks 1986, p. 16.

33. Quibell 1902, p. 17, pl. 68.

34. Quibell and Hayter 1927, pp. 40–41. From above, the support looks very much like a potter's wheel, but a side view (ibid., p. 40, ill.) shows that the object is broad and rounded in shape.

35. Lucas and Harris 1962, p. 423.

36. For the use of sand and emery as abrasives, see ibid., pp. 72–74.

37. Schoske 1990.

38. Moret 1902, pp. 199–200; Posener-Kriéger 1976, vol. 2, pp. 537–38; Martin-Pardey 1984b, cols. 367–69; C. Müller 1984, col. 666, n. 10.

39. Schoske 1990, pp. 10–13. For temple vases, see also E. Schott 1972, pp. 34–50.

40. Dreyer 1986, p. 86, with earlier bibliography.

41. Hayes 1959, p. 85, figs. 46, 47.

42. Brier 1994, pp. 42–43, 133, 140. See also Nigel Strudwick in D'Auria, Lacovara, and Roehrig 1988, pp. 81–82, no. 12.

43. C. Müller 1984b; see note 38 above.

44. Bourriau 1984, cols. 362–66.

45. Reeves 1990, pp. 198–99.

46. See note 1 above.

47. For a few of the many examples, see Spencer 1993, p. 74, fig. 51; Emery 1949, pls. 4–7, 18, 38; Emery 1954, pls. 18, 19; and Emery 1958, pls. 91, 95, 118, passim.

48. Reisner (1931, pp. 178–99) discusses vessels that are overwhelmingly of Archaic date. For fragments of earlier vases from the precincts of Fourth Dynasty kings, see Porter and Moss 1974, p. 21 (Khafre).

49. Borchardt 1910, pp. 113–18, figs. 146–63. For Neferirkare and Niuserre, see Reisner 1931, p. 201, n. 1.

50. Jéquier 1934, pp. 97–105; Jéquier 1935, p. 160; Jéquier 1936, pp. 6–8, fig. 6. Interestingly, the top right vase is an imitation in stone of a Canaanite jar. Clay versions of such jars were commonly imported at the time (Jéquier 1929, p. 26, fig. 25). For another stone vase of the same type, see Valloggia 1986, vol. 1, p. 79, pl. 80, no. 1130.

51. For Djoser's vessels, see note 1 above; for Pepi II's vases inscribed for Pepi I, his grandfather, and Merenre, his father, see note 50 above. An alabaster bowl fragment found in the burial chamber of Merenre appears to have a pre–Sixth Dynasty date (Labrousse 1996, p. 68, fig. 122b). A piece-by-piece study of the stone vessels found in the valley temple of Menkaure (Reisner 1931, pp. 178–201, figs. 45–60) with a determination of which are of pre-Menkaure date has not yet been undertaken. That the majority of Menkaure's vessels and many of Sahure's may be early is suggested by comparing them to inscribed vases from the Djoser precinct and other early complexes, which show similar shapes and materials (Aston 1994, pp. 91–132).

52. Helck (1979, p. 124) considers the possibility that some of the Djoser vessels came from the storerooms of sanctuaries. A number of them must even have been taken from groups belonging to nonroyal persons, as evidenced by a vessel inscribed "gift from the king" found in the Djoser stores (see note 55 below).

53. For other vases inscribed with names of Old Kingdom rulers now in museums, see, for instance, Kaiser 1967, nos. 238–41,

ills.; Hayes 1953, pp. 126–28, figs. 77, 78; and Porter and Moss 1974, pp. 21, 333, 338.

54. For queens, see Jéquier 1933, pp. 30, 32, figs. 12, 15. For female members of court, the royal family, and the upper class, see Jéquier 1929, p. 91, fig. 103; and British Museum 1964, p. 175 (British Museum, EA 57 322). For male officials, see Valloggia 1986, pp. 78–81, nos. 1018, 1130, 1042, 1046, pls. 80, 81; and Minault-Gout 1992, pp. 81–83, nos. 1930, 1969, 1991. For the middle class, see Fischer 1993, p. 3, no. 8, p. 7, n. 21. A grave at Badari (Brunton 1927, p. 30, pl. 26, no. 29, pl. 49, with entry in the find list: Brunton 1928, pl. 57) contained a vessel inscribed for the mother of Pepi II, Ankh-nes-pepi (see also cat. nos. 172, 184). The gender of the occupant of this grave is not known.

55. *inw ḥr nswt* (gift from the king) is written on a stone vessel in the subterranean galleries of Djoser's complex (Lacau and Lauer 1965, no. 5; Helck 1979, p. 126). For the considerable number of female recipients, see note 54 above, and note that among the middle-class burials cited by Fischer (1993, pp. 3, 7, n. 21), grave no. 3202 at Badari (Brunton 1927, pl. 26, no. 28, pl. 45; Brunton 1928, pl. 57) and both graves at Matmar (Brunton 1948, pls. 25 [3243], 27 [3058]) were those of women.

56. Altenmüller 1977, col. 837.

57. Minault-Gout (1997, pp. 307–8) believes that the practice evolved over time, theorizing that officials gave stone vases to the king in the Third Dynasty and that the king made gifts of them to officials in later eras. This may indeed have been the general trend but is not entirely the case: a vase with the inscription "gift from the king" in Djoser's galleries clearly indicates that rulers gave stone vessels to officials in early periods (see note 55 above). Such vessels found their last resting place in the king's pyramid because they were returned to him on the occasion of his funeral or because they were never delivered to the intended recipients.

58. Helck 1979, pp. 129–30. Helck correctly cites the gifts of *shawabti* figurines made in the name of high officials in the tomb of Tutankhamun (Reeves 1990, p. 139). The terracotta pots given by officials to their deceased counterparts at Aswan may represent an Old Kingdom parallel of a sort; see Edel 1970b, esp. pp. 85–93.

59. Minault-Gout (1997, pp. 305–14) adds examples to the considerable number of such inscriptions that are known, for some of which see notes 50, 54, 55 above.

60. For the painting of the eyes of cows about to be slaughtered, see Borchardt 1913, p. 56, pl. 47. For the anointing of the king himself, see Martin-Pardey 1984b, col. 368.

61. See note 75 below.

62. For instance, Jéquier 1936, p. 7, fig. 6; Valloggia 1986, pp. 78–80, nos. 1018, 1130, pls. 64, 80; Minault-Gout 1992, pp. 81–83, nos. 1930, 1969, 1991.

63. Westendorf 1991, pp. 427–34, with earlier bibliography.

64. Smith 1946, p. 37, fig. 12.

65. Borchardt 1913, pp. 45–46, fig. 48. For a column of the same type but with vertical images, see ibid., p. 64, fig. 81.

66. For the double-headed earth god Aker, see Hornung 1975, cols. 114–15.

67. On the confrontation of hieroglyphs, see Fischer 1977b, pp. 9–13.

68. Ziegler 1997b, pp. 461–64, figs. 2–4, with parallels from Edfu and Byblos cited on p. 469, nn. 30, 31. A late Middle Kingdom to Second Intermediate Period example of an anhydrite vessel with sculpted vultures is reminiscent of the Old Kingdom vessels with incised falcons (Bourriau 1988, pp. 140–41, no. 142).

69. Ziegler 1997b, p. 463.

70. See Aldred 1971, pls. 42, 50, 140, 145 (simple borders); 92–97 (the Tutankhamun pectorals); 25, 26, 41, 80, 81 (plants); 100 (shrine roofs carried by columns).

71. Ibid., pls. 37, 38. For a design with flanking signs denoting millions of years, see ibid., pl. 108.

72. Andrews 1990, pp. 136–37, fig. 119. The base here is identified as water because the central motif is a boat. A Middle Kingdom pectoral with a sky emblem on which King Amenemhat IV presents ointment vases to the god Atum of Heliopolis is interesting (ibid., p. 91, fig. 65a on p. 89).

73. Feucht 1967, pp. 61–77.

74. Epigraphic Survey 1980, pp. 54–58, pl. 51.

75. Aldred 1971, pp. 185–96. See also Morgan 1895; Morgan 1903; Brunton 1920; and Winlock 1934. For connections to the Heb Sed, see Feucht 1967, pp. 74–77.

76. For an upper-middle-class burial with a royal-name pectoral, see, for instance, Engelbach 1915, p. 12, colorpl. 2.

77. Feucht 1967, pp. 61–77.

78. For beliefs about female powers of rebirth benefiting kings, see Troy 1986.

79. Osing 1977, cols. 815–16.

80. Fischer 1993, p. 9. On Punt as the main source for the importation of baboons and monkeys, see Naville 1898, pl. 74.

81. Desroches Noblecourt 1995, esp. pp. 30–34.

82. Some of these inscriptions, like those on vessels mentioned above, also provide names of nonroyal individuals, including one or two women, who received the vases as gifts (Fischer 1993, pp. 3–6).

83. Valloggia 1980, pp. 143–51, pls. 12–18, esp. pl. 12b; Valloggia 1986, pp. 80, 116–17, pls. 29c, 61, 64, 81. For the titles of Medu-nefer, the governor of the oasis, see ibid., pp. 71–73.

84. Brunton 1948, p. 49, pl. 27, no. 3058, pl. 34, no. 17; Fischer 1993, p. 3, fig. 2.

85. Dreyer 1986, pp. 96, 152, no. 455, pl. 58.

86. Montet 1928, pp. 72–75, pls. 40, 41, 45; Valloggia 1980, p. 146, with earlier bibliography; Minault-Gout 1997, p. 307.

87. See also Minault-Gout 1997, p. 308.

88. For Egypt's connections with Byblos during the Old Kingdom, see Redford 1992, pp. 37–43.

89. Borchardt 1913, pp. 25–28, 86–88, pls. 11–13. Bietak (1988, pp. 35–40) has argued that the Asiatics shown onboard these ships were not slaves but sailors employed by the Egyptians. Such sailors might have brought stone vessels back to Byblos from Egypt to present as votives.

90. In addition to the monkey vases, the Byblos finds included cylindrical stone ointment jars with the names of Sixth Dynasty kings (Montet 1928, pp. 68–72, 74; Minault-Gout 1997, pp. 306–7) and uninscribed vessels of Sixth Dynasty date (Montet 1928, pp. 76–77).

91. For Egyptian objects found at Byblos and inscribed for nonroyal individuals, see Redford 1992, p. 42.

92. We cannot entirely exclude the possibility that some vessels found their way to Byblos by means of tomb robbers, who were always eager to trade their spoils outside Egypt. In fact, a monkey vessel, a fragment of which is preserved in the National Archaeological Museum, Athens (inv. 2657), may well have come to Mycenae in this manner. This fragment shows the left leg and back of a monkey and is made of veined Egyptian alabaster. The position of the leg differs from that of the monkey vessels under consideration here (cat. no. 178a–c) and makes it appear that the animal was seated on a low stool or other object, no trace of which remains. On the basis of this difference, Fischer (1993, p. 3, no. 15) correctly suggests that it may be of later date (New Kingdom) than the Sixth Dynasty. For Egyptian stone vessels of Old Kingdom date found at Aegean sites, see Warren 1969, pp. 110–12.

93. For the date of deposition of the vessels, see Dunand 1939, pp. 63–64, 79–81, 84, 87, 157; Dunand 1937, pls. 205, 206; and Valloggia 1980, p. 146.

94. Dunand 1939, pp. 82 n. 1, 156–57.

EXCAVATING THE OLD KINGDOM

From Khafre's Valley Temple to the Governor's City at Balat

NICOLAS GRIMAL

Before the French Egyptologist Auguste Mariette started to clear the Serapeum at Saqqara in the balmy autumn of 1850; before Howard Vyse and John Shae Perring joined forces to study the pyramids of Giza and Giovanni Battista Caviglia began to dig out the Great Sphinx there; before Bonaparte sent Louis Costaz, Jean-Baptiste Fourier, François Jomard, Le Père, and many other scientists and savants to the Nile Valley on an information-gathering mission unmatched to this day; and before curious visitors and amateurs in ancient times and our own tried to follow in the footsteps of the pyramid builders—the Egyptians themselves became archaeologists and restorers in order to save their most important royal necropolis. During the New Kingdom King Ramesses II himself commissioned his son Khaemwase, who at the time was supervising the Ptah priests at Memphis, to restore the royal necropolis at Saqqara. Thanks to him, Mastabat Faraoun and the precinct of King Unis were saved from oblivion.

In the wake of Bonaparte's expedition to Egypt, both individuals and great nations (usually acting through their consuls) threw themselves into archaeological pursuits. Since this chapter is devoted to French achievements, the first name to mention is that of Auguste Mariette, who systematized Egyptian archaeology. Mariette undertook his first real dig at Saqqara; however, it was his discovery of the Serapeum and the Hemicycle of Greek Philosophers, and not an Old Kingdom monument, that won him lasting fame. These discoveries brought Mariette new authorizations to excavate and, in a curious twist of fate, the following year he unearthed

the tomb of Khaemwase himself in the Serapeum! By comparison, Mariette's clearance of the valley temple of Khafre at Giza—after postponing the project for want of funds—may seem insignificant, especially since he just missed one of the most beautiful finds the site contained, the statue of King Khafre with the Horus falcon (fig. 28).

Things began in earnest in 1857, when the viceroy of Egypt, Said Pasha, on the advice of Ferdinand-Marie de Lesseps, persuaded Mariette to return to Egypt. The imminent arrival from France of Prince Napoleon—and assuredly also the need to replenish the stock of khedivial antiquities, exhausted since 1855, when Archduke Maximilian of Austria received gifts from the pasha—made Said look warmly on the idea of appointing Mariette to guarantee the smooth progress of excavations and preserve Egypt's archaeological patrimony. The fortunate excavator of the mastaba of Khufu-ankh at Giza and of Mastabat Faraoun at Saqqara thus became *mamur* of antiquities in 1858.

For nearly a century France was intimately associated with the Antiquities Service, and the work sites of the two nations overlapped to some degree, at least with regard to the professional staff. This meant that excavations were more often undertaken in response to the urgency of the situation than as part of a rational scientific program. The starting point for excavation was, in essence, a list of sites likely to furnish important documentation, which the decipherer of the Rosetta Stone, Jean-François Champollion, and others after him had drawn up. That is why French archaeologists—beginning with Mariette—turned their attention to such later

Fig. 78. Pyramid Text fragment. The Syndics of the Fitzwilliam Museum, Cambridge, 55.2 (cat. no. 177c)

sites as Tanis, Karnak, and Deir el-Medina, where work continues to this day. These huge complexes have produced the most spectacular finds, which are often better known to the general public than Old Kingdom monuments, apart from some exceptional pieces.

As for the Old Kingdom, in 1859 Mariette found the prize he had missed several years earlier in the valley temple of King Khafre. The marvelous statue of the king that he unearthed is today one of the jewels of the Egyptian Museum in Cairo (fig. 28). Other great French finds are, at Saqqara, the mastabas of Ti and Ptah-hotep, the extraordinary serdab statues of Ti and Ra-nefer, the Sheikh el-Beled (fig. 34), and the Scribe in the Louvre (fig. 33); and, at Meidum, in the mastaba cleared by Albert Daninos, the splendid statues of Ra-hotep and Nofret (fig. 31) and the celebrated painting of geese from the tomb of Itet (cat. no. 25). All of these marvels are today in the Egyptian Museum, Cairo. Among the excavations conducted by the Antiquities Service at Abydos perhaps the most notable are those in the southern area: the temples of the kings Seti I and Ramesses II and of the god Osiris. But important, too, was Mariette's discovery of the Sixth Dynasty tomb of Weni with its important biographical inscription. After Mariette's death in 1881, his successor at the Antiquities Service, Gaston Maspero, saw to it that his colleague's manuscript on the mastabas of the Old Kingdom was published. This early compendium inspired interest in a more systematic excavation of the Memphite necropolis.

Chance decreed that the first Pyramid Texts were not found until 1880, at Saqqara (fig. 78; cat. no. 177). Terminally ill, Mariette had, as Pierre Montet said, "this final satisfaction." But it was Maspero who excavated the funerary chambers of King Merenre I and then the other pyramids with these funerary texts. Overnight some monuments that had previously seemed quite disappointing to archaeologists gained a new interest. Research at the royal Old Kingdom cemeteries proceeded apace, and soon the private cemeteries around them began to yield a wealth of treasures. To this day the great Old Kingdom sites, especially the Memphite cemeteries, continue to reward research, at mastabas as well as at the pyramids of kings and queens, about whom fresh discoveries are continually being made.

After Mariette's death the activities of the Antiquities Service increased in scope, and new organizations appeared on the archaeological horizon. Among these, the French Institute of Near Eastern Archaeology (IFAO) was to play a primary role, often taking charge of excavations that the Antiquities Service had neither the opportunity nor the time to carry out. And the task sharing was not restricted to French circles. Although they were at the mercy of international events, the Egyptological institutions of many nations—including Great Britain, Germany, the United States, and Italy—cooperated in the international archaeological endeavor.

Until 1886 Maspero was especially involved in excavating the pyramids at Saqqara with funerary inscriptions—the monuments of Unis, Teti, Pepi I, Merenre I, and Pepi II—and he published the results in the *Recueils des Travaux* from 1882 onward. The other French archaeologists concentrated their attention on Saqqara as well. Notable among them was Jacques de Morgan, who cleared a number of large mastabas in 1893, including the tombs of Mereruka and Ka-gemni. Victor Loret took over in 1899, making great discoveries at the first queen's pyramids uncovered at Saqqara, in the vicinity of the complex of King Teti. Loret pioneered systematic research at Saqqara by working in sections, just as Morgan had done for the Middle Kingdom structures at Dahshur—with extraordinary success.

In 1901 the IFAO began work on the pyramid at Abu Rawash. The director, Émile-Gaston Chassinat, identified the owner as Djedefre, the third king of the Fourth Dynasty, and uncovered splendid fragmentary statues of the pharaoh, which are today preserved in the Louvre (cat. no. 54) and at the Egyptian Museum, Cairo. Until the eve of World War I Chassinat tried to clear the pyramid's funerary chambers, but without success because the technical means at his disposal were insufficient. Not until 1995 did the IFAO resume the work at Abu Rawash, this time in collaboration with the University of Geneva, the Swiss National Foundation for Scientific Research, and the Supreme Council for Egyptian Antiquities.

Another royal site was the step pyramid at Zawiyet el-Aryan, probably belonging to King Nebka. Morgan discovered the entrance in 1900 and A. Barsanti excavated the crypt in 1904. Although they are outside the scope of this exhibition, the very rich Predynastic excavations of Morgan at Naqada, Émile Amélineau at Abydos, and Montet at Abu Rawash must be mentioned here.

Except for the re-excavation and restoration of the Great Sphinx undertaken by Émile Baraize in 1925, during the first decades of the twentieth century the Italians, Americans, and Germans (succeeded by the Austrians) divided the work at Giza among themselves. At Saqqara, Cecil Mallaby Firth and then James E. Quibell led digs until 1936, the year when Jean-Philippe Lauer assumed the directorship of the Djoser-complex excavations. The stunning results he achieved there—at the Southern Tomb and in the burial chamber of Djoser, as well as in the reconstruction of some of the chief elements within the complex—are well known. Also at Saqqara, during the same period but in the southern part of the site, we must mention the work of Gustave Jéquier, whom our Swiss colleagues will pardon us for associating with French achievements. Jéquier completed the excavation of Mastabat Faraoun and also cleared the funerary complex of Pepi II and those of Pepi's queens, Neith, Iput, Wedjebten, and Ankhes-en-pepi. His work at two

Thirteenth Dynasty pyramids, one belonging to King Khendjer, must be mentioned, although they are outside the compass of this exhibition. At Dahshur in 1925 Jéquier began to clear the Bent Pyramid of Snefru, a task finished some twenty years later by Alexandre Varille, Abdel Salam Hussein, and Ahmed Fakhry.

The years immediately before and after World War II were marked by great discoveries. The royal necropolis at Tanis is perhaps the most memorable example, although this Late Period site postdates the Old Kingdom by many centuries. Closer to the subject at hand is the fruitful cooperation in the 1930s between Polish and French teams. Together they excavated the Old Kingdom cemetery at Edfu.

After the 1952 Revolution the archaeological landscape became truly international and collegial. The years that followed were successful ones for the Antiquities Service, and in 1954 a truly extraordinary discovery was made at Giza. Featured in a special issue of the *Revue du Caire*, the royal boat unearthed from a pit south of Khufu's pyramid excited worldwide attention.

The international campaign conducted during the 1960s to save the Nubian monuments from the rising waters of Lake Nasser forced into the background long-term archaeological excavations that would otherwise have been considered of primary importance. Among the Old Kingdom sites to which French teams return year after year, Saqqara must be cited first of all. Lauer still works at the precinct of Djoser, and a museum is being set up on the site, the focus of which will be a presentation of the results of discoveries made by this senior colleague of ours during the course of a long and distinguished career.

At South Saqqara in the early 1960s, working within the framework of the National Center for Scientific Research (CNRS), affiliated with the University of Paris–Sorbonne and supported by the Ministry of Foreign Affairs and the IFAO, Jean Sainte Fare Garnot and then Jean Leclant and his associates resumed excavation of the royal funerary complexes. Today directed by Audran Labrousse, the mission continues research in the complex of Pepi I, which is now completely cleared and open to the public. It is no exaggeration to say that almost every year the team manages to discover a new pyramid belonging to one of the queens of Pepi I, and with it a significant amount of new information.

Analysis and reconstruction of the Pyramid Texts continues, and at some pyramids the work has reached completion. Publications based on this endeavor, and a new edition of the Pyramid Texts as well, are in preparation at the IFAO. Labrousse continues to oversee many collaborative projects with his Egyptian colleagues, notably in the area of the pyramid of Unis.

Also at Saqqara, the Musée du Louvre has started excavations at the Unis causeway, under the direction of Christiane Ziegler. Initially, the team found vestiges of the mastaba of Akhet-hotep still in place; later, a wealth of material was uncovered, as this area proved to be particularly rich in Old Kingdom tombs. The splendid achievements of Ziegler's team thus far offer hope of many new discoveries to come.

I have already mentioned in passing the excavations resumed in the mid-1990s at Abu Rawash. There the IFAO, in association with the Supreme Council for Egyptian Antiquities, the University of Geneva, and the Swiss National Foundation for Scientific Research, has cleared rubble from Djedefre's funerary chambers and begun to survey and conduct a preliminary examination of the neighboring cemetery and elements of the royal complex.

Since 1976 the study of the Old Kingdom has undergone, at least as far as French research is concerned, a renaissance as unexpected as it is spectacular, thanks to digs conducted in the oases of the Western Desert by the IFAO, at sites chosen by the late Serge Sauneron. Today Georges Soukiassian is digging at Balat, the Sixth Dynasty town of the governors of the Dakhla Oasis. This virtually unique site bears comparison only with settlements at Elephantine brought to light by the German Archaeological Institute. Balat has produced data that would be impossible to find in the heavily populated Nile Valley. Within the vast necropolis the mastabas of the local governors still thrust their enormous bulk against the sky, and thousands of administrators' tombs dot the landscape. A town site exists, too, with civic buildings and with palaces that are remarkably well preserved.

Meanwhile, the IFAO continues to disseminate the findings of French Egyptologists through monographs, excavation reports, complete publications of monuments, and paleographic studies of inscriptions from such sites as Giza and Saqqara.

Necessarily incomplete, this overview cannot do justice to the scope of present-day research on the Old Kingdom. To give a more accurate idea of these endeavors, it would be necessary to take into account the work of the Egyptians themselves, and of the Germans, Americans, Italians, Czechs, British, Australians, and other national groups. Although this chapter is dedicated to the French achievements, it is nevertheless appropriate to emphasize how internationalized the field has become, with teams from many countries, of course, but also with new methods—such as colloquia, study groups, and so forth—that facilitate the analysis of data accumulated from many discoveries and serve to open new avenues of study.

EXCAVATING THE OLD KINGDOM

The Giza Necropolis and Other Mastaba Fields

PETER DER MANUELIAN

The Giza necropolis, doubtless the most famous archaeological site in the world, has experienced two golden ages. The first took place in the Fourth Dynasty, when the pharaoh Khufu (Cheops) and two of his successors, Khafre (Chephren) and Menkaure (Mycerinus), chose the plateau on the desert's edge west of the Nile for their monumental pyramid complexes and the surrounding private, or nonroyal, cemeteries. The second dates some 4,500 years later, to the twentieth century C.E., when the first scientific archaeological investigators excavated the necropolis, revealing countless treasures and invaluable information about all aspects of Egyptian culture during the Old Kingdom. This second golden age continues to the present day, and, indeed, the spectacular discoveries at Giza show no signs of abating. These remarks will concentrate on the new golden age, the era of scholarly discovery at the Giza pyramids.

Giza (figs. 79, 80), Saqqara,[1] and Abusir were clearly the most important necropolises for Egyptian royalty and the upper echelons of officialdom during the Old Kingdom.[2] While the principal royal tombs at Giza, the three pyramids themselves, date to the Fourth Dynasty, the necropolis continued to function as a huge bureaucratic institution, serving both the living and the dead, right through the Sixth Dynasty, whose conclusion marked the end of the Old Kingdom. But between the Old Kingdom and our own century Giza saw relatively little use and change.[3]

In later antiquity, however, the site was never completely abandoned. Evidence of post–Old Kingdom activity at Giza includes the New Kingdom temple of Amenhotep II (1427–1400 B.C.E.), built beside the Great Sphinx of the Fourth Dynasty; the so-called Dream Stela of Thutmose IV (1400–1390 B.C.E.), a colossal statue that may have been set up under Ramesses II (1279–1213? B.C.E.);[4] and the Saite Period (Twenty-sixth Dynasty, 672–525 B.C.E.) temple to Isis, mistress of the pyramids, east of the Great Pyramid of Khufu itself; along with various Late Period burials scattered throughout the site. But these later monuments are scanty indeed compared with the daunting amount of chronologically homogenous Old Kingdom material at Giza. In later centuries the site certainly attracted its share of tourists, historians (such as Herodotus during the fifth century B.C.E.), and pyramidologists (for example, astronomer Charles Piazzi Smyth [1819–1900]).[5] The only major event prior to the twentieth century C.E. that we will stop to mention here is the removal of many of the pyramids' exterior casing stones. These were reused in the construction of medieval Cairo in the eleventh and fourteenth centuries C.E.

Aside from some early clearance work by Auguste Mariette (1821–1881),[6] head of the first national service to monitor and safeguard Egyptian antiquities, the earliest activity at Giza resembling anything like modern scientific investigation took place in 1842–43. At this time a Prussian expedition led by Karl Richard Lepsius (1810–1884) cleared and numbered several private tombs, entered the Great Pyramid, and drew maps and plans of the site.[7] In December 1842 Lepsius excavated one particularly well-preserved painted and carved chapel, belonging to Mer-ib, an official of the early Fifth Dynasty, and in

Fig. 79. Aerial view of the Giza plateau, with the Great Pyramid of Khufu in the foreground and the pyramids of Khafre and Menkaure behind, looking southwest. The mastaba tombs of the Eastern and Western Cemeteries are visible on either side of the Great Pyramid, and the Great Sphinx appears at the center left edge of the image.

1845 he received permission to ship all the decorated blocks to Berlin. The first of five Giza tomb chapels that came to be exported to Europe, today it awaits reconstruction on Berlin's soon-to-be-restored museum island.[8]

In 1880 the pioneering British archaeologist W. M. F. Petrie (1853–1942) set out for Giza, responding to the various fantastic contentions of the day about the true significance of the dimensions of the Great Pyramid and their possible relation to the circumference of the earth. Using an elaborate series of triangulations over the entire site, in 1881 Petrie was able to provide the most accurate measurements of the ancient monuments produced up to that time.[9] He also investigated a few isolated private tombs in the Western Cemetery (fig. 81), and even lived at the site in an abandoned rock-cut tomb, frightening off unwanted tourists by unceremoniously appearing before them in his pink underwear.

By the end of the nineteenth century the bases of the three large pyramids had long since lain covered with sand and debris, the Great Sphinx was buried up to its neck, and the extensive cemeteries surrounding the Great Pyramid were visible only in barest outline. It was under these conditions that Giza's second golden age, the age of discovery, began. While a dozen or more scholars are primarily responsible for unlocking many of Giza's secrets in this enlightened period, the American George Reisner (1867–1942), the Germans Georg Steindorff (1861–1951) and Hermann Junker (1877–1962), and the Egyptian Selim Hassan (1886–1961) made the greatest

contributions to the field. Reisner led the largest and longest-running expedition of all, working almost uninterrupted on the Giza plateau (in addition to investigating twenty-two other Egyptian and Nubian sites) from 1902 until his death at Harvard Camp, just west of the pyramids (fig. 82).

After earning his B.A., M.A., and Ph.D. degrees at Harvard University, Reisner left the United States to study Semitics in Berlin, which at the close of the nineteenth century was the primary center for serious philological and historical learning. He found himself drawn away from his original interest in Assyrian and Babylonian texts and toward the realm of ancient Egypt. Studying under Egyptologists such as Kurt Sethe, Reisner was exposed to the meticulous analysis and thorough scholarship that were to become defining elements in his approach to academic problem solving.

In 1899, after returning to the United States and then proceeding to Cairo to assist with the Egyptian Museum's catalogue raisonné project, the Catalogue Général, Reisner received funding for archaeological fieldwork from Phoebe Apperson Hearst, mother of the well-known American newspaper publisher William Randolph Hearst. The Hearst Expedition became affiliated with the University of California at Berkeley and first concentrated on the great cemeteries of Nag el-Deir, which date from the Predynastic era through the First Intermediate Period, and later the sites of Quft and Deir el-Ballas. Armed with a few years of digging experience

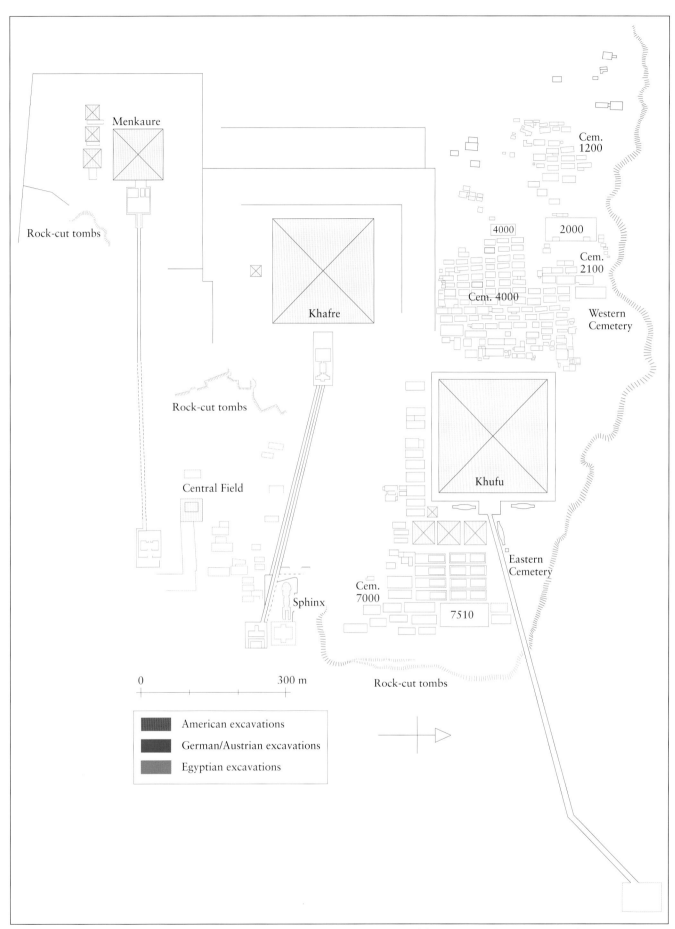

Fig. 80. Overview map of the Giza necropolis, showing the excavation concessions of the major expeditions. Drawing by Liza Majerus, modified by Peter Der Manuelian

Fig. 81. View down a street of mastaba tombs in cemetery 4000, looking south toward the pyramid of Khafre

Fig. 82. Four giants of Egyptology meet in the garden of the Continental Hotel, Cairo, November 15, 1935. Left to right: Hermann Junker, George Reisner, James Henry Breasted, and Ludwig Borchardt.

and a clear methodological approach, in 1902 Reisner obtained the most important site concession of his career, at the Giza necropolis.

Too much illicit digging had been eroding the Old Kingdom cemeteries surrounding the three great pyramids of Giza. The last straw was probably provided unknowingly by one Montague Ballard, M.P., who discovered the beautifully painted slab stela of Nefret-iabet that is now in the Louvre (cat. no. 51) but tore through portions of the cemetery west of the Great Pyramid in 1901–2. Ballard's depredations prompted Gaston Maspero, Director of the Egyptian Antiquities Service, to invite trained professionals to excavate the site before more irreparable damage could be done. Maspero suddenly had a number of archaeologists eager to win the concession: an Italian team led by Ernesto Schiaparelli (1856–1928) of Turin, a German mission with Ludwig Borchardt (1863–1938) representing Steindorff of Leipzig, and Reisner standing for the American expedition. In Reisner's own words, from his unpublished autobiographical notes in the Museum of Fine Arts, Boston, the site of the Giza pyramids was divided thus:

In December, 1902, the three concessionaires met on the veranda of the Mena House Hotel. Everybody wanted a portion of the great Western Cemetery. It was divided in three strips East-West. Three bits of paper were marked 1, 2, and 3 and put in a hat. Mrs. Reisner drew the papers and presented one to each of us. The southern strip fell to the Italians, the middle to the Germans and the northern strip to me. Then we proceeded to divide the pyramids. I perceived that the Italians were interested in the First Pyramid [Khufu's] and the Germans in the

Second [Khafre's]. I kept my mouth shut and let them wrangle. When they had adjusted the line between the First and Second Pyramid the Italians thinking that I might insist on a ballot resigned to me the northern part of the area east of the First Pyramid, if I would accept the Third Pyramid [Menkaure's]. I was perfectly willing to have the Third Pyramid but of course accepted his offer.[10]

The Italian mission set to work on both sides of the Great Pyramid in 1903–4 and investigated a number of important tombs.[11] But by 1905 Schiaparelli's talents were needed at other sites, and Giza became merely one of a number of famous necropolises this most energetic scholar helped to unearth. His concession was passed on to Reisner and the American team, which thus ended up with the lion's share of the necropolis (see map, fig. 83).[12] From 1902 to 1905 the Hearst Expedition made a solid beginning in the task of unraveling the development of the great Western Cemetery, which contains the tombs of Khufu's highest officials; during this period as well, thanks to the official division of finds, many fine examples of Egyptian relief and three-dimensional sculpture reached the Lowie Museum, Berkeley, now the Phoebe Apperson Hearst Museum, as well as the Egyptian Museum, Cairo. The standard tomb, or mastaba (after the Arabic word for the bench of similar form), usually consists of a large rectangular superstructure with sloping sides formed of limestone blocks surrounding a rubble core, a stela or chapel with a false door (cat. no. 155) serving as the offering place, and a burial shaft cut through the superstructure down into the underlying bedrock. At the bottom of the shaft is the burial chamber, housing a sarcophagus constructed of stone or wood (fig. 14).

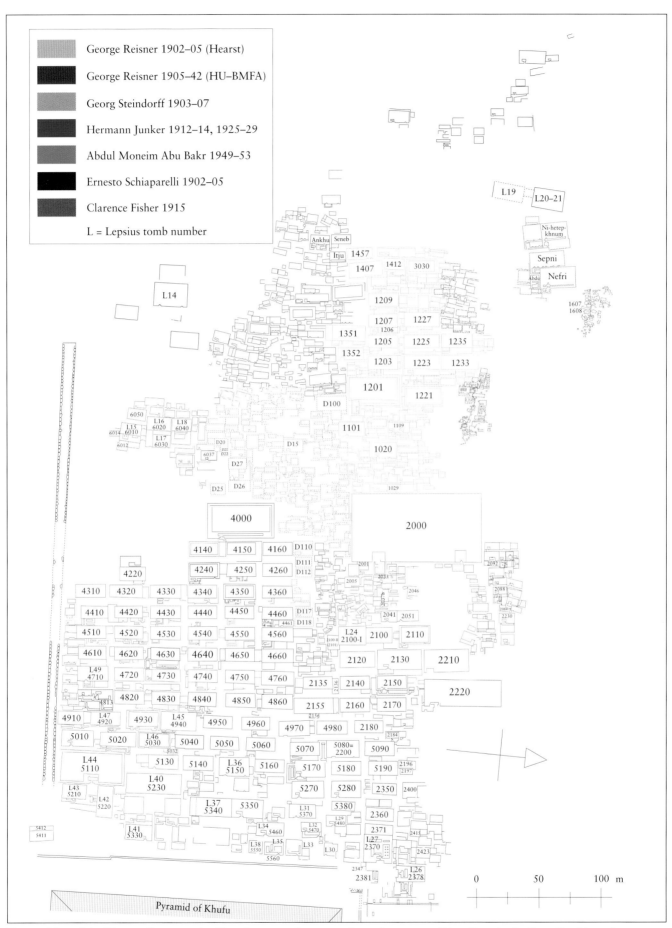

L19   L20–21

Ni-hetep-khnum

Sepni

Abdu   Nefri

1607
1608

Ankhu   Seneb

Itju   1457

1407   1412   3030

1209

1207   1227
1206

1351   1205   1225   1235

1352   1203   1223   1233

1201   1221

D100

1101   1109

1020

L14

6050

L16   L18
6020   6040

L15   6010
6014

L17
6012   6030

D20
D22
6037   D23

D15

D27

D25   D26

1029

4000

2000

4140   4150   4160   D110

D111
4240   4250   4260   D112

4220

4310   4320   4330   4340   4350   4360

2092

2001

2005   2033

4410   4420   4430   4440   4450   4460   D117
4461   D118   2046

4510   4520   4530   4540   4550   4560   2041   2051   2088

4610   4620   4630   4640   4650   4660   L24   2230
100 II
2100-I   2100   2110
2101

L49
4710   4720   4730   4740   4750   4760   2120   2130   2210

L47
4813   4820   4830   4840   4850   4860   2135   2140   2150

L45
4910   4920   4930   4940   4950   4960   2155   2160   2170   2220

2156
5010   5020   5030   5040   5050   5060   4970   4980   2180
L46
5032   2184

L44   5130   5140   L36   5160   5070   5080=   5090
5110   5150   2200

L40   5170   5180   5190   2196
5230   2197

L43   5270   5280   2350   2400
5210   L42
5220   L37   5350   5380
5340   2360

5412   L31
5411   5370   2371

L34   L32   L29
L41   5460   5470   5480   2413
5330   L27
L38   L35   L33   L30   2370   2423
5550   5560

2347   L26
2381   2378

0   50   100 m

Pyramid of Khufu

Fig. 83. Map of the Western Cemetery, detailing the excavation concessions of every expedition. Drawing by Peter Der Manuelian.

Fig. 84. East half of the great Western Cemetery, December 1906, looking north from the pyramid of Khafre. At this early stage only portions of cemeteries 2000 and 2100 (far left, center) have been excavated by Reisner. The famous Mena House Hotel appears near the center of the image.

Reisner correctly surmised that construction in the great Western Cemetery had most likely begun in an area farthest from the Great Pyramid and in time had progressed eastward toward the pyramid's west face. The earliest mastaba tombs were laid out along a prearranged grid, giving the necropolis a regularity and rational organization absent from all earlier Egyptian cemeteries. Only later in the Old Kingdom did subsidiary burials and minor mastabas choke the symmetrical plan, turning Giza into a chronological jigsaw puzzle for the archaeologist. Reisner devised a numbering system for the hundreds of tombs located along what are best described as the streets and avenues of the necropolis, proceeding from the 1000s in the far west across the site to the 7000s east of the Great Pyramid. This numbering system is still used for Giza by Egyptologists today.

Among the more spectacular early discoveries in the far west of the Western Cemetery were a series of rectangular slab stelae. The slab stelae (cat. nos. 51–53), each of which was set into an emplacement in the exterior east face of a mastaba, were critical in helping to identify the owners of the monuments they embellished.

The decorative scheme that Khufu apparently introduced at Giza was so reduced, contrary to the practice of previous pharaohs, that the stelae represent the only ornamented or inscribed portion of these early Fourth Dynasty tombs. (For a somewhat different interpretation, see "The Tombs of Officials" by Peter Jánosi in this catalogue.) Clearly products of the highest quality from the royal workshops, they provide a primary source of information on early Old Kingdom funerary ritual, decoration, and artistic style.[13] Since they were often plastered over and effectively sealed when alterations to the mastabas' exteriors were carried out, several slab stelae even preserve much of their original polychromy, revealing hieroglyphs and figures in all their original colorful brilliance (see cat. nos. 51, 52).

By 1905 Mrs. Hearst was unable to continue supporting Reisner's work, and thus his expedition's American home base moved east to become the Joint Expedition of Harvard University and the Museum of Fine Arts, Boston. The new arrangement called for objects of artistic value to be divided between the Boston and Cairo museums (as determined by the Egyptian antiquities

Fig. 86. Statuettes of Menkaure in various stages of completion, as found in the king's valley temple, July 14, 1908

Fig. 85. The Harvard University–Museum of Fine Arts Expedition's discovery of four triads of Menkaure, from the king's valley temple, looking north, July 10, 1908. One of the triads is in the exhibition (cat. no. 68).

authorities), while the publication of the scientific results was made Harvard's responsibility. Reisner became curator of the Boston Museum's Egyptian Department soon thereafter.

In 1906–7, after clearing major portions of the Western Cemetery, both west and east of the great anonymous mastaba numbered G 2000 (fig. 84), Reisner turned his attention to the royal pyramid complex of Menkaure.[14] In addition to the pyramid itself, the smallest of the three king's pyramids at Giza, this group included three subsidiary pyramids, the king's pyramid temple and valley temple, which are connected by a long causeway, and even an associated cemetery of rock-cut tombs hewed into the adjacent quarry. The area yielded countless treasures of Fourth Dynasty royal sculpture, including calcite, or alabaster, colossi from the pyramid temple and numerous graywacke triads from the valley temple depicting Menkaure with the goddess Hathor and minor provincial deities (fig. 85; cat. no. 68).[15] Here too was found in a so-called robber's hole the famous uninscribed dyad, or pair statue, of Menkaure and his mother or one of his queens (cat. no. 67).[16] One of the greatest masterpieces ever discovered in Egypt, the dyad embodies the supreme confidence of a powerful, semidivine monarchy at the head of a prosperous nation. A series of unfinished seated statuettes of the king also unearthed in

the valley temple displays in frozen moments all the stages of the sculptor's creative process, from the red outlining on a block of stone to the nearly finished and polished final product (fig. 86; cat. no. 73).

Reisner's explorations of the site also uncovered post–Menkaure era finds, for the king's valley temple area was occupied subsequent to his own reign. Originally built by Menkaure with limestone foundations and completed in mud brick by his successor, Shepseskaf, it later flooded and was restored during the Sixth Dynasty by Pepi II. The houses of the adjacent pyramid town eventually expanded into the temple precincts themselves, and thus Reisner's stratigraphic excavations revealed thousands of ceramic and calcite vessels, implements of all sorts, and, ironically, invaluable evidence of domestic architecture despite the building's funerary context.

Working on behalf of the University of Leipzig, Reisner's German colleague Steindorff began clearing the western portion of the central strip of the Western Cemetery in 1903, supported in part by Hildesheim businessman and collector Wilhelm Pelizaeus (1851–1930).[17] The first student of the great philologist Adolf Erman (1854–1937) in Berlin, Steindorff enjoyed a full and varied career that encompassed seventy years of publications ranging from Coptic-language studies to art-historical treatises. He founded Leipzig's Egyptological Institute, whose collections came to include the fruits of his excavations. After immigrating to the United States during World War II, Steindorff assumed responsibility for the Egyptian holdings at the Walters Art Gallery, Baltimore. His Giza concession focused on a still imperfectly understood area that is choked with mastabas smaller and later than those built under Khufu in the Fourth Dynasty. This area came to be known in the scholarly literature as the Steindorff cemetery.

After digging only a few seasons, through 1906–7, Steindorff decided to relocate his excavations south to ancient Nubia (modern Sudan). At the opening of the Roemer- und Pelizaeus-Museum in Hildesheim on July 29, 1911, Steindorff and his younger German colleague Hermann Junker agreed to trade concessions: Steindorff would take on part of Junker's Vienna Academy of Sciences concession at Aniba in the Sudan, between the Nile's first and second cataracts, and in return Junker would obtain Steindorff's Giza concession. This arrangement led to many years of German and Austrian productivity at Giza, as well as to official permission to transport three complete mastaba chapels to Europe.[18] All of Steindorff's excavation records were thought to have been lost in World War II; however, many have turned up in recent years, resurrecting basic information on 134 mastabas of the Western Cemetery.[19]

As for Steindorff's compatriot Junker, he originally hoped to join the Catholic priesthood but had a change of heart and trained in Berlin as a philologist. He eventually went to Austria, filling a recently vacated professorial post at the University of Vienna in 1907. This position in turn led him to take up fieldwork in Egypt and Nubia, which culminated in his assumption of Steindorff's Giza concession in 1912. Eight seasons were required to complete the Junker concession, but only three were concluded before the outbreak of World War I put a halt to all German activity at Giza in 1914. In fact, Junker was unable to resume his excavations until 1926, by which time his earlier finds must surely have suffered considerable loss due to exposure and deterioration. Nevertheless, he continued working at the site from 1926 through 1929, finishing the clearance of the central portion of the Western Cemetery, as well as that of the southern row of mastabas located just south of the Great Pyramid. It was a mere accident of archaeology that he barely missed two of Khufu's funerary boat pits squeezed in between these tombs and the pyramid itself; their discovery and the excavation of one boat would have to wait until the 1950s.[20]

Among Junker's many spectacular finds was the huge and exquisitely built tomb of the Overseer of All Construction Projects, Hemiunu, nephew to Khufu and most likely the man responsible for supervising the erection of the Great Pyramid. Hemiunu's lifesize statue (cat. no. 44), depicting a corpulent and clearly successful bureaucrat seated and gazing into eternity, is, like the pair statue of Menkaure and his mother or queen, one of the greatest treasures of Old Kingdom sculpture in the round.[21] Another mastaba Junker discovered not far away belonged to a woman named Nen-sedjer-kai and is justly famous for its imitation of an Egyptian house, now converted into a stone mansion of eternity, complete with a courtyard, an enclosure with rounded walls, and a pillared portico.[22] In 1913 his efforts brought to light the superbly carved and painted mastaba chapel of Ka-ni-nisut I, which was subsequently removed to the Kunsthistorisches Museum, Vienna.[23] Junker also excavated one of the earliest burial chambers decorated with paintings, in the tomb of a treasury official named Kai-em-ankh.[24]

One of the most enigmatic groups of objects unearthed at Giza, in both Reisner's and Junker's concessions, is a series of so-called reserve heads (see "Reserve Heads" by Catharine H. Roehrig in this catalogue), traditionally thought, for lack of a better explanation, to be substitute homes for the spirit provided in case any misfortune befell the mummy. Forty or so of these carved limestone heads have been discovered, most of them at Giza and all in an unclear context at or toward the bottom of burial shafts. Never part of complete statues, they often show plaster modeling and what appear to be scratches or incisions that scholars have interpreted in countless ways—calling them everything from simple sculptor's guidelines to ritual mutilations intended to magically damage the spirit of the deceased.[25] Although the last word on the precise function of the reserve heads is perhaps yet to be written, it is clear that in their depiction of individual likenesses they offer a striking departure from the stylized features represented in most two- and three-dimensional Egyptian works of art.

While Reisner concentrated on Menkaure's precinct, the third pyramid complex at Giza, and while generations of explorers focused their efforts on Khufu's Great Pyramid, other archaeologists have conducted their own explorations of the necropolis. Thus in 1909 the second pyramid complex, that of Khafre, was first systematically cleared and studied by German Egyptologist and architect Uvo Hölscher (1878–1963).[26] The Egyptian Antiquities Service cleared the Great Sphinx under the direction of Émile Baraize from 1925 to 1934 and again under Selim Hassan from 1936 to 1938.[27] And Herbert Ricke,

Mark Lehner, James Allen, and Zahi Hawass are among those who have studied, mapped, restored, and extended excavations around the Great Sphinx and its accompanying temples in recent years.[28] Moreover, various Egyptian archaeologists have worked at Giza as well as in the larger Memphite area (a subject discussed by Hawass in "Excavating the Old Kingdom" in this catalogue).

By the mid-1920s much of the great Western Cemetery had been cleared by the Reisner and Steindorff-Junker expeditions. Tons of debris had been removed by Decauville railway carts from the mastaba fields, and an ever clearer picture of the ancient evolution of the cemetery was emerging (fig. 87). Reisner's recording and documentation system had become a well-oiled machine, consisting of photographers using large-format-plate cameras, draftsmen, excavation diaries, object registers, and countless numbering systems. And so in 1924 Reisner relocated his expedition to the cemetery east of the Great Pyramid (fig. 88). This area houses mastabas originally built as individual tombs that were later joined together in pairs to form great double mastabas for members of Khufu's immediate family and for high officials. The Eastern Cemetery also contains numerous rock-cut tombs at the eastern edge of the plateau and a host of Late Period burials peppering the Old Kingdom necropolis. Thus this field boasts tombs both older and more recent than those in the Western Cemetery, with some dating as early as 2500 B.C.E. and others as late as 600 B.C.E.

As tantalizing clues to the complicated history and possibly tumultuous succession of the Fourth Dynasty royal family came to light in the course of Reisner's explorations, numerous artistic masterpieces also surfaced in the Eastern Cemetery. These included a bust displaying the arresting facial features of Khafre's vizier, Ankh-haf,[29] whose mastaba is the largest at Giza after the anonymous tomb G 2000; the vibrant painted reliefs and engaged statues from the rock-cut chapel of Queen Mer-si-ankh III, granddaughter of Khufu (fig. 89); and the subterranean chapels of the Sixth Dynasty officials Qar and Idu (cat. nos. 195, 196).

Fig. 87. General view of the Giza necropolis, showing (far to near) the pyramids of Khufu (right) and Khafre (left), the Central Field mastabas excavated by Selim Hassan, the pyramid tomb of Queen Khent-kawes, the causeway and mud-brick houses from the Fifth and Sixth Dynasties, the valley temple of Menkaure, and a modern cemetery in the foreground, looking northwest, August 22, 1937

Fig. 88. The Harvard University–Museum of Fine Arts Expedition removes a sarcophagus from the burial shaft of the mastaba of Nefer-maat (G 7060B), Eastern Cemetery, looking northwest, October 26, 1929. The Great Pyramid of Khufu and satellite pyramid GI-c are in the background.

Fig. 89. Painted architrave, pillars, and engaged statues in the Fourth Dynasty rock-cut tomb of Queen Mer-si-ankh III, Eastern Cemetery, looking north

Perhaps the greatest Eastern Cemetery discovery, however, was made in 1925, during one of Reisner's rare stays in the United States. This was the accidental find of the tomb of Queen Hetep-heres I, wife of Snefru and probable mother of Khufu. Built twenty-seven meters (almost ninety feet) below the surface, her unmarked tomb was placed twenty-eight meters to the south of the queen's satellite pyramid as the result of a change in that monument's plans, and whether it represents a preliminary burial or a reburial remains unclear. It is certain,

however, that Hetep-heres' shaft tomb, discovered three years after the opening of the tomb of Tutankhamun at Thebes by Howard Carter, is the most intact royal burial of the Old Kingdom yet encountered. Intricate jewelry (cat. nos. 31, 32) and some of the earliest examples of furniture from the ancient world (cat. no. 33) were recovered from the jumbled mass on the burial-chamber floor, documented, and reconstructed; even the canopic vessels bearing the queen's internal organs still bore their contents in liquid state, over four thousand years after the

Fig. 90. The Great Sphinx, with the restoration scaffolding of Émile Baraize, looking northwest, December 26, 1925. The pyramids of Khufu (right) and Khafre (left) are in the background.

last Egyptians ascended from her resting place.[30] The find consumed 280 days of excavations and was recorded in 1,057 photographs and 1,701 pages of notebook listings.

Material archaeological remains have their own powerful way of speaking to us (fig. 90). But the inscriptions on the tomb walls at Giza, with their ritual, biographical, and legal texts, communicate even more directly than the cemetery's artifacts and architecture the aspirations of the Egyptians who constructed this great city of the dead. Among the more interesting texts from the Western Cemetery are legal decrees, such as that of one Pen-meru, Overseer of Mortuary Priests, designating individuals and institutions to service his mortuary cult and restricting interference with it.[31] The biographical texts offer all manner of information. Those of Nekhebu (tomb G 2381), for example, describe this man's years of loyalty and promotion in the architectural service of the pharaoh.[32] Copies of royal letters written to Senedjem-ib Inti (tomb G 2370) tell how pleased the king was with his

services as chief architect. Senedjem-ib Inti's son Mehi (tomb G 2378) completed his father's tomb, in which he included an extremely rare example of an inscription that states how long the construction process took (fifteen months in this case).[33] And another official, named Ra-wer, proudly recounts how the king accidentally struck him with his staff during a ceremony and then interceded on his subject's behalf.[34] Indeed, these inscriptions are just a few of the thousands of texts at Giza that provide revealing glimpses into administrative, legal, religious, and historical aspects of Egyptian society of the third millennium B.C.E.

The above remarks have touched upon some of the major figures who excavated in the Giza necropolis during the twentieth century. It should be noted, however, that many other individuals also made significant contributions to our understanding of the site, among them not only Selim Hassan,[35] who has been mentioned, but Abdel Moneim Abu Bakr,[36] Karl Kromer,[37] Clarence

Fig. 91. William Kelly Simpson (right) with Zahi Hawass in front of the Dream Stela of Thutmose IV, situated between the paws of the Great Sphinx, August 1977

Fig. 92. The Harvard University–Museum of Fine Arts Expedition's discovery of Fifth Dynasty statues of Raramu and his family in the serdab of mastaba tomb 2099, looking east, January 31, 1939. From Roth 1995

Fisher,[38] Ahmed Fakhry,[39] and Alexander Badawy as well.[40] The primary-source publications produced by these scholars have spawned a host of Egyptological dissertations and treatises about Giza concerning topics as various as the evolution of tomb architecture and decoration, religious ritual, ancient textiles and costume, hieroglyphic grammatical constructions, and mummification in the Old Kingdom.

Since the 1970s those who have followed Reisner at the Museum of Fine Arts, Boston, most notably William Kelly Simpson (fig. 91), have initiated the tomb-by-tomb mastaba publication series originally envisaged by Reisner and his successor as curator at the museum, William Stevenson Smith (1907–1969). To date Simpson and colleagues Dows Dunham (1890–1984), Kent R. Weeks, and Ann Macy Roth have produced six volumes of the Giza Mastabas Series, and additional volumes are in preparation (fig. 92).[41] Moreover, new excavations at Giza have revealed much that was missed by the original archaeologists and have also investigated previously unexplored regions of the necropolis. In this vein we have already mentioned the famous Khufu funerary boat just barely overlooked by Junker south of the Great Pyramid and discovered in 1954. Additional boat pits, belonging to both Khufu and Menkaure, await further excavation.[42]

In recent years Hawass's excavations in the far west of the Western Cemetery have revealed a number of tombs unknown to Reisner, specifically the beautifully painted chapel of an official named Kai and the tomb of the dwarf Per-ni-ankhu (see cat. no. 88), as well as other burials in a small cemetery. And in the Eastern Cemetery, clearance work near the southeast corner of the Great Pyramid uncovered the so-called satellite or cult pyramid of Khufu, overlooked by Reisner, raising the number of pyramids found at Giza to a total of eleven.

Newly discovered areas include the region of South Giza, where a vast cemetery of late Old Kingdom burials at the desert's edge has yielded all manner of unusual architectural forms. The individuals buried here were both workers and foremen associated with the construction of the royal pyramid complexes, as is shown by their administrative titles, their statuary, and the occasional physical injuries associated with heavy lifting displayed by their skeletal remains. In meticulous interdisciplinary excavations in this same area, an American expedition directed by Lehner has unearthed evidence of large-scale institutions of types that could have serviced the community engaged in pyramid construction. At this writing the dig has documented bakeries, fish-processing works, and a variety of other food-production establishments, as well as pigment-grinding and copper-working facilities, all of them royal and some accompanied by sealings that name King Menkaure. And finally, in conjunction with various development and sewage projects, survey and salvage explorations of the area east of the Giza plateau have delineated the original location of Khufu's valley temple beneath the modern suburb of Nazlet es-Samman, where archaeologists have also found a number of other Old Kingdom structures.

Thanks to the work of such scholars as Hawass, Lehner, and Michael Jones, it can now be postulated that during the Old Kingdom the Memphite region was not so much a series of towns and cemeteries punctuating the area as it was a continuous development along the desert's edge. And we should remember that Giza and Saqqara are surrounded by additional sites that continue to yield their own spectacular discoveries. Thus Meidum[43] and Dahshur, both south of Saqqara, provide key links between the Archaic Period cemeteries of the earliest dynasties and the established mortuary canon from the Fourth Dynasty onward found at Giza and elsewhere. Excavated for many years by Rainer Stadelmann and his colleagues from the German Archaeological Institute,[44] Dahshur is home to two of Snefru's three pyramids (his first being at Meidum), as well as a few organized rows of mastaba tombs that foreshadow the cemeteries east and west of the Great Pyramid at Giza. At Abusir, to the north of Saqqara, the Czech expedition under Miroslav Verner has for several decades been expanding on original excavations by Borchardt[45] and investigating the Fifth Dynasty pyramid complexes of King Neferefre, Neferirkare (the south side), and Queen Khent-kawes II, as well as the massive mastaba of King Niuserre's vizier, Ptahshepses (see "The Tombs of Officials" by Peter Jánosi in this catalogue, pp. 34–36), and other tombs from subsequent periods.[46] Inscribed papyrus documents from the pyramids of Neferefre, Neferirkare, and Khent-kawes have given us a wealth of information on the administration of Old Kingdom royal mortuary complexes, including their personnel schedules, inventories, and accounts.[47] And

additional Old Kingdom cemetery sites such as Abu Rawash, where Khufu's son and successor Djedefre constructed his pyramid complex, continue to broaden our overview of the Memphite cemetery in its widest definition.[48]

New technologies are now revealing more and more about the Giza necropolis and surrounding cemeteries, helping Egyptologists document and preserve the monuments with greater speed and accuracy in the face of accelerating deterioration.[49] Rising water tables, crystallization of salts on decorated wall surfaces, vandalism, and increased tourist activity have taken a heavy toll on the age-old monuments all along the Nile. Egyptologists, archaeologists, and conservators are engaged in a desperate race to preserve Egypt's ancient heritage. But this race against time actually serves to increase the value of the archaeological work carried out earlier in the twentieth century, whose scientific investigation and meticulous recording have preserved Old Kingdom data that have long since disappeared from the sites themselves. For example, Reisner's archive of large-format glass negatives, produced between 1902 and 1942, includes tens of thousands of views of ancient Giza monuments, many of which either no longer survive or retain merely a portion of their original information, whether it be relief carving, inscriptions, mud-brick architecture, or stone casing blocks; moreover, new technologies are helping at last to reassemble this material, as well as many other elements gathered during the earlier archaeological process, and reconstructions, often made with the aid of computers, are reviving the ancient sites as never before.

As the twentieth century draws to a close, Old Kingdom archaeology holds as much promise as it did for Reisner and his colleagues over a hundred years ago. Certainly the methods have changed: expedition teams of ten or twenty have replaced armies of one or two hundred; computers, remote sensing, and careful stratigraphic procedures are replacing the massive clearance projects of the past; and the search now focuses on ancient cultural patterns instead of museum-quality treasures, although extraordinary artifacts still emerge from the desert sands in abundance. Today's finds, and the knowledge to be gained from them, will continue to fascinate and educate us about life in the Pyramid Age for generations to come.

1. For a general overview of this site, see Lauer 1976.
2. This essay will hardly do justice to Saqqara and other fascinating Old Kingdom cemeteries such as Meidum, Dahshur, Abu Rawash, Abusir, and the oases. However, a few words on these sites will appear at the end of the text; see also "Excavating the Old Kingdom: The Egyptian Archaeologists" by Zahi Hawass

and "Excavating the Old Kingdom: From Khafre's Valley Temple to the Governor's City at Balat" by Nicolas Grimal in this catalogue. For popular overviews of the Old Kingdom, pyramids, and tombs and temples, see Roberts 1995; Stadelmann 1995a; Der Manuelian 1997; Hawass 1997c; and Lehner 1997.

3. For valuable collections of material relating to Giza in the New Kingdom and the Late Period, see Zivie 1976 and Zivie-Coche 1991.

4. On the colossal statue of Ramesses II (?) accompanied by a deity, recently discovered by Hawass adjacent to the pyramid of Menkaure, see Hawass 1997a, pp. 289–93; and Hawass 1997d, p. 20.

5. A small selection of early explorers at Giza might include: Caliph al-Mamun (736–833), the first to break his way into the Great Pyramid in 820; Napoleon Bonaparte, whose military campaign of 1798 included savants who measured the interior of the Great Pyramid and produced views of the Great Sphinx and the site; Giovanni Battista Caviglia (1770–1845), the first to attempt to dig out the Great Sphinx and the discoverer of the Dream Stela of Thutmose IV between its paws; Giovanni Battista Belzoni (1778–1823), who first penetrated the upper entrance of Khafre's pyramid; and Richard William Howard Vyse (1784–1853) and John Shae Perring (1813–1869), who in 1837 removed the sarcophagus from Menkaure's pyramid for transport to England (it was later lost at sea) and entered the five relieving chambers in the Great Pyramid, but unfortunately were not averse to blasting their way into passages and burial chambers. For recent summaries of these and other explorers' exploits, see Lehner 1997.

6. For more on this subject, see "Excavating the Old Kingdom" by Grimal in this catalogue; and Mariette and Maspero 1889, pp. 488–571. Mariette discovered the valley temple of Khafre in the 1850s, a find that included the king's famous seated statue with the protective Horus falcon, now in the Egyptian Museum, Cairo (fig. 28) and certainly one of the greatest works of three-dimensional sculpture from any Egyptian site or period; see Saleh and Sourouzian 1987, no. 31.

7. For a highly readable and well-illustrated account of the Lepsius expedition, see Freier and Grunert 1984, esp. pp. 13–43. The results of the expedition were published by Naville in Lepsius's monumental series *Denkmäler aus Aegypten und Aethiopien* (1897–1913).

8. A painted-plaster replica of the four walls of Mer-ib's chapel (G 2100-I) was prepared in the 1980s. The other four mastabas, in the order they were found, are those of Ii-nefret, now in Karlsruhe (Menkaure cemetery; discovered sometime prior to 1897, the year of accession by Karlsruhe; on display in Karlsruhe 1911); Wehem-ka, now in Hildesheim (D 117; discovered in 1906; 1925 in Hildesheim); Seshem-nefer III in Tübingen (G 5170; discovered in 1910 with the support of the Ernst von Sieglin Expedition; 1911 in Tübingen); and Ka-ni-nisut I, now in Vienna (G 2155; discovered in 1913; 1914 in Vienna). See Kayser 1964; Schürmann 1983; and Priese 1984; along with Schmitz 1986, pp. 46–49; Brunner-Traut 1995; and Gamer-Wallert 1998. Many other private tomb chapels from Saqqara were sent to museums in Boston, Brussels, Chicago, Copenhagen, Leiden, New York, Paris, and Philadelphia.

9. See Petrie 1883, revised and updated by Hawass in 1990.

10. Reisner, unpublished diary (n.d.), stored in the Museum of Fine Arts, Boston. I am grateful to Rita E. Freed, Norma-Jean Calderwood Curator, Department of Egyptian, Nubian, and Ancient Near Eastern Art, Museum of Fine Arts, for permission to quote from Reisner's notes.

11. These Eastern and Western Cemetery tombs were eventually published by Silvio Curto in 1903.

12. Appearing the year of his death, Reisner's monumental *A History of the Giza Necropolis*, vol. I (1942) was perhaps the greatest testament to his decades of meticulous excavations on the Giza plateau. He attempted to summarize the evolution of private tombs prior to the Fourth Dynasty in *The Development of the Egyptian Tomb down to the Accession of Cheops* (1936).

13. On the Giza slab stelae, see Der Manuelian 1998a. For remarks on Fourth Dynasty artistic style, see Stadelmann 1995b, pp. 155–66; and Stadelmann 1998a, pp. 353–87.

14. The excavations were published by Reisner in 1931.

15. For a study of the king's triads, see Wood 1974, pp. 82–93.

16. For recent remarks on the identity of the woman standing with Menkaure (who has been considered a goddess, Kha-merer-nebti II, or an unnamed queen), see Fay 1998, pp. 164–66; and Rzepka 1998, pp. 77–90.

17. For a lively account of Pelizaeus's Egyptological life, see Schmitz 1996, pp. 8–48.

18. See note 8 above. For an excellent summary of Junker's many productive years at Giza, see Jánosi 1997; as well as Junker's own *Leben und Werk in Selbstdarstellung* (1963).

19. Steindorff and Hölscher 1991.

20. On the first funerary boat of Khufu, see Abu Bakr and Mustafa 1971, pp. 1–16; and Jenkins 1980. The second still awaits final excavation.

21. See Junker 1929, pp. 132–62, pls. 18–23; and Schmitz 1986, pp. 36–41.

22. Junker 1934, pp. 97–120, pls. 1–4.

23. Junker 1931; Junker 1934, pp. 135–72, pls. 5–10; Satzinger 1994, pp. 90–93. See also note 8 above.

24. Junker 1940.

25. See Tefnin 1991; Assmann 1996, pp. 55–81; Bolshakov 1997; Lacovara 1997, pp. 28–36; and Wildung 1998, pp. 399–406.

26. Hölscher 1912.

27. Hassan 1949.

28. Ricke 1970, pp. 1–43; Lehner 1991, pp. 32–39; Lehner 1992, pp. 3–26; Hawass 1997b, pp. 245–56; and in general see the Great Sphinx Symposium 1992. For a recent argument assigning the Great Sphinx to Khufu rather than Khafre, see Stadelmann 1998a, pp. 353–87; and Stadelmann 1998b, pp. 73–75.

29. See Bolshakov 1991, pp. 5–14; Junge 1995, pp. 103–9; and Lacovara 1996b, pp. 6–7.

30. See Reisner and Smith 1955, pp. 21–22, pl. 44. A recent publication on the complicated history of the tomb is Lehner 1985.

31. See Simpson 1980, p. 24.

32. See Dunham 1938, pp. 1–8.

33. New transcriptions and translations of these inscriptions are scheduled for publication by Edward Brovarski in volume 7 of the Giza Mastabas Series.

34. See Allen 1992, pp. 14–20.

35. Hassan published his *Excavations at Giza* from 1932 to 1960.

36. Abu Bakr 1953. For more on the contributions of Egyptian scholars, see "Excavating the Old Kingdom" by Hawass in this catalogue.

37. Kromer 1978; Kromer 1991.

38. Fisher 1924.

39. Fakhry 1935.

40. Badawy 1978.

41. Forthcoming volumes are in preparation by Brovarski, Der Manuelian, Roth, and Simpson.

42. For more on the second funerary boat of Khufu, see El-Baz 1988, pp. 513–33.

43. On this site, see Petrie 1892; Mackay and Wainwright 1910; and El-Khouli 1991.

44. See Stadelmann 1991; along with a series of archaeological reports in Stadelmann 1982; Stadelmann 1983; Stadelmann et al. 1993; and Alexanian 1995, pp. 1–18.

45. Among Borchardt's important publications on this site are Borchardt 1909; Borchardt 1910; and Borchardt 1913.

46. For an excellent summary of Czech excavations at Abusir, see Verner et al. 1990; Verner 1994a; and Verner 1994b,

pp. 295–305. Recent publications on his work at the site include Verner's *Pyramid Complex of Khentkaus* (1995).

47. Posener-Kriéger and Cenival 1968; Posener-Kriéger 1976.

48. For recent excavations at Abu Rawash, see Valloggia 1994, pp. 5–17; Grimal 1996, pp. 494–99; Grimal 1997, pp. 317–26; and Valloggia 1997, pp. 417–28. A summary of information on the royal pyramid is provided by Lehner 1997, pp. 120–21.

49. On new approaches to producing facsimile line drawings of Egyptian tomb and temple wall reliefs and paintings using computer technology, see Der Manuelian 1998b, pp. 97–113.

EXCAVATING THE OLD KINGDOM
The Egyptian Archaeologists

ZAHI HAWASS

I n Egypt today it is generally believed that most of the archaeological discoveries that have been made in the country were achieved by foreign expeditions. Very little has been written about the efforts and successes of native archaeologists, yet numerous Egyptians have excavated at sites throughout the land and have contributed substantially to the field of Egyptology by means of their discoveries and research. Three generations of Egyptian scholars have worked in the Memphite region, mostly at sites within the cemeteries at Giza, Saqqara, and Dahshur, and this essay takes a number of their explorations as examples to shed light on native contributions to the study of the Old Kingdom.[1]

BRIEF DESCRIPTION OF THE MEMPHITE REGION

The cemeteries of Memphis extend from Abu Rawash in the north to Meidum in the south and house tombs of kings, queens, and officials from the time of the Archaic Period to the end of the Old Kingdom.[2] Abu Rawash, which includes a large cemetery dating back to the First Dynasty, is dominated by the unfinished pyramid complex of King Djedefre of the Fourth Dynasty.[3] Farther south is the necropolis of Giza, site of the pyramid complexes of Khufu, Khafre, and Menkaure of the Fourth Dynasty and of many nonroyal tombs from the Old Kingdom. Presiding over Giza is the Great Sphinx, the first colossal statue known from pharaonic Egypt. As an archetype of antiquity, the image of the Sphinx has stirred the imagination of poets, writers, adventurers, and tourists for centuries. Originally a symbol of Egyp-

tian kingship, in modern times it has come to stand for the Egyptian nation itself.[4]

The Layer Pyramid, built by Khaba in the Third Dynasty and characterized by a superstructure typical of the period, stands at Zawiyet el-Aryan, seven kilometers to the north of Saqqara. And about one kilometer to the northwest of the Layer Pyramid the so-called Unfinished Pyramid is found. This monument's ownership remains in dispute, with some Egyptologists maintaining that it belonged to Djedefre of the Fourth Dynasty and others attributing it to Nebka of the same dynasty.

South of Zawiyet el-Aryan is Abusir, encompassing the pyramids of most of the kings and queens of the Fifth Dynasty, among which the pyramid complex of Sahure is the best preserved. The remains of two sun temples stand near Abusir, one of them at Abu Ghurab. As inscriptions reveal that six or more kings of the Fifth Dynasty had sun temples, we know that at least four such monuments have yet to be discovered.[5]

Saqqara, south of Abusir, one of the principal cemeteries of the Archaic Period, was chosen by Djoser, of the Third Dynasty, as his eternal home. It was in what later became the central section of this necropolis that the architect Imhotep constructed Djoser's imposing Step Pyramid complex. A large step pyramid was begun nearby for Sekhemkhet, Djoser's successor; this structure, which was never finished, lies southwest of Djoser's complex and is known as the Buried Pyramid. Userkaf and Unis, the first and last kings of the Fifth Dynasty, built their own pyramid complexes near Djoser's Step Pyramid, and in the Sixth Dynasty others were erected in the northern and southern parts of the necropolis, the most important being those of Teti, Pepi I, and Pepi II. Most

Fig. 93. Zakaria Ghoneim (left), Selim Hassan (fourth from left), and Zaki Saad (third from right), Saqqara, January 16, 1927

of these Fifth and Sixth Dynasty pyramids are associated with cemeteries for officials and nobles of the same period, some of whose tombs have beautifully carved or painted chapels.

South of Saqqara are two other Old Kingdom cemeteries, the fields of Dahshur and Meidum. Snefru, the first king of the Fourth Dynasty, built three pyramids at these sites, the first at Meidum, the second and third at Dahshur.[6] Important officials and relatives of the pharaohs of the early Fourth Dynasty were buried in cemeteries not far from these pyramids.

THREE GENERATIONS OF EGYPTIAN ARCHAEOLOGISTS

The following list records some of the most important scholars among the three generations of Egyptian archaeologists who have conducted excavations in Memphite cemeteries between Abu Rawash and Meidum from the late 1920s to the present day. The names are arranged according to the chronology of their activity.

First Generation: *Selim Hassan*; Zaki Saad; *Zakaria Ghoneim*; Abdel Hafiz Abdel-al; *Kamal el-Mallakh*;

Hag Ahmed Youssef; Hakiem Abou Seif; Abdel Salam Hussein; *Ahmed Fakhry*; *Abdel Moneim Abu Bakr*; Mounir Basta; *Abdel Aziz Saleh*; Mohamed Zaki Nour; Abdel Taweb el-Heta; Rizkall Makra-Malla

Second Generation: *Ali Radwan*; *Gaballa Ali Gaballa*; *Said Tawfik*; *Ahmed Moussa*; Sami Farag; Mahmoud Abdel Razik; Ali el-Khouli; Abdallah el-Sayed

Third Generation: *Zahi Hawass*; Said el-Fikey; Holeil Ghali; Khaled Daoud; Mohammed Hagrass; Magdy el-Ghandour; Orban E. Abu el-Hassan; Ahmed Abdel Hamied

The collective achievements of these men form a rich corpus of material that would be an appropriate subject for a future book. Here, however, space permits reference to only the few Egyptologists whose names are italicized, together with a brief discussion of some of the important discoveries they had the good fortune to make over the past eighty years.

The First Generation

Selim Hassan (1886–1961) (fig. 93) was appointed assistant curator at the Egyptian Museum, Cairo, in 1921 and later studied Egyptology in Paris. He was the first Egyptian appointed professor of Egyptology in the Faculty of Arts at Cairo University. Well into his career as an archaeologist he read for his doctorate in Vienna, completing his studies there in 1939.[7]

In 1928 Hassan commenced his archaeological activities, working with the German Egyptologist Hermann Junker, who was excavating west of the Great Pyramid at Giza. Within a year Hassan was leading his own team from Cairo University, which undertook important and extensive explorations at both Giza and Saqqara that lasted until 1939. It is estimated that Hassan discovered more than two hundred tombs and thousands of related artifacts. Among his most important finds at Giza were the tomb of Queen Khent-kawes I and its associated temples and pyramid city. He also uncovered the tombs of Khafre's sons and courtiers, as well as the solar boat pits of Khafre himself.[8] In addition Hassan pursued excavations around the Great Sphinx, where he unearthed the temple of Amenhotep II.[9]

At Saqqara, Hassan excavated the Fifth Dynasty valley temple and causeway of King Unis.[10] In the vicinity he uncovered many Old Kingdom tombs, as well as two large tombs that are of particular interest because they date much earlier, to the Second Dynasty. Toward the end of his career as an active archaeologist, at age sixty-eight, Hassan participated in the campaign to salvage monuments in Nubia, a project whose success he lived to see.

Without doubt Hassan ranks as one of the most important of all Egyptian archaeologists by virtue of his numerous discoveries at Giza and Saqqara as well as his many scholarly publications.[11] The rare and beautiful stela of Ra-wer (cat. no. 144), which he found at Giza, appropriately represents this great Egyptologist's contribution to Old Kingdom studies.

Zakaria Ghoneim (1911–1959) (fig. 93) was awarded a Diploma in Egyptology at Cairo University in 1934. At the age of twenty-six he became Hassan's assistant during the excavations of 1937 in and around the pyramid complex of Unis at Saqqara. In 1939 Ghoneim was appointed Inspector of Antiquities at Aswan; he spent more than a decade working in southern Egypt and became Chief Inspector of Upper Egypt in 1946. He held this post until 1951, when he was made Chief Inspector at Saqqara, where he discovered the unfinished pyramid of Sekhemkhet (fig. 94). Undoubtedly Ghoneim's greatest discovery, the king's pyramid was an important landmark in the study of Old Kingdom royal tombs and their

Fig. 94. Gamal Abdel Nasser visiting the pyramid of Sekhemkhet at Saqqara, June 30, 1954

contents.[12] It yielded much valuable material, including a seemingly intact sarcophagus made of alabaster discovered within the king's burial chamber. Once opened, however, it was found to be empty, and in fact not a trace of Sekhemkhet's mummy was ever located. Three bracelets belonging to Sekhemkhet (cat. no. 19) exemplify Ghoneim's finds in the present exhibition.

Ghoneim's life ended tragically when, in a state of acute depression after he had been held responsible for the disappearance of an artifact, he drowned himself in the Nile. Barely a week later the object in question, which had been accidentally misplaced, was located.

Kamal el-Mallakh (1918–1987) (fig. 95) unearthed the boat of Khufu south of the Great Pyramid. His remarkable find, made in 1954 when boat pits were revealed below the surface of debris that was being removed from the area, ranks as one of the greatest discoveries in Egyptian archaeology. Its implications involve not only the burials of kings and the cult of Khufu[13] but practical issues as well: the bark excavated by el-Mallakh and another that still remains in a second pit

Fig. 95. Kamal el-Mallakh

Fig. 96. Hag Ahmed Youssef

provide direct information relating to the construction of large-scale wood boats in antiquity, a subject formerly understood primarily from depictions in tombs.[14]

Other Egyptian archaeologists, including Mohamed Zaki Nour, Zaki Iskander, and Salah Osman, played roles in the discovery of Khufu's bark, and we cannot speak of el-Mallakh's accomplishments in this realm without mentioning our great restorer and conservator, Hag Ahmed Youssef.

Hag Ahmed Youssef (1912–1999) (fig. 96) started his career as a restorer with American Egyptologist George Reisner during the excavation of the tomb of Queen Hetep-heres I (see cat. nos. 31–33) and subsequently pursued his extraordinary craft at the Egyptian Museum, Cairo. As the individual chiefly responsible for the restoration of Khufu's boat, Hag Ahmed spent almost twenty-eight years working on its 650 parts and fitting together some 1,224 pieces of cedarwood. During the course of these labors he lived in a rest house near the tomb of Debhen and produced many beautiful photographs of the boat as it underwent reconstruction. His work saw its culmination in the display of the reassembled bark at the Cheops [Khufu] Boat Museum, which opened in Giza on March 6, 1982. The present essay can offer only a glimpse of Hag Ahmed's achievements; indeed, an

entire volume should be devoted to the life and accomplishments of this extraordinary man.

Ahmed Fakhry (1905–1973) graduated from the Faculty of Arts at Cairo University in 1928 and continued his education in Belgium, England, and Germany for the next four years. On his return to Egypt in 1932 he joined the Department of Antiquities, initially as an inspector at Giza, then at Luxor, and, finally, starting in 1938, as Chief Inspector of Middle Egypt, the oases, and the Delta. He also worked for a period in the Egyptian Museum, Cairo. In 1952 Fakhry was appointed Professor of Ancient History in the Faculty of Arts at Cairo University.[15] During his tenure he served as a visiting professor at many foreign institutions and became well known abroad.

Fakhry excavated extensively, conducting his most significant work at the oases, Giza, and Dahshur.[16] In 1951 Gamal Mokhtar, then head of the Egyptian Antiquities Organization, appointed him Director of the Pyramid Studies Project, with Giza as its center. Dahshur, however, became the site of Fakhry's greatest discoveries. There, in October 1952, he found the so-called valley temple, or statue-cult temple, of the Bent Pyramid, in which he uncovered some 1,400 inscribed blocks, statues, and stelae.[17] Fakhry's Dahshur finds are his most important legacy, both for irrevocably establishing Snefru as the

Fig. 97. Abdel Moneim Abu Bakr

owner of the Bent Pyramid and for providing Egyptolo-gists with information about the content of particular scenes as well as their positions within early Old King-dom pyramid complexes. The valley temple reliefs from the Bent Pyramid complex, two of which (cat. no. 22) are included in the present exhibition, are arguably the most illuminating of Fakhry's discoveries.

Abdel Moneim Abu Bakr (1907–1976) (fig. 97) stud-ied at Cairo University under Alexander Golenischeff and read for his doctorate in 1938 at Berlin University under the guidance of Kurt Sethe. In 1939 he began his teaching career at Alexandria University, moving to Cairo University in 1954. He taught the present author Egyp-tian archaeology as a visiting professor at Alexandria University in 1968. Between 1939 and 1953 numerous sites in the Giza necropolis, especially in the area to the west of the Great Pyramid, were excavated by Abu Bakr, who also participated in the Nubian salvage cam-paign between 1960 and 1965. Only a portion of Abu Bakr's work saw publication during his lifetime,[18] and additional detailed studies of his expeditions would

Fig. 98. Abdel Aziz Saleh (center) with (left to right) Dieter Arnold, Werner Kaiser, Peter Grossman, and Jutta Kaiser

contribute much to our knowledge of Old Kingdom tombs at Giza.

Abdel Aziz Saleh (b. 1921) (fig. 98) received his Diploma in Egyptology from Cairo University in 1951. His fieldwork career commenced shortly thereafter, with excavations at Tuna el-Gebel in 1954–55. Subsequently he taught at Riyadh University and King Abdel Aziz University in Gada, Saudi Arabia, and then, in 1977, he became Dean of the Faculty of Archaeology at Cairo University. He is currently a member of many important archaeological committees. The topic of his dissertation, "Upbringing and Education in Ancient Egypt," is of particular interest today, and his contributions to the field of Egyptian history, which he taught the present author, are original and important.

Perhaps Saleh's most intriguing discoveries were made at Giza, just south of the causeway of Menkaure's pyramid; here he found unique structures of stone rubble mixed with mortar that he calls "foundation embankments" and believes to be ramps that were used to transport blocks to building sites.[19] He also uncovered what he has suggested is an open-air altar. Saleh found as well fifteen buildings made from rubble and mortar that in his view served as living and working quarters for an industrial community preoccupied with activities connected with the cult of Menkaure. Later study of the site by the present

writer has confirmed this theory. Material evidence shows that the area was used for the manufacture of objects and foodstuffs essential to maintain the cult: ovens and fireplaces indicate the existence of a bakery and public kitchens, while other structures have been identified as workshops and official buildings, including a hall for scribes. These finds provide Egyptologists with new insight into the practical efforts that sustained a royal cult in antiquity. Although communal buildings of the kind Saleh uncovered are rare, it can be assumed that they must have existed in association with other pyramid complexes in the Memphite region and that more may yet be found.

The Second Generation

Ali Radwan (b. 1941) (fig. 99) read for his doctorate at Munich in 1968 and became the Head of the Egyptian Department of Cairo University in 1980. Seven years later he was appointed Dean of the Faculty of Archaeology, a position he maintains in 1999. At present he is a member of a number of Egyptian and foreign committees concerned with education and Egyptology.

Radwan's most significant contribution to Egyptian archaeology has been his work at Abusir, which commenced in 1988 and continued until 1993. He also

Fig. 99. From left to right, Said Tawfik, Gaballa Ali Gaballa, Ali Radwan, and Tohfa Handussa

Fig. 100. Ahmed Moussa
(left) and Mamdouh Yacoub
(second from left) during the
uncovering of the tomb of
Nefer and Ka-hay, Giza,
1969

applied modern excavation techniques to the site and trained young Egyptian archaeologists in the new methods. Most of his efforts in the area were concentrated in a location northwest of the sun temple of Niuserre, because the initial intention of his expedition was to search the area for other sun temples that were unknown except for mention of their names in the Abusir papyri and priestly titles. It came as a surprise, therefore, when he discovered a large cemetery dating back to the Predynastic Period (Naqada III) and the First Dynasty.[20] (The earliest king named at Abusir is Den, of the First Dynasty, who is cited in inscriptional material.) The importance of Radwan's achievement is based on the information uncovered about a cemetery dating to the Predynastic and Archaic Periods in a region not thought to contain such early burials.

Gaballa Ali Gaballa (b. 1939) (fig. 99) is currently the General Secretary of the Supreme Council for Antiquities, a position he has held since 1997. He received his doctorate from Liverpool University in 1967 and on his return to Egypt joined the teaching staff of the Faculty of Archaeology at Cairo University, first as a lecturer and then as Dean of the Faculty. Gaballa is well known as the author of two useful books, the earlier one entitled *Narrative in Egyptian Art* and the later *The Memphite Tomb-Chapel of Mose*. The chapel of Mose, at Saqqara, was of partic-

ular interest to him primarily because it houses significant legal texts, which he translated and analyzed.[21]

The most important aspect of Gaballa's explorations at the ancient capital Memphis, a project he began in 1987, was his use of modern scientific methods. Gaballa's excavations commenced in the southeast corner of Memphis, about ninety meters from the Ptah temple, where he uncovered mud-brick walls, ovens, hearths, and granaries. Although detailed study of the area is still in progress, evidence gleaned so far from various sources indicates that the settlement dates between the late Eighteenth Dynasty and the beginning of the Nineteenth Dynasty.[22]

Said Tawfik (1936–1990) (fig. 99) studied Egyptology under Siegfried Schott and read for a doctorate at Göttingen before returning to Egypt. In 1980 Tawfik was elected Dean of the Faculty of Archaeology at Cairo University, and in 1989 he became Chairman of the Egyptian Antiquities Organization, a post he filled until his death the following year.

His explorations pursued for Cairo University on a rich site south of the causeway of Unis at Saqqara beginning in January 1984 resulted in the unique and unexpected find of two cemeteries of widely separated periods, one lying above the other: Ramesside tombs in the upper level and beneath it others from the Old Kingdom.[23] The Old Kingdom tombs, built of stone and mud brick, range in date from the Third Dynasty to the end of the Old Kingdom. Almost all of the material associated with this site remains unpublished, owing to Tawfik's sudden death while excavations were in progress. It is hoped that, after a lapse of almost ten years, efforts will soon be made to ensure full publication of the tombs and artifacts he uncovered and to begin the considerable restoration and conservation of an expert nature that are required at the site.

Ahmed Moussa (1934–1998) first worked as Inspector of Antiquities at Saqqara, where he later became Chief Inspector, a post he held from 1962 to 1980. From 1980 to 1987 he served as Director General at Giza and Saqqara, but most of his activity was concentrated in the Saqqara necropolis. Perhaps his best-known discovery is the rock-cut tomb of Nefer and Ka-hay (fig. 100), uncovered south of the causeway of Unis, containing nine burials and, in a shaft below the east wall of the chapel, a wood coffin with an extremely well preserved mummy.[24] Notable features of this tomb are its wonderfully bright and fresh painted reliefs, which include spirited depictions of daily life as well as more sober funerary scenes and inscriptions.

In addition Moussa made major discoveries relating to an Old Kingdom rock-cut tomb excavated in an area just south of Unis's causeway in 1964 by Mounir Basta, then Chief Inspector at Saqqara. The inscriptions in the tomb reveal that it belonged to Ni-ankh-khnum and Khnum-hotep, who lived in the Fifth Dynasty during the reigns of Niuserre and Menkauhor and were palace officials, both married men with children who were perhaps brothers or related in some other way. Digging near the middle of the causeway of Unis in 1965, Moussa found the entrance to the extensively decorated chapel of Ni-ankh-khnum and Khnum-hotep, inside a unique stone mastaba connected by an undecorated open court to the rock-cut rooms Basta had uncovered.[25]

Moussa excavated part of the valley temple of Unis and also undertook important work at Memphis.[26] His most remarkable accomplishments were in the field of Old Kingdom architecture and tomb decoration, as embodied primarily in his discovery of two of the best-preserved tombs of the Fifth Dynasty unearthed at Saqqara in recent years.

The Third Generation

The third generation of Egyptian archaeologists concerned with the cemeteries of Memphis is represented here by the present author and the team working under his direction. The efforts of this group, composed not only of archaeologists but also of architects, draftspersons, pottery specialists, and conservators, have resulted in many discoveries at Giza and Saqqara and, most important, the training in excavation techniques of those who will constitute the fourth generation of native Egyptologists. A number of our finds are included in this exhibition. The following summary is meant to place these objects, which were unearthed at three sites, in context.

1. Tombs associated with the workmen's community at Giza

On April 14, 1990, the chief of the pyramid guards, Mohammed Abdel Razek, reported that an American tourist was thrown from her horse when the animal stumbled on a previously unknown mud-brick wall, located to the south of the colossal stone wall known as the *heit el-ghorab,* or "wall of the crow"—an accident that led to the discovery of tombs associated with what was presumably the workmen's community at Giza.[27] The mud-brick wall turned out to be a portion of a tomb, with a long, vaulted chamber and two false doors inscribed with the name Ptah-shepsesu. While not in the style of the great stone mastabas of nobles that lie beside the pyramids, Ptah-shepsesu's tomb and courtyard are grand in comparison to the others we uncovered around it. Pieces of granite, basalt, diorite, and other stones of the kind used in the pyramid temples were incorporated into the walls of these more modest structures, suggesting that some tombs in the cemetery may belong to the pyramid builders or succeeding generations of workers who made use of material left over from the construction of the pyramids, temples, and great mastabas at the site.

The lower part of the cemetery contains about six hundred such graves, which presumably served workmen, and thirty larger tombs, which perhaps belonged to overseers. The tombs take a variety of forms: stepped domes, beehives, and gabled roofs. The domes, which are two to six feet high, cover simple rectangular grave pits and follow the configuration of the pyramids in an extremely simplified manner. An interesting example we came upon during our excavations in this portion of the cemetery is a small mastaba built of limestone that is similar in style to the tombs of the Fourth Dynasty. This tomb has six burial shafts and two false doors carved into its east face. Attached to the mastaba, but separate from it, is a room cut into the bedrock, which contained an intact burial, with pottery. A niche carved

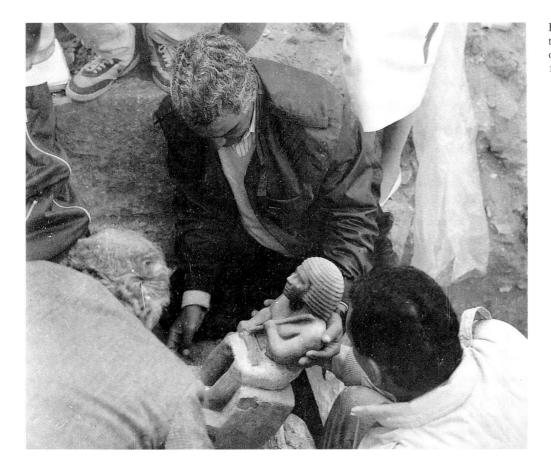

Fig. 101. Zahi Hawass with the newly discovered statue of the dwarf Per-ni-ankhu, 1990

into the west side of the chamber was sealed, except for a small hole, with limestone, mud bricks, and mud mortar. We peered inside and were astonished to see the eyes of a statue staring back at us. We were even more surprised when we removed the mud bricks and limestone blocks and found not one sculpture but four limestone statues and the remains of another in wood. The four complete examples are inscribed for the "Overseer of the Boat of the Goddess Neith, the Royal Acquaintance, Inti-shedu."[28] The entire group of five, four of which are included in the present exhibition (cat. nos. 89–92), recalls the five statues of the pharaohs placed in most pyramid temples from the time of Khafre to the end of the Old Kingdom.

2. Tombs in the great Western Cemetery, west of Khufu's pyramid at Giza

Our expedition was initially meant to publish the tomb of Nesut-nufer (G 1457) in the great Western Cemetery at Giza, but our explorations led to other finds. Nesut-nufer's tomb was discovered by Reisner[29] but had remained unpublished despite the owner's very interesting titles and its proximity to the famous tomb of the dwarf

Seneb, found by Junker.[30] The area west of G 1457 was covered with excavation debris disposed of by Reisner and Junker, which perhaps accounts in part for the neglect of the tomb; in any event, our architect requested clearance of the debris in order to complete his drawing of the mastaba's plan. During this clearing the tomb of the dwarf Per-ni-ankhu was discovered.

On the east facade of this mastaba's superstructure we encountered two false doors on whose drums Per-ni-ankhu's name is inscribed. We also discovered the openings of three burial shafts; two housed artifacts and the skeletons of two women, and in the third was the skeleton of a dwarf, Per-ni-ankhu himself. Attached to the north side of the tomb the expedition found a serdab with a niche containing the statue of the seated Per-ni-ankhu (fig. 101; cat. no. 88).[31] A rare example of a private statue carved in basalt, this is sculpted with such care and skill that it must be regarded as a masterpiece of Old Kingdom art.

For several reasons, the tomb and statue of Per-ni-ankhu have been dated to the Fourth Dynasty. For one, the serdab, which is very similar to the external serdab of King Djoser of the Third Dynasty, is situated outside the mastaba rather than within the superstructure, as in examples from the Fifth and Sixth Dynasties. Moreover, the use of basalt is indicative of an early date. This stone was employed extensively in the funerary complex of Khufu, the second king of the Fourth Dynasty, and no doubt there were large cast-off fragments available for statues in the sculptors' workshops at Giza. The superb technical achievement of the sculptor who worked the hard stone with great confidence suggests an early date as well, as do the delicacy of detail and the strong facial features the piece exhibits. Indeed, the upper part of Per-ni-ankhu's body shows strong affinities with the statuary of King Khafre (cat. no. 56), which is also carved from hard stone.

It is instructive to situate Per-ni-ankhu in relation to two other famous dwarfs of the Old Kingdom: the Fourth Dynasty Seneb, who was the prophet of Khufu and Djedefre, tutor of a king's son, and director of dwarfs in charge of dressing;[32] and Khnum-hotep, of the Sixth Dynasty, who bore the titles Ka Servant and Overseer of the Ka Servants. Seneb's titles are more important than those of both Per-ni-ankhu and Khnum-hotep, and the remarkable decorated false door of his tomb suggests high status as well. Per-ni-ankhu's fine statue is superior in quality to that of Khnum-hotep and also displays more elevated symbols of office. This evidence indicates Seneb ranked highest, Per-ni-ankhu second, and Khnum-hotep third. Additional archaeological testimony allows further interesting speculation regarding Per-ni-ankhu's place in society. His mastaba is quite close to that of Seneb, and the name of Seneb's wife, Senet-ites, is inscribed in the tomb of the official Ankh-ib situated just north of Per-ni-ankhu's monument. On the basis of the proximity of these burials and the connections indicated by the appearance of Senet-ites' name in Ankh-ib's tomb, we can surmise that the families of Seneb, Per-ni-ankhu, and Ankh-ib may have been related.

3. Excavations near the pyramid of Teti at Saqqara

The first project undertaken by our expedition at Saqqara was pursued in 1996 at the site of the pyramid of Queen Iput I, the wife of King Teti and mother of King Pepi I of the Sixth Dynasty. Here our aim was to clean and re-excavate the queen's mortuary temple, located about one hundred meters to the north of the pyramid temple of Teti, and then to enter her pyramid.[33] Numerous artifacts were uncovered during the excavation of the temple, the most significant of which was an object made from limestone that had been broken in two and incorporated in the pavement of a room north of the offering chamber.

When the two pieces were joined it became clear that they formed a doorjamb (cat. no. 3). The shape of the reconstituted object and the relief decoration and inscriptions it bore led us to conclude that we had probably discovered an architectural element from King Djoser's funerary complex, dating back to the Third Dynasty, that had been removed from its original context and reused in the temple we were exploring.[34]

Our excavations of 1997 led us to the tomb of Teti-ankh, northeast of the pyramid of Teti. This tomb has a very simple layout, with an entrance on the south side, a hall and burial shaft, and a second long hall and passage leading to the offering room. The burial shaft near the north wall of the hall leads to the burial chamber, which is cut into the north side of the shaft. Inside the room we discovered an unpolished limestone sarcophagus containing a mummy in poor condition.[35] The expedition found evidence that robbers had penetrated the tomb in antiquity—a hole they had driven through the north side of the sarcophagus, just large enough for a small child to squeeze through—and came upon lampblack that may have come from lamps used by these thieves.

Although this summary of the accomplishments of three generations of Egyptian archaeologists in the region of Memphis concludes here, it should be stressed that it would be possible to discuss many more if space permitted. It is worth noting as well that native expeditions made discoveries of parallel importance at other sites. While the present writer welcomes the opportunity to shed light on examples of the work of his Egyptian colleagues and of his own expeditions at Giza and Saqqara, he must also emphasize that the numerous accomplishments of the many native scholars who have contributed to Egyptian archaeology over the years should be recorded more extensively for posterity. As for the future, there are rich possibilities for Egyptian archaeologists to build on their past achievements, not only in the realm of excavations but also in the increasingly vital fields of survey, restoration, conservation, and the detailed recording of exposed monuments.

1. In 1983 the permanent committee of the Egyptian Antiquities Organization decreed that no more foreign expeditions would be allowed to excavate at sites in the Memphite region. However, the committee still gives permission to excavate to both Egyptian and foreign expeditions, although, in my opinion, work at Saqqara in particular should focus upon the restoration, conservation, and recording of monuments that have already been excavated.

2. For summary descriptions of the Old Kingdom pyramid sites, see Stadelmann 1985a, pp. 105–28; and Lehner 1997, pp. 95, 107.

3. Hawass 1980, pp. 229–42. A French, Swiss, and Egyptian expedition is currently working at the site.

4. See Hawass 1992b; Hawass 1996a; and Hawass 1997c, pp. 168–91. See also Lehner 1997.

5. Verner 1994a; Hawass and Verner 1996, pp. 177–86.

6. Stadelmann 1980, pp. 437–49; Stadelmann 1985a, pp. 164–72.

7. Dawson and Uphill 1995, pp. 192–93.

8. Hassan's *Excavations at Giza* was published in ten volumes from 1932 to 1960.

9. Hassan 1949. He also found rock-cut tombs north of the Great Sphinx.

10. Hassan 1955, pp. 136–44.

11. Hassan's extremely valuable publications comprise sixteen volumes on the history of ancient Egypt and more than fifty-three other books and articles.

12. Ghoneim 1957.

13. See Hawass 1987, pp. 53–86.

14. Jenkins 1980; Hawass 1990, pp. 24–26.

15. Dawson and Uphill 1995, p. 147.

16. Fakhry 1935; Fakhry 1942–50; Fakhry 1993.

17. Fakhry 1959; Fakhry 1961b.

18. Abu Bakr 1953.

19. Saleh 1974, pp. 131–54.

20. Radwan 1991; Radwan 1995, p. 312.

21. Gaballa (1977) noted that Mose's tomb had not been located. However, subsequent to the publication of that volume, during the present writer's excavation east of the pyramid of Queen Khuit at Saqqara, the tomb's burial shaft, which contained blocks inscribed with the name of Mose, was discovered.

22. Gaballa 1989, pp. 25–27.

23. Tawfik 1991, pp. 403–9.

24. Moussa and Altenmüller 1971.

25. Moussa and Altenmüller 1977.

26. Moussa 1981, pp. 75–77; Moussa 1985, pp. 33–34.

27. Hawass 1996b, pp. 53–67; Hawass and Lehner 1997, pp. 30–43.

28. Hawass 1991a, pp. 29–32; Hawass 1991b, pp. 33–35; Hawass 1998, pp. 187–208.

29. Reisner 1942, p. 210, fig. 12; Porter and Moss 1974, p. 64.

30. Hawass 1987, p. 679.

31. Hawass 1991c, pp. 157–62.

32. Porter and Moss 1974, p. 101; El-Aguizy 1987, pp. 53–60.

33. Loret excavated here from 1897 to 1898; Firth and Gunn followed him, and Labrousse has recently undertaken work in the area. See Loret 1899, pp. 85–86; Firth and Gunn 1926, vol. 1, pp. 11–14; and Labrousse 1994, pp. 231–43.

34. Hawass 1994, pp. 45–55.

35. A full report on the mummy will be included in the forthcoming publication of this monument.

THIRD DYNASTY

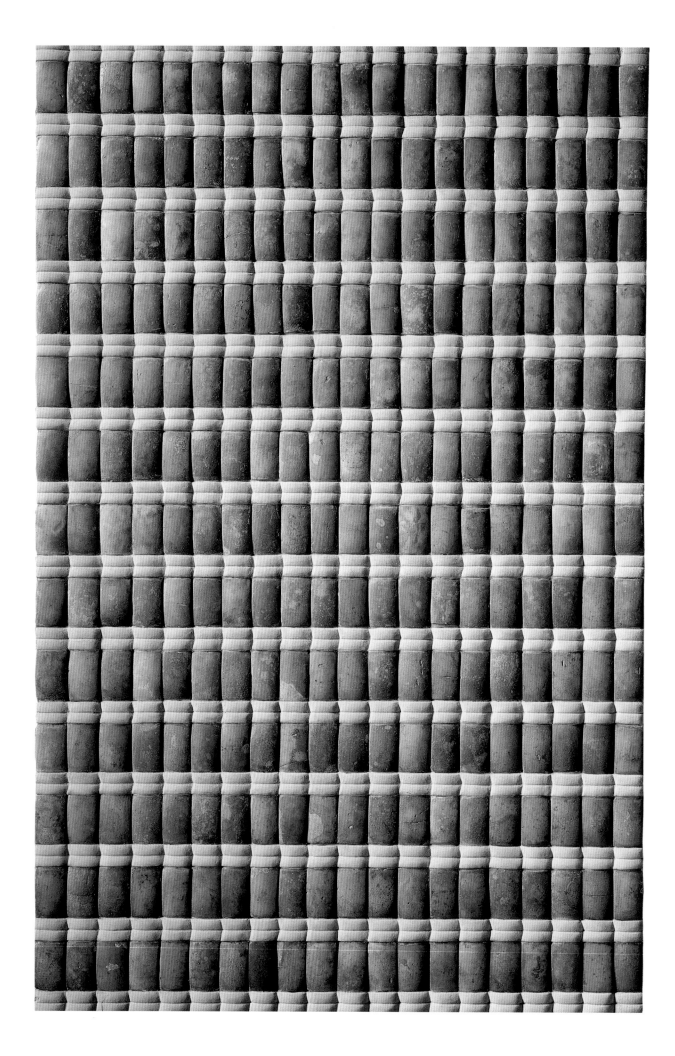

1. WALL DECORATION FROM THE FUNERARY APARTMENTS OF KING DJOSER

Third Dynasty, reign of Djoser
Blue-green Egyptian faience
H. 113 cm (44½ in.); w. 73.5 cm (29 in.); each tile
ca. 6.5 x 4 cm (2⅝ x 1⅝ in.)
The Metropolitan Museum of Art, New York,
Rogers Fund, by exchange, 1948 48.160.1

Within Djoser's funerary complex at Saqqara apartments were carved out beneath both the king's pyramid and a building called the Southern Tomb. The rooms around the king's burial chamber—reserved for his use and located 28 meters (92 feet) belowground—and in the Southern Tomb include a series of chambers whose walls are faced with sculpted limestone blocks, into which thousands of small faience tiles were fitted. The vivid color of this covering gave these apartments their name: the Blue Chambers of Djoser, which can no longer be visited.

In the Blue Chambers under the pyramid, one wall has four panels surmounted by *djed* pillars (the hieroglyph meaning "stability") supporting an arch; another, probably representing the palace facade, is decorated with three niches and small windows sculpted in limestone, which stand out from the blue wall tiled with faience. The backs of the niches are magnificently decorated in relief. Here, King Djoser is seen performing rites, most importantly, running the Heb Sed race. The royal apartments of the Southern Tomb display the same decoration.

The tiles have different shapes and dimensions. Those surrounding the windows are much smaller than the others and form a tight grid. At the top, *djed* pillars, with their elongated shapes, curves, and representations of veins, evoke stylized plant elements, such as reed grass. Probably the decoration on these walls depicts reed matting and captures the appearance of the lightweight constructions of the era. Yet it should perhaps be seen as more than an evocation of architecture. The symbolic value of the blue-green color (signifying regeneration) and the mention in the Pyramid Texts (cat. no. 177) of a "field of reeds" located in the next world suggest that this decoration also alludes to the destiny of the deceased king.

Like most of the tiles discovered in the Blue Chambers, the examples in this exhibition are rectangular and are sometimes marked on the back with a hieroglyphic sign. The slightly convex face is covered with blue glaze; the flat back, which is white and unglazed, has a rectangular tenon with a hole through it to accept a string for attachment. These are among the oldest examples of molded Egyptian faience.

The limestone facing was prepared and sculpted to house the tiles. In this example, bands of molding represent the ties holding bundles of upright reeds. Channels serve to house the tiles: a tenon on the back of each tile fits into a mortise in the side of the limestone channels. At regular intervals, small conduits were drilled into the stone moldings. A brace was passed through them, holding a sequence of four to eight tiles in place until the plaster mortar dried.

The Step Pyramid of Djoser contained no fewer than thirty-six thousand of these tiles, and many examples of this type have been found in other monuments dating to the early dynasties, including royal tombs, the temple at Elephantine, and even non-royal mastabas.[1]   CZ

1. Friedman 1998, p. 181.

PROVENANCE: Saqqara, Step Pyramid of Djoser

BIBLIOGRAPHY: Borchardt and Sethe 1892, pp. 86–87 (for marks on the back); Lauer 1936–39, vol. 1, p. 36; Hayes 1953, p. 60; Porter and Moss 1978, pp. 401, 408; Friedman 1995, pp. 1–42; Friedman 1998, pp. 180–81, nos. 17–20

2. Model of the Third Dynasty Complex of King Djoser at Saqqara

Architectural class project, Ryerson Polytechnic
University, Toronto, 1990; completed by Georgia
Guenther, Royal Ontario Museum, Toronto,
ca. 1991
Wood, cardboard, and plaster of paris
H. 109.2 cm (43 in.); w. 467.4 cm (15 ft. 4 in.);
d. 161.1 (63⅜ in.)
Royal Ontario Museum, Toronto 992.285.1

The present model, which shows the complex of the Third Dynasty king Djoser in
the necropolis of Memphis, is based on the
results of excavations conducted by Jean-
Philippe Lauer, beginning in 1927. The enclosure wall of the actual complex, measuring
277 by 544 meters, replicates in stone the
paneled brick wall of the royal palace. It
has fifteen gates, but only one, at the south
end of the east side, functions as a real
entrance. The central focus of the complex
is a six-step mastaba usually called the Step
Pyramid (although it is not a true pyramid),
which rises over underground apartments.
These apartments reproduce elements of a
royal palace. A second royal underground
palace (the Southern Tomb) lies below the
center of the enclosure's south wall. Both
underground apartments contain chambers
covered with blue-green faience tiles. A
palace or templelike structure of unknown
cultic purpose adjoins the north side of the
step mastaba.

The complex's eastern area is filled with
rows of smaller sanctuaries belonging to deities who apparently visit the king. Twenty-
five to thirty chapels for these deities are
arranged around an elongated court. Two
larger and apparently more significant sanctuaries lie north of the court. A large open
area south of the step mastaba probably
served as a festival court. The western and
northern parts of the complex are filled
with buildings that seem to be giant store-
houses for the royal possessions.

The complex is the earliest large-scale
stone monument of ancient Egypt. It is a
copy of the king's earthly residence, cult,
and administration center intended for his
eternal use. In it early Egyptian buildings
that were constructed of brick, wood, and
reed were simplified and translated into
stone. Most structures are massive mock
buildings that have no interior rooms, and
their function is for the most part open to
speculation. Apparently no rituals were
performed in the complex. It seems that
the replica had the power to produce the
intended reality.

The interior's clustered organization is
partially the result of several building phases.
However, it is clear that the designers were
not attempting to achieve the rigid orientation, frontality, and symmetry typical of
later Egyptian architecture.   DA

BIBLIOGRAPHY: Firth and Quibell 1935; Lauer
1936–39; Lauer 1962

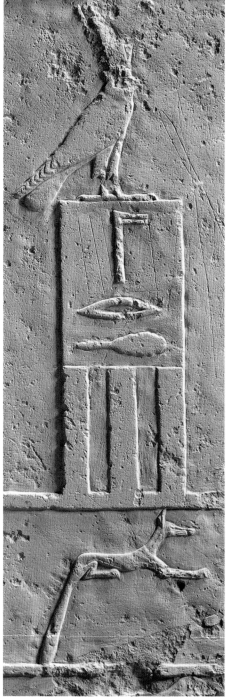

Detail, cat. no. 3

3. DOORJAMB OF KING DJOSER

Third Dynasty
Limestone
Total h. 211.3 cm (83¼ in.); w. 30.5 cm (12 in.);
d. 25.4 cm (10 in.)
Egyptian Museum, Cairo JE 98951a,b

During excavations in 1992–93 at Saqqara, two interesting reused blocks were uncovered in the pavement of the funerary temple of the Sixth Dynasty queen Iput I. When subsequently fitted together, the pieces were found to form a doorjamb that dated to the reign of the Third Dynasty king Djoser, builder of the Step Pyramid.

The jamb has a flat top, decorated front and sides, and a blank back. Its front was divided into twenty compartments. The uppermost compartment is large and has a curved top. It contains a rectangular *serekh* surmounted by a falcon wearing the crown of Upper and Lower Egypt, which represents the god Horus. The *serekh* encloses hieroglyphs spelling Netjeri-khet, the Horus name of Djoser. Below the *serekh* are twelve compartments, alternately large and small; each of the large registers contains a recumbent jackal, while in each small one there appears a recumbent lion or lioness. Below these compartments is another *serekh*, beneath which is another sequence of jackals, lions, and lionesses. Only six registers of the lower sequence are preserved. Given the Egyptian love of symmetry, it is likely that the second block also contained twelve registers; the monument may even have contained a third identical block.

The recumbent jackal and lion/lioness figures have been carefully arranged within different-sized compartments tailored to fit the animal depicted. The lion/lioness, positioned slightly off center in each compartment, displays a lashing tail that suggests an alertness belied by its recumbent pose. The jackal is more centered in its compartment, but its carefully rendered tail extends to the bottom line, while its ears touch the top. Unlike the lion/lioness, the jackal is thus connected with its frame.

Each of the side panels is divided into two long, vertical compartments, the upper round-topped, the second rectangular. The undulating body of a snake with a protruding forked tongue, portrayed as if slowly sliding across the sand, fills each compartment. The artist emphasized the importance of these serpents by carving them in higher relief than the decoration on the front and by crosshatching their bodies to give the appearance of skin.

This block may have come either from Djoser's Heb Sed court or from a lost ceremonial gate, which perhaps gave access to a valley temple some distance from the Djoser complex as it exists today.   ZH

PROVENANCE: Saqqara, Hawass excavation, 1992–93

BIBLIOGRAPHY: Hawass 1994, pp. 44–55

4. Boundary Stela of King Djoser

Third Dynasty, reign of Djoser
Limestone
H. 29.5 cm (11⅝ in.); w. 22.5 cm (8⅞ in.);
d. 6 cm (2⅜ in.)
Lent by the Oriental Institute of The University of
Chicago 13652

The large court south of Djoser's Step Pyramid has yielded a number of stelae bearing the name of the king and of two "daughters of the king," Inet-kaes and Hetep-her-nebti. (These women are also depicted on reliefs from Heliopolis [cat. no. 7b] and on small curved-top stelae found near the serdab north of the pyramid.) Present opinion holds that these stelae were erected at the start of construction on the pyramid, perhaps to mark off the sacred area or to delimit the vast space between the pyramid and the Southern Tomb.

There are nearly forty of these stelae, which were reused in the paneled revetment walls that line the south court. They look like truncated cones and are about 2 meters (80 inches) high with a base measuring 1 meter (40 inches) in diameter. Composed of several stacked half-drums of limestone, each bore a sculpted inscription arranged in a frame measuring about 20 centimeters (8 inches) per side. These inscriptions, carefully executed in the type of raised relief carved on the stelae in the Blue Chambers at Saqqara (cat. no. 1), are all identical. This fragment is one of the best preserved.

Near the center, "Netjeri-khet," Pharaoh Djoser's Horus name, is inscribed in three hieroglyphs on the walls of a palace surmounted by a divine falcon. On the right, the *imiut* fetish holds out its beneficent signs to the figure, symbolizing life and strength. Above the fetish is the dog of Anubis, the god associated with the *imiut* fetish, and his epithet, "He Who Presides over the Sacred Land." The names of the two princesses are inscribed at the left.

CZ

PROVENANCE: Saqqara, precinct of Djoser, Great Southern Court; purchased by James Henry Breasted 1926

BIBLIOGRAPHY: Firth and Quibell 1935, vol. 2, pl. 87(6); Lauer 1936–39, vol. 1, pp. 187–89, fig. 209; Porter and Moss 1978, p. 407

5. VASE WITH ROPE DECORATION

Third Dynasty
Egyptian alabaster
H. 63.5 cm (25 in.); diam. 19.1 cm (7½ in.)
Egyptian Museum, Cairo JE 65423

This vase, quite extraordinary in its dimensions, was discovered in an underground gallery of the Step Pyramid of Djoser at Saqqara. While excavating the complex, the archaeologists James E. Quibell and Jean-Philippe Lauer were surprised to discover about forty thousand vases of various shapes and materials. Since the ceilings of the corridors had collapsed, most of the vessels were broken. The fact that they were often arranged one inside another strongly suggests that they were placed there for safekeeping by Djoser, either after earlier tombs had been plundered or because such tombs were in poor condition. In any case, many of these vases do not date to the reign of Djoser but to the First or Second Dynasty, as inscriptions on certain vases attest. They are all of high quality, reflecting the skill and patience of the artisans, who had only modest tools available for hollowing out and decorating different types of stone, some of which—such as graywacke, granite, and amethyst—are very hard.

The decoration on the present example imitates rope, or rather a sling made of rope, that encircles the vase and creates a geometric motif. It probably represents a device designed to transport the vase, translated into a purely ornamental pattern. The knots and twills of the rope are rendered very realistically.   SL-T

PROVENANCE: Saqqara, Step Pyramid of Djoser, underground galleries, Egyptian Antiquities Service excavation

BIBLIOGRAPHY: Unpublished; for comparisons, see El-Khouli 1978; Saleh and Sourouzian 1987, nos. 19, 20

6. Statue Base with Enemy Heads

Third Dynasty
Egyptian alabaster
H. 19.5 cm (7¾ in.); w. 35 cm (13⅞ in.); d. 23 cm
(9⅛ in.)
Staatliche Sammlung Ägyptischer Kunst, Munich
ÄS 6300

On two faces of this alabaster block a pair of human heads has been sculpted side by side in high relief. Their features reflect two ethnic types that were depicted throughout the pharaonic period: the Near Eastern with full beard, aquiline nose, and high cheekbones, and the Libyan with round face and a goatee. Among the list of the pharaoh's traditional enemies only the Nubians are missing.

A rectangular cavity carved in the top of the block suggests that this object was the pedestal of a statue. The viewer must imagine it surmounted by the figure of a triumphant pharaoh, symbolically trampling his defeated enemies. This evocative theme, first introduced on Predynastic palettes,[1] was treated again on the pedestals of royal statues from the Archaic Period. These latter statues depict the sovereign in the costume of the Heb Sed, the ceremony in which he ritually renewed his strength.[2] From Djoser's complex at Saqqara came several statue bases very similar to this one in both form and decoration.[3] There,

chiseled faces emerge from the block of stone in an identical arrangement, and the features are individualized without compromising the general meaning of the group. For stylistic reasons, too, this work may be assigned to the Third Dynasty. The prominent cheekbones, thick mouths, and brutal energy of the foreign enemies of the pharaoh suggest the large statue of Djoser (fig. 29), and the flatness of the faces characterizes the nonroyal statuary of his era (see cat. nos. 11–13).   CZ

1. Midant-Reynes 1992, pp. 228–34.
2. For example, the statue of King Khasekhemui in the Egyptian Museum, Cairo, JE 32161; Saleh and Sourouzian 1987, no. 14.
3. Firth and Quibell 1935, pl. 57.

PROVENANCE: Unknown

BIBLIOGRAPHY: Wildung 1980a, p. 6; Wildung 1980b, pp. 260ff.; Schoske and Grimm 1995, p. 44, fig. 43; Grimm, Schoske, and Wildung 1997, no. 6; Donadoni Roveri and Tiradritti 1998, p. 265, no. 248

7A–C. DECORATED FRAGMENTS FROM THE CHAPEL OF KING DJOSER AT HELIOPOLIS

Third Dynasty, reign of Djoser
Limestone
a. H. 20 cm (7⅞ in.); w. 50 cm (19¾ in.)
Not in exhibition

b. H. 13.5 cm (5⅜ in.); w. 7 cm (2¾ in.)
c. H. 13 cm (5⅛ in.); w. 27 cm (10⅝ in.)
Soprintendenza al Museo delle Antichità Egizie,
Turin (a) 2671/15, (b) 2671/21, (c) 2671/20

Executed with exquisite refinement and precision, these reliefs once decorated a chapel built by Pharaoh Djoser at Heliopolis, not far from modern Cairo. Thirty-six fragments belonging to the same monument were discovered by the Italian archaeologist Ernesto Schiaparelli in the foundations of a later building, where they had been reused. It is not known what Djoser's temple looked like initially or why it was destroyed. The images and texts carved on the fragments are primarily invocations to the assembly of the nine creator gods of Heliopolis (the Ennead); they suggest that the chapel was dedicated to the jubilee feast, or Heb Sed, during which the pharaoh ritually renewed his strength (cat. no. 121). Images of the primordial gods are separated by columns of text immortalizing the words of protection they direct to the sovereign.

One fragment (a), which bears wishes

a

c

b

for "life, stability, dominion, and happiness" in a vertical column at left, shows, in the center, a palace facade with double doors. According to very old conventions, above the palace appears the pharaoh's Horus name, Netjeri-khet, of which only the last two signs survive. On each leaf of the door, two other elements of the royal titulary are finely sculpted: "King of Upper and Lower Egypt" and "He of the Two Ladies."

A second fragment (b), on which only the lower part of the scene has been preserved, depicts Djoser seated on a throne, one hand on his knees, the other holding the ceremonial flail, whose dangling ends are visible at the top of the block. Three small female figures are kneeling at the pharaoh's feet. Texts give the identity of the first two: "daughter of the king, Inet-kaes," followed by the queen, "she who sees Horus and Seth, Hetep-her-nebti." The identity of the third is unknown. She encircles the pharaoh's leg with her arm, in a pose that was later imitated in royal and nonroyal statuary (see cat. nos. 126, 130).[1]

The third fragment (c) depicts a seated god wearing a long wig and the "divine" beard, with curled tip. The powerful face, thick lips, and coarse profile of the deity are reminiscent of Djoser as he is depicted at Saqqara. A broad collar embellishes the plain, clinging garment from which one hand emerges to rest on the knees. The hieroglyph for "b," which appears above the figure and is probably the last sign of his name, suggests this is the god named Geb. A column of hieroglyphs records the deity's wishes for Pharaoh Djoser: "I give life, stability, dominion, and happiness eternally."

These fragments, which have extraordinary historical and religious importance, may be compared with the admirable stelae in the funerary complex of Djoser at Saqqara (see cat. no. 4). There is the same subtlety in the way the relief stands out against the background, the same precision in the details, and the same mastery in the carving and arrangement of the large hieroglyphs

CZ

1. Fay 1998, pp. 160–61, nos. 2 (Snefru), 3 (Djedefre).

PROVENANCE: Heliopolis, temple area, Schiaparelli excavation, 1903–6

BIBLIOGRAPHY: Schiaparelli, inv. ms. 1903–6, n. 2671; Weill 1911–12, pp. 9–26; Sethe 1933, pp. 153–54; Porter and Moss 1934, p. 61; Smith 1946, pp. 133–39; Roccati 1987, fig. 1; Curto 1988, fig. 48; Leospo 1989, pp. 199–201, figs. 301, 302; Kahl, Kloth, and Zimmermann 1995, pp. 114–19; Donadoni Roveri and Tiradritti 1998, pp. 260–61, nos. 239–41

8. STELA OF KING ZANAKHT

Third Dynasty, reign of Zanakht
Sandstone
H. 33 cm (13 in.); w. 41 cm (16⅛ in.)
Trustees of the British Museum, London, Egypt Exploration Fund 1905 EA 691

The image of a pharaoh beating the head of an enemy with his club as he grabs him by the hair is among the common themes that express the omnipotence of the sovereign of Egypt, great warrior and subduer. It appeared during the Archaic Period, on the tablets of King Den, for example (fig. 102).[1] The theme was repeated extensively

102. Ivory tablet of King Den, from Abydos. British Museum, London, EA 55586. Drawing by Thomas Scalise after Spencer 1996

on the pylons of temples, boundary stelae, and the most precious jewelry.[2] This is one of the earliest examples, rendered in relief. King Zanakht, Djoser's shadowy predecessor, or perhaps successor, is slaying a warrior (no longer visible) who personified the tribes of the Eastern Desert. The sovereign, whose name is inscribed at right on the wall of a palace surmounted by the falcon god Horus, is wearing the red crown, symbol of his power over Lower Egypt. In front of him on a shield was the emblem of the god Wepwawet, now lost. The few hieroglyphs surviving in the right corner of the fragment signify "turquoise," a highly prized stone, which the Egyptians went to the mountains of the Sinai peninsula to extract.

This relief, a large stela carved in the red sandstone of Wadi Maghara, comes from that region. Executed in the cliff itself under difficult conditions, and exposed to the elements for more than four millennia, it does not display the same sculptural qualities as reliefs almost as old from Saqqara or Heliopolis (cat. nos. 4, 7).

It belongs to a series of inscriptions with the names of kings Djoser, Sekhemkhet, and Zanakht that commemorate the first expeditions launched by the pharaohs to the so-called turquoise terraces. Distinguished from nonroyal inscriptions by their bellicose iconography, they magically mark the limits of the pharaoh's domain and immortalize his appropriation of the world. A text from the time of Djedkare-Isesi, a Fifth Dynasty pharaoh, reveals that royal troops also came to Wadi Maghara to seek another very precious resource, copper.[3]

CZ

1. See the palette in the British Museum, London, EA 55586.
2. Bonhême and Forgeau 1988, pp. 196–235.
3. Valbelle and Bonnet 1996, p. 3.

PROVENANCE: Wadi Maghara, Sinai

BIBLIOGRAPHY: Porter and Moss 1951, p. 340; Gardiner, Peet, and Černý 1952–55, vol. 2, p. 56; James 1961, p. 1, no. 1, pl. 1; Spencer 1993, p. 101, fig. 77

9. STELA OF KING QAHEDJET

Third Dynasty
Fine-grained limestone
H. 50.5 cm (19⅞ in.); w. 31 cm (12¼ in.); max. d. 2.8 cm (1⅛ in.)
Musée du Louvre, Paris E 25982

Aside from an inscription, the only decoration on this stela carved in low relief is the image of a sovereign in the embrace of a god with a falcon's head. The scene is framed by a relief border that is widest at the left and across the bottom of the slab.

The pharaoh is depicted standing, wearing the white crown, a false beard, a corselet, and a kilt adorned with an animal's tail. A dagger is passed through his belt. In his right hand he holds a mace with a pear-shaped head and in his left a long staff with a pointed tip and a flange in the middle, a type of staff well documented for the Old Kingdom.[1] The falcon-headed god Horus faces him, clasping the king's forearm with his left hand, while the right arm encircles the sovereign's shoulders as a sign of protection. This is one of the oldest known representations depicting Horus as a man with a falcon's head.

The two figures are identified by the hieroglyphs above them. At left the falcon perched atop the palace facade gives the king's Horus name, "Horus Qahedjet," while the facing hieroglyphs read "Horus in the Residence." The pharaoh is thus called by one of the many names that place him under the protection of Horus, tutelary god of royalty. Horus is depicted in the form worshiped in Heliopolis, a city near Cairo. Nothing is known about Qahedjet, who is sometimes identified with Huni, last king of the Third Dynasty.[2]

In its very shallow relief, which blends into the background, this stone carving is comparable to six stelae adorning the niches under Djoser's pyramid and Southern Tomb at Saqqara.[3] There is the same subtlety in the treatment of the human body, whose forms are rendered through slight gradations of the surface. The subtle modeling indicates the structure of the king's face, the more pronounced facial features of the divine falcon, the articulation of the knees,

and the musculature of the legs. This simple, perfectly ordered composition is echoed
in the large hieroglyphs that surmount the
scene. Even though the work is smaller
than the stelae of Djoser, we can assume
that, like them, it occupied the back of a
niche and stood out against a background
of blue-green faience (see cat. no. 1).   CZ

1. Fischer 1978, p. 24; Stewart 1979, fig. 2.
2. Vandier 1968b, pp. 16–22.
3. Firth and Quibell 1935, pls. 15–17, 40–42.

PROVENANCE: Unknown; purchased 1967

BIBLIOGRAPHY: Cenival 1968, p. 14; Vandier
1968a, p. 108; Vandier 1968b, pp. 16–22; Wildung
1969, p. 101, n. 4; Vandier 1974, p. 165, N4;
Beckerath 1984, p. 51c; Ziegler 1990a, pp. 21, 23;
Ziegler 1990b, pp. 54–57, no. 4; De Putter and
Karlshausen 1992, p. 66; Fischer 1992, p. 143;
Manniche 1994, p. 48; Michalowski 1994, fig. 28;
Ziegler 1994, p. 535, n. 43; Clayton 1995, p. 25;
Berman and Letellier 1996, pp. 36–37, 94; Val-
belle 1998, p. 38

10. MALE DEITY

Third Dynasty
Gneiss
H. 21.4 cm (8½ in.); w. 9.7 cm (3⅞ in.); d. 8.9 cm
(3½ in.)
Brooklyn Museum of Art, Charles Edwin Wilbour
Fund 58.192

This is one of the oldest surviving Egyptian
statues of a standing deity. The figure is
sculpted in a rare stone, anorthosite gneiss,[1]
known as Chephren's diorite, which Egyptians went searching for on the borders
of distant Nubia (see "Royal Statuary"
by Krzysztof Grzymski in this catalogue,
p. 53). The figure has his back to a broad
support with a curved top, whose shape is
suggestive of the royal stelae of Abydos.
Standing with his left leg forward, arms at
his sides, he is depicted in an attitude that
later became customary for statues of men.
His left fist is clenched, and his right hand
holds a knife. Its wide blade, pressed against
his thigh, stands out in sharp relief. The
torso is modeled with care, as are the bones
of the rib cage and knees. The figure is nude
except for a wide belt knotted in front, from
which a penis sheath is suspended. The full
face, framed by a broad, round wig, is organized in horizontal bands: the eyes, their
upper lids emphasized by a large pouch of
fat; the short, wide nose; and the horizontal
mouth, bordered at the bottom by the false
beard, which falls low on the chest. The
god's palpable strength is concentrated in
the broad shoulders, on which the head
seems to rest directly.

As the provenance of this work is unknown and there are no hieroglyphic inscriptions, dating must rest on stylistic criteria.
The unusual treatment of the knife, sculpted

partly in high relief, may be compared with
the carving of the scepter tipped up against
Sepa's right arm in the two large statues of
him from Saqqara (cat. nos. 11, 12). The
voluminous wig and the proportions of
the back support suggest a date prior to
the Fourth Dynasty. The archaic form of
the penis sheath and the long beard, which is
different from the one ordinarily worn by
pharaohs, suggest this is the statue of a deity,
Old Kingdom examples of which are very
rare. The god represented may be Onuris,
who is depicted in Egyptian iconography
with a penis sheath and round wig and who
sometimes brandishes a weapon. The statue
probably came from a sanctuary; possibly it
was part of a group of divine figures[2] placed
in small niches tucked away in the back of
chapels belonging to Djoser's funerary complex at Saqqara.   CZ

1. For this material, see Aston 1994, pp. 62–64.
2. The head of a similar statue is in the collection
of the Musées Royaux d'Art et d'Histoire,
Brussels, E 7039.

PROVENANCE: Unknown; Levy de Benzion
collection

BIBLIOGRAPHY: Wildung 1972, pp. 145–60;
Fazzini 1975, p. 24, no. 12; Vandersleyen 1975a,
no. 120; Karig and Zauzich 1976, no. 9; Smith
1981, p. 61, fig. 46; *Neferut net Kemit* 1983,
no. 11; Fazzini et al. 1989, no. 7; Seipel 1992,
p. 82, no. 7

Cat. nos. 13, 12, 11

11. Sepa Standing

Third Dynasty, before or during reign of Djoser
Painted limestone
H. 165 cm (65 in.); w. 40 cm (15¾ in.); d. 55 cm
(21⅝ in.)
Musée du Louvre, Paris N 37 (=A 36)

Purchased for the Louvre in 1837 with
the reliefs of Aa-akhti from Saqqara (cat.
no. 18), two large statues of Sepa (see also
cat. no. 12) and one of Lady Nesa (cat.
no. 13) undoubtedly originated at the same
site. All three statues are sculpted in a bioclastic limestone produced by bivalves and
gastropods; the quarry from which it was
cut may be at Helwan. The three figures
have retained abundant traces of colored
paint: black for the hair and eyes, and
green for the wide cosmetic bands used
in the Archaic Period.

They are the oldest known examples of
large Egyptian nonroyal statuary. The date
proposed is based on the inscription on a

shard found in the Step Pyramid of Djoser,
which mentions a titulary identical to
Sepa's, although the name has been lost.

Sepa is standing, and he apparently is
walking because his body weight seems to
fall on the advancing left leg. With his left
arm bent across his waist, he grips a staff.
In his open right hand he holds a scepter
with an elongated tip, which stands out in
sharp relief against his arm. The statue has
no back support, and, although its proportions are close to lifesize, it has a certain
massiveness and rigidity that are accentuated by such features as the very short
neck, the broad shoulders, the position of
the arms held tightly against the body, and
the thick legs and ankles.

A short, voluminous wig hugs the contours of the round face, concealing the ears
and extending to the base of the neck but
leaving the forehead uncovered. The carefully detailed rows of curls are all of equal
length. The top of the head has a circular
depression from which the locks of hair

radiate, forming a circle that organizes the
rest of the hairstyle. A wide band of green
cosmetic is drawn under the eyes, and the
upper lid of each eye forms a ridge that was
once highlighted in black; the inner corners
are drawn with a certain naturalism. On
the right eye the ridge extends to the outer
corner and around part of the lower lid.
The upper lids are indicated by a fold; the
fine eyebrows curve gently. The nose has
been restored. The upper lip of the sharply
outlined mouth is notched in the center by
a clearly defined philtrum. The placid face
is expressionless.

The modeling of the body is not pronounced. Such anatomical details as the
tendons in the neck and the individualized
clavicle shown as an almost horizontal
ridge are carefully rendered, however. On
the rounded pectorals the nipples are indicated by two circles in relief. The curve of
the abdomen is captured, with a recessed
round navel and the hipbones showing. No
muscles are visible on the flat arms. The

treatment of the back is even more under-stated: the upper body emerges from the plain kilt, a furrow represents the spinal column, and, more unusually, the shape of the shoulder blades is indicated by two symmetrical semicircles.

Seen from the front, the short kilt, fastened by a plain belt with an oval knot, is pleated along the right side; the pleats on either side of the staff are treated differently. On the statue's thick legs emphasis is given to the left knee with its quadrangular cap, flanked toward the top by two protuberances and accentuated by a ridge in the shape of a chevron, which joins the ridge of the tibia. The space between the legs has not been cut away, and only the external line of the right leg is sculpted. Like the left leg, it is treated with great simplicity: muscles are schematized as a vertical ridge, and a bump indicates the anklebone. The left-profile view reveals the silhouette of the thigh extending up beneath the kilt.

The inscriptions, which stand out in relief on the top of the pedestal, give the titles and name of Sepa: "Chief of the Tens of the South, Priest of Nezer and Kherty, Royal Acquaintance, *hery seqer*, Staff of the White Bull, Sepa." According to a practice that dates to the very beginning of the Old Kingdom, the inscriptions do not face the beholder but are arranged to be read from the side, from the front to the back of the statue. The right-profile view, which shows both legs, is the most important, as it is on reliefs of the same period.   CZ

PROVENANCE: Probably North Saqqara; Mimaut collection; purchased 1837

BIBLIOGRAPHY: Weill 1908, pp. 257–59, pl. 5; Bissing 1914, p. 5, pl. 5; Bénédite 1923, p. 276; Steindorff 1923, p. 316, pl. 176; Schäfer and Andrae 1925, p. 219; Boreux 1932, vol. 1, pp. 223–29, pl. 30; Weill 1938, p. 125; Scharff 1940, p. 46; Desroches 1941; Capart 1942, vol. 2, pl. 126; Hornemann 1951–69, no. 202; Shoukry 1951, pp. 58–59, fig. 9; Wolf 1957, pp. 131, 133, fig. 97; *Merveilles du Louvre* 1958, p. 44; Vandier 1958, pp. 41 n. 2, 61, 102, 126, fig. 664; Du Bourguet and Drioton 1965, pp. 115, 117, pl. 19; Michalowski 1968, figs. 201, 202; Vandier 1970, p. 10; Vandier 1974, p. 161, n. 2; Vandersleyen 1975a, pp. 218, 219, fig. 119a; Aldred 1978, pp. 182–83, figs. 177, 178; *Naissance de l'écriture* 1982, no. 27; Helck 1984, col. 590, n. 7; Ziegler 1990b, pp. 21, 24; De Putter and Karlshausen 1992, p. 65; Franke 1992; Manniche 1994, pp. 45–46; Tietz 1995, p. 100; Ziegler 1995b, pp. 167–69; Eaton-Krauss and Loeben 1997, pp. 83–87; Ziegler 1997a, pp. 141–44, no. 39, with earlier bibliography

11

12. SEPA STANDING

Third Dynasty, before or during reign of Djoser
Painted limestone
H. 169 cm (66⅝ in.); w. 44 cm (17⅜ in.);
d. 50.5 cm (19⅞ in.)
Musée du Louvre, Paris N 38 (=A 37)
Paris only

This statue is somewhat taller than the other
figure of Sepa in this exhibition (cat. no. 11)
but is identical in pose, costume, and features, as well as in style. There are a few
differences in treatment, however, some
attributable to the effects of wear.

Although they are not as clearly delineated, the eyebrows are more pronounced
than those of Nesa (cat. no. 13). The hori-
zontality of the mouth is tempered by the
notch in the upper lip. The modeling of
the wings of the nose, indicated by a slight
groove, is particularly well done. The indication of the shoulder blades with symmetrical semicircles is emphasized by two
curving furrows on either side of the spinal
column, which is rendered with a broader
and deeper groove. Old photographs of the
statue taken before it was restored show
two vertical ridges running the length of
the leg. The details of the knees are less
pronounced than in the other statue of
Sepa. The line of the clavicles also seems
more curved; it is continuous and forms a
ridge in the center. There are no nipples.
The left forearm forms an acute angle with
the upper arm. The left thumb is very flat
and more awkwardly carved.

The inscriptions, which stand out in relief on the top of the pedestal, give Sepa's
titles and name, and they are very similar to
those carved on his other statue.   CZ

PROVENANCE: Probably North Saqqara;
Mimaut collection; purchased 1837

BIBLIOGRAPHY: Weill 1908, pp. 257–59, pl. 5;
Boreux 1932, vol. 1, pp. 228–29, pl. 30; Vandier
1951, p. 3; Vandier 1970, p. 10; Ziegler 1990b,
pp. 21, 24; De Putter and Karlshausen 1992,
p. 65; Ziegler 1995b, pp. 167–69, pl. 63b,f;
Eaton-Krauss and Loeben 1997, pp. 83–87;
Ziegler 1997a, pp. 145–47, no. 40, with earlier
bibliography

13. NESA STANDING

Third Dynasty, before or during reign of Djoser
Painted limestone
H. 154 cm (60⅝ in.); w. 41 cm (16⅛ in.); d. 39 cm
(15⅜ in.); h., base 11 cm (4⅜ in.)
Musée du Louvre, Paris N 39 (=A 38)
Paris only

This statue of a woman named Nesa was
found covered to the hips with saltpeter;
treated in 1966, it remains extremely fragile. Nesa is standing with her feet together,
the traditional pose of female statue subjects. Her right arm is at her side; her left
arm is bent at a right angle and resting
on the stomach. Her sheath dress, with a
wide V-neck, reveals a body curiously similar to the figures of Sepa purchased for the
Louvre in the same year at Saqqara (cat.
nos. 11, 12): the head is set deep into the
shoulders; the shoulders and chest are very
wide, merging imperceptibly into a barely
indicated waist and hips; the ankles are thick
and the feet short. The identical treatment
flattens the figure's natural curves and accentuates the rigidity of the pose.

Only the slight swelling of the chest, the
nipples that show through the fabric, and
the discreet indication of the pubic triangle
reveal the subject's femininity, which is
attested primarily through the accessories:
the long wig and dress and the many rows
of bracelets, eleven on the left wrist and
twelve on the right.[1]

The broad, flat face with high forehead
is framed by an opulent tripartite wig.
Parted down the center of the crown, the
hair falls in three great masses of parallel
striated locks, each ending in tiers that give
the illusion that the hair is cut in three different layers. The view from above reveals
a part ending in a small round depression,
which divides the hair into three sections.
A wide band of green cosmetic extends
under the eyes, which are wide open; the
upper part of each eye is bordered by a
slight pouch highlighted in black. The eyelid is indicated by a fold; the fine eyebrows
molded in relief taper to a point at the temples. The tip of the nose has been restored.

There is a broad, well-marked groove
between nose and lips; the upper lip of the
small mouth, clearly outlined, its median
line curving slightly downward, is somewhat fuller than the lower lip. Like Sepa's,
the face is expressionless.

Although the contours of the body are
not pronounced, the clavicle has been carefully individualized with a V-shaped ridge
in the middle. The modeling is extremely
rudimentary on the flat arms and hands,
but the nails are delicately sculpted. The
left-profile view reveals an elegant silhouette that contrasts with the frontal view in
its slenderness, displaying the flat belly and
the curves of the thigh. The back is treated
with even more restraint: the head seems
to sink under the weight of the wig, whose
dark and imposing mass contrasts with the
body and makes it seem more svelte.

The inscriptions, which stand out in
relief on top of the pedestal, give the subject's title and name: "Royal Acquaintance,
Nesa." As with the statues of Sepa, the inscription stands out in relief in a rectangular frame, since the surface of the stone
has been carved away around it. The hieroglyphs are rather roughly shaped, with
very few details.   C Z

1. During the Fourth Dynasty, the representation
   of multiple bracelets came to an end. Their
   presence thus constitutes a criterion for dating
   an artwork. The tomb of Queen Hetep-heres I,
   wife of Snefru, has yielded a rich set of bracelets
   (cat. nos. 31, 32).

PROVENANCE: Probably North Saqqara; Mimaut
collection; purchased 1837

BIBLIOGRAPHY: Capart 1904, p. 257, fig. 183;
Weill 1908, pp. 259–60, pl. 5; Steindorff 1923,
p. 316, pl. 176; Boreux 1932, vol. 1, pp. 228–29,
pl. 30; Desroches Noblecourt 1941; Smith
1946, pl. 4c; Pijoán 1950, p. 128; Shoukry
1951, pp. 58–59, fig. 9; Vandier 1951, p. 3; Wolf
1957, p. 131, fig. 97; Vandier 1958, pp. 41, 63,
fig. 664; Fischer 1963, p. 32, n. 15; Vandier 1970,
p. 10; Vandier 1974, p. 161, n. 2; Vandersleyen
1975a, pp. 218, 219, fig. 119b; Ziegler 1990b,
pp. 21, 24; Hart 1991, p. 98; De Putter and Karlshausen 1992, p. 65; Vogelsang-Eastwood 1993,
p. 113; Manniche 1994, pp. 45–46; Ziegler
1995b, pp. 167–69, pl. 63c,d,g; Eaton-Krauss
and Loeben 1997, pp. 83–87; Ziegler 1997a,
pp. 112–15, no. 31, with earlier bibliography

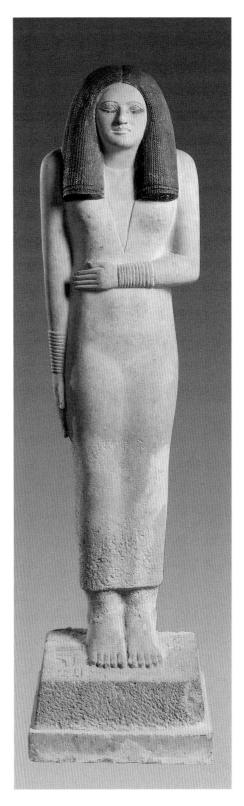

14. Ankh Seated with Hands Clasped

Third Dynasty, reign of Djoser
Gray porphyroid granite
H. 62.5 cm (24⅝ in.); w. 20.5 cm (8⅛ in.);
d. 32.5 cm (12⅞ in.); h., seat 24 cm (9½ in.),
including 6 cm (2⅜ in.) base
Musée du Louvre, Paris N 40 (=A 39)

Although the place where this statue was found is not known, Ankh can be identified as the high official whose name appears in a tomb at Beit Khallaf, not far from Abydos,[1] where an impression of the seal of King Djoser was also found. The Rijksmuseum van Oudheden in Leiden houses two statues that are probably of the same individual (see cat. no. 15).

The style of this statue is characteristic of the Third Dynasty. Ankh is shown sitting on a backless cubic seat that is decorated on three sides in imitation of the kind of stool with bentwood supports that was in use during the Third Dynasty. Dressed in a plain kilt with the end of a belt emerging from the waist, the figure has a stocky body that conforms to the cubic block of stone from which it was cut. Ankh's shoulders are very high, and his head is larger than lifesize. The pose with hands clasped on the lap is very rare in Egyptian art. Tilted slightly up, the round face is framed by a tripartite wig of medium length that conceals the ears. The locks that frame the subject's face fall in parallel rows from a central part. The hair does not follow the contours of the back of the head but hangs straight, and the ends are cut at an angle. The eyes are flush with the head; the upper

eyelid is emphasized by a slight fold ending at the outside corner, but no emphasis is given to the internal canthus. The eyebrows are thin and arched, and each is indicated by a ridge. The short, broad nose is unusually narrow at the base. The line of the full mouth is very schematic, especially the upper lip, which is not notched. The roundness of the face with its indefinite contours is accentuated by the carefully indicated depression under each eye and the puffiness around the eyelids, the heavy cheeks, the round chin, and the fatty neck. The torso is flat, with very high pectorals that are subtly accentuated; the nipples are executed in relief. No muscle structure is evident in the arms. The very flat hands—the right one placed on the palm of the left—are roughly outlined, and the thumbnail is indicated by a flattened tip. The heavy legs are close together and have thick ankles. The ridge of the tibia is pronounced, and the massive knees have been rendered as geometric shapes, with the patella emphasized by a chevron. Except for the toenails the feet are free of anatomical details, and these are summarily indicated by depressions. There is no support behind the figure, making it easy to see the back, which is divided by a vertical furrow and lacks indication of the shoulder blades.

Certain details were added after the statue was polished, including the rare *shenu* necklace, which resembles one found on a relief from King Snefru's time,[2] the bracelet adorning the right wrist, and the inscription on the knees: "Stolist (priest) of Horus, *medjeh ames*, Ankh." Like the inscriptions on the statues of Sepa and Nesa (cat. nos. 11–13), these are arranged to be read from the side, from the front to the back of the statue on the right leg, and from back to front on the left.   CZ

1. Garstang 1903, pp. 15–16.
2. Tomb of Iy-nefer, Dahshur, Egyptian Museum, Cairo, CG 57121.

PROVENANCE: Beit Khallaf?; Salt collection; purchased 1826

BIBLIOGRAPHY: Weill 1908, p. 181, n. 1; Spiegelberg 1918, p. 109; Keimer 1931, pp. 176–79; Boreux 1939a, pl. 1; Wolf 1957, pp. 49, 131, fig. 93; Vandier 1958, pp. 64, 126, fig. 661; Kanawaty 1985, p. 38, pl. 1a; Helck 1987, pp. 241–42; Kanawaty 1990, p. 268; Ziegler 1990b, pp. 21, 23; Seipel 1992, pp. 88, 89, no. 10; Tietz 1995, p. 103; Ziegler 1995b, pp. 172–73, pl. 64; Eaton-Krauss 1997, pp. 7–21; Ziegler 1997a, pp. 79–82, no. 22; Baud 1998, p. 76

15. ANKH WEARING TWO FELINE PELTS

Third Dynasty, reign of Djoser
Granodiorite
H. 79 cm (31⅛ in.)
Rijksmuseum van Oudheden, Leiden AST 18, D93

Although this statue of Ankh is slightly larger than the one in the Louvre (cat. no. 14), in several respects the two works are very similar: there is the same flat, round face framed by a tripartite wig of medium length, the same bentwood stool, the same high quality of workmanship, even the same granitic look to the stone. But the treatment of the face is not the same. Whereas the eyebrows of the Louvre statue are more arched and more prominent, in the Leiden statue the philtrum is more pronounced and the modeling is less vigorous. And, although Ankh's pose here—with his right hand on his knee and left hand on his chest—is more conventional than the very unusual pose of the Louvre statue, the accessories to his costume are unique in the whole of Old Kingdom statuary.

Here Ankh wears two feline pelts. The first is pulled over his left shoulder, and one paw hangs over his left knee. The second, lying on top of the first, covers his right shoulder, with one paw and the tail hanging on either side of his legs. Together, the two pelts form a V-neckline. The semicircular toggle pins depicted on Ankh's shoulders are regularly associated with a feline-pelt garment on reliefs.[1] Before the Fifth Dynasty this costume was apparently related to the royal cult and royal ceremonies, but in the famous Palette of Narmer in the Louvre, the king's sandal bearer is wearing the same type of pelt. The unusual feature here is that the toggle pins placed on the figure's chest like a coat of arms serve as a frame for the carved hieroglyphs that mention his name and titles. To his right they read "Ankh," and to his left, "high official, attendant to [the city of] Nekhen."

In the corpus of Third Dynasty statuary, then, these two statues of Ankh are distinguished by some very original characteristics. Should these features be seen as the mark of a specific function? According to a recently proposed hypothesis, the two statues of Ankh were housed not in a tomb but in a temple, so that they could continue to participate actively in the cult of a god or pharaoh.[2]

CZ

1. For example, a relief of Prince Iy-nefer in the Egyptian Museum, Cairo, CG 57121.
2. Eaton-Krauss 1997, pp. 12–13.

PROVENANCE: Beit Khallaf?; Anastasi collection; purchased 1829

BIBLIOGRAPHY: Leemans 1840, pt. 2, no. 93, pl. 20; Wiedemann 1898, pp. 269–73; Capart 1902, pl. 3; Boeser, Holwerda, and Holwerda 1905, pp. 10–11; Weill 1908, p. 181, n. 1; Keimer 1931, pp. 176–79; Vandier 1952b, p. 984, fig. 660; Vandier 1958, p. 64; Helck 1987, pp. 241–42; Tietz 1995, p. 103; Eaton-Krauss 1997, pp. 7–21; Schneider 1997

16. PRINCESS REDJIEF SEATED

Third Dynasty
Basalt
H. 83 cm (32¾ in.)
Soprintendenza al Museo delle Anitchità Egizie,
Turin C 3065

Sculptures of women from the Third Dynasty are rare. Best known are the painted limestone statue of Nesa (cat. no. 13) and the Lady of Brussels (Musées Royaux d'Art et d'Histoire, Brussels, E 752). This statue of Redjief is distinguished from both of these works by the subject's seated pose[1] and by the medium, a hard, dark stone commonly used during the same period for statues of men, which are much more numerous.[2]

The princess is sitting on a blocklike seat with decoration on four sides that evokes the bentwood chairs of the Archaic Period; the low back against which she leans is ordinarily reserved for sovereigns. Her feet together, she rests her right forearm on her thigh and holds her left arm, bent at a right angle, against her chest. Her sheath dress with a wide V-neck reveals a stocky body with very broad shoulders and chest; thick waist, hips, and ankles; and short feet. As in the statue of Nesa, the subject's natural curves are flattened and the rigidity of her pose is accentuated. Redjief's femininity is conveyed primarily by her costume: the long wig and dress and the bracelets adorning both forearms. Her head is set deep into her shoulders. Her face, broad and flat with a high forehead, is framed by an opulent tripartite wig characteristic of the Third Dynasty:[3] parted on the crown, the masses of hair fall outward and down in parallel striated locks that end in tiers, giving the wig a three-layered look. The upper part of the large eyelids is rimmed. The fine, raised eyebrows narrow to points at the temples. The mouth is large and wide. The precise treatment of the resolute face, highlighted by the polish on the dark stone, gives the piece a severity that makes it resemble more closely the statue of Pharaoh Djoser than that of Lady Nesa.

Inscriptions, which stand out in raised relief on the top front of the pedestal, give the title and name of the figure: "true daughter of the king, Redjief." This is the oldest surviving example of an inscribed statue depicting a woman from the Egyptian royal family. The rank of its owner explains the high quality of the sculpture and, no doubt, the form of the seat as well.   CZ

1. An Archaic Period statue, popularly titled Lady of Naples, that depicts a figure in the same attitude (Museo Archeologico Nazionale, Naples, 1076), actually represents a man.
2. Eaton-Krauss 1998, pp. 209–25.
3. See Cherpion 1998, pp. 97–142.

PROVENANCE: Unknown; Drovetti collection

BIBLIOGRAPHY: Seipel 1992, p. 86, no. 9; Cherpion 1998, pp. 103 n. 25, 134, fig. 14; Donadoni Roveri and Tiradritti 1998, p. 259, no. 238; Eaton-Krauss 1998, p. 210; Fay 1998, pp. 159–60, 170–71, no. 1, figs. 1, 2; Sourouzian 1998, pp. 322, 346, fig. 37

17. RELIEF OF HESI-RE

Third Dynasty, reign of Djoser
Acacia wood
H. 86 cm (33⅞ in.); w. 41 cm (16⅛ in.)
Egyptian Museum, Cairo CG 1430

This panel is one of a group of six in the Egyptian Museum, Cairo. Five were found by Auguste Mariette and transported to the museum in 1866. The sixth was discovered by James E. Quibell in 1912. All are from the mastaba of Hesi-re, a high official of King Djoser, whose titles included Greatest of the King's Scribes, Chief of the Tens of Upper Egypt, and Chief of Dentists. His mastaba, located north of the funerary complex of Djoser at Saqqara, was built primarily of unbaked brick. Hesi-re's offering chapel takes the form of a long corridor and includes, on one side, very unusual paintings depicting funerary furnishings (among them vases, chests, and games) and, on the other, eleven niches. A carved wood panel was fitted into the back of each of these niches. Five have disappeared; the other six depict Hesi-re seated or standing, wearing different hairstyles and costumes but always with the royal scribe's insignia (a palette with two compartments for ink, a long pen case, and a small bag), indicating the importance of his position at a time when the corps of scribes was still small. The lower part of the present panel is badly damaged and incomplete. A large crack mars the upper section.

Sculpted in low relief, Hesi-re is seen standing with his right arm at his side; in his left hand, held up at chest level, is a staff. The scribe's palette is placed on his right shoulder. He is wearing a short, round wig with straight locks at the crown and rows of curls below. His nose is slightly hooked, and he has a mustache. The rest of the panel's surface is covered with hieroglyphs. The upper section gives Hesi-re's name and titles; below, in front of him, an offering formula enumerates the food and drink the deceased will need in the afterlife (bread, beer, beef, fowl, and other essentials), accompanied by the sign for "one thousand," which is intended to multiply them magically.

Because it can be precisely dated, and because the proportions of the figure are elegant and its details and expression realistic,

the panel is considered one of the most important reliefs from the Old Kingdom.

SL-T

PROVENANCE: Saqqara, mastaba of Hesi-re (Mariette mastaba A 3), Mariette excavation, 1866

BIBLIOGRAPHY: Quibell 1913, p. 40, pl. 30; Borchardt 1937, p. 110, pl. 27; Capart 1937, pl. 407; Pijoán 1945, fig. 110; Porter and Moss 1978, p. 439; Saleh and Sourouzian 1987, no. 21 (for comparison)

18. RELIEF BLOCK WITH THE FIGURE OF AA-AKHTI

Late Third Dynasty
Fine-grained limestone with faint remains of paint
H. 184 cm (72½ in.); w. 83 cm (32¾ in.); d. 18 cm
(7⅛ in.)
Musée du Louvre, Paris B 1

This beautiful relief decorated a door recess
that provided access to a mortuary chapel.
The block is sculpted on two perpendicular
faces, and the narrower one simply bears
the titles of the deceased. The main face
still has traces of red and black paint. The
owner of the tomb, Aa-akhti, is depicted
on foot, walking out of the chapel, a long
staff in one hand and a *sekhem* scepter in
the other. He is wearing a short wig with
curls distributed in even rows.[1] His long
tunic is of an unusual type; it leaves the
left shoulder bare and is decorated with a
pleated panel in the front, adorned with
a large knot.

The figure may appear odd to modern
eyes because it combines different perspec-
tives: the profile face with a frontal eye;
the frontal shoulders twisting into a profile
view of hips and legs; the inner profile of
the foot with an arch and a single toe. In
short, the image does not reproduce reality
but, by using conventions that were established very early, recapitulates the most
characteristic aspects of the individual represented. It is these conventions, linked to
the purpose of the artwork in question—
the image must be effective and recognizable so that it can magically replace the
human model—that give Egyptian relief
its inimitable originality.

The columns of hieroglyphs above the
figure complement the representation and
identify the important dignitary. His name
is given, and Royal Governor and Chief
Architect to the King are among the numerous titles he bears.

Although the location of Aa-akhti's
tomb is unknown, there are strong reasons
to believe it was situated in the necropolis
of North Saqqara, since two of its blocks
were reused in the modern village of Abusir,
which is north of the site. An effort has
been made to rebuild the Archaic Period–
style cruciform chapel from the fragments
dispersed among several museums.[2] The
lower part of a statue of the same individual, also in the Archaic Period style, is in

the Ägyptisches Museum und Papyrussammlung, Berlin (14277). Aa-akhti bears
the title Priest of the Temple of Nebka and
thus could not have lived before the reign
of this sovereign. His monuments are usu-

ally dated to the Third Dynasty. This relief
is one of the finest of the period. With its
large masses clearly set off from the background and the vigor with which the silhouette stands out, it contrasts with the

stelae of Djoser. The particular sharpness of the outlines and the terseness of the style are manifest even in the large, closely spaced hieroglyphs, each made with an incisive stroke.   cz

1. With high and tapering crown; see Cherpion 1989, pp. 55–56, criteria 28, 30.
2. Louvre, Paris, B1, B2; Ägyptisches Museum, Universität Leipzig, 2897; Ägyptisches Museum und Papyrussammlung, Berlin, 1141, 1142, 15302, 15303 (Smith 1942, pp. 518–20).

PROVENANCE: North Saqqara; Mimaut collection; purchased 1837

BIBLIOGRAPHY: Weill 1908, pp. 262–73; Capart 1914b, pp. 27, 28, pl. 14; Boreux 1932, vol. 1, pp. 238, 239; *Encyclopédie photographique* 1935, pp. 8, 9; Reisner 1936, pp. 206, 282, 364; Capart 1942, pl. 422; Smith 1942, pp. 518–20; Smith 1946, pp. 149–51, pl. 35; Jelinkova 1950, pp. 335, 339–40; Vandier 1951, p. 11; De Wit 1956, pp. 94–95; Wolf 1957, p. 203, fig. 171; Smith 1958, pp. 36, 37; Kaplony 1963, pp. 450 n. 672, 467; Smith 1971, p. 16; Goedecken 1976, pp. 128–30; Martin-Pardey 1976, p. 235; Leclant et al. 1978, p. 284, fig. 288; Porter and Moss 1978, p. 500; Strudwick 1985, p. 217; Chevereau 1987, p. 36, no. 184; Harpur 1987, p. 272, no. 336; Ziegler 1990b, pp. 96–100, no. 14, with earlier bibliography; Fischer 1992, p. 143; Bietak 1996, p. 198, n. 12; Sourouzian 1998, pp. 323, 347, fig. 40

19A–C. THREE BRACELETS

Third Dynasty, reign of Sekhemkhet
Gold
a. Diam. 7.5 cm (3 in.); w. 1.4 cm (½ in.)
b. Diam. 5.6 cm (2¼ in.); d. 1.1 cm (⅜ in.)
c. Diam. 7.3 cm (2⅞ in.); d. 1.6 cm (⅝ in.)
Egyptian Museum, Cairo JE 92655–53, 92655–56, 92655–70

Sekhemkhet, King Djoser's successor, undertook the construction at Saqqara of a vast funerary complex similar to that of his predecessor. Excavations conducted inside Sekhemkhet's uncompleted step pyramid at that site led to the discovery of a very fine group of jewelry. Among the items found in the shaft leading to the funerary chamber were a small, shell-shaped gold box and a bracelet made up of 388 gold beads arranged in ten rows and held together by five bead spacers, as well as many other beads of gold, faience (sometimes covered with gold), and carnelian scattered on the ground. Twenty-one bracelets—closed gold-leaf hoops, their

edges curled slightly inward and most formed into a beautiful, regular shape—complete the group. The large number of bracelets found can be explained by the fact that Egyptians of the time liked to wear several bracelets piled up on the forearms (see cat. no. 13).

Perhaps originally housed in a chest that had disintegrated by the time of discovery, this jewelry is the only extant group from the Third Dynasty and must have belonged to a woman from the royal family. It is tempting to compare these pieces to the set from the early Fourth Dynasty belonging to Queen Hetep-heres I, which also includes several bracelets (cat. nos. 31, 32) and similarly attests to the virtuosity of artisans at the beginning of the Old Kingdom.

PR

PROVENANCE: Saqqara, pyramid of Sekhemkhet, Egyptian Antiquities Service excavation

BIBLIOGRAPHY: Ghoneim 1957, pp. 13–14, pls. 31–34

20A–C. THREE BRACELETS

Third Dynasty
Ivory
Diam. 4.7–5.1 cm (1⅞–2 in.)
Trustees of the British Museum, London
EA 68316, 68317, 68318

Their small size suggests that these brace-lets, reconstructed from fragments found in the ruins of a Third Dynasty mastaba, probably belonged to a child. Simple, regu-lar hoops, flat on the inside and slightly rounded on the outside, they resemble the thin ivory or stone bracelets worn in earlier periods. In the Old Kingdom such bracelets were worn, alone or in combination, on one or both arms. Altogether comparable exam-ples dating from the Fourth Dynasty have been found at Mostagedda, in the tomb of a child buried with three ivory bracelets on the right arm and four on the left.[1]

Ivory hoops were common in the Old Kingdom,[2] but bracelets were also made of bone,[3] tortoiseshell,[4] horn,[5] calcite,[6] and metal (for examples of the last, see cat. nos. 19, 166).   PR

1. Mostagedda, tomb 2821; see Brunton 1937, p. 96, pl. 63.

2. For other examples, see Brunton 1948, tombs 800 and 817, p. 32 (Sixth Dynasty); and Reis-ner 1932, tombs N 579, N 760, pls. 39d,e.
3. Brunton 1948, pl. 35.25, tomb 865 (Sixth Dynasty).
4. Petrie 1901a, p. 38, cemetery N, tomb N 19 (Sixth Dynasty).
5. Brunton 1937, tombs 243, 3540, pp. 97, 98 (Fifth Dynasty), tombs 677, 10002, p. 99 (Sixth Dynasty).
6. Valloggia 1986, vol. 2, pl. 72, inv. no. 1128 (Sixth Dynasty).

PROVENANCE: Saqqara, Egypt Exploration Soci-ety excavation

BIBLIOGRAPHY: Spencer 1980, p. 77, no. 566, pl. 62; Andrews 1981, p. 38

FOURTH DYNASTY

21. COLOSSAL HEAD

Late Third or early Fourth Dynasty
Red granite
H. 54.3 cm (21⅜ in.); w. 29 cm (11½ in.)
Brooklyn Museum of Art, Charles Edwin Wilbour
Fund 46.167

This larger-than-lifesize head is generally dated to the beginning of the Old Kingdom, between the end of the Third Dynasty and the reign of Khufu near the beginning of the Fourth. Unfortunately, because there is no inscription and the provenance is unknown, the subject's identity can be discussed solely on the basis of style. The head is unusually large. Few colossal statues were made in the Old Kingdom, but the earliest of them date from the Third Dynasty, in Djoser's time, when monumental architecture in stone began to flourish. King Khafre also was a great builder (cat. no. 65) and left monumental sculptures depicting members of his family.

This statue is carved in a hard red granite whose surface has never been polished. Traces of a white coating on the crown suggest it was painted. The very broad face evokes the countenance of a tiny ivory statuette inscribed with the name of Khufu in the Egyptian Museum, Cairo (JE 36143). The stern expression and deep lines around the mouth are reminiscent of such austere images of Djoser and his contemporaries as the large Cairo statue (fig. 29), reliefs in the Step Pyramid complex at Saqqara, and panels with Hesi-re (cat. no. 17) and Kha-bau-sokar (see "The Human Image in Old Kingdom Nonroyal Reliefs" by Nadine Cherpion in this catalogue, pp. 104–7). The small, wide-set eyes, treated naturalistically, also bring to mind the images of Djoser and his court, as do the broad nostrils with sharply pronounced contours. The pharaoh is wearing the white crown, symbolizing his sovereignty over Upper Egypt. The tabs on either side of the disproportionately large ears belong iconographically to the Second Dynasty and are identical in type to those depicted on the ivory statuette of Khufu mentioned above. The mantle, which rises high on the neck and conceals the bottom of the crown, is probably the kind worn during the Heb Sed, when the pharaoh ritually renewed his strength.[1]

With its muscular neck and impassive face, the head is one in a series of early large royal statues that evoke the absolute power of the king of Egypt in a fairly brutal manner. It anticipates the more subtle and accomplished artworks produced in large numbers during the reigns of Djedefre, Khafre, and Menkaure. Although there is still room for uncertainty, this colossal head can be called, with a high degree of probability, a likeness of the builder of the Great Pyramid.   CZ

1. Sourouzian 1995, pl. 42, n. 39.

PROVENANCE: Unknown

BIBLIOGRAPHY: Cooney 1948, pp. 1–12; Fazzini 1975, no. 15a; *Neferut net Kemit* 1983, no. 9; Fazzini et al. 1989, no. 9; Stadelmann 1998a, p. 365, n. 63

b

a

22A,B. TWO RELIEF FRAGMENTS FROM DAHSHUR

Fourth Dynasty, reign of Snefru
Limestone with faint remains of paint
a. H. 93 cm (36⅝ in.); w. 24 cm (9½ in.)
b. H. 55 cm (21⅝ in.); w. 50 cm (19¾ in.)
Egyptian Museum, Cairo (a) JE 98949,
(b) JE 98950

Ahmed Fakhry discovered many important inscribed blocks during his 1952 excavations at the statue-cult temple of the Bent Pyramid of Snefru. Among them were these two fragments depicting female figures, found near the eastern wall under the debris of the central hall. The women, who represent royal estates from the nomes of Egypt, are all similarly depicted. Each wears a wig and a long, tight dress; each balances on her left hand a *hetep*-shaped offering table that holds loaves of bread and a *heset* vase; and each bears the ankh hieroglyph in her right hand.

Carved in low relief and originally painted, the figures still reveal traces of pigment indicating that the skin was yellow and that the dresses had a geometric pattern of red, blue, yellow, and black squares familiar from tomb paintings of the Fourth and Fifth Dynasties.

Fakhry determined that the original temple was a simple rectangular structure with a north-south axis. A narrow hall was entered through a doorway on the south side, and friezes decorated the long eastern and western walls. The western friezes showed royal estates from the nomes of Upper Egypt, the eastern ones from those of Lower Egypt; together they assured that offerings for the king were provided perpetually from all the provinces. Surmounting these representations of the estates was a large-scale depiction of the king in the company of various gods, clearly intended to demonstrate the direct relationship the sovereign enjoyed with the divinities.   ZH

PROVENANCE: Dahshur, statue-cult temple of Snefru, Fakhry excavation, 1952

BIBLIOGRAPHY: Fakhry 1961b

23. Scenes from a King's Thirty-Year Jubilee

Fourth Dynasty, probably reign of Snefru
Limestone with remains of paint
H. 73.6 cm (29 in.); w. 149.8 cm (59 in.)
The Metropolitan Museum of Art, New York (left fragment) Rogers Fund and Edward S. Harkness Gift, 1922 22.1.1; (right fragment) Rogers Fund, 1909 09.180.18

When King Amenemhat I (about 1991–1962 B.C.E.), first ruler of the Twelfth Dynasty, decided late in life to build a pyramid for himself close to his new capital at Lisht, about thirty miles south of present-day Cairo, he ordered his workmen to collect stones from decaying Old Kingdom pyramid precincts and incorporate them into the inner structure of his own monument.[1] Many of these blocks, which still carry relief decoration made for their original owners, were discovered by archaeologists of the Metropolitan Museum when they excavated Amenemhat's funerary precinct and pyramid at Lisht between 1906 and 1922. The origin of the reused blocks can sometimes be determined from the names of the kings that appear in their inscriptions. However, these two blocks from a representation of the thirty-year jubilee ritual of a pharaoh (the Heb Sed, or Sed festival)[2] do not furnish

the name of a king, and their attribution to a specific Old Kingdom building must, therefore, be based on the style of the relief. Goedicke, who first studied the two blocks in detail, believed they were originally carved for Khufu's pyramid temple at Giza, but this cannot be correct, as the reliefs differ markedly from examples dated to Khufu's reign by inscriptions (for instance, cat. nos. 38, 41).[3]

In terms of both the height and style of relief the present blocks are comparable only to works from the time of Khufu's father, Snefru. The figures stand out boldly in high relief and are entirely surrounded by straight edges that meet the background at right angles. These characteristics were common to works of the Third Dynasty (cat. nos. 17, 18) and continued to appear during Snefru's reign, as demonstrated by the estate reliefs from this king's statue-cult temple at Dahshur (cat. no. 22);[4] the reliefs of Khufu's monuments are considerably lower and make use of edges of this kind only around certain parts of the figures, for instance, along the backs of the cattle in cat. no. 38. Especially close to the present scenes in height and roundness of sculptured surface are the reliefs from the tomb of Ra-hotep, who was a high official of Snefru and would have had his tomb decorated late in that pharaoh's reign or at the

very beginning of the reign of Khufu.[5] Iconographic details corroborate a close relationship between the Ra-hotep reliefs and the Heb Sed blocks. In Ra-hotep's tomb there is, for instance, a representation of a man with a rope over his shoulder whose right arm overlaps his head, and the arm of the standard-bearer in the jubilee relief is shown in a similar way.[6] Such overlaps are usually avoided in Egyptian art.

It is not easy to determine from which building of Snefru's later reign the jubilee blocks could have derived. The preserved reliefs of Snefru's statue-cult temple are somewhat flatter and cruder than the relief on the Lisht blocks. However, very fragmentary remains of reliefs showing a Heb Sed that once adorned the temple at Snefru's latest funerary monument, the northern stone pyramid at Dahshur, recently excavated by Stadelmann, display a roundness similar to that of the present reliefs.[7] The Lisht blocks can, therefore, be tentatively assigned to Snefru's pyramid precinct at the northern stone pyramid at Dahshur, although his name does not appear on a reused block from Lisht. We have no knowledge of any building erected by Khufu during the very first years of his reign.

The figures on the Lisht blocks are playing parts in the thirty-year jubilee, that important occasion for the rejuvenation of

Egyptian kings through ritual. On the left block the goddess Meret stands in the middle of the remaining three registers, left of center on a rectangle bearing the hieroglyphic sign for "gold."[8] She is described in the inscription behind her as "Meret of the Upper Egyptian lands." Meret's role in the Heb Sed rituals was to invigorate the king; acting as a kind of divine cheerleader, she raises her arm in a gesture that recalls the clapping of hands that was a customary part of Egyptian musical performances. The inscription in front of the goddess provides the words of her chant: "Recitations spoken: Come and bring, come and bring." The figure of the king to whom she addresses her words is broken off the left edge of the block. The evidence provided by other representations of the festival tell us that he towered over two registers: the one in which mortals and Meret are depicted and the one above it, of which little remains. In this scene the king performed a ritual race that was a major feature of all Heb Seds.[9] His movement is mirrored here in the pace of the standard-bearer, who precedes him. The artist has, moreover, positioned this man in rich priestly costume on a ground line higher than that of the other figures to ensure that the top of his standard, with its sacred emblem, is held above the head of the running king. The standard-bearer's ritual title "Servant of

the Bas (ancestral spirits) of Nekhen (an ancient city in Upper Egypt)" was written behind him; however, only part of one hieroglyph remains.

The proceedings are attended by various court officials. In front of the standard-bearer kneels a man whose title the inscription gives as "courtier." The importance of the courtier's presence is underlined by the fact that a representation of the sky spreads over him as well as Meret. To the right of the goddess is a group of six men, the first three of whom are identified, from left to right, as "lector-priest," "celebrant," and "chamberlain," while the last three, dressed in especially elaborate costumes, are labeled "Controllers of the Palace."[10]

There are scant remains of a register above and a register below the one showing Meret and the courtiers. The lowest register was crowned by a sky emblem decorated with stars, and the remnants of an inscription here refer to "coming forth from . . . ," doubtless part of the depiction of another ritual. The uppermost register was more closely connected with the one in which Meret and the courtiers appear. There is only a simple horizontal band between these two registers. The torso and head of the large figure of the running king must have been level with the uppermost register. Of the elements in that register,

only part of an inscription is preserved. It states that some spell or other is being spoken "four times." Still visible to the right are the legs of a man and a portion of a staircase that probably ascended to a throne upon which the king would sit at the conclusion of the ritual.

This scene in which a pharaoh is so pointedly encouraged and protected by a divine personage and various court attendants bears witness to both the sacred nature and the vulnerability of Egyptian kingship. When contemplating the monumental pyramids of the Old Kingdom, we should remember that kings needed protection at least as much as confirmation of their power.   DOA

1. Goedicke 1971, pp. 1–2, 4–7. The most recent discussion of Amenemhat's use of Old Kingdom building blocks is Jánosi 1988, p. 74.
2. For this festival and its representations in Egyptian art, see in general, Kaiser 1971, pp. 87–105; and Martin 1984, cols. 782–90, with earlier biography.
3. Goedicke (1971, pp. 35, 38) accounted for this difference by assigning the jubilee blocks to the pyramid temple and the reliefs bearing the name of Khufu to the valley temple (see ibid., pp. 11, 13, 16, 18, 19, 20). However, in no other Old Kingdom pyramid precinct do the reliefs of the valley temple, causeway, and pyramid temple differ from one another in style to the extent observed here.
4. Fakhry 1961b, pls. 13–32.

Detail, cat. no. 23

5. For the date of the Ra-hotep reliefs, see Smith 1946, p. 149 (dating the tomb firmly to Snefru); Martin-Pardey 1984a, col. 83 (rejecting the date to the reign of Khufu maintained in Schmitz 1976, p. 142); and Harpur 1987, pp. 177 (dating the tomb to Khufu), 373 (to the time of Snefru and Khufu). Harpur points out (ibid., pp. 178–79) that the reliefs of Ra-hotep and Nefer-maat are closely related in terms of iconography and furnishes evidence that Ra-hotep's are further advanced than Nefer-maat's. The famous statues of Ra-hotep and Nofret indicate without doubt that his tomb dates before the majority of the works created in the reign of Khufu. For the group, see Russmann 1989, pp. 16–19. For relatively good illustrations of some of the Ra-hotep reliefs, see Smith 1946, pls. 34, 35; and Quirke and Spencer 1992, p. 36, fig. 23.

6. Petrie 1892, pl. 10. See also Smith 1946, pp. 315–16, and Harpur 1987, p. 179. For a Fifth Dynasty version of the standard-bearer, see cat. no. 121.

7. Stadelmann 1983, pp. 233–34, pl. 73. For the date of the northern pyramid in relation to other monuments of Snefru, see ibid., p. 235; and Stadelmann 1991, p. 100.

8. Berlandini 1982, cols. 80–88. For the costume and base of the goddess, see Goedicke 1971, pp. 37–38, with the interesting suggestion that the sign for "gold" on the pedestal of the goddess was originally gilded.

9. See Bissing and Kees 1923, no. 33b, pl. 13; and Jéquier 1938, pl. 12.

10. For details and parallels in other works, see Goedicke 1971, pp. 38, 40.

PROVENANCE: Lisht North, pyramid of Amenemhat I, core of pyramid on north side, Metropolitan Museum of Art excavation, 1908–9 (left fragment); pyramid of Amenemhat I, precise find spot not noted, Metropolitan Museum of Art excavation, 1920–22 (right fragment)

BIBLIOGRAPHY: Goedicke 1971, pp. 35–41, nos. 16, 17

24A–C. Paste-Filled Reliefs from the Tomb of Itet

Fourth Dynasty, reign of Snefru
Limestone with paste fill of gypsum (white and
black-gray) and ocherous clay (red and yellow)
mixed with small amounts of organic matter[1]

a. H. 100 cm (39⅜ in.); w. 114 cm (44⅞ in.)
Ny Carlsberg Glyptotek, Copenhagen AEIN 1133 A

b. H. 61 cm (24 in.); w. 122 cm (48 in.)
Ny Carlsberg Glyptotek, Copenhagen AEIN 1133 B

c. H. 52 cm (20½ in.); w. 115 cm (45¼ in.)
Staatliche Sammlung Ägyptischer Kunst, Munich
GL. 103e–f

Nefer-maat, vizier and, according to the
inscription on his tomb, "eldest son" of
King Snefru, was buried in a huge mastaba
close to Snefru's pyramid at Meidum.[2]
Nefer-maat's wife, Itet, was buried in the
same mastaba, where she had her own
chapel for her funerary cult (fig. 103). Among
the inscriptions in Itet's chapel is one that
has always intrigued Egyptologists.[3] Carved
in front of a figure of Nefer-maat—who is
fairly conspicuously represented in his wife's
tomb—it boasts that "he made his pictures
in a [kind of] drawing that cannot be erased."
This statement appears to refer to the technique of filling reliefs with paste that was
used in the innermost tomb chapels of both
Nefer-maat and Itet. In this technique figures
and hieroglyphs were carved into limestone
blocks as recessed areas that the artist filled
with colored paste. Undercut edges along
the outlines of small figures and signs, as well
as rows of deep cells divided by diagonally
drilled ridges inside larger ones, helped
anchor the paste. Pastes were formed of
ocherous clay, gypsum, and other pigments,
which were consolidated with a binder of
resin; when colors were made of more valuable materials, such as malachite (for green),
these were applied in thin layers over an
ocherous-clay substratum. Pastes of different
colors were packed beside one another, and
small amounts of one paste were inlaid into
large areas of another to achieve a variety
of effects. In the final stage of the process,
a fatty substance appears to have been
employed to polish the surface of the pastes
and enhance their colors.[4] Unfortunately,
Nefer-maat's claim that he had invented a
method for producing especially long-lasting
tomb decoration proved to be incorrect; the
pastes did not survive well, and the technique was abandoned—except for use in a
few inscriptions (cat. nos. 44, 45)—after

a

b

c

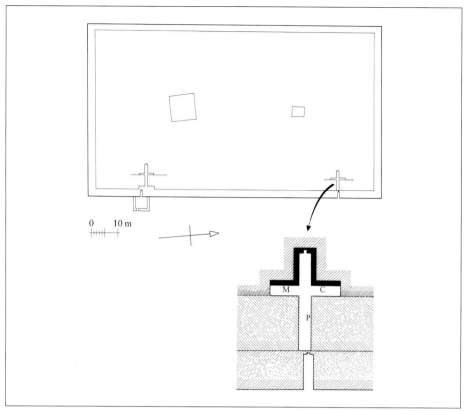

103. Plan of mastaba of Nefer-maat and Itet, Meidum, showing in detail three building phases of chapels of Itet. Drawing by Dieter Arnold after Gerald Wainwright in Petrie, Mackay, and Wainwright 1910, pl. 3, and Petrie, Wainwright, and Mackay 1912 and after Smith 1937, fig. 2

the one attempt in the tomb of Nefer-maat and Itet.

The paste-filled reliefs were, however, a failure only in the area of technique. Stylistically and iconographically they constitute an important step in the development of Egyptian art. Indeed they introduce images and motifs that became common in succeeding Old Kingdom representations and in works of later times as well. Moreover, the number of scenes included is impressively large in comparison with the tomb of Metjen (cat. no. 29), for instance, which was decorated earlier in the reign of Snefru than these reliefs; in fact, the richness of detail in the Itet reliefs has given rise to the suggestion that many more pictorial works existed in the time before the reign of Snefru than are preserved. (Most of these may well have been paintings [see cat. no. 25].[5])

The blocks from Copenhagen and Munich clearly reveal the quality and intriguing content of the paste reliefs. One of the Copenhagen reliefs (b) formed the uppermost of six registers that decorated the north outer face of Itet's stone-lined chapel (fig. 103c).[6] The two offering bearers seen marching toward the chapel entrance

constitute an image characterized by a remarkable combination of formalism and variety. An inscription in front of the first man states that the scene depicts the "taking the wine of the washing of the mouth," that is, breakfast, in this context a part of the offering ritual.[7] Another inscription, at the right end of the block, identifies as figs the small round fruits on two tables. The first man supports a pair of jars on his right hand while balancing a single vessel on his left.[8] Pairs of wine jars joined together in a single basket were commonly depicted during the Old Kingdom and indeed constituted a hieroglyph.[9] In fact, the unrealistically thin, elongated shape of the jars and the impossible balancing act the offering bearer is performing here suggest that the artist was more concerned with representing the hieroglyphic sign than actual vessels. Only one arm of the second man is shown; on it, in the manner of a fertility figure (cat. no. 113), he bears a low table covered with figs. The contrasting poses of the two bearers not only create variety but also produce a sense that the men are moving away from the table on the floor. Pieces of red and yellow paste remain.

The second Copenhagen relief (a) formed the lowest part of the wall that was surmounted by the block showing the men with wine and figs (fig. 103c).[10] Its two registers are of unequal heights. In the upper and taller one, two men draw shut a clapnet in which they have caught three ducks, while another bird, which has escaped, flies off. The inscription reveals that the men are not ordinary fowlers but "the courtiers Seref-ka and Wehem-ka," who are known from other images in the tomb to have been sons of Nefer-maat and Itet.[11] The image has a close parallel in a paste-filled relief on the front of Nefer-maat's stone-lined inner chapel,[12] where, however, all four birds are caught in the net and two grazing geese and a few plants are also included.[13] Itet's clapnet scene, like the depiction of the wine bearer, shows a close relationship to writing. The three symmetrically grouped overlapping ducks, for instance, almost certainly stand for the plural of the word "duck," which in hieroglyphics is as a rule indicated by the repetition of three signs or three strokes. The group of the two figures drawing the trap closed is a remarkably skillful composition, with its intricate yet clearly disposed interaction of four arms and legs. The kneeling posture of the men eloquently expresses the strength they bring to bear on the rope; it is, however, also a clever device that allowed the artist to avoid a large discrepancy between two tall standing figures and the small clapnet and enabled him to fit the scene into a fairly narrow register. The flying bird, although damaged, can still be appreciated as a strikingly naturalistic image untouched by the conventionalism that marks many later pictures of this type.

The lower register on the second Copenhagen block is narrower than the upper; here the potential discrepancy in height between the human and animal figures, as well as the need to fit them into the allotted space, is dealt with by introducing a child, identified as such by his nudity, as the keeper of the monkeys shown. In the parallel scene from Nefer-maat's tomb, monkeys are pictured with two children who are identified by their names and the title of courtier as sons of Nefer-maat and Itet.[14] We can, therefore, safely assume that the child on this Copenhagen block is also a son of Itet. The image has the special flair of a court scene at a great family's residence. It is well known that Egyptians derived great joy from their pet monkeys, and Smith has correctly pointed out how much humorous appreciation of the species is encapsulated in this group of a child with two naughty animals, one of which is pulling at a crane's tail feathers.[15] "The bird's hinder leg is suspiciously raised," writes Petrie, "as if he was just going to let fly with it right into the monkey's face."[16] More paste is preserved here than on the other two blocks under discussion, and the crane presents a well-preserved example of the joining of different colored pastes within one cutout area.

The Munich block (c) was located south of the entrance to the stone-lined portion of Itet's tomb (fig. 103m), where it formed the middle register of a five-register wall. Here three men are engaged in building a boat from papyrus reeds. The two workers in the boat are pulling on the ropes with which they are tying the reeds, while the third man helps them shape the vessel by standing outside it and pressing his back against the prow.[17] The inscription reads "binding." The motif of men tying a papyrus

skiff together was quite popular in tomb reliefs of the Old Kingdom but was never again presented with such intense concentration upon the actions and positions of the figures.[18]

DOA

1. F. C. J. Spurrell in Petrie 1892, pp. 24–25, 29.
2. Simpson 1982, cols. 376–77. For building phases of the mastaba, see entry for cat. no. 25.
3. Petrie 1892, pl. 24.
4. Spurrell in ibid., pp. 24–25, 29; Wildung 1982c, col. 913.
5. Smith 1946, pp. 154–55.
6. Petrie 1892, pl. 24.
7. El-Metwally 1992, p. 46.
8. Is the single vessel a water jar for the "washing of the mouth"?
9. Balcz 1934, pp. 51–53.
10. Petrie 1892, pl. 24.
11. Ibid., pls. 17, 18, 20, 22, 24, 26; El-Metwally (1992, pp. 42–47) understands the presence of the sons to underline the fact that all food represented in the tomb decorations was dedicated to the cult of the deceased. This would mean that the images present not pure scenes of daily life but rather depictions that are at least in part ritual scenes.
12. Petrie 1892, pl. 18.
13. Harpur 1987, pp. 178–79; Saleh and Sourouzian 1986, no. 25b.
14. Petrie 1892, pl. 17.
15. Smith 1946, p. 340.
16. Petrie 1892, p. 26.
17. Dürring 1995, pp. 15, 26–28.
18. For parallels, see Harpur 1987, pp. 152–53, figs. 107–9; and Dürring 1995, pp. 15–25, pls. 3–6.

PROVENANCE: Meidum, tomb of Nefer-maat and Itet (mastaba 16), stone-lined chamber of Itet (fig. 103c,m), Mariette excavation, 1871,* Petrie excavation, 1891**

BIBLIOGRAPHY: Petrie 1892, pp. 24–27, pls. 23, 24; Mogensen 1930, pp. 87–88; Jørgensen 1996, pp. 36–39; H. W. Müller 1972, p. 38, no. 24; Harpur n.d.

*Mariette and Maspero 1889, pp. 473–77; for the date of the work, see Rowe 1931, pp. 8–9.

**At the request of Gaston Maspero, Director of the Egyptian Antiquities Service, Petrie removed the reliefs and paintings in the tomb to the Egyptian Museum, Cairo, and various European museums. See Petrie 1892, pp. 26–27, 39, pls. 23, 24; Petrie, Mackay, and Wainwright 1910, pp. 4–5, pls. 3, 4; and Wainwright in Petrie, Wainwright, and Mackay 1912, pp. 24–26, pls. 15, 16.

Detail, cat. no. 24a

104. Reconstruction, north wall of outer chapel of Itet, mastaba of Nefer-maat and Itet, Meidum. From Smith 1946 (fig. 61)

25A–C. Fragments of Paintings from the Tomb of Itet

Fourth Dynasty, reign of Snefru
Tempera on thin layer of fine plaster over coarser plaster mixed with chaff, originally applied to sun-dried brick wall[1]

a. Left side, h. 26 cm (10¼ in.); w. 18 cm (7⅛ in.); right side, h. 17 cm (6¾ in.); w. 15 cm (5⅞ in.)
Museum of Fine Arts, Boston, Gift of British School of Archaeology in Egypt 91.286a,b

b. H. 26 cm (10¼ in.); w. 37.5 cm (14¾ in.)
Museum of Fine Arts, Boston, Gift of British School of Archaeology in Egypt 91.285

c. H. 41 cm (16⅛ in.); w. 91 cm (35⅞ in.)
The Manchester Museum, University of Manchester 3594

Like many other large mastabas, the tomb of Nefer-maat and his wife, Itet, underwent various building phases. The original massive brick structure of this tomb was enlarged twice by the addition of new layers of brickwork on all four sides.[2] Thus in stage two of the building process the stone-

a

c

lined chapels of Nefer-maat and Itet with their paste-filled reliefs (cat. no. 24) became the rear portions of cruciform chambers whose new front sections were formed by a brick corridor.[3] The walls of this corridor were covered with plaster and painted (fig. 103p). Although the ravages of time left most of these paintings severely damaged, William Stevenson Smith was able to reconstruct one large area from the north wall of Itet's chapel with some certainty. The fragments from the Museum of Fine

Arts, Boston, and the Manchester Museum were once part of this wall.

The painting had two main registers and a subregister (fig. 104). The scenes—painted on a light blue-gray background—unfolded in front of a large figure, doubtless a representation of the tomb owner's husband, Nefer-maat (see entry for cat. no. 24), wearing a shoulder ornament that was part of the priestly leopard garment,[4] which is preserved on one of the Boston fragments (a, 91.286a). Itet was probably also de-

picted.[5] In the uppermost register a man offers two pintail ducks[6] to the large figure. Two joined Boston fragments (a, 91.286a,b) show the hand of this man and part of one of the ducks. The wings of the duck are black on top and gray with feathers delineated in black below. The gray must have been obtained by mixing white with black. The neck and head are also gray, and the body has a vermiculated effect, typical of the species, that was achieved with black brushstrokes over a gray area.[7] To the right of the man with the pintails is a group of three running men who pull the rope of a clapnet bird trap that has been set out in a pond in which lotus flowers grow.[8] The third Boston fragment (b) shows part of the torso and the left arm of the man in the middle of this group. According to an inscription that Smith places above the Boston fragment (fig. 104), this might have been Nefer-maat and Itet's son Ankh-er-fened. Part of the right arm of the next figure (possibly their son Wehem-ka) and a bit of the rope are also visible. The rather thick brush lines that outline the limbs and torso are hardly distinguishable from the rest of the painted area, but they help to define such details as the angular elbow and the soft flesh on the inside of the arm of the figure on the right.[9]

Below the men catching ducks and perhaps other birds with a clapnet is the subregister, which contains the famous geese panel now in the Egyptian Museum, Cairo.[10] From the bottom register, where the sowing of grain was represented,[11] the Manchester

b

fragment (c) has preserved the upper part of the sower and the heads of two cattle that pull a plow. "Plowing" says the inscription above the cattle. "Sowing" must have been written in front of the sower. In his left hand this man holds the typical whip of Old Kingdom farmers and herdsmen, which is made from braided strips of leather with a single strip at the end. Here the sower raises the whip as a token of his superiority—there was no room on the wall to show other cattle under his command in front of him.[12] With his raised right hand, held even higher than the left, he throws the seeds onto the earth. The seed bag[13] has two elaborate loops at the top that hold a string with which the container is fastened around the sower's neck and shoulder. With rather striking naturalism the artist allowed the string to disappear behind the sower's upper right arm.[14] According to Smith's reconstruction, a second plow followed the one whose draft cattle are partially preserved on the Manchester fragment. The two plows are positioned behind the sower; they do not break the ground but work the earth to cover the seeds the sower throws.[15]

Like all the men still visible in the painting, the sower wears a flimsy plant fillet around his head and a black-outlined band around his neck from which two lotus flowers hang. As Smith has observed, the ornaments worn by all the men appear to be made of the same plants shown in the geese scene and in and around the pond in which the bird trap is set out. He notes that these ornaments and plants contribute "an attractive unity" to the picture.[16] The ubiquitous plants with their fresh green also serve to create a festive atmosphere in which the outdoor activities of the men take place. The cattle are differentiated by color: the nearer animal is a dark red-brown, the one behind it a yellowish light brown.[17] Their eyes are round and have large brown pupils and black lashes.

These few fragments from a once-magnificent large image provide an inkling of the level of quality the art of painting had reached in the early Fourth Dynasty.[18] It was a level seldom equaled in later Egyptian art.[19]   DOA

1. For painting techniques, see Williams 1932, pp. 20–37; N. M. Davies 1936, pp. XXIII, XXXI–XLVI, 4–5; and more recently, with analyses, Jaksch 1985.
2. See Petrie 1892, pp. 14–15; Petrie, Mackay, and Wainwright 1910, p. 4; Reisner 1936, pp. 221–22, 280, 284; and Smith 1937, pp. 18, 20, fig. 2.
3. In a third stage the cruciform chapel disappeared, and a simple niche was built into a new brick layer, now the outermost layer (Petrie 1892, p. 15). No decoration is reported to have been found in the niche of the last stage.
4. This ornament is now white but originally was yellow; compare ibid., pl. 23. For the ornament, see Staehelin 1966, pp. 57–60, pl. 8.
5. Smith 1937, p. 20.
6. Houlihan 1986, pp. 71–73.
7. Meinertzhagen 1930, p. 468. For similar effects attained by a Middle Kingdom painter, see Terrace 1967, pls. 7, 26.
8. See Smith 1937, pl. 8; and Harpur 1987, p. 178.
9. For outlines in Old Kingdom painting, see Williams 1932, p. 22; N. M. Davies 1936, pp. XXXV–XXXVII; and Smith 1946, pp. 265–66.
10. Saleh and Sourouzian 1986, no. 26.
11. Harpur 1987, pp. 159–60, 204.
12. See Smith 1937, p. 20, for dimensions.
13. Indicated as yellow by Petrie (1892, pl. 28).
14. There is an interesting detail to be observed about this string: where it would have run, if it did not disappear behind the arm, a band of lighter red crosses the dark red limb. A lighter band of the same kind also runs below the string where it crosses the man's breast to the right of the flower ornament. We can deduce from these traces only that an artist originally intended to show the string in front of the right arm and that this position was changed by the painter who did the final work.
15. Harpur 1987, p. 161.
16. Smith 1937, pp. 19–20.
17. See Smith 1946, p. 266, on the use of different colors for pairs of cattle.
18. A glimpse of a predecessor of the Itet paintings is provided by the Third Dynasty tomb of Hesi-re (Quibell 1913, pp. 4–9, pls. 4–6, 9–23).
19. Examples of later works of like mastery are provided by the Middle Kingdom Bersha Coffin (Terrace 1967); and the New Kingdom tomb of Kenamun (N. de G. Davies 1930, esp. pls. 34, 50).

PROVENANCE: Meidum, tomb of Nefer-maat and Itet (mastaba 16), north wall of inner brick-lined chamber of Itet (fig. 103p), Mariette excavation, 1871,* Petrie excavation, 1891**

BIBLIOGRAPHY: Petrie 1892, pp. 27–28, pl. 28; Smith 1937, pp. 17–26

*Mariette and Maspero 1889, pp. 473–77; for the date of the work, see Rowe 1931, pp. 8–9.

**At the request of Gaston Maspero, Director of the Egyptian Antiquities Service, Petrie removed the remaining painting fragments to the Egyptian Museum, Cairo, and various European museums. See Smith 1937, pp. 17–26, esp. p. 18, on the provenance of fragments in Boston and other locations.

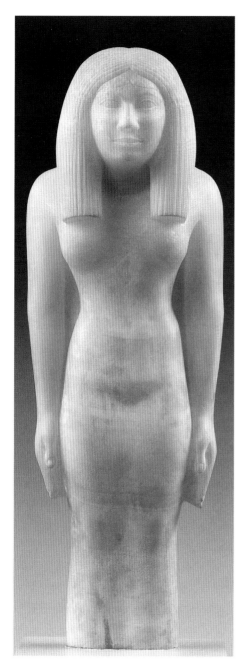
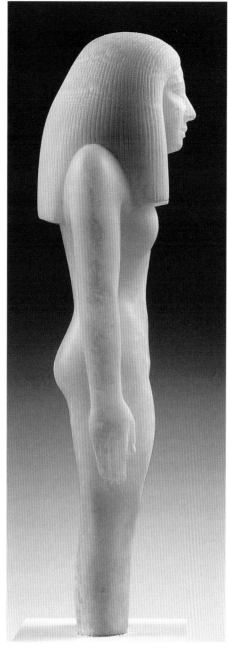

their unusually supple fingers and nails carefully defined, the hands give an impression of extreme refinement. The lines of the dress are not visible on the upper torso, and the body under the imperceptible fabric, which conceals fine anatomical details, is treated with great attention. The careful modeling of the body and the plasticity of the flesh are of a quality rarely attained, although they are matched in the statue of the lady Hetep-heres, mother of Ra-wer (cat. no. 131), which is very probably of later date. The treatment of the body of this unknown woman, broad of shoulder and narrow of hip, has also been compared to the group of Hetep-heres II and her daughter Mer-si-ankh.[1]

Certain stylistic features are helpful in dating this work. Rarely after the reign of Menkaure does a subject's natural hair appear on her brow under the wig in this way.[2] The tripartite wig, worn in the Third Dynasty by Princess Redjief (cat. no. 16) and Lady Nesa (cat. no. 13), is very rarely depicted in statuary after the beginning of the Fourth Dynasty. Two other features— the absence of a back support and the position of the head, set deep into the shoulders as if weighed down by the abundant hair— are reminiscent of the so-called precanonical sculptures of the Third Dynasty. For all these reasons, the sculpture should be dated to the very beginning of the Fourth Dynasty. But what a distance has been traveled in the treatment of the female body, from the bulky silhouette of Nesa to this harmonious construction, which the translucent stone admirably enhances!   CZ

1. Museum of Fine Arts, Boston, 30.1456;
   Vandier 1958, p. 55; Fay 1998, p. 162, fig. 7.
2. Cherpion 1998, p. 100.

PROVENANCE: Unknown; purchased 1893

BIBLIOGRAPHY: Budge 1922, p. 128; Hall 1925, p. 1, pl. 1; Smith 1946, pl. 16b; Vandier 1958, pp. 2, 55, 58, 63, 111, 131, 138, pl. 15; Eaton-Krauss 1998, pl. 2a–d

26. STANDING WOMAN

Early Fourth Dynasty
Egyptian alabaster with faint remains of paint
H. 48.7 cm (19¼ in.)
Trustees of the British Museum, London EA 24619

Although individual statues of women from the Old Kingdom are rare, a few, like this alabaster figure in the British Museum, are among the finest works of the period. Once painted, it has traces of black on the wig. The pedestal, feet, and bottom of the dress have disappeared. The subject is standing in the classic pose of a woman, her feet together, arms falling naturally at her sides, and hands open against her thighs. There is no support behind the woman, and although her back is modeled with care it is very stylized. A long tripartite wig frames the delicate face, and each strand is carefully separated from the others by a groove. The subject's natural hair appears on her forehead below the wig. In its expression the full face is extremely gentle. The large eyes are almond shaped, and a horizontal incision accentuates the corners. The upper eyelids are indicated by a fine fold, and the eyebrows are barely suggested. The nose is wide and the mouth soft, with full lips that seem to bear the trace of a smile. A profile view reveals the extreme slenderness of the body and the imposing mass of the wig, which seems to weigh down the head. With

Detail, cat. no. 26

27. STANDING MAN

Early Fourth Dynasty
Painted quartzite
H. 89.5 cm (35¼ in.)
The Metropolitan Museum of Art, New York,
Harris Brisbane Dick Fund, 1962 62.200

The formal structure of this figure—defined by the base, the back pillar, and the interplay between the strictly vertical body and the oblique line of the striding left leg—reflects the basic rules that Old Kingdom artists observed in creating statues of men. In its proportions and style, however, the statue differs considerably from other works of the period. The oversize feet, the boldly modeled musculature of the legs, arms, and chest, the short neck, and the low forehead have no parallel in contemporary statues found at Saqqara and Giza, for example. Also unlike works from the Memphite region is the face, with its large eyes, broad, flat nose, deeply incised furrows between nose and mouth, broad mouth, and prognathous jaw.

The unusually bold style of the statue suggests a provenance in Upper Egypt, and this supposition is confirmed when the work is compared with another, excavated between Luxor and Aswan, at El Kab.[1] Although the head is missing, this second work, today in the Museum of Archaeology and Anthropology at the University of Pennsylvania in Philadelphia (EJ 16160), is so close to the Metropolitan Museum's statue in all its essential aspects that it may safely be called a duplicate. The Philadelphia statue was found in a tomb of the early Fourth Dynasty, and there is little doubt that the Metropolitan statue was created at the same time and in the same place.

An independent style influenced by Nubia, Egypt's southern neighbor, existed in Upper Egypt at the beginning of the Middle Kingdom. This statue appears to provide evidence of a similarly influenced style in the early Fourth Dynasty. Such examples impressively substantiate the African roots of the ancient Egyptian culture.   DW

1. Quibell 1898, p. 5, no. 8, pl. 3; Smith 1946, pp. 45, 142; Vandier 1958, pp. 56–57; Wildung 1996, p. 46.

PROVENANCE: Probably El Kab

BIBLIOGRAPHY: Fischer 1963, p. 18, n. 6; Hayes 1963, p. 65; Schoske 1986, p. 222, n. 6; Russmann 1995a, p. 277; Wildung 1996, pp. 46–48; Wildung 1999

28. METJEN SEATED

Fourth Dynasty, reign of Snefru
Red granite
H. 47 cm (18½ in.)
Ägyptisches Museum und Papyrussammlung,
Staatliche Museen zu Berlin 1106

This statue was discovered in the serdab
tucked behind the north wall of Metjen's
mortuary chapel (see entry for cat. no. 29).
Sculpted in red granite (the front of the
pedestal is cracked), it depicts the high official sitting on a cubic seat, his right hand
closed in a fist and pressed against his chest,
his left hand flat on his knee. There is no
back support. The head set deep into the
shoulders, the slender limbs, the abnormally small proportions of the lower body,
and the thin face give the statue an almost
sorrowful expression, which is quite unusual in Egyptian art. The face is framed by
a round wig that covers the ears, closely
hugs the skull, and falls very low in back,
concealing the nape of the neck; the rows
of curls are indicated by simple concentric
grooves. The upper lids of the deep-set
eyes are rimmed and extended by cosmetic
lines, which, like the eyebrows, are in

relief. A marked cleft separates the prominent mouth from the protruding chin. The
chest is narrow and the pectorals do not
jut out. There are careful indications of
the details of the feet and hands. The plain
kilt is described simply by the ridge of the
belt and an incision for the lower border.
The modeling of the back is rudimentary.
On the sides and back of the seat large
hieroglyphs in relief, inscribed within a
rectangular frame, give Metjen's name and
a few of his titles, one of them relating to
the cult of the king's mother.[1]

Like the chapel reliefs, the statue can be
dated to the reign of Snefru. It marks a very
important stylistic division between works
from the beginning of the Old Kingdom
and the austere statuary of the first part of
the Fourth Dynasty. It has certain characteristics of the earlier period: the modest
dimensions, the hard stone, the disproportionately large head, and the inscriptions in
relief.[2] But the position of the hands—right
hand on chest, left on knee—is reversed,
perhaps inspired by the change of pose
introduced into royal statuary by Djoser.[3]
Finally, the seat is different from those preferred in Third Dynasty statuary, which
reflect wood furniture of more ancient
times (see cat. no. 15).

A comparison of this statue of Metjen to his likeness in relief illustrates how, at the same historical moment, Egyptian artists could offer very dissimilar interpretations of reality. How different is this compact, almost disproportionate image carved in granite from the elegant silhouette freely inscribed on the chapel walls that dominates the procession of offering bearers! Nevertheless, there are a few points in common between these two representations destined for immortality, such as the slightly raised chin and the wig that covers the nape of the neck. CZ

1. Helck 1987, pp. 268–74.
2. Eaton-Krauss 1998, pp. 209–27.
3. Sourouzian 1998, p. 327.

PROVENANCE: Saqqara, north of Step Pyramid of Djoser, tomb of Metjen (L.S. 6), Prussian expedition led by Lepsius, 1842–45; gift of Mohammed Ali Pasha 1845

BIBLIOGRAPHY: Lepsius 1849–58, vol. 2, p. 120 (a–e), vol. 3, p. 288 (1); Smith 1946, p. 18; Porter and Moss 1978, p. 494; Sourouzian 1998, p. 351, fig. 46a,b

Detail, a

29. RELIEF BLOCKS FROM THE MORTUARY CHAPEL OF METJEN

Fourth Dynasty, reign of Snefru
Limestone
H., each block ca. 50.5 cm (19⅞ in.)
Ägyptisches Museum und Papyrussammlung, Staatliche Museen zu Berlin 1105.54, 1105.55, 1105.84, 1105.85, 1105.130, 1105.131, 1105.132

The chapel of Metjen is generally dated to the beginning of the Fourth Dynasty, during the reign of Snefru. Among Metjen's many titles as governor and head of expeditions, some include the names of the pharaohs Huni and Snefru. Inscriptions at the chapel also mention offerings from "the funerary estate of the mother of the king [Snefru], Ni-maat-hapi."

Metjen's chapel, whose many decorated blocks were dismantled and are now housed in the Ägyptisches Museum in Berlin, is therefore one of the oldest of the period.

It is of modest dimensions, about 265 centimeters (9 feet) long, 75 centimeters (29.5 inches) wide, and more than 300 centimeters (10 feet) high; it was entered through a corridor 215 centimeters (7 feet) long. The structure is cruciform in plan, as the chapel and corridor are at right angles to each other. The blocks of limestone are entirely covered with sculpted columns of inscriptions and with scenes that would become standard in Old Kingdom mastabas. On the rear wall is a false door, a passageway between the world of the living and that of the dead. Metjen appears there, sculpted in the embrasure, moving to the right. Above, he is depicted sitting in front of a table laden with offerings. There is another image of him seated, a middle-aged man with a flabby chest, receiving invocation offerings. On the other side, priests are performing the glorification rite and the Opening of the Mouth ceremony, which will allow him to recover the use of his senses in the next world. He is

E   F

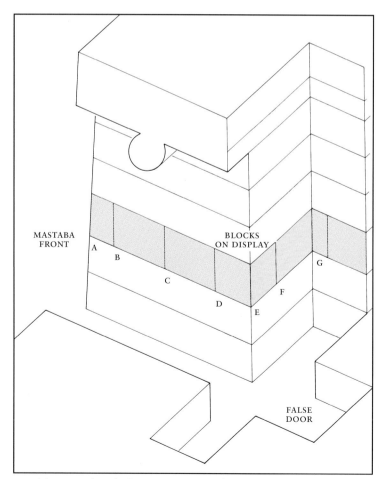

105. Mortuary chapel of Metjen, Saqqara, showing location of blocks
exhibited. Isometric drawing by Dieter Arnold

Labels in drawing: MASTABA FRONT; BLOCKS ON DISPLAY; A; B; C; D; E; F; G; FALSE DOOR

represented four times in large scale, leaving the chapel. Processions of servants come
to meet him, bringing the products of his
many properties as well as furnishings and
clothes; desert animals parade before him
in a stylized hunting scene.

In the corridor and above the false door,
magnificently sculpted inscriptions record
the seemingly endless litany of his titles and
immortalize the official documents relating
to his estates. These are contracts of sorts,
accompanied by excerpts from royal decrees, having to do with the deceased's
landholdings. Metjen's estates maintained
his funerary cult after his death: in particular, their products supplied the dead man
with food and paid the priests employed at
his tomb. These texts, among the oldest
and most detailed that survive from ancient
Egypt, have interested scholars even more
than the pictorial decoration.[1] Important
for the study of law, they are also of general historical interest, as they retrace the
career of the man and precisely describe
some of his farms, with their ornamental
lakes, orchards of fig trees, and vineyards
surrounded by enclosure walls.

The decoration in this tomb, one of the
few found intact, is unfinished.[2] The scenes

G

are sculpted in high relief and the sharp outlines are drawn with precision. The details are executed with greater care than those in the contemporary mastaba of Ra-hotep (Egyptian Museum, Cairo, temp 19-11-24-3). A great deal of attention was given to the modeling of the heads, faces, and hair.

The blocks shown here come from the south wall of the corridor and from the east and south walls of the chapel; they were located along the lower third of the monument's elevation. One block (A) was placed at the entryway (see fig. 105), set into the sloping facade of the mastaba. A servant enters carrying a basketful of food on his head: this is one of three figures, one above another, representing the "endowments of Metjen." Eleven columns of hieroglyphs separated by vertical lines (B–D) are part of a large inscription that extended from floor to ceiling and which reads from right to left. Reminding the reader that this is property guaranteed by royal decree, it enumerates the twelve endowments of Metjen located in different nomes (provinces) of Lower Egypt. In the fourth column the nome of the goddess Neith, recognizable by

Detail, b

A

B   II   10   9   8   7

her emblem (detail, b), is mentioned immediately above the nome of the wild bull (detail, a). The sixth column cites offerings from the "funerary estate of the mother of the king, Ni-maat-hapi." In the tenth column, hieroglyphs depicting a rectangular lake and trees from an orchard evoke one of the deceased's properties (detail, c). The very large signs, in the spacious arrangement characteristic of the period, are sculpted in careful detail.

On the chapel's east wall, a man is carrying a Dorcas gazelle (E). The artist has shown a great deal of talent in capturing the animal's quivering muzzle. The gazelle is offered to Metjen, whose impassivity contrasts with the animal's suppressed impatience (F). Standing with a long staff in one hand, a scepter in the other, his tall silhouette dominates two registers of offering bearers. His fine profile stands out with simplicity against the background and contrasts with the elaborate wig, with its high crown and radiating locks. The eyes—lined with green cosmetic and rimmed around the upper eyelids—the short, pointed nose,

and the well-drawn mouth constitute what seems to be a lifelike portrait.

Is the hunting scene (G) depicted behind Metjen to be attributed to his title, Official of the Desert and Commander of Hunters? The same theme is treated in the tombs of Ra-hotep and Nefer-maat (see entries for cat. nos. 24, 25). The block shown here illustrates a motif repeated on five consecutive registers in Metjen's tomb: processions of oryx, gazelles, and ibex are sculpted in single file side by side or are shown being attacked by a hunting dog, which is cruelly biting their hindquarters.   CZ

1. Goedecken 1976.
2. Smith 1946, pp. 151–53.

PROVENANCE: Saqqara, north of Step Pyramid of Djoser, tomb of Metjen (L.S. 6), Prussian expedition led by Lepsius, 1842–45; gift of Mohammed Ali Pasha, 1845

BIBLIOGRAPHY: Naville 1897–1913, vol. 1, pp. 142–44; Goedecken 1976; Porter and Moss 1978, pp. 493–94; Priese 1991, no. 14, pp. 24–25; Wildung in Donadoni Roveri and Tiradritti 1998, p. 275, no. 266

Detail, c

C 6   5   4   D 3   2   1

TRANSLATIONS

Egyptian text runs from right to left. Italics indicate the text on the illustrated columns

1. (Document of record) the land administrator, nome ruler, Overseer of *Commissions in the Kynopolite nome, Overseer of* Messengers:

2. (Re:) the Mendesian nome, town of Ram's Area: *a field of 4 aruras (2.7 acres), the people, and everything in* the funerary-estate decree of the scribe of stores (Metjen's father). They have been given to one son (Metjen), and he (Metjen) has been made to get the funerary-estate decrees from him (his Father). For he has a document

3. that has been assigned to him at his disposal. To the Overseer of Commissions of the *Western Saite nome:*

4. There have been founded for him (Metjen) 12 Metjen-foundations of the *Saite, Xoite, and Letopolite nomes,* whose yield he shall have on festivals.

5. There have been bought for him *from many landholders a field of 200 aruras* (136 acres),

6. so that offering-hall bread might come forth every day in the *ka chapel of the King's Mother* Ni-maat-hapi,

7. and an estate 200 cubits long by 200 cubits wide (344.5 x 344.5 feet), with a wall equipped and *set with good wood, a very big pool made in it,* and planted with figs and grapes.

8. A record of it is in the royal archive, and *their names* (of the landholders from whom Metjen purchased the land) are in the royal archive.

9. Very many trees and vines have been planted, *from which much wine might come.*

10. A vineyard of a hundredth of an arura (297 square feet) has been made for him *inside the wall, planted* with vines.

11. I-meres, a Metjen-*foundation* (the name of the 200-arura field), *and Sobek's Mound,* a Metjen-foundation (the name of the estate).

Translated from the ancient Egyptian by James P. Allen

30. MODEL OF THE GIZA PLATEAU

Prepared for exhibition "The Sphinx and the Pyramids: One Hundred Years of American Archaeology at Giza," held in 1998 at Harvard University Semitic Museum
H. 15 cm (6 in.); w. 130 cm (51¼ in.); d. 130 cm (51¼ in.); scale 1:2,000
Harvard University Semitic Museum, Cambridge, Massachusetts

The exhibition for which this model was prepared traced the history of excavations on the plateau of Giza conducted by George Reisner over a forty-year period at the beginning of the twentieth century, and those undertaken more recently by Mark Lehner. The scale model shows the results of these excavations, offering the most accurate picture possible of the plateau in antiquity.

The first true pyramid, built in Dahshur, south of Saqqara, belonged to Snefru, the immediate predecessor of King Khufu. Thereafter, the tombs of Old Kingdom sovereigns took the form of true pyramids, with one exception, the tomb of Menkaure's successor, Shepseskaf, who for unknown reasons had himself buried in an enormous stone mastaba, today called Mastabat Faraoun. Khufu chose the plateau of Giza for his tomb, the Great Pyramid, and its colossal size and perfect proportions have fired imaginations since antiquity. Khufu's son Djedefre built his pyramid at the neighboring site of Abu Rawash (see entry for cat. no. 54), but Khafre and Menkaure returned to Giza to construct their gigantic funerary complexes. Together with Khufu's pyramid, their monuments are universally acknowledged to be the most extraordinary architectural achievements of all time.

The internal plan of these three pyramids is simple. A corridor beginning at the north face leads to the funerary chamber, where the mummy lay in a sarcophagus placed against the west wall. The straight passageways and ramps required for the workmen and for ventilation were built into the mass of the monument. This was composed of enormous stacks of limestone blocks held together by plaster mortar. Once the funeral ceremony was over, the passages were blocked with huge slabs of granite, designed to prevent access to the burial vault. The exterior was covered with fine, carefully smoothed limestone slabs, giving the monument a sparkling brilliance.

Removed for reuse during the Roman Period, this revetment has now almost totally disappeared, as has the pyramidion, a block carved in the shape of a pyramid, which crowned the edifice. By happy chance, the summit of the pyramid of Khafre still has part of its limestone facing, and the base of Menkaure's pyramid is still adorned with sixteen rows of red granite, allowing us to imagine the original splendor of these monuments.

The measurements themselves convey only a poor idea of the impressiveness of the pyramids. The tallest of these, which bore the name Horizon of Khufu, was originally 146.59 meters (481 feet, 3 inches) high. The length of the sides is 230 meters (755 feet), with a slope of 51°56′. The technical achievements of Khufu's architects are extraordinary, and it is difficult to know which to admire most: the transportation on clay ramps and logs of more than two million blocks, some weighing more than two metric tons; the accuracy of the assemblage (the joints between the facing stones were nearly invisible, less than one millimeter in breadth); the extremely level rows of stone (there is a difference of only 2.1 centimeters [⅞ inch] between opposite ends of a single side); the once-perfect orientation of the faces in relation to the cardinal points; or the alignment of the southeast corner of the three pyramids along a single diagonal, which reveals that the site was conceived as a whole. The existence of a master plan is also attested by the arrangement of the mastabas of princes and courtiers along streets beside the pyramid. They form a veritable city of the dead around each royal tomb, in a grid reflecting the organization of the royal court.

Located northwest of the valley temple of Khafre, the Great Sphinx[1] is part of that king's funerary complex and gives it a unique character. The fabulous animal, a reclining lion with a king's head, is

sculpted entirely from the limestone rock of the plateau, whose strata are quite visible in the monument. It may represent the pharaoh as an aspect of the god Horus, whose name was among the royal titles of the Fourth Dynasty.

The monuments of Khufu, Khafre, and Menkaure at Giza display in perfected form the royal funerary complex characteristic of the Old Kingdom, which had begun to take shape during the reigns of Huni and Snefru at Meidum. The layout changed little thereafter. The pyramid was protected by an enclosing wall, where over time depots and stores of liturgical material accumulated. Structures necessary for the cult and afterlife of the king and his family surrounded the pyramid. The north-south axis of the building was marked on the north by the long descending access route leading to the burial chamber and on the south by the presence of a small structure, often a satellite pyramid, the pharaoh's Southern Tomb. Khufu's Southern Tomb has recently been found, and there are still questions about its ritual role, just as there are about Djoser's Southern Tomb at Saqqara. The east-west axis, which reflected the solar cycle, became the more important of the two beginning in the Fourth Dynasty and underwent a significant architectural development. An upper temple was attached to the east face of the pyramid; it was the principal site of the royal cult, and its most secret chamber contained a room for statues and a sanctuary. It was connected to a covered causeway leading to the Nile; once decorated with reliefs, the causeway ended at a second temple, called the lower temple or valley temple. This building was the starting point for the funerary procession leading up to the pyramid, and the sovereign was worshiped there before his death. Closer than other structures of the complex to the world of the living, this valley temple was equipped with a wharf overlooking a canal, an actual

funerary port where boats could dock and unload cargo and passengers bound for the necropolis. Not far away was "the city of the pyramid." Here lived the priests and the many employees involved in the day-to-day maintenance of the king's cult. Very often it was still active centuries after his death. At Dahshur, south of Saqqara, stelae have been exhumed bearing decrees that exempt its inhabitants from corvées and taxes for all eternity.

At Giza, some of the funerary monuments have been excavated. They are among the most magnificent in existence, particularly the valley temple of Khafre, with its harmoniously austere spaces adorned with monu-

mental pillars in red granite. The buried causeway, valley temple, and port of Khufu's pyramid are threatened by the encroaching western suburbs of Cairo. However, excavations continue, and recent ones have brought to light the workshops and cemetery of both the foremen and the workers who built the great pyramids.

Boats made of brick, stone, or wood were buried near the royal tomb to accompany the deceased king on his last journey. Five have been found at the foot of Khufu's pyramid; the most spectacular of these, made of cedar from Lebanon, were deposited disassembled in enormous pits dug to the south of the pyramid. One of these barks has been re-

built, and it measures more than 43 meters (141 feet) in length. More modest pyramids nearby house the tombs of the king's wives and mother. The precinct of Khufu has three well-preserved tombs of this sort, and the funerary furnishings of Hetep-heres I, his mother, were discovered in a shaft not far from the northernmost of the small pyramids (cat. nos. 31–33).   CZ

1. H. 20 m (66 ft.); l. 72.55 m (238 ft.). Porter and Moss 1974, pp. 3, 5–38; Zivie-Coche 1997.

BIBLIOGRAPHY: Porter and Moss 1974, pp. 7–47; Edwards 1979; Hawass 1987; Stadelmann 1990; Lehner 1997, pp. 106–37; Adam and Ziegler 1999, pp. 127–30

31. Two Bracelets of Queen Hetep-heres I

Fourth Dynasty
Silver, turquoise, lapis lazuli, and carnelian
a. Diam. 9 cm (3⅝ in.); w. 2.4 cm (1 in.)
b. Diam. 8.8 cm (3½ in.); w. 2.4 cm (1 in.)
Egyptian Museum, Cairo (a) JE 53271,
(b) JE 53273

PROVENANCE: Giza, tomb of Queen Hetep-heres I (G 7000X), Reisner excavation, 1925

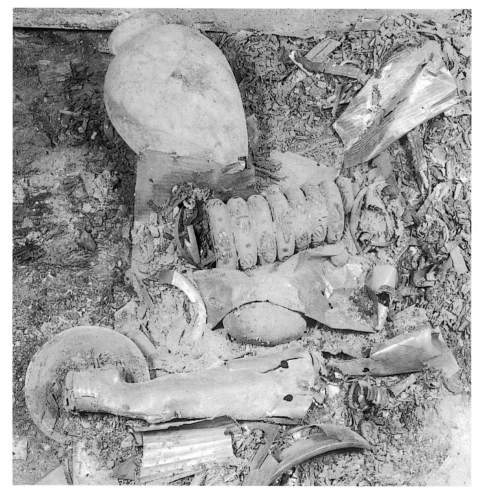

106. Bracelets as found in debris, tomb of Queen Hetep-heres I (G 7000X), Giza

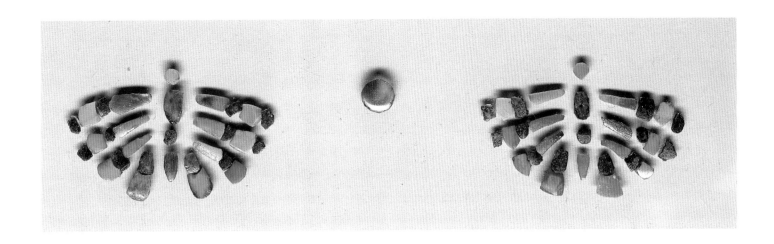

32. Inlays from a Silver Bracelet of Queen Hetep-heres I

Fourth Dynasty
Turquoise, lapis lazuli, and carnelian
L. 12.7 cm (5 in.)
Museum of Fine Arts, Boston, Harvard University–
Museum of Fine Arts Expedition 47.1701

The bracelets of Queen Hetep-heres I, mother of King Khufu, were found among the remains of a large wood box (fig. 106), now restored, that was covered inside and out with gold leaf. The lid of the box bears a hieroglyphic inscription in raised relief identifying it as a "box containing rings" and naming the owner as "Mother of the King of Upper and Lower Egypt, Hetep-heres." The twenty silver hoops inlaid with semiprecious stones were still arranged in two rows, as they had been originally. The bracelets would have been extremely valuable: silver, which was relatively rare in Egypt, was thought more precious than gold. Most of them are today in the collection of the Egyptian Museum, Cairo, but two complete bracelets and the inlays of a third, in the present exhibition, were given to the

Museum of Fine Arts in Boston by the Egyptian government.

Composed of silver combined with gold (nearly 9 percent) and copper (1 percent), all the hoops are wide and relatively thin. Their diameters range from 6.8 to 7.7 centimeters, and their edges curve slightly inward. Their decoration is unusual both technically and thematically. The placement of the inlays within cavities made in the metal itself, in a technique similar to champlevé, does not appear often in Egyptian jewelry, which in later periods did employ cloisonné. Equally distinctive are the four highly refined stylized butterflies on each bracelet—a rare design achieved through the use of turquoise, lapis lazuli, and carnelian of superior quality[1]—which are separated by small carnelian disks.

Owning twenty bracelets of the same design may seem surprising, but it must be remembered that several of them, piled up on one or both arms, were commonly worn at the same time. A representation of Queen Hetep-heres, engraved on a chair covered in gold leaf, depicts her with fourteen bracelets on her right arm.[2] The practice has been documented as early as the Third Dynasty (Lady Nesa is depicted wearing numerous

bracelets on her arms; see cat. no. 13), was in great favor in the Fourth, and remained in use, although less popular, at least through the Fifth.[3] Furthermore, the representations of men with their arms laden with multiple bracelets attest that the practice was not confined to women.[4]

Other bracelets with inlaid decoration appear in a few Old Kingdom representations,[5] but only those of Queen Hetep-heres I have been recovered.   P R

1. Keimer 1934, p. 194, pl. 15.
2. Reisner and Smith 1955, pl. 30.
3. See the examples given in Cherpion 1989, pp. 70, 194.
4. For example, in the Fourth Dynasty mastaba of Nefer, the deceased is pictured seated at his table of offerings with seven bracelets on his right arm. See Junker 1944, fig. 75a,b; and Cherpion 1989, pl. 9.
5. For example, a bracelet worn by Snefru, husband of Queen Hetep-heres, is decorated with an emblem of the god Min and with rosettes, probably inlaid. See Fakhry 1961b, figs. 134, 135.

PROVENANCE: Giza, tomb of Queen Hetep-heres I (G 7000X), Reisner excavation, 1925

BIBLIOGRAPHY: Reisner and Smith 1955, pp. 43ff., pls. 36–38

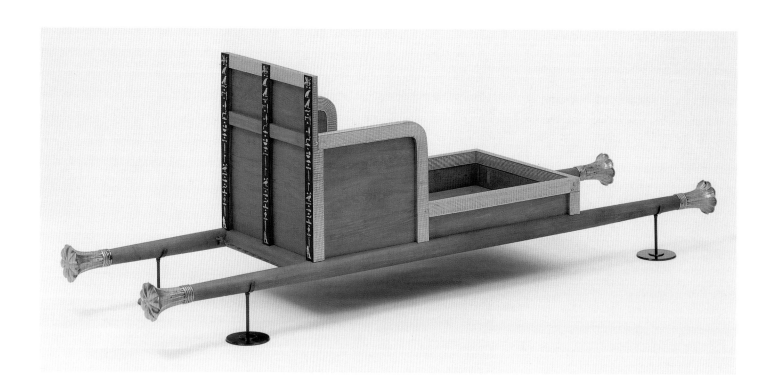

33. REPRODUCTION OF THE CARRYING CHAIR OF QUEEN HETEP-HERES I

Modern reproduction of Fourth Dynasty original
Cypress, ebony, gilded copper, and gold-plated
copper electrotypes
L., poles, 207.5 cm (81¾ in.); h., seat back, 52 cm
(20½ in.); max. w., seat, 53.5 cm (21⅛ in.)
Museum of Fine Arts, Boston, Gift of Mrs. Charles
Gaston Smith & Group of Friends 38.874

An elegant carrying chair was found at Giza
among the decayed remains of other furniture, including a bed, portable canopy, two
armchairs, and several boxes, within the
hidden tomb of Queen Hetep-heres I, wife
of Snefru and mother of Khufu (fig. 107). Its
cypress and ebony woods were poorly preserved, but they were restored by members
of the Harvard University–Museum of Fine
Arts Expedition; the same team also created the replica shown in this exhibition.[1]

Examples of Old Kingdom furniture are
rare, and Hetep-heres' original chair is
truly outstanding for its clean lines, simple
form, excellent craftsmanship, and lavish
use of gold. The elements of the frame were
connected by mortise-and-tenon joints, and
the interior of the frame was rabbeted to
allow the seat boards to be set in place.
The occupant of the chair rode on the seat
boards with knees drawn up, a pose that
may be represented in later block statues.

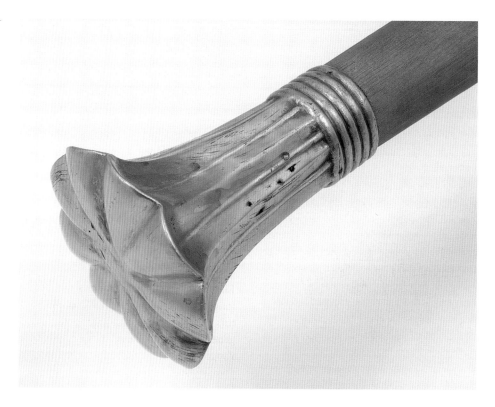

The carrying poles were further secured
by leather thongs lashed to copper cleats
both in front of and behind the seat. Gold
sheathing impressed with a matte design
covered the edges of the chair, while gold
palmiform capitals—a shape rarely used in
furniture—were employed to finish the
ends of the carrying poles.

Four identical inscriptions, presented

in finely detailed gold hieroglyphs inlaid in
ebony panels and probably secured by gesso,
give the name and titles of the chair's owner.
Three are vertical and located on the backrest, while the fourth runs horizontally
across the chair front. The inscriptions read:
"Mother of the King of Upper and Lower
Egypt, Follower of Horus, Director of the
Ruler, the Gracious One, Whose every

utterance is done for her, Daughter of the God's body, Hetep-heres."

The depiction of sedan chairs in reliefs from the Old Kingdom mastaba tombs of Mereruka and Queen Mer-si-ankh III suggest that this form of transportation was not uncommon for members of the Egyptian nobility.[2]　　　　JA

1. The reconstruction of the original chair is now in the collection of the Egyptian Museum, Cairo, JE 52373.
2. Duell 1938, pt. 1, pls. 14, 53; Dunham and Simpson 1974, fig. 5. For carrying chairs, see also Vandier 1964, pp. 328–51.

PROVENANCE: Original, Giza, tomb G 7000x, Reisner excavation, 1925

BIBLIOGRAPHY: Reisner and Smith 1955, pp. 33–34, pls. 27–29, figs. 20, 34; Porter and Moss 1974, pp. 180–81; Lehner 1985; Saleh and Sourouzian 1987, p. 29

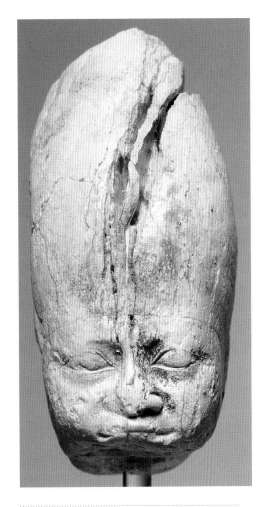

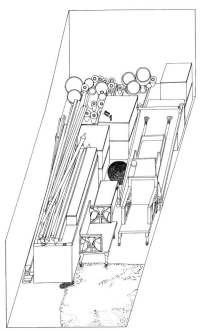

107. Isometric drawing showing objects in their original positions, tomb of Queen Hetep-heres I (G 7000x), Giza. From Reisner and Smith 1955 (fig. 20)

34. SMALL HEAD, PERHAPS OF KING KHUFU

Late Third or early Fourth Dynasty
Limestone
H. 5.7 cm (2¼ in.); w. 3.4 cm (1⅜ in.)
Staatliche Sammlung Ägyptischer Kunst, Munich
ÄS 7086

Like the colossal granite head of a king who may have been Khufu himself (cat. no. 21), this small head sculpted in soft limestone is generally dated to the beginning of the Old Kingdom, between the end of the Third Dynasty and the reign of Khufu. It, too, has no inscription, and its origins remain a mystery. Again we must look to stylistic criteria for clues to its subject.

There is a large crack across the crown, and the chin has disappeared; however, the line of the mouth remains visible. The very broad face evokes the visage of a minuscule ivory statue inscribed with the name of Khufu in the Egyptian Museum, Cairo (JE 36143). Its fragmentary state and mutilation accentuate the geometric organization of the features: the vertical line of the nose, extended by the fracture, and

the horizontal lines of eyes and mouth. Remains of a back support are discernible behind the head. The prominent, wide-set eyes are treated naturalistically, as are the eyebrows. Particular attention was given to the zygomatic muscles, which are pronounced, and to the area under each eye, which is recessed. The strong nostrils have a firm outline, as does the prominent mouth, which is deeply inset at each corner. The pharaoh wears the white crown of Upper Egypt, the eartabs of which are identical to those on the ivory statuette of Khufu and the colossal head.

Despite the differences in scale and material, the similarities between this piece and the colossal head are striking. Here, as in the case of the large example, the securely dated minuscule statuette of Khufu offers suggestive points of comparison. It is gratifying that the series of statues that can be linked to the most famous of all Egyptian kings is becoming ever richer and more diversified.　　CZ

PROVENANCE: Unknown

BIBLIOGRAPHY: Schoske and Grimm 1995, p. 44, fig. 42; Grimm, Schoske, and Wildung 1997, p. 56, no. 39; Donadoni Roveri and Tiradritti 1998, p. 266, no. 249

108. Pyramid of Khufu, Giza

35. Block from the Pyramid of King Khufu

Fourth Dynasty, reign of Khufu
Limestone
H. 25 cm (9⅞ in.); w. 72.5 cm (28½ in.);
d. 35 cm (13¾ in.)
Trustees of the British Museum, London EA 491

The Great Pyramid (fig. 108), built on a superhuman scale, is the tomb of King Khufu. It is the oldest and most imposing pyramid on the plateau of Giza. Between 449 and 430 B.C.E., the Greek traveler and historian Herodotus described the monument, with its causeway in "polished stone, with figures carved on it." His informants, Egyptian priests, depicted Khufu as a tyrant who reduced the country "to a completely awful condition. . . . [Egyptians] worked in gangs of 100,000 men for three months at a time. They said it took ten years of hard labour for the people to construct the causeway along which they hauled the blocks of stone. . . ."[1] The legend persisted in the popular imagination and was reinforced three centuries later by a different version from another ancient historian, Flavius Josephus, who cited the construction of the pyramids as among the labors the Hebrews performed during their captivity in Egypt. All this has no historical foundation, and we now know that the laborers were free peasants, drafted by the king for the great construction projects.

Although it has lost its apex, the Great Pyramid, which originally measured 146.59 meters (481 feet, 3 inches) in height, is still colossal. The number of stone blocks used in its construction has been estimated at 2.3 million; some weigh 2.5 metric tons. During his expedition to Egypt, Napoleon Bonaparte, who was an accomplished mathematician, calculated that the blocks of Khufu's pyramid could be used to build a wall 3 meters (10 feet) high and 30 centimeters (a foot) thick around France. Although that may be an exaggeration—we do not know the size of the blocks inside the monument, for example—these often-cited figures are staggering.[2] The casing, made of blocks of fine limestone from Tura and long since plundered, must also be mentioned: certain blocks still in place weigh as much as 15 metric tons. The enormous granite slabs, which form the ceiling of the King's Chamber and cap the five weight-relieving chambers above it, are estimated to weigh between 50 and 80 metric tons each. Based on a reign of about thirty years for Khufu and the scope of the construction undertaken at Giza, Rainer Stadelmann's calculations show that laborers would have had to set in place 230 cubic meters (300 cubic yards) of stone per day. That means an average of one block set in place every two or three minutes during a ten-hour workday.

And what is there to say about the extreme precision of the execution? The largest difference in the length of the sides, which measure 230 meters (755 feet), is only 4.4 centimeters (1¾ inches); the height varies by only 2.1 centimeters (⅞ inch); and the orientation of the faces in relation to the cardinal points differs by only 0°3'6".

The block illustrated here was brought to England by Richard William Howard Vyse. It serves as mute testament to the extraordinary feat of engineering achieved by King Khufu's construction team. Vyse was the moving force behind the largest program of scientific explorations at Giza. His first excavations were conducted in 1837 with Giovanni Battista Caviglia and the second with the engineer John Shea Perring. Vyse discovered the casing block shown, along with two others, which are carved of fine limestone, among the accumulated debris at the foot of the north face of the Great Pyramid. They demonstrate that the angle of the sides was a bit more than 51°.   CZ

1. Herodotus, *History* 2.124 (1998, pp. 144–45).
2. Many scholarly books have been devoted to the pyramids and their construction, most recently Lauer 1988; Stadelmann 1990; and Lehner 1997.

PROVENANCE: Giza, rubble from pyramid of Khufu; gift of Colonel Richard William Howard Vyse 1838

BIBLIOGRAPHY: Budge 1909, p. 5, nos. 10–12

36. POUNDER

Probably Fourth Dynasty, reign of Khufu
Stone
Diam. 6.9 cm (2¾ in.)
Trustees of the British Museum, London EA 67818

The Great Pyramid at Giza is traversed by
mysterious passages known as air shafts.
During his exploration of the lower part
of the air shaft leading from the so-called
Queen's Chamber, Waynmann Dixon discovered three tools: this small stone pounder, a
small wood board, and a copper object in
the shape of a dove's tail (cat. no. 37). Now
thought to be offerings dating to the age of
Khufu, they were either genuine tools or
models of tools and are similar to objects
discovered in foundation deposits. They
may have been placed in the air shaft at
Giza to allow the deceased king to magically
open the passage and return to heaven.

CZ

PROVENANCE: Giza, pyramid of Khufu, north
air shaft of Queen's Chamber, discovered by
Waynmann Dixon 1872

BIBLIOGRAPHY: *Graphic*, December 7, 1872,
pp. 530, 545, figs. 1, 2, 4; *Nature*, December 26,
1872, pp. 146–47; Smyth 1880, p. 429; Stadelmann 1994, pp. 287–88, pl. 55; Lehner 1997,
p. 112

37. FORKED INSTRUMENT

Probably Fourth Dynasty, reign of Khufu
Copper
H. 4.5 cm (1¾ in.); w. 5.2 cm (2⅛ in.); d. 1.1 cm
(½ in.)
Trustees of the British Museum, London EA 67819

This object was probably attached to a wood
handle. Sometimes identified as a sculptor's
tool, it was more probably used to manipu-
late ropes, as were similar instruments from
the Roman Period.

CZ

PROVENANCE: Giza, pyramid of Khufu, north
air shaft of Queen's Chamber, discovered by
Waynmann Dixon 1872

BIBLIOGRAPHY: *Graphic*, December 7, 1872,
pp. 530, 545, figs. 1, 2, 4; *Nature*, December 26,
1872, pp. 146–47; Smyth 1880, p. 429; Stadelmann 1994, pp. 287–88, pl. 55; Lehner 1997,
p. 112

38. KING KHUFU'S CATTLE

Fourth Dynasty, reign of Khufu
Limestone
H. 46 cm (18⅛ in.); w. 137.5 cm (54⅛ in.)
The Metropolitan Museum of Art, New York,
Rogers Fund and Edward S. Harkness Gift,
1922 22.1.3

On this relief block three cattle march
sedately one behind the other; of a fourth
only the tip of the horn is preserved at the
right. The animals are of a lean, long-legged
breed with extremely long horns, which the
artist has depicted in a beautiful lyre shape.
In ancient Egypt such cattle were kept in
herds that grazed on the open grasslands in
the Delta and at the desert margins under
the tutelage of herdsmen who shared their
half-wild life. Sometimes longhorn cattle
were used as working animals on farms,
especially for plowing (however, see the
shorthorn breed in the plowing scene [cat.
no. 25c]), and, like their fatter counterparts
that lived in stables, they were also butch-
ered for offerings and to provide meat for
the tables of the wealthy.[1] Castration of
animals to improve the quality of meat
was probably customary, and the cattle
on this Fourth Dynasty relief reused at Lisht
appear to be oxen.[2]

In the tombs of officials of high status
processions of cattle were a common theme;
the animals were depicted driven to slaugh-
ter as offerings to the dead or being counted
and inspected by the tomb owner in life.[3] In
the royal monuments the cattle were shown
either assembled among the booty from military campaigns or presented as offerings.
Judging from preserved scenes, booty animals were often grouped closely together so
that they overlapped one another.[4] Cattle
in single file appear for the most part in the
context of a presentation of offerings for
the funerary cult of a deceased king.[5] Thus,
the beasts in this relief probably belonged
to a scene of the latter kind.

Elaborate names are written above the
animals on the Lisht block, a feature that is
unique in known representations of this
type. These names are difficult to translate,
and scholars have advanced various versions of them. Goedicke tentatively translates the first name from the left as "the
tribute from Tefrer belonging to Khufu"
(Tefrer being the source of lapis lazuli);[6] the
second ox he calls "the surrounding terri-
tories serve (Khufu),"[7] and the third "the

surrounding lands act for Khufu."[8] Whatever these rather high-sounding appellations
may signify in terms of literal meaning, they
are strikingly similar to the names of the
estates whose personifications frequently
appear in rows in pyramid temples and
causeways (cat. nos. 22, 41). Perhaps each
of the dignified oxen represented an economic entity, such as a particular herd that
Khufu had designated to provide meat for
his funerary cult in eternity.

Stylistically the cattle relief takes its
proper place beside the fragment of a relief
with the head of an estate personification
from Lisht (cat. no. 41). The outlines of the
animal figures are well rounded, and the
modeling of the musculature is especially
sensitive. Judging from finds in other pyramid precincts, this cattle *défilé* could have
been located at Giza, either in Khufu's valley temple or in his pyramid temple.[9] The
oxen would have been placed on a wall in
the north half of one of these buildings so
that their heads faced the pyramid.

The relief was originally in two parts,
which were subsequently joined at the
middle of the center cow.   DOA

1. Störk 1984a, cols. 257–63, with earlier bibliography; Houlihan 1996, pp. 10–21.
2. Vandier 1969, pp. 9–10. Representations do
   not always make a clear distinction between
   bulls and oxen; see ibid., pp. 13–27.
3. Ibid., pp. 13–58.
4. Perhaps the most famous example of this type
   is from the pyramid temple of Sahure; see Borchardt 1913, pl. 1. But see also Labrousse and
   Moussa 1996, p. 97, doc. 57; and Jéquier 1940,
   pls. 36, 37, 40.
5. Jéquier 1940, pl. 55.
6. Goedicke 1971, p. 19, n. 44. Dobrev (1992,
   pp. 403–4) tentatively interprets this inscription
   as referring to trees of certain types (*trrw[t]*)
   that were lifted up (*f[ȝ w]*), presumably for the

building of the king's pyramid. I would like to
thank Salima Ikram for her assistance in securing the relevant pages from the author and for
obtaining his permission to use them here.
7. In this appellation Khufu is identified not by
   his familiar name but by his so-called gold
   Horus name, which consists of two falcons on
   a gold hieroglyph; see H. Müller 1938, pp. 54–
   62; and Beckerath 1984, pp. 21–26. Dobrev
   (1992, p. 402, nn. 2, 3) follows Iversen (1987,
   pp. 54–59), who understood *hȝw nbw(t)*,
   translated by Goedicke as "surrounding terri-
   tories," to indicate islands near the shore of
   the Nile Delta.
8. Goedicke 1971, p. 19.
9. Labrousse and Moussa 1996, p. 78, doc. 26
   (valley temple); Borchardt 1913, pl. 55 (pyramid temple). A fragment found near Khufu's
   pyramid temple between the small pyramids
   G I a and G I c shows the head of a bull or an
   ox and the remains of the arm of a man who

leads this animal by a rope; see Reisner and
Smith 1955, p. 5, n. 6, fig. 7: 26-2-24. The
muzzle of the animal, if drawn correctly,
is broader than the strikingly small muzzles on
the Lisht block.

PROVENANCE: Lisht North, pyramid enclosure
of Amenemhat I,* foundation of a large mastaba
at southwest corner, Metropolitan Museum of
Art excavation, 1920–22

BIBLIOGRAPHY: Hayes 1953, p. 63, fig. 39;
Goedicke 1971, pp. 18–19

*This was called the "French Mastaba" because it had
been explored by the French expedition of 1895–96;
see Gautier and Jéquier 1902, pp. 100–103. The
Metropolitan Museum expedition used the numbers
372 and 384 for this mastaba. The name Rehu-er-
djersen on a block found here may identify the tomb
owner; see Mace 1922, pp. 10–13, with plan on p. 5.

39. Man with a Sunshade

Fourth Dynasty, reign of Khufu
Painted limestone
H. 38 cm (15 in.); w. 40 cm (15¾ in.)
Royal Ontario Museum, Toronto 958.49.2

Goedicke has convincingly demonstrated that this fragment,[1] found reused in the pyramid of the Twelfth Dynasty pharaoh Amenemhat I, was originally part of the relief decoration of King Khufu's pyramid temple at Giza.[2] Indeed, it has the roundness and smooth surfaces typical of the reliefs of Khufu's pyramid precinct (cat. nos. 38, 41) and shows many similarities with the fragment of an estate personification that carries the name of this king (cat. no. 41). The differentiation between the smooth surfaces of the man's body and the main part of the shade and the grooved wig, for example, is comparable to the play between areas of contrasting texture on the estate relief.

The man grasps the pole of a lotus-leaf-shaped sunshade,[3] which rests on his shoulder, and enough is preserved of another shade behind him to tell us that he is the first of at least two shade bearers. Of an inscription on the right only parts of the hieroglyphs for "Upper Egypt" and "protection" remain, which are not sufficient to allow us to reconstruct the whole. Lotus-leaf-shaped sunshades were customarily carried by attendants of the pharaoh in Old Kingdom Egypt, especially at performances of rituals.[4] We can assume, therefore, that the scene to which the Toronto fragment belonged involved a ritual and that a large figure of the king was depicted close by. The sky

symbol with rather large stars that crowns the relief is a common feature in wall representations of religious character.

The Toronto relief is one of only a few reused blocks from Lisht on which substantial amounts of color remain. The black in the wig and the dark red of the skin alone have survived, but the intensity of these colors helps us imagine the original impression that was conveyed when the traditional bluish gray background and the probable green of the shade and blue and yellow of the sky were still in place.   DoA

1. The fragment was formerly in The Metropolitan Museum of Art, New York, 22.1.22.
2. This attribution is convincing even though the eyebrow and wig shapes that Goedicke (1971, pp. 56–57) cites also appear in Fifth Dynasty reliefs; see, for example, Cherpion 1989, pls. 43–45.
3. The only difference between a sunshade and a fan of the type that imitates the form of a lotus leaf is size; see Fischer 1977a, col. 81; and Fischer 1984b, col. 1104. The object in the present relief is large enough to be called a shade. In practice, one and the same instrument may have provided movement of air and served as a shield against the sun.
4. See Borchardt 1907, p. 84, fig. 62c; Bissing and Kees 1923, frontis., pls. 9 (foot washing of king), 11 (king being carried in palanquin), 16 (king on throne being adorned), 17 (throne), 18 (king on throne); and Bissing and Kees 1928, pl. 3 (king carried by officials in priestly garment and with insignia). For the early history of the shade, see Goedicke 1971, p. 57 n. 147.

PROVENANCE: Lisht North, pyramid of Amenemhat I, west side of core, Metropolitan Museum of Art excavation, 1920–22

BIBLIOGRAPHY: Needler 1959, pp. 32ff.; Goedicke 1971, pp. 56–57

40. Woodcutter among Trees

Fourth Dynasty, probably reign of Khufu
Limestone with remains of paint
H. 28 cm (11 in.); w. 90 cm (35⅜ in.)
The University of Pennsylvania Museum of Archaeology and Anthropology, Philadelphia
58-10-3

Ancient Egypt, although not rich in trees, nevertheless had enough wood to supply material for the manufacture of furniture, coffins, and many other commonly used articles. And although most ships of state were probably made from imported cedar,[1] the overwhelming number of vessels that sailed the Nile must have been made of indigenous wood.[2] No wonder that time and again Old Kingdom depictions of ship-building include scenes of lumbermen cutting trees for the men who make the boats. Often we see herds of goats that have come to feed on the foliage of trees (see entry for cat. no. 42), which are felled and trimmed by lumbermen and then transported to the shipyard.[3] The present relief block[4] comes from such a representation. It preserves only part of the uppermost register of the original scene and shows the leafy tops of two magnificent trees whose trunks must have been carved on the block below. Like the traditional figure of the pharaoh, the trees towered over two or more registers; in these registers their felling and trimming and the eventual building of a ship (or ships) must have been depicted. A man whose head and raised arms were carved on the block above strides with legs far apart and left foot lifted from the ground. He was undoubtedly engaged in a forceful action— probably the swinging of an ax over the fallen tree trunk whose end is visible behind his forward leg.

As Goedicke has noted, the detailed depiction of the foliage is without parallel in Old Kingdom art.[5] Remarkable also is the liveliness of the plants. The tips of the branches at the left side of the tree nearest the man are more loosely distributed than those on the right, as if a wind was blowing them toward the left, and the central branch of the other tree is bent in an utterly natural way. There can be no doubt that a master sculptor was at work here. Taking this into account and considering that the original composition must have been of large size, given the remains of the trees

that extended over two or even three registers, we almost certainly can assign the relief to a royal monument. There is also enough evidence to indicate that the monument in question belonged to the pyramid complex of Khufu at Giza: the roundness of the sculpted areas and their subtle relationship to the background, as well as the sparsely indicated musculature of the fully rounded limbs and torso of the woodcutter, firmly place the work in the same group of reliefs from Khufu's pyramid precinct that includes representations of a procession of cattle, a man with a sunshade, and a personification of an estate (cat. nos. 38, 39, 41).[6]

Assigning the woodcutter relief to the funerary complex of Khufu—most likely the pyramid temple—runs counter to the general belief that full representations of shipbuilding did not belong to the repertoire of scenes included in royal funerary structures. It is true that no monument from a royal funerary complex has a similar scene that is preserved, and it seems that in the tombs of officials depictions of woodcutters began to appear only about the time of Sahure's reign, in the Fifth Dynasty.[7] Boat building, however, was already widely shown in the reliefs and paintings of the Meidum tombs from the time of Khufu's father, Snefru (cat. no. 24c).[8] And among the tantalizingly small relief fragments found near the site of Khufu's pyramid temple and upper causeway were some bits that indicate the presence of scenes with boats.[9]

DOA

1. In addition to cedar, Nour et al. (1960, pp. 45–46) note that juniper and thorn-tree wood, which are indigenous, are present in the royal boats.
2. Lucas and Harris 1962, p. 442; Haldane 1992, p. 104.
3. Vandier 1969, pp. 86–90, 661–64; Dürring 1995, pp. 92–95. The most important parallels to the scene discussed here are Hassan 1943, p. 115, fig. 60 (tomb of Seshemkare, time of Sahure); Moussa and Altenmüller 1971, p. 27, pls. 20, 21, 22b (early Niuserre); Moussa and Altenmüller 1977, p. 74, pls. 20, 21, fig. 8 (late Niuserre to reign of Menkauhor); Lepsius 1849–58, vol. 2, pl. 108 (Sixth Dynasty); and Varille 1938, pl. 16 (Sixth Dynasty).
4. The fragment was formerly in The Metropolitan Museum of Art, New York, 22.1.11.
5. Goedicke 1971, p. 120.
6. For examples of royal reliefs of the Fifth Dynasty, see cat. nos. 112, 113.
7. See note 3 above.
8. See, above all, Petrie 1892, pls. 11, 25.
9. Reisner and Smith 1955, p. 5, fig. 7: 24-11-889, 24-12-14, 24-12-545.

PROVENANCE: Lisht North, pavement west of pyramid of Amenemhat I, Metropolitan Museum of Art excavation, 1920–22

BIBLIOGRAPHY: Goedicke 1971, pp. 118–20

41. HEAD OF A FEMALE PERSONIFICATION OF AN ESTATE

Fourth Dynasty, reign of Khufu
Limestone
H. 30 cm (11⅞ in.); w. 22 cm (8⅝ in.)
The Metropolitan Museum of Art, New York,
Rogers Fund and Edward S. Harkness Gift,
1922 22.1.7

Like the scenes from a ksing's Heb Sed (cat. no. 23), this fragment is from the group of Old Kingdom blocks that was reused in the core of the pyramid of the Twelfth Dynasty king Amenemhat I at Lisht. Preserved here is the upper part of a female figure, a woman who carries on her head the cartouche of King Khufu resting on a horizontal staff or board with a feathery protuberance in front and two streamers at the back.

From earliest times in Egypt horizontal bars of the kind that carry the king's cartouche here were shown mounted on poles; instead of hieroglyphs they usually supported sacred emblems. Such standards served at ritual and state functions to establish the presence of superhuman forces.[1] From the Third Dynasty onward not only sacred powers but also administrative entities such as the nomes were represented by images on standards,[2] and a similar device was used to denote royal agricultural foundations, usually called estates. In the latter representations human figures were substituted for the poles of the standards, thus transforming each image into a personification of the estate. In place of the sacred emblem the name of the estate's founder, most often a king, crowned the configuration; this name was inscribed in either a cartouche or the rectangular hieroglyph designating "house" or "walled farmstead" (cat. no. 22a).[3] The royal name was part of the estate's own name, and the rest of the word was written behind the figure. In the present fragment the estate name reads from right to left, "Perfect Is Khufu,"[4] and the personification is female because the estate in question is a *niwt*, or village, a word of feminine gender in ancient Egyptian.[5]

Old Kingdom estates were either villages of long standing or new foundations established (some of them on recently reclaimed land) by a royal or a private owner; all were dedicated to provide in perpetuity for the funerary cult of the founder or for a temple.[6] The personifications of estates that appeared as rows of many figures, therefore, did not merely demonstrate wealth: they represented an economic reality and served magically to preserve this reality in eternity. Because of this magical function it was important to provide a name with each estate personification.

A comparison of the present Khufu estate figure and predecessors from the time of Snefru (cat. no. 22) reveals the considerable development of Old Kingdom relief art from the reign of the first king of the Fourth Dynasty to that of his successor. In the Snefru examples the estate figures stand out sharply against their backgrounds, the relief surface is relatively flat, and all details are outlined with almost graphic precision. The Khufu figure meets the background with a rounded edge, except where the outline is straight, and as a result figure and background appear to be more unified. An overall roundness in the relief lends soft- ness to the figure and the details, and there is a sensitive differentiation between the grooved area of the wig and the smooth skin and garment. Intricate detailing in the hieroglyphs and the double-rope pattern of the cartouche (compare cat. no. 176) are also notable in this fine royal relief, which probably once adorned Khufu's pyramid temple or the upper part of his causeway at Giza.[7] Since the figure would certainly have faced toward the inside of the temple, we can assume that this estate personification was placed on a wall in the south half of the monument.   DoA

1. Curto 1984b, cols. 1255–56.
2. Helck 1977, cols. 422–26.
3. For concepts of personifications of abstract terms, see Baines 1985.
4. For the names of estates, see Jacquet-Gordon 1962, pp. 43–79.
5. For male estate personification figures and the reasons for a predominance of female figures, see ibid., pp. 26–28.

6. See ibid., pp. 3–7; and Jacquet-Gordon 1977, cols. 919–20.
7. Goedicke (1971, p. 16) tentatively assigned the piece to the valley temple. For his reasons, see entry for cat. no. 23, n. 3. However, in the pyramid precincts in which relief decoration is preserved, estate personifications were usually placed in the pyramid temples or at the very top of the causeway; see Jacquet-Gordon 1962, pp. 140 (Userkaf pyramid temple), 144 (Sahure pyramid temple), 152 (Niuserre pyramid temple), 158 (sun temple of Niuserre), 160 (Isesi pyramid temple), 168 (Unis, upper part of causeway), 183 (Pepi II, upper part of causeway).

PROVENANCE: Lisht North, pyramid of Amenemhat I, west side of core, Metropolitan Museum of Art excavation, 1920–22

BIBLIOGRAPHY: Smith 1946, p. 157, pl. 39; Jacquet-Gordon 1962, p. 138; Goedicke 1971, pp. 16–17

42. BILLY GOAT

Fourth Dynasty, probably reign of Khufu
Limestone
H. 28 cm (11 in.); w. 50 cm (19¾ in.)
The Metropolitan Museum of Art, New York,
Rogers Fund and Edward S. Harkness Gift,
1922 22.1.20

Goats are satisfied with all manner of plant food that cattle and sheep do not eat, and they adjust easily to dry climates.[1] No wonder that herds of goats were kept routinely in ancient Egypt and that many representations in tombs show them roaming the countryside with their herdsmen. They are often pictured under trees trying to feed from the foliage. But there are also images of mating goats (cat. no. 120), goats giving birth, and goats in rows in the open countryside grazing with their young.[2] As Goedicke has pointed out, the animal in this relief—a fragment found at Lisht—has an unusual twisted horn that differs from most other goat horns shown in paintings and reliefs. The usual horns have an undulating shape and are spread farther apart.[3] The closest parallel to the horns of the goat of the present relief appears in a fragment that was discovered in the debris of King Khufu's

causeway at Giza, near the point at which it enters the pyramid temple.[4]

The Lisht goat is, moreover, closely related stylistically to reliefs bearing Khufu's name, such as fragments showing a procession of cattle and a personification of an estate (cat. nos. 38, 41). In all three the relief is well rounded and the sculpted areas rise smoothly toward their highest points. To be sure, the carving is somewhat higher here than in the two other examples; the head especially has an almost three-dimensional quality, with the eye deeply carved and the bones around the eye emphasized. There are, however, notable parallels in the treatment of the goat and the cattle: the skin and musculature between the front legs sag in like manner, and very similar elongated muscles at the base of the neck in all the animals are indicated with shallow depressions.

If the goat relief, like the cattle fragment, originally came from Khufu's valley or pyramid temple, the two scenes may have carried a similar meaning: the goat and its companion,[5] whose head is now missing, perhaps belonged to a row of animals representing the offering of meat in perpetuity for the cult in the king's temple. The goats must have been positioned on a wall in the south half of the building,

whereas the cattle relief would have been placed in the north part of the monument.

DOA

1. Störk 1986, cols. 1400–1401; Houlihan 1996, p. 25.
2. Vandier 1969, pp. 86–92.
3. Goedicke 1971, p. 134.
4. Reisner and Smith 1955, pp. 4–5, n. 6, fig. 7: 37-3-4b.
5. Goedicke (1971, p. 134) reconstructs this animal as a female antelope, but it could well be another goat—for which the tail is more suitable.

PROVENANCE: Lisht North, pyramid of Amenemhat I, west side of core, Metropolitan Museum of Art excavation, 1920–22

BIBLIOGRAPHY: Mace 1922, p. 13, fig. 13 (detail); Goedicke 1971, pp. 133–34

43. SOLDIERS RUNNING WITH A ROPE

Fourth Dynasty, possibly reign of Khufu
Limestone
H. 27.1 cm (10⅝ in.); w. 45 cm (18⅛ in.)
The Metropolitan Museum of Art, New York, Rogers Fund, 1913 13.235.2

Like other fragments in this exhibition (cat. nos. 105–107), this piece of a relief probably belonged to a scene with sailing ships and small companies of running troops; the figures here, however, are larger than those of the related objects. All were found reused in the pyramid of Amenemhat I at Lisht. Preserved in part on the present fragment are the figures of two men supporting on their shoulders a carrying pole from which a heavy coil of rope is suspended. Much of the body of the lead man is still visible, but only the forward arm and part of the breast of his companion remain. The first man grasps the pole with his left hand, while his right arm curves awkwardly behind him; his long fingers and somewhat thick wrist overlap the coils of rope. His

legs are spread apart, indicating that he and his companion are running, a difficult task considering the instability of the load balanced between them. The soldier wears an apron composed of three very short, wide strips, which are separated by incised lines. The left arm of the second man is draped over the pole so that the inside of his elbow rests against it and his arm hangs down.

Like depictions of running troops dated to the reign of the Fifth Dynasty king Userkaf (cat. nos. 103, 104), this fragment is rendered in low relief. However, stylistic features indicate that the work probably predates the Fifth Dynasty. The contour lines that define the rope bearers slope gradually toward the surface of the stone and are sharply outlined where they join the background. This type of surface treatment is characteristic of early Fourth Dynasty reliefs and suggests that the piece may have originated at the pyramid complex of Khufu at Giza.[1] In contrast to the relatively graceful proportions and poses typical of figures in early Fifth Dynasty works, the arms of these men seem thick and their contorted positions appear strained and uncomfortable.

A close parallel to the composition of this piece is found in a relief from the tomb of Prince Ka-ni-nisut at Giza, which probably dates from the Fourth Dynasty.[2] In this scene, where soldiers are seen running in front of a sailing ship, the lead figure swings his right arm over the pole while the second man grasps it with both hands. Given that Ka-ni-nisut's tomb is located not far to the west of Khufu's pyramid, we are left with the intriguing possibility that the prince's artists copied at least one of the figural arrangements found in the temple of his royal ancestor.   AO

1. See Smith 1946, pp. 157–58.
2. Junker 1934, p. 156, fig. 22, pl. 9. The parallel was recognized by Goedicke (1971, p. 104). For a discussion of the date of this tomb, see entry for cat. no. 106. For a later example of this type of figural grouping, see Ziegler 1993a, pp. 66, 69, 142.

PROVENANCE: Lisht North, core of pyramid of Amenemhat I, Metropolitan Museum of Art excavation, 1912–13

BIBLIOGRAPHY: Goedicke 1971, p. 104

44. HEMIUNU SEATED

Fourth Dynasty, later reign of Khufu
Limestone with remains of paint
H. 155.5 cm (61¼ in.); w. 61.5 cm (24¼ in.);
d. 104.7 cm (41¼ in.)
Roemer- und Pelizaeus-Museum, Hildesheim 1962

Hemiunu—as the colored-paste inscriptions on the base of his statue tell us and as this remarkable statue and his huge mastaba beside Khufu's pyramid testify—was one of the most important individuals of the Old Kingdom:

> Member of the elite, high official, vizier, king's seal bearer, attendant to Nekhen, and spokesman of every resident of Pe, (2) priest of Bastet, priest of Shesmetet, priest of the Ram of Mendes, (3) Keeper of the Apis Bull, Keeper of the White Bull, whom his lord loves, (4) elder of the palace, high priest of Thoth, whom his lord loves, courtier, (5) Overseer of Royal Scribes, priest of the Panther Goddess, Director of Music of the South and North, Overseer of All Construction

44

Projects of the King, king's son of his own body, Hemiunu.[1]

The title "king's son of his own body" seems to have been used with some latitude. Hemiunu of Giza is generally considered to be the same Hemiunu who was the eldest son of Nefer-maat of Meidum (see entry for cat. no. 24), himself a "king's son."[2] As "Overseer of All Construction Projects of the King," Hemiunu would have directed the building of the Great Pyramid. His mastaba seems to have been built during the later years of Khufu's reign.[3]

When the statue of Hemiunu was found by Hermann Junker in a serdab of mastaba G 4000 (figs. 109, 110), it was largely intact except for the face, which had been badly damaged around the eyes and nose, apparently by thieves digging out the inlays (particularly the casings of gold)[4] from the eyes. Fortunately, a reasonable restoration could be made from a number of fragments found in the sand filling the serdab chamber.[5] While the animation of the original eyes (probably rock crystal) could hardly be duplicated, their general shape was deemed recoverable; the line of the browridge seems to have been unambiguous, but the treatment of the eyebrow as a natural ridge rather than a plastically raised strip was a decision of the restorers. The shape of the nose was re-created from traces of its original contours on the face and from the relief depiction of Hemiunu (cat. no. 45) and is perhaps less satisfactory. Traces of color noted by Junker indicate that the statue had been fully painted.

Sitting unusually far forward on a wide, block-shaped seat, Hemiunu wears a kilt that is tied with a rare type of knot.[6] His hands rest on his knees, the right hand formed into a fist and the left with open and downward-facing palm. His head is small for his large body. The natural hair is indicated, rounded and full, and is separated from his face by a raised edge. Distinctive features are rendered: an oblong face, full cheeks, a small, rather thin-lipped, slightly turned-down mouth with muscle ridges marked at each corner, and a small, sharp chin over a heavy throat.

The body is modeled with great particularity: certain articulations, such as the clavicle and elbows, are closely observed, and details such as the cuticles of the nails, the wrinkles at the joints of the fingers, and even the creases on the underside of the fingers of the flattened left hand are meticulously rendered.

109. Head and shoulders of statue of Hemiunu, seen through hole in serdab, mastaba of Hemiunu (G 4000), Giza

110. Statue of Hemiunu in opened serdab

Most remarkable—indeed inescapable—is the flesh that suffuses his form. The muscles are minimally modeled, as though they were slack and overwhelmed by the weight of the flesh. From the front the great sagging breasts and chest, heavy belly, and crushed navel are impressive. In side view the effect of these features is magnified: the large breasts hang in great soft mounds; the folds of sagging flesh visible on the chest continue around the sides of the body in long, curved laps ending only on the back, as they do on extremely obese or very aged persons. At the same time a slight discordance arises for the modern viewer; in fact, the extreme marks of obesity are applied as signs of importance to a torso whose mass is not really quite sufficient to justify them physically.

Similar attention to indications of obesity can be seen in a few other statues. The scribe statue of Setka, son of Djedefre

(cat. no. 55), has the same crushed navel, while the Scribe in the Louvre (fig. 33) and the figure of Peher-nefer in the Louvre (N 118) have strikingly similar puffy skin, slack muscles, and distinctive laps of flesh running under the arms and onto the back.[7] It may well be that these statues, which exhibit a hyperrealistic modeling of flesh, belong to a school of the early to mid-Fourth Dynasty.[8]

The pastes inlaying the inscription, here show unusual tones. Junker noted that the original signs probably had the more usual colorations and that their present appearance is due to the loss of paste layers.[9]

MH

1. Translation by James P. Allen.
2. The titles and relationship of Hemiunu and Nefer-maat were first addressed by Junker 1929, pp. 148–53, and have often been dis-

cussed since then; see Strudwick 1985, p. 117, for a recent discussion.
3. Strudwick (1985, p. 117) cites the evidence.
4. Junker (1929, pp. 153–54) noted that a small piece of the gold framing remained.
5. Junker (ibid., pp. 155–56) and Schmitz (1986, p. 38) discuss the restoration.
6. The knot is also seen on the statue of Nesut-nefer in the Roemer- und Pelizaeus-Museum, Hildesheim (2143).
7. See Ziegler 1997a, pp. 64–67, 204–8, 116–19; she dates both the Scribe in the Louvre and the figure of Peher-nefer to the Fourth Dynasty.
8. Compare the later statue of Ankh-haf (fig. 32) with its stronger interest in musculature and structure (Smith 1946, pls. 14, 15).
9. See the discussion of the paste-filled reliefs from the tomb of Itet in the entry for cat. no. 24 in this catalogue.

PROVENANCE: Giza, Western Cemetery, mastaba G 4000, Junker excavation

BIBLIOGRAPHY: Junker 1929, pp. 153–57, pls. 18–23; Porter and Moss 1974, p. 123; Schmitz 1986, pp. 36–38

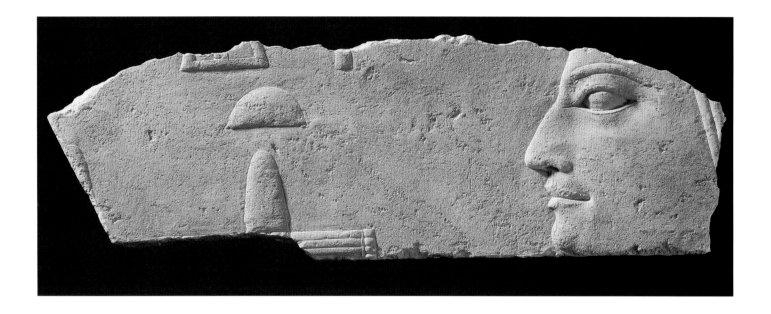

45. Relief of Hemiunu's Face

Fourth Dynasty, reign of Khufu
Limestone
H. 12.1 cm (4¾ in.); w. 39.5 cm (15½ in.)
Museum of Fine Arts, Boston, Harvard University–
Museum of Fine Arts Expedition 27.296

His high rank as prince, vizier, and Overseer of All Construction Projects enabled Hemiunu to obtain for his burial a large mastaba at Giza, in the center of the cemetery west of Khufu's pyramid, the construction of which Hemiunu may have supervised (see entry for cat. no. 44).[1] Initially this mastaba[2] was the solid rectangular stone structure customary during Khufu's reign. However, when the original building was enlarged on all sides but the west, an elongated corridor was added to the east. This corridor housed two false doors, each in front of a serdab chamber, the northern one containing the magnificent statue of Hemiunu (cat. no. 44).

Both the corridor and the doorway leading into it were decorated with reliefs, of which a few fragments remain.[3] The present piece comes from a depiction of the seated tomb owner on the south, or left, reveal of the doorway. Preserved at the right edge is the face of Hemiunu, with traces of ridges representing the strands of his shoulder-length wig. Hieroglyphs in front of the face are part of the traditional offering formula: "An offering that t[he king] gives." The outline of a side of a loaf of bread at the left suggests that a prayer for a thousand loaves of

bread and a thousand jars of beer, among other texts, once filled the space in front of the seated figure.[4]

The remarkable qualities of the relief fragment showing Hemiunu become apparent when it is compared with faces from earlier reliefs, such as those showing Metjen (cat. no. 29) and Aa-akhti (cat. no. 18). Both the Metjen and Aa-akhti pieces are carved in the high relief common in the Third Dynasty and the early Fourth. The Hemiunu relief is somewhat lower but does share a number of important traits with these antecedents and works contemporary with them. For instance, all delineate the outline of the upper face in one way and that of the lower in another.[5] Forehead and nose above the tip are separated from the background by the same angular edge that was used in early Old Kingdom reliefs to set off not only faces but also other parts of figures, such as the torso, kilt, and legs. However, nostrils, philtrum, mouth, and chin curve smoothly into the background. In each of the earlier works the combining of these two techniques to delineate the face produces a well-defined profile and a soft, youthful expression around the mouth. The

differentiation between Hemiunu's upper and lower face is carried out in a manner that is identical to that seen in the reliefs of Metjen and Aa-akhti except for the use of a very thin edge along the upper area. The result is the image of a self-confident and determined person in whose face a bony, slightly curved nose contrasts with a faintly smiling mouth that is surrounded by soft, subtly modeled musculature. A strong, broad jaw ends in a round chin, leaving no doubt about the powerful will of this official.

It is clear that Hemiunu's face exhibits a number of features reminiscent of sculpture in the round. Among them are the three-dimensional treatment of the eye, with its rounded eyeball,[6] the fine lines enhancing both upper and lower lids, the cosmetic line added to the outer corner of the eye,[7] and the faint but determined indication of the cheekbone. In view of the highly sculptural quality of the relief it is understandable that scholars have repeatedly commented that its face and that of the statue of Hemiunu are closely related.[8] However, the two faces, although both unmistakably individualized, are not so similar. The pointed chin of the statue, for instance, is separated from the mouth by a rather long, flat area, whereas only a soft indentation intervenes between the chin and the mouth in the relief. And beyond such differences in detail, the Hemiunu of the relief is younger and less forbidding than the man represented in the statue. Perhaps their expressive characters are at variance because the relief figure was depicted seated at a table with offerings and receiving eternal sustenance, while the statue was lodged in a serdab as a representative of the living man;[9] certainly the two works were made by different groups of artists. The vizier and Overseer of All Construction Projects evidently commanded the best talents in both relief sculpture and statuary.

DoA

1. Junker 1929, pp. 148–50. For the possibility that Hemiunu was the son of Nefer-maat, son of Snefru, see ibid., pp. 151–53; and cat. no. 24.
2. Junker 1929, pp. 132–45, figs. 18–21; Porter and Moss 1974, pp. 122–23, pls. 7, 15.
3. Junker 1929, pp. 145–48, fig. 23, pls. 15b, 16b, 17; Smith 1942, pp. 525–30; Martin 1978, nos. 2146, 2380.
4. For the offering formula in the Fourth Dynasty, see Junker 1955, pp. 82–86, with earlier references on p. 25a: "Totengebet"; Barta 1968, pp. 3–11.
5. The wood reliefs of Hesi-re (cat. no. 17 and Quibell 1913, pls. 29–32) are much earlier examples that display this differentiation between the outlines of the upper and lower parts of the face. The Hemiunu relief, however, has greater subtlety, as a comparison with these antecedents reveals.
6. The very rounded eyeball is seen in a number of mid-Fourth Dynasty reliefs of high quality. See, for instance Smith 1946, pls. 40e (Ankh-haf), 41 (Meret-ites), 42b, 43 (Khufu-khaf).
7. For comparable sculpture in the round, see especially a head of Khafre (cat. no. 61); for a parallel in relief, see the head of Mer-ib from mastaba G 2100 Annex in Berlin (ibid., pl. 46c).
8. Steindorff 1937, pp. 120–21; Smith 1946, pp. 303–4.
9. Schulz (1995, pp. 119–20) has remarked on the fact that Hemiunu's statue may depict an old man in the evening of his life.

PROVENANCE: Giza, near southeast corner of mastaba of Hemiunu (G 4000), Reisner excavation, 1925

BIBLIOGRAPHY: Steindorff 1937, pp. 120–21; Smith 1946, pp. 22–23, pl. 48c; Smith 1952, p. 33, fig. 16 on p. 37; Smith 1960, p. 37, fig. 20 on p. 45; Schmitz 1986, pp. 38, 39, ill.

THE RESERVE HEADS OF THE OLD KINGDOM: A THEORY

Of all categories of ancient Egyptian sculpture that of the so-called reserve heads, one must say, has always constituted one of the most puzzling. These limestone heads, found almost without exception in the Western Cemetery at Giza, and all apparently dating to the early part of the Fourth Dynasty,[1] were so named by Hermann Junker when he first encountered them early in the century (*Ersatzköpfe*, in German, literally "substitution heads"). It was his theory, and it has been one followed by most scholars after him, that such stone heads were intended to take the place of the actual perishable head of the person represented if it should be damaged in any way.

The characteristics of this group of sculptures are easily described but have proved difficult to account for. In the first instance, they reproduce only the head and neck of a figure, making them quite unusual among Egyptian funerary statues, where the representation of a complete figure is for magico-religious reasons the norm; secondly, they are not shown with coiffures of any sort, there being usually only an engraved indication of the hairline; and thirdly, the gaze of the person represented is somewhat raised from the horizontal, which is also unusual, although sometimes encountered in Pharaonic statuary.[2] But added to these peculiarities, which are common to all of the group, are a number of other features that occur in many examples.

The sculptors' treatment of certain of the facial features is not only odd, but odd in such ways that the variations from the norm must be explained away. The peculiarities were listed by Smith in his chapter on the heads in his work of 1946.[3] They consist of (1) the appearance in some of the examples of deep cutting around the eyeballs, separating them from the lids to a degree unusual in Egyptian sculpture, (2) the occasional presence of a fine carved line around the roots of the alae of the nose, where the lateral portions, or wings, of the nostrils join the cheeks, emphasizing the join in an unnatural way, and (3) the quite peculiar and equally unrealistic treatment of the philtrum, the groove down the center of the upper lip, which, instead of being a mere shallow depression, is rendered as a

shallow trench with vertical walls. This is so utterly strange both in terms of the marked naturalism of the portraits themselves and of the Egyptian sculptor's own tradition—both before and after the period with which we are dealing—that some explanation must be sought.

Even stranger and more puzzling are the odd mutilations that many heads have suffered. Most noticeably, some examples have had a rough groove hacked in the back along the median line from the crown of the head to the lower end of the neck. Another mutilation visible on many heads is damage to, or complete removal of, the ears; oddly enough, in one or two of the examples where the ears are missing, considerable care has been taken to dress down and smooth the areas where they once were.

Much ink has been spilled over the question of the purpose of these heads, which seem to make nonsense of many of the principles we see, or believe we see, in Egyptian art of this or any other period. But any hypothesis that seeks to explain the purpose of a discrete and clearly definable group of artifacts must surely take into account all extraordinary characteristics found within the group, whether or not these characteristics are all present in all members of the group.

A theory was suggested by the present writer several years ago in which the reserve heads were seen as artists' prototypes of the type exemplified by the famous head, now in the Ägyptisches Museum und Papyrussammlung, Berlin, of Nefertiti, and the other stone and plaster heads found in the reknowned sculptor's workshop at Amarna.[3] In other words, they were models for the use of sculptors engaged in producing several representations of the same person, whether in sculpture in the round or in two-dimensional art.[4] The peculiar treatment of the heads' features was there explained as intended to facilitate the use of a successful molding medium—the one suggested was fine linen soaked in water with some sort of glue or size, the kind of medium later used for cartonnage masks and coffins—to enable the sculptors of the royal workshops to produce copies in clay or gypsum plaster. Indeed, one such head in the Museum of Fine Arts, Boston (21.329), still has its left cheek partly covered with a thick wad of plaster, suggesting that a direct mold in gypsum plaster had been attempted and had proved a failure.

This theory assumes, of course, that several copies would be needed, that statues would be worked on at various venues, and that the chapel relief carvers might make use of them as well; the highly individualistic relief portraits of Nefer and Hemiunu from their Giza chapels suggest the artists responsible had prototypes of some sort to work from.[5]

A related sculpture was also referred to in the aforementioned article by the present author; this is the famous bust of Ankh-haf (fig. 32). This superbly realistic work, executed in limestone with a plaster coat of varying thickness, is that of a man of middle years, with the suggestion of a rather fuller figure than the usual Egyptian ideal; the ears, which had apparently been added in plaster, are missing. Unlike the reserve heads, it has been given a coat of red-brown paint; the eyes were picked out in black and white, but only traces remain. Unlike the heads, it was found not in a tomb shaft but in the inner room of the chapel of mastaba G 7510 in the Eastern Cemetery at Giza, where it had apparently been set up on a low mud-brick stand. When it fell from its position, it crushed several pottery offering vessels, showing that, unlike the heads, it had been actively used as a focus for the funerary cult.

Not the least of the problems surrounding the heads is that of their original location in the tombs in which they were found. This question has been lately much addressed;[6] apart from the fact that the objects were mostly deposited somewhere at the foot of the vertical shaft leading to the actual burial chamber, nothing very certain can be said on this point.

Although attempts have been made to explain the creation of reserve heads as artifacts intended solely for magical purposes—representations of the deceased that could be ritually killed, as by the previously described incision down the back of the head—these founder on the fact that the killing of funerary gifts to enable them to accompany the deceased has never been reliably inferable from the Egyptian archaeological record and would almost certainly have been alien to the Egyptian way of thought; this would of course have particularly been true with regard to representations of the honored dead. Such fanciful theories, one must conclude, deserve only to be dismissed out of hand.   NBM

46

1. Smith 1946, pp. 23–30.
2. Bothmer 1970, pp. 37ff.
3. Smith 1946, pp. 28–29.
4. Millet 1981, pp. 129ff.
5. Smith 1946, pp. 23, 29, 303–4.
6. See Kelley 1974 and Lacovara 1997.

46. RESERVE HEAD

Fourth Dynasty, probably reign of Khufu
Limestone
H. 26.7 cm (10½ in.)
Phoebe Apperson Hearst Museum of Anthropology,
University of California at Berkeley 6-19767

111. Reserve
head (cat. no.
46) as found
in burial cham-
ber, mastaba
G 1203, Giza

This head was discovered in 1904 during
George Reisner's excavations at Giza undertaken for the University of California and
sponsored by Phoebe Apperson Hearst.
It was lying on its left side in debris above
the canopic pit in the burial chamber of
mastaba G 1203 (fig. 111). A broken slab
stela in the tomb's offering chapel identified
the monument's owner as the Overseer of
Commissions and Director of Bowmen Ka-
nefer.[1] The head has sometimes been identified as depicting Ka-nefer's wife, but it
probably represents Ka-nefer himself.[2]

Of all the known reserve heads, this is
one of the most carefully finished and displays some of the finest modeling.[3] The
hairline is shown around the entire skull,
and the eyebrows are carved in low relief.
The eyes, with long, tapering inner canthi,
are crisply delineated. An incised line describes the natural fold of each of the upper
lids, which bulge slightly above rounded
eyeballs.[4] The lips are relatively thin, and
the philtrum, indicated by a slight depression beneath the nose bordered on either
side by a fine ridge, makes only a slight
indentation in the center of the upper lip.
Instead of turning down at the corners,
as it does on many reserve heads, the
mouth is entirely horizontal and suggests
an almost beatific smile.[5]

In 1904 only two reserve heads were
known, one found at Dahshur and one at
Abusir. The excavators working at Giza at
this time would not have expected to come
across such a head and may have inflicted
a number of small gouges on its right side
during digging.[6] Unlike ancient damage,
which has acquired the same buff-colored
patina as the well-preserved surfaces, these
abrasions are stark white, revealing the
original color of the fine-grained limestone.
The ears, like those of most reserve heads,
seem to have been damaged on purpose.
On each ear the outer edge has been chipped
away, but the outline of the unusually long
lobe and the decorative intersecting curve
that defines the helix are still visible. The
damage to the nose may be accidental, as
broken noses are comparatively rare on

reserve heads.[7] Several imperfections in
the surface appear to have been filled with
plaster in ancient times: the odd pattern of
concentric fissures on the right cheek looks
like plaster fill that has dried unevenly; the
center of the left eyebrow was probably finished in plaster that has disappeared; and
two large abrasions behind the left ear have
traces of what seems to be ancient plaster.[8]

Ka-nefer's offering chapel was the typical
simple mud-brick structure built to surround
a slab stela (fig. 14).[9] Such chapels have no
serdab, and one would not, therefore, expect
to find statues associated with them. However, there is a pair statue in the Louvre
(E 6854)[10] that is inscribed for a Ka-nefer
who has the same titles that appear on the
slab stela in the offering chapel in mastaba
G 1203. Stylistically, the statue is consistent
with Fourth Dynasty sculpture from Giza
and may well represent the owner of G 1203
and his wife. It may also have stood originally in the offering chapel of G 1203,[11]
yet there are other possibilities. Professions
were often passed from one generation to
the next in ancient Egypt. Ka-nefer's two
titles are not particularly common, but they
appear in inscriptions in several other
mastabas in Giza, including G 2150, which
has a serdab and was probably used late in
the Fourth Dynasty or even early in the Fifth
Dynasty. The owner of G 2150, another
Ka-nefer, may be a descendant of the Ka-
nefer of G 1203.[12] Ka-nefer the younger
may have commissioned the Louvre statue
to represent his parents or grandparents
and placed it in the serdab of G 2150, thus
allowing his forebears to benefit from his
own funerary offerings.[13] It is also possible
that the statue was moved from G 1203 to

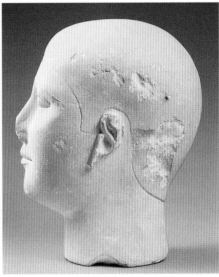

46

G 2150 after the funerary cult of the earlier
tomb was discontinued.[14]

CHR

1. For the slab stela, see Reisner 1942, p. 390,
   pl. 17b. For the titles Overseer of Commissions (*imy-rȝ wpwt*) and Director of Bowmen
   (*ḫrp tmȝ [ty.w]*), see Eichler 1993, pp. 205–6;
   Fischer 1959, p. 267; and Chevereau 1987,
   p. 35.
2. G 1203 was intended for a single burial.
   Because the head was found in the burial
   chamber rather than in the shaft, where it
   might have been thrown with debris from
   another tomb, it most likely belongs with this
   tomb; for the moment, therefore, it seems best
   to identify the piece as a representation of the
   mastaba's owner, Ka-nefer. Microscopic remnants of black and yellow paint have been
   found on the head, but the amounts are so
   small, and the function of reserve heads is still
   so little understood, that it is not possible to
   conclude with any certainty that the yellow
   color, as a rule used for female skin, indicates
   the sex of the person represented.
3. For an entirely different view, see Vandier
   (1958, p. 47), who describes this head as
   "d'un style nettement inférieur."

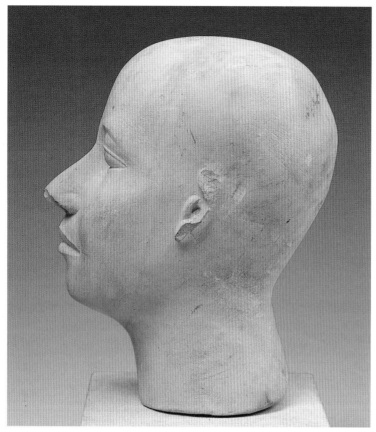

47

4. The incised line indicating the fold of the upper lid has a more natural appearance than on most heads. The line is more deeply incised than usual and does not surround the entire lid but ends a few millimeters short of the inner canthus.

5. Tefnin (1991, pp. 14–15) quite aptly compares the otherworldly quality of this face to that of images of angels in Western art. The Dahshur reserve head in the Egyptian Museum, Cairo (CG 519), and the head of Meret-ites from mastaba G 4140, also in Cairo (fig. 46e), close parallels to this one, have very similar expressions.

6. At the time it was generally supposed that in the Old Kingdom Egyptians did not place statuary in the subterranean burial chamber but in the serdab, a secret room that was part of the offering chapel in the superstructure.

7. Only three of the well-preserved heads from the great Western Cemetery of Giza have broken noses: this one; JE 46217 (G 4140, fig. 46e); and Egyptian Museum, Cairo, JE 67569 (G 5020). However, Museum of Fine Arts, Boston, 21.328 (cat. no. 47) shows another type of damage to the nose, which appears to be intentional.

8. The description of these areas is based on careful examination by the author, but none of them has been tested for the presence of plaster.

9. The chapel of G 1203 was particularly well preserved and is drawn in Reisner 1942, pp. 187, 188, fig. 94a,b.

10. See Ziegler 1997a, pp. 100–104.

11. Although evidence is scanty, it appears that freestanding statues were sometimes placed in the offering chapels of nonroyal individuals during this period. An example is the pair statue of Iai-ib and Khuaut (cat. no. 83).

12. On the basis of the titles, Junker (1938, p. 5; 1944, pp. 161–63) suggested that there was a connection between the two Ka-nefers. It can be assumed that the Louvre statue probably does not represent the Ka-nefer who owned G 2150 for two reasons: in G 2150 Ka-nefer is spelled using the *kȝ* hieroglyph, but on the statue and on the slab stela from G 1203 *kȝ* is spelled phonetically with the basket and vulture hieroglyphs; the name of the woman on the statue is not among those of female relatives recorded in the offering chapel of G 2150.

13. Serdabs at Giza often held more than one statue. Some of these statues represent family members whose relationship to the tomb owner is recorded on the statue itself or in the texts inscribed in the offering chapel; most often, however, no relationship is noted, probably because it was understood.

14. G 1203 is in cemetery 1200, in the Western Desert, more than four hundred meters beyond Khufu's pyramid, while G 2150 is in cemetery 2100, less than half that distance from the pyramid. It is possible that the descendants of Ka-nefer the elder decided to move his cult statue from his tomb on the edge of the great Western Cemetery to a more convenient location in the tomb of his son or grandson in order to consolidate the family funerary cult.

PROVENANCE: Giza, Western Cemetery, mastaba G 1203, Reisner excavation for University of California, Hearst Expedition, 1903–4

BIBLIOGRAPHY: Reisner 1942, p. 390 (where the height is given as 25.5 cm), pls. 21f (in situ), 22a–e; Smith 1946, pl. 9b; Porter and Moss 1974, p. 57; Tefnin 1991, pp. 97–98, pl. 1a–d

47. RESERVE HEAD

Fourth Dynasty, probably reign of Khufu
Limestone
H. 26.3 cm (10⅜ in.)
Museum of Fine Arts, Boston, Harvard University–
Museum of Fine Arts Expedition 21.328

This piece is usually identified as depicting a woman because the features are perceived as delicate compared to those of many other reserve heads. However, when it is seen in profile, the prominent nose and jaw give an entirely different impression. In fact, like all but two of the known reserve heads, it presents no indication of whether a male or a female is represented.[1] Moreover, there are no inscriptions in the mastaba's offering chapel to provide a clue to the owner's identity.[2]

The head is striking because it lacks any suggestion of a hairline, which on other excavated heads is outlined at least along the forehead.[3] The browridges have been sharply cut and end with deep depressions near the nose. The resulting shadows create the illusion of pencil-thin eyebrows, although none exist.[4] Above these ridges, on either side of the nose, the surface has been roughened where eyebrows would have been carved in relief. While the effect may not have been intentional, this treatment of the brows combined with the slightly downturned mouth produces a hint of a frown, in contrast to the smile of the Berkeley head (cat. no. 46). The eyelids are sharply cut, and the upper lids show an incised line. Undercutting along the lower lids accentuates the roundness of the eyeballs, which bulge from the sockets—as is evident in a profile view—and seem to be held in place by the upper lids.[5] The nose is straight and narrow and comes to a point at the end. The philtrum is bordered by sharp ridges and leaves only the slightest indentation in the full upper lip. The crisply outlined mouth is slightly to the left of center. When the piece is seen from the side, it is apparent that the neck juts forward, unlike the neck of the Berkeley head, which is absolutely vertical. The chin of the present example and of a number of others is slightly raised, a feature that has led some scholars to assert that all reserve heads gaze upward.[6] However, profile views of this piece and nearly every other reserve head reveal that they look straight ahead even if the chin is raised.[7]

The surface of this head has been carefully smoothed and is in nearly pristine condition, heightening the impact of the clearly intentional damage it bears. Although the most prominent parts of the ears have been chipped off, enough remains to suggest that they were not as large and did not lie as close to the head as the ears of most other examples.[8] The groove gouged down the back of many reserve heads is absent here, but there is a surprising injury to the nose. Whereas the noses of a few other reserve heads have sustained apparently accidental breakage at the tips (for example, cat. no. 46), the nostrils of this head seem to have been intentionally slit from the inside out, a form of defacement unique among the types of damage documented for these objects. CHR

1. The best-known exception, Roemer- und Pelizaeus-Museum, Hildesheim, 2384, was found in G 4650, the mastaba of a woman named Iabtit. Here the single indication of gender is the hairline above the brow, which displays the part in the coiffure found only on statues of women. Without this element, the head would probably be identified as male by virtue of the rather heavy features. The second example, Egyptian Museum, Cairo, JE 46217 (fig. 46e), was discovered in the burial chamber of G 4140 and identified as the tomb's owner, Princess Meretites. On this head, too, a woman's parted hair is shown; this hairline has been unevenly scratched rather than gouged as on the head of Iabtit, but it can be seen clearly in a photograph published in Michalowski 1968, p. 361, fig. 193.

2. Small specks of what may be red paint (usually employed for men's skin) are preserved on the edge of the right brow ridge and near the end of the nose, but these may not be original to the piece and do not necessarily indicate the sex of the subject. There appear to be traces of paint on several of the reserve heads in the Museum of Fine Arts, Boston. However, these remnants have not been tested, and they occur on areas such as cheeks, brow, and neck, which might have rubbed against another object or might have been splattered (either in ancient or in modern times). Moreover, no color is visible in the deep lines around the eyes and the nostrils and at the corners of the mouth, where one would expect small traces of original paint to be preserved.

3. The one possible exception is Kunsthistoriches Museum, Vienna, ÄS 9290, which is too badly damaged to be evaluated in this respect.

4. Two other heads, Museum of Fine Arts, Boston, 14.717 (G 4140; fig. 46f), and Egyptian Museum, Cairo, JE 46218 (G 4340; fig. 46c), display a similar but less exaggerated treatment of the browridges. These two heads also share other features with the present example, Boston 21.328: 14.717 and 21.328 have similar profiles and comparatively small ears with the same tilt; the mouths of 21.328 and JE 46218 have a similar shape and are both slightly off center;

and all three show hairlines with the same outline across the brow and around the sideburns.

5. This effect is also seen, albeit to a lesser degree, in Museum of Fine Arts, Boston, 14.717, and Egyptian Museum, Cairo, JE 46218.

6. Millet 1981, p. 130; Vandersleyen 1977, cols. 11–14.

7. Many photographs of Egyptian Museum, Cairo, JE 46217, the head of Meret-ites, are taken from below eye level, and this creates the impression that she looks up. However, when the piece is seen in profile, she appears to look straight ahead. Even Cairo JE 45216 (fig. 46a), whose face is set at the sharpest angle, seems to look straight ahead in a profile view.

8. The ears on this head were attached to an area much smaller than the comparable surfaces of other examples such as Museum of Fine Arts, Boston, 14.718, and Egyptian Museum, Cairo, JE 46215 (Snefru-seneb; fig. 46d). Boston 14.717, however, seems to have had fairly small ears with a shape similar to those of the present work.

PROVENANCE: Giza, mastaba G 4540 A, Reisner excavation, 1913–14

BIBLIOGRAPHY: Reisner 1942, pls. 49e (in situ), 55a; Smith 1946, pl. 7d; Porter and Moss 1974, p. 131; Tefnin 1991, pp. 103–4, pl. 9a,b

48. RESERVE HEAD

Fourth Dynasty, probably reign of Khufu
Limestone
H. 30 cm (11⅞ in.)
Museum of Fine Arts, Boston, Harvard University–
Museum of Fine Arts Expedition 14.719

In any group of reserve heads this example
would stand out, as fig. 46 demonstrates.
At 30 centimeters in height, with its long,
broad face, the head is slightly over lifesize
and the most massive of the group.[1] The

eyes, showing no line along the upper lid,
are almost unique.[2] The nearly perfect condition of the piece, which reveals no intentional damage of the kind documented on
most examples, is exceptional, particularly
in view of the fact that it was found in a
violently disturbed context.[3]

When this example is seen in the company of other reserve heads, its resemblance
to Egyptian representations of Nubians
becomes apparent, although it shows none
of the tendency toward caricature that
marks later portrayals of Nubians.[4] At the

same time it is nearer in its physiognomy to
royal statues than are any of the other heads,
by virtue of the shape of the face, with its
high cheekbones and fleshy cheeks, and its
round, wide-set eyes.[5] These features bring it
especially close to the gneiss statue of Khafre
(fig. 112).[5] However, in some respects this
face differs markedly from Khafre's. For
example, the unusually short nose juts out
sharply and turns up at the end, allowing a
full view of the nostril openings.[6] The fullness of the cheeks accentuates the naso-labial
folds. The distance from nose to upper lip is

remarkably long, and the philtrum makes only a slight, uneven indentation in the full upper lip. The two halves of the lip join in a sharp seam down the middle of the mouth, a feature found on no other reserve head.

Although the head is in excellent condition, the surface has not been smoothed as carefully as that of other examples. Patches of plaster adhere to the helix of the left ear, and a trace of red paint is visible on the right one.[7] The ears slant backward slightly and are set quite close to the head. The browridges have been subtly modeled to arch above the wide-open eyes, but the eyebrows have not been sculpted. There is a clear indication of the hairline across the forehead, but this disappears toward the temples, and the sideburns are not outlined.

This head was found with another in the single shaft of mastaba G 4440, and George Reisner concluded that they represented the Egyptian owner of the tomb and his Nubian wife. Reisner's identification was based on a series of seemingly logical assumptions: that G 4440 belonged to a man; that both heads were originally placed in this mastaba; that one head must represent the male owner of the monument and therefore the other had to depict his wife. These assumptions, however, are based on faulty reasoning. First, although the majority of identified Giza tomb owners were men, a number of the core mastabas in the Western Cemetery belonged to women.[8] Second, there is no evidence that this mastaba was intended for more than one burial, and the owner's spouse, whether male or female, could have been entombed in a neighboring mastaba. Third, neither head displays any features that indicate the sex of the subject. In fact, had this head been found alone in the shaft, Reisner would undoubtedly have identified it as the male owner of the tomb.

Why there were two reserve heads in mastaba G 4440 remains a question. The simplest answer is that one is intrusive, having been thrown in with debris from another mastaba, perhaps G 4450 to the north, which contained no reserve head.[9] As the heads were found lying close together near the bottom of the tomb shaft, surrounded by debris containing broken pottery and fragments of a limestone sarcophagus (fig. 113), this seems a reasonable assumption. Which head belonged to G 4440 is a matter of speculation, but the exceptionally good condition of the example illustrated here suggests that it was handled

less and, thus, is the one more likely to have originated in this tomb.   CHR

1. Museum of Fine Arts, Boston, 14.718 (fig. 46g), and the head of Snefru-seneb (Egyptian Museum, Cairo, JE 46215; fig. 46d) also measure about 30 centimeters high, but their faces, although quite long, are extremely narrow. And while the head of Meret-ites (Cairo JE 46217; fig. 46e), with its exceptionally long neck, stands about 30.5 centimeters tall, the dimensions of its face are similar to those of most of the other examples, whose average height is 26 centimeters.
2. The head found in G 5020 (Egyptian Museum, Cairo, JE 67569; see Reisner 1942, pl. 56) appears to have large eyes very similar to those of the present piece, but the available photographs are not very clear. The head found by Hassan (1953, pls. 3, 4) seems to have true buttonhole eyes. The clay head from G 4840 (Cairo JE 44975; Junker 1929, pl. 14) has eyes that are more almond shaped and have no outline. The poorly carved head found in G 4940 (Museum of Fine Arts, Boston, 21.329; Reisner 1942, pl. 56), which may have been finished in plaster, shows eyes that have been recarved.
3. Tefnin (1991, p. 103) sees symmetrical damage to both ears, but in my opinion the minimal damage on this head appears to be entirely accidental.
4. This is not surprising since the subject is not interpreted as one of the traditional enemies of Egypt but as an Egyptian, albeit a distinctly individual one.
5. This comparison is not meant to imply a date for the head because there are no well-preserved lifesize statues of Khufu against which it can be judged.
6. This slightly upturned nose is a feature found on many reserve heads.
7. The curve of the helix where it turns toward the center of the ear is less exaggerated here than in other examples (cat. no. 46).
8. Reisner himself had excavated four women's tombs, one of them the mastaba of Meret-ites (G 4140). Meret-ites' mastaba also contained two reserve heads, identified by Reisner as the female tomb owner and her husband. In fact, the head depicting the "husband" may have

112. Detail, King Khafre Seated with the Horus Falcon behind His Head. Egyptian Museum, Cairo, CG 14

come from the neighboring mastaba to the north (G 4150), which contained no reserve head (see "Reserve Heads" by Catharine H. Roehrig in this catalogue, pp. 76–77).

9. G 4430, the mastaba south of G 4440, contained a fragmentary clay head, and there is no reason to suppose that it would have housed another example. Furthermore, the majority of reserve heads were found in the three northern, east-west-oriented rows of cemetery 4000 (fig. 47). And finally, the mastabas to the east and west of G 4440 each contained one reserve head, leaving G 4450 as the most likely home for the second head.

PROVENANCE: Giza, mastaba G 4440 A, Reisner excavation, 1913–14

BIBLIOGRAPHY: Reisner 1942, pls. 49c (in situ), 54b; Smith 1946, pl. 8c,d; Porter and Moss 1974, p. 128; Tefnin 1991, pp. 102–3, pls. 7c, 8a–c

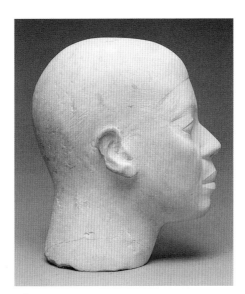

48

113. Two reserve heads (Boston 14.718 and cat. no. 48) as found in shaft A, mastaba G 4440, Giza

49. RESERVE HEAD

Fourth Dynasty, probably reign of Khufu
Limestone
H. 27.7 cm (10⅞ in.)
Kunsthistorisches Museum, Ägyptisch-Orientalische
Sammlung, Vienna ÄS 7787

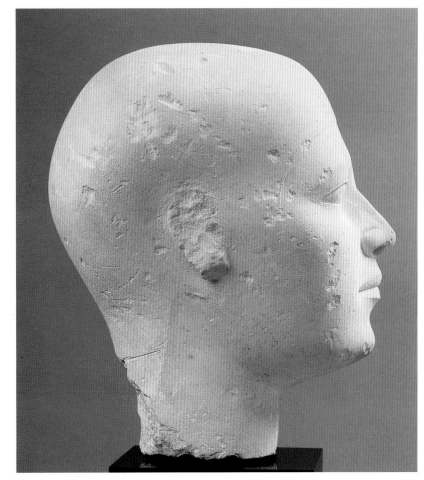

49

Hermann Junker found this piece in 1914, by which time more than a dozen reserve heads had been uncovered. It was lying on its left side at the entrance to the passage leading from the shaft to the burial chamber of mastaba G 4350. Junker identified the head as representing a prince, although the tomb contained no inscriptions or other material that might offer information about the owner. Some years later William Stevenson Smith described it as "the beautiful head of a princess."[1] As in most other examples, no element of the head indicates the sex of the subject, and the finely formed features and well-proportioned profile could as easily belong to a man as to a woman.

The planes of the nose are quite angular and almost unfinished looking, especially in comparison with the other features, which are rather finely modeled, and the rest of the surface, which is carefully smoothed. The hairline has been carved in very low relief across the forehead and around the sideburns, disappears over the area of the ear, and is indicated with an incised line across the back of the neck. The preserved outlines of the missing ears indicate that they were well placed in relation to the facial features and were normal in size. The browridges are softly modeled, but no eyebrows have been carved. The upper and lower lids of the almond-shaped eyes have similar curves. An incised line bounds the entire length of each upper lid. The eyeballs have been modeled, but the profile view reveals that they are quite flat compared with those of the other reserve heads in the exhibition (cat. nos. 46–48) and slope markedly from top to bottom; this inward slant, by no means unique among reserve heads, is more exaggerated here than in other examples. The mouth is very symmetrical, with upper and lower lips of the same fullness. The lips are well defined but not as sharply outlined as on some heads. The philtrum is marked by a soft ridge on either side and makes only a slight indentation in the upper lip.

This head exhibits more damage than the three other examples in the catalogue, some of it probably accidental, some undoubtedly intentional. Most of the gouges in the surface and the breaks on the neck are most likely due to rough handling inflicted when the tomb was robbed, whereas the pitting on the left side of the face was perhaps caused by some element in the soil in which the head lay for thousands of years. The missing ears, however, were removed with extreme care, indicating a well-considered, intentional act rather than an accident or random vandalism. The same is true of the line that is deeply scored along the top of the head and becomes fainter as it extends down the back of the skull to the break in the neck. Although it has been suggested that the groove is a sculptor's guideline,[2] this seems unlikely because it appears to have been cut after the surface was carefully smoothed and, moreover, is slightly off center to the right on the top and curves even farther to the right in the back.

The removal of the ears and the gouging of a groove down the back of the skull are the most widespread forms of intentional damage inflicted on reserve heads. Neither type is universal, however, nor do the two always occur together, as is clear from the examples in this exhibition, one of which has almost perfectly preserved ears and three of which have no groove at the back of the head.   CHR

1. Smith 1946, p. 28.
2. See Lacovara 1997.

PROVENANCE: Giza, mastaba G 4350, Junker excavation, 1914

BIBLIOGRAPHY: Junker 1929, p. 198, pls. 9b (in situ), 12; Porter and Moss 1974, p. 126; Tefnin 1991, pp. 127–28, pls. 27a–d, 29a,b; Seipel 1992, pp. 90–93

50. PRINCESS NEFRET-IABET?

Fourth Dynasty, reign of Khufu
Limestone
H. 37 cm (14⅝ in.); w. 11 cm (4⅜ in.); d. 20 cm
(7⅞ in.)
Staatliche Sammlung Ägyptischer Kunst, Munich
ÄS 7155

Representations of women are relatively
rare in Old Kingdom statuary. Tradition
has it that this pretty statue was discovered
at the same time as the slab stela showing
Princess Nefret-iabet (cat. no. 51), a member
of King Khufu's family. The results of Montague Ballard's excavations at Giza were
never published, and it is not known whether
the statue was actually found near the princess's mastaba. But no stylistic argument has
been advanced to contradict that assumption,[1] and the work can safely be dated to
the beginning of the Fourth Dynasty.

The young woman is sitting on a cubic
seat, hands flat on her knees, and it is easy
to see how her body was cut out of the
original block of stone. Her sheath dress,
suggested only by the indication of the
lower border above the ankles, envelops
a stocky body with very simplified modeling; no details show through the fabric.
The neck is short and the head is set almost
directly into the round shoulders. The
ankles and feet are very thick. The sculptor
has focused all his attention on the heavy,
energetic face. The eyes are strongly outlined, the nose is broad and thick, and the
mouth is strong and slightly asymmetrical.
The chin and cheeks are pronounced. This
somewhat rustic face, with irregularities
that are not without charm, is framed by a
wig of medium length parted in the center
and falling in large, parallel, and obliquely
striated locks. The three ridges high on the
forehead probably represent the woman's
natural hair.

As in the case of Metjen (see cat. nos. 28,
29), there are striking differences between
the relief and the three-dimensional representations of this person. As in Metjen's case,
too, the statue has a less refined appearance
and a stronger personality than the relief.
The woman with the fine profile and graceful silhouette depicted on the stela in no
way resembles the figure seen here. Even the
accessories are different: the long tripartite
wig, which persisted in reliefs, disappeared
in statuary at the beginning of the Fourth

Dynasty, and the feline pelt depicted in the
stela is never seen in sculptures of women.
In addition, the jewelry shown in the relief
is not evident on the statue; however, such
details may have been added in paint that
has disappeared.   CZ

1. Cherpion 1998, p. 101, n. 20.

PROVENANCE: Giza, Western Cemetery, probably mastaba of Nefret-iabet (G 1225), Ballard
excavation, 1902; Sambon collection

BIBLIOGRAPHY: Porter and Moss 1974,
p. 59; Wildung 1980a, pp. 8–9; Ziegler 1990b,
pp. 188–89; Ziegler 1995b, pl. 64c; Sotheby's
(London), sale cat., July 2, 1996; Cherpion
1998, p. 133, fig. 10

51. SLAB STELA OF PRINCESS NEFRET-IABET

Fourth Dynasty, reign of Khufu
Painted limestone
H. 37.7 cm (14⅞ in.); w. 52.5 cm (20¼ in.);
d. 8.3 cm (3¼ in.)
Musée du Louvre, Paris E 15591
Paris only

This delicate stela is one of the so-called slab
stelae from Giza. At left is the traditional
scene of the funeral meal; on the right is a
list of fabrics. The whole decoration is bordered on four sides by a relief band.

Nefret-iabet, wearing a long striated
wig, dressed in a feline pelt, and adorned
with a choker, arm bracelet, and ankle
bracelet, is seated on a stool with bull's
legs, decorated with a papyrus umbel. Her
left hand is placed on her chest, and her
right is extended toward the offering table
laden with loaves of bread. Above the

Detail, cat. no. 51

51

table, food offerings are depicted: a foreleg of beef, ribs, a basket surmounted by three grains, and fowl. On either side of the foot of the table, a formula is inscribed naming the offerings the deceased woman will enjoy for eternity: "a thousand loaves of bread and jugs of beer, a thousand head of cattle and of game, a thousand fowl." At the level of Nefret-iabet's chest the ideogram for "lustration" is visible, and in front of her face that for "libation" appears. Above her are her title and name, "daughter of the king, Nefret-iabet." The texts inscribed above the table record the ritual offerings: incense, oil, green and black eye paint, figs, wine, cakes, and carob.

The fabrics noted on the right side of the stela are no doubt related to mummification. The different types are listed by name (*idemi, sesher, aa*) and then by quality and quantity.

This work has been dated on the basis of its very special style and its provenance, the ancient heart of the Giza necropolis.

The same mastaba yielded a statue that also probably depicts the princess (cat. no. 50). Given the location of her tomb near the pyramid of Khufu, Nefret-iabet is undoubtedly the sister of the great pharaoh. The extreme freshness of the colors—red for the pupils of the eyes, animals, and loaves of bread; yellow for the skin, feline pelt, and seat; green for hieroglyphs; and black for hair and details—can be explained by the fact that the stela was protected by masonry that was added later. Nefret-iabet's stela is one of the best preserved of such works. The wafer-thin relief and the simple carving, primarily concentrated on the face, show a return to the traditions of the age of Djoser. Shapes are indicated by an outline circled with a brushstroke, and volumes are suggested by the slightly convex surface that gently blends into the background. The princess's countenance, with its protruding forehead, small, straight nose, and delicately rounded lips and nostrils, expresses a new softness, and a radiant femininity emanates

from the body wrapped tightly in a feline pelt, a femininity found also in the statuary of the Fourth Dynasty (see cat. nos. 80, 83).

CZ

PROVENANCE: Giza, Western Cemetery, mastaba of Nefret-iabet (G 1225), Ballard excavation, 1902; Louise Ingeborg and Atherton Curtis collection; their bequest 1938

BIBLIOGRAPHY: Boreux 1925, pp. 5–14, pl. 2; Reisner 1942, pp. 65, 113, 403–5, pl. 19; Barta 1963, pp. 42, 43; Schäfer 1963, pl. 11; Brunner 1965, pl. 1; Porter and Moss 1974, pp. 59–60; Vandier 1974, p. 164, n. 1; Worsham 1979, p. 7, pl. 1; Delange-Bazin 1980, p. 3; Málek 1986, p. 78; Ziegler 1986, pp. 41, 42, n. 33, fig. 6; Maruéjol and Julien 1987, p. 116; Germond 1989, p. 52, n. 7; Laclotte 1989, p. 77, fig. 5; Delange 1990, p. 5; Ziegler 1990a, pp. 22, 25; Ziegler 1990b, pp. 187–89, no. 29; Dunand and Lichtenberg 1991, p. 60; Hart 1991, p. 130; Maruéjol 1991, p. 88; Schmidt 1991, p. 344, n. 48; Aufrère, Bossons, and Landes 1992, p. 117, n. 7, fig. 34; Franco 1993, p. 66; Manniche 1994, p. 57; Der Manuelian 1998a, pp. 123–24

52. SLAB STELA OF PRINCE
WEP-EM-NEFRET

Fourth Dynasty, reign of Khufu
Painted limestone
H. 45.7 cm (18 in.); w. 66 cm (26 in.); d. 7.6 cm
(3 in.)
Phoebe Apperson Hearst Museum of Anthropology,
University of California at Berkeley 6-19825

This magnificent stela showing Wep-em-
nefret owes its extraordinarily fine state of
preservation to a slab of stone that was set
against the decorated side; in 1905, some
four thousand years later, archaeologists
found it still in place (fig. 114). This good
fortune has made it possible to admire not
only the artist's brilliant palette but also his
delicate touch, which carefully describes the
iridescent plumage of a bird, the marbled
skin of a frog, the detail of basketwork,
and the colored grain of an exotic wood.

Here, as on all the slab stelae that have
been recovered (see cat. nos. 51, 53), the
deceased is depicted seated in front of a
table laden with bread. He is wearing a

Detail, cat. no. 52

Detail, cat. no. 52

114. Stela of Wep-em-nefret as found set into mastaba facade, mastaba G 1201, Giza

rather unusual medium-length wig, a mustache, and a short beard. Like Princess Nefret-iabet (cat. no. 51), he is dressed in a long feline pelt, attached at the shoulder by a ribbon. Five columns of hieroglyphs arranged above the table and to the right of it list the offerings necessary for survival: incense, green eye-paint, unguents, wine, bread, beer, fruit, and "all sweets." On the right, three falcons, each perched on a separate standard, introduce the list of various fabrics he will have available for eternity. The two columns of text inscribed at far right, the horizontal band above, and the line over the image of Wep-em-nefret give his identity. This is a very important personage, a prince, Overseer of Royal Scribes, Chief of the Tens of the South, admiral,

and priest of many deities, such as the frog goddess Heket. In addition, he owned the largest tomb in cemetery 1200 at Giza, and his stela is exceptionally large. But his family connection to Khufu is not as clear as the excavator George Reisner suggested when he identified core areas 1200, 2100, and 4000 as cemeteries belonging to three different branches of Khufu's family.[1] It has recently been suggested that Wep-em-nefret was the husband of Nefret-iabet.[2] Both persons were royal, and their mastabas are very close to each other. By a happy chance, theirs are the best-preserved slab stelae, and this exhibition has made it possible to compare the two works, which are among the most beautiful and most accurately dated from the Old Kingdom.   CZ

1. Reisner 1942, pp. 27, 77.
2. Helck 1994, p. 221.

PROVENANCE: Giza, Western Cemetery, tomb of Wep-em-nefret (G 1201), Reisner excavation for University of California, Hearst Expedition, 1903–5

BIBLIOGRAPHY: Lutz 1927, no. 1 (48), pl. 1; Reisner 1942, pp. 385–87; *Ancient Egypt* 1966, p. 42; Porter and Moss 1974, p. 57; Der Manuelian 1998a, pp. 122, 124

53. SLAB STELA OF NEFER

Fourth Dynasty, reign of Khufu
Limestone with faint remains of paint
H. 38.1 cm (15 in.); w. 50.8 cm (20 in.); d. 8.3 cm (3¼ in.)
Phoebe Apperson Hearst Museum of Anthropology, University of California at Berkeley 6-19801

The cemetery west of Khufu's pyramid at Giza has yielded no fewer than fifteen slab stelae, either whole or in fragments.[1] Except for Nefret-iabet's (cat. no. 51), the first to be discovered, all were found during excavations conducted by archaeologists George Reisner and Hermann Junker. They come from the largest mastabas, where in each case they were fitted in on the south end of the east facade. In three cases they were found hidden behind a limestone slab that protected the decorated surface.[2] A small offering chapel of unbaked brick, built against the east facade of the mastaba in front of the stelae (fig. 115), was the principal cult site of these tombs, whose superstructures did not have any other decorations.

In addition to the evidence they provide regarding the evolution of funerary customs during the Fourth Dynasty—when for a brief period all other decoration disappeared from private tomb chapels—the slab stelae are particularly interesting for the history of Old Kingdom art. They date to the reign of Khufu and occur in the same context as reserve heads (see "Reserve Heads" by Catharine H. Roehrig in this catalogue). Because the relief carving is of exceptionally high quality, it is probable that they were gifts from the king.

115. Offering chapel with stela of Nefer in place, mastaba G 1207, Giza

Detail, cat. no. 53

This stela comes from the tomb of Lady Nefer, where one of the blocks bore a mason's mark naming Khufu. In its dimensions and in the arrangement of the decoration, it is very similar to the stela of Nefret-iabet. Nefer is seated in front of a table laden with bread, her left arm on her chest and the right extended toward the offering table. The hairstyle, fine profile, and stool are the same as Nefret-iabet's. Only the clothing is different: Nefer wears a sheath dress cut low on the chest. The list of offerings, arranged in columns above the table and at its feet, is shorter than

53

Nefret-iabet's. But the fabrics listed at the right—probably used in mummification—are of better quality. To modern eyes the difference between the two works lies essentially in the almost complete disappearance from Nefer's stela of the vivid colors that once highlighted the delicate relief. In fact, deterioration has set off the exquisite work of the sculptor, who with consummate mastery played on the imperceptible undulations of the surface and the simplicity of the outlines.   CZ

1. Western Cemetery, cemeteries 1200, 2100, and 4000.
2. Tomb of Nefret-iabet (G 1225); tomb of Wep-em-nefret (G 1201; cat. no. 52); and tomb of Iunu (G 4150).

PROVENANCE: Giza, Western Cemetery, tomb of Nefer (G 1207), Reisner excavation for University of California, Hearst Expedition, 1903–5

BIBLIOGRAPHY: Lutz 1927, p. 15, no. 2, pl. 2; Reisner 1942, pp. 394–96; Hassan 1944, pp. 107–10, fig. 18; *Ancient Egypt* 1966, pp. 50–51; Porter and Moss 1974, p. 58; *Journey to the West* 1979, p. 4; Spanel 1988, pp. 48–49, no. 5; Der Manuelian 1998a

54. HEAD OF KING DJEDEFRE

Fourth Dynasty, reign of Djedefre
Red quartzite (silicified sandstone) with remains of paint
H. 26.5 cm (10⅜ in.); w. 28.8 cm (11⅜ in.); d. 38.5 cm (15¼ in.)
Musée du Louvre, Paris E 12626

The site of Abu Rawash, located a few miles north of the pyramids of Giza, was excavated by the French Institute of Near Eastern Archaeology (IFAO), in neighboring Cairo, between 1901 and 1924. With the exception of a Coptic convent, the ruins date to the beginning of Egyptian history. An Archaic Period necropolis of the First and Second Dynasties was discovered there, as was a nonroyal cemetery with tombs from the Third and Fourth Dynasties and the tomb of Pharaoh Djedefre, Khufu's son and successor. Unfortunately, Djedefre's enormous pyramid had been largely demolished by Cairo entrepreneurs, who came in search of high-quality stones and took away the fine limestone of the casing as well as the red granite of the temples. According

to an early-nineteenth-century observer, up to three hundred camel loads were removed every day. Using the most recent technology, IFAO and University of Geneva teams have recently uncovered an impressive sloping shaft leading to the unexplored burial chamber. Thousands of terracotta jars and small dishes have also been found, attesting to the cult the sovereign enjoyed. No doubt other surprises await excavators in the years to come.

In 1924 archaeologists discovered a series of magnificent works adorning the funerary temple. Among them were works received by the Musée du Louvre: this head of Pharaoh Djedefre, a statue of Prince Setka, son of Djedefre, represented as a scribe (cat. no. 55), and a very beautiful female torso, probably Nefer-hetepes, daughter of Djedefre (E 12628).

There are only four known portraits depicting Djedefre, including this example, which is the largest and sculpturally the most accomplished.[1] However, more than twenty statues once adorned his funerary complex and his pyramid. Archaeologists discovered fragments of them, piled into a large boat-shaped pit. The recent resump-

tion of excavation has allowed a tenacious legend to be put to rest: their destruction was not the act of the king's successors, who for some unknown reason sought to eradicate the memory of Djedefre, but was the handiwork of quarriers of the Late Period who were seeking construction materials.

The king is wearing the royal headcloth, called *nemes*. This plain example is bordered on the forehead by a flat band, which is indicated by two incised lines, the upper one displaying some corrections. In the center of the band the royal cobra, or uraeus, rears up with its hood extended; there is no detail on the very broad central band that delineates the snake's body. The tail is coiled along the top of the king's head in a sinuous S-shape. In back, visible on the right side of the statue, the *nemes* extends into a lappet, the angle of which suggests that this head belonged to a sphinx and not to a seated or standing figure of a king. The face, whose bone structure is visible under the flesh, is rectangular. The left profile clearly shows the stone bridge that supported the false beard. A painted black line extending from the temples to the chin indicates the strap

that attached the beard to the king's face in real life. The fairly large ears are carefully detailed, although the stylized antihelix has no fossa. The inner canthi are emphasized with a horizontal line, and the upper eyelids are rimmed with an incised line, while the lower lids are in slight relief. There is no trace of the cosmetic line, which, according to the excavator, encircled each eye and extended toward the temple. Seen from the side, each eyeball, still bearing the traces of an iris in black paint, does not display a regular curve: the lower eyelid, recessed in relation to the upper lid, delimits an oblique, slightly bulging surface. The eyebrows, treated in low relief, are highlighted in black and follow the curves of the upper eyelids. The thin nose, which has been damaged, is separated from the mouth by a very marked philtrum. The wide, full mouth is encircled

by a sharp ridge that does not end at the corners of the lips; a vertical incision divides the lower lip in the middle. The lip is puffy and recedes slightly.

The extraordinary rendering of notable anatomical features—the receding line of the chin, strong jaw, high cheekbones, full mouth, and structure of the forehead perceptible under the taut skin—gives the work a sharp expressiveness that is tempered by more subtle notations, such as the depressions under the eyes and the puckering of the muscles at the corners of the mouth. This likeness of Djedefre is very different from the impassive images of his successor, Khafre.

CZ

1. The others are: Louvre, Paris, E 11167, wearing the white crown (?), h. 12 cm (4¾ in.); Egyptian Museum, Cairo, JE 35138 = Suez, Port Tawfiq

S.10, wearing the *nemes* headcloth, h. 14 cm (5½ in.), see Smith 1946, pl. 2d, and Vandier 1958, pl. 1.3; and Egyptian Museum, Cairo, JE 35139, wearing the white crown, h. 19 cm (7½ in.), see Smith 1946, pl. 2c, and Vandier 1958, pl. 1.1.

PROVENANCE: Abu Rawash, pyramid of Djedefre, east face, under thick layer of rubble in large boat-shaped pit, five meters southeast of mortuary chapel court, Chassinat excavation, winter 1900–1901; gift of the Egyptian Government as part of the division of finds, 1907

BIBLIOGRAPHY: Chassinat 1921–22, pp. 53–76, pls. 8, 9; Boreux 1932, vol. 2, pp. 444–45, pl. 59; Bissing 1934a, vol. 1, pp. 84, 163, pl. 66 [403a,b], text 1; *Encyclopédie photographique* 1935, pl. 10; Smith 1946, pl. 11; Steindorff 1951, pp. 9–10 [20]; Vandier 1951, p. 7; Vandier 1952c, p. 35; Wolf 1957, p. 142, fig. 105; Reuterswärd 1958, pl. 3 ("E 47"); Vandier 1958, pp. 16, 17, 28, 54, 574, pl. 1 [2]; Pirenne 1961, pp. 148–49, pls. 46, 47; H. Müller 1964, p. 129; Aldred 1965,

fig. 115; Bourguet and Drioton 1965, pp. 116,
118, fig. 20; Maragioglio and Rinaldi 1966,
pp. 27, 39; Porter and Moss 1974, p. 2; Vandersleyen 1975a, p. 221, fig. 124; Aldred 1978,
p. 185, fig. 181; Edwards 1979, pl. 12b; *Siècle
de fouilles* 1981, pp. 46–47, no. 53; Smith 1981,
p. 116, fig. 112; Zivie 1984, p. 1145; Romano
1985, p. 39; Aldred 1988a, p. 42, n. 8; Johnson
1990, pp. 83–84, figs. 137–39; Stadelmann 1990,
fig. 155; Ziegler 1990a, pp. 21, 25; Hart 1991,
p. 138; De Putter and Karlshausen 1992, p. 97,
pl. 30; Manniche 1994, p. 53; Valloggia 1994,
pp. 7, 10; Clayton 1995, p. 25; Valloggia 1995,
p. 65, fig. 1; Berman and Letellier 1996, pp. 38,
39, 94; Fay 1996, pp. 19 n. 72, 62 nn. 308, 309,
95, pl. 82; Ziegler 1997a, pp. 42–45, no. 1, with
earlier bibliography

55. SETKA, ELDEST SON OF KING DJEDEFRE, AS A SCRIBE

Fourth Dynasty, reign of Djedefre
Statue: red porphyroid granite with megacrystals
of feldspar, remains of paint around eyes
Interior pedestal: wood
Exterior pedestal: low-grade dolomitic, bioclastic
limestone, streaked with gypsum veins (possible
quarry: plateau of Gaa in Abu Rawash); remains
of white mortar inside and along edges of semicircular cavity, dark fill in inscription
Statue: h. 30 cm (11⅞ in.); w. 23 cm (9⅛ in.);
d. 19 cm (7½ in.)
Interior pedestal: h. 4.6 cm (1⅞ in.); w. 30.5 cm
(12 in.); max. d. 17.5 cm (6⅞ in.)
Exterior pedestal: h. 17 cm (6¾ in.); w. 64 cm
(25¼ in.); d. 66 cm (26 in.)[1]
Musée du Louvre, Paris (statue) E 12629,
(pedestals) E 12631

The first scribe statues appeared during the
Fourth Dynasty. They represent the sons of
kings as scholars who have mastered the
complex use of hieroglyphs and gained
immortality by composing literary works.[2]
This is the pose assumed by Setka, King
Djedefre's son, whose statue was found at
the foot of his father's pyramid at Abu
Rawash. In an unusual assembly arrangement, the granite statue with a hole in the
semicircular base is fitted into nested pedestals, the interior made of wood, the exterior of limestone. Each pedestal has a hole
through the center. Presumably a peg was

inserted through the holes to hold all three
parts together. The prince is sitting cross-
legged, his hands on his knees, holding an
unrolled papyrus; much of its writing surface blends into his plain kilt. A short titulary designating the figure as "eldest son of
the king, Setka"[3] is inscribed on the papyrus, complemented by the text carved in the
limestone pedestal: "eldest bodily son of the
king, Unique Associate of his father, Setka;
son of the king, lector-priest of his father,
Governor of the Palace, Setka; member of
the elite, son of the king, Initiate of the
Morning House." The same method of inlaying hieroglyphs was used on the statue
of Hemiunu (cat. no. 44) and can be linked
to the decorative techniques employed at
the tombs of Nefer-maat and Meni.[4]

On Setka's lap, the papyrus stands out
in slight relief, and its rolled end is firmly
clasped in the scribe's left hand, placed palm
up. The thumb and index finger of the right
hand are joined, as if grasping a brush, suggesting the act of writing. But the sculptor
went no further: there is no sign that a detachable element was fixed to the fingers.

Viewed from the front, the statue can be
envisioned within an isosceles triangle, with
the wood pedestal forming its base. The
side view reveals that the work tilts notice-

ably backward. Setka has his head lifted
and is looking up. His face is round, with a
low, sloping forehead, a thick nose, and
eyes flush with the head. Eyebrows are not
marked. Characteristic features are carefully observed: the depression under the eye
and puffiness around the eyelids; heavy
cheeks set off by the deep furrow between
nose and lips; and round chin. By comparison, the sculptor has taken little care in
rendering the mouth, which has undefined
outlines and turned-down corners. The
medium-length wig, which leaves the earlobes visible, is flared, and the locks are
divided by a central part. The head is
attached to the shoulders almost without
transition. Three rolls of flesh around the
torso and abdomen indicate the scribe's
plumpness, which is accentuated by the
careful modeling of his fan-shaped navel,
sunk deep into a fold of fat. The arms,
separated from the trunk by wide fissures
that give the illusion of depth, have received detailed treatment. The upper arms
curve slightly to show the smooth shapes of
shoulder and biceps; below the sharp bend
at the elbow, the almost flat surfaces are
broken by the protrusion of a muscle. On
the right leg, the musculature of the calf
and the ridge of the tibia are individualized.

However, the aligned toes of the right foot, seen on the underside, are treated with extreme simplicity.

Simplicity also keynotes the treatment of the back, which is divided by a shallow vertical furrow. The nipped-in waist is relatively slender. A ridge indicates the upper edge of the plain kilt that envelops the lower body, which is treated summarily with full, round forms.   CZ

1. For further dimensions, see Ziegler 1997a, pp. 64–68, nos. 17, 18.
2. Eight scribe statues indisputably date to the Fourth Dynasty (G. Scott 1989, vol. 1, p. 21). Three are well preserved: this one and two others, representing Khuen-re (cat. no. 72), son of King Menkaure, and Ba-baef, a contemporary of King Shepseskaf (Museum of Fine Arts, Boston, 21.931). Five others are very fragmentary. They represent Kawab, son of King Khufu (three statues, all Museum of Fine Arts, Boston, 27.1127, 34.4.1, 24.12.1105); Ankh-haf, a contemporary of King Khufu (Egyptian Museum, Cairo, 27-2-304); and Her-net, son of King Djedefre (Egyptian Museum, Cairo, temp. 5-11-24-16). In addition, there are two semicircular pedestals from Abu Rawash that probably once supported scribe statues. They are in the names of Prince Her-net (Louvre, Paris, E 12639) and Baka (Egyptian Museum, Cairo, temp. 5-11-24-8). All these subjects bear the title "eldest son of the king": this type of statue seems to have been created for princes and reserved for their exclusive use during the Fourth Dynasty (ibid., pp. 22 ff.). In the statue of Setka, the right leg is crossed over the left, the

reverse of other examples from the Fourth Dynasty (ibid., p. 23).
3. The inscription faces the viewer and not the scribe, as is the case with one of the scribal statues of Prince Kawab (Museum of Fine Arts, Boston, 34.4.1), who is depicted in the same attitude.
4. Cherpion 1989, p. 94.

PROVENANCE: Abu Rawash, pyramid of Djedefre, east face, in a chamber "almost at the northeast corner" of mortuary chapel court,* Chassinat excavation, winter 1900–1901; gift of the Egyptian Government as part of the division of finds, 1907

*Chassinat 1921–22, p. 64.

BIBLIOGRAPHY: Chassinat 1921–22, pp. 66, 67, fig. 3; Boreux 1932, vol. 1, p. 230; Smith 1946, pl. 10D; Vandier 1948, p. 9; Vandier 1952c, p. 10; Vandier 1958, pp. 46, 48, 69–71, 103, pl. 13.5; Bothmer 1960, p. 23; Porter and Moss 1974, p. 3; Siècle de fouilles 1981, pp. 50–51, no. 55; Wildung 1982d, col. 1118, n. 20; Vandersleyen 1987, p. 196; G. Scott 1989, no. 6, pp. 14–16, vol. 1, pt. 1, pp. 9–11; De Putter and Karlshausen 1992, p. 83, pl. 21; Clayton 1995, p. 51; Ziegler 1995b, p. 144; Ziegler 1997a, pp. 64–68, nos. 17, 18

THE STATUES OF
KING KHAFRE

More than one hundred statues may originally have adorned the funerary complex
of King Khafre at Giza.[1] Some have come
down to us as undamaged masterpieces,
but most have been reduced to humble
fragments of alabaster, quartzite, anorthosite gneiss, black granite, or schist. The first
and most spectacular find—which included
the famous seated statue of Khafre with the
Horus falcon in the Egyptian Museum, Cairo
(fig. 28)—was made by Auguste Mariette
in 1860. This trove of statues was found
in a shaft dug in the vestibule of the valley
temple of Khafre's pyramid. Seventeen
works, complete or fragmentary, appear in
the Cairo Catalogue Générale, but many
fragments have not been published. The
expedition headed by Ernst von Sieglin in
1909–10 discovered royal heads and the
remains of statues, some of them inscribed,
lying for the most part in the debris at the
south entrance to the pharaoh's valley
temple. Different sections of the nonroyal
necropolis explored by archaeologists Hermann Junker, George Reisner, and Selim
Hassan have yielded nearly fifty fragments
from workshops. A few pieces from old
collections such as the MacGregor collection should be added to them.[2] The royal
funerary complex was thus crammed full
of statues of very high quality, executed in
the most diverse materials.

The definitive study of Khafre statues is
still the one published by Reisner, who also
studied the sculpture of Khafre's successor,
Menkaure. Reisner was able to distinguish
between two workshops, that of Sculptor A
and Sculptor B. The first, true to tradition,
worked in a severe style[3] characterized by
more extensive modeling, especially around
the mouth; eyebrows with an accentuated
arch (inherited from the Archaic Period);
and a preference for an ideal type rather
than a realistic portrait. The style of the
sculptors of the second school, who may
have been younger than those of the first
and who worked for a longer period, is
characterized by gentler modeling and a
more realistic rendering.[4] That distinction
has been refined by William Stevenson
Smith, who takes into account variations
in treatment resulting from the nature of
the stones used and who observes that during the same reign the shape of the eyebrows
could be completely different from one
statue to the next.[5]   CZ

1. According to Reisner (1931, p. 126), the figure
   is between one hundred and two hundred.
2. Porter and Moss 1974, pp. 21–25.
3. Stadelmann 1995b, pp. 154–66.
4. Reisner 1931, chap. 7.
5. Smith 1946, pp. 35–36, reprinted in Vandier
   1958, pp. 26–27.

56. KING KHAFRE SEATED

Fourth Dynasty, reign of Khafre
Graywacke
H. 120 cm (47¼ in.)
Egyptian Museum, Cairo CG 15

This splendid royal statue, portions of
which are restored, was found in 1860 by
Auguste Mariette's workers. Along with
other statues, it had been thrown into a pit
within Khafre's valley temple. This king, a
son of Khufu, succeeded his brother Djedefre under obscure circumstances. Khafre's
pyramid was the second constructed at
Giza, and the Great Sphinx, built next to
his pyramid complex (see cat. no. 30), is
thought to reflect his features.

In this statue Khafre is seated on a low
throne. Its sides are decorated with the
sema-tawi, which combines the hieroglyph
sema ("union") and the symbols for the
two lands of Egypt, each land represented
by a plant—the papyrus for the north and
a flower for the south. This motif is a
reminder that the union of the two lands
created Egypt and that the king is forever
the guarantor of the country's unity.

Simply dressed in a finely pleated *shendyt*
kilt, the king is wearing a *nemes* headcloth
surmounted by a uraeus, which is carved
nearly flat against the headcloth; a false
beard, like the headcloth and the uracus an
attribute of his office, is attached to his chin.
His left hand lies flat on his knee, and his
right fist is closed around an enigmatic
object. Khafre's well-defined musculature
conveys a strong sense of power. On the
front of the seat, to either side of his legs,
two symmetrical columns of hieroglyphs
give the king's titulary: in addition to
Khafre, his Horus name, User-ib. This piece
is part of a group of about twenty similar
statues, many of which were found in fragmentary condition. The most remarkable
of these, sculpted in gneiss and housed in
the Egyptian Museum, Cairo, places the
king under the protection of the god Horus,
depicted in the form of a falcon spreading
its wings around the king's neck (fig. 28). It
is easy to imagine the majestic effect produced by these statues, the emplacements
of which can still be seen in one of the halls
of the valley temple. They were lined up
between granite pillars and illuminated
so that their dark mass was reflected in
the alabaster floor (fig. 49).   SL-T, CZ

PROVENANCE: Giza, valley temple of Khafre,
Mariette excavation, 1860

BIBLIOGRAPHY: Borchardt 1911, pp. 16–17,
pl. 4; Maspero 1912a, fig. 121; Maspero 1915b,
p. 79 [179]; Vandier 1958, pp. 19–21; Porter and
Moss 1974, p. 22; Saleh and Sourouzian 1987,
no. 31 (for comparison to another seated Khafre)

57. FRAGMENTS OF A ROYAL HEAD

Fourth Dynasty, reign of Khufu or Khafre
Egyptian alabaster
H. 32 cm (12⅝ in.)
Museum of Fine Arts, Boston, Harvard University–Museum of Fine Arts Expedition 27.1466 (field number 25-1-587)

These three connecting fragments of a royal head were discovered east of the pyramid of King Khufu in debris above mastaba G 7102. They come from a statue similar to the famous gneiss figure of Khafre in the Egyptian Museum, Cairo (fig. 28), which depicts him seated on a high-backed throne with the Horus falcon standing behind his head, its wings spread protectively along

the sides of a *nemes* headdress.[1] The bird's tail and right leg and wing are visible in the photograph above, as are part of the king's right shoulder and the back of his pleated headcloth.

A number of statues belonging to Khafre were found broken up in the area east of the Great Pyramid, and these three pieces may belong to a representation of this king, who commissioned various lifesize alabaster figures. However, since the fragments were uncovered in the vicinity of Khufu's mortuary temple, it is equally possible that Khufu was the first Egyptian king to be depicted in this powerfully symbolic pose as the living Horus. This possibility is supported by an image carved in relief on one of the limestone fragments uncovered in 1938–39 by Selim Hassan while he was excavating

Khufu's mortuary complex.[2] The scenes depicted on these fragments relate to Khufu's Sed festival, and one preserves the back of the king's head covered by an early form of the *khat* headcloth. A tiny Horus falcon, perhaps a piece of jewelry, is attached to the cloth where it is tied at the back of the king's neck.   CHR

1. For a reconstruction drawing of the head, see Simpson 1976, fig. 43.
2. Hassan 1960b, p. 23, pl. 6B; see also Lauer 1949, pl. 2; and Reisner and Smith 1955, p. 4, fig. 6a.

PROVENANCE: Giza, east of the pyramid of Khufu, Reisner excavation, 1925

BIBLIOGRAPHY: Smith 1946, p. 20 (4), pl. 5a; Simpson 1976, p. 30, fig. 43

58. HEAD OF KING KHAFRE

Fourth Dynasty, reign of Khafre
Egyptian alabaster
H. 20.5 cm (8⅛ in.)
Museum of Fine Arts, Boston, Harvard University–
Museum of Fine Arts Expedition 21.351

This lifesize head was discovered in the rubble of the Western Cemetery at Giza, at the northeast corner of mastaba G 5330. Found with it was workshop debris, including some fragments bearing the cartouche of Khafre.[1] The face of the sculpture is broader than most representations of this pharaoh. The sovereign is shown wearing the *nemes* headcloth, of which only the plain headband, executed in high relief, survives. In the center of the band, which is almost flush with the eyebrows, is a uraeus cobra with a flat body. The king's curved eyebrows are treated like ribbons. The eyes are very large, with relatively flat eyeballs, and the inner corners are emphasized by a horizontal incision. The upper lids are rimmed, and a cosmetic line, sculpted in relief, extends to the temples. The fleshy nose is, unfortunately, mutilated. The wide and slightly smiling mouth is completely encircled by a clean ridge. A piece of the striated false beard survives at the chin.

The head as a whole is majestic, and the striking stylization of shapes and their treatment as simple, rounded forms justifies George Reisner's attribution of the piece to the workshop of Sculptor A.[2] The statue, particularly the eyes and eyebrows, was probably enhanced with color, to judge from the remains of blue-green paint on a similar work in the Roemer- und Pelizaeus-Museum, Hildesheim (5415). The delicate modulations of the flesh found on another fragmentary alabaster head of a king (cat. no. 60) are absent here.

The slightly translucent Egyptian alabaster chosen for this work seems to have been much in vogue during the reigns of Khafre and Menkaure. Representations of Khafre in this medium include an undamaged statue discovered in Memphis, which depicts the sovereign seated (Egyptian Museum, Cairo, CG 41); an impressive mask, larger than life, from the king's valley temple;[3] and a face in a more vigorous style, housed in the Ny Carlsberg Glyptotek in Copenhagen (cat. no. 59)—not to speak of numerous fragments, many of which have never been published.   CZ

1. Reisner 1931, p. 128 (4).
2. Ibid.
3. Egyptian Museum, Cairo, CG 41, and Roemer-
   und Pelizaeus-Museum, Hildesheim, 5415.

PROVENANCE: Giza, Western Cemetery, near
mastaba G 5330, Reisner excavation, 1921

BIBLIOGRAPHY: *Bulletin of the Museum of
Fine Arts, Boston*, 23, no. 140 (1926), p. 72;
Ranke 1936, pl. 54; Smith 1946, p. 34, pl. 12a;
Smith 1960, fig. 21; Porter and Moss 1974,
p. 24; Vandersleyen 1975a, fig. 125; Seipel 1992,
p. 96, no. 13

59. FACE OF KING KHAFRE

Fourth Dynasty, reign of Khafre
Crystalline limestone[1]
H. 15.5 cm (6⅛ in.)
Ny Carlsberg Glyptotek, Copenhagen AEIN 1599

This piece and another face of Khafre once
in the collection of the Reverend William
MacGregor (cat. no. 60) were said to have
been found in the area of the king's pyramid
complex at Giza.

The face is preserved from the frontlet
almost to the lower end of the ribbed beard.
The upper part of the face is relatively open,
with a good distance between frontlet and
brows and with wide eyes. The cheeks are
long and smooth, with slight indications of
musculature around the nose and mouth.
Neither the underside of the nose nor its
juncture with the face is clearly modeled.
The upper lip shows a sharp central dip
from which the top edges of the lips form
straight diagonals out to the corners. The
wide, curved lower lip gives the mouth a
mild expression.   MH

1. According to Jørgensen (1996); a similar
   stone, when closely examined, was found
   to be alabaster (see entry for cat. no. 60,
   note 1).

PROVENANCE: Said to be Giza

BIBLIOGRAPHY: MacGregor sale 1922,
lot 1657, pl. 44; Jørgensen 1996, pp. 42–43

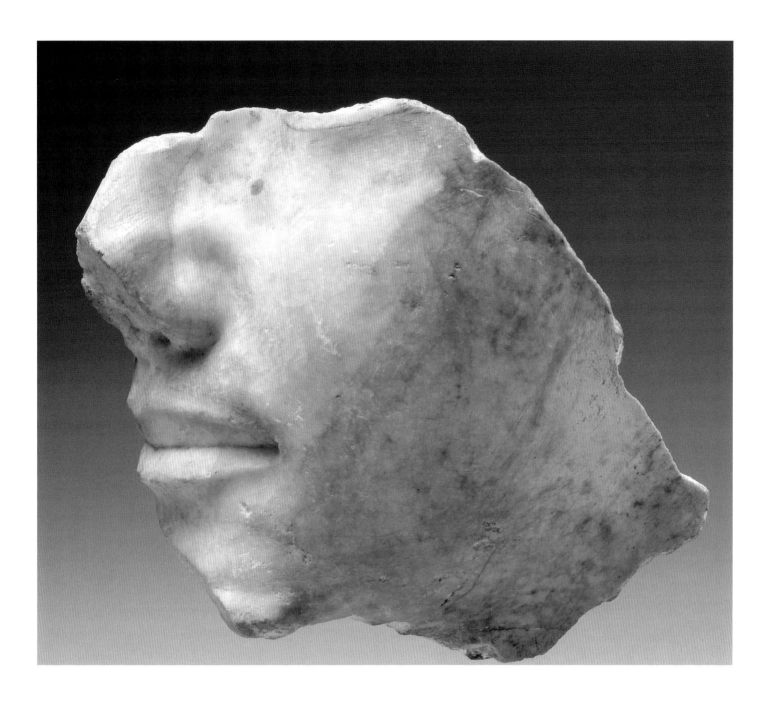

60. Fragmentary Face of King Khafre

Fourth Dynasty, reign of Khafre
Egyptian alabaster[1]
H. 8.5 cm (3⅜ in.)
The Metropolitan Museum of Art, New York,
Purchase, Edward S. Harkness Gift, 1926
26.7.1392

This piece, once in the collection of the Reverend William MacGregor, was said to have been found at Giza in the "pyramid" or "temple" of Khafre along with the more complete face in Copenhagen, ascribed to that king (cat. no. 59), and two fragmentary mace heads bearing names of Khafre.[2]

Dense Egyptian alabaster was used for many of the statues from the Khafre pyramid complex. This piece, carved in an almost marblelike stone with only a slight translucence, preserves part of the left cheek, part of the nose, mouth, and chin, and the root of the royal beard.

The surface is very fine and the modeling delicate: the flesh thickens where the nose abuts the cheek above the nasal ala, and there is a pronounced muscle over the upper lip that appears more faintly below at the corners of the mouth. The mouth is small, and its lines are more curved and delicate than in many depictions of Khafre. The shape of the lower lip, which is narrower than the upper,[3] is closer to that of the face in Boston (cat. no. 58) than to that in Copenhagen (cat. no. 59).   MH

1. Determined by Deborah Schorsch, Associate Conservator, The Sherman Fairchild Center for Objects Conservation, Metropolitan Museum.
2. MacGregor sale 1922, lots 1657, 1658, pl. 44.
3. The Ägyptisches Museum, Universität Leipzig, has a related fragment in graywacke (8249; Krauspe 1997b, p. 19, no. 16, pl. 8.3).

PROVENANCE: Said to be Giza

BIBLIOGRAPHY: MacGregor sale 1922, lot 1658; Hayes 1953, p. 65, fig. 42

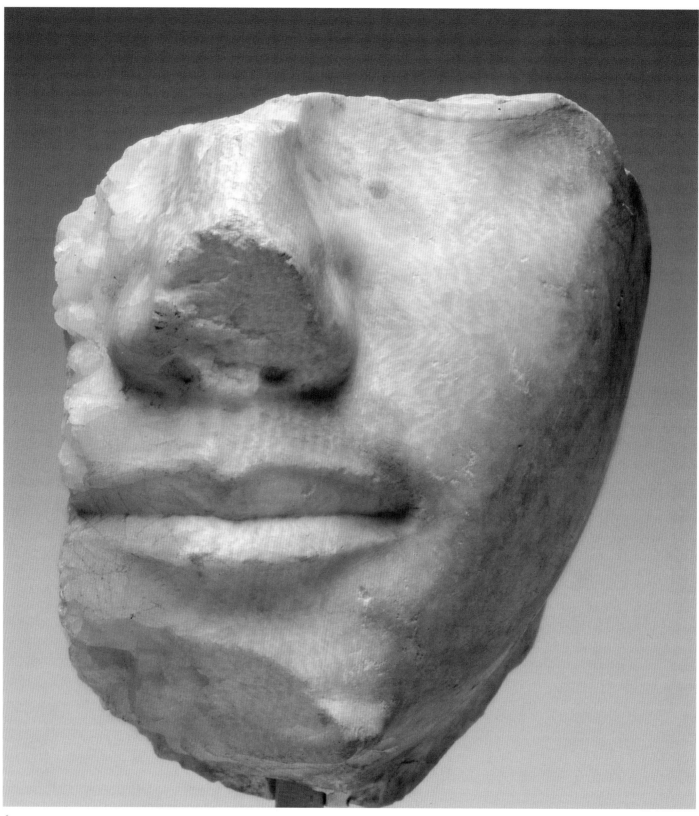

60

61. HEAD OF KING KHAFRE

Fourth Dynasty, reign of Khafre
Gneiss
H. 17.2 cm (6¾ in.); w. 7.3 cm (2⅞ in.); d. 7.2 cm
(2⅞ in.)
Ägyptisches Museum, Universität Leipzig 1945

This little masterpiece has been reconstituted from six scattered fragments discovered in a hundred-meter strip in front of Khafre's pyramid temple. The context in which the work was discovered, the style, and the material—anorthosite gneiss,[1] known as Chephren's diorite—leave no doubt about the sovereign's identity: it is, in fact, Khafre. The pharaoh is wearing the *nemes* headcloth. The brow band stands out in relief against his forehead, revealing his natural hair at the temples, and above it rears a delicately sculpted uraeus, symbol of kingship. The arched eyebrows are treated as wide ribbons; they extend to the temples, following the cosmetic line, which emphasizes the external corners of the eyes. The upper lids are rimmed and the eyeballs extremely con-

vex. The nose is straight and fleshy, differing from that of the seated statue of Khafre with the Horus falcon in the Egyptian Museum, Cairo (fig. 28). The slightly sinuous mouth is prominent. The shape of the cheeks, which swell beneath the eyes, is particularly understated and refined. The narrow beard is ridged, and the profile view reveals it is attached to the neck by a bridge of stone whose triangular form is characteristic of the Fourth Dynasty.[2] George Reisner attributed this extraordinary head, which

exudes majesty and serenity, to the workshop of Sculptor B.   CZ

1. For this material, see Aston 1994, pp. 62–64.
2. Stadelmann 1998a, p. 367.

PROVENANCE: Giza, precinct of Khafre, in front of pyramid temple, von Sieglin expedition, 1909–10

BIBLIOGRAPHY: Hölscher 1912, p. 91, no. 1, figs. 80, 81; Vandier 1958, p. 20; Porter and Moss 1974, p. 23; Krauspe 1987, p. 29, ill. p. 28; Johnson 1990, p. 90; Krauspe 1997a, pp. 29–30, ill.; Krauspe 1997b, pp. 13–14, no. 1

62. SMALL HEAD OF KING KHAFRE WITH THE RED CROWN

Fourth Dynasty, reign of Khafre
Red limestone with inlaid eyes of stone mounted in copper cells (black stone modern)
H. 9.9 cm (4 in.); w. 4.3 cm (1¾ in.); d. 4.8 cm (1⅞ in.)
Ägyptisches Museum, Universität Leipzig 1947

Although small, this royal head has an impressive presence. The subject is a pharaoh wearing the red crown of Lower Egypt and a horizontally striated beard, which is attached to the neck by a bridge of stone. The face is broad and square. The eye sockets are inlaid with white stone held in place by copper cells, now very corroded. The inlays representing the corneas had already disappeared when the head was discovered; they were probably inserted by the same technique used for the statue of Kai (cat. no. 124) and the Scribe in the Louvre (fig. 33). A peg, visible on each temple, held the eye inlay in place. The eyebrows, which, like the chin strap, were once emphasized by a black brushstroke, are indicated by browridges. The ears are broad and curved, with a particularly well developed lobe. The nose is unusually short and its wings

are framed by very pronounced grooves. The crown and the upper part of the face are carefully polished and display only light parallel streaks, but the area around the wide, horizontal mouth shows large chisel marks. The red crown is set very low on the forehead and the base circles around the ears. On its flat top are vestiges of a copper rod, an element of the red crown frequently depicted on reliefs but seldom seen in statuary.

The extremely short nose, the inlaid eyes, and the unusual crown have led some specialists to rule out the association with Khafre, whose features have been preserved in many statues.[1] A very late date has been proposed for this piece and for a statuette of Khufu in the Egyptian Museum, Cairo (JE 36143), which is similar to it. But the site at which it was discovered and a number of elements argue for an early date. The inlaid eyes are attested in royal statuary since the time of Djoser, and a magnificent statue of him (fig. 29) now displays only empty eye sockets. The method used to hold the eyes in place was employed for a series of statues from the Old Kingdom whose date is still in dispute, including the famous Sheikh el-Beled (fig. 34).[2] Although fairly rare in statuary, the red crown first appeared during Khufu's reign (Egyptian Museum,

Cairo, JE 36143), and a few fragmentary examples have been dated to the reign of Khafre.[3] Finally, although it has not been possible to establish a definite connection between this head and two fragments bearing the cartouche of Khafre,[4] the similarities among the pieces are arresting: the provenance is the same, the type of limestone is identical, and the scale is similar.   CZ

1. Hölscher 1912. Vandier (1958) rejects the association a priori but acknowledges that his judgment is primarily based on the inlay of the eyes.
2. Egyptian Museum, Cairo, CG 34. Fischer 1989b, pp. 213–14.
3. Stadelmann 1998a, p. 365.
4. Hölscher 1912, p. 101, nos. 48, 49, figs. 130, 131; Krauspe 1997b, nos. 69, 70.

PROVENANCE: Giza, valley temple of Khafre, in rubble east of door, von Sieglin expedition, 1909–10

BIBLIOGRAPHY: Hölscher 1912, p. 93, no. 3, figs. 83, 84; Reisner 1931, p. 129; Abu Bakr 1937, p. 12; Spiegel 1938, p. 23; Smith 1946, p. 35; Vandier 1958, pp. 20, 21, 571; Porter and Moss 1974, p. 25; Cooney 1975, p. 79; Blumenthal 1984, p. 550; Krauspe 1987, p. 27, no. 26/4; Krauspe 1997b, p. 15, no. 3; Stadelmann 1998a, p. 365, n. 66

63. SMALL HEAD OF A KING, PROBABLY KHAFRE, WEARING THE WHITE CROWN

Fourth Dynasty, probably reign of Khafre
Dense beige limestone with inlaid eyes; sclera in
white stone surrounded by now-oxidized copper,
left pupil in black stone, right pupil missing
H. 8 cm (3⅛ in.); w. 2.7 cm (1⅛ in.); d. 5 cm (2 in.)
Collection of Nanette B. Kelekian, New York

This beautiful piece, whose inherent monumentality belies its small size, shows the head, proper right side of the neck, and most of the high white crown of a king. A protuberant stone element at the back once connected it to a high slab, possibly representing the upper part of the back of a seat.[1] The crown fits the head tightly, leaving only the ears free. Its simple lower edge embraces the king's forehead, curves around the temples, and clings to the neck. In front of each ear is a small rectangular slot below which the rounded and partially flattened end of the crown extends toward the face to cover part of the cheek. The king wore a round ceremonial beard attached to the tip of his chin. Horizontal indentations on the front of the beard created the impression of wavy hair. Part of the uppermost indentation is preserved.

The face is remarkable for its austerity. An expression of openness and clarity is conveyed by means of the dominance of two main axes, maintained by the emphatic carving of the elements disposed along them: the vertical that runs from the bridge of the nose to the chin and beard, and the horizontal formed by the ears, eyes, and nose. Features outside these axes—cheeks, chin, and neck—are only sparsely modeled. Most expressive are the mouth and eyes. The mouth is surrounded by a sharp edge (the so-called vermilion line), inside which the lips are softly rounded. The straight chin rounds gently into the lower lip, and the mouth owes much of its fullness and sensitivity to the delicate forward thrust that results from this small curve. A slight groove delineates the muscles above the upper lip at both sides of the damaged philtrum. The king's eyes below their brows in shallow relief look straight ahead, their wide-open gaze enhanced rather than diminished by the oxidized state of the copper margins of the lids.

The piece is doubtless closely related to the small head with a red crown in Leipzig (cat. no. 62). Both are made of dense limestone of the same consistency, although the material of the present head is less reddish. And they are almost identical in size, as well as in the technique used for the eye inlays: in both the eyelids are secured from behind by wires whose tips emerge through holes in the temples, where they were attached with patches of plaster (?). The facial features differ only slightly. The Kelekian head has ears that are less fleshy and more closely attached to the skull, a beard more rounded in front, and a leaner, more elongated face. Moreover, the area around the mouth is not reworked as it is in the Leipzig example and the execution is more sensitive, with more delicate rendering of features such as the ears and mouth. Despite these distinctions, the heads are so similar that we may say they were surely made in the same workshop—although by two different sculptors, which accounts for their variations. We can also conclude that the heads were probably placed in the same sanctuary, namely the valley temple of Khafre at Giza, where the Leipzig example was discovered.

In her entry on the Leipzig head, Ziegler rejects the various arguments previous scholars have invoked to show that that piece is not contemporary with the reign of Khafre.[2] Her position is correct in the view of this writer, and it is reinforced by the links between the Leipzig and Kelekian works: there can be no doubt that the Kelekian head was made during the Fourth Dynasty, and the form of the mouth in particular points strongly to its identification as an image of King Khafre. Moreover, a comparison of the Kelekian head with the head in the Metropolitan Museum that indisputably represents Khafre (cat. no. 60) suffices to demonstrate the striking similarity of the two pieces, particularly in the area around the mouth and nostrils.

Another royal head, that of Khafre's immediate predecessor, Djedefre, in the Louvre (cat. no. 54), is also remarkably close to the Kelekian piece. They are connected by the shape of the ears and the mouth and above all by their strongly axial structure. Both images present the pharaoh as a superhuman being who towers over ordinary men and women by virtue of his rigorous clarity of vision and an austerity untouched by mortal fears or desires. It is conceivable that the small statuette of Khafre to which the present head belonged was created early in the king's reign, and by a sculptor with connections to the artist who produced the Louvre head of Djedefre.

DoA

1. Other fragments of the same dense limestone material excavated at the valley temple of Khafre are from seated figures wearing the Heb Sed garment; Krauspe 1997b, p. 35, no. 71, pl. 24.1,4; British Museum, EA 69216, see note 2 below.
2. To the authors Ziegler lists add Biri Fay, who in her lecture at the 1994 Old Kingdom conference at the French Institute for Near Eastern Archaeology, Cairo, cited a headless figure in the British Museum (EA 69216) and a head in the Egyptian Museum, Cairo, as members of the group of limestone works excavated from the valley temple of Khafre. Fay suggested a Middle Kingdom date for these pieces, based primarily on her contention that supports for beards that slant downward to the chest, which are present in the group, were not used in the Old Kingdom. This argument, however, is contradicted by the evidence of the statue of Sahure and a god in the Metropolitan Museum (cat. no. 109; frontis., p. 2), in which a support of this kind appears. I thank Fay for allowing me to read the manuscript of her lecture.

PROVENANCE: Probably valley temple of Khafre, Giza

BIBLIOGRAPHY: Unpublished

64. HEAD OF A QUEEN

Fourth Dynasty, probably reign of Khafre
Egyptian alabaster
H. 10.2 cm (4 in.); w. 12.2 cm (4⅞ in.); d. 8.6 cm (3⅜ in.)
Ägyptisches Museum, Universität Leipzig 1965

This small head probably represents a queen of the Fourth Dynasty, who may have lived during the reign of Khafre, since the head was discovered near his pyramid. The broad face is framed by wavy hair falling very low over the forehead and parted in the center. The lids above the large eyes are emphasized by cosmetic lines extending to the temples like flat ribbons, and the sinuous eyebrows are treated in the same fashion. The lower eyelids form a pronounced edge. The wide nose has been mutilated. The straight mouth with full lower lip is delicately modeled. The ears, large and broad, stand out against a smooth surface that represents the body of a vulture, whose wings stretch over the woman's temples. The bird's head is barely visible above her hair.

Throughout Egyptian history vulture headdresses were traditionally worn by queens and many goddesses. In the Old Kingdom this attribute was apparently reserved for use by queen mothers,[1] who played a particularly important role.[2] For example, Queen Ankh-nes-meryre is depicted in a Sixth Dynasty statue with that headdress, holding her son Pepi II on her knees (cat. no. 172). But the motif occurs in the Fourth Dynasty as well. In addition to this small head, the mortuary complexes of Khafre and Menkaure have yielded remnants of wigs adorned with the same decoration.[3] They are the only remaining vestiges of now-lost queen statues.

In fact, there are very few Old Kingdom statues depicting women of the royal family.

116. Architrave of King Khafre as currently located in entrance corridor, pyramid of Amenemhat I, Lisht

A study by Fay lists nine examples where the head has survived and the identity of the subject is certain.[4] For the Fourth Dynasty, the rock-cut statues in the tomb of Mer-si-ankh and numerous unidentified fragments should be added to the list,[5] as well as the colossal statues of Kha-merer-nebti I, wife of Khafre, the most spectacular of which presents her draped in a pleated mantle (Egyptian Museum, Cairo, JE 48828).[6]

CZ

1. Sabbahy 1982, p. 317.
2. As is attested, for example, by the cult of statues of queen mothers. See Posener-Kriéger 1976, pp. 527–33; and Troy 1986.
3. Hölscher 1912, pp. 102–3; Reisner 1931, pl. 17.
4. Fay 1998, pp. 160–86.
5. See Smith 1946, pp. 41–44.
6. Daressy 1910, pl. 1.

PROVENANCE: Giza, pyramid temple of Khafre, in rubble near east facade, von Sieglin excavation, 1909–10, discovered by Steindorff, February 3, 1909

BIBLIOGRAPHY: Hölscher 1912, p. 102, no. 56, fig. 140; Reisner 1931, p. 128; Smith 1946, p. 42; Porter and Moss 1974, p. 25; Brunner-Traut 1977, col. 515, n. 2; Blumenthal 1984, p. 550; Krauspe 1987, p. 27, no. 26/1; Krauspe 1997a, p. 31, fig. 29; Krauspe 1997b, p. 39, no. 86, pl. 28/1–4; Fay 1998, p. 168, n. 43

65. CAST OF AN ARCHITRAVE OF KING KHAFRE

Cast of original Fourth Dynasty red granite architrave taken by Ronald Street, Molding Studio, The Metropolitan Museum of Art, New York, 1998
Fiberglass-reinforced epoxy resin
H. original, 90 cm (35⅜ in.); w. 405 cm (159¾ in.); d. 85 cm (33½ in.)
The Metropolitan Museum of Art, New York
N.A. 1999.1

The present object is a cast of a red granite architrave made in the Fourth Dynasty and reused in the entrance corridor of the pyramid of Amenemhat I (Twelfth Dynasty,

66

about 1970 B.C.E.) at Lisht. The original architrave (fig. 116) is located so deep within the structure that it cannot be removed. The front of the architrave is inscribed with the horizontal cartouche of Khafre, which reads: "The King of Upper and Lower Egypt Khafre, Son of Re." The inscription was deliberately damaged, probably before the block's reuse in the pyramid. At both ends of the block are remains of two seated falcons with cobras in front of them, forming the top of the vertically written Horus name of the king; the Horus name would have continued on the piers that supported the architrave. The extreme left and right ends of the architrave also include two flying falcons facing outward and rendered in shallow incised lines. These remains suggest that the architraves lacked a continuous inscription and that the pattern of cartouches flanked by the Horus name and two flying falcons either repeated or alternated with another, unknown text.

Ricke recognized that the architrave was originally part of the court of Khafre's pyramid temple at Giza. The court was surrounded by a sequence of sixteen narrow doorways and twelve wide piers with over-lifesize seated figures of Khafre inset into them. According to Ricke, the architrave bridged the doorways between the piers. He also suggested that representations of flying falcons faced toward and protected the royal statues (see fig. 20). Small discrepan-cies in the measurements of his reconstruction can no longer be addressed because of the poor state of preservation of the temple.

A more cautious evaluation would therefore assert that the architrave belonged either to that court of Khafre's pyramid temple or to a similar locale in another, unknown temple. DA

PROVENANCE: Original, Lisht North, entrance corridor, pyramid of Amenemhat I, Maspero survey, 1883, and Metropolitan Museum of Art excavation, 1907–8

BIBLIOGRAPHY: Naville 1891, pl. 31[B]; Ricke 1950, pp. 50–52, pl. 2, figs. 17–19; Goedicke 1971, pp. 23–24

66. GROUP OF ARCHERS

Fourth Dynasty, reign of Khufu or Khafre
Painted limestone
H. 25.4 cm (10 in.); w. 37.5 cm (14¾ in.)
The Metropolitan Museum of Art, New York,
Rogers Fund and Edward S. Harkness Gift,
1922 22.1.23

This relief fragment, which was reused in the pyramid of Amenemhat I at Lisht, shows one of the most intricate groups of figures extant from Old Kingdom art. Close examination reveals that parts of five archers are preserved on it. We see two complete heads in the center of the carved area. The slightly upturned forehead, eye, and nose of a third man appear at the bottom edge below the head of the man on the right. The outstretched arm and the hand above this third head belong to a fourth man, whose figure is otherwise lost. At the extreme right edge of the fragment the hand and arrow of a fifth man are visible. Of the two arms below the head of the archer on the left, the upper belongs to the second man with a complete head and the lower belongs to the third archer. Thus the group originally consisted of at least three men standing in a row, one behind the other, and another archer kneeling in front of them.

All the men hold longbows with arms stretched out straight in front of them at shoulder height. Each grasps a bow shaft between his thumb and the last three fingers of his left hand,[1] while the index finger keeps the front section of an arrow in place. With his right hand each archer draws the string of the bow, with the notched end of the arrow set against it, toward his shoulder. The bowstring is held between the thumb and the index finger of the right hand, and the arrow between the index and second fingers. The thumb of the same hand also holds two reserve arrows. The bows are of the simple type (self bows) most prevalent during the Old and Middle Kingdoms.[2] The arrows have a tapering conical point and are split at the end for the insertion of a leaf-shaped piece of feathering that is tied to the butt in three places. All the archers would have worn the military equipment that can be seen on the first man: two crossed bands over the torso and a rectangular quiver fastened with a cord above the waist. The quiver is of a typical Old Kingdom kind,[3] and the crossed bands were part of every archer's uniform at the time.[4]

The date of the archer relief has been disputed by various scholars. Goedicke, although well aware that "the style matches the best examples of the IV Dynasty," was nevertheless inclined to assign the piece to the early Fifth Dynasty.[5] Smith, however, advocated a date in the reign of Khufu,[6] and Dorman followed, calling it a work of the Fourth Dynasty.[7] If we accept a Fourth Dynasty date, which seems probable, the question of placing the fragment in a specific monument still remains difficult. Ascribing the piece to Khufu's pyramid complex presents a problem, because its style is not exactly that of the reliefs securely assigned to this king's funerary monuments (cat. nos. 38, 41). The figures of the archers stand out harshly against their background, and the modeling of details, although of the first quality, lacks the subtlety and smoothness of the Khufu reliefs. The archers' facial features and ears are more deeply carved and more boldly, even naturalistically conceived.

There are, however, other reliefs of Khufu's time whose style comes closer to that of the archers scene. The fragment from the tomb of Hemiunu (cat. no. 45) is a good example of this style, and even more closely related to the present work are the reliefs in the tomb of Khufu-khaf I, who was a son of King Khufu.[8] Both tombs date from the end of Khufu's reign and their decorations embody a style bolder than that of the king's known pyramid complex reliefs. Can the archers relief be assigned to an official's tomb that was decorated in this bolder style? To answer this question it is necessary to consider the iconographic context of the fragment.

During the Old Kingdom the hunt with bow and arrow was a royal privilege in the Memphite region, and in reliefs of the period only the king himself is shown using this weapon.[9] The archers in the Metropolitan relief cannot, therefore, be identified as hunters. Moreover, the crossed bands pictured here unquestionably indicate that the archers wearing them are not hunters but

men engaged in a military campaign. They are thus part of the earliest battle scene known from the Old Kingdom. The other preserved battle scenes from the period date to the reign of Unis in the Fifth Dynasty and to the Sixth Dynasty.[10] The Fifth and Sixth Dynasty scenes, however, present their martial theme with much less concision and monumentality than the archers relief; Goedicke has, therefore, correctly maintained that the archers scene is by far the earlier version and that the others must be understood as dependent on it.[11] It is very unlikely that such an early prototype would have been carved in the tomb of a mere official rather than in a royal context. Two possibilities for this context present themselves: the pyramid precinct of Khufu, for which it would have been produced by sculptors who practiced the bold style known from tombs of officials, or the pyramid temple or causeway of Khafre, the next king after Khufu who had his pyramid built at Giza.[12]

Indeed, a relief block found in the debris of Khafre's valley temple shows a bound prisoner confronted by an Egyptian who wears the same crossed bands as the archers on the Metropolitan relief.[13] As the block is known only from an old photograph, its style is difficult to judge, but it seems to show deeply carved eyes and ears and well-modeled features, especially in the captive's face. On the evidence of this block, then, we can tentatively assign the archers relief to King Khafre's pyramid temple or perhaps his causeway.[14] We can also propose that the battle under way was probably a siege of an Asiatic fortified city because most later battle scenes employ archers in this context, leading the attack and providing protection for soldiers armed with axes, who are better equipped for hand-to-hand combat.[15] Since this appears to be the earliest depiction of a siege in Old Kingdom art, it is very likely that an actual historical event is shown. We do not know which of the fortified towns of Early Bronze Age Canaan might be under attack,[16] but there

Details, cat. no. 66

can be no doubt about the pride with which the soldiers of the pharaoh are presented as a formidable military machine: the men stand well aligned, their weapons poised in unison.　　　　　　　　　　　DoA

1. Recognizing which is the right and which the left arm and hand is somewhat problematic because the modern viewer is tempted to understand Egyptian figures that are turned toward the left as if they showed the backs of the subjects. This modern reading is, however, not correct. Egyptian artists presented the right arm behind the left to avoid overlapping them. The issue has been variously discussed, especially by Fischer (1958, p. 34); see also G. Scott 1986, p. 60.
2. They are not composite bows as maintained by Goedicke (1971, p. 76, n. 187). For simple or self bows, see McLeod 1982, esp. pp. 50–52; for examples, see Hayes 1953, p. 279, fig. 181. For the arrows, see ibid., fig. 182; and McLeod 1982, pp. 58–60.
3. Goedicke 1971, p. 76, n. 186.
4. Jaroš-Deckert 1984a, pp. 28, 38, n. 213.
5. Goedicke 1971, pp. 76–77.
6. Smith 1965, p. 150.
7. Dorman in Dorman, Harper, and Pittman 1987, p. 13.
8. Simpson 1978, pls. 22–26. For the style and date of Khufu-khaf's reliefs, see Smith 1981, p. 111, figs. 105, 106.
9. Vandier 1964, pp. 800–801.
10. Hassan 1938, p. 520, pl. 15 (causeway of King Unis); Petrie 1898, pl. 4 (nonroyal tomb of the Sixth Dynasty); Quibell and Hayter 1927, frontis. (nonroyal tomb of the Sixth Dynasty). For an extensive discussion of Old Kingdom battle scenes, see Schulz 1999.
11. Goedicke 1971, p. 77.
12. There are no indications that the quarrymen of King Amenemhat I who collected stone material from Old Kingdom pyramid sites went as far north as Abu Rawash, where Djedefre, who ruled between Khufu and Khafre, built his pyramid (see entry for cat. no. 54).
13. Hölscher 1912, p. 110, figs. 162, 163. Goedicke (1971, p. 10) ascribed the Khafre valley-temple piece showing the prisoner to Khufu's precinct, but his statement that its style is the same as that of one of the Khufu reliefs cannot be accepted. Note elements at variance with the Khufu decoration: the more detailed indication of musculature in the legs of the men in the upper register, the intricate modeling of the foreigner's face and arms, and the complex depiction of the cords, which is reminiscent of the same detail in the archers relief.
14. The valley temple of Khafre was built of granite and had no relief decoration; see Hölscher 1912.
15. See the two Sixth Dynasty examples cited in note 10 above and the post–Old Kingdom examples cited by Jaroš-Deckert (1984a, pp. 44–46).
16. On Egypt and its eastern neighbors during the Old Kingdom, see Redford 1992, pp. 29–32, 51–55.

PROVENANCE: Lisht North, pyramid of Amenemhat I, west side of core, Metropolitan Museum of Art excavation, 1920–22

BIBLIOGRAPHY: Goedicke 1971, pp. 74–77; Dorman, Harper, and Pittman 1987, pp. 12–13

67. KING MENKAURE AND A QUEEN

Fourth Dynasty, reign of Menkaure
Graywacke with faint remains of paint
H. 139 cm (54¾ in.); w. 57 cm (22½ in.); d. 54 cm
(21¼ in.)
Museum of Fine Arts, Boston, Harvard University–
Museum of Fine Arts Expedition 11.1738

[*Giza, January 18, 1910*] . . . In the evening, just before work stopped a small boy from the gang at the thieves' hole in strip 1 appeared suddenly at my side and said "come." In the lower part of the hole the female head of a statue (¾ life size) of bluish slate had just come into view in the sand. It was too late to clear it. But immediately afterwards a block of dirt fell away and showed a male head on the right,—a pair statue of king and queen. A photograph was taken in failing light and an armed guard of 20 men put on for the night.[1]

In those five sentences George Reisner related the discovery of one of the most important masterpieces of Egyptian sculpture. Found in the valley temple of Menkaure's pyramid, the statue was not in its original location and had probably been thrown there by tomb plunderers after the Arab conquest.[2]

In its size and majesty the statue is comparable to the great seated statue of Khafre in the Egyptian Museum, Cairo (fig. 28). But this king is not depicted in divine isolation. Although the base never had an inscription, the sovereign is unquestionably Menkaure, whose face looks thinner than it does in other sculptures from Giza. Beside him is his principal wife,[3] probably Kha-merer-nebti II.[4] The two figures stand with their backs against a wide slab that comes to their shoulders. Treated as two juxtaposed individuals, they are joined by the affectionate gesture of the queen, who embraces her royal spouse. The pharaoh is adorned with the insignia of power: *nemes* headcloth, here appearing without the uraeus cobra, revealing the natural sideburns; a false beard with horizontal striations; a plain *shendyt* kilt fastened by a wide belt. His left leg forward, the monarch has his arms at his sides and each hand closed around an enigmatic object. The queen, slightly smaller than her spouse, is at his left, her left foot slightly advanced. Like goddesses in triad statues with Menkaure (cat. no. 68),[5] she is wearing a long wig, but the artificial hair is smooth and reveals the natural hair, with its central part, on the temples and forehead. Wearing a sheer sheath, her left arm across her midriff in a pose seen in Third Dynasty statues (cat. no. 13), the queen has placed her left hand on Menkaure's arm and is encircling his waist with her right arm. That attitude, which gives a new humanity to the royal couple, served as a model for private statuary.[6]

Detail, cat. no. 67

The simplicity of the forms and composition is combined with an extraordinary delicacy in the modeling of the body and an unmatched precision in indications of musculature. Although the treatment of the features is identical—compare, for example, the precisely outlined eyes and their naturalism, the carefully realized inflections of the mouths, and the firmness of the flesh—the two faces are individualized in the manner of portraits. The square, mature face of the king, who is turning slightly to the right, has a noticeably firm mouth, whereas the queen's face is all youthful roundness. Remnants of red paint still highlight the king's face, ears, and neck; the queen's hair still retains traces of black. Oddly, the work is unfinished, perhaps because of Menkaure's premature death (his funerary complex was hastily completed). Only the faces and upper bodies received a final polishing. Below, the torsos display an irregular surface, and tool marks are visible on both bodies. Citing the severe features of Menkaure, whom alabaster statues (cat. no. 70) and one of the triads show with full cheeks and a very round nose, Reisner attributed this masterpiece to the workshop of Sculptor A (see introduction to cat. nos. 56–63).[7]   CZ

1. Reisner, excavation journal, January 18, 1910, p. 9; see Der Manuelian 1996, p. 64.
2. Reisner 1931, p. 110.

3. Nothing about the attributes suggests this is a representation of the goddess Hathor. See Fay 1998, p. 166.
4. For a cautious view, see Seipel 1980, pp. 165ff.
5. Egyptian Museum, Cairo, JE 40678, JE 40679, JE 46499 (cat. no. 68), and Museum of Fine Arts, Boston, 09.220. All these statues have the same provenance.
6. For gestures of affection as a dating criterion, see Cherpion 1995, pp. 33–47.
7. Reisner 1931, pp. 128–29.

PROVENANCE: Giza, valley temple of Menkaure, Reisner excavation, 1910

BIBLIOGRAPHY: Reisner 1931, p. 110, no. 17, pls. 54–60; Smith 1946, p. 38, pl. 13; Vandier 1958, p. 24; Porter and Moss 1974, p. 29; Aldred 1978, pp. 188–89; Fay 1998, pp. 164–66, no. 7, figs. 11, 12

68. TRIAD OF KING MENKAURE

Fourth Dynasty, reign of Menkaure
Graywacke
H. 96 cm (37⅞ in.)
Egyptian Museum, Cairo JE 46499

Discovered by George Reisner in 1908, this statue depicts King Menkaure flanked by two female figures. On his right stands the goddess Hathor, Lady of the Sycamore, identifiable by the cow's horns surrounding a sun disk that she wears on her head. On his left is the personification of the nome (province) of Diospolis Parva, with the emblem of the goddess Bat above her head. Bat is depicted as a woman with cow's horns, whose face is resting on an elaborate knot. The three figures stand against a back slab that joins the base of the statue. All three are standing with their arms at their sides, and Hathor holds the king's right hand in her left. An enigmatic object, identical to those held by the nome goddess, is visible in the sovereign's left hand. Menkaure's left leg is advanced, in the walking pose traditionally reserved for male figures. He is wearing the *shendyt*, or tripartite pleated royal kilt, and the white crown of Upper Egypt. No chin strap is visible. The treatment of the upper corners of the beard seems characteristic of the Fourth Dynasty. The two women are dressed in identical long, close-fitting sheaths, which partly reveal the details of their bodies beneath the sheer fabric. Each is wearing a tripartite wig with carefully incised locks. Despite their strong resemblance, a few differences are apparent: the left foot of the goddess Hathor is slightly advanced, and her face is turned to the side; the nome goddess faces straight ahead, her feet together and arms at her sides, and she is wearing a necklace. The artist has rendered the shapes and musculature, especially of the king's torso and legs, with a great deal of care and has paid particular attention to the harmony of the composition. Enhanced by the stone—a dark, perfectly polished graywacke—this triad is one of the masterpieces of Old Kingdom sculpture.

The group was found in the valley temple of Menkaure along with three other complete triads and one that is fragmentary. One complete triad and the fragmentary group (fig. 117) are housed in the Museum of Fine Arts in Boston; two other complete examples are in the Egyptian Museum in Cairo.

Although very similar at first glance, the triads differ in a number of their details. The inside arms of the figures standing beside the king sometimes hang straight down but sometimes are wrapped around the king's torso, with the hand resting on his arm. The deities may hold either *shen* signs or enigmatic objects in their hands. In the complete triad in Boston the goddess Hathor is seated in the middle of the group, between the king and the nome personification.

Scholarly opinion about the number and purpose of these triads has changed since they were discovered. It was first thought that there must have been about forty triads—one group for each Egyptian nome. Now it is supposed there were eight triads in all, symbolizing the principal sites where the goddess Hathor was worshiped.

ST, CZ

PROVENANCE: Giza, valley temple of Menkaure, Reisner excavation, 1908

BIBLIOGRAPHY: Maspero 1915b, p. 72 [158]; Reisner 1931, pp. 109–10 [12], pls. 38[d], 44, 45, 46[a,b]; Pijoán 1945, fig. 141; Vandier 1958, pp. 22, 24, 26, 33, 77, 100, 105, 117, pl. 4-4; Hornemann 1951–69, vol. 5 (1966), pls. 1388, 1389; Michalowski 1968, fig. 204; Porter and Moss 1974, p. 28; Aldred 1978, p. 190; Saleh and Sourouzian 1987, no. 33 (for comparison with another triad)

69. HEAD OF MENKAURE

Fourth Dynasty, reign of Menkaure
Graywacke
H. 22 cm (8¾ in.)
Musées Royaux d'Art et d'Histoire, Brussels
E 3074
Paris only

The formal perfection of this head is only slightly compromised by its mutilation. This is very probably a portrait of Menkaure, depicted with the attributes of kingship: the white crown, symbolizing his power over Upper Egypt, and the false beard, traces of which are visible on the right side of the chin. The subtle modeling of the magnificently polished stone may well faithfully capture the features of the king. The impression of fatigue conveyed by the drooping lower lids and the heavy cheeks bordered by folds in the surface of the skin is belied by the firmness of the straight mouth. The eyes are treated naturalistically: there is no cosmetic line extending to the temples, no ribbon-shaped eyebrows, but simply an outline emphasizing the upper eyelids.

The material, dimensions, and style of the work led Gilbert to link this head to a fragmentary triad in the Museum of Fine Arts, Boston (fig. 117). It is now generally accepted that this triad depicted Menkaure

117. Fragmentary Triad of King Menkaure. Museum of Fine Arts, Boston, 11.3147

between two figures, probably a goddess and the male personification of a province, or nome, of Egypt.[1] The Boston fragment, which is carved in a remarkable style, comes from the valley temple of Menkaure. It belongs to an extraordinary series of statues representing the pharaoh in the company of the goddess Hathor and a male or female nome deity, recognizable by the emblem worn on the head. This theme was repeated in statues of other Old Kingdom sovereigns.

Four admirable triads with Menkaure have been found intact at Giza: three of them, in the Egyptian Museum, Cairo, depict the king standing with Hathor on his right and on his left, respectively, the nomes of Thebes (JE 40678), Cynopolis (JE 40679), and Diospolis Parva (JE 46499; cat. no. 68);[2] the fourth triad, in the Museum of Fine Arts, Boston (09.200), is dominated by a representation of Hathor seated between two standing figures, the king on her left and the goddess of the Hare nome on her right. This series of triads is notable for the high slab against which the figures stand. Several fragments of similar groups were discovered in Menkaure's valley temple. We do not know how many there once were: perhaps more than thirty, each correspond-

ing to a different nome, or, according to current opinion, perhaps as few as eight, one in each of the chapels in the foretemple, to represent the principal cities where Hathor was worshiped.

The group to which this head belongs is distinguished by the splendid modeling of the goddess's body; she is standing to the right of the king and holding his hand. The king is also depicted standing, dressed in a *shendyt* kilt with fine pleats. The third figure has his arm around the king's shoulders. The subtle treatment of this male figure's bones and musculature, like the treatment of Menkaure's head, attests to the sense for sculptural form attributed to the workshop of Sculptor B (see introduction to cat. nos. 56–63).   CZ

1. Tefnin 1988, p. 19.
2. See Stadelmann 1998a, p. 376.

PROVENANCE: Giza, valley temple of Menkaure; gift of Baron Édouard Louis Joseph Empain 1910

BIBLIOGRAPHY: Reisner 1931, p. 110 (13), pl. 46f (on the body); Gilbert 1961, pp. 49–52, figs. 2, 3 (on the relationship between the body and this head); Porter and Moss 1974, pp. 28–29; Tefnin 1988, p. 19, no. 2 (on this head)

70. HEAD OF KING MENKAURE AS A YOUNG MAN

Fourth Dynasty, reign of Menkaure
Egyptian alabaster
H. 28.5 cm (11¾ in.); w. 16 cm (6⅜ in.)
Museum of Fine Arts, Boston, Harvard University–Museum of Fine Arts Expedition 09.203

In July 1908 this head and two others (in which the king is shown wearing a *nemes* headcloth) were uncovered during George Reisner's excavations in the valley temple of Menkaure's pyramid complex at Giza. Other statue fragments, including four bases inscribed for the king, were also discovered.[1] Only one figure could be fully reconstructed, but the similarities of stone and scale suggest that this head belonged to one of at least four lifesize seated statues of Menkaure that were set up in the offering hall of the temple.[2] Although the three heads were carved in slightly varying styles, they clearly represent the same person. The knobbed chin, well-formed mouth, full cheeks, and prominent eyes are seen in other representations of Menkaure, such as that in the pair statue in this catalogue (cat. no. 67). The profile, with its prominent browridge, rounded nose, and deeply undercut lower lip, is especially recognizable as belonging to this king.[3]

Menkaure wears the ceremonial royal beard and has a uraeus at his forehead. The cobra's head, which has been reattached, juts out from the surface of the stone, but its open hood is carved almost flat against the king's hair, without any delineation of the reptile's body down the center of the hood.[4] Behind the hood, extending across the top of the king's head almost to its crown, the serpent's thick body forms six compressed curves.[5] The piece is unusual because it represents Menkaure with short-cropped hair instead of a crown or *nemes* headcloth. The hair is indicated by irregular striations that do not extend to the sideburns and have not been completed at the back of the skull. This way of representing short hair is occasionally seen in nonroyal sculpture, as, for example, in the wood statue known as the Sheikh el-Beled (fig. 34). By contrast, the hairstyle when shown in royal statuary is usually indicated in a more formal fashion, using a series of concentric bands, as in a fragmentary royal head in the Petrie Museum, London (cat. no. 101). However, the more irregular

70

pattern can be found in some royal reliefs, such as the hunting scene of King Sahure (cat. no. 112).

Most of the face and the right side of the head are in excellent condition, but the left ear has been damaged, and a large section of the lower left side of the head is missing. The short-cropped hair and the shape of a break at the back of the king's head encourage a comparison between this piece and the fragmentary statuette of King Neferefre discovered in his funerary complex at Abusir (Egyptian Museum, Cairo, JE 98171).[6] The statuette depicts Neferefre seated, with a falcon behind his head. In a better-known example of this pose, a lifesize gneiss statue of King Khafre (fig. 28), the falcon stands on the high back of the throne and actually peers over the king's head, but in the Neferefre example the bird perches on the king's shoulders and its eyes are level with the middle of the pharaoh's head. It is at least possible that the present head came from a similar statue. Since three fragments of a lifesize Egyptian alabaster statue showing a falcon at the back of a royal head adorned with a *nemes* headcloth (cat. no. 57) were found just east of the pyramid temple of Khufu,[7] and since the well-known Khafre statue was discovered in that king's valley temple, it is likely that Menkaure would have had a similar type of statue in his mortuary complex at Giza.[8]

CHR

1. The bases were lined up within the western portico of the offering hall; their exact locations are noted in Reisner 1931, plan 9.
2. Reisner (ibid., p. 112) suggested that the head might belong to statue 21, although he felt that it was too small. Considering the relatively small size of the head that was rejoined to statue 18 (ibid., pl. 48, now in the Egyptian Museum, Cairo), this objection seems unfounded.
3. After tentatively describing the head as a youthful portrait of Menkaure, Reisner (ibid., p. 112) suggests that it may have belonged to a statue of King Shepseskaf, one fragment of which was found in Menkaure's temple. However, the similarity of the features to other representations of Menkaure makes the connection with Shepseskaf unlikely.
4. This piece is discussed in Johnson 1990, p. 108, figs. 195–97. It is the only known example of a uraeus with a complete head in Old Kingdom statuary; it is also the earliest instance in which the uraeus appears on a royal head that is not adorned with a *nemes* headcloth.
5. I would describe these curves as compressed rather than semicompressed, as does Johnson (ibid.).
6. Verner 1985a, pls. 45–47; Verner 1994a, pp. 143–45, ills. For another fragmentary statue of the same type, see Verner 1985a, pl. 44.
7. Found in debris above mastaba G 7102. See Smith 1946, p. 20, pl. 5a.
8. For another opinion about this head, see Lacovara 1995, p. 126, where the author proposes that it has been recarved.

PROVENANCE: Giza, valley temple of Menkaure, Reisner excavation, 1909

BIBLIOGRAPHY: Reisner 1931, p. 112, pls. 52, 53; Smith 1960, pp. 46, 51, fig. 27; Godron 1964, pp. 59–61; Lacovara 1995, pp. 126–27, ills.

71. FRAGMENTS OF A RECLINING ANUBIS

Fourth Dynasty, reign of Menkaure
Greenish basalt (schist?)
Head and neck: l. 12.8 cm (5 in.); w. 7.9 cm (3⅛ in.)
Haunches: l. 22.7 cm (9 in.); w. 12.8 cm (5 in.)
Estimated original dimensions: l. 56 cm (22 in.);
h. 30 cm (11⅞ in.)
Museum of Fine Arts, Boston, Harvard University–
Museum of Fine Arts Expedition 11.721ab

The head and hindquarters are all that remain of a canid with upraised head shown
reclining on a thick plinth. The snout and
ears are missing, and only the stump of the
tail is left at the back of the plinth; the rest
of the hanging tail was perhaps originally
carved as part of a separate base. The modeling of the eyes, bones, and tendons of the
head and neck and of the musculature of
the legs is subdued but very fine. The eyes
are both more frontal and more ovoid than
true canine eyes, and thus appear more
human. Apparently unfinished, the piece is
worn from reuse as a grindstone.

These fragments were found in the later
levels of Menkaure's valley temple, where
they and many other unfinished statues and
fragments had apparently been deposited
during the temple's history of rebuilding
and decay.[1]

Divine statuary from the Old Kingdom
is rarely preserved, and little is certain about
temples of the gods during this period.[2]
Most of what is extant comes from Fourth
Dynasty royal pyramid complexes, where
certain gods were present to support the
king's cult: in addition to this statue of
Anubis, group statues of kings with the great
goddesses Bastet (perhaps also Sakhmet)
and Hathor were found in the valley temples of the Fourth Dynasty kings.[3] In fact,
Anubis and Hathor both had particularly
important if not entirely clear roles in royal
cult temples from the Old Kingdom through
the Middle Kingdom and certainly into the
New Kingdom; it has been suggested that
in the New Kingdom the two might be
understood as counterparts—Anubis as
the embalmer who brought the king to life
eternally and Hathor as the goddess who

could ensure his eternal rebirth and youthfulness.[4] Perhaps already in the Old Kingdom the presence of Anubis was similarly
basic to the king's cult.   MH

1. One of the nearby fragments was a base on
   which Menkaure was named "beloved of
   Sokar," another god with funerary associations; Reisner 1931, p. 113 (39).
2. See Grimm, Schoske, and Wildung 1997,
   p. 146, for a statue fragment of Khnum as a
   ram, inscribed for Khufu. For recent investigations regarding early divine temples, see
   O'Connor 1992, pp. 83–98, and D. Arnold
   1996, pp. 39–54.
3. Seidel 1996, pp. 10–49. The small face of an
   alabaster baboon was found in front of the
   pyramid temple of Khafre (Krauspe 1997b,
   pp. 120–21).
4. Quirke (1997, pp. 44–45) discusses New Kingdom evidence and reflects on its meaning for
   the erratic evidence of the Old and Middle
   Kingdoms.

PROVENANCE: Giza, valley temple of Menkaure,
room (II/III)2, Reisner excavation

BIBLIOGRAPHY: Reisner 1931, pp. 36, 114 (45),
pl. 64a; Holden 1981, pp. 99–103; Grimm,
Schoske, and Wildung 1997, p. 146

72. PRINCE KHUEN-RE

Fourth Dynasty, reign of Menkaure
Hard yellow limestone
H. 30.5 cm (12 in.); w. 21.5 cm (8½ in.); d. 16 cm
(6¼ in.)
Museum of Fine Arts, Boston, Harvard University–
Museum of Fine Arts Expedition 13.3140

Although uninscribed, this statue was found in the tomb of Khuen-re, son of Kha-merer-nebti II and Menkaure (?),[1] and certainly represents him. The prince sits cross-legged on a base that is straight in front and rounded in back. On the kilt stretched taut between his legs he rests his left hand palm downward; his right hand is broken away but was probably clenched and turned downward on his lap.[2] The toe of his right foot is seen from the front and its nail and cuticle are carefully indicated.[3] Differences between the finish of the face and that of the body have been thought to indicate that the piece was not completed. In any case, it is clear that the stocky neck, body, and legs are minimally modeled.

The head sits low on the short neck, and the face is slightly raised. The smooth, flaring wig emphasizes the roundness of the face. Beneath smoothly curved natural brows,

the eyes are finely drawn, with slightly puffy eyelids and rimmed upper edges. The nose and mouth are similarly well defined, the latter drooping noticeably on the left.

Fine-grained hard yellow limestone—a material that lends itself to clarity of detail and the illusion of warm, soft texture—has been employed for the statue. This stone was used at various periods but always rarely, another such instance apparently being the fragmentary statue of Princess Nefer-hetepes, daughter of King Djedefre, in the Louvre (E 12628).[4]

The cross-legged sitting position shown here was reserved during the Fourth Dynasty for men who styled themselves "king's eldest son."[5] Some figures, such as this one, adopt the simple pose with no other attributes, while others add the papyrus and implements of a scribe; since both variations existed from the beginning, it is not possible to be sure that the occupation is necessarily

implied with the attitude, which may also suggest ease or dependence.[6]   MH

1. See Callender and Jánosi 1997, pp. 20–21, for a discussion of these relationships.
2. G. Scott 1989, vol. 2, p. 23.
3. Ibid., p. 24.
4. Ziegler 1997a, pp. 60–61.
5. G. Scott 1989, vol. 1, pp. 22–23. See also Ziegler 1997a, pp. 66–67, for discussion and references regarding the title. If the Scribe in the Louvre (fig. 33) is to be identified with Peher-nefer, and that official is to be dated to the Fourth Dynasty as suggested by Ziegler (ibid., p. 208), this point must be qualified.
6. G. Scott 1989, vol. 1, pp. 3–8. Roth (1997) discusses the "scribe statue" in relation to serving statuettes.

PROVENANCE: Giza, Menkaure cemetery, MQ 1, found in sand in outer chamber of tomb of Khuen-re, Reisner excavation

BIBLIOGRAPHY: Porter and Moss 1974, pp. 293–94; G. Scott 1989, vol. 1, pp. 12–13, vol. 2, pp. 23–25

SCULPTOR'S TOOLS

The subject of sculptors at work is frequently represented on the walls of Old Kingdom tomb chapels. Sharing the same shops as joiners and smiths, sculptors and painters do not seem to have enjoyed special status.[1] Although all of them did not vanish into anonymity—sometimes a proper name is written over the figure of a busy artist—they did not sign their work, with the possible exception of a statue of King Djoser, the remains of which bear the name "Imhotep."[2] Most often, the statues shown in such scenes are completed, although the artisans are still actively at work. In the tomb of Ti, two men are shown beside a wood statue. They are using joiners' tools: adze, hammer, chisel, and coarse stone for polishing the work of art. Nearby, comfortably seated, sculptors are depicted roughing out a stone statue with heavy pieces of rock attached to handles.[3] They will shape the forms with a chisel and mallet or with stone pounders; then the work will be polished with pebbles and an abrasive paste with a sand or emery base. Finally, the finishing touches: color will be applied. A scene from the tomb of Mer-si-ankh depicts an "outline draftsman" named Rahay, with a brush in one hand and a shell-shaped palette for mixing pigments in the other.[4]

But there is no picture of the extraction and transportation of the stone block, which was cut from the quarry with stone picks and wood wedges, and no information on the initial roughing out in the workshop. There is no depiction of the preparation and assembly of wood statues either; generally, different parts were shaped separately and then put together. Along with the tools found by archaeologists (see cat. nos. 74, 75), it is the unfinished pieces that allow us to understand how the work progressed. In the valley temple of Menkaure a sculptors' workshop was discovered, still filled with stone statues that had been abandoned at different stages in their execution (see entry for cat. no. 73).

By examining completed statues, archaeologists have been able to confirm and clarify the nature of this work. Limestone statues show that the stone pounder was used only for the first roughing out; the rest of the work was done with a copper chisel, held either at a slant—thus functioning as a stonemason's point—or level, as was generally the custom. Numerous striations resulting from abrasion can be seen on the surface of statuary. The artist did not exploit the properties of soft stone: there is no openwork, no lacework, no hollowing out, nor are there pronounced effects of shadow and light.[5] Limestone is carved as if it imposed the same constraints on the artist as granite or diorite. Identifiable on statues made of hard stone are marks from such tools as pounders and burins, which were used to strike the stone directly. It is these stone tools, probably fashioned from dolerite, that gave working in granite its specificity. Furthermore, it is known that Egyptian artists of forty-five hundred years ago had copper saws and drills capable of shaping hard stone. Looking at the perfect polish and fine details of works in granite, we can only marvel at the Egyptian sculptor's technical mastery.

Examination of wood statues reveals chisel marks running in all directions; particularly pronounced on certain statues, they reinforced the adhesiveness of the plaster that was applied to the statue as a whole. Elements generally executed separately, namely, the arms and front part of the feet, were attached to the body of the figure by mortise and tenon. Small pegs filled in surface irregularities. These pegs were concealed by a layer of plaster, which might be quite thick. Plaster was used to accentuate details of nose or mouth and sometimes changed the proportions of the statue. Plaster might also be applied to stone statues, especially on the kilt, where thick layers of it were sometimes used to form narrow pleats. Color completed the work and gave it a realistic quality. In fact, however beautiful and well finished the stone or wood, most Egyptian statues display traces of original paint.[6] The grain and warm tones of quartzite naturally mimic the texture of skin, yet King Djedefre's portraits in this medium were nonetheless covered with vibrant colors. Large areas painted in red still survive on the forehead and temples of the head now in the Louvre (cat. no. 54); and on other fragments hieroglyphs display abundant traces of blue-green paint.

CZ

1. Drenkhahn 1976, pp. 65–69, 159–61; Eaton-Krauss 1984; D. Arnold 1991; Vercoutter 1993, pp. 70–83.
2. Pedestal, Egyptian Museum, Cairo, JE 49889.
3. Eaton-Krauss 1984, KIV 26.
4. Ibid., pls. 1, 3.
5. Zuber 1956, p. 161.
6. Reuterswärd 1958.

Unfinished statuettes of King Menkaure. Left, stage one; center, the work exhibited, stage two; right, stage six

73. Unfinished Statuette of King Menkaure

Fourth Dynasty, reign of Menkaure
Diorite
H. 35.2 cm (13⅞ in.); w. 18 cm (7⅛ in.)
Museum of Fine Arts, Boston, Harvard University–
Museum of Fine Arts Expedition 11.730

While exploring Menkaure's valley temple at Giza, an expedition from Boston uncovered a sculptors' workshop containing no fewer than fourteen unfinished statuettes of the king, some hardly begun, others ready to receive their final buffing. All depict the pharaoh in the same pose, seated on a cubic throne with his hands on his knees. He wears the *nemes* headcloth, and the statuettes nearest completion show the two hands in different positions—the right in a closed fist, the left flat. All the figures wear a false beard and the *shendyt* kilt. This is the classic image of the pharaoh, which famous works such as the seated statue of Khafre with the Horus falcon (fig. 28) and the colossal alabaster figure of Menkaure (Museum of Fine Arts, Boston, 09.204) immortalize on a majestic scale. These statuettes in different stages of completion clearly illustrate how the sculptor, beginning with a quadrangular block of hard stone, gradually carved out the figure of a seated man. The base preserves the dimensions of one side of the block, and the seat conveys an impression of its shape.

After a careful study of the series, George Reisner identified eight different stages in the work. Using red paint, the artist began by sketching a geometric silhouette on a block of diorite. This first stage is illustrated by one of the statuettes (above left), which displays no details. At the second stage, illustrated by the present example (center), the protuberance of the head, the contours of the right arm, and the seat are visible. Next, the artist again used red lines, this time to mark out the face, arms, and hands. By the sixth stage (above right), the details were complete. The statuette had only to be polished and the inscriptions carved. The end product seems all the more remarkable when one realizes that Egyptian sculptors used extremely rudimentary tools to work their exceptionally hard stone. cz

PROVENANCE: Giza, valley temple of Menkaure, Reisner excavation

BIBLIOGRAPHY: Reisner 1931, pp. 112–13, pls. 62, 63; Anthes 1941, pl. 17a; Porter and Moss 1974, pp. 30–31; Davis 1989, p. 96, fig. 5.1

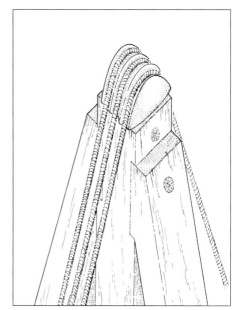

74A,B. SCULPTOR'S CHISELS

Sixth Dynasty
Copper
a. L. 13 cm (5⅛ in.)
b. L. 12.2 cm (4¾ in.)
Museum of Fine Arts, Boston, Harvard University–
Museum of Fine Arts Expedition (a) 13.3428,
(b) 13.3426

PROVENANCE: Giza, tomb of Impy (G 2381 Z),
Reisner excavation

BIBLIOGRAPHY: Petrie 1917, pl. 22; Scheel 1989,
pp. 47–58; Seipel 1992, pp. 456–57, no. 187

75. STONE HAMMER

Fourth to Fifth Dynasty
Granite
L. 13 cm (5⅛ in.); w. 9 cm (3½ in.)
Museum of Fine Arts, Boston, Harvard University–
Museum of Fine Arts Expedition 27.1550

This stone was used as a hammer.

CZ

PROVENANCE: Giza, debris above tomb G 7242,
Reisner excavation, 1927

BIBLIOGRAPHY: Seipel 1992, pp. 456–57, no. 187

76. BEARING STONE FOR ROPES

Fourth Dynasty, probably reign of Menkaure
Dark slate
Max. l. 12 cm (4¾ in.); max. w. 8 cm (3⅛ in.);
max. d. 11 cm (4⅛ in.)
Museum of Fine Arts, Boston, Harvard University–
Museum of Fine Arts Expedition 11.34910

During his excavations in the valley temple
of Menkaure, George Reisner found this
stone implement, which appears to be a fore-
runner of the pulley (fig. 118). In its rounded
head are three smooth grooves to guide
thick ropes. In the broken shaft is a hole for
a peg.[1] An undamaged tool of this type was
discovered at Giza during Selim Hassan's
excavations in the pyramid city of Khent-
kawes I.[2] Judging from the shape of their
heads, these tools were used to shift ropes,
altering the direction of the pull by approx-

imately 45 degrees, using Hassan's example,
and 90 degrees using Reisner's example.
They were probably set into wooden poles
or scaffolding and secured by means of
pegs through holes in the shaft. Depending
on whether this device was set vertically
or horizontally, it could have been used to
raise and lower heavy objects or to pull
them into position in a confined space.

CHR

1. The estimated original dimensions of this piece
   are recorded in D. Arnold 1991 as 37 centimeters long and 16 centimeters wide.
2. Hassan 1943, p. 44, pl. 18a,b; also mentioned
   in Lehner 1997, p. 211.

PROVENANCE: Giza, valley temple of Menkaure,
Reisner excavation

BIBLIOGRAPHY: Reisner 1931, p. 272, pl. A [6];
D. Arnold 1991, pp. 282–83, fig. 6.45

118. Possible use of bearing stone. Drawing
by Dieter Arnold, from D. Arnold 1991
(fig. 6.46)

77. MEMI, WAB PRIEST OF THE KING

Fourth or Fifth Dynasty
Painted limestone
H. 63.6 cm (25⅛ in.)
Ägyptisches Museum, Universität Leipzig 2560

The extraordinarily well preserved red and black paint and the vivacity of the gaze give this statue a very engaging quality. Memi is sitting on a cubic support, both hands on his knees, right hand flat, left fist closed around an enigmatic object. The head and upper body are slightly turned to the left, in a movement rather unusual in Egyptian art. The priest is dressed in a plain, immaculately white kilt and wears a *wesekh*, or broad collar, and a bracelet around the left wrist. His expressive face is framed by a short, curly wig that closely hugs the temples and falls low on the neck in back. The very large eyes and the eyebrows are emphasized with black paint. There is a fine mustache. The modeling of the torso is very rudimentary, and the legs are heavy and thick. The disproportionate size of the head, the hairstyle, and the disorder in the hieroglyphs carved in the seat contribute a touch of archaism that calls into question the Fifth Dynasty date usually assigned to the statue.

Each side of the seat bears an inscription. To the right of the figure can be read: "*Wab* Priest of the King, Memi, who walks on the beautiful paths on which the honored walk." To the left: "The *Wab* Priest of the King, Memi, who says: 'I had these statues made by the sculptor, who was satisfied by the payment I gave him.'" The second inscription is particularly interesting, since it indicates that the ancient Egyptians were concerned with asserting their property rights. The custom of noting them in writing goes back to the Fourth Dynasty.[1] Quite often inscriptions on mastabas attest that the tomb and its equipment belong to the deceased, either as a gift from the pharaoh or as a duly remunerated private commission.

A second statue sculpted for Memi, now in the Roemer- und Pelizaeus-Museum, Hildesheim (2) is known; like this one, it was discovered in a niche of his chapel.

CZ

1. See the inscription of Prince Neb-em-akhet, son of Khafre (Porter and Moss 1974, p. 230);

for an example from the Fifth or early Sixth Dynasty, see cat. no. 154.

PROVENANCE: Giza, Western Cemetery, section known as Steindorff cemetery, found March 22, 1905, in niche of mastaba chapel D 32A, University of Leipzig–Pelizaeus-Museum excavation, 1903–7; gift of the Egyptian Government as part of the division of finds

BIBLIOGRAPHY: Steindorff 1910, p. 156; Sethe 1933, vol. 1, p. 225 (4); Junker 1950, p. 74; Helck 1956, p. 66; *Ikuinen* 1973, p. 121, no. 281; Porter and Moss 1974, p. 110; Blumenthal 1984, p. 550; Eaton-Krauss 1984, p. 80; Krauspe 1987, no. 18; Steindorff and Hölscher 1991, p. 41; Steinmann 1991, p. 157; Krauspe 1997a, pp. 34–35, fig. 31; Krauspe 1997b, pp. 51–53, no. 101

78. RELIEF OF MER-IB

Fourth Dynasty
Painted acacia wood
H. 83 cm (32¾ in.); w. 41.5 cm (16⅜ in.);
d. 4.7 cm (1⅞ in.)
Musée du Louvre, Paris N 3389

This rare acacia panel is bordered by two
vertical moldings that frame the image of a
man moving to the left, holding a *sekhem*
scepter in his left hand and supporting himself with a long staff in his right. He is
wearing a short curly wig that conceals his
ears, a kilt with knotted belt, and a feline
pelt fastened to the right shoulder with a
large knot. Two bracelets and a short necklace with a pendant flanked by two tubular
beads complete his costume. The ideogram
for "libation" is sculpted in front of his
face. At the top of the panel a horizontal
text carved in large hieroglyphs indicates
his identity: "Royal Acquaintance, Mer-ib."
There are abundant traces of paint—green
to outline the eye, red for the face—applied
over a plaster coating.

In the lower right corner a second figure
is depicted in very reduced dimensions.
Only his head and body above the waist
have been preserved. This man with crudely
modeled features is moving to the left, as
Mer-ib does; his hair is close-cropped and
he wears a pendant like Mer-ib's. The vertical inscription says this is "the steward
Nedjem-ib," son or servant of Mer-ib.

Because of their fragility, Egyptian reliefs
on wood are rare. Those of Chief of Dentists Hesi-re, a contemporary of Djoser (cat.
no. 17), are the most famous. They look like
stelae and were inserted into brick architecture following the same principle as decorations in the royal tomb. The relief with
Mer-ib was long compared to this sort of
independent panel, but as the orientation of
the figures and the assembly holes on the
back suggest, it seems probable that the relief is the right jamb of a false door. Many
characteristics suggest a date for this work
in the Fourth Dynasty: the large hieroglyphs,
pronounced relief, simplicity of forms, pendant,[1] and wig with a high crown.[2]   CZ

1. Cherpion 1989, p. 87, criterion 35.
2. Ibid., p. 55, criterion 28.

PROVENANCE: Giza or Saqqara; Clot Bey
collection; purchased 1852

BIBLIOGRAPHY: Weill 1908, pp. 235–36;
Junker 1944, p. 181; Smith 1946, pp. 172, 276;
Porter and Moss 1979, p. 746; Ziegler 1990b,
pp. 104–7, no. 16

79. RELIEF OF NEFER

Fourth Dynasty, late reign of Khufu to mid-reign
of Khafre
Limestone
H. 95 cm (37⅜ in.); w. 109.5 cm (43⅛ in.)
Museum of Fine Arts, Boston, Harvard University–
Museum of Fine Arts Expedition 07.1002

This relief comes from the chapel of G 2110,
one of the core mastabas located in cemetery 2100, to the west of the Great Pyramid
at Giza. It was excavated during the 1905–6
field season and was reexamined in 1932–37.
The chapel had been partially dismantled

by the late 1850s, when relief blocks were
presented to Prince Napoleon by the viceroy of Egypt,[1] but a number remained in
place, including this one, which was part of
the north doorjamb of the chapel entrance.
The angle of the right edge of the block
reflects the slope of the chapel facade. The
decoration depicts the tomb owner, Nefer,
facing out of his mastaba. In front of him
are three columns of hieroglyphs that give
his name and titles. The text began on the
block above, which has never been located.
Nefer's name and principal title, Overseer
of the Treasury, are written in the two lines
of hieroglyphs directly in front of his face.[2]

At the lower right, the smaller figures of
four scribes face Nefer, who was also an
overseer of two categories of scribes.[3]
The figure of Nefer is carved in relatively low relief, with very little indication
of musculature except around the knees.
More attention was paid to the face, where
the eye has been modeled and the nose has
been accentuated by the careful rounding
of the front of the cheek.
Like the larger figure of Nefer, the bodies of the four scribes are relatively flat,
except around the faces and knees. However, they are noteworthy because of the
details included by the sculptor. Each scribe

is named: Neferu, Weni,[4] Khenti-kauef, and Senenu-ka. The last was the owner of a small mastaba (G 2041) adjoining Nefer's tomb. Each man is shown with individualized scribal equipment: Neferu and Khenti-kauef both carry a supply of ink in a shell, whereas the other two men bear the customary rectangular ink holder. Because all four face left, the artist represented them in a most interesting manner. In typical Egyptian fashion, the last three in the line are shown with the upper torso facing the viewer. Each has his right arm forward and his left arm back. The pose of the first scribe is different, however, because he is shown writing. In order to avoid depicting him as left-handed, the artist has twisted his torso so that the viewer sees the back of his shoulders, thus shifting his left arm forward and allowing him to write with his right hand. The same type of representation occurs on a block from inside the chapel, where four squatting scribes who are facing left also have their shoulders twisted so that they can be depicted as right-handed.[5]

Nefer's tomb has been dated convincingly to the years between the end of Khufu's reign and the middle of Khafre's.[6] When the tomb was excavated, a reserve head (see "Reserve Heads" by Catharine H. Roehrig in this catalogue and cat. nos. 46–49) was found in the burial chamber. Taken by itself, this fact suggests a date during the reign of Khufu, since the majority of the reserve heads in the Western Cemetery at Giza are apparently of his time. But reserve heads are almost always found in association with a mud-brick chapel containing a simple slab-stela type of relief decoration (cat. nos. 51–53),[7] and Nefer's tomb has an extensively decorated stone offering chapel. In fact, G 2110 is the only mastaba that has both a decorated offering chapel and a reserve head. Although Nefer's reserve head and decorated chapel may be contemporary, it is also possible that the chapel was a later addition, built after Nefer's burial. In a recent article on slab stelae Der Manuelian

has suggested that there may be a slab stela or a slab-stela emplacement in the mastaba's core, behind the massive outer casing stones, which were not removed when Reisner excavated the tomb.[8] Whether or not this proves to be the case, the presence of the reserve head does not necessarily suggest a date for the chapel, nor do the reliefs necessarily indicate a date for the reserve head.

CHR

1. Smith 1942, pp. 509–10; Ziegler 1990b, p. 167.
2. For a full list of his titles, see Reisner 1942, p. 422; and Strudwick 1985, p. 109.
3. Overseer of Scribes of Crews [or Sailors] and Overseer of Scribes of the King's Documents.
4. Weni was Scribe of the House of the Master of Largesse; see Gardiner 1938, p. 88.
5. This block, now in the Ny Carlsberg Glyptotek, Copenhagen, is illustrated in a drawing in Reisner 1942, fig. 242; see also Jørgensen 1996, pp. 46–47. This is not an example of the pseudo-rear view, as described by Fischer (1984a, cols. 187–91), but rather a conscious attempt to indicate the right-handedness of the scribes. Another tomb in which this occurs is G 7948 (Lepsius 1849–58, vol. 2, pl. 9). The artist responsible for a relief in the Saqqara tomb of Ra-shepses (ibid., pl. 64) took the opposite approach: the scribes facing left are right-handed, those facing right are left-handed, and in both cases the result is very awkward. It is interesting to note that in scenes where an artisan is using a tool that requires some degree of manual dexterity, that person, whether facing left or right, is usually depicted holding the tool in the right hand. Except in the case of a scribe, who must hold his palette in front of him, the artisan's torso almost never had to be twisted so that the back of the shoulders faces the viewer.
6. Reisner 1942, pp. 306–7; Smith 1946, p. 163. See Strudwick 1985, pp. 109–10; and Cherpion 1989, pp. 119–20, among others.
7. Two other reserve heads have been found in mastabas whose chapels contained decorated false doors (Iabtit's, G 4650, and Snefru-seneb's, G 4240), but see "Reserve Heads" by Catharine H. Roehrig, note 40, in this catalogue.
8. Der Manuelian 1998a, p. 121, n. 31.

PROVENANCE: Giza, Western Cemetery, mastaba G 2110, Reisner excavation

BIBLIOGRAPHY: Reisner 1942, pp. 422–25, pls. 29–33; Smith 1946, p. 163, pl. 48e

80. LADY KHENTET-KA AND HER SON

Fourth Dynasty, probably reign of Khafre
Limestone with remains of paint
H. 53 cm (20⅞ in.); w. 26 cm (10¼ in.); d. 38 cm (15 in.)
Kunsthistorisches Museum, Vienna ÄS 7507

Lady Khentet-ka is posed on a high-backed seat, her hands pressed flat on her knees and her legs parallel to each other. At her right, depicted on a smaller scale, stands her son Rudju, his back against the seat. The lady's radiant face is framed by a medium-length wig, with every lock finely scored. Her natural hair, parted in the center, appears on the forehead. Although her face is plump, the features—small, full mouth and almond-shaped eyes with rimmed upper eyelids—are delicately shaped. Her neck is short, her shoulders are broad, and her chest is minimally modeled. Seen through the tight dress, which is clearly perceptible only at the lower edge, is a stocky body with a stout waist; the ankles are exceptionally heavy. Traces of color are still visible. They indicate the outline of a broad collar (wesekh) on the chest and supply the yellow tone conventional for women's skin.

The little boy has the usual attributes of childhood: he is nude, wears his hair in the braid called "the sidelock of youth," and holds his index finger to his mouth. The sculptor has captured particularly well the chubby body of early childhood, with its round belly, in which the navel is deeply inscribed, and the plump face. On either side of the figures two vertical inscriptions incised on the front of the seat give their identity: "Royal Acquaintance Khent, daughter of Khent," and "Royal Acquaintance Rudju, son of the Royal Acquaintance Khent." "Khentet-ka," the lady's real name as it is written on the walls of her offering chapel, has been shortened here.

The statue was discovered in a mastaba at Giza by Austrian archaeologists. The tomb belonged to Khentet-ka's husband, the high official Nesut-nefer, one of whose titles was "priest of Khafre." Although the chapel was shared by husband and wife—its decoration tells us that Nesut-nefer and Khentet-ka had eight sons and nine daughters—they each had their own serdab. The statue of Nesut-nefer (Roemer- und Pelizaeus-Museum, Hildesheim, 2143)

Detail, cat. no. 80

depicts him seated, wearing a round wig that hugs his head.[1] His skin was painted a vivid red, a color traditionally reserved for men.

The tomb has been dated to the Fifth Dynasty since its discovery; however, the style of the subject's own hair and the fact that she has the same name as King Djedefre's wife strongly suggest a date in the Fourth Dynasty, probably in the reign of Khafre, Djedefre's successor.[2]   CZ

1. Compare with the statues of Peher-nefer (Louvre, Paris, N 118) and of Huti (cat. no. 86).
2. Cherpion 1989, p. 114.

PROVENANCE: Giza, Western Cemetery, mastaba of Nesut-nefer (G 4970), German-Austrian excavation, 1913–14; gift of the Egyptian Government as part of the division of finds

BIBLIOGRAPHY: Junker 1938, pp. 185–87, pl. 19b; 5000 Jahre Ägyptische Kunst 1961, no. 44; Komorzinsky 1965, fig. 17; Hornemann 1951–69, vol. 5 (1966), no. 1290; Porter and Moss 1974, p. 144; Satzinger 1987, p. 16, fig. 4; Kunsthistorisches Museum Wien 1988, p. 21; Cherpion 1989, p. 114; Seipel 1992, pp. 126–27, no. 28; Jaroš-Deckert and Rogge 1993, pp. 61–67; Cherpion 1998, pp. 100, 115, 131, fig. 5

81. HEAD OF AN OLDER MAN

Mid-Fourth to early Fifth Dynasty
Painted limestone
H. 10.2 cm (4 in.); w. 10.7 cm (4¼ in.); d. 8.5 cm
(3⅜ in.)
The Metropolitan Museum of Art, New York,
Dodge Fund, 1947 47.105.1

This head was originally part of a statue
that was probably standing and that had a
back pillar ending just below the hair. At the
rear, part of the surface and left side of the
pillar are preserved (this is not visible in
the photograph), but there are no clear indications of any termination on its right side.

The man wears the long flaring wig popular from at least the mid-Fourth Dynasty.
The wig has particularly high and square
contours on the top, flares out in a very
shallow curve from a central part low on
the forehead, and descends well below the
upper edge of the shoulders in the back.
Both its upper surface and undersurface
are neatly striated. The lobes of the ears
project beneath it.

The man's quadrangular, slightly prognathous face is realistically depicted and
marked by signs of age. Vertical creases
and a roll of flesh appear above the nose,
which juts outward just above the break.
Eyebrows were added in paint over the low,
flat natural brow line. The eyes are small,
with plastic rims that extend in points beyond their outer corners; the right inner
canthus is carved onto the nose, the left
only indicated in paint. There are pouches
beneath the eyes, and the cheeks are hollow.
From the lower corners of the nose, two
carved lines on each side curve down toward
pouches of flesh at the corners of the mouth.
The broad, flat lips, their contours indicated by a fine raised line, come together
in a sharp point at the outer corners. The
upper lip is slightly thicker than the lower
and shows a deep dip in the center below
the philtrum.

This very fine head belongs to a rather
small group of realistic images of aged officials from the Old Kingdom, each unique
in its own way. The earliest and best dated
are those of Hemiunu (cat. no. 44) and

Ankh-haf.[1] While the use of carved lines to
mark facial furrows seen here is not apparent in any of the other realistic images, the
high, square shape of the upper part of the
wig and the shape of the face and mouth
suggest a date in the mid-to-late Fourth or
very early Fifth Dynasty.[2]   MH

1. Other examples include the Scribe in the Louvre
   (fig. 33), for which Ziegler (1997a, pp. 204–8)
   suggests a Fourth Dynasty date, and a piece
   found in very mixed debris in a shaft of a tomb
   with the name of Osiris in offering formulas
   (Egyptian Museum, Cairo, JE 72221; Russmann
   1989, p. 37).
2. The image of Ra-nefer (Saleh and Sourouzian
   1987, no. 45) provides a parallel for the shapes
   of the wig and face, and that of Ankh-haf
   (fig. 32) for the face shape and general modeling. The form of the mouth, with its accentuated dip in the upper lip, is similar to that of
   kings from Khafre (cat. nos. 59–63) through
   Userkaf (head from the sun temple; Russmann
   1989, p. 29).

PROVENANCE: Unknown

BIBLIOGRAPHY: Hayes 1953, p. 110, fig. 63

82. Pair Statue of Katep and Hetep-heres Seated

Fourth Dynasty
Painted limestone
H. 47.5 cm (18¾ in.)
Trustees of the British Museum, London EA 1181

Pair statues depicting a man and woman were frequently placed in the serdabs of Old Kingdom private tombs. This one shows the Royal Acquaintance Katep and his wife, the Royal Acquaintance Hetep-heres, whose names appear on the statue and also on a false door[1] and other inscribed architectural fragments[2] from an offering chapel. The location of Katep's tomb is unknown, but his titles, which include Director of Phyle Members, Administrator of the Northern Settlements,[3] Director of the King's *Wab* Priests, and Priest of Khufu,[4] suggest a location in the Giza necropolis.[5] Stylistic features of the relief decoration also argue for a Giza provenance.[6]

Katep and Hetep-heres sit on a bench with a back that rises to midshoulder height. This arrangement allowed their shoulders and heads to be sculpted entirely in the round. From the front, even the lower torsos, arms, and legs give the illusion of being freed from the stone. While Hetep-heres is slightly smaller than her husband, the difference between them is less than one would expect in life. Consequently, she appears almost as Katep's equal, although his is marginally the dominant figure. This near equality in the size of paired male and female figures is common in the Fourth Dynasty and occurs in both nonroyal and royal sculpture.

Katep's torso is well modeled, with the nipples indicated in paint. His shinbones and knees are sharply defined. Hetep-heres sits to his right. Her body is set slightly apart from her husband's, but her left arm extends around his back and her hand wraps around his waist. Her slim body is short waisted, and the left breast is smaller and higher than the right, as if to show the backward pull of her arm and shoulder. Her lower legs, her navel, and the lower edge of her rib cage are visible beneath the fabric of her sheath dress, but her nipples are not defined. The nails on the fingers and toes of both figures are carefully carved and rounded.

As is common in pair statues, the faces are similar, with full cheeks, knobby chin, short, slightly upturned nose, and well-

defined mouth, which in Katep's case is bordered by a thin painted mustache. The browridges are delicately modeled, and the eyebrows are indicated in black paint. The inner edges of the eyelids are also lined with black and the pupils are painted so that Hetep-heres gazes to her right, while Katep looks ahead.

Both figures originally wore jewelry, but the blue and green paint that indicated it have vanished almost entirely, except for traces on Hetep-heres' anklets. A bracelet on her right wrist is outlined with faint black lines, and a broad collar, now almost indistinguishable from her white dress, is still faintly indicated by concentric light and dark bands.[7] The absence of yellow paint, the color used for women's skin, around her neck suggests that Hetep-heres also wore a choker, or "dog-collar," necklace. The faint black outline of an inverted triangle between the woman's breasts defines the bottom of the broad collar and the inner edges of her dress straps,[8] the outer edges of which are also outlined.

In certain respects the style of the pair statue and the relief decoration from Katep's offering chapel suggest a date in the Fourth Dynasty.[9] The hairstyles are of particular interest. Katep's short, curled wig touches his shoulders and back. It also forms a curved frame for his face, a feature that appeared in the Fifth Dynasty but was most common in the Fourth Dynasty.[10] The locks of Hetep-heres' wig are twisted inward, toward her face, and join in a softly defined part along the crown of her head. Beneath the wig one sees her natural hair, which is also parted

in the center. This detail seems to disappear after the reign of Menkaure, in the late Fourth Dynasty.[11]

CHR

1. British Museum, London, 1173–74, 1288; see Scott-Moncrieff 1911, pl. 9; James 1961, pp. 5–6, pl. 5; and Fischer 1976b, fig. 9 on p. 33.
2. Field Museum of Natural History, Chicago, 31709–31711; see Fischer 1976b, pp. 34–37, pls. 9–11, figs. 10–14.
3. The full form of this title, *ꜥd-mr grgt mḥtt*, is recorded on British Museum, London, 1288, and on Field Museum of Natural History, Chicago, 31709. Both are illustrated in Fischer 1976b, figs. 9, 10.
4. This title is recorded on British Museum, London, 1288, and Field Museum of Natural History, Chicago, 31709.
5. This is also proposed in James 1961, p. 5. One of Katep's titles, *ḥrp imiw sꜣ*, although recorded in several tombs at Giza, is unattested at Saqqara; see Roth 1991, p. 79.
6. On the Field Museum fragments (see note 2, above), Hetep-heres wears only a choker, or "dog-collar," without the more common broad collar. This seems to be characteristic only of reliefs found in the Giza necropolis, according to Cherpion (1989, p. 69).
7. The circles of the broad collar are more clearly visible in Budge 1914, pl. 2, as are the bands of Katep's collar.
8. In ibid., p. 7, this inverted triangle is described as a cord on which an amulet was suspended.
9. For the dating criteria, see Cherpion 1989, p. 225, bottom.
10. Cherpion (1998, pp. 104–5) would prefer to date this hairstyle to the reign of Niuserre or earlier.
11. See ibid., p. 100.

PROVENANCE: Probably Giza

BIBLIOGRAPHY: Budge 1914, p. 7, pl. 2; Budge 1920, p. 338; Porter and Moss 1979, p. 693; Quirke and Spencer 1992, p. 155, fig. 119

83. PAIR STATUE OF IAI-IB AND KHUAUT STANDING

Fourth Dynasty
Painted limestone
H. 73.5 cm (29 in.); w. 31 cm (12¼ in.);
d. 30.8 cm (12⅛ in.)
Ägyptisches Museum, Universität Leipzig 3684

The pair statue of Iai-ib and Khuaut was discovered early in 1927 during Hermann Junker's excavation at Giza of a group of mastabas located 500 meters (550 yards) from the pyramid of Khufu, at the outer edge of the great Western Cemetery. The statue was in front of the southern false door, in a vaulted corridor that served as an offering chapel for Itju's mastaba (fig. 119). The statue had been broken when the vault collapsed, but it appears to have been in its original place, and the excavator suggested that Iai-ib and Khuaut were the parents of the mastaba's owner.[1] The relationship is not mentioned in any inscriptions in the mastaba, however, and although at least one of these individuals was probably related to Itju, he or she could be his child, grandchild, sibling, or even cousin.[2]

This superb pair statue—one of the finest of its type—was probably somewhat overshadowed by the unique group of the dwarf Seneb and his family,[3] which Junker discovered in an adjacent mastaba. The two statues actually have a great deal in common stylistically and were probably made at about the same time, during the middle of the Fourth Dynasty.[4]

Iai-ib displays the typical striding pose of a standing male figure. Khuaut echoes his striding stance with her left foot, which is slightly advanced in a pose that is unusual, but not unique, among standing female figures in Old Kingdom statuary.[5] She is a fraction shorter than Iai-ib and stands slightly behind him, with her right arm around his back and her hand resting behind his right shoulder. They stand so close together that Khuaut's right breast is pressed against and slightly obscured by Iai-ib's left arm, which in turn is pushed slightly forward by her body. Both figures hold their outer arms tightly against their bodies, and Khuaut's open left hand closely follows the curve of her thigh. The fingernails and toenails of the couple are well carved and slightly pointed. Their faces are similar, although not identical.

Their bodies are well proportioned and carefully modeled, and Khuaut's is clearly

visible beneath her sheath dress. Unlike the majority of Egyptian statues, both royal and nonroyal, they have been freed exten-

sively from the stone. The back pillar rises only to hip level and engages merely the right leg and hip of each figure. Iai-ib's extended

83

119. Pair Statue of Iai-ib and Khuaut as found in mastaba of Itju, Giza

left leg has been sculpted in the round below his kilt as has Khuaut's left ankle below her dress. Because the size of the pillar behind the pair has been kept to a minimum, the sculptor has devoted unusual attention to the backs of the two figures. Khuaut's right arm is carved in high relief against her husband's back, and the area of negative space between the two bodies is painted both black and red, to indicate Iai-ib's left arm. There is also a fine black line extending from Khuaut's waist to her armpit, separating her body from her husband's red-painted arm. The back of each figure is slightly modeled, and Khuaut's spine is clearly indicated by the depression down the center of her back.[6]

The texturing of Khuaut's wig is very detailed, the locks twisting out from either side of her face. This pattern continues around to slightly right of center behind the head, where two locks twisted in opposite directions converge in a braid pattern. A circular area at the top of the head (slightly right of center) has been left smooth. Khuaut's natural hair, parted in the middle, is visible beneath the front of the wig. This feature, too, suggests that the pair statue was executed during the Fourth Dynasty, probably no later than the reign of Menkaure.[7] CHR

1. Junker 1941, p. 146.
2. The relationships between individuals whose names appear on statues in Old Kingdom tombs are frequently unstated. A serdab in mastaba G 2009 contained four statues representing eight individuals with different names, and offering basins in an adjacent chamber yielded two more names. No relationships were given. See Brovarski in D'Auria, Lacovara, and Roehrig 1988, pp. 88–90.
3. Egyptian Museum, Cairo, JE 51280; see Saleh and Sourouzian 1987, no. 39.
4. On the basis of the relief decoration, Cherpion (1984) dates Seneb's tomb to the reign of Djedefre and Itju's to the reign of Khufu. However, the date of Itju's mastaba does not necessarily correspond to that of this pair statue: since it was found in the offering chapel and not in a sealed serdab, it could have been made and placed in the tomb at a somewhat later time.
5. The most famous example of the pose is the queen's in the pair statue of Menkaure (cat. no. 67), but see also Louvre, Paris, E 6854, in Ziegler 1997a, pp. 100–104; and Kunsthistorisches Museum, Vienna, ÄS 7788, in Jaroš-Deckert and Rogge 1993, pp. 87–94.
6. This depression ends about where one would expect to see the upper edge of Khuaut's dress. There is a similar depression down the back of the statue of Seneb's wife and it ends in the same place.
7. See Cherpion 1998, p. 100.

PROVENANCE: Giza, mastaba of Itju, Junker excavation, 1927

BIBLIOGRAPHY: Krauspe 1997b, pp. 47–48, pls. 36.1–4, 37.1, with a full discussion and earlier bibliography

84. PAIR STATUE OF MEMI AND SABU STANDING

Fourth Dynasty
Limestone with remains of paint; ancient repair on man's right arm and back slab
H. 62 cm (24⅜ in.); w. 24.5 cm (9⅝ in.); d. 15.2 cm (6 in.)
The Metropolitan Museum of Art, New York, Rogers Fund, 1948 48.111

Until recently this statue was thought to represent the Royal Acquaintance Memi-Sabu and his wife; however, there is reason to believe that the inscription names two individuals, Memi (the man) and Sabu (the woman).[1] Although the text does not specify a relationship, they were probably husband and wife, as is usual for the subjects of Old Kingdom pair statues whose relationship is stated.

The statue is exceptional because Memi returns Sabu's embrace by draping an arm around her shoulders. This restricting gesture may account for the fact that he stands with his feet together, rather than striding forward in the normal masculine pose. In spite of these departures from the norm, Memi is clearly the dominant figure. Not only is he larger than Sabu but he also stands slightly ahead of her, his right heel a full three centimeters (one inch) out from the back slab. Although a ridge of stone attaches Memi to the back slab, his body does not lean against it. Instead, he is carved in high relief, separated from the slab by at least one centimeter (three-eighths of an inch) along the entire length of his back. His right arm hangs at his side, separated from his body by a narrow ridge of stone. His hand clutches a rod that extends through the fist to the back slab.[2]

From Sabu's side of the statue, Memi's left arm is visible behind his wife's head. Drawn back to encircle her shoulders, his arm touches the back pillar. Memi's forearm hangs over Sabu's shoulder, and his open palm rests on her breast. This unusual gesture has only two parallels in Old Kingdom statuary: one royal, and one nonroyal.[3]

Although Sabu stands closer to the slab than Memi, she is separated from it by at least a few millimeters along her entire back, and her left heel is one centimeter away from the pillar. Although markedly shorter than Memi, she is not improbably small. Her diminutive size may have been dictated in part by her husband's embrace, which is far less awkward than the other

examples of this pose, where the two figures are more nearly equal in height. Sabu's right arm is wrapped around Memi's waist, and the left hangs straight at her side, the tips of the fingers held out from her thigh by a ridge of stone. Her slim body is well proportioned and clearly defined beneath her sheath dress. Memi is also well proportioned. His torso and arms are modeled with care, and his shinbones and knees are sharply defined.[4] His kilt, with its fan-pleated flap, and his carefully depicted tie-belt are exceptionally detailed. The fingernails and toenails of both figures are slightly pointed. Their faces are similar, although not exactly alike. Sabu's eyes are larger in proportion to her face, and her mouth is fuller than Memi's. Her browridge is also more sharply modeled above the nose, which gives her profile some resemblance to images of King Menkaure. Unlike Memi, who looks straight ahead, Sabu's face and gaze turn slightly to her left. The thick locks of her wig are twisted away from her face and meet in a soft, untextured part along the top of her head. Her natural hair, parted at the center, is visible beneath the wig.

Like most Old Kingdom nonroyal statues, this pair has been dated to a period extending from the late Fifth Dynasty to the late Sixth Dynasty. In recent years, however, a careful study of Old Kingdom

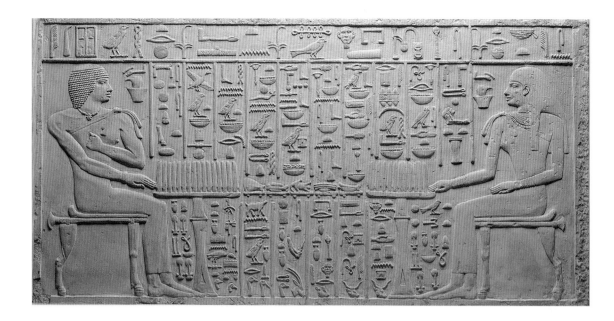

reliefs and statuary has made a date in the Fourth Dynasty, probably not later than the reign of Menkaure, seem plausible. This new date is based both on Sabu's coiffure[5] and on the intimacy of the couple's embrace.[6] The fact that one of the Old Kingdom statues depicting the same embrace dates early in the reign of Menkaure[7] reinforces the probability of an early date for this statue.   CHR

1. Donald Spanel in Capel and Markoe 1996, p. 53, n. 15.
2. For one explanation of this rod and a photograph of Memi's right side, see Fischer 1976a, pp. 9–21, fig. 9.
3. Both statues are in the Museum of Fine Arts, Boston. For 30.1456, Hetep-heres II and Mer-si-ankh III, see Smith 1946, pl. 16c; and Capel and Markoe 1996, p. 131. For the nonroyal example, 13.3164, see Smith 1946, pl. 25f.
4. For a fuller description of Memi's anatomy, see Fischer 1965, pp. 172–73.
5. Cherpion 1995, p. 100.
6. Ibid., p. 37.
7. Hetep-heres II and Mer-si-ankh III (see note 3 above). Mer-si-ankh seems to have been buried early in the second year of Menkaure's reign, and the statue was probably completed at about that time.

PROVENANCE: Probably Giza

BIBLIOGRAPHY: N. Scott 1948, pp. 95–100; Dorman, Harper, and Pittman 1987, p. 20; Spanel in Capel and Markoe 1996, pp. 51–53, ill. p. 51

85. RELIEF BLOCK WITH FUNERARY MEAL OF HUTI AND KETISEN

Fourth Dynasty, no later than reign of Djedefre
Limestone
H. 48 cm (19 in.); w. 95 cm (37½ in.)
Egyptian Museum, Cairo CG 1392

The funerary meal was the central element of decoration in Egyptian tombs. Through the magic of its image and its writing, the representation allowed the deceased to benefit eternally from the offerings depicted and named. The scene often decorates the panel over the false doors of Old Kingdom funerary chapels. Such is the case with this extraordinary relief from a nonroyal tomb at Saqqara. A broad band frames the scene, which stands out sharply from the background. The high official Huti and Lady Ketisen, probably his wife, are shown facing each other. They are seated on stools with bull's legs, each decorated with a papyrus umbel at the back and equipped with a cushion. With equivalent gestures, they hold out their right hands to grasp the bread placed on the two offering tables in front of them.

Huti, his left arm to his chest, is wearing a long kilt made of a feline pelt. The garment, attached at the left shoulder by a large knot, leaves the right shoulder and left breast bare. The short, curly wig that covers his neck is similar to the one shown on his statue (cat. no. 86). His right wrist is adorned with a wide bracelet, and he wears a short neck-

lace with a central pendant shaped like a stylized flower and bracketed by two tubular beads. Certain details of Huti's musculature and bone structure are carefully rendered, particularly in the areas of the arms and shoulders, and the curve of the calves shows through the long kilt.

Ketisen wears a long tunic, but it reveals nothing of her body except the right breast, which is high and firm; a large knot fastens the garment at the right shoulder. Her long, sleek tripartite wig leaves the left ear clearly exposed. Her eyebrow curves sharply over the temple. Her wrists are adorned with many bracelets, similar to those worn by Nesa (cat. no. 13) and Hetep-heres I (cat. no. 31). Her elaborate neck ornaments include a choker and a broad collar with pendants.

Horizontal inscriptions above the figures give their names and titles: "Overseer of Scribes in the Office of Offerings Distribution, Overseer of the *Wer* Team, and Overseer of Royal Documents, Royal Acquaintance, Huti," and "Royal Acquaintance, Ketisen."

In addition to the two offering tables holding bread, there is a very long inscription, divided into columns, that enumerates an impressive quantity of additional offerings:[1] incense, eye paint, unguents, wine, fruit, and grains. In the lower register the list contains the classic offerings: a thousand loaves of bread, pitchers of beer, cuts of meat, and fabrics—all destined for the afterlife of the deceased. With the exception of the name and title of Ketisen, all the hieroglyphs are oriented in the same direction as the figure of Huti.

Many stylistic criteria make it easy to date this remarkable piece, which is characterized by the balance of its composition, the attention given to rendering the anatomy, and the extraordinarily precise detail of the jewelry, curls of Huti's hair, and even the joins securing the parts of the stools. The characteristic form of Huti's wig, the type of necklace he wears, and his long garment are not found in representations dating after the death of King Djedefre.[2] The relief cannot postdate his reign, nor can the large statues of Huti (cat. no. 86) and Ketisen[3] found in the same mastaba.   SL-T,CZ

1. For this noncanonical list, see Strudwick 1985, p. 26.
2. Cherpion 1989, p. 112.
3. Egyptian Museum, Cairo, CG 48; Borchardt 1911, pp. 43–44.

PROVENANCE: Saqqara, mastaba 88 (Mariette mastaba B 9)

BIBLIOGRAPHY: Borchardt 1937, p. 53, pl. 134; Vandier 1954, p. 425, fig. 282; Porter and Moss 1978, p. 489; Desroches Noblecourt 1986, p. 47, no. 18; Cherpion 1989, pp. 111–12; Roth 1991, p. 16

86. Huti Seated

Fourth Dynasty, no later than reign of Djedefre
Limestone with faint remains of paint
H. 110 cm (43⅜ in.)
Egyptian Museum, Cairo CG 64

This male statue is unusually large. Huti is seated, his right hand placed flat on his knee, his left fist closed around a cylindrical object, and his feet together on a rectangular base. He is dressed in a plain kilt knotted under the navel. The short wig that conceals his ears closely hugs his face and falls low over his neck. Despite its mutilation, there is no doubt that the broad face, in particular the mouth, was carefully modeled. The eyeballs were once inlaid but have been gouged out; like those of Kai (cat. no. 124) and the Scribe in the Louvre (fig. 33), they were probably made of crystal and stone mounted in copper cells.

Huti's stocky, thick-waisted body is notable for its highly developed pectorals. The heavy ankles contrast with the carefully fashioned toes and toenails. Two columns of hieroglyphs, carved on the seat at either side of Huti's legs, give his name and titles: "Royal Acquaintance, Scribe in the Office of Offerings Distribution and of Royal Documents and Fields, Huti." Huti's tomb, discovered by Auguste Mariette north of the Step Pyramid of Djoser, also contained a large seated statue of Lady Ketisen, probably Huti's wife,[1] whose stocky silhouette, wig, and head—which is set deep into the shoulders—are reminiscent of those of the figure believed to represent Nefret-iabet (cat. no. 50). The stela depicting Huti and Ketisen (cat. no. 85), which is from the same tomb, is certainly of the Fourth Dynasty, and none of the details of this statue of Huti, such as his hairstyle,[2] suggest a different date.   SL-T, CZ

1. Egyptian Museum, Cairo, CG 48; Borchardt 1911, pp. 43–44.
2. Cherpion 1998, p. 121.

PROVENANCE: Saqqara, mastaba 88 (Mariette mastaba B 9)

BIBLIOGRAPHY: Borchardt 1911, p. 56, pl. 16; Vandier 1958, p. 66; Porter and Moss 1978, p. 489; Cherpion 1998, p. 121

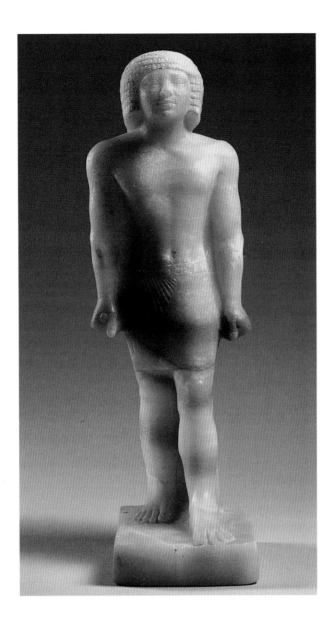

Construction Projects for the King, Ba-baef."
Only about sixty of the very high officials
with this title are known in the Old Kingdom; they combined the abilities of an architect and a public-works engineer. Entrusted
with digging canals for shipping, these chief
overseers coordinated activities at all the
major work sites; in particular, they were
responsible for the construction of the pyramids.[1] That important assignment, which
gave them authority over the quarries and
over the best sculptors, explains the abundance and high quality of the statues found
in the tomb of Ba-baef (the tomb itself is
oddly lacking in decoration, however).
Archaeologists found several dozen statues
there; both whole and fragmentary, these
are executed in a wide range of stones,
including red granite, diorite, limestone,
alabaster, graywacke, and basalt.[2] Their
inscriptions tell us that Ba-baef performed
the duties of vizier as well as Overseer of
All Construction Projects and bore the
unusual titles of son of the king "of his
body" and "Unique Associate of his father,"
usually conferred on the pharaoh's sons
(see entry for cat. no. 55). Unfortunately,
this king is not mentioned by name. Ba-baef
is generally considered a contemporary of
the Fourth Dynasty king Shepseskaf. The
type of wig Ba-baef wears is compatible with
this date[3] and the technique used to inlay
the eyes in an alabaster head found in the
same tomb also supports it.[4]   CZ

1. The title of these officials is the subject of several unpublished studies. See, for example,
   Pfirsch 1990, pp. 32–35. For Ba-baef, see
   Strudwick 1985, pp. 82–83, no. 42.
2. Austrian excavators found this statue and
   an alabaster head next to two granite torsos
   (Junker 1944). The American expedition
   uncovered a statue of the tomb owner as a
   scribe, plus ten limestone statues and a multitude of fragments. On the basis of this evidence Smith (1946, p. 50) estimated that
   the number of statues in the tomb must have
   totaled thirty to fifty. Most of them have
   not been published.
3. Cherpion 1998, pp. 103–4, table 8 on
   pp. 120–21.
4. Kunsthistorisches Museum, Ägyptisch-
   Orientalische Sammlung, Vienna, AS 7786.

PROVENANCE: Giza, Western Cemetery, mastaba
G 5230, in tomb rubble northwest of serdab,
Junker excavation, 1914

BIBLIOGRAPHY: Junker 1944, pp. 152–56,
pls. 30, 31, fig. 64; Smith 1946, pp. 46, 50–51;
Porter and Moss 1974, p. 156; Seipel 1992,
p. 108, no. 19; Jaroš-Deckert and Rogge 1993,
pp. 72–76; Seipel 1993, p. 82, no. 36; Satzinger
1994, p. 114, fig. 80

87. PRINCE BA-BAEF STANDING

Probably late Fourth Dynasty
Egyptian alabaster
H. 49.7 cm (19⅝ in.); w. 16.3 cm (6½ in.);
d. 22.5 cm (8⅞ in.)
Kunsthistorisches Museum, Ägyptisch-Orientalische
Sammlung, Vienna ÄS 7785

This standing figure of Ba-baef is supported
by a back pillar that rises from his feet to
the middle of his head. As was the custom
for male statues, the left leg is advanced,
but in this case a particularly vigorous forward movement infuses the whole body.
The face is turned slightly to the figure's
left. Ba-baef's arms are at his sides, and in
each fist he clasps a cylindrical object. He
wears a kilt pleated at the side, fastened by
a belt knotted horizontally. His round face
is closely framed by a curly wig that conceals the ears and falls very low over the
nape of the neck. The facial features have
been modeled with care: the eyebrows follow the curve of the eye; the upper lids are
rimmed; the cheeks are high and round; the
nostrils are delicately marked on the broad,
short nose; and the mouth is full and sinuous. The body is executed with the same
care, and, like the face, it has been polished
to a remarkable smoothness made possible
by the nature of the stone. The broad shoulders, with clavicle precisely indicated, and
the muscular, solid limbs—the ankles are
abnormally thick—contrast with the narrow waist. Details such as the nipples and
nails are finely sculpted.

On the back, a vertical inscription runs
down the support: "Prince, Overseer of All

88. THE DWARF PER-NI-ANKHU SEATED

Fourth Dynasty
Painted basalt
H. 48 cm (18⅞ in.); w. 14 cm (5½ in.)
Egyptian Museum, Cairo JE 98944

The statue of the dwarf Per-ni-ankhu (*pr-n[i]-ʿnḫ[w]*) is a rare example of non-royal statuary carved in basalt. Executed with great care and skill, it must be regarded as a masterpiece of Old Kingdom sculpture. It was discovered on January 11, 1990, inside a serdab attached to the deceased's tomb, located at the southern end of the cemetery that is west of the Great Pyramid of Khufu at Giza. Seated on a backless chair, the dwarf wears a traditional short, curled wig, which reaches to his shoulders. The details of this wig have been very carefully crafted, and traces of its original brown paint are preserved. Per-ni-ankhu's short, bright white kilt has a black belt.

Special care has been taken to depict the dwarf's round face realistically. Its well-defined features include black eyebrows, meticulously carved eyes with white eyeballs and black pupils and rims, and an accurately modeled nose and mouth. The forehead bears traces of the same brown color found on the wig.

The pectoral muscles, short neck, and powerful shoulders and arms effectively indicate Per-ni-ankhu's strength. The dwarf's right hand rests on his thigh and clutches a *sekhem* scepter; in his raised left hand he holds a long staff close to his chest. While the torso is of normal proportions, the upper arms are quite short, although well muscled. Per-ni-ankhu's deformity is clearly indicated by his short, slightly bowed legs, exceptionally thick ankles, and flat feet. The modeling of the left leg, especially the knee, is exaggerated, and its variation from the right one suggests that the dwarf had suffered injuries. These may also have been responsible for the apparent swelling or inflammation of the lower part of the left leg. Alternatively the swollen leg may denote a moderately advanced case of Bancroftian filariasis, bet-ter known as elephantiasis. If so, the statue would be the earliest record of this disease. The back view reveals that the right shoulder is higher than the left and that the spine curves slightly to the left, seemingly as a result of Per-ni-ankhu's sitting position.

On the front of the chair, at either side of the figure's legs, are two vertical lines of incised hieroglyphs identifying the sitter as "one who delights his lord every [day], the king's dwarf Per-ni-ankhu of the Great Place."[1] To gladden the king's heart by dancing and performing for him was usually a task reserved for the court pygmies, but dwarfs sometimes acted as their substitutes. Per-ni-ankhu must have pleased the king so well in the performance of this function that he gave the dwarf the authority to hold the staff and scepter of power. The hieroglyphs of the inscription do not accord well with the fine artistic style of the statue—the text is poorly written and curiously divided between the left and right sides of the chair—and it is possible that they were added later by another artist. An irregular diagonal crack across the back of the seat from left to right was repaired, probably by the same artist who made the statue.   ZH

1. *sḫmḫ-ib nb.f [rʿ] nb nmi nswt Pr-n(i)-ʿnḫ(w)*.

PROVENANCE: Giza, Western Cemetery, tomb of Per-ni-ankhu, Hawass excavation, 1990

BIBLIOGRAPHY: Hawass 1991c, pp. 157–62.

Cat. nos. 92, 89, 90, 91

89–92. FOUR STATUES OF THE ARTISAN INTI-SHEDU

The statues of Inti-shedu ('*Inti-šdw*) were found in the serdab of his tomb, located in the area of higher elevation at the work-men's cemetery at Giza. They were in a niche concealed by a wall built of three courses of limestone, topped with mud brick and mud mortar. At the top of the wall was a small hole through which the face of the tallest statue, with its large, bright eyes, was visible (fig. 120). When the blocking was removed, four well-preserved statues and

the remains of a fifth were found instead of the one originally expected. The main statue, a large seated figure (cat. no. 89), was placed in the middle; at its left were two more, one a seated figure, the other standing (cat. nos. 90, 91). At its right there was another seated figure (cat. no. 92), beside which were the remains of a wood statue that had probably been another standing figure but had disintegrated into a pile of powder.

The four surviving statues, all of painted limestone, differ slightly in style and greatly in size. All dating to the end of the Fourth Dynasty, they represent one person, identi-fied by inscriptions on each as Inti-shedu.

Although the statues were made for the tomb of an artisan, the sculptor followed the same conventions used in works created for officials, noblemen, and even the king.

The deceased may have intended to have himself represented at different ages: the larg-est statue (cat. no. 89) shows him at the time of his death, the standing statue and small seated statue (cat. nos. 91, 92) depict him in his youth, and the medium-sized seated statue (cat. no. 90) presents him at an intermediate age. Each face is carved to indicate its respec-tive stage of life, and the muscles and shoul-ders are sculpted to show the level of strength corresponding to that stage.   ZH

120. Serdab of Inti-shedu at time of discovery, with one statue (cat. no. 89) visible, Western Cemetery, Giza

89. INTI-SHEDU SEATED

End of Fourth Dynasty
Painted limestone
H. 75 cm (29½ in.); w. 26 cm (10¼ in.);
d., base, 27 cm (10⅝ in.)
Egyptian Museum, Cairo JE 98945

The large central statue in Inti-shedu's tomb, showing the owner seated on a backless chair, was clearly the most important of the group. It depicts the artisan wearing a short kilt with a pleated overlapping panel and a belt tied in an elaborate knot carefully carved in relief; both kilt and belt are painted white. His head is covered with a flaring black wig, parted down the middle, each lock carefully depicted as a separate curled strand. A broad collar is outlined in black paint around the short, thick neck and its three rows of beads are indicated by brown and blue lines.

The reddish brown paint on the skin has not been evenly applied, and brush marks are visible where the pigment is thin. The artist has attempted to reproduce the effect of the prominent brow bone on the wide, rather low forehead, which slopes gradually from the wig to the eyebrows. The eyebrows are black and carefully outlined but not quite symmetrical. The similarly asymmetrical eyes are emphasized by a thick black outline that may be intended to represent kohl. The eyeballs are white, the pupils black with a thin reddish brown

outline, and the inner canthi a light brown. The straight nose has been simply modeled, as has the mouth, which is topped by a thin black line indicating a mustache.

The muscles of the shoulders, chest, and stomach have been indicated by the artist. The broad shoulders and heavy arms convey the impression of strength, but the chest is modeled in a rather stylized manner, the nipples are placed too close to the arms, and the juncture of chest and arms is unnaturally sharp.

Inti-shedu is shown holding a linen cloth or a leopard skin in his clenched right hand; the long fingers of his left hand lie flat on his thigh. The negative spaces between the arms and the chest and between the legs are painted black. Both legs, particularly the knees, are carefully modeled. The feet, which have long, thin toes, rest on some sort of stand.

A hieroglyphic inscription written on the right side of the seat, which is otherwise undecorated, reads "Overseer of the Boat of the Goddess Neith, Royal Acquaintance, Inti-shedu."[1]   ZH

1. *imy-rꜣ wiꜣ n Nt rḫ nswt 'Inty-šdw.* The title has no parallels but suggests that Inti-shedu was a carpenter making boats for Neith, who was worshiped at Giza by both priests and priestesses.

PROVENANCE: Giza, Western Cemetery, tomb of Inti-shedu, Hawass excavation, 1990

BIBLIOGRAPHY: Hawass 1998, pp. 187–208

90. INTI-SHEDU SEATED

End of Fourth Dynasty
Painted limestone
H. 40.5 cm (16 in.); w. 12.2 cm (4¾ in.)
Egyptian Museum, Cairo JE 98946

Inti-shedu is shown here sitting on a chair without a back. His head is covered with the flaring wig traditional in the Old Kingdom, and he wears a simple kilt, painted white. The belt of the kilt, which has an elaborately tied knot, bears a pattern of alternating blue and white vertical stripes. Inti-shedu's broad collar was originally painted blue, but some of its paint has flaked away to reveal the white limestone underneath. Apparently of religious significance, this type of collar may be connected with the Ennead of Heliopolis.

The face is quite unusual when compared with those of other statues dating to the Old Kingdom in that the features, particularly

the widely spaced eyes, are noticeably larger. The heavy black eyebrows follow the line of the wig. The eyes (the right is smaller than the left) are outlined in black, and the pupils, which are not entirely circular, are painted black against the white eyeball. As on the larger seated statue of Inti-shedu (cat. no. 89), there are traces of dark reddish brown paint encircling the pupils. The nose is straight, rather short, and slightly snub, its well-defined nostrils painted black. The mustache is a single black line above the lips.

The head is thrust forward on the short, thick neck. This statue has a more relaxed air than the larger seated one, for the shoulders are not as broad and the muscles of the torso not so well defined. The nipples are painted black and emphasized by a ring of black dots. Both hands are placed on the knees: the right hand clutches a linen cloth and the long fingers of the left lie flat. The modeling of the muscles and shinbones of the sturdy legs is clear and rather stylized.

This statue shows a much darker brown skin than the others of Inti-shedu. Its paint was applied carelessly, especially beneath the left arm, where it spills onto the kilt. The negative space around the legs has been painted black, but the rest of the seat, which was restored in ancient times, is dotted with red and black paint meant to imitate granite.

The subject of this statue seems to be strong and confident, still youthful yet rich in life's experiences. On the right side of the seat he is identified as "Overseer of the Boat of Neith, Inti-shedu."[1]   ZH

1. *imy-rꜣ wiꜣ n Nt 'Inty-šdw.*

PROVENANCE: Giza, Western Cemetery, tomb of Inti-shedu, Hawass excavation, 1990

BIBLIOGRAPHY: Hawass 1998, pp. 187–208

91. INTI-SHEDU STANDING

End of Fourth Dynasty
Painted limestone
H. 31 cm (12¼ in.); w. 5.8 cm (2¼ in.)
Egyptian Museum, Cairo JE 98948

Found next to the medium-sized seated statue (cat. no. 90) on the north side of the serdab niche in Inti-shedu's tomb, this figure stands with his left leg advanced, both arms close to his sides, and hands clutching rolls of linen or leather. He wears a short, curly

black wig and a short, belted white kilt. The collar around his neck is outlined in red and has three rows of beads painted white, blue, and white respectively.

The facial features are more delicate than those of the other three statues in the group from this tomb. The forehead is broad. Modeled and outlined in black paint, the eyes slope downward near the temples, as do the eyebrows. The eyeballs are painted white with black pupils, and the right eye is slightly smaller than the left. The straight nose has only a summary indication of nostrils, and the lopsided mouth is not fully developed. Above the upper lip a mustache is indicated by a thin black line of which only the left part is preserved. The chin is small. The overall effect of the face is square rather than rectangular or round.

Inti-shedu's short, thick neck sits on broad, strongly muscled shoulders and a simply modeled torso. The muscles of the legs are crudely indicated, although the left is better modeled than the right. The legs are attached to the back pillar, which extends to the middle of the figure's back. The negative spaces between the arms and the body and between the legs and the back pillar are painted black. When the statue was found, its lower right arm and hand were broken and the right side of its base was chipped.

An inscription on the base, in front of the right leg, identifies the subject as "Overseer of Neith, Inti";[1] another, at the left side of the base, gives the second half of his name, "shedu" (*šd*).   ZH

1. *imy-rꜣ Nt 'Inty.* The hieroglyphic sign *n* and the boat hieroglyph found on the other three statues do not appear here.

PROVENANCE: Giza, Western Cemetery, tomb of Inti-shedu, Hawass excavation, 1990

BIBLIOGRAPHY: Hawass 1998, pp. 187–208

92. INTI-SHEDU SEATED

End of Fourth Dynasty
Painted limestone
H. 32 cm (12⅝ in.)
Egyptian Museum, Cairo JE 98947

Here Inti-shedu sits on a backless chair, his forearms resting on his thighs. Painted the same reddish brown as the large seated statue of the artisan (cat. no. 89), this figure

women on a block to the left; their motionless pose contrasts with the animation of their companions. Wearing long dresses, heads crowned with lotus flowers, adorned with necklaces held in place by heavy counterpoises, they sing and clap their hands.

The ballet takes place during a banquet attended by the deceased, his wife, Henutsen, and two members of the family identified as Niwi-netjeru Junior and Henutsen Junior. Scenes of music and dance began to be shown in similar contexts during the Fourth Dynasty, and it is not easy to date this relief, since the dancers, whose faces are rather crudely drawn, have been considered comparable to figures in Sixth Dynasty works. A few indications, such as the necklace worn by Henutsen[2] and the type of offering table laden with food,[3] suggest a date between the middle of the Fourth Dynasty and the middle of the Fifth.   CZ

1. This is one of the oldest representations of a naos sistrum; compare it with another depicted in the tomb of Ihy at Thebes dating to the Sixth Dynasty (Saleh 1977, pl. 17).
2. It is a "dog collar" associated with a *wesekh* collar; see Cherpion 1989, criterion 46 (Fourth Dynasty to Fifth Dynasty, attested until the reign of Djedkare-Isesi).
3. Ibid., criterion 22 (attested from the reign of Khafre to the reign of Niuserre).

PROVENANCE: Giza, Cemetery GIS, south of pyramid of Khufu, tomb of Niwi-netjeru, Junker excavation, 1928–29

BIBLIOGRAPHY: Junker 1951, pp. 113–36, pl. 18, figs. 44–46; Vandier 1964, pp. 403–4; Porter and Moss 1974, p. 217; Satzinger 1994, p. 108, fig. 74

---

wears a black wig that flares out at the sides and reaches his shoulders. His broad collar is delineated with three rows of paint—white, blue, and white respectively— but the details of the beads are not represented. On the back of the statue, beneath the wig, the knot of the collar has been painted white. The short, belted kilt is also of the same color.

The features of the round face are fine and well defined. Black paint has been used for the eyebrows and for the outlines of the eyes, which have white eyeballs and black pupils showing traces of a red outline. The nose is long, and the well-formed lips show a slight smile that is emphasized by the fullness of the cheeks. Above the mouth is a thin black mustache.

As on the other three statues of Inti-shedu, the muscles have been modeled. Black paint has been used to indicate the navel. The right hand clutches a linen cloth, painted white, and the left hand lies flat on the thigh.

An inscription on the right side of the chair identifies the subject as "Overseer of the Boat of Neith, Inti-shedu."[1]   ZH

1. *imy-rꜣ wiꜣ n Nt 'Inty-šdw.*

PROVENANCE: Giza, Western Cemetery, tomb of Inti-shedu, Hawass excavation, 1990

BIBLIOGRAPHY: Hawass 1998, pp. 187–208

93. FEMALE DANCERS AND MUSICIANS

Mid-Fourth to mid-Fifth Dynasty
Limestone
H. 78 cm (30¾ in.); w. 190 cm (73¾ in.)
Kunsthistorisches Museum, Ägyptisch-Orientalische Sammlung, Vienna ÄS 8028

The musical interlude shown is part of a large scene sculpted on a wall of Niwi-netjeru's offering chapel. Two groups of female dancers are turning with one leg raised; between the groups, a female dwarf wearing a crown of lotus flowers makes an identical movement. The women on the right turn their heads gracefully backward, one hand on hip, the other held over the head. Their partners move in the opposite direction, marking time with a sistrum, a musical rattle (cat. no. 182) they shake above their heads.[1] In the other hand they hold clappers. Are the two groups turning in opposite directions, circling around the dwarf? Or is each dancer describing her own circle, striking her neighbor's clapper with her own as she passes? Opinion is divided on this point. In any case, this relief represents a ballet with skilled choreography, danced by alert young girls in short skirts, their chests encircled by flowing sashes. The music is performed by kneeling

JEWELRY IN THE OLD KINGDOM

The many representations of jewelry in Old Kingdom reliefs, stelae, and statues reveal that both men and women of the period wore diadems, necklaces (primarily broad collars), and bracelets. In addition to this artistic evidence, a few examples of such jewelry have been recovered through archaeological excavations of tombs. While only a tiny part of the total produced during the period, the extant pieces allow us to appreciate the quality, originality, and diversity of Old Kingdom jewelry, which could vary greatly depending on the place of origin. The pieces found in the modest cemeteries of the provinces hardly resemble those retrieved from the tombs of officials in the large necropolises that surround the royal tombs. For the most part, provincial cemeteries have yielded simple strings of beads and amulets; although no doubt worn in everyday life, such adornments appear very rarely in artistic renderings. In contrast, the sites of Giza and Saqqara have yielded ensembles similar to those represented in the art of the period. Most noteworthy among these are the several complete funerary diadems (and fragments of many others) that have come from Giza. One type of diadem, consisting of a simple copper or wood band covered with gold leaf and adorned with one or two clusters of papyrus umbels set off by a circular element on either side, was clearly worn every day and is often represented on reliefs. A more sophisticated type, apparently reserved for women's use, depicts two ibis[1] poised on umbels, sometimes flanking an ankh, symbol of life.[2] Such diadems, which are never represented on reliefs, seem to have been purely funerary, with the ibis intended to evoke the spirit of the deceased.

Also found at Giza and Saqqara are several examples of broad collars composed of several rows of beads joined together. Worn by the elite of Egyptian society beginning in the Fourth Dynasty, these splendid necklaces may have been gifts from the king or rewards given by high officials to deserving servants. Several tombs from the Old Kingdom, including the mastaba of Akhet-hotep in the Louvre, are decorated with scenes showing the distribution of necklaces and diadems.[3] As an ornament with protective powers, the broad collar rapidly became an integral element of funerary equipment. Object friezes from Middle Kingdom sarcophagi depict it; chapter 158 of the Book of the Dead was later devoted to it; and it persisted into the Late Period, by which time it had been transformed into a small gold amulet. The oldest surviving examples date from the Fourth Dynasty and often combine gold, hematite, turquoise, and carnelian beads, whereas later examples are primarily made of faience, which is sometimes partially covered with gold leaf. Broad collars frequently had matching beaded bracelets, and those for women might be accompanied by an anklet and a choker, a narrow band of several rows of beads that closely encircles the throat. Among the other types of bracelets in use during the Old Kingdom, the finest were made of metal and decorated with inlaid semiprecious stones.   PR

1. This so-called crested ibis served as a model for hieroglyph *ȝẖ*, meaning "spirit." See Keimer 1930, pp. 24ff.
2. Museum of Fine Arts, Boston, 37606A: diadem in gilded copper inlaid with carnelian, from tomb G 7143 B in Giza, Fifth Dynasty; Ägyptisches Museum, Universität Leipzig, 2500: diadem in gilded copper and wood, from mastaba G 208 in Giza, end of the Fifth Dynasty.
3. For such award scenes, see Ziegler 1993a, pp. 120–22; and Junker 1941, pp. 55ff.

NECKLACES

From the Predynastic Period through the end of the Old Kingdom, Egyptians wore simple strings of beads that often included amulets and pendants as well. Many artistic renderings from the Fourth Dynasty depict men wearing short necklaces composed of a cord strung with one or two cylindrical or barrel-shaped beads and having an amulet in the center (cat. nos. 78, 85). The object represented by that amulet is usually difficult to identify: it is sometimes oval with bulges on either side[1] and sometimes elongated, suggesting part of a plant, perhaps a bud or stylized leaf.[2] Depictions of the same individual on different reliefs may show him with such a necklace or with the broad collar, which appeared during the same dynasty. In the Fifth Dynasty men were represented wearing another type of ornament—a long cord with two or four widely separated tubular beads and a round amulet at the center.[3] Of the various interpretations of this amulet, the most convincing describe it as a small fabric sack containing an object or a closed fist holding an object; in both cases, however, the object in question has yet to be identified.[4] Until the early Sixth Dynasty this type of necklace was worn either over or under the broad collar and seems to have been reserved primarily for men, representations of women wearing such ornaments being very rare.[5]

A few necklaces, either alone or in combination with the broad collar, have been found at Giza and Saqqara. These are of two types: a complete row of cylindrical, round, or barrel-shaped beads usually made of gold, carnelian, lapis lazuli, turquoise, and faience[6] or a simple gold strand on which a few beads have been strung.[7] These necklaces do not contain any of the amulets found in contemporary representations.

Conversely, among the countless amulets found in provincial cemeteries, there is a relatively small one (generally interpreted as a closed fist) that has clear similarities to those in artistic renderings.[8]

The modest tombs of provincial cemeteries have yielded many necklaces composed of simple rows of beads combined with all sorts of amulets designed to protect the deceased. Some of these amulets, such as the falcon, hippopotamus, and recumbent dog, had already been used during earlier periods; others, such as the frog, double lion, hare, tortoise, scorpion, and different types of human figures, made their appearance later. Many of them are so schematic and crudely executed that they cannot be identified. Only a few are found in burials from the Third and Fourth Dynasties, but they are plentiful in those from the Sixth Dynasty.

Beads and amulets are made of many types of materials, primarily carnelian, turquoise, feldspar, ivory, steatite, serpentine, agate, quartz, limestone, diorite, basalt, Egyptian faience, and shells. The most common metals are gold, silver, electrum, and copper. Gold leaf was sometimes applied to the surface of the beads.

The necklaces discovered in provincial cemeteries are rarely illustrated in artistic representations, the most notable exception being a depiction of Kawab, son of Khufu, who is shown wearing a necklace adorned with several amulets.[9] Such necklaces, which are often accompanied by arm bracelets and anklets of a similar kind, have most frequently been excavated in the tombs of women and children. PR

1. See, for example, the Mer-ib panel (Louvre, Paris, N 3389, cat. no. 78; in Ziegler 1990b, pp. 105–6); Ra-hotep (Egyptian Museum, Cairo, CG 3; in Saleh and Sourouzian 1987, p. 27); and the false door of Nefer from Giza (Cherpion 1989, pl. 9).

2. See, for example, amulets shown in representations of Irery, British Museum, London, EA 1168; and Metjen, Ägyptisches Museum und Papyrussammlung, Berlin, 1105.
3. The presence of such ornaments in a few mastabas containing the name of Menkaure is noteworthy; see Cherpion 1989, pp. 60–62.
4. For a detailed study of these amulets, see Staehelin 1966, pp. 100ff.
5. The wife of Ka-gemni is one of the few women to be depicted wearing this necklace. See ibid., pl. 10, fig. 15.
6. See, for example, Junker 1938, pp. 223ff., fig. 45 (Ra-wer); Junker 1944, p. 180, fig. 74 (Kȝjswdȝ); and Museum of Fine Arts, Boston, necklace found in tomb G 2381 A (Impy).
7. See Junker (1944, pp. 178–79), who gives a list of ten items falling within these two types of necklaces. Notable among necklaces of the second type are those found in shaft 559 (gold strand with two beads in carnelian and faience) as well as in the tombs of Iput (gold strand with seven cylindrical beads in gold, lapis lazuli, and faience; see Firth and Gunn 1926, vol. 2, pl. 15B); Seshemu (gold strand with seven cylindrical and round beads in gold, carnelian, turquoise, faience, diorite, and white stone; see Hassan 1941, p. 87, pl. 26 [2]); Ankh-haf (gold strand with four cylindrical beads in gold, carnelian, and faience; see ibid., p. 142); and Ptah-hotep (gold strand with two beads in faience and carnelian; see Junker 1944, p. 227, fig. 92).
8. See, for example, Petrie 1994, pls. 1, 12a–c; Valloggia 1986, p. 86, nos. 934/7, 934/8, 936/7, 962/1, fig. 12, Sixth Dynasty; Brunton 1928, pl. 94, 8 T 3, 6, 9; and Brunton 1937, pl. 56, 8 T 2, 8, 10.
9. Dunham and Simpson 1974, fig. 4.

EGYPTIAN FAIENCE

Beginning in the Predynastic Period, Egyptians developed a beadmaking technique in which certain stones such as steatite were covered with either a blue or a green glaze. Although that technique continued to be used in subsequent periods, a new type of material, called faience, was soon invented. This substance, which is specific to Egyptian civilization, is composed of a core of pulverized quartz or sand covered with a vitreous glaze of various hues, most commonly blue, green, and black in the Old Kingdom. Easy to model and mold, faience was widely used by jewelers of every era. Its brilliant appearance and the intensity of its colors made it a good substitute for semiprecious stones, which were more expensive and difficult to obtain. PR

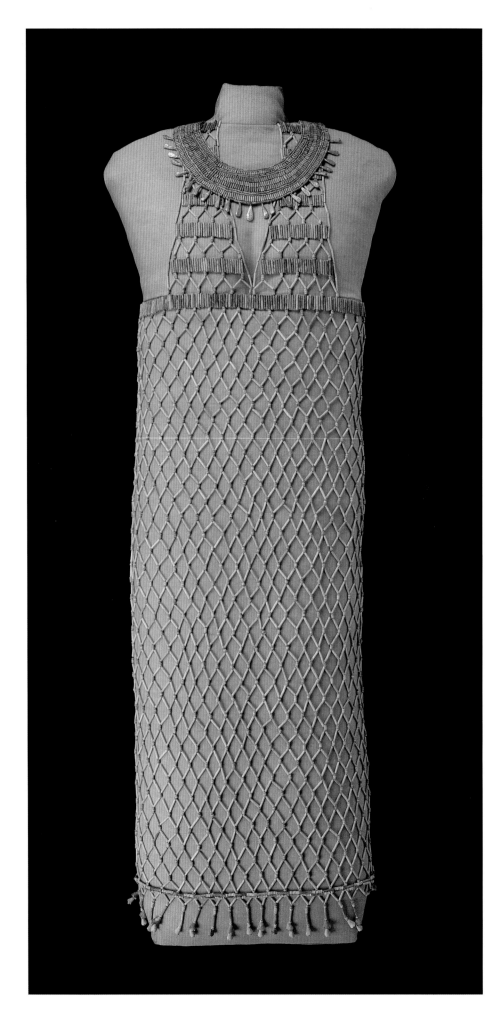

94. DRESS IN BEADED NETTING

Fourth Dynasty
Egyptian faience
L. 113 cm (44½ in.); w. 44 cm (17⅜ in.)
Museum of Fine Arts, Boston, Harvard University–
Museum of Fine Arts Expedition 27.1548

The various elements of this extraordinary dress in beaded netting were found in an intact tomb on the mummy of a female contemporary of the great King Khufu. They were reassembled by restorers from the Museum of Fine Arts, Boston, who relied on the meticulous sketches, surveys, and photographs produced on the site by excavator George Reisner and his team.

The approximately seven thousand cylindrical and ring-shaped faience beads, originally in contrasting shades of pale and dark blue, have lost much of their color. The main part of the dress is a net formed by beads arranged into regular diamond shapes, each point of which is marked by three small ring-shaped beads. The body of the dress is separated from the straps, which covered the breasts, by a row of vertically arranged cylindrical beads, originally dark blue. Wide at the bottom and relatively narrow at the shoulders, the straps consist of three rows of vertical cylindrical beads with half-diamond shapes inserted between them. Unlike the only other extant bead-net dress, now in the collection of the Petrie Museum in London,[1] this one did not possess faience "breastplates," although excavators did discover similar elements fashioned in linen among the bandages underneath the dress. Rows of beads adorned with small faience flowers mark the hemline, which must have fallen just above the ankles. As a funerary garment, the dress would have covered only the front of the body. A famous tale recorded in the Westcar Papyrus relates that King Snefru's oarswomen dressed themselves in such netting,[2] which is also represented in reliefs and statues. It is not clear whether, in everyday life, the bead-net dress was sewn onto or simply pulled over its underlying garment. The present example apparently had no fabric underneath it apart from the bandages.[3]

A broad collar made of several alternating rows of cylindrical and ring-shaped faience beads, colored blue, light green, and beige, is set over the netting. Its teardrop pendants are covered with gold leaf, as are its terminals.

A relatively large number of bead-net shrouds, used to wrap mummies from the Twenty-first Dynasty on, have been preserved, but only two bead-net dresses of this type have come down to us. Nevertheless, there is no doubt that many female mummies of the Old Kingdom were provided with them. PR

1. Petrie Museum, London, UC 17743, from tomb 978 in Qaw el-Kebir, dating to the Fifth Dynasty.
2. Lefebvre 1982, pp. 77ff.
3. In certain cases, it seems that excavators have found remnants of clothing onto which beads had been sewed. See, for example, Brunton 1948, tomb 839, p. 33.

PROVENANCE: Giza, tomb G 7440Z, Reisner excavation, 1927

BIBLIOGRAPHY: Jick in D'Auria, Lacovara, and Roehrig 1988, pp. 78–79, no. 9; Jick 1996, pp. 73–74

95. NECKLACE WITH FROG AMULET

Fourth Dynasty
Egyptian faience, serpentine, steatite, feldspar, limestone, Egyptian blue, and shell
L. 24.5 cm (9¾ in.)
Trustees of the British Museum, London EA 62563

Found in a woman's tomb, this necklace is composed of about sixty beads of various shapes and materials, arranged in a fairly regular pattern. The cylindrical beads, primarily in green and blue faience, are the most numerous and alternate with small ring- and disk-shaped beads, three of which are made of green feldspar and reddish limestone. A few are composed of greenish gray serpentine and steatite. Three beads are of a substance called Egyptian blue, whose basic constituents are identical to those of faience (quartz or sand, copper oxides, and alkaline elements). This material, of a consistent, deep blue hue similar to that of lapis lazuli, could be molded to fabricate beads and amulets.

A small Conus shell is integrated into the necklace, and two serpentine beads are sculpted to imitate Nerita shells. Almost from the time that shells were first used to make jewelry, in the Predynastic Period, their forms were copied in various materials. Thus, although natural shells (most often Nassarius, Conus, Nerita, and cowrie) were still found in necklaces, bracelets, and anklets throughout the Old Kingdom, equivalents made of agate, carnelian, feldspar, and sometimes even gold also occur frequently. Finally, this necklace contains a small serpentine amulet in the shape of a frog, symbol of fertility and regeneration, which was no doubt intended to strengthen the deceased woman's guarantee of life after death. Common in the Old Kingdom, frog-shaped amulets are found in Egypt up to the Roman Period. PR

PROVENANCE: Mostagedda, tomb 2625, British Museum expedition, 1928–29

BIBLIOGRAPHY: Brunton 1937, pl. 45; Andrews 1981, p. 41, no. 207, pl. 20

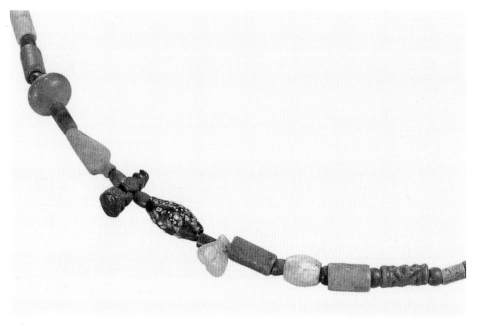

96

NECKLACES FROM TOMB 312 AT MOSTAGEDDA

Tomb 312 at Mostagedda was the small, modest burial place of a woman. Around her neck were many beads of various materials and three amulets: a falcon, a crude human figure, and the figure of an indeterminate subject. These various elements have been reassembled and displayed as two separate necklaces (cat. nos. 96, 97).

96. NECKLACE WITH AMULETS

Fourth Dynasty
Egyptian faience, carnelian, Egyptian alabaster, quartz, feldspar, glazed steatite, and crumb beads
L. 32.5 cm (12¾ in.)
Trustees of the British Museum, London EA 62443

The first necklace from tomb 312 comprises almost all the nongold beads and amulets found in this burial. Most numerous are large, cylindrical beads (one of which is twisted) made of carnelian and blue faience. Among the others are small cylindrical or barrel-shaped beads of carnelian, feldspar, and blue or green faience; a large, round bead in light brown faience; two crumb beads of dark blue faience adorned with lighter faience crumbs (some lost from one bead); a jar-shaped faience bead; and three Nassarius shells. Crumb beads, which appear in many pieces from the Old Kingdom, were fabricated using a highly original technique. Small, baked crumbs of faience were incorporated on the surface of a faience bead of a different color, producing a very decorative effect.

The two amulets of this piece are of lesser quality than the gold falcon found on the other necklace from tomb 312 (cat. no. 97). One, composed of blue faience, represents a squatting man[1]—men are represented in the Old Kingdom in many guises, but depictions of women and children are less common. The subject of the second amulet, made of Egyptian alabaster (calcite), is difficult to identify but may be a piece of fruit.[2]   P R

1. Brunton 1937, Amulet Corpus, pl. 1 D5.
2. Ibid., pl. 11 H3, which suggests testicles as the subject.

PROVENANCE: Mostagedda, tomb 312, British Museum expedition, 1928–29

BIBLIOGRAPHY: Brunton 1937, p. 94, pl. 1, 5, Tomb Register, pl. 45, Bead Register, pl. 49, Bead Corpus, pls. 56.1.D5, 11 H3, 58, 76 D 16, 89 A6; Andrews 1981, p. 44, no. 234, pl. 20

97. NECKLACE WITH FALCON AMULET

Fourth Dynasty
Gold and turquoise
L. 17.4 cm (6⅞ in.)
Trustees of the British Museum, London
EA 62444

The second necklace from tomb 312 is composed primarily of the gold elements found there: cylindrical, ring-, and barrel-shaped beads of this material, plus a few turquoise beads. A magnificent gold amulet in the shape of a falcon constitutes its central element. The bird is made of three different parts—molded body, gold-leaf feet, and flat base—which have been soldered together, and the details of its plumage are rendered with small incised strokes. The refinement of this amulet contrasts with the cruder technique of the large beads, which were made by simply rolling up pieces of gold leaf and letting the edges overlap.

The earliest falcon-shaped amulets, from the Predynastic Period, depict the bird with folded legs, while those representing standing falcons made their appearance a little later, during the Old Kingdom. These objects are often made of faience, semiprecious stones such as feldspar, or metal; however, one Fifth Dynasty tomb at Naga el-Deir, near Abydos in Upper Egypt, contained five made of copper, and other examples in gold have been discovered, especially at Qaw el-Kebir, in the northern part of Upper Egypt.[1] This amulet, of exceptionally high quality, somehow managed to escape plunderers and is one of the finest examples known.   P R

1. Qaw el-Kebir, tomb 4914; see Brunton 1928, pls. 45 F3, 97.

PROVENANCE: Mostagedda, tomb 312, British Museum expedition, 1928–29

BIBLIOGRAPHY: Brunton 1937, p. 94, Tomb Register, pl. 45, Bead Register, pl. 49, Bead Corpus, pls. 45 B4, 57; Andrews 1981, p. 45, no. 243, pl. 20; Andrews 1990, pp. 86, 87

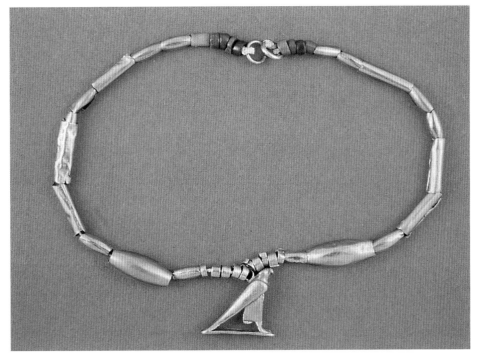

97

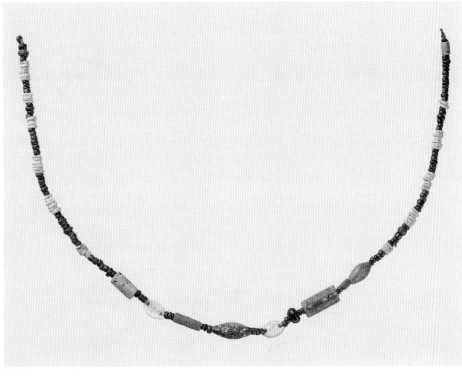

98

98. NECKLACE

Fourth Dynasty
Egyptian faience, bone or shell, glazed steatite,
and carnelian
L. 37 cm (14⅝ in.)
The Syndics of the Fitzwilliam Museum,
Cambridge E 25-1923

At the center of this necklace are three long,
cylindrical blue faience beads, a round carnelian bead, two beads of bone or shell that
imitate cowries, and two biconical green
faience beads—all separated from one
another by groups of small, ring-shaped
faience beads. On either side of this central
area, small groups of ring-shaped beads,
made of shell and dark blue faience, alternate in a regular pattern.

The necklaces found at excavations are
of two types: long strings of beads in identical materials and shapes[1] or, as here,
assemblages of various elements in which
beads of different sizes, materials, and
shapes seem to be randomly combined.
Despite the absence of any precise order in
the latter type, it seems that certain arrangements were favored. For example, excavators who examined partly preserved strings
at Naga el-Deir noted a pattern of prefer-
ences: some necklaces featured alternating
groups of different-colored beads, others
contained large beads of different materials, while still others had amulets and large
beads separated by small groups of beads.

PR

1. See, for example, the necklaces found in tombs
N 591 (Third to Fourth Dynasty), N 607 (Fifth
Dynasty), and N 734 (Sixth Dynasty) at Naga
el-Deir, in Reisner 1932, pls. 40, 44.

PROVENANCE: Qaw el-Kebir, tomb 628; gift
of the British School of Archaeology to the
Fitzwilliam Museum

BIBLIOGRAPHY: Brunton 1928, vol. 2, Tomb
Register, pl. 50

99. Bowl with Turned-in Sections of Rim

Fourth Dynasty or earlier
Gneiss
Diam. 20 cm (7⅞ in.)
Phoebe Apperson Hearst Museum of Anthropology,
University of California at Berkeley 6-19784

The seemingly incongruous shape of this intriguing gneiss[1] bowl would appear to the modern-day viewer to be more in keeping with a ceramic vessel than one of stone. However, in ancient Egypt bowls of this type were made of stone as early as the First Dynasty.[2] Indeed, the idea of producing an inward-turned rim on a stone object may have originated with the Archaic Period's predilection for the representation in stone of objects usually made from flexible materials.[3] Terracotta vessels with decorative turned-in rim sections were rare[4] before the very end of the Old Kingdom and the following era, the so-called First Intermediate Period, when they became rather common.[5] The longevity of the almost unchanging stone type and the lack of terracotta parallels for comparison during most of the Old Kingdom make it extremely difficult to precisely date an individual piece such as the present bowl. George Reisner dated the mastaba, G 1024, in which this bowl was found to the Fourth Dynasty,[6] and a similar date for the vessel is supported by the object's strong links to Archaic Period stone vessels. However, it is possible that the piece was not contemporary with the tomb but was an heirloom of earlier date inherited by the people buried there. The piece cannot date to the Sixth Dynasty because examples of stone bowls of the same type made during this period and found in the pyramid of

Queen Neith, daughter of King Pepi I and wife of King Pepi II,[7] show more angular edges along the folded-in parts.

This bowl's superb workmanship speaks for its manufacture in a royal shop by a first-class craftsman. The walls are astonishingly thin, and the folds in the rim are shaped so naturally that any viewer who did not know the vessel was stone would surely think its material was flexible.

The function of the rim with turned-in sections was largely decorative, although its origins may lie in the custom of producing a spout in vessels of pliable clay by pushing the rim in at two closely spaced points.[8] If this treatment is repeated at even intervals around the rim of a vessel, and the indentation made is transformed into a fold, the decorative wavy rim of the present bowl results. Paintings and reliefs often show vessels with such wavy rims among the paraphernalia of a prepared meal. Covered by lids and no doubt holding choice dishes, the containers are displayed on tables or stands, their contents ready to be consumed. Some bowls of the type are depicted holding flower arrangements at table.[9] The stone version accompanying a burial would have perpetuated, through the magic of its material, the availability of a lavish meal throughout eternity.   DoA

1. For this material, see Aston 1994, pp. 62–64.

2. Ibid., pp. 115–16, no. 61.
3. See "Stone Vessels" by Dorothea Arnold and Elena Pischikova in this catalogue, p. 121.
4. An example can be found in the Fourth Dynasty tomb of Hetep-heres; Reisner and Smith 1955, fig. 61.
5. Brunton 1928, pl. 82, nos. 70, 8z; Petrie and Brunton 1924, pl. 30, nos. 38a,b. They are even more common on jars. For examples, see Brunton 1928, pl. 88, nos. 91C, 91F, 91G, 91W, 91Y, 92F, 93K, pls. 91, 92.
6. See Reisner's unpublished manuscript, n.d., Giza Necropolis 3, chap. 7, pp. 4–5. In this manuscript Reisner never directly gives a precise date for G 1024, but he clearly implies its placement in the Fourth Dynasty. He first describes nucleus cemetery G 1200, which lies to the west of nucleus cemetery G 2000 in the Western Cemetery of Giza (see map "Western Cemetery" in Reisner 1942). Nucleus G 1200 he places in the reign of Khufu. Here he also notes that G 1024 belongs to a group of tombs "not obviously of types of Dynasty V" that were added to nucleus G 1200 at an "early date." I thank Rita E. Freed and Peter Der Manuelian for generously making this manuscript available to me.
7. Jéquier 1933, pp. 30–31, figs. 11, 13; Jéquier 1934, pp. 105–13, ills.
8. Petrie 1892, pl. 30, nos. 1, 3; Brunton 1928, pl. 76, nos. 7M, 7N, 13S; on jars: ibid., pl. 88, nos. 90C, 90E.
9. Balcz 1932, pp. 106–8, figs. 21, 22.

PROVENANCE: Giza, Western Cemetery, mastaba G 1024, Reisner excavation for University of California, Hearst Expedition, 1903–4

BIBLIOGRAPHY: Reisner and Smith 1955, p. 101, pl. 45a,b, fig. 147; Elsasser and Fredrickson 1966, p. 32, ill.

FIFTH DYNASTY

100. HEAD OF KING USERKAF

Fifth Dynasty, reign of Userkaf
Red granite
H. 75 cm (29⅝ in.)
Egyptian Museum, Cairo JE 52501

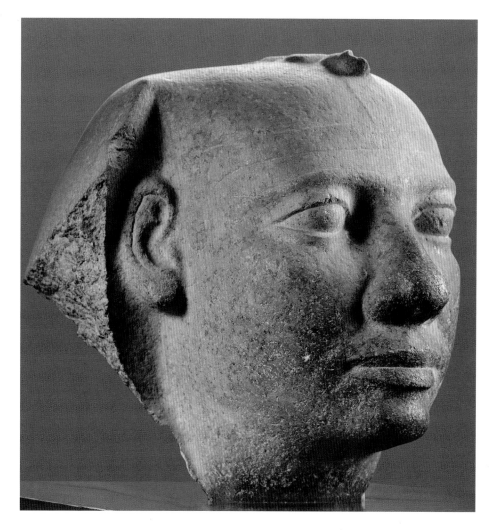

This imposing head of Userkaf, first king of the Fifth Dynasty, was discovered by Cecil Firth in 1928 in the sovereign's funerary complex. Userkaf chose to be buried at Saqqara, not far from the Step Pyramid of the illustrious Djoser. King Shepseskaf of the previous dynasty had already abandoned the plateau of Giza for South Saqqara, where he built a strange tomb in the form of a monumental mastaba, Mastabat Faraoun. This head was found in the court of Userkaf's pyramid temple, which, contrary to the usual practice, was attached to the south and not the east face of the pyramid. Many fragments of small statues of Userkaf in diorite and granite, bearing the king's cartouche and Horus name, come from the same site. They are the only remnants of an elaborate program of statuary that decorated this temple, which is today in ruins.

This is the head of one of the few colossal statues from the Old Kingdom. It is the largest, the most beautiful, and the oldest of Fifth Dynasty royal statues. All the others are small, including the extraordinary series recently discovered at Abusir in the funerary complex of King Neferefre. The face of the king, set off by the *nemes* headcloth, is striking in its simplicity and stylization: these qualities can be explained by the dimensions of the work, which is monumental and sculpted to be seen from a distance. If we assume the king was seated, like the figures of Khafre from Giza, the total height of the statue exceeded four meters (thirteen feet) and thus prefigures works from later periods in Egyptian history, in particular, New Kingdom colossi. It has been suggested that the fragment was part of a sphinx, but the back of the statue's neck, which would identify it as a sphinx, is poorly preserved, and the arguments advanced are therefore not very convincing.[1] Its dimensions are unique for Old Kingdom statuary, but our knowledge is dependent on random excavations and the state of preservation. Apart from the "caryatids" in Djoser's funerary

complex at Saqqara,[2] only a few statues at royal complexes were much larger than lifesize. These include a representation of Djoser, of which the pedestal and a few fragments have survived;[3] the engaged statues of Snefru in Dahshur;[4] and an alabaster colossus depicting Menkaure.[5]

Despite a dearth of precedents, the sculptor of Userkaf's head was able to render an expressive face, treated with sensitivity, in granite, a very hard stone. The eyes and eyebrows jut out, the nose is strong, the ears protrude, the chin and jaw are broad: all these elements contribute to a severe expression. There is no detail on the *nemes* headcloth; the uraeus barely stands out from the king's forehead. This representation of the sovereign perpetuates the refined style established by statues of Menkaure, with which it shares certain characteristics.

SL-T,CZ

1. Kozloff 1982, pp. 211–23.
2. Adam and Ziegler 1999, p. 58.
3. Egyptian Museum, Cairo, JE 49889, pedestal; see ibid., p. 24.
4. Stadelmann 1995b, pp. 164–65, pl. 60.
5. Museum of Fine Arts, Boston, 09.204, h. 235 cm (92½ in.); see Vandier 1958, pp. 21–22, 25–26, pl. 4.4; Adam and Ziegler 1999, p. 159.

PROVENANCE: Saqqara, pyramid temple of Userkaf, southwest corner of court, Firth excavation for Egyptian Antiquities Service, 1928–29

BIBLIOGRAPHY: Firth 1929, p. 65, pl. 1; Smith 1946, p. 46, pl. 17a; Lange and Hirmer 1957, pls. 50, 51; Vandier 1958, pp. 14, 29–30, pl. 7.6; Edwards 1961, pl. 22; Michalowski 1968, fig. 214; Donadoni 1969, ill. on p. 37; Porter and Moss 1978, pp. 397–98; Kozloff 1982, pp. 211–23; Saleh and Sourouzian 1987, no. 35 (for comparison); Lauer 1988, pp. 82, 83; Aldred 1992, p. 118; Lehner 1997, p. 140; Adam and Ziegler 1999, p. 71

101. FRAGMENTARY HEAD OF A KING

Mid-Fifth Dynasty, perhaps reign of Neferefre
Hard yellow limestone with remains of paint
H. 8 cm (3⅛ in.); w., face, 5.8 cm (2¼ in.)
Petrie Museum of Egyptian Archaeology, University
College London UC 14282

This small royal head is about one-third lifesize. It was uncovered beneath the pavement of a Twelfth Dynasty temple during excavations conducted by W. M. F. Petrie at Coptos. Part of a small throne cut from the same hard yellow limestone was discovered in the vicinity of the head, and it is probable that both fragments were part of a seated statue of an unknown king.[1]

The king has a tightly fitting wig, or skullcap, worn very low across his forehead and incised with concentric rings that may indicate hair. A damaged uraeus is visible at the center of his brow. His chin is missing, but the end of a chin strap in black paint is visible in front of the right ear, indicating that he wore a false beard. The ears are naturally placed in relation to the features, and the right ear is well preserved. The left ear has been described as unfinished, but in fact it appears to have been chipped away almost entirely, and below it something else has also been consciously chipped away at an angle behind the jawbone.

The surface of the face, especially the right side around the eye and across the cheek, has been badly abraded, obscuring much of the detail. The surface of the left side is in better condition, although a large piece of the cheek is missing. Details around the left eye suggest the beginning of a cosmetic line. The eyes themselves are large and wide open. The eyeballs have been modeled and the eye sockets are deeply hollowed out along the edge of the nose, creating dark shadows below the brows. The brows have been indicated in low relief. The nose is well formed, but the nostrils have been indented only slightly.

The head has been dated to the Fourth Dynasty based on comparisons with statues of kings Khafre and Menkaure;[2] however, the face is not as full or as broad as that of Khafre in the gneiss statue of him in the Egyptian Museum, Cairo (fig. 28), and the browridge and nose are not as pronounced as they are in representations of Menkaure.[3] This head in the Petrie Museum, London, does have features in common with the

small head of an unknown king in the Musées Royaux d'Art et d'Histoire, Brussels (E 7117).[4] Although the eyes of the London head are much larger, the faces are similarly shaped, and both subjects wear the same short wig or skullcap incised with concentric circles and resting low on the forehead.

Both the London and the Brussels heads have been dated to the Fourth Dynasty, but closer parallels for both works can be found

102. Two Birds

Fifth Dynasty, reign of Userkaf
Painted limestone
H. 14.5 cm (5¾ in.)
Egyptian Museum, Cairo TEMP 6-9-32-1

This little fragment from Userkaf's ruined mortuary complex was part of a large scene depicting life in a marsh along the Nile. It is not unusual to find hunting and fishing scenes or simple depictions of nature in the reliefs within Fifth Dynasty royal temples. Such reliefs reflect a long tradition, attested by a few fragments from the temple of the Bent Pyramid, built by Snefru in Dahshur (cat. no. 22). The traces of green paint on the papyrus stalks behind these birds are a reminder that all such scenes were painted in bright colors. The finely sculpted relief in soft limestone shows the technical skill and gifts of observation possessed by early Fifth Dynasty artists. In particular, note how the plumage on the birds' wings and heads gives a lifelike appearance to the charming scene as it unfolds before our eyes.   SL-T,CZ

PROVENANCE: Saqqara, precinct of Userkaf

BIBLIOGRAPHY: Firth 1929, p. 66; Wreszinski 1936, pl. 105 [B]; *5000 ans* 1960, p. 22, fig. 11; Gilbert 1960, pp. 153–55, fig. 38; Lauer 1976, pl. 119; Porter and Moss 1978, p. 398; Smith 1981, p. 127; Saleh and Sourouzian 1987, no. 36 (for comparison with another marsh scene from the same temple, in the Egyptian Museum, Cairo, JE 56001)

in the Fifth Dynasty, especially among the royal statuary uncovered in the 1980s at Abusir.[5] Of special interest are two fragmentary limestone statuettes of Neferefre in which the king is depicted wearing a wig dressed in concentric rows of textured locks.[6] The comparison is particularly interesting for the present head because the Neferefre statuettes are both protected by the Horus falcon. On the better preserved of the two, the bird hugs the back of the king's wig. Its beak is well below the crown of the king's head, and its wing tips end just behind the back edge of his jawbones. Considering the broken areas on the Petrie Museum head, it is at least possible that a similar falcon protected this king.

Two other statues in the Neferefre group also provide interesting comparisons for this head: one a statue of the standing king wearing the white crown, the other a seated statue in which he wears the *nemes* head-cloth.[7] In both, the headdresses are worn low on the forehead and the ears roughly resemble in size and shape those of the Petrie Museum head; moreover, the eyes of the seated king are large and wide open like those of this king. Although it might be unwise to identify the London head as Neferefre, on the basis of similarities with the Abusir group, it seems safe to date it to the middle of the Fifth Dynasty, when Neferefre ruled. It seems likely that the Brussels head belongs to this period as well.

CHR

1. Petrie 1896, p. 11; Murray 1930, pp. 8, 10; Page 1976, p. 4.
2. Murray 1930, pp. 8–10; Page 1976, pp. 4–5.
3. Compare profile views of the present head and the head of Menkaure in the Museum of Fine Arts, Boston (cat. no. 70). For a profile view of the present head, see Petrie 1896, pl. 5 [9]; and Murray 1930, fig. 4.
4. As is pointed out in Page 1976, p. 5. The Brussels head is published in Capart 1927, pp. 7–8, pl. 5.
5. Verner 1985a, pp. 267–80, pls. 44–59; Verner 1994a, pp. 143–50.
6. Verner 1985a, pls. 44–47.
7. Ibid., pls. 49–53.

PROVENANCE: Coptos, Petrie excavation, December 3, 1893–February 26, 1894

BIBLIOGRAPHY: Petrie 1896, pl. 5 [9]; Murray 1930, pp. 8–10, figs. 1, 4; Page 1976, pp. 4–5

103. CAST OF A BLOCK WITH RUNNING TROOPS AND AN INSCRIPTION WITH THE NAMES AND TITLES OF KING USERKAF

Cast of original Fifth Dynasty, reign of Userkaf, painted limestone block taken by Ronald Street, Molding Studio, The Metropolitan Museum of Art, New York, 1998
Plaster
H. 91 cm (35⅞ in.); w. 146 cm (57½ in.)
The Metropolitan Museum of Art, New York
N.A. 1999.2

Four Old Kingdom pharaohs are named on stone blocks that were found early in this century and reused in the Middle Kingdom pyramid of Amenemhat I at Lisht: Khufu, Khafre, Unis, and Pepi II.[1] During the 1991 excavation season at Lisht, the Egyptian Expedition of The Metropolitan Museum of Art discovered a large block with names of Userkaf, first king of the Fifth Dynasty; it is a cast of this object that is exhibited here. Middle Kingdom builders had removed the block from a temple erected by Userkaf at Saqqara and used it to fill a deep trench dug while they were constructing the burial chambers below Amenemhat's pyramid. The block was placed upside down on the west side of the trench (fig. 123). The carved figures had been systematically defaced in order to deprive them of their magical efficacy, and the block employed simply as building material.[2]

The relief work is generally of good quality, but the incomplete state of a few of the hieroglyphs indicates that the decoration was left unfinished. Particularly noticeable is the imperfect palace facade below the king's Horus name, where details were added only at the far right.

The carving on the preserved part of the block is oriented in two directions, marking a transition between scenes. The right third is filled with the ends of three registers of running troops who face toward the right, while the left two-thirds are covered with inscriptions, which for the most part read from left to right. Running soldiers often accompany ships, and the inscription at the far left mentions a ship, revealing that the presumably related scenes had nautical subject matter.

The troops are clad either in aprons with three lengths of cloth hanging down in front, or kilts. Simple staves are carried by six of the soldiers, and four or five hold long bundles with bows protruding from their tops. One man in the central register supports a bundle of sticks with his right hand, while two figures in the bottom row carry weapons wrapped in tied sacks.[3] Two men appear to be empty-handed. The lowest register has fewer troops than the upper two, and there is a relatively large empty space behind the last figure, perhaps indicating that the complete scene contained a numerically faithful representation of different units of troops, rather than a tightly knit arrangement of human figures dictated by aesthetic concerns alone.

Dominating the center of the block is a large vertical rectangle enclosing the names, titles, and epithets of Userkaf and three deities who protect him. At the top is an image of the flying Horus falcon, with an identifying line of text above. In reliefs such as this, flying falcons generally hover near the top of a wall and above a depiction of the king, who was believed to receive protection from Horus's outstretched wings. At the bottom left and right sides of the rectangle, respectively, are images of the cobra goddess Wadjet and the vulture goddess Nekhbet; their names and epithets are inscribed above them. In the center of the rectangle are two of Userkaf's five names, as well as epithets relating to the king. Beneath the panel is a horizontal line of text that states, "She is giving life, stability, dominion, all joy and health forever." The recipient of this commonly used blessing is the king himself, and the bestower is probably Wadjet, who is shown directly above the beginning of the text.

At the far left of the block are two partial columns of inscription that include the names of two feline goddesses. The left column preserves part of the name of a goddess who is probably Bastet,[4] followed by the name of the goddess Shesmetet.[5] The right column identifies the now-lost scene that filled the wall below and/or to the left as "Returning from (?) the temple of Bastet in the ship (called) 'He Who Controls the Subjects.'"[6] The owner of the ship is the king himself, who was presumably depicted on board the vessel and below the flying Horus falcon.

This relief presents a juxtaposition of figures and an unusual text that provides tantalizing clues to the missing decoration of the entire wall.   AO

1. Goedicke 1971, pp. 8–28.
2. Although Goedicke (ibid., pp. 5–7) argued that Amenemhat I reused decorated Old Kingdom blocks in the structures of his pyramid complex because of their magical properties, several observations suggest otherwise. Many of the animal and human figures carved on the blocks, including the running troops, appear to have been deliberately mutilated, suggesting that a conscious attempt was made to deprive them of their spiritual power. Decorated blocks were randomly laid in the pyramid structure, and some were even placed upside down. Finally, it is difficult to accept Goedicke's suggestion that Amenemhat I intended to honor his predecessors by reusing elements of their constructions in his own buildings—for Amenemhat's builders were in reality contributing to the decay and destruction of Old Kingdom monuments.
3. For a similar sack, see Fischer 1979, p. 8, fig. 3.
4. The two deities are related; see Schmitz 1984, cols. 587–90.
5. The name of this goddess was found among the fragments excavated in the Userkaf pyramid temple. An unpublished drawing of the fragment by William Stevenson Smith is in the archives of the Museum of Fine Arts, Boston. I wish to express my appreciation to Rita E. Freed and Peter Der Manuelian for allowing me access to this material. The goddess also appears in the pyramid temple of King Niuserre at Abusir (Borchardt 1907, p. 94).
6. I would like to thank James P. Allen for his advice about the inscription. The closest parallel to the name of the ship comes from the mastaba of Mer-ib (G 2100-I-annex) at Giza, where the tomb owner is referred to as the god's treasurer on the "ship of the Lord of the Subjects." See Jones 1988, p. 106, no. 243, p. 235, no. 23, with earlier bibliography; and Porter and Moss 1974, pp. 71–72. For the identification of the "Lord of the Subjects" with the king, see Kaplony 1980, col. 418.

PROVENANCE: Original, Lisht North, pyramid of Amenemhat I, Metropolitan Museum of Art excavation, 1991

BIBLIOGRAPHY: D. Arnold in Leclant and Clerc 1993, p. 212, fig. 24

Opposite, top: 121. Block with Running Troops and Inscription of King Userkaf (cat. no. 103). Drawing by Jo Ann Wood after Lara Bernini

Opposite, bottom: 122. Block with Running Troops (cat. no. 104). Drawing by Thomas Scalise

104. RUNNING TROOPS

Fifth Dynasty, reign of Userkaf
Limestone with faint remains of paint
H. 85 cm (33½ in.); w. 127 cm (50 in.)
The Metropolitan Museum of Art, New York,
Rogers Fund, 1915 15.3.1163

The 1991 discovery at Lisht of a reused block decorated with running soldiers and inscribed with names of King Userkaf (fig. 123; cat. no. 103) has allowed the assignment of this relief with running troops to the same king's reign. Both works are executed in delicate low relief. The compositions are extremely similar, and the size and spacing of the figures are nearly identical. This reused piece was found in 1914 by the Metropolitan Museum's Egyptian Expedition in the same general area as the block inscribed with Userkaf's name.[1]

At first glance the scene seems to consist of two somewhat monotonous registers of closely spaced, repetitively posed soldiers who run to the viewer's left. However, closer inspection reveals that the composition is actually quite varied, complex, and full of closely observed detail. Although the soldiers' limbs are similarly positioned, subtle variations in the poses are found throughout the work. Particularly intriguing is the intricate overlapping of the figures, which does not follow a discernible pattern and in places defies logical spatial arrangement.[2] Although the fine workmanship has been somewhat obscured by erosion and ancient vandalism, subtle modeling is still evident on the legs and abdomens of many of the figures, and traces remain of rimmed upper eyelids and eyebrows raised slightly above the surface of the faces.

The troops are organized in two groups of ten, behind each of which a kilted figure runs. A short inscription precedes and follows each group and serves to identify the units or their individual commanders.[3] The men wear either aprons or kilts and grasp the same kinds of weapons and implements as the soldiers on the block inscribed in the name of Userkaf—with the exception of the sixth man from the right in the

upper register, who carries the tools of a scribe, and the fifth man from the right on the lower register, who holds a stick with a semicircular disk.

The upper edge of the present block retains bits of the vertically oriented, zigzagging lines traditionally used to represent water, indicating that the running troops belonged to a nautical scene. Beneath the lower register is a horizontal band with five-pointed stars, which symbolize the sky and mark the transition to the scene below. For unknown reasons, the left side of the band and, immediately above it, the ground line under the soldiers' feet were left unfinished, as were elements of the inscription on the block with Userkaf's name.

The left side of the relief slopes inward from top to bottom, indicating that it was placed at the left end of a wall in an inside corner and that it adjoined a wall with a distinct batter. In Egyptian architecture batters are customarily found on exterior walls, and they are used as well on interior walls that mark the connection between adjoining buildings. In pyramid complexes battered interior walls occur where the valley temple joins the causeway and where the causeway joins the pyramid temple. Thus, the sloping side of this block must belong to one of the few areas of architectural transition in the Userkaf pyramid complex.[4]

A block with a sloping left edge that depicts running troops accompanying a ship was found at Abusir by Ludwig Borchardt in the valley temple of Sahure, Userkaf's immediate successor. Borchardt's reconstruction places the block on the north wall of the innermost room of the valley temple, an area that marks the transition into the causeway.[5] Unfortunately, nothing is yet known about the valley temple of Userkaf. The upper temples of the complex have been

excavated, but final reports on the architecture and the relief decoration have not been published.[6] Relief fragments that belong to a scene depicting rowers and running soldiers were found in the southeast part of Userkaf's main temple,[7] so it is possible that this block came from a transitional area at the temple entrance.

The numerous parallels between this block and the one with Userkaf's name make it likely that the two belonged to the same wall; the Userkaf relief would have been higher up and to the right of the present corner block. In the latter block, the troops ran in registers beneath the king's ship, while the soldiers on the Userkaf relief ran in the opposite direction and belonged to a different scene. Since the inscription on the Userkaf relief indicates that the ship is returning from the temple of Bastet, which was located in the Delta and to the north of Userkaf's pyramid complex in Saqqara, the scene was probably placed on the north wall of whichever temple it once graced.

AO

1. During the New Kingdom, blocks removed from the same wall of an older building were sometimes placed close together in a new structure; see Romano 1979, pp. 106–7.
2. For a discussion of overlapping figures in Egyptian art, see Schäfer 1986, pp. 177–89. It should be noted that the troops probably ran in short rows of three or four across rather than in single file. For three-dimensional representations of marching soldiers dating from the early Middle Kingdom, see Saleh and Sourouzian 1987, nos. 72, 73.
3. For a detailed discussion of the inscriptions, see Goedicke 1971, pp. 68–74.
4. Similar scenes with ships and running men are found in Old Kingdom nonroyal tombs, where they are often placed at the entrance. Their iconography and location within the tomb are probably copied from prototypes in royal temples; see Harpur 1987, pp. 56–57.

5. See Borchardt 1913, pp. 21–22, fig. 4.
6. Information about the architecture has been collected and summarized in Maragioglio and Rinaldi 1970, pp. 10–43. See also Porter and Moss 1978, pp. 397–98. None of the available sources addresses the question of battered walls. However, it must be noted that intrusive Saite Period tombs damaged much of the Userkaf complex, possibly obliterating any evidence of such features.
7. Lauer 1955, p. 120. For a line drawing of the fragments, see Smith 1981, pp. 128–29, fig. 122.

PROVENANCE: Lisht North, pyramid of Amenemhat I, above entrance of robbers' tunnel, Metropolitan Museum of Art excavation, 1914

BIBLIOGRAPHY: Hayes 1953, pp. 68–69, fig. 45; Goedicke 1971, pp. 68–74

123. Block with Running Troops and Inscription of King Userkaf (cat. no. 103), as currently located in pyramid of Amenemhat I, Lisht

104

105. Ship under Sail

Mid-to-late Fourth or early Fifth Dynasty
Limestone with faint remains of paint
H. 72.8 cm (28⅞ in.); w. 77 cm (30⅜ in.)
The Metropolitan Museum of Art, New York,
Rogers Fund and Edward S. Harkness Gift, 1922
22.1.13

An elaborate arrangement of nautical
equipment dominates this relief depicting a
ship under sail, one of the rare types of Old
Kingdom scene in which human figures are
dwarfed by inanimate objects.[1] Most imposing are the tall, tapering mast with a tightly
wound truss at the bottom and the large,
sweeping sail, the undifferentiated expanse
of which is broken up by an array of ropes.
The two men at the bow are probably pilot-
ing the craft,[2] while the man behind them
adjusts the sail. Slender oars rest along the
side of the ship. At the prow are three bladelike objects, vertical in front and curved in
back, each of which is decorated with a representation of the sacred *wedjat* eye, a protective symbol usually associated with the
falcon deity Horus. The device probably
serves to protect the vessel physically[3] and
spiritually, as well as magically allowing it
to see where it is going.[4] At the right end of
the fragment is part of the last figure aboard
the preceding vessel and a line of indecipherable text. In front of the better-preserved
ship a partially restored column of inscription states, "Sail well like this, hurry."[5]

The scene is most notable for its fine,
detailed execution and complex series of
overlapping forms. Particularly striking is
the tangle of legs, oars, and ropes on the

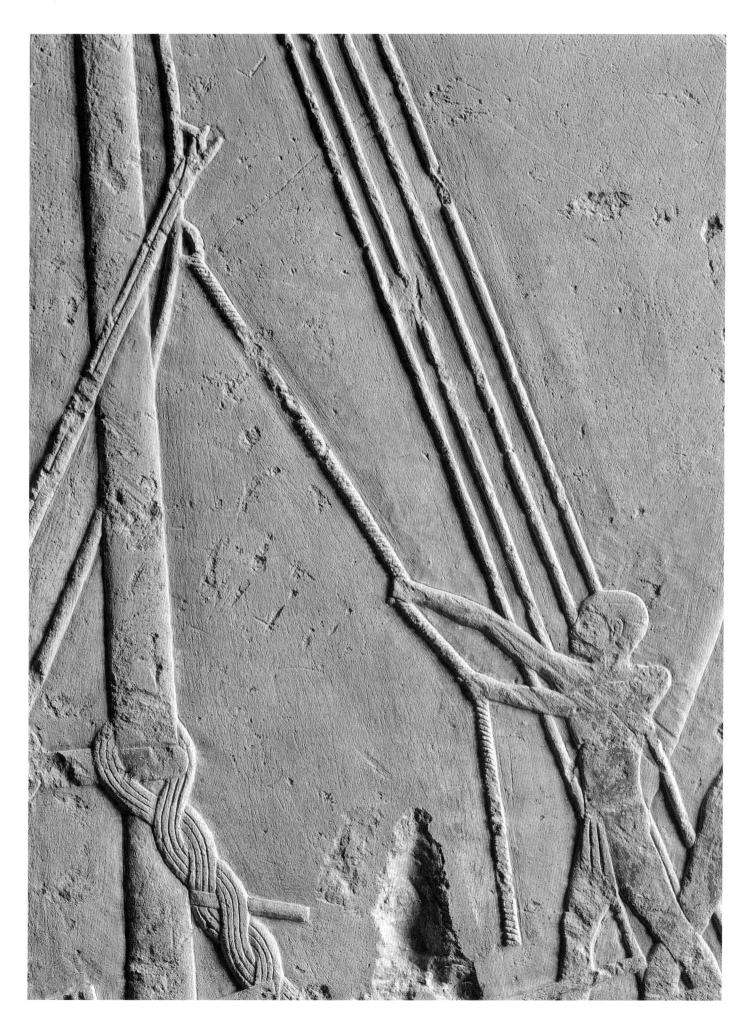

ship's deck. Although relatively small, the figures are carefully rendered and include such features as eyebrows raised above the surface of the faces and delicately rounded cheeks. In places where overlapping occurs, the area around the forward object is carved back completely, creating a sense of depth and demonstrating the artist's control of the stone surface. Such interest in the three-dimensional possibilities of a relatively flat plane is most striking in the small *wedjat* eyes, which appear to float on top of the bladelike objects.

A significant number of the reused blocks found at Lisht depict ships fitted with sails or oars.[6] Because of their similar stylistic features and their scale, a group of the sailing-ships reliefs (including this one and cat. nos. 106, 107) has been recognized as belonging to a single scene.[7] The group was originally dated between the mid-to-late Fourth Dynasty and the early Fifth Dynasty, but in light of the recent discovery at Lisht of a block inscribed in the name of Userkaf (cat. no. 103), it may now be possible to refine this date. That the sailing-ships group is earlier than the nautical scenes found in the pyramid complex of King Sahure at Abusir is confirmed by such stylistic criteria as the subtly handled musculature of the running figure in the relief from the Art Museum, Princeton University (cat. no. 107), and the triple aprons worn by some of the sailors. Figures from the Sahure pyramid-complex reliefs have much more explicitly rendered musculature (cat. nos. 112–114), and nearly all the aprons there have four strips of hanging cloth.[8] Moreover, relief representations after the time of Sahure tend to be flatter, with overlap indicated by means of either incised lines or surfaces carved back only in the area immediately around the contour line of the forward object.[9]

A comparison of the sailing-ships fragments and the reliefs dated to the reign of Userkaf shows that there are strong similarities between the two groups as well as several differences. The same intricate spatial relationships characterize the sailing-ships scene and the reliefs from Userkaf's complex, including those showing running troops (cat. nos. 103, 104) and two birds (cat. no. 102). Especially notable are the animated poses of the sailors, who are captured during an instant of their work. A striking parallel to this liveliness is found in a unique representation of rowers from the Userkaf pyramid temple.[10] Here the poses of the figures are arranged to show every moment in the sequence of an oar stroke; each man is depicted in a position that could only be held for a split second. The method of carving that represents overlapping objects entirely on top of each other is also paralleled on securely dated Userkaf blocks, particularly one famous image of birds in a marsh.[11]

The sailing-ships group is rendered in somewhat bolder relief than the Userkaf running-soldiers blocks, and the long, narrow objects in it have rounder surfaces, suggesting that if the ships scene belongs to the Userkaf pyramid complex, it may not come from the same wall as the running troops.[12] However, it should be noted that other relief fragments from Userkaf's temple, particularly the marsh scene, are also carved in bolder relief than the running troops. Another difference is found in scenes with strips of water. Securely identified Userkaf reliefs omit the narrow ground line that is usually placed directly beneath a zigzagging expanse of water,[13] but this line is included on the block of the sailing-ships group in the Royal Ontario Museum, Toronto (cat. no. 106). Thus, while it seems likely that the sailing scene originated at the pyramid complex of Userkaf, a mid-to-late Fourth Dynasty date cannot be completely ruled out.   AO

1. For a general discussion of scale in two-dimensional Egyptian art, see Schäfer 1986, pp. 230–34.
2. Goedicke 1971, p. 110.
3. Jones (1995, p. 40) states that the bladelike objects provided protection for seagoing vessels. The group of sailing ships under discussion here are probably not seagoing vessels, as they lack hogging trusses, an essential feature of seagoing ships (ibid., pp. 40–42). However, the differences between riverine and seagoing vessels are not marked during the Old Kingdom; see Landström 1970, p. 64.
4. As noted by Goedicke (1971, p. 109), similar symbols are found on ships carved in reliefs found in the pyramid temple of King Sahure at Abusir and the causeway of Unis at Saqqara. The so-called ship of state from a relief in the valley temple of Sahure has a *wedjat* eye applied to the side of its prow; Borchardt 1913, pl. 9.
5. Goedicke 1971, pp. 111–12. For a similar inscription, see Ziegler 1993a, pp. 125, 140.
6. Goedicke 1971, pp. 86–118. The use of sails or oars does not indicate the type of ship being depicted, but rather the direction in which the vessel is traveling. Vessels going up the Nile sailed with the prevailing north wind, while those moving down the Nile were rowed.
7. Ibid., pp. 106–18; only three of these reliefs are included in this catalogue.
8. Borchardt 1913, pls. 9–14, 17, 24, 28–30, 52–53, 55.
9. For a discussion of style in early Fifth Dynasty royal relief, see Smith 1946, pp. 176–85.
10. Smith 1981, pp. 128–29, fig. 122.
11. Smith 1946, pl. 52.
12. For the existence of different relief heights on the same wall during the Fourth Dynasty, see ibid., pp. 161–62, 165. In the Sahure complex nautical scenes are found in both the pyramid temple and the valley temple; see Borchardt 1913, pp. 23–28, pls. 9–14.
13. These include the Metropolitan Museum block with running troops (cat. no. 104), a scene with rowers (Smith 1981, pp. 128–29, fig. 122), and pieces known to this author through unpublished drawings by William Stevenson Smith in the Museum of Fine Arts, Boston.

PROVENANCE: Lisht North, pyramid of Amenemhat I, west side of core, Metropolitan Museum of Art excavation, 1920–22

BIBLIOGRAPHY: Goedicke 1971, pp. 109–12

106. HULL OF A SHIP UNDER SAIL

Mid-to-late Fourth or early Fifth Dynasty
Limestone
Reconstructed h. 42 cm (16½ in.); w. 59 cm
(23¼ in.)
Royal Ontario Museum, Toronto 958.49.3

Among the reused blocks found at Lisht were a number of carved fragments—including these—that belong to a single scene of sailing ships. Two other sections are in this exhibition, one from the Metropolitan Museum (cat. no. 105), the other from the Art Museum, Princeton University (cat. no. 107). Our understanding of the original appearance of the entire scene is enhanced by this fragmentary relief. Here we see the slightly concave prow of one ship, the entire side of the hull, the area behind the mast, and the representation of the water on which the vessel floats. The

legs of two sailors are shown at the prow of the ship, indicating that the activities taking place on this vessel differ from those visible on the fragment in the Metropolitan Museum, where three sailors stand in front of the mast of another ship.

In the present relief four sailors, whose figures are incomplete, remain behind the mast, and the one who stands second from the right seems to be adjusting the sail. This second group of sailors is placed amid a complex tangle of ropes and oars. The gesture of the third figure from the right is uncommon, although not unknown. This man holds his right arm vertically, while grasping what appear to be two short lengths of rope. His left hand bends sharply behind his back and grasps the right arm just above the wrist, in a gesture that is said to signify respect.[1] The same gesture is made by a larger, apron-clad figure in a relief from the pyramid temple of Userkaf,[2] but it is uncertain whether this man was part of a nauti-

cal scene. A scribe in a relief in the tomb of Prince Ka-ni-nisut at Giza,[3] which probably dates to the Fourth Dynasty, assumes what may be the earliest preserved example of this pose.[4] Boatmen in the Fifth Dynasty tombs of Akhet-hotep and Ti also make the gesture.[5]

It seems safe to say that this vessel lacks the *wedjat* eye standards found on the Metropolitan Museum fragment, as the bases of these objects would be visible if they had existed. The end of a braided rope belonging to the rigging of the ship is attached to the deck above the prow. Two rectangular objects can be seen just behind the prow on the side of the vessel; their function remains uncertain.[6]   AO

1. Dominicus 1994, pp. 5–9.
2. Drawing by William Stevenson Smith in the Museum of Fine Arts, Boston. This figure faces to the left.
3. Junker 1934, fig. 18, pl. 6b.

124. Ship under Sail and Running Troops (cat. no. 107). Drawing by Lindsley F. Hall, from Goedicke 1971

4. Junker (ibid., pp. 136–37) ultimately dated the tomb to the early Fifth Dynasty (that is, the time of Userkaf), although he had initially placed it earlier. Harpur (1987, p. 270, no. 265) dates the tomb within the first three reigns of the Fifth Dynasty. However, Cherpion (1989, pp. 118–19) assigns it to the Fourth Dynasty, no later than the reign of Djedefre. The reliefs do have a decidedly archaic appearance. For example, there are almost no overlapping figures and the inscriptions are arranged in the relatively undefined registers that are characteristic of the Fourth Dynasty.

5. Ziegler 1993a, p. 142. See also Steindorff 1913, pls. 78–81. This parallel to Ti had been noted by Goedicke (1971, p. 108, n. 269), who had learned from Smith about the appearance of the same gesture in a relief from the pyramid temple of Userkaf.

6. Landström 1970, pp. 40–42. The rectangular shapes on the ships illustrated by Landström are similar, but not identical, to those on this sailing ship.

PROVENANCE: Lisht North, pyramid of Amenemhat I, core, Metropolitan Museum of Art excavation, 1908–9

BIBLIOGRAPHY: Goedicke 1971, pp. 106–8

107. SHIP UNDER SAIL AND RUNNING TROOPS

Mid-to-late Fourth or early Fifth Dynasty
Limestone
H. 57 cm (22⅝ in.); w. 75 cm (29½ in.)
The Art Museum, Princeton University 1950-128

This fragment of a reused block of stone was found in an unspecified location within the pyramid of Amenemhat I at Lisht. The relief formed part of a scene of sailing ships. Other sections of the scene are today in the Metropolitan Museum (cat. no. 105) and the Royal Ontario Museum, Toronto (cat. no. 106). Here, in what must be an upper section of the composition, we see a huge expanse of billowing sail and a piece of the horizontal top of the mast of one ship. At left, the sail is crossed by an elaborate array of ropes, the individual strands of which are filled with short incised lines, a detail that is omitted on the Metropolitan Museum relief.

To the right of the sail are parts of two vertical lines of inscription; the reading of the column at right is uncertain. The left column states that the ship is "steering to port."[1] Below and to the right, small pieces of the ship sailing ahead of this one and two of its sailors can be seen. The figure to the left may have a short beard, perhaps indicating that he is a foreigner, but the poor condition of this section of the block makes a certain identification impossible. Above the inscription are parts of two soldiers running on a ground line of a subregister.

Examination of the three blocks of the sailing scene included in this exhibition permits us to evaluate the appearance of the whole composition. It must have been dominated by a series of ships with billowing sails, which were manned by a varying number of sailors engaged in a variety of activities. Although the ships all belonged to the same category of riverine vessel, they were not identically rendered. Above the front and back of each ship was a vertical line of text that contained a brief statement concerning the progress of the voyage; an empty vertical band separated the last column of one ship's inscription from the first column of text associated with the following vessel's. Above the inscriptions were subregisters with running or striding figures who presumably carried nautical implements or weapons. Columns of text with figures above them are not found in scenes of rowing ships, which occupy a more compact space than the tall sailing ships.[2] The total number of sailing ships remains uncertain, and the number of registers that contained them and the purpose of their voyage are unknown as well.

The original scene must have been one of striking beauty and visual interest. Although now only a few traces of green remain on the sail of the Metropolitan Museum relief, this and other large expanses were once brightly painted, perhaps with elaborate patterns similar to those on the sail of Sahure's so-called ship of state seen in a relief from his valley temple.[3] Contributing to the sense of movement were the varied poses of the sailors carrying out different tasks aboard ships under full sail. Perhaps most impressive, from the point of view of the ancient Egyptian, was the spectacle of so many elaborately outfitted vessels cruising in a stately procession up the Nile.

A O

1. Goedicke 1971, p. 112.
2. For well-preserved boating scenes of the Fifth Dynasty, see Ziegler 1993a, pp. 66–70, 140–43. See also Steindorff 1913, pls. 74–76 (rowing), 77–81 (sailing).
3. Borchardt 1913, pl. 9.

PROVENANCE: Lisht North, pyramid of Amenemhat I, core, Metropolitan Museum of Art excavation, 1908–9

BIBLIOGRAPHY: Goedicke 1971, pp. 112–13

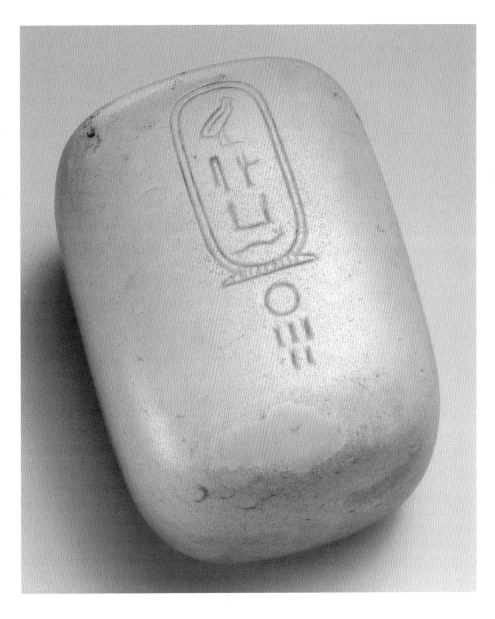

108. WEIGHT

Fifth Dynasty, reign of Userkaf
Opal jasper with traces of deposit in inscription
L. 3.8 cm (1½ in.); w. 2.5 cm (1 in.); d. 2.5 cm (1 in.)
The Metropolitan Museum of Art, New York, Gift of Edward S. Harkness, 1935 35.9.5

This piece of polished stone is inscribed with the name of King Userkaf, founder of the Fifth Dynasty. Beneath his cartouche, the hieroglyphs indicate that the weight is equal to five *deben*. The official weight of the *deben*, a standard measurement for metals, was established in each king's reign and it changed quite dramatically over time, from approximately 13.6 grams (about ½ ounce) during the Old Kingdom to about 91 grams (about 3 ounces) during the New Kingdom.[1] This example is unbroken, and its weight is 68.22 grams—which means that the weight of the *deben* during the reign of Userkaf was 13.64 grams.[2]

CHR

1. Helck 1980, col. 1202.
2. A second weight in the collection of the Metropolitan Museum, 14.2.3, inscribed for a man named Akhet-hotep, probably also dates to the Fifth Dynasty. The inscription gives its weight as eight *deben*. This polished piece of basalt actually weighs 126.5 grams (about four and one-half ounces), yielding a value for the *deben* of 15.8 grams.

PROVENANCE: Unknown

BIBLIOGRAPHY: Bull 1935, p. 142, fig. 1; Hayes 1953, p. 5, fig. 47; Kozloff 1982, p. 219, fig. 17

109. KING SAHURE AND A NOME GOD

Fifth Dynasty, reign of Sahure
Gneiss[1]
H. 64 cm (25¼ in.); w. 46 cm (18⅛ in.);
d. 41.5 cm (16⅛ in.)
The Metropolitan Museum of Art, New York,
Rogers Fund, 1918 18.2.4

Against a high back slab the king sits on a block-form seat, with a smaller divine figure standing to his right. The latter is identified as the god of the Coptite nome located in Southern Egypt, by signs carved above his head. In his left hand, which rests on the edge of the throne, he holds an ankh toward the king; in his right he clasps a *shen* ring.

The king's Horus name and prenomen are inscribed identically on either side of his legs. A large, rectangular area of the base is broken off in front of the god, leaving only traces of his speech, which can, however, be reconstructed as promising the good things of the South to the king.

A recent study suggesting that this statue was reused from a series planned for the valley temple of Khafre cites a perceived contrast between the lightly incised, abbreviated inscription and the fine, careful workmanship given the king's physiognomy; it also notes that the style and particularly the statue type are conceptually at home in the period of Khafre and Menkaure.[2]

Examined at first hand, however, the statue cannot represent Khafre or Menkaure—both because of its more direct spirit and because of stylistic details of the rendering. Compared to the very confidently worked hard-stone statuary of the Fourth Dynasty kings, this statue actually manifests a certain hesitation: for example, while the facial details, particularly of the god, are very fine, other areas, such as the ears and the *shen* ring, are only schematically rendered, and the body forms are minimally differentiated from the connective stone behind them.[3] Moreover, although the kings of the

Detail, cat. no. 109

early Fifth Dynasty are only erratically preserved, they certainly used gneiss;[4] the wide, long beard with a nonacute lateral profile finds parallels in representations of Neferefre;[5] and the heavy lower face and broad, arching upper lip with its shallow central dip bear similarities to the face of the statue of Userkaf from his pyramid temple (cat. no. 100) or to that found in one preserved Sahure fragment—not to Khafre's face and mouth with its distinctive sharp dip in the center of the upper lip, and certainly not to Menkaure's.[6]

It is not impossible that Sahure might have completed a statue that had been only roughed out by a predecessor. He might have intended it for the valley temple of his own pyramid complex at Abusir, where during

the previous dynasty such statues had represented the gathering of the divinities of the country around the king.[7] Or, if speculations concerning the southern origin of the statue are taken seriously, it might have been a gift to a temple in the Coptite nome.[8] In either case, the statue is an imposing image of forceful, direct majesty attended by the gods of the country.   MH

1. For this material, see Aston 1994, pp. 62–64.
2. Seidel 1996, pp. 50–53, 57–58.
3. For Khafre, compare the gneiss statue in the Egyptian Museum, Cairo (fig. 28); for Menkaure, see cat. no. 68; for the *shen* ring of Khafre, see Krauspe 1997b, p. 120, no. 237; for ears similar to those of Sahure and the nome god seen on gneiss fragments of Neferefre, see Verner 1985a, pls. 54, 55.

4. Verner 1985a, pls. 54, 55. For possible use of gneiss in Sixth Dynasty royal sculpture, see Romano 1998, nos. 12, 14.
5. See Verner 1994a, pp. 145–47, 150, where the original length and width of the beards are visible or traceable. Menkaure's similar beards are smaller and more angled.
6. For Sahure, see Borchardt 1913, p. 150, fig. 197. For comparison with Khafre and Menkaure, see cat. nos. 58–63, 67–70.
7. See, for example, D. Arnold 1997, pp. 51–52.
8. Seidel (1996, pp. 50–53) is, of course, right to question such suppositions if they are based simply on place of purchase; however, decontextualizations can occur, and involvement with the southern part of the country was surely greater than present evidence would allow (compare cat. no. 27).

PROVENANCE: Unknown

BIBLIOGRAPHY: Seidel 1996, pp. 50–533

Small model

110. MODELS OF THE PYRAMID COMPLEX OF KING SAHURE AT ABUSIR, FIFTH DYNASTY

Berlin, 1910. Made by Stegemann Brothers; restored by Ann Heywood, The Sherman Fairchild Center for Objects Conservation, and Ronald Street, Molding Studio, The Metropolitan Museum of Art, New York, 1998
Wood, plaster, sand, and cardboard
Large model: h. 62 cm (24½ in.), w. 200 cm (78½ in.), d. 160 cm (63 in.); small model: h. 12 cm (5 in.); w. 110 cm (43 in.), d. 80 cm (31½ in.); scale 1:75
The Metropolitan Museum of Art, New York, Dodge Fund, 1911 11.165

The Deutsche Orient-Gesellschaft under Ludwig Borchardt excavated the pyramid complex of Sahure at Abusir in 1907–8. Built in 1910, the present models (see p. 332) are complete reconstructions of the exterior architecture of the complex, including such details as wall decoration. Two of several identical models made for museums, they are important examples of architectural model building as well as valuable historical artifacts. They were recently restored by Ann Heywood of The Sherman Fairchild Center for Objects Conservation and Ronald Street of the Molding Studio of the Metropolitan Museum (a mechanism to lift the temple's center part has not been reactivated).

The models show the spatial organization of an Old Kingdom pyramid complex, which consists of the smaller valley temple and the larger pyramid temple adjoining the 50-meter-high pyramid. The 235-meter-long causeway (A, D) connecting the structures was omitted because of limited space. The valley temple, rising above a harbor basin connected to the Nile, may be analogous to the landing station of a royal palace, where the barks of visiting deities and dignitaries landed to be received by the deified king. It is not known whether the royal funerary procession also landed here.

The tall front part of the pyramid temple protrudes from the enclosure wall. This section, which may represent the festival halls of the royal palace, contains an entrance hall and a court surrounded by palm columns (E). The actual mortuary cult section of the temple, with a lower roof, is hidden behind the enclosure wall. The main feature of this rear temple is its offering hall (identifiable by its raised roof [G]) with the false door and the altar for the mortuary offerings. As is usual, a small subsidiary pyramid of unknown purpose is located behind a separate wall in the southeast corner of the main enclosure.

The large model shows the inaccessibility so characteristic of Egyptian sacred architecture. The vast undecorated limestone wall surfaces emphasize the sense of exclusion. Even the red granite colonnades in the valley temple are exterior additions that offer no direct access to the interior.

In the model the rear halves of the pyramid and the enclosure wall are cut away to reveal the structure's interior. The pyramid's core masonry is built in six immense steps, covered with roughly dressed blocks. The steps are filled with rough backing stones cased with blocks of smoothed Tura limestone. It is not known whether the pyramid was crowned by a capstone of white limestone or dark hard stone. Below, at court level, is the entrance to the funerary apartments. A gradually descending corridor, lined with heavy limestone blocks, leads to the burial chamber in the pyramid's center. The chamber's roof is constructed of three layers of enormous limestone blocks probably weighing fifty tons each. The access to the chamber was barred by three granite portcullises.   D A

BIBLIOGRAPHY: Borchardt 1910; Borchardt 1911

Large model

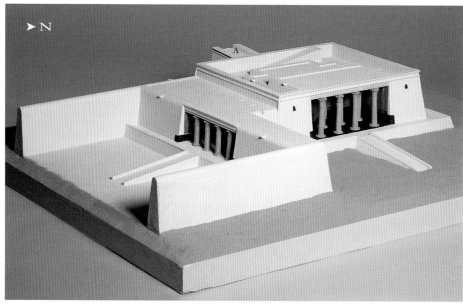

A Beginning of causeway (model, right)

B Subsidiary pyramid

C Side entrance: location of cat. no. 113

D End of causeway

E Location of cat. no. 111

F Location of cat. no. 112

G Roof of offering hall

Small model

111. BOOTY ANIMALS AND A VASE FROM THE NEAR EAST

Fifth Dynasty, reign of Sahure
Painted limestone
H. 38.5 cm (15⅛ in.); w. 35 cm (13¾ in.)
Ägyptisches Museum und Papyrussammlung,
Staatliche Museen zu Berlin 21828

This fragment from the pyramid temple of Sahure is remarkable for both its content and its style. It was once part of an ensemble of reliefs celebrating the military exploits of the king that decorated the walls under the porticoes surrounding the temple's central courtyard. In the section under the southern portico the king was depicted slaying a chief of the Libyans and receiving booty of thousands of cattle, donkeys, sheep, and goats.[1] (The military feats of the Old Kingdom were either raids into neighboring countries carried out to obtain booty or expeditions that had something of the character of trading ventures. Territorial conquest was not the aim of these enterprises; rather it was the acquisition of raw materials, animals, and sometimes people.) Shown under the northern courtyard portico was booty from the Levant. The bears and the jar holding oil represented on the present fragment exemplify the exotic animals and precious goods among the Near Eastern booty.

Here Syrian bears (*Ursus arctos syriacus*) are tethered to looped objects, possibly pierced stones, in the ground. These animals were quite common in Levantine mountain regions in antiquity,[2] and Egyptians liked to keep them in their royal zoos. Large jugs of the type depicted are known to have been imported from Canaan into Egypt beginning in the Archaic Period. Examples were found in the tombs of the kings of the first two dynasties at Abydos,[3] and one was among the grave goods of Queen Hetep-heres I, mother of King Khufu, at Giza.[4] When they arrived in Egypt, such jugs must have been filled with the precious oils valued by upper-class Egyptians.

This fragment epitomizes the structural clarity and sensitive surface qualities that distinguish the reliefs of the Sahure pyramid complex. The figures blend beautifully with the background because most edges bordering the raised relief areas are rounded and the carved elements rise smoothly from their lowest to their highest points. Nevertheless the animals and the vase stand out clearly, as modeling is kept to a minimum. The effect is enhanced by the rather well preserved color: dark reddish brown on the vase and yellowish brown on the bears' fur.

DOA

1. Borchardt 1913, pp. 10–15, 73–78, pl. 1.
2. Boessneck 1988, p. 53.
3. Amiran 1969, pp. 58–66, pl. 17.
4. Reisner and Smith 1955, pp. 64–65, fig. 61, pl. 46d.

PROVENANCE: Abusir, pyramid temple of Sahure, north side of courtyard, Borchardt excavation for Deutsche Orient-Gesellschaft, 1907–8

BIBLIOGRAPHY: Borchardt 1913, pp. 16–17, pl. 3; Priese 1991, no. 24; Grimm, Schoske, and Wildung 1997, no. 23

Above and opposite, details, cat. no. 112

112. The Hunt in the Desert from the Pyramid Temple of King Sahure

Fifth Dynasty, reign of Sahure
Limestone with faint remains of paint
Two adjoining blocks with figure of king: total
h., left side 159 cm (62⅝ in.), right side 123.5 cm
(48⅝ in.); w., top 113 cm (44½ in.), bottom
108.5 cm (42¾ in.); d. 7–14.5 cm (2¾–5¾ in.)
Fragment with animals: H. 130 cm (51⅛ in.);
w., top, from right corner 30 cm (11⅞ in.),
bottom, from left corner 71 cm (28 in.);
d. 14–15 cm (5½–5⅞ in.)
Ägyptisches Museum und Papyrussammlung,
Staatliche Museen zu Berlin 21783

112, fragment with animals

These three blocks from a group housed in Berlin are fragments from one of the great masterpieces of Old Kingdom royal relief art. In the complete relief, which originally must have measured 8 by 3 meters, the Fifth Dynasty king Sahure was depicted hunting desert animals that had been driven into a netted stockade (fig. 54). The trapezoidal fragment shows a wild cow and its calf, and, below it, antelopes and a hyena. Only the feet of two hoofed animals are preserved at the top edge, and the head of a second antelope appears at the lower left. The scene takes place on the undulating surface of the desert, where only sparse plants grow. All the animals except the calf are pierced by arrows. The cow has been shot in the head just above the eyes, and another arrow has penetrated the flesh on its breast. The antelope is pierced through the eye, and the hyena is clawing at an arrow that has been driven into its mouth, breaking the back end of the shaft in the process. The remorseless precision with which these injuries are described was never equaled in Egyptian art.

The king's striding figure seen on the blocks on the left towers over the victims, not only in height but also by virtue of its aura of physical strength and royal bearing. Sahure's cropped hair befits the athlete, but his ceremonial beard, bead collar, and pleated kilt characterize the impeccably attired courtier. Muscular strength is emphasized in the knees. The arms and shoulders are full and rounded, and their soft-looking skin underlines the hunter's youth. The king holds three arrows in reserve in his right hand, the same that draws the string of the bow. His eye was once inlaid with rock crystal and stone.

On a pole behind the king stands a complicated emblematic representation of his ka (life force). The king's birth name (Sahure, "He Whom Re Has Touched") and his Horus name (Neb-khau, "Lord of Appearances") are inscribed within an abstract image of the royal palace, atop which stands the falcon god of kingship, Horus. The bottom of the emblem is embraced by two upraised arms (the hieroglyph for "ka") below which two other, more flexible arms appear. The hand of one of the latter arms holds a standard with the king's head; the other carries an ankh (life) sign and the feather of Maat, goddess of world order and justice. At the lower left edge of the block appears the foot of a smaller figure and the barely visible cartouche of Sahure's successor, King Neferirkare. When the relief was originally carved, this figure represented the heir to the throne, who accompanied the king on the hunt; the royal name was inserted when Neferirkare became king.

The Sahure relief style has reached its peak here. The height of the sculpted figures varies according to their importance and size: the figure of the king stands out most prominently in the highest relief, the ka representation behind him is barely raised, and the animals project at an intermediate level. Sahure's figure also has the most detailed interior modeling and the most carefully rounded edges along its outline. Overlapping parts of his body such as the right arm are delineated with delicately rounded grooves rather than sharply incised lines, and numerous inventive surface treatments enrich the characterization. The irregular grooves in the close-cropped hair,[1] the radiating pleats and pointed end of the front of the kilt, and the undulating pleats that follow the outline of the right thigh all contribute to the creation of a formidable image of Pharaoh Triumphant. Even the strictly vertical reserve arrows add weight to the figure.

This representation of the desert hunt from Sahure's pyramid temple is the earliest example of its kind preserved from a royal monument.[2] In the tombs of nonroyal persons of high rank the hunting of desert animals with the help of dogs had already been depicted in the early Fourth Dynasty,[3] and the lassoing of stockaded animals was often represented in the Fifth Dynasty (cat. no. 147). None of these scenes possesses a hunter as imposing as Sahure or shows equal daring in the depiction of the wounded animals.[4] The frequent reappearance of the hyena that claws at the arrow in its muzzle in reliefs and paintings of the Middle and New Kingdoms[5] is impressive evidence of the debt later Egyptian art owed to the inventive masters of the Sahure relief.

DOA

1. Cropped hair was already indicated in this manner on the head of Menkaure (cat. no. 70).
2. Altenmüller 1980a, cols. 224–30.
3. Petrie 1892, pls. 9, 17, 27; Harpur 1987, p. 82.
4. Smith (1946, p. 179) has argued that three blocks from Lisht that were reused from Old Kingdom royal monuments show earlier desert hunts of the Sahure type. However, Goedicke (1971, pp. 47–48) has correctly shown that one of these, now in the Art Museum, Princeton University, belonged to a scene of the smiting of enemies; of the others, one now also at Princeton (ibid., pp. 135–38) that depicts the lassoing of animals may not be earlier than the time of Sahure; indeed, its lack of indication of musculature makes a Sixth Dynasty date probable (see entry for cat. no. 193), an attribution favored by Goedicke (ibid., p. 138). Finally, a fragment of especially high quality (ibid., pp. 132–33) representing two felines marching one behind the other, although possibly of Fourth Dynasty date, need not be from a hunting scene but could well have been part of a nature scene, such as that in Niuserre's Room of the Seasons (cat. no. 120), or a row of booty animals (compare cat. no. 111).
5. Smith 1946, pp. 179, 181, fig. 70; Ikram 1999.

PROVENANCE: Abusir, pyramid temple of Sahure, east end of south wall in south corridor, Borchardt excavation for Deutsche Orient-Gesellschaft, 1907–8

BIBLIOGRAPHY: Borchardt 1913, pp. 30–35, pl. 17; Porter and Moss 1974, p. 327; Aldred 1996, p. 83, fig. 41 (figure of king)

113. RELIEF BLOCK WITH DEITIES AND FECUNDITY FIGURES

Fifth Dynasty, reign of Sahure
Limestone with remains of paint
H., left side 137.5 cm (54⅛ in.), right side 132 cm
(52 in.); w., top 202 cm (79½ in.), bottom
209.5 cm (82½ in.); d. 16–19 cm (6¼–7½ in.)
Ägyptisches Museum und Papyrussammlung,
Staatliche Museen zu Berlin 21784

The southern, subsidiary entrance of Sahure's pyramid temple was adorned with a portico that had two simple shaftlike columns of granite ending in simple square abaci. Basalt was used for the floor of the portico and for the dado; above that the limestone walls were decorated with brightly colored reliefs.[1] The present block was once positioned south of the doorway, its left side forming the southwest corner of the portico, and the patterned border on the right joining the edge of the doorway into the temple. Of the original four relief registers the two lowest are preserved.

On three walls of the subsidiary entrance portico were representations of long rows of deities, nome and estate personifications, and fecundity figures marching into the temple. On the right edge of the Berlin block large hieroglyphs proclaim the words spoken to the king by all the figures on this portion of the wall: "[We give you all life, stability, and dominion], all joy, all offerings, all perfect things that are in Upper Egypt, since you have appeared as king of Upper and Lower

Egypt alive forever." Appropriately, this declaration on the south side of the doorway reaffirms the allegiance to the king of the gods and institutions of the south (Upper Egypt).

The upper register of this block depicts five gods and two goddesses carrying scepters and ankh (life) signs. These deities must remain anonymous because the inscriptions above the figures are missing and their clothing and accoutrements are not differentiated enough to provide clues to their identities. In the lower register are personifications of abstract terms related to Upper Egypt. From right to left they are, according to their inscriptions: "Upper Egypt as he gives life and all stability," "Liquid (a feminine word in ancient Egyptian) as she gives all life and dominion," "Food as he gives all life and health," "Offerings as she gives all life and dominion," "Sustenance: as he gives all life, stability, and dominion," "West (the place of burial, and thus rebirth) as she gives life and dominion." The figures named in this litany—so reminiscent of the fairies in "Sleeping Beauty"—were complemented on

the north side of the doorway by portrayals of gods and personifications of fecundity relevant to Lower (northern) Egypt.[2]

The artists differentiated the deities in the upper register from the personifications in the lower one by posture: the former stand or walk upright, while the latter bow toward the king in his temple. However, the divine nature of the personifications is marked by the scepters they all hold and by the curled ceremonial beards of the male figures.[3] In accordance with Egyptian iconographical convention the male symbols of fecundity and prosperity are portrayed as extremely obese, with pendulous breasts and abdomens that hang over their girdles.[4] Except for "Liquid," who is depicted as a pregnant woman, the female figures are slender.[5] The personifications carry offering mats from which ankh signs dangle. The skin of the males was painted red, that of the females yellow; "West" wears a green dress.

The block is a perfect example of the Sahure relief style. All edges along the outlines of the raised figures are fully rounded, and fine modeling shapes important details such as the muscles and sinews in the legs and knees of the male figures, the strained muscles at their waists, which support the inflated abdomens, and the muscles at the sides of their necks. The expressively detailed male bodies contrast with the smooth, elegant figures of the females, and together these auspicious spirits present a beautifully varied image that aptly visualizes the abundance of fertile Egypt.   DoA

1. Borchardt 1910, pp. 24–25, 62–65, pl. 1.
2. Baines 1985, p. 147.
3. Ibid., pp. 38–39.
4. Ibid., pp. 84–99.
5. Ibid., pp. 110–11.

PROVENANCE: Abusir, pyramid temple of Sahure, southern subsidiary entrance, Borchardt excavation for Deutsche Orient-Gesellschaft, 1907–8

BIBLIOGRAPHY: Borchardt 1913, pp. 45, 108–9, pl. 29

Detail, cat. no. 113

114. RUNNING TROOPS

Fifth Dynasty, reign of Sahure
Limestone
Larger section: h. 69 cm (27⅛ in.), w. 48.5 cm
(19⅛ in.); smaller section: h. 17 cm (6¾ in.),
w. 20 cm (7⅞ in.)
Sammlung des Ägyptologischen Instituts der
Universität Heidelberg HD 900

These fragments of a relief of troops running to the right were found in Sahure's valley temple and may have belonged to a scene similar to the one there that depicts the so-called ship of state, which sails to the left.[1] These troops would have been in a register below a ship sailing or being rowed to the right. The partial figures of five men are visible; three are clad in kilts, but the types of garments the others wear cannot be determined. The first soldier carries a sack (visible behind the head of the second), which is similar to those seen in

the reliefs from the pyramid complex of Userkaf (cat. nos. 103, 104). The second man holds a stick. Each of the three following men holds a staff with a uraeus cobra wrapped around the top. Semicircular disks are preserved on two of them. The pattern of alternating narrow and wide stripes below the men indicates that we have reached the bottom of the wall's figural decoration.

Userkaf reigned for only seven years and was succeeded by his son Sahure, who ruled for twelve years. The relatively short interval between the construction and decoration of the pyramid complexes of the two kings makes it likely that some of the same artists worked on both projects. Yet a comparison of Userkaf's and Sahure's reliefs reveals that several developments in representing running troops took place during those years. By the reign of Sahure, the composition of troop-unit scenes had become standardized and monotonous. Almost every soldier here is identically posed, with both arms bent at the elbow and the hands curled into fists; weapons are carried in the fist of the hand that overlaps the torso. The complex, almost indecipherable, arrangement of overlapping figures in Userkaf's reliefs has given way to a repetitive, rhythmic pattern that is more easily understood but lacks the dynamism and visual interest of the earlier compositions.

Although there has been a decline in compositional inventiveness, Sahure's artists have imparted a new sense of vigor to the male body.[2] Most striking is the greater interest in powerful musculature and finely detailed modeling. On each face the curving line of the jawbone is well defined, and there are deep depressions in front of and beneath the eye and at the corner of the mouth. Ear and eyebrow are distinctly raised above the surface of the face. The muscles of the abdomen are indicated by two roughly vertical depressions, and a third depression curves around the hip area. Undulating surfaces on the legs, around the knees, and on the ankles delineate the rippling muscles of the running men. The artists' increased attention to anatomy has resulted in a stylized depiction that not only serves to

enliven the surface of the relief but also conveys a vivid impression of well-built young soldiers rushing forward to serve their pharaoh. AO

1. Borchardt 1913, pp. 23–24, pl. 9. In Borchardt's opinion, these men are not sailors because they do not wear aprons; however, within the same groups, some sailors wear aprons and others wear kilts, even in the case of the men beneath Sahure's ship of state.

2. Photographs in the Museum of Fine Arts, Boston, of several unpublished reliefs from Userkaf's pyramid complex indicate that the emphasis on musculature may have already appeared during this king's reign.

PROVENANCE: Abusir, valley temple of King Sahure

BIBLIOGRAPHY: Borchardt 1913, pp. 24–25, pl. 10; Feucht 1986, pp. 34–37

115A,B. INLAID WOOD VASE AND FAIENCE TILES

Fifth Dynasty, reign of Neferirkare
a. Vase: sycamore wood, Egyptian faience, mortar, plaster, and gold leaf
H. 45 cm (17¾ in.); max. diam. 18 cm (7⅛ in.)
Ägyptisches Museum und Papyrussammlung, Staatliche Museen zu Berlin 18807
b. Tiles: Egyptian faience, plaster, and gold leaf
Ägyptisches Museum und Papyrussammlung, Staatliche Museen zu Berlin 18808, 18813, 18815, 18816, 35550–35552, 35610–35614

The neck, body, and foot of the vase (a), a *heset* type, were probably fashioned from a single piece of wood from a sycamore fig tree (*Ficus sycomorus*).[1] Its partially hollowed interior begins as a straight shaft but narrows slightly at the shoulder, the cavity reaching a depth estimated at between twelve and fifteen centimeters. Pitting, the result of decay, mars much of the vessel's surface, but part of the original decoration was still attached when it was discovered in the funerary temple of Neferirkare at Abusir.

The excavator, Ludwig Borchardt, made a modern reconstruction of this vessel by studying the original find and the many faience pieces (b) located in nearby debris. Remains of a greenish gray mortar, which originally held the small faience tiles in place, are still visible on the vessel's body (a),[2] although only a few tiles remain attached to the vase's shoulder, body, and foot. Borchardt's reconstruction proceeded from his belief that these traces gave an inadequate impression of the object's original appearance. He restored a row of large tiles around the shoulder, following the curve of the vessel's surface and spelling out Neferirkare's titles and name as well as a wish for "life, stability, dominion, and health forever" (b1). Below this text, a second row, partially preserved on the vase, displays repeating *shen* signs and symbols of the god Min. At the base of the neck, just above the shoulder, Borchardt positioned a large *wedjat* eye on either side of the vase (detail, a, p. 347). The surviving tiles at midbody and on the foot clearly show that the decoration replicated various types of bird feathers (a, b7–9, 11, 12).[3] Borchardt's reconstruction thus views the original vase as a representation of a falcon, its eyes near the mouth of the vessel, its wing feathers covering the body, and its tail plumage

around the foot. The *wedjat* eyes suggest that the avian model was the Horus falcon.[4]

This vessel's decorative scheme involved more than the simple application of faience tiles to a wood form. The large inscribed tiles (b1, 3–5), for example, show traces of white gypsum plaster applied to the surface between the raised hieroglyphs. In addition, Borchardt discovered that gold leaf had been applied to the surface of this plaster while moist (b1). Remains of the plaster can also be seen between the feathers, where it was employed to outline each one. In antiquity the vessel would therefore have been bright blue with details in black and white and would have been embellished with two wide bands of gold bearing a turquoise inscription.

Borchardt discovered three other inlaid wood vessels in the treasury at Neferirkare's funerary temple, apparently in association with this, the best-preserved example.[5] The other three share this vessel's overall shape and method of ornamentation, but differences in technique suggest that, although stored together, they were not all made at the same time or by the same craftsman. A smaller vessel in the Ägyptisches Museum und Papyrussammlung, Berlin, for example, was crafted from two separate pieces of wood pegged together. This technique allowed the carver to create a hollow interior, which was not possible using the method employed by the craftsman responsible for the present piece.[6] The smallest vase, in the Egyptian Museum, Cairo, is made from fir, not sycamore fig, and has the remains of a layer of yellow paint under its gilding.

Representations of the *heset* vase type that Borchardt reconstructed seem not to have survived on temple walls, or perhaps they were never depicted there. Vessels of similar shape, most of which have spouts, are shown in offering scenes, but none possess more than a few blocks of color or

decorative bands around the shoulder.[7] Borchardt theorized that the Neferirkare *heset* vases were not designed for use but were instead intended during funerary rituals to symbolize the functioning vessels made of precious materials that were employed in cult temples.[8]

Small objects were decorated with inlay as early as the first two dynasties in Egypt.[9] The first examples were inlaid with ivory, which was later combined with other materials such as exotic woods and faience. A marvelous wood box from an Archaic Period burial at Helwan was completely covered with patterned ivory tiles and strips.[10] Excavations at Minshat Abu Omar in the Delta yielded another box, again elaborately decorated with ivory strips.[11] The early royal tombs at Abydos contained fragmentary ivory strips, probably once used as inlays. Among the elite burials at Saqqara, that of Hemaka yielded an ebony box with a lid entirely covered in ivory and wood tiles.[12]

An early example of the use of faience as an inlay material is found on a fragment of a box or furniture element from the tomb of the First Dynasty king Semerkhet at Abydos, in which triangles of this material were embedded in the wood. Loose faience tiles and pieces of various shapes have been excavated at temple and tomb sites mostly dating to the Old Kingdom,[13] but none of these can be clearly associated with specific object types.

By the end of the Old Kingdom Egyptian artisans had developed at least four methods for using small faience tiles as inlays. The first consisted of setting faience pieces, usually geometric shapes or hieroglyphs, into fitted cavities in the surface of a wood object such as a coffin.[14] In the second method the craftsman carved a set of desired shapes into the surface of a faience plaque, filled the resulting cavities with

b. Top to bottom, left to right: first two rows, 1 (18808); third row, 2 (18813), 3 (35551), 4 (35552), 5 (35550); fourth row, 6 (18816), 7 (35612), 8 (35614, long vertical piece), 9 (35610); fifth row, 10 (18815, two pieces), 11 (35613), 12 (35611)

plaster, and then applied gold leaf.[15] The third inlay technique involved the application of small faience elements, often with tiles of another material, to the surface of a box (usually the lid) in order to produce a pattern resembling a mosaic. This procedure, which clearly derived from the technique used in decorating Hemaka's box, is superbly executed in chests from Gebelein and El Kab.[16]

Artisans employing the fourth approach completely covered the entire surface of an object with tiles, using mortar as the adhesive and plaster to hold the smaller elements in place. With this technique a simple form could be transformed into an elaborately decorated vessel, as exemplified by the four inlaid wood vases from Neferirkare's treasury. These vessels also display a variation

of the second technique: cavities in the faience tiles were filled with plaster and covered with gold leaf so that the faience hieroglyphs appeared inlaid into gold.[17]

The Neferirkare vessels lack clear parallels in the Old Kingdom, although several finds of faience tiles may be from similar vases. The small fragments found by George Reisner at Menkaure's valley temple probably belonged to a similar vessel, but not enough of them have survived to allow a detailed comparison.[18] In the rooms under Djoser's pyramid at Saqqara, Cecil Firth and James E. Quibell discovered three small faience pieces that they maintained were marked with feather patterns. If the Saqqara finds did originally come from a vessel of avian form, its style differed significantly from that of the Menkaure and Neferirkare

examples. Such a difference is hardly surprising given the early date of the Djoser materials.[19] Recent discoveries in the magazines of Neferefre's funerary temple at Abusir most likely belonged to ritual containers decorated with inlay.[20]   DCP

1. Borchardt 1909, p. 61.
2. Ibid., p. 60.
3. Three other faience fragments (Berlin 18813, 18815, 18816) do not fit into the reconstructed scheme for this vessel. One of these may belong to another vase, which, following Borchardt's reconstruction, shows such a tile (ibid., pl. 3, no. 3). Borchardt clearly states that numerous faience inlay fragments were found throughout the excavation and perhaps intends to suggest that these come from other contexts (ibid., p. 59). Verner (1984, pp. 74–76) indicates that some faience pieces can be associated with certain types of furniture.
4. Sokar, another falcon deity, is closely associated with the funerary zone surrounding Memphis and therefore could be the god represented on this vessel. The Abusir papyri state that *heset* vessels were used in his feast (Posener-Kriéger 1976, p. 184). However, the presence on the vase of the name of Min, an ancient fertility god whose responsibilities tied him closely to the pharaoh and to Horus, in conjunction with the vessel's *wedjat* eyes, makes Horus a more likely candidate (Frankfort 1948, p. 189). Additionally, Horus and Min could represent the balance between Egypt's northern and southern regions.
5. One of these, also in the Ägyptisches Museum und Papyrussammlung, Berlin (35615; Borchardt 1909, pl. 6, no. 1), is similar to the vase under discussion, although less well preserved. Another (Berlin 18806; ibid., pl. 6, no. 3), lost in World War II, was smaller and less elaborately decorated. The last is in the Egyptian Museum, Cairo (ibid., pl. 6, no. 4).
6. Ibid., pl. 5F.
7. For example, see offerings by the Nile gods or representations of gifts in Sahure's funerary temple (Borchardt 1913, pls. 24, 62).
8. Borchardt 1909, pp. 59–60.
9. Scholars now widely recognize that the contact between Egypt and Mesopotamia during the fourth millennium was complex. Thus, the antiquity of the Mesopotamian tradition of elaborately inlaying vessels must be mentioned when discussing the development of inlay in Egypt. By about 3200 B.C.E. spouted stone vases from Uruk depicted complex designs in tiles of colored stones and shell (Heinrich 1936, pp. 35–36, pls. 26, 27). In Egypt the tradition of inlaying boxes and vessels appears already developed in the archaeological record. This lack of tradition may be due to accidents of preservation rather than interconnections with the ancient Near East; either way, the finds from Egypt do have their own distinctive character.
10. Saad 1969, pls. 60, 61. Other Helwan tombs produced a coffin covered in shell tiles and two other boxes covered, respectively, in small ivory tiles and decorated ivory strips.
11. Kroeper and Krzyzaniak 1992, pp. 209–13.

Detail, cat. no. 115a

12. Emery 1938, p. 41, pl. 23a.
13. Deposits at the temple of Khenti-amentiu at Abydos (Petrie 1903, p. 32, pl. 21, nos. 17–22); main chamber at the end of tomb gallery 3 and other passageways in Djoser's Step Pyramid at Saqqara (Firth and Quibell 1935, pl. 94).
14. Emery 1954, p. 38, fig. 16, p. 44, pl. 27, no. 160, pl. 31c; Reisner and Smith 1955, pp. 25–26, 36–40; H. W. Müller 1972, p. 43 (ÄS 4224); Friedman 1998, p. 17, fig. 5.
15. A piece in the Museum of Fine Arts, Boston, described in detail by Lacovara (1996a, pp. 487–91) illustrates this method. Such plaques may have then been mounted onto another surface, possibly a box or shrine.
16. For Gebelein, see Leospo 1988, p. 137,

pl. 182; and for El Kab, see Quibell 1898, p. 19, pl. 8, no. 2.
17. The covering of plaster with gold leaf is documented in other Old Kingdom contexts (Petrie 1903, p. 32). The boxes in the tomb of Hetep-heres I, inlaid with faience and covered with gold or silver leaf, would have offered the same visual impression as the bands on the Neferirkare vase, but their method of manufacture was quite different. For the Hetep-heres boxes, the metal leaf was glued to the wood and pressed down into the cutouts for the faience inlays (Reisner and Smith 1955, pp. 25–26).
18. Reisner (1931, p. 236, pl. 65c) illustrates a small fragment in his excavation report. This unaccessioned piece, along with the edge from

a faience tile perhaps from the same vessel, resides in the permanent collection of the Museum of Fine Arts, Boston.
19. Firth and Quibell 1935, p. 35, pl. 94, no. 1.
20. Verner 1984, p. 74; Verner 1986b, p. 158; and Verner 1994a, p. 142.

PROVENANCE: Abusir, funerary temple of Neferirkare, treasury, Borchardt excavation

BIBLIOGRAPHY: (a) Borchardt 1909, pp. 61–62, pls. 3, no. 2, 5E, 6, no. 2, 7; Porter and Moss 1974, p. 339. (b) Borchardt 1909, pp. 64–66, pls. 7, 8, no. 1

116. Fragment of the Royal Annals

Fifth Dynasty?
Diorite
H. 8.5 cm (3⅜ in.); w. 8 cm (3⅛ in.); d. 5.3 cm
(2⅛ in.)
Petrie Museum of Egyptian Archaeology, University
College London UC 15508

A few ancient inscriptions mention the existence of royal annals, the official record of events during the successive reigns from the beginnings of Egyptian history. Pieces of these annals survive—among them this small chip—and they have proved invaluable in fleshing out the scant information gleaned from other sources; however, because of their fragmentary nature they can no longer recount for us the whole history of pharaonic Egypt. In the annals every reign marked a new era, which ended with the pharaoh's death. Thus, in order to construct a chronology it is necessary to establish the succession of the kings and the sequence of cultural events and then situate them within a universal calendar, in this case, our own.

The largest fragment of the royal annals —and the most important text for the Old Kingdom—is called the Palermo Stone, after the city where it has been housed since 1877. This is a diorite slab 43 centimeters (17 inches) in height and inscribed on both faces. The events it relates concern the sovereigns of Egypt, from the earliest to those of the Fifth Dynasty; the last pharaoh mentioned is Neferirkare. The surface of the stone is divided into horizontal bands, each with three registers. The upper register gives the names of a king and his mother. The next two registers are divided into compartments, one for each regnal year. In each compartment the first line lists the outstanding events of the year: religious ceremonies, wars, construction of buildings, and periodic inventories of wealth. The second gives measurements, probably the height of the annual inundation of the Nile, on which the life of the country depended, expressed in cubits (1 cubit is 52.4 centimeters [20⅝ inches]), palms

(1 palm is 7.48 centimeters [3 inches]), and digits (1 digit is 1.87 centimeters [¾ inch]).

Similar fragments have been found, but they may not all come from the same document; five are currently in Cairo,[1] and this one is in London. On the best-preserved surface of the present text, two rows of compartments are visible—those in which memorable events are mentioned and those recording the height of the inundation over a series of years. The upper line, where the pharaoh's name was inscribed, has unfortunately disappeared. Nonetheless, judging from the dimensions of the compartments, we can determine that the inscription is part of the fifth band of the Palermo Stone, which deals with the Second Dynasty. The inscription is fragmentary and obscure:

1. Upper register, compartments from right to left (events): (a) ". . . the first [occasion] . . . gold"; (b) ". . . the second census"; (c) ". . . the bas of Pe"; (d) "the third [?] census."
2. Second register (height of the inundation): (a) [   ]; (b) "3 cubits 6 palms 2 digits"; (c) "3 cubits 1 palm"; (d) "1 cubit. . . ."

Below, remnants of a register can be discerned, beginning another series, with the top of the bent stalk recording the years, and the hieroglyph *aha*.

Very recently a slab measuring 234 centimeters (92⅛ inches) in height, the lid of a sarcophagus in the Egyptian Museum, Cairo (JE 65908), has been published. Carved on its surface are the annals of Sixth Dynasty sovereigns, complementing the information given in this first series of documents.[2]

CZ

1. Egyptian Museum, Cairo, JE 39734, JE 39735, JE 44859, JE 44860, and an unnumbered fragment; Cenival 1965, pp. 13–17.
2. Baud and Dobrev 1995, pp. 23–92.

PROVENANCE: Probably Memphis (Mitrahina)

BIBLIOGRAPHY: Petrie 1916, pp. 115, 119–20; O'Mara 1979; Stewart 1979, p. 6, no. 17; Helck 1982, cols. 652–54; Roccati 1982, pp. 36–52

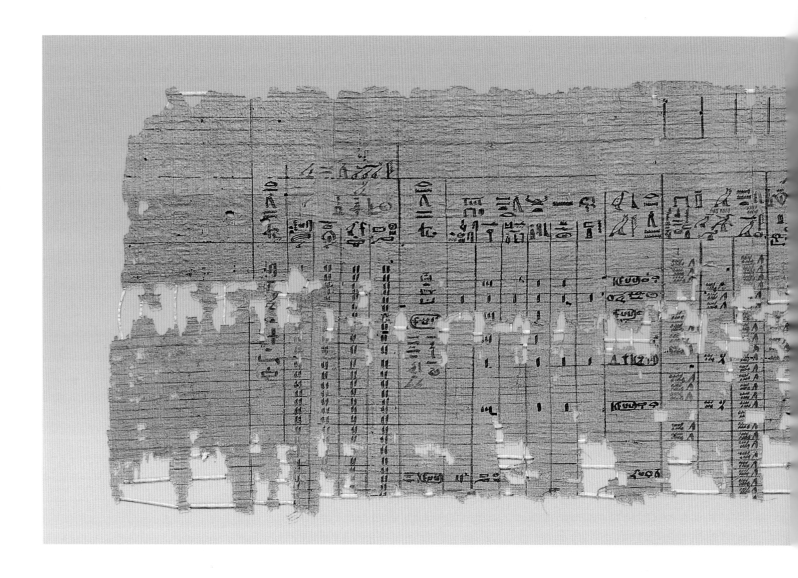

117. DOCUMENT FROM THE ROYAL RECORDS OF ABUSIR

Fifth Dynasty, reign of Djedkare-Isesi
Papyrus, with hieratic and hieroglyphic script in black and red ink
H. 19.2 cm (7⅝ in.); w. 64.5 cm (25⅜ in.)
Musée du Louvre, Paris E 25416c

In 1893 Egyptian peasants discovered a large bundle of inscribed papyri at Abusir and immediately sold it. The Egyptian Museum in Cairo bought part of the trove, and the rest was divided among the British Museum, London, the Petrie Museum, London, the Musée du Louvre, Paris, and the Ägyptisches Museum und Papyrussammlung, Berlin. The exact origin of the papyrus sheets has been known since Ludwig Borchardt's excavations in 1903 because Borchardt found more of them in situ near the pyramid of Neferirkare.[1] These extraordinary documents, which are among the oldest from pharaonic Egypt, were part of the archives of the royal mortuary temple. They include lists of personnel recruited for daily tasks—watchmen, laborers, and torchbearers—registers of receipts and expenses, reports of inspections of temple furnishings, inventories, the schedules of priests celebrating feast days, notes concerning damage to liturgical objects, lists of officials, many bookkeeping accounts, and correspondence. Because they are much like modern business records, they bring to life with exceptional clarity the daily routine at a temple nearly forty-five hundred years ago. A similar group was discovered, also at the site of Abusir, by archaeologists from the universities of Giza and Prague.[2] And very recently, members of the Musée du Louvre's archaeological expedition at Saqqara exhumed a fragment north of the causeway of Unis that bore the name of Isesi and proved to be the same sort of document.[3]

On the recto of this sheet, there is a record of the monthly accounts of the mortuary temple. At the top the heading is inscribed horizontally: "Offerings brought to the mortuary temple of King Neferirkare from his sun temple." A very clear table follows. Indications of provenance, names of provisions entered in the accounts (bread, beer, meat, fowl), and names of transport chiefs serve as vertical subheads. Each product is given three columns, the first for the quantity that was supposed to be delivered, the second for the quantity actually delivered, and the third for the difference between the two. On the thirty lines for the thirty days of the month, the figures corresponding to these quantities are recorded. The offerings required by the royal cult arrived daily from "Set-ib-re," the sun temple. Located a few miles from the pyramid, this building warehoused the products from various estates and from the palace and served as a redistribution center.

The verso of the sheet bears four texts written by the same scribe, whose handwriting is recognizable. This must be a copy consolidating various documents,

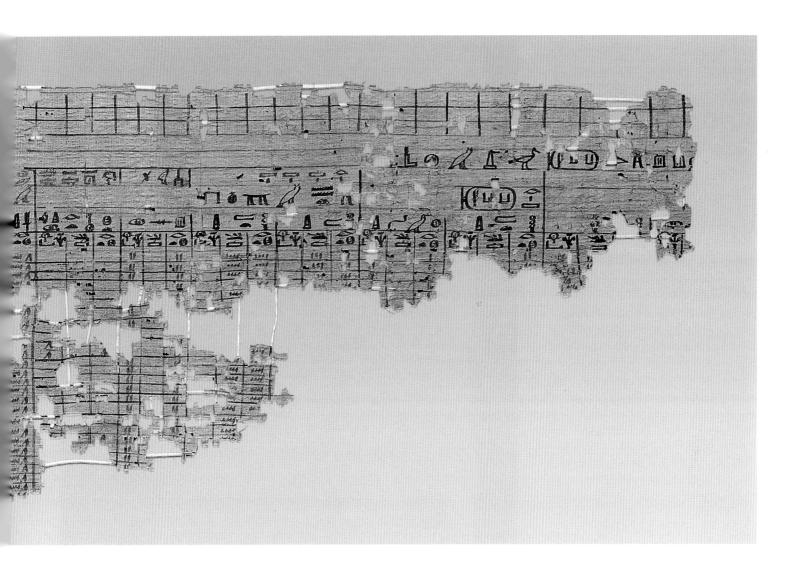

since the dates span more than ten years. At right is a duty roster for a religious feast (text 1), followed by an inventory of liturgical objects (text 2); at left is an accounting of the distribution of grain (text 3). The bookkeeping note scrawled at the bottom is undoubtedly a memorandum.

Text 1

This duty roster has to do with the feast of Sokar, god of the Memphite region; it was a very important annual observance, often mentioned in the tombs of private individuals who received offerings on that occasion. In this case the funerary meal was to be offered to King Neferirkare. At the top are the date and the heading: "The year of the third census, fourth month of the season of the inundation, twenty-fifth day: makeup of the duty roster for the feast day of Sokar, Tawer team, *was* section." Below are several columns, divided into three sections by vertical strokes, enumerating the employees for the different tasks. At right: "Those

who are assigned to purify in the temple," followed by three proper names. In the middle: "Those who are assigned to the two *wekh* fetishes and the *teba* scepters," followed by seven proper names. At left: "Those who are assigned to the funerary meal in the hall of offerings."

There follows a list of liturgical objects (silver basin, ewer, and goblet, table of offerings, copper brazier, and so on) used during the meal, and, across from each utensil, the proper name of the individual in charge.

Text 2

This text gives an inventory of liturgical objects and their condition. At the top are the date and the heading:

The year following the tenth census, fourth month of the season of harvest, twenty-first day: inspection of the *wekh* fetish, brought out for the occasion of the litany offering of rejoicing, in the presence of the lector-priest Ka-hotep:

gold—the fetish: a great deal of damage on it . . .
the sun disk: damage on four points . . .
the two cobra uraei: missing sections
. . . damage . . .
the stand: missing some of the . . .

Text 3

This text is not related to the two previous ones. At the top are the date and the heading: "Year of the fourteenth census, third epagomenal (intercalary) day. Division of wheat received as nourishment." Two proper names and a quantity follow.   CZ

1. Posener-Kriéger and Cenival 1968, pp. ix–xii.
2. Verner 1979, pp. 98–100.
3. Ziegler et al. 1997, p. 279.

PROVENANCE: Abusir, mortuary temple of Neferirkare; purchased

BIBLIOGRAPHY: Posener-Kriéger and Cenival 1968, pls. 33A–35 (recto), 13A, 14A,B (verso); Posener-Kriéger 1976, pp. 257–72 (recto), pp. 59–80, 336–39 (verso)

118. Lion-Headed Goddess Suckling King Niuserre

Fifth Dynasty, reign of Niuserre
Limestone with patches of ancient plaster and
faint remains of paint
H. 112.2 cm (44¼ in.); w. 63 cm (24¾ in.)
Ägyptisches Museum und Papyrussammlung,
Staatliche Museen zu Berlin 17911

A number of reliefs in pyramid complexes depicted the king being suckled by a goddess. These were located in important positions beside the central doorways leading from the valley temple into the causeway, and from the transverse corridor of the pyramid temple into the hall containing statue chambers (see "Royal Reliefs" by Dorothea Arnold in this catalogue, p. 94). The goddesses in these scenes take different forms. The deity of entirely human shape preserved on a relief from the valley temple of Niuserre's ancestor Sahure[1] had the name Semat-weret written beside her. Semat-weret, the Great Wild Cow, was a mother goddess with connections to the Upper Egyptian town of El Kab, whose main goddess was Nekhbet, patroness and guardian of Upper Egypt.[2] The present relief does not preserve a name for the suckling lion-headed deity. There were various goddesses of the type in the Egyptian pantheon, Sakhmet and Bastet foremost among them,[3] and any one of these could be depicted here. It appears that the specific identity of the suckling figure was less important than her function as the divine mother and protectress of the king.[4] While her identity is unclear, there can be no doubt that her lion's head contributes considerably to the awe experienced even by the present-day viewer when confronted with this image of the pharaoh intimately associated with a creature that is half human, half animal.

The inscription above the heads of goddess and king contains the Horus name of Niuserre, "Darling of the Two Lands," and words spoken by the deity to the king: "[Recitation by (name of goddess) I have given you] all life and stability, all happiness. . . ." Behind the goddess are remains of another inscription: "Recitation: 'S[uckle from me, my son . . .']." As in all Old Kingdom scenes of this type, the goddess does not bend her head toward the king—who, although clearly an adult, barely reaches her shoulder—nor does the king lift his head to look into her face.[5] On the contrary, with her now-missing inlaid eye the deity gazes to the left, far above the king's head, while he looks directly to the right with an eye that was also once inlaid. Without eye contact the only expression of the emotional relationship between the figures would have been the gently endearing gesture of the goddess's right arm, now missing, which must have encircled the king's neck, and his tender grasp of her forearm. In the absence of eye contact the suckling becomes the main focus of the scene, and it is perhaps no accident that one of the rare instances of naturalism in Egyptian art occurs here. As Smith has pointed out, the goddess's fingers disappear behind her breast as she holds it to the king's mouth.[6] This represents a break with the Egyptian convention that does not allow important parts of the human body to disappear from sight. But it is precisely this deviation from the norm that enabled the artist to emphasize the goddess's full breast and thus draw attention to the central subject, the furnishing of the king with

divine nourishment.[7] On the evidence of the preserved remains, it appears that the unusual treatment of the goddess's hand on her breast was an invention of the artists of Sahure's reign that continued in use during the time of Niuserre.[8] Sixth Dynasty sculptors reverted to a more conventional rendering of the gesture and depicted all fingers of the hand.

Like the scene of King Sahure hunting (cat. no. 112), this piece from the valley temple of Niuserre exhibits relief executed at varying levels. The goddess's lion head stands out fiercely as the most deeply sculpted and richly modeled area: especially the thick bones above the eye contribute to its awe-inspiring effect. In the other areas of the figures most emphasis is given to the contours, with those of the king's swelling arm and the musculature of his torso contrasting expressively with the smooth silhouette of the goddess's slender body, which is in part overlapped by his form. The inscriptions are the shallowest part of the image, and their flat quality is enhanced by the considerable losses in the uppermost part of the block, where the relief was carved on fragile plaster that repaired an ancient damage.

Most of the following remains of pigment noted by Borchardt in 1907 are still visible: red on the body of the king and every fourth strand of the goddess's hair; green on the deity's garment, the lion face, and choker; blue on her collar; and yellow on her body.[9]   DOA

1. Borchardt 1913, pp. 35–36, 94, pl. 18. For beautiful photographs of part of this block, see Jéquier 1938, pls. 30–33; Smith 1946, p. 176, pl. 54; Labrousse, Lauer, and Leclant 1977, p. 84, pl. 29; Leclant 1979a, p. 23, pl. 17, fig. 25; and Stadelmann 1991, pl. 65.
2. Verhoeven 1984, cols. 836–37.
3. Rössler-Köhler 1980, cols. 1081–83.
4. Leclant 1951, pp. 123–27; Leclant 1961, p. 275.
5. For examples of scenes in which the goddess lowers her head to the king and he looks up, see, for the Middle Kingdom, Habachi 1963, p. 26, pl. 8, fig. 8; and, for the New Kingdom (Nineteenth Dynasty), Lepsius 1849–58, vol. 3, pls. 150b, 177f, g; and Sotheby Parke Bernet, New York, sale cat., May 22, 1981, lot 39, currently on loan to the Metropolitan Museum (L 1996.46). For Late Period scenes without eye contact, see Capel and Markoe 1996, pp. 117–18, nos. 50, 51; and Wildung 1996, p. 196, no. 221, with earlier bibliography.
6. Smith 1946, pp. 281, 299.
7. It is interesting to note that in his description of the scene, Borchardt (1907, p. 41) showed great difficulty in understanding the position of the right breast of the goddess, which she seems to be drawing out of the side of her garment under her right armpit: a somewhat awkward way to suckle a child if the image is interpreted as a naturalistic rendering. However, it is not naturalistic but combines more than one view (garment from the front, breast in profile, for example) in a manner that has become familiar to the modern viewer, thanks to the breakthrough work of Heinrich Schäfer in 1919 (see 1986 ed., pp. 287, 297, and passim).
8. For these reliefs, see note 1 above.
9. Borchardt 1907, p. 41, n. 3.

PROVENANCE: Abusir, valley temple of Niuserre, Borchardt excavation for Deutsche Orient-Gesellschaft, 1902–4

BIBLIOGRAPHY: Borchardt 1907, pp. 39–41

119. EARLY SUMMER IN THE NILE VALLEY

Fifth Dynasty, reign of Niuserre
Painted limestone
H. 72 cm (28⅛ in.); w. 66 cm (26 in.)
Ägyptisches Museum und Papyrussammlung,
Staatliche Museen zu Berlin 20038

The sun god—under his various names, Re, Khepri, Atum, and Aten—was without doubt one of the most important deities of ancient Egypt, and much of the thankful delight of the Nile Valley dwellers in their environment's rich fauna and flora found expression in the thoughts and beliefs of the solar religion and the art it inspired. Witnesses to these beliefs in Old Kingdom art are innumerable representations of out-door life executed in tombs; however, the most direct surviving statement is provided by the so-called season reliefs from the sun temple of King Niuserre at Abu Ghurab, just north of the Fifth Dynasty pyramids of Abusir.

Owing to their fragmentary state of preservation, no full reconstruction of the reliefs in the Room of the Seasons (fig. 125) has yet been possible. It is generally agreed, however, that various representations of two seasons, the *akhet* (inundation) and the *shemu* (harvest),[1] were displayed on the chamber's two long walls.[2] A large per-sonification of each of the two seasons, in the guise of a fertility figure with offerings in its hands, stood at the head of several registers with scenes depicting the natural events that took place in the Nile Valley during the time of year appropriate to the figure.[3] There were also smaller fertility figures and nome personifications in undeter-mined places in the room.[4] The present blocks and three others in the exhibition (cat. no. 120) derive from two preserved clusters of nature scenes. Both groups are concerned with events that unfold under the aegis of the *akhet*:[5] those discussed here involve the time of the onset of the inundation in early sum-mer,[6] while the complementary fragments are concerned with late summer and early fall, when the floods are beginning to recede.[7]

In its uppermost register the present relief shows the fish-filled water of the inundation (symbolized by vertical zigzag lines in a blue area) covering the land (represented by a narrow strip painted pink with black dots), as it did every year between July and October before modern river dams at Aswan intro-

duced totally controlled irrigation. Above the floodwaters only the highest points of the alluvial land remained dry, forming islands on which animals and humans could con-tinue to live. In the uppermost register of this relief one such island is depicted as an area of rectangular shape.[8] It shelters a nest of birds' eggs, from one of which a chick

has emerged begging food from its parents.[9] In the middle register on the left we see a calf and cow and, just behind them, the muzzle of yet another cow. These animals belong to a herd ("herd of cattle" is written above them)[10] that is roaming the savanna at the margins of the desert where rich vegetation has sprouted during inundation.

The rest of the relief is dedicated to the depiction of men catching birds. The inscription above the two men to the right of the cattle says "putting birds into a cage."[11] Both are designated "fishermen" by the boat-shaped signs above their heads. Below them six men pull a long rope attached to a bird trap represented on the block adjoining at the right (which is not illustrated here).[12] Following usual practice, the trap has been laid behind a bush so that the birds do not notice the men who will close it. The hieroglyphs above the four individuals to the right proclaim "catching *khetta* ducks (geese?)[13] in a trap." And the man to the left cries "bring it (the rope) in with me, dear!" according to the inscription above his head and that of his companion.[14]

The relief, although carefully laid out,[15] is executed with a certain nonchalance. The heads of the two men catching birds in the middle register are too large for their bodies, and the relief surface is remarkably uneven for a work from a royal monument. The emphasis is clearly on the illustrative value of the picture, and as an illustration the scene has great charm. By deviating only slightly from the usual conventions the artist has impressively evoked the breezy atmosphere and airy freshness of the Nilotic landscape at the time of inundation. He achieved this by depicting watery areas, plants, humans, and animals at almost equal size, instead of allowing the figures to overpower the landscape, as is usually the case in Egyptian art. Also contributing to the effect is the great importance given to the color green, which dominates the image thanks to the two large bushes. The bush at the left separates the men catching birds from the cattle and also marks the division between savanna on the left and agricultural land on the right, a division that provides one of numerous important references to the actual landscape of the Nile Valley. Youth and new life are visualized through the baby bird[16] and the calf, the fish swim freely in various directions, and the air is filled with the cries of the men.   DOA

1. Edel (1964, pp. 202–3) translates *shemu* as time of "heat." For the translation as "harvest," see Guglielmi 1975, cols. 1271–72; see also *Wörterbuch der Aegyptischen Sprache*, vol. 4 (1930), p. 481.
2. The ancient Egyptian calendar was divided into three seasons. For the complicated questions surrounding omission of the *peret*, the third season, as well as the implications

of the discrepancies between the natural cycle and the civic calendar, see Edel 1964, pp. 185–89; Smith 1965, pp. 142–43; Wenig 1966, pp. 10–11; and Edel and Wenig 1974, pp. 10–11.
3. Edel and Wenig 1974, pls. 1–3.
4. Ibid., pls. 4–7.
5. It is not clear why Edel and Wenig (ibid., pp. 21–22) placed the events shown on the present block in the *shemu* season, after Edel (1964, p. 191) had correctly pointed out that it unmistakably depicts the inundated land.
6. The events depicted here can be placed in the early summer on the evidence of the scene that adjoined it on the right (Egyptian Museum, Cairo; Edel and Wenig 1974, p. 22, pl. 12), which shows the arrival of mullet at Elephantine in the course of their annual migration (Edel 1961, pp. 214–18, 249–50; Edel 1964, pp. 118–26). In antiquity the mullet started to swim from the Mediterranean Sea southward up the Nile in January and, as far as can be ascertained, arrived at Elephantine about June of each year. After the construction of the Nile dam north of Cairo in 1885–90 this migration ceased. See Edel 1964, pp. 160–63, esp. p. 161.
7. For the date of the events depicted on this block, see Edel 1964, pp. 176–85.
8. With its oblique green lines, the border at the bottom of the rectangle is not easy to explain. It is possible that the lines represent grass, but they can also be interpreted as portraying a kind of reed binding because of their regular slant. If binding is indeed shown, the rectangular area may be an artificial floating island set on the water to shield young birds.
9. James P. Allen (personal communication) tentatively identifies the hieroglyphs above the young bird as part of the word *nwi*, "to care for." See *Wörterbuch der Aegyptischen Sprache*, vol. 2 (1928), p. 220.
10. Edel 1961, pp. 246–49.
11. Ibid., pp. 245–46.
12. See note 7 above.
13. Edel 1961, p. 236, n. 54.
14. Edel 1964, p. 142.
15. Ibid., pp. 134–37.
16. Compare the three-dimensional figure of a young bird in the same posture from the tomb of Tutankhamun; see Desroches Noblecourt 1963, pl. 47.

PROVENANCE: Abu Ghurab, sun temple of Niuserre, east wall of Room of the Seasons (fig. 125),* Borchardt and Schäfer excavation for Königliche Museen, Berlin, 1898–1901

BIBLIOGRAPHY: Edel and Wenig 1974, pp. 21–22, colorpl. A, pl. 12; Priese 1991, no. 23, pp. 37–38

*For the most probable position of this relief on the east wall of the room, see Edel 1964, p. 159. Edel supposes that all the deities and emblems pictured were shown proceeding toward the north side of the room (and thus toward the temple's large obelisk). One of these emblems, a large elephant head directed toward the left, was portrayed on a block that originally adjoined the present relief. See ibid., fig. 13.

120. Late Summer in the Nile Valley

Fifth Dynasty, reign of Niuserre
Limestone with remains of paint
H. 51 cm (20⅛ in.); total w. 283 cm (111⅜ in.)
Ägyptisches Museum und Papyrussammlung,
Staatliche Museen zu Berlin 20035

Represented on these three blocks from the Room of the Seasons (fig. 125; see entry for cat. no. 119) are events that occur in nature during the late summer and early fall months. Before the Nile dams were constructed this was the time when the waters of the annual inundation began to recede from the agricultural areas, and migratory creatures were on their journeys, the birds traveling south and the fish north. The middle register is complete, but half of the one below it and most of the upper one were carved on adjoining blocks. In the top register we can see the lower portion of a row of trees of species native to various parts of the country.[1] In the bottom register are four scenes separated by vertical lines. The two on the left and the one on the far right portray birds, while the depiction at center right concerns the northward journey of mullet.

The preserved parts of the scenes of birds show the creatures in flight and, in two places, the tops of papyrus thickets. In the compartment at center left a man pulls a bird trap shut. The birds on the far left are, from left to right, a duck, a goose, a tern, and a pigeon. Above the clapnet and one of the papyrus thickets pigeons are

depicted, and in the vignette on the far right there are, reading from the left, an ibis, a tern, and two ducks. All the birds shown are wild migratory species that visit Egypt on their journeys south and north. The inscriptions, written in the concise manner of the Old Kingdom, have been translated and elucidated by Edel.[2] A somewhat modernized version of the one above the birds on the far left reads: "When the land emerges [from the floods of the inundation?], the *fekhen* (ibis), *bedju* (pigeon), *khat* (tern), *sa* (goose), and *pekhet* (duck)[3] come into the Delta, the tern[4] to catch fish in the cool water."[5] Written above the scene with the man at the trap, who is designated as a "fisherman," is "the coming into the Delta by the *aba* and the *shesemtj* birds (two kinds of pigeons)," and on the right three more varieties of pigeon are named,[6] followed by an explanation of their activity: "the coming forth [from the papyrus thicket]."[7] Inscriptions[8] above the scene on the far right announce that this also shows "the coming to the cool water of the Delta by the *kheret* and *wekhat* (two kinds of ducks), *khat*, and *gemet* (a variety of ibis) birds."[9] This careful enumeration of names of bird species and their portrayal in compartments whose main scenic elements are repetitive, rather uniformly conceived papyrus thickets strongly suggests that the designer's aim was to create a kind of instruction book in natural history rather than a visualization of actual events unfolding in a Nile landscape. The row of trees in the upper register certainly belongs to the same category of didactic presentation.

The scene of fish is essentially of the same nature. The inscription here informs us that this is a representation of "the coming forth from the nomes of Upper and Lower Egypt[10] by the *kheskemet* and the *heba* fish (two kinds of mullet)[11] while they journey northward in order to eat *sha*-herbs in the waters of the Delta."[12] Before the great dam was built north of Cairo between 1885 and 1890, mullet swam "in the spring up the river [Nile] to spawn, and came back down the river shortly before the setting of the Pleiades [in early November], at which occasion they were caught and became victims of weirs in great numbers," as Strabo (64/63 B.C.E.– after 23 C.E.) wrote.[13] Several other scenes in the Room of the Seasons depicted stages in this journey of the mullets, which was, of course, a rich opportunity for fishing that was, in the fullest sense of the term, a godsend for the ancient Egyptians.[14]

The center register is divided into two parts. On the left the harvest of honey is shown.[15] Tubular jars stacked one above the other house the bees. A man kneels and blows into a similar jar that he holds in his hands (the inscription reads "blowing")— presumably to provoke a reaction from the queen bee that will tell him whether she is ready to initiate a swarming of the hive. Farther to the right a man empties a jar that resembles the containers holding the bees into a large vat. It has been suggested that he is pouring out the best and purest honey, which separates easily from the honeycomb. The inscription above the next two men tells us that they are "filling"; one holds a

tall, slender jar into which the other pours a liquid, possibly water, to wash out honey of lesser quality. The group that follows, which is only partially preserved, contains men who, according to the inscription, are "pressing." They may be extracting the last and poorest of the honey from the remaining broken honeycombs.[16] The last man on the right ties a knot in the binding over a dome-shaped lid that closes the chalicelike containers into which the honey has been emptied for storage ("sealing the honey" announce the hieroglyphs). To the right of this harvest scene a herd of copulating goats and sheep appears. An inscription above each animal identifies it as male or female, and the word "swelling" above the female goat in the center, at whose hindquarters a male is sniffing, indicates that she is in heat.[17] Visible on the far right are a man picking figs from a tree and, preserved at the very edge of the block, the arm and foot of a second man.[18]

The scenes of honey harvest, copulating animals, and fruit picking are clearly more than simple enumerations for didactic purposes. Although landscape elements are scarce, in keeping with the instructional presentation here, the atmosphere of a fall season in the Nile Valley is unmistakably conveyed. Main actors in the drama are the animals shown following their natural procreative instincts. The ancient Egyptians saw their unhampered activity as guaranteeing new births in spring, a meaning underlined by the presence of two young kids in the middle of the scene. The arrangement of the

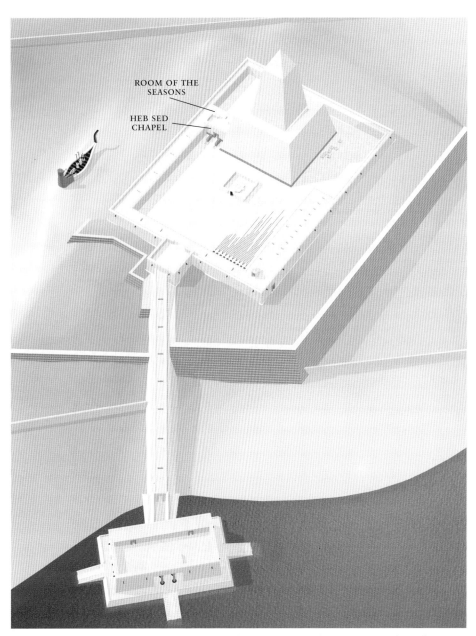

ROOM OF THE
SEASONS

HEB SED
CHAPEL

125. Computer reconstruction of sun temple of Niuserre, Abu Ghurab. By David S. Johnson

honey harvesters in groups of two mirrors the pairing of the animals and thus links man and beast together. And the balancing of the honey harvest and the picking of figs on either side of the animals connects the two scenes that speak of the provision of sweet substances in the year to come. DOA

1. Edel 1961, pp. 250–53.
2. Ibid., pp. 220–24.
3. For all these birds, see ibid., pp. 254–55.
4. As Edel (ibid., p. 223) has remarked, among these birds only the tern catches fish. Thus, this part of the sentence can relate only to the tern.
5. More literally, and reading the hieroglyphs in both directions from the sign of the two legs in the center, Edel (ibid.) translated the text from the center to the left: "The coming into the Delta by the *bedju* bird, in order to catch fish in the cool water by the *khat* bird, [the coming into the Delta] by the *sa*-goose, the coming into the Delta by the *pekhet* duck"; and from the center to the right: "the coming into the Delta by the m . . . bird, the *tekhen* bird, when the *seb* (unknown word) of the land comes forth."
6. Ibid., p. 230: *shem, khesef,* and *menut.*
7. Ibid., pp. 229–30.
8. Ibid., pp. 221, 223–24.
9. For the birds, see ibid., pp. 254–55.
10. Ibid., pp. 212, 214–15.
11. Ibid., pp. 211–14.
12. Ibid., pp. 217–18.
13. *Geography,* book 17, II.5; see Edel 1964, pp. 161–62.
14. Edel 1961, pp. 211–18; Edel 1964, pp. 118–63, esp. pp. 153–63.
15. Edel 1964, pp. 177–79; Kuény 1950, pp. 84–93; Leclant 1975, cols. 786–89, with earlier bibliography.
16. According to Kuény (1950, p. 92) they are making a sweet drink, but it seems more probable that the scene depicts the third stage in the production of honey (pressing the honeycomb mass) that Kuény himself described (ibid., p. 91).
17. Edel 1964, pp. 180–81.
18. Ibid., pp. 179–80.

PROVENANCE: Abu Ghurab, sun temple of Niuserre, east wall of Room of the Seasons (fig. 125), Borchardt and Schäfer excavation for Königliche Museen, Berlin, 1898–1901

BIBLIOGRAPHY: Edel and Wenig 1974, p. 21, colorpls. E, F, pl. 9, nos. 255, 256

a

121A,B. SCENES FROM THE THIRTY-YEAR JUBILEE OF KING NIUSERRE

Fifth Dynasty, reign of Niuserre
Limestone
a. Left block: h. 86 cm (33⅞ in.); w. 56 cm (22 in.)
b. Right block: h. 80 cm (31½ in.); w. 80 cm (31½ in.)
Staatliche Sammlung Ägyptischer Kunst, Munich
(a) Ä 180, (b) Ä 181

Throughout their long history Egyptians believed firmly that their kings, however divine in nature, needed periodic rejuvenation and strengthening effected by a special encounter with divine forces and by the practice of rituals. The primary occasion for this renewal was the Sed festival, or Heb Sed.[1] Ideally this festival was celebrated after thirty years of a king's reign. However, since many rulers did not live long enough to observe a thirty-year jubilee, the mere depiction of the ritual, or indeed the simple mention of a jubilee in an inscription, became a potent means of ensuring renewal of the kingly powers for eternity. The earliest and most elaborate of such representations of which large portions remain are the Heb Sed reliefs found in the Fifth Dynasty king Niuserre's sun temple at Abu Ghurab.

Sed festival scenes were depicted in three places in Niuserre's sun temple (fig. 125). One series was carved on the walls of the corridor that led from the sanctuary's entrance and along its enclosure wall to the platform with the obelisk, the temple's central cult object. Another set was placed in the passage that ascended to the obelisk platform. Only relatively small fragments of these two groups are preserved.[2] Considerably more remains of the reliefs from a chapel (fig. 125) that was situated parallel to the Room of the Seasons (see entries for cat. nos. 119, 120). It is from this third group that the Munich blocks derive. These reliefs show the moment in the Heb Sed proceedings at which the king, who has undergone various rites indoors, appears in the open for the first time and, clothed in the characteristic short Heb Sed cloak, sits upon the double throne.[3]

b

To correctly understand the narrative of the Munich reliefs it is necessary to be aware that they present only a portion of a series of scenes in which the figure of the king was repeated at regular intervals. The figure of the enthroned pharaoh preserved on the left block belongs to the scene on the block adjoining at the left. Only the four men in the lower register who turn left are connected with this image of the king. Most of the other attendants turn their attention to the now-missing enthroned king on the adjoining block on the right. This clarified, we can proceed to describe some of the scenes in detail. In the upper register a row of standards bearing sacred emblems is carried toward the missing king on the right. The inscription in front of the standards calls them "followers of Horus (god of kingship)," an ancient name for the pharaoh's divine entourage. Appearing four times at the head of the procession are the standards of Wepwawet, literally the "Way Opener," who appears in the form of a jackal. The image is followed by two falcon standards and other emblems that are as yet unexplained.

Marching at the end of the procession is a man whom the inscription identifies as a representative of Heliopolis, the sacred city of the sun god just north of the capital, Memphis. Near the throne on the right are the remains of another inscription.

A highly dramatic action takes place in the middle register. Three "great ones," or chiefs, have prostrated themselves in front of a Wepwawet standard, which is surrounded by warlike symbols, namely a bow and an archer's equipment. Behind them a man, called a "ramherd" in the inscription, raises a twisted magical instrument or amulet. The prostrate chiefs are confronted by two officials with crooked staves and scepters.[4] The second official appears to approach in haste,[5] while the first raises his scepter and cries "Back." To whom this imperious injunction is directed is unclear: it is probably the prostrate chiefs who are ordered to keep back, and it may be this command that has induced them to fall flat on their faces. At the right edge, separated from the other figures by a vertical line, stood two priests (only one is preserved)

accompanied by an inscription that reads "Recitation: hurry! hurry!" Of the attendants in the lower register one man, who faces right below the ramherd, is preserved; the inscriptions here read "going round" and "sitting down," doubtless a description of ritual performances of some kind. The men shown below the preserved figure of the king on his throne are, from left to right, a "[lector] priest," according to the partially preserved inscription, followed by a standard-bearer; the "master of largesse," identified in another inscription; the king's sandal bearer; and a person who holds above his head a symbol of Min, the Upper Egyptian vegetation god (see entry for cat. no. 176). Kaiser, who has made the most thorough study of the Heb Sed representations, maintains that the inclusion of this emblem indicates that the king will visit a Min sanctuary in a ritual depicted on the block adjoining to the left.[6]

The relief of the Niuserre Heb Sed representations is wafer thin, and their paint is now completely gone. Although much of the effect of these scenes must have depended on their now-vanished colors, these pieces still convey a sense of the highly developed ancient Egyptian art of narrative description of rituals. Most striking in the present images is the intensity with which all attendants are shown to perform their tasks and the isolation, even loneliness, of the pharaoh on his throne.   DOA

1. Martin 1984, cols. 782–90, with earlier bibliography.
2. Bissing and Kees 1928.
3. Kaiser 1971, pp. 94, 96, offering many reinterpretations of the earlier analyses of Bissing and Kees 1928, p. 5.
4. See Kaplony 1986, cols. 1376, 1386 n. 66.
5. See Bissing and Kees 1922, p. 81.
6. Kaiser 1971, p. 95. The emblem is not discussed in McFarlane 1995; see, however, ibid., p. 76.

PROVENANCE: Abu Ghurab, sun temple of Niuserre, Heb Sed chapel (fig. 125), Borchardt and Schäfer excavation for Königliche Museen, Berlin, 1898–1901

BIBLIOGRAPHY: Bissing and Kees 1923, pl. 11; Kaiser 1967, p. 25, no. 226 (on loan from Munich); Grimm, Schoske, and Wildung 1997, pp. 120–21, no. 91 (right block)

122. STARVING BEDOUIN

Fifth Dynasty, reign of Unis
Limestone with faint remains of paint
H. 38 cm (15 in.); w. 20 cm (7⅞ in.); d. 1.4 cm
(⅝ in.)
Musée du Louvre, Paris E 17381

This fragment of a relief, original in its
theme and the vividness of its treatment,
attests that on occasion the Egyptian artist
did not hesitate to abandon his habitual
serenity in favor of a dramatic style. Emaciated bedouin are shown on different registers of the relief. The plain, wide band at
top indicates it is the upper part of the scene
that has been preserved. All that remains
here are two prostrate, shockingly thin men.
The sculptor was able to render with striking realism the tragedy of starvation: flesh-
less clavicles, sunken shoulders, torso scored
with a series of parallel lines that suggest
protruding ribs, and shrunken waists and
bellies. The two unfortunate individuals no
longer have the strength to stand; they are
seated, legs bent in front of them. The figure depicted on the upper register extends
his hand to the left, perhaps to offer help to
another starving man; only the feet of the
latter are still visible. On the lower register
an arched back with horribly protruding
vertebrae can be made out at far right; the
remnants of yellow paint, traditionally used
to indicate female skin color, suggest this is
a woman.

The scene is difficult to interpret, since
we lack a text and since until recently the
only point of comparison was a scene on a
block also from the causeway of Unis.[1] We
now know, however, that there is an older
example. Very recently, a joint mission of
the universities of Giza and Prague uncovered a block bearing a similar decoration
among the reliefs from the funerary complex of King Sahure at Abusir.[2] The unusual
hairstyle of the figures and, on the Cairo
fragment, the fringe of beard along the jaw-
lines of the old men seem to indicate these
are not Egyptians but bedouin living in the
Eastern Desert on the border of Egypt.
According to the most commonly accepted
hypothesis, the theme illustrates the generosity of the sovereign coming to aid desti-
tute populations.[3] The relief from Abusir,
which mentions the pyramidion atop the
pharaoh's tomb, suggests another interpretation, however: the scene may evoke the
difficulties encountered by Egyptians in

finding the most suitable stones for building.
During their quest for construction materials, they may have been forced to venture
into inhospitable deserts, traveled exclusively
by half-starved bedouin.   CZ

1. Drioton 1943, pp. 45–54.
2. Hawass and Verner 1996, pp. 184–85.
3. Vercoutter 1985, pp. 327–37.

PROVENANCE: Saqqara, causeway of pyramid of
Unis; purchased 1949

BIBLIOGRAPHY: Vandier 1950, pp. 27, 28, fig. 4;
Keimer 1957, pp. 116, 117; S. Schott 1965, pp. 7–
13; Amiet 1967, no. 72; Leclant et al. 1978, p. 147,
figs. 146, 147; Porter and Moss 1978, p. 420; Vercoutter 1985, p. 329, n. 16; Málek 1986, p. 121;
Ziegler 1990b, pp. 48–49, no. 2; Hart 1991, p. 200;
Hawass and Verner 1996, p. 180, n. 33; Andreu,
Rutschowskaya, and Ziegler 1997, pp. 66, 251,
no. 19; Bianchi 1997, p. 37, n. 27

123. Jar Inscribed with the Name of King Unis

Fifth Dynasty, reign of Unis
Egyptian alabaster
H. 17 cm (6¾ in.); diam. 13.2 cm (5¼ in.);
diam., neck 4.7 cm (1⅞ in.); w., cartouche 3.9 cm
(1⅝ in.)
Musée du Louvre, Paris E 32372

Old Kingdom jars with incised decoration are rare. The images and inscriptions on this large, globular receptacle are displayed in two symmetrical groups on the belly. Exploiting the characteristic qualities of the stone, the artist centered the principal images over especially translucent areas. On one side "King of Upper and Lower Egypt" is written above the name Unis, which appears inside a cartouche imitating a knotted double cord. The inscription includes not only the royal name, accompanied by a short protective formula as on traditional models, but in addition symbolic images that are also written signs. On either side of the royal name, two ankh signs, rendered in a naturalistic manner, give the sovereign the guarantee of eternal life. They are presented by two cobras, hoods spread, which are linked to the bird depicted on the back: a falcon with spread wings.

The entire decoration can be read as a promise of renewed life granted to King Unis by Horus, the falcon god, through the mediation of the two solar cobras. It was an artistic vocabulary familiar in later periods: for example, it is found in jewelry from the Middle Kingdom, with a similar placement of the ankh sign. It is very rare on objects from the Old Kingdom.

Although this jar is remarkable for its dimensions and the artistic play among text, form, and material, it can be assigned to a little-known group of decorated vases dating to the end of the Fifth Dynasty and the Sixth Dynasty. Those most like it have been found in the necropolis of Edfu. On the belly of one, inscribed with the name of King Teti, is a decoration of two birds, missing their heads, with outstretched wings, and the bottom is inscribed with a lotus in bloom. The other jar comes from the tomb of the nomarch Izi, whose career ended in the time of King Teti: its incised decoration includes two uraei, separated by a vertical ankh sign. Two fragments uncovered in Byblos (present-day Jabayl) bear the name of Unis, inscribed horizontally and surmounted by

a falcon's wing, which the excavator of the object identified as a winged disk. Finally, a jar made of an ostrich egg with a falcon decoration has just been discovered in the Dakhla Oasis, at Balat. There is no doubt that, like other precious objects with royal inscriptions (see cat. nos. 178–180), this was a gift from the pharaoh. CZ

PROVENANCE: Unknown; acquired at auction, Hôtel Drouot, Paris, December 7, 1995, lot 226

BIBLIOGRAPHY: Ziegler 1996, p. 88; Ziegler 1997b, pp. 461–89, figs. 2–4

124. KAI SEATED

Probably early Fifth Dynasty
Painted limestone with inlaid eyes of rock crystal, calcite, and magnesite mounted in copper cells
H. 77 cm (30⅜ in.); w. 34 cm (13⅜ in.); d. 52 cm (20½ in.)
Musée du Louvre, Paris N 117 (= E 3024 = A 106)

Scholars have long believed that the famous Scribe in the Louvre (fig. 33), which bears no inscription, is another representation of the man named Kai seen here, although there was no evidence for this attribution except that the eyes in both works are inlaid. Recent analyses show that the two sets of eyes were executed using the same technique and in both cases are held in place by large copper cells, whose visible flat edge outlines the eye like a cosmetic band. Each eye is composed of a chunk of white stone for the sclera, into which is inserted a crystal iris, perforated at the back. It is this complex structure, partly reproducing the actual anatomy of the human eye, that gives such a lifelike appearance to the faces; moreover, in both pairs of eyes the pupils are slightly off center in the irises, as are the irises in the scleras, and this irregularity makes the eyes seem to be constantly in motion.

The vizier Kai was a very high official who probably lived in the early part of the Fifth Dynasty; his tomb, containing this statue, was discovered by the French archaeologist Auguste Mariette.[1] Kai began his career as Administrator of the Jackal and rose to occupy the most coveted post in the land—that of vizier, whose powers can be compared to those of a prime minister. Kai's importance explains the high quality of this statue, which has retained some of its paint: on the body red—the conventional color for a man's skin; black for the wig, necklace, hieroglyphs, and negative spaces; white for the kilt; and blue for the broad collar.

Kai is depicted sitting on a cubic seat whose high back rises almost to the top of his head; on the right side of the seat, a column of hieroglyphs is inscribed, giving his mother's name, his name, and their titles: "Royal Acquaintance, Mesehet; her son, Administrator of the Jackal, Kai." On the front of the seat, illegible traces of two other columns of writing are visible, painted on either side of Kai's legs and feet.

Kai is dressed in a kilt with pleated side panel, fastened with a belt knotted horizontally. On his chest he wears a broad collar with several blue and black rows that are still visible in outline. The man's legs are parallel, and he sits with his arms at his sides and hands on his knees, the right palm down, the left in an upright fist, holding a folded cloth. The face is framed by a round wig that conceals the ears and follows the curves of the cheeks; the curls, separated by grooves, are arranged in circular tiers whose common center is marked by a large rosette at the top of the head. The face is broad with pointed chin and rounded cheeks. The eyes are large, and the eyebrows are indicated by a band in very low relief that follows the curve of the eye and tapers at the temple. The nose is thin. The philtrum is marked, and furrows border the cheeks.

The full mouth is precisely outlined, with no clear median notch in the upper lip. The neck is short. There is a very slight depression that indicates the clavicles. The torso is broad and flat, with high pectorals and no nipples; the fold of the armpit extends onto the arm. The deep, circular hollow of the navel is inserted into the flat abdomen; a vertical furrow runs above it. The waist is nipped in and the hips are flat. The rectilinear pleats of the kilt are triangular in cross section. The musculature of the arms at shoulder level is shown, and the muscles of the forearms are elegantly rendered as a triangular structure on the inside of the arm. The elbows are well modeled. The hands are flat with very long fingers and barely delineated nails around the cuticle. The legs, planted slightly apart, are relatively slender despite their thick ankles; the muscles of the calves are rendered with a very smooth indentation; and the ridges of the tibia and knees are subtly modeled. In spite of their massiveness, the feet display subtle details: anklebones, thin, supple toes, and tapering almond-shaped nails.

The statue is remarkable for its large size and for the vividness of the gaze, attributable to the skillfully inlaid eyes that give life to the otherwise impersonal physiognomy.

CZ

1. Porter and Moss 1978, p. 479, n. 63, pl. [46]. Inscriptions on two altars from the same tomb give the title Administrator of the Jackal, but not the title of vizier (Borchardt CGC 1299 and 1303).

Detail, cat. no. 124

PROVENANCE: Saqqara, north of avenue of sphinxes in the Serapeum, Mariette excavation; discovered November 1850; gift of the Egyptian Government as part of the division of finds, 1854

BIBLIOGRAPHY: Capart 1902, pls. 6, 7; Capart 1921, pp. 186–90, pl. 31; *Encyclopédie photographique* 1935, pls. 32, 33; Ranke 1935, p. 164; Reisner 1936, pp. 402–3, study no. 54; Capart 1942, vol. 2, pp. 217, 244; Cerny 1943, p. 346; Smith 1946, p. 47; Harris 1955, pp. 122–23; Vandier 1958, pp. 66, 122, 124, pl. 19.6; Du Bourguet and Drioton 1965, p. 133; Vandier 1974, p. 162, n. 1; Leclant et al. 1978, p. 289, fig. 308; Porter and Moss 1978, p. 458; *Rites de l'éternité* 1982, no. 51; Vandersleyen 1983, pp. 62, 63; Bolshakov 1990, p. 106b; Ziegler 1997a, pp. 104–8, no. 29

125. PAIR STATUE OF DEMEDJI AND HENUTSEN

First half of Fifth Dynasty
Limestone with remains of paint
H. 83 cm (32⅛ in.); w. 50.8 cm (20 in.); d. 51 cm
(20⅛ in.)
The Metropolitan Museum of Art, New York,
Rogers Fund, 1951 51.37

Demedji was Overseer of the Desert, Overseer of the King's Hunters, and Herdsman of the King's Flocks. His wife, the Royal Acquaintance Henutsen, was priestess of the goddesses Hathor and Neith. The couple's pair statue was dedicated by a son, Ti, who was senior administrator, Chief of the Tens of the South, Master of Secrets, and Overseer of Marshes. It is possible that he was the same Ti who owned a well-known tomb at Saqqara.[1] If so, it is possible that Demedji's tomb was also located there.[2]

Demedji sits on a block seat with no back support. His upper body is carved in the round, except for the arms, which are attached to his torso. Details of his kilt have been exceptionally well executed. The wraparound flap was carved with sharply creased fan pleats that are crosshatched to indicate double pleating, and the lip of cloth pulled up from behind his tied belt is also pleated. His body is well proportioned, but there is somewhat less definition in the modeling of torso and legs than, for example, in the statue of Memi and Sabu (cat. no. 84). This is partly due to the rougher surface of the stone, which is of lesser quality and shows marked deterioration in places.

Henutsen stands to her husband's left. Their arms touch, but there is no other physical contact. She is supported by a narrow back pillar to midshoulder height.

Detail, cat. no. 125

The negative space between her arms and torso is filled with a layer of stone so thin that it has been breached at a point between her right elbow and waist, leaving a small hole. Her hands do not hug the curve of her body, but hang straight at her sides, supported by a ridge of stone about two centimeters thick. The contours of her body are visible beneath her sheath dress, and at first glance she appears to be well proportioned. However, her head and neck are offset slightly to her right, and her arms are unnaturally long, the fingers reaching nearly to the level of her knees. Her fingernails and toenails are carefully carved and slightly rounded.

Henutsen's coiffure is unusually intricate. The interior locks of the wig—those closest to her cheeks—twist inward, toward her face. The outer layer of locks twist away from her face in a pattern that continues around her head. However, instead of meeting at the back of her head, the opposing locks meet just behind her right shoulder. A fairly distinct part creases the top of her wig, and there is no indication of the natural hairline along her forehead.

The faces of the man and his wife, although on different scales, are quite similar. The browridges are more deeply modeled near the nose and above the outer corners of the eyes, but they blend into the eyelids. The mouths are sharply delineated, with full lower lips and clearly defined philtrums that create distinct notches in the upper lips.

This statue was originally dated to the second half of the Fifth Dynasty;[3] however, if the couple's son is, in fact, the famous Ti of Saqqara, it must have been made in the first half of the dynasty. Even if one discounts this relationship, several features argue in favor of an earlier date. Demedji's wig hangs down to his shoulders, reinforcing his neck, a device that seems to disappear in the reign of Niuserre.[4] While the distinctly subordinate position of the unnaturally small Henutsen may argue for a date in the Fifth Dynasty, the intricate detailing of her coiffure, the absence of cosmetic lines around the eyes and brows, and the exquisitely delineated upper lips suggest an early date in this dynasty, as does the resemblance of Demedji's profile to that of Userkaf, the dynasty's first king.

CHR

125

1. This was suggested in N. Scott 1952, pp. 116–17. The Ti buried at Saqqara shared some titles with Demedji's son, and an inscription in Ti's tomb mentions a son named Demedji.
2. Unfortunately, a neutron-activation study of limestone objects including this statue could conclusively establish the origin of the stone by region but not by site; see Myers and Van Zelst 1977.
3. N. Scott 1952, p. 116. This is odd, since Scott herself suggests that Demedji was the father of Ti, who served Niuserre, a king whose reign ended at the midpoint of the Fifth Dynasty.
4. Cherpion 1998. The profile of Demedji's wig is similar to those of Ni-ankh-re's (ibid., fig. 28) and Ka-em-heset's (ibid., fig. 17), although it has a slightly sharper angle at the temples.

PROVENANCE: Unknown

BIBLIOGRAPHY: N. Scott 1952, pp. 116–19, ills.; Porter and Moss 1979, p. 729

126. FAMILY GROUP

Fifth Dynasty, probably first half
Limestone with remains of paint
H. 73.5 cm (29 in.); w. 23 cm (9 in.); d. 25 cm
(9⅞ in.)
Brooklyn Museum of Art, Charles Edwin Wilbour
Fund 37.17E

Although the group is uninscribed, it was
said to come from the same tomb as a
number of offering stands bearing the name
and various titles of Iru-ka-ptah and thus
would probably represent that official and
his family.

The tomb owner stands with hands
clenched at his sides and left leg advanced.
On the base beside that leg sits a woman, presumably his wife, carved at a much smaller
scale than the man; her legs are tucked under
her to her left, her left hand touches his shin,
and her right arm is wrapped around his leg.
Beside his right leg stands his small, naked
son, who wears the sidelock of youth and
holds his forefinger to his mouth.

The owner's large, helmetlike wig and
somber expression contrast pleasingly with
his almost childishly round cheeks and chin.
His figure is skillfully modeled, considerable
attention having been given to the structure
of the muscles and bones of the arms and
legs and to fine details such as the meeting
of the collarbones at the base of the neck
and the upcurving forefingers of the fists.

The wife's form is less modeled, but her
small face with its faintly clouded expression holds the attention of the viewer; the
child is not as distinctively rendered as
either of his parents.

The striking disposition of this family
group, with the smaller figures flanking the
legs of the standing man, is not very frequently used—perhaps because, although it
is formally very attractive, the disparities of
scale and pose are cumulatively jarring.[1]

The form of the owner's hairstyle points
to a date in the Fifth Dynasty, and that
of the woman's would suggest a limit not
much later than the reign of Niuserre;[2] the
plump yet delicate features of the owner
are certainly not out of place in the first
half of the same dynasty.[3]   M H

1. Most similar are two works in the Egyptian
   Museum, Cairo (CG 37 [Fay 1998, fig. 15] and
   CG 62)—both, by their appearance, Fifth
   Dynasty works from Saqqara. Vandersleyen
   (1973, pp. 14–15) discusses the formal aspects
   of family groupings.
2. Cherpion 1998, pp. 105, 120–21 (the man),
   116 (the woman).
3. Compare the statue of Neferefre in Saleh and
   Sourouzian 1987, no. 38.

PROVENANCE: Said to be from Saqqara

BIBLIOGRAPHY: Cooney 1952, pp. 10–15;
Porter and Moss 1979, pp. 691–92

FOUR STATUES OF THE GRANARY SCRIBE NI-KA-RE

The location of the tomb of Ni-ka-re is unknown, but most probably it was at Saqqara, perhaps in an area south of the Step Pyramid of Djoser that was explored and then covered with rubble.[1] Four of the statues from the tomb were acquired early in the twentieth century by different collectors (cat. nos. 127–130), and during the same period some blocks from the mastaba appeared on the art market.[2] On them were carved the titles Priest of Re in the Sun Temple of King Niuserre and Priest of Kings Sahure and Niuserre;[3] they indicate that Ni-ka-re's career was contemporary with or followed the reign of the Fifth Dynasty sovereign Niuserre. Ni-ka-re's principal occupation was related to the royal granary, and it is mentioned on all the documents concerning him that he was Chief of the Granary or Overseer of Granary Scribes.

Two reliefs in the Cleveland Museum of Art (64.91) show Ni-ka-re standing, accompanied by his eldest son, Ankh-ma-re, Chief of the Granary. Among Ni-ka-re's numerous titles, four names of Fifth Dynasty kings appear: Sahure, Neferirkare, Neferefre, and Niuserre.[4] Sculpted in limestone highlighted with red, the two symmetrical reliefs are executed with great simplicity.[5]

The four surviving statues differ in size, material, theme, and level of sculptural refinement. The temporary grouping of these relatively accurately dated works in this exhibition thus illustrates the diversity of nonroyal art from the Fifth Dynasty, immortalizing the deceased in a multiplicity of ways.   CZ

1. N. Scott 1952, p. 118; Spanel 1988, p. 53.
2. Cooney 1952, p. 8.
3. N. Scott 1952, p. 119.
4. Andreu 1997, p. 24.
5. Ibid., pp. 21–30.

127. NI-KA-RE, HIS WIFE, AND THEIR SON

Fifth Dynasty, reign of Niuserre or later
Painted limestone
H. 57.5 cm (22⅝ in.)
Brooklyn Museum of Art, Charles Edwin Wilbour Fund 49.215

This statue depicting Ni-ka-re between two members of his family is as fine in quality as the group sculpture of Ni-ka-re, his wife, and their daughter (cat. no. 130), although it is in a different style. Here Ni-ka-re is flanked by his wife, Khuen-nub, and his son Ankh-ma-re, both of whom are standing. Despite the different postures of the figures, the three heads are aligned; thus, the central

series of rosettes, perhaps stylized curls, is surmounted by horizontal grooves.[2] The modeling is precise, revealing arched eyebrows, the fold of the upper eyelid, the shape of the mouth, and the fleshy cheeks, which individualize the physiognomy. The very round and placid face is that of a young woman. Standing with her feet together and her left arm at her side, she wears a clinging, almost entirely sheer dress; only the V-shaped line of the bodice is visible. Although concealing certain anatomical details, the thin fabric reveals the curves of her high bosom, the vertical groove above the navel, the detail of the hipbone, and the pubic triangle.

By its symmetrical placement, the figure of Ankh-ma-re, who is also standing with feet together, establishes a balance, which is subtly broken by the movement of his right hand to his mouth, a gesture symbolizing childhood. Other conventional attributes of childhood are his nudity and the braided sidelock. The extensive modeling captures the chubbiness of a child's body—with its round belly and short arms. The plump face, made heart-shaped by the hairline, has a very individual quality, with its almond-shaped eyes, emphasized by a rim around the upper eyelid, arched eyebrows, short nose, and small mouth with dimples on either side. The contrast between the vividness of the secondary figures and the more conventional look of the central figure gives this group a very unusual charm, which the abundant remnants of red, yellow, and black paint reinforce.

In addition to the damage to Ni-ka-re's face, there are wide fractures in the base of this group.   cz

1. On the different proportions of the figures in the Ni-ka-re groups, see Vandersleyen 1973, pp. 13–25.
2. On this hairstyle, see Cherpion 1998, p. 117.

PROVENANCE: Probably Saqqara, south of precinct of Djoser

BIBLIOGRAPHY: *Brooklyn Museum Annual Report* 1949–50, ill. on p. 4; Brooklyn Museum 1952, no. 16; Cooney 1952, pp. 2–11; N. Scott 1952, ill. pp. 118, 120, 122; Vandier 1958, p. 82, pl. 31; Hornemann 1951–69, vol. 5 (1966), pl. 1412; Fischer 1973, p. 8, n. 8, fig. 9; James 1974, p. 13, no. 36, pl. 19; Aldred 1978, p. 197, fig. 194; Porter and Moss 1979, p. 697; Romano 1990, p. 4; Feucht 1995, p. 406, n. 2004

figure is almost twice as large as the others.[1] It is not his figure that attracts attention, whether because the secondary figures are proportionally bigger, or because Ni-ka-re's face has been damaged, or because the details of his body—for example, the pectorals— are rendered more schematically. Ni-ka-re wears a kilt with pleated side panel and knotted belt. A short, curly wig frames his

face. His cubic seat is set against a wide slab that preserves the form of the original block.

Wife and son embrace Ni-ka-re tenderly, but with a distinction suggested by the position of the hands, Khuen-nub's right hand on her husband's shoulder and Ankh-ma-re's left around his father's waist.

Khuen-nub wears a medium-length wig, parted in the center. Along her forehead a

128. Ni-ka-re Seated

Fifth Dynasty, reign of Niuserre or later
Red granite
H. 54 cm (21¼ in.)
The Cleveland Museum of Art, Leonard C. Hanna
Fund 1964.90

Ni-ka-re is depicted alone, sitting on a
backless cubic seat; on top of the base in
front, two columns of hieroglyphs are
inscribed with his title and name: "[Chief]
of Granaries, Ni-ka-re." He is dressed in a
simple kilt. His legs are parallel and his
arms are at his sides. His right hand grasps
an enigmatic object, and his left is flat on
his knee. The figure was carved from a
quadrangular block of stone, whose original shape is suggested by the base of the
seat. The face is framed by a short wig that
follows the curve of the cheeks and conceals the ears. The curls are arranged in
concentric rows separated by grooves.
Ni-ka-re has large eyes, and the upper lid is
emphasized with a slight fold, which ends
at the external corner; the shapes of the eye
and the iris were once highlighted in black
paint. The face, with its schematically
treated full mouth, short nose, and plump
cheeks, has an accentuated roundness.
The man's torso is slim, however, and flat,
with very high pectorals that are subtly
modeled. The muscles of the arm are barely
visible, except at shoulder level. The hands
are modeled schematically. The legs, treated
with simplicity, are stocky, and the ankles
are thick. A very shallow vertical groove
runs the length of the back, and there are
no shoulder blades. The compactness of the
statue and the paucity of details can be explained by the hardness of granite, a highly
prized stone, which the artist worked with
extremely simple tools (cat. nos. 74, 75).

CZ

PROVENANCE: Probably Saqqara, south of
precinct of Djoser

BIBLIOGRAPHY: *Art Quarterly* 27 (1964), ill.
p. 379; *Bulletin of the Cleveland Museum of Art*
51 (1964), ill. pp. 236–37, 263; Kozloff [1970],
pp. 4–5; Porter and Moss 1979, p. 697; Spanel
1988, pp. 52–53, no. 7, pl. 7

129. NI-KA-RE AS A SCRIBE

Fifth Dynasty, reign of Niuserre or later
Red granite with painted details
H. 31 cm (12¼ in.)
The Metropolitan Museum of Art, New York,
Rogers Fund, 1948 48.67

In this scribe statue Ni-ka-re is shown reading a long papyrus rolled at the ends. He is
sitting cross-legged on a semicircular base,
his left leg crossed over the right, as was
the custom.[1]

The edge of the papyrus stands out in
slight relief, and Ni-ka-re holds the ends
firmly as though lingering over his reading.
But the text is inscribed in such a way as
to be readable by the viewer, not the scribe.
It gives the identity of the figure: "Chief
of the Granary, Ni-ka-re."

Viewed from the front, the statue seems
to be inscribed within an isosceles triangle,
with the pedestal forming the base. A side
view reveals the attentive expression of the
reader, head bent over the text placed on
his raised knees. His square face has a low
forehead; his oblique eyes, like his eyebrows and fine mustache, are outlined in
black. The tip of the nose has broken off.
The wig, also highlighted in black, is different from that worn by Ni-ka-re in other
statues: it is flared, and the hair is divided
by a central part, leaving the earlobes uncovered. The forms of the body are ample,
and the arms are separated from the trunk
by a wide space, giving the illusion of
depth. On the legs, the musculature of the
right calf and the ridge of the tibia, which
are barely visible, are individualized. The
toes of the left foot, seen from the underside, are treated with extreme simplicity.

It is interesting to compare this representation of an important Fifth Dynasty
official with the oldest Egyptian scribe statues, sculpted for sons of kings during the
Fourth Dynasty. For example, the face of
Prince Setka has much more clearly individualized features, and the anatomical details
of his body are more richly satisfying (cat.

no. 55). Nonetheless, this statue of Ni-ka-re,
carefully executed in the very hard material
granite, is remarkable for the subject's
attentive expression (rare in Egyptian art)
and for the touches of black paint emphasizing the details, which have disappeared
from most other statues.   CZ

1. G. Scott 1989, vol. 1, p. 23.

PROVENANCE: Probably Saqqara, south of
precinct of Djoser; Benzion collection

BIBLIOGRAPHY: Hayes 1948, p. 61; Cooney
1952, pp. 7–9; Hayes 1953, p. 110; Vandier 1958,
pp. 69–71, 575; Metropolitan Museum 1962,
fig. 11; Porter and Moss 1979, p. 697; Hibbard
1980, p. 40, fig. 70; *Profil du Metropolitan
Museum* 1981; Spanel 1988, p. 53; G. Scott 1989,
vol. 1, pt. 2, pp. 56–57, no. 22

130. NI-KA-RE, HIS WIFE, AND THEIR DAUGHTER

Fifth Dynasty, reign of Niuserre or later
Painted limestone
H. 57 cm (22½ in.); w. 22.5 cm (8⅞ in.);
d. 32.5 cm (12¾ in.)
The Metropolitan Museum of Art, New York,
Rogers Fund, 1952 52.19

Painted in red, yellow, and black, this very fine limestone group depicts Ni-ka-re flanked by two members of his family, who are represented on a much smaller scale (their heads reach only to the top of his seat). At his left, Ni-ka-re's wife, Khuen-nub, is kneeling on the ground, her legs folded to the side in an attitude first adopted for royal couples in the Third Dynasty.[1] Turned slightly away from him, she is affectionately embracing Ni-ka-re's leg with her right arm (the left has been lost). Their daughter, Khuen-nebti, stands on the other side, making a gesture similar to her mother's with her left arm.[2] Like her mother's, Khuen-nebti's exterior arm has been damaged.

Ni-ka-re is seated on a cubic seat. He is dressed in a kilt with a pleated side panel. Only traces of the broad collar that once adorned his chest remain. His legs are parallel to each other and his arms are at his sides. With his right hand he grasps a cylindrical object; his left is flat on his knee. The figure was cut from a quadrangular block whose proportions were those of the base of the seat. The latter is unusually wide, supporting the two small figures. Ni-ka-re's short hair, which leaves the ears exposed, is treated as a series of concentric grooves, and the locks are not detailed. His face is broad, with round, high cheeks. The eyes are large, and the upper lid has a clearly delineated fold that ends at the outer corner. The lower lid forms a horizontal rim encasing the eyeball, which curves upward. The eyebrows are arched, with each indicated by a wide relief band that follows the curve of the eye and tapers to a point at the temple. The philtrum is prominent, and a shallow fold originating at the base of the nose delimits the cheek.

The full mouth with turned-up corners is precisely outlined, and the notch in the upper lip is clearly drawn. A slight depression indicating the clavicle appears under the necklace. The torso is thin and flat, with very high pectorals and nipples in relief. The semicircular navel has a vertical groove

above it. The musculature of the arm is visible at shoulder level, and it appears again in the forearms, rendered through a play of horizontal and vertical planes. The shape of the arm is explored in unusual detail, and the elegance of the artist's style is also notable in the full treatment of the thin wrist and the precisely shaped elbow. The hands are carefully modeled, even though the left one is shown flat on the knee. The closed legs are relatively slender despite their thick ankles; the inner musculature is rendered

with slight vertical grooves, which make the ridge of the tibia stand out. Although they are massive, the feet display subtle details, such as the delicate nails, the external curve of the foot pad, and the fine articulation of the toes and of the tendons just below the skin. The back, which does not rest against any support, is divided by a very slight vertical groove separating the shoulder blades. Finally, the notation of two very precise anatomical details shows how very careful was the treatment of the

Detail, cat. no. 130

body: the contracted deltoid muscles and the individualized seventh cervical vertebra, at the base of the neck.[3]

Despite their small size, the two female figures received just as much attention from the sculptor. The face of Khuen-nub, plump and friendly like Ni-ka-re's, is framed by a medium-length wig that is parted in the center. Her natural hair is treated as it is in the other Ni-ka-re family group (cat. no. 127). A plain dress clings to the woman's body, revealing with a certain refinement her broad chest, slender hips, and a rounded belly marked with a depression for the navel. The young girl is depicted in the conventional nudity of childhood, even though she has an adolescent's body. Her face, which is less well preserved than her body, is set off by a charming hairstyle, often seen in tomb decorations: the hair is gathered into a braided ponytail from which a disk is suspended.   CZ

1. For the Fourth Dynasty, the most famous example is the statue of Djedefre and his wife (Louvre, Paris, E 12627; see Ziegler 1997a, pp. 47–49, no. 3).
2. The group displays many similarities to the Sekhem-ka group (Louvre, Paris, N 116, probably of the same period; see ibid., pp. 134–38, no. 37).
3. Fischer 1965, pp. 171–72.

PROVENANCE: Probably Saqqara, south of precinct of Djoser

BIBLIOGRAPHY: N. Scott 1952, p. 116; Hayes 1953, frontis.; Fischer 1965, pp. 171–72, figs. 4, 5; *Masterpieces of Fifty Centuries* 1970, p. 82, no. 11; N. Scott 1973, p. 126, fig. 4; Fischer 1974, p. 8, n. 8; Fischer 1978, p. 90, n. 21, pl. 5B; Porter and Moss 1979, p. 697; Dorman, Harper, and Pittman 1987, p. 18; Spanel 1988, p. 53; Feucht 1995, p. 405

131. LADY HETEP-HERES STANDING

Fourth Dynasty, reign of Shepseskaf, or Fifth Dynasty, reign of Neferirkare
Limestone
H. 137 cm (54 in.)
Worcester Art Museum, Massachusetts, Museum purchase 1934.48

This splendid statue of a woman belonged to a five-figure family group carved from a single block of stone. After a meticulous investigation, John Cooney demonstrated that the statue came from a tomb in Giza, plundered in the distant past and later excavated by Selim Hassan, who published the decorated walls of the chapel and the many statues found in situ. In the serdab, Hassan discovered the pedestal of an unusually large group, which bore traces of five pairs of feet and the names of the subjects. It was clear that the left leg of the female figure standing at the right side of the pedestal was advanced—a very unusual feature, for a walking pose was ordinarily reserved for men. This figure, too, advances on the left leg, and it obviously occupied the right end of the pedestal since the left side of the figure is complete and the end of the missing right arm is resting on a back support. The subject is Lady Hetep-heres, mother of Ra-wer, the owner of the rich mastaba. An autobiographical inscription mentions an incident that brought him much honor: during the reign of Neferirkare, it recounts, the sovereign's scepter accidentally touched Ra-wer's leg.[1] Despite this evidence pointing to a Fifth Dynasty date, the age of the tomb is controversial: the inscription may have been incised on the external slab after the tomb was closed; it is the name of Shepseskaf, who reigned at the end of the Fourth Dynasty, that appears within.[2]

The statue of Ra-wer from the five-figure group is today in the Nelson-Atkins Museum of Art, Kansas City (38.11); that of his father is in the Brooklyn Museum (37.365); the two other figures, which are of children, have appeared on the art market. Originally, in its size and the disposition of its figures, the group was similar to that of Pen-meru in the Museum of Fine Arts, Boston (12.1484).

The accidental isolation of the large female statue and the disappearance of her head, feet, and right arm focus attention on the extraordinary modeling of the body. It conforms to the Old Kingdom canon: broad shoulders, round breasts, narrow hips, flat belly, and horizontal band delimiting the pelvic area. In accordance with custom, the subject is clothed in a long dress so sheer that its only line is at the hem.[3] The rare sensuality of the work, resulting from a subtle play between the subject's near nudity and the varying thickness of the garment, makes the sculpture one of the masterpieces of the period.   CZ

1. Hassan 1932, pp. 15, 18, pl. 18; Roccati 1982, pp. 101–2.
2. Cherpion 1989, p. 227, n. 376.
3. Tefnin 1987.

PROVENANCE: Giza, Central Field, tomb of Ra-wer

BIBLIOGRAPHY: Hassan 1932, pp. 1–61 (on the tomb); Smith 1946, pp. 42–43, pl. 16(a); Cooney 1949b, pp. 54–56, pl. 1; Porter and Moss 1974, pp. 265–67 (on the tomb), 267–68

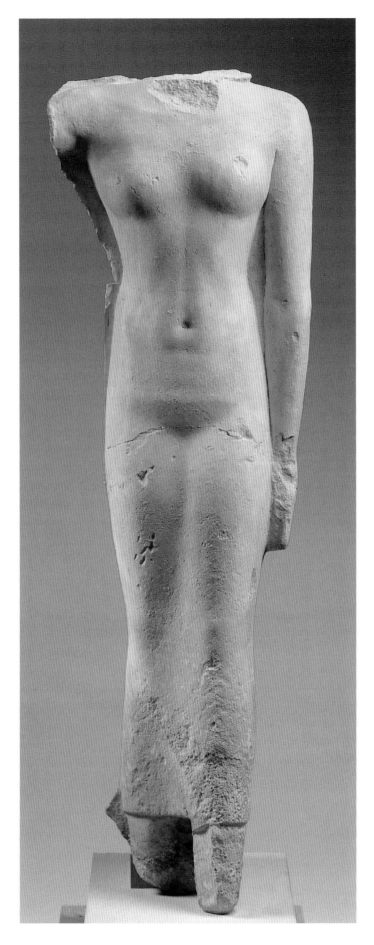

132. SEKED-KAW, HIS WIFE, AND THEIR SON

Fifth Dynasty, no later than reign of Niuserre
Painted limestone
H. 51 cm (20⅛ in.)
Egyptian Museum, Cairo CG 101

The charm of this pretty, rather simple statue is owed to the excellent state of preservation of the colors, which are of mineral origin, with the exception of the carbon-based black paint. The red and yellow skin tones; the black hair, details of the eyes, negative spaces, and pedestal; and the blue and green jewelry all contrast attractively with the pure white of the clothing.

This group, like many others from the Old Kingdom, represents a family. It immortalizes the image of the deceased tomb owner as paterfamilias, and by reuniting him with his wife and their son it allows him to continue the cycle of generations in the next world. Both parents are sitting on a high rectangular bench, their backs against a support that rises to mid-head height. On the front of the pedestal an inscription identifies the principal figure: "Overseer of the Sealed Documents, Seked-kaw." He is the subject of another statue in the Egyptian Museum, Cairo,[1] but his tomb has not been located. Their son is standing next to his mother, and as he is almost as tall as his seated father, he pleasingly balances the composition. The clothing traditionally worn in the Old Kingdom—a short kilt with pleated side panel for the men and a long, tight-fitting sheath with straps for the women—is highlighted here with painted details and accessories. Of particular interest are the stripes and concentric circles decorating the lady's dress straps, a pattern also found on a beautiful example of blue-beaded netting from Giza (cat. no. 94). All three subjects are wearing necklaces with several rows of beads: Seked-kaw's, with its small transverse bead spacers, is the most elaborate; his wife's consists of a choker combined with a broad collar. The adults are wearing wigs—a row of tight curls adorns the lady's forehead—and the boy has close-cropped hair.

Reflecting the custom of the time, it is the wife who expresses her affection: in a reserved but unambiguous gesture, she has extended her arm around her husband's shoulder, and she draws him to her by placing her right hand in the crook of his elbow. That particular token of affection,[2] as well as her hairstyle,[3] has made it possible to date the work to the first part of the Fifth Dynasty.   SL-T, CZ

1. CG 208; Borchardt 1911, p. 140.
2. Cherpion 1995, pp. 33–47, esp. p. 36.
3. Cherpion 1998, pp. 97–117, esp. p. 117.

PROVENANCE: Saqqara

BIBLIOGRAPHY: Borchardt 1911, pp. 79–80, pl. 63; Maspero 1915a, p. 73 (166); Ranke 1935, p. 321; Vandier 1958, pp. 79, 82, 111, 114, 119, pl. 29.2; Hornemann 1951–69, vol. 5 (1966), pl. 1376; Porter and Moss 1979, p. 724

133. Pair Statue of Ka-pu-ptah and Ipep Standing

Fifth Dynasty
Painted limestone
H. 56 cm (22 in.); w. 28 cm (11 in.); d. 22.3 cm
(8¾ in.)
Kunsthistorisches Museum, Ägyptisch-
Orientalische Sammlung, Vienna ÄS 7444

Hermann Junker uncovered the pair statue of Ka-pu-ptah and Ipep in 1912 while excavating in the vicinity of mastaba G 4460 in Giza's cemetery 4000. The statue was lying in debris inside the offering chapel of G 4461, one of numerous secondary tombs that gradually filled in the streets separating the great core mastabas of the nucleus cemeteries laid out during the reign of Khufu. The chapel was equipped with a serdab, but this had been broken into and the contents removed and reused or discarded.[1]

Ka-pu-ptah stands in the usual masculine striding pose, with his left leg advanced and his arms at his sides, but his left arm is held noticeably forward, in a manner similar to Iai-ib's in the pair statue that shows him (cat. no. 83). Iai-ib's left arm is pushed forward by his wife's body, which is directly behind it, but this is not the case with Ka-pu-ptah and Ipep, who stand slightly apart. Ipep's right arm is around Ka-pu-ptah's back and her hand is just visible curving around his waist. This traditional feminine gesture keeps her shoulders close to the back pillar, but her feet are set almost level with her companion's advanced left foot. As a result, Ipep leans back noticeably when seen from the side, unlike the standing women in other pair statues illustrated in this catalogue (cat. nos. 83, 84, 125). Although the back pillar rises above their shoulders, it is narrower than the width of the two figures, creating the illusion from the front that their bodies are more three-dimensional than is the case.

Ka-pu-ptah is only half a head taller than Ipep, a natural size difference between a man and woman. His body is well proportioned, but Ipep is very long waisted and has unusually short, slim legs, which makes her head seem unnaturally large. Ka-pu-ptah wears the standard short, curled wig and a short kilt that once had a pleated overlapping panel indicated in paint, only traces of which remain.[2] The knot of his belt has been carved in detail,

and the pleating of the flap of cloth pulled up behind the belt has been carved in relief. Ipep wears a shoulder-length wig of untextured locks that meet in a well-delineated part that extends to the back of her head, ending just above the back pillar, where the strands of hair meet in an inverted V. Her sheath dress reveals the shape of her body and clings especially tightly around her knees. In a photograph taken shortly after the statue was excavated, the straps of the dress are visible and it is clear that both figures wore broad collars.[3] The outline of Ka-pu-ptah's is still visible, and a small section of darkened green (perhaps blue) pigment, showing five rows of beads, is visible near his left shoulder. Substantial amounts of red paint are preserved on Ka-pu-ptah's body, and dark yellow paint remains on Ipep's left arm, feet, and ankles. Black paint is preserved on the wigs and on the base and back pillar.

The faces of both figures have been carefully modeled. The noses and crisply delineated mouths are similar, and the philtra are well defined. The large eyes of

both are rimmed along the upper lids, but Ka-pu-ptah's browridges are more sharply modeled than his companion's. Ipep's face is also rather pear shaped, with very full cheeks. In profile, Ka-pu-ptah's head and features are rounder than those of Ipep.

Junker dated mastaba G 4461 to the late Fifth Dynasty, but a date earlier in the dynasty is also possible.[4] Ka-pu-ptah's name appears in the inscriptions in his tomb chapel and on the base of this statue in front of his right foot. Ipep's name is inscribed next to her right foot. She is not mentioned in the tomb texts, and she may have been either Ka-pu-ptah's wife or his mother.   CHR

1. Junker 1943, p. 224.
2. Jaroš-Deckert and Rogge 1993, p. 26.
3. Junker 1943, pl. 22.
4. Ibid., p. 220; Harpur 1987, pp. 270, 317.

PROVENANCE: Giza, mastaba G 4461, Junker excavation, 1912

BIBLIOGRAPHY: Junker 1943, pp. 224–26, pl. 22, fig. 90; Porter and Moss 1974, p. 129; Seipel 1992, pp. 124–25; Jaroš-Deckert and Rogge 1993, pp. 26–31, with earlier bibliography

134. SCRIBE

Fifth Dynasty
Painted limestone
H. 49 cm (19⅜ in.)
Egyptian Museum, Cairo CG 78

Like Setka (cat. no. 55), this very handsome scribe is seated on the ground in the
traditional pose of the high official reading:
head slightly bent, one hand about to unroll
the papyrus scroll, the other hand at rest.
He is dressed in a simple, immaculately
white kilt knotted below the navel and is
wearing a broad collar, whose silhouette
is set off by his red skin. Unfortunately, the
blue and green colors and touches of white
that enlivened the rows of beads have partly
disappeared. The flaring black wig with
meticulously crafted striated locks frames
a rather heavy face, leaving the earlobes
exposed. The stocky body with large round
forms was sculpted separately from the semicircular base, and the two parts were assembled with a piece of wood forming a dovetail
joint. The spaces between the torso and the
arms are painted black. The anatomical
details—the lashes, eyebrows, and pupils,
the nostrils, a fine mustache darkening the
upper lip, and the nipples—are carefully
indicated with strokes of dark paint. A dark
brown stroke outlines the kilt and belt.

Because there is no inscription, we do not
know the name or title of this man, but the
statue is stylistically similar to Fifth Dynasty
works. In 1911 Ludwig Borchardt was able
to discern columns of hieroglyphs—unfortunately illegible—traced in black on the
yellow papyrus.   SL-T,CZ

PROVENANCE: Saqqara

BIBLIOGRAPHY: Borchardt 1911, pp. 63–64,
pl. 18; Vandier 1958, pp. 69–70, 72, 103, 112,
134, pl. 23.3; 5000 ans 1960, p. 22 (13), fig. 14;
Porter and Moss 1979, p. 724; G. Scott 1989,
no. 28

135. SNEFRU-NEFER STANDING

Late Fifth Dynasty[1]
Painted limestone
H. 78 cm (30¾ in.); w. 23.7 cm (9⅜ in.);
d. 28.5 cm (11¼ in.)
Kunsthistorisches Museum Ägyptisch-
Orientalische Sammlung, Vienna Äs 7506

Snefru-nefer is depicted nude, his back against a support, which has suffered damage from top to bottom. His left leg advances in the customary pose for male figures, and both arms are at his sides, a cylindrical object clasped in each fist. Rigid and strictly frontal, the compact and muscular body exudes strength. Although it is usually children (cat. no. 80) and adolescents (cat. no. 188) who are shown unclothed, here the subject is an adult depicted nude, probably as an entreaty to be born again in the next world.[2] Yet Snefru-nefer has kept his ornaments: a broad collar, or *wesekh*, and a pendant hanging on his chest from a long strand of beads.

Snefru-nefer wears no wig. His full face is accentuated by his own short hair, outlined by the incision marking the hairline and once painted black. The forehead is low and the large eyes are surmounted by sinuous eyebrows in sharp relief. The upper lids are rimmed, and an incision sets off the inner corners. The subject's nose is short and round. The mouth—wide and full beneath a well-defined philtrum—is outlined by a chisel mark and cut deeply in at the corners. The very short neck rests on broad shoulders. Like the muscles of the arms and legs, Snefru-nefer's pectoral muscles are clearly marked. Particular attention has been given to small anatomical details: the cuticles are indicated on the oval nails, and the notch characteristic of circumcision appears on the penis.[3]

An inscription carved in sunk relief on the pedestal identifies the subject: "honored by the great god, Overseer of Palace Singers, Snefru-nefer." Texts inscribed in the tomb where the statue was found give a second title, Overseer of Entertainments. The professional activities represented by these titles, which may seem frivolous, were, in fact, entrusted to high-ranking individuals. Old Kingdom records preserve the names of several of these artists and teachers— among them Khufu-ankh, not only Overseer of Palace Singers but also Chief of Flutists, to whom the pharaoh gave a funerary monument.[4] Two other Overseers of Palace Singers are known. They, too, were named Snefru-nefer, which suggests the existence of a dynasty of court musicians transmitting their duties from father to son, like the Couperins in seventeenth- and eighteenth-century France. The decoration of their tombs and the solicitude shown them by sovereigns attest to their importance, as do the size and remarkably high quality of this sculpture.   CZ

1. Jaroš-Deckert and Rogge 1993, p. 55. The date is suggested by the type of pendant Snefru-nefer wears and the shape of the seat depicted on the architrave of the tomb from which the statue comes.
2. On these statues, see Junker 1944, p. 40 (eighteen examples are listed); and Schulz 1999.
3. De Wit 1972, pp. 41–48, fig. 4.
4. Hickmann 1952, pp. 79–101; Manniche 1991, pp. 120–22.

PROVENANCE: Giza, Western Cemetery, serdab of tomb of Snefru-nefer, Junker excavation, 1913

BIBLIOGRAPHY: Smith 1946, p. 73; Porter and Moss 1974, p. 146; Seipel 1992, pp. 106–7, no. 18; Jaroš-Deckert and Rogge 1993, pp. 15, 54–60; Seipel 1993, pp. 80–81, no. 35; Satzinger 1994, pp. 113–14, fig. 79

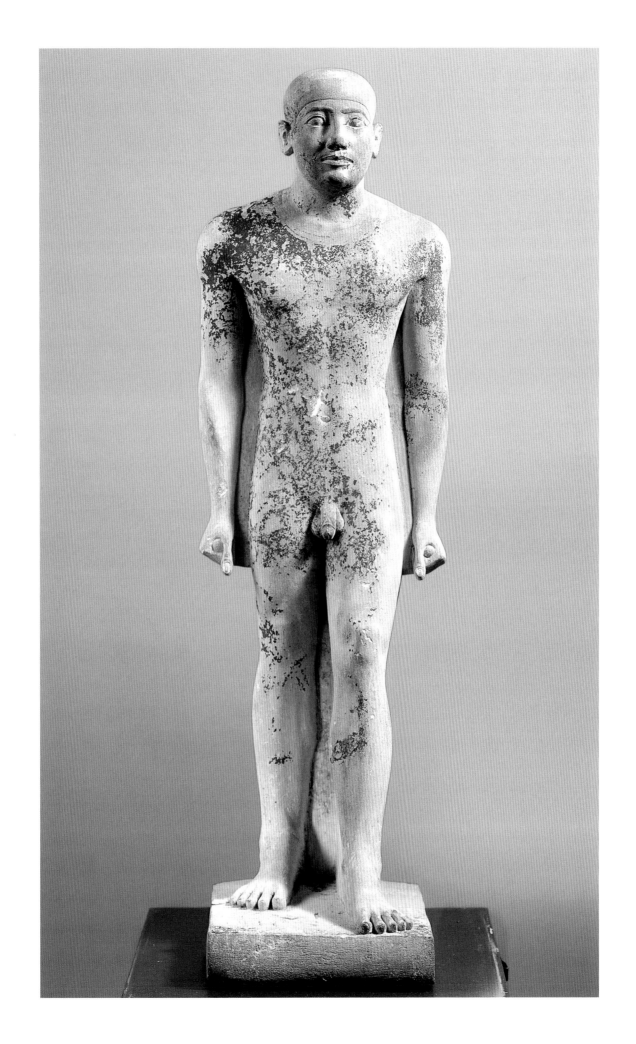

NOTE ON THE DATING OF CERTAIN STONE SERVING STATUETTES[1]

Recent studies of datable features of the Old Kingdom mastabas and tombs at Giza make it feasible to begin to establish groups and suggest phases in the development of at least the Giza stone serving statuettes.[2]

GROUP A

The earliest such figures with datable contexts were found in the Giza burials of two Fourth Dynasty queens whose funerary equipment must date to the late Fourth or early Fifth Dynasty. Three headless statuettes were discovered in the debris of the main chamber of the tomb of Mer-si-ankh, the granddaughter of Khufu, who was probably married to Khafre and who appears to have died in the second year of the reign of an unnamed king, perhaps Menkaure. These figures—a brewer, a butcher, and a woman holding a sifting basket—originally measured between 22 and 28 centimeters in height, and all had back supports and substantial bases. In the tomb of Kha-merer-nebti II, a queen (perhaps of Menkaure) and the mother of Prince Khuen-re, were found fragments of two female millers—all millers seem to be women—and of a figure pounding a round, flat bread.[3]

A third tomb with an early serving statuette may be that of Tep-em-ankh, which has been dated by Cherpion to the time of Khufu, although some criteria suggest it may be as late as the reign of Isesi. Resting on a substantial rectangular base, Tep-em-ankh's miller has an unusually positioned thrown-back head with proportional features, small, schematic ears, and a bulging headcloth tied with an uncommon low-relief knot.[4]

GROUP B

A number of serving statuettes can be dated within a restricted chronological range, extending from a point probably in the early Fifth Dynasty through the mid-Fifth Dynasty, on the basis of stylistic datings for reliefs in the tombs in which they originate.

Two tombs at Giza that produced statuettes, those of Ni-wedja-ptah[5] and Mer-su-ankh,[6] are dated by Cherpion at the latest to the reign of Niuserre or not long after; the tomb of Weri and Meti[7] and that of Medu-nefer[8] would seem to be similarly datable. Ni-wedja-ptah's miller (22 centimeters high) has a proportional head and features with small ears, the forward gaze that becomes standard (although occasionally varied by a turned-down gaze; see entry for cat. no. 136), and a substantial rectangular base. Although rather crude and with large shoulders and arms, Mer-su-ankh's female brewer (28 centimeters high) has a proportional head and features. Weri and Meti's tomb yielded a female baker (23.8 centimeters high) and a very fine large female miller (28.2 centimeters high), with heads that are perhaps slightly large but with proportional features and substantial bases. Two female millers (16.5 and 17 centimeters high) found in an area between the tombs of Medu-nefer and Sed-hotep, and probably from one of them, have large heads, features, and ears, odd, thin bases, and—for the first time in this listing—one foot crossed over the other.

GROUP C

A third group seems to date near Group B but probably can be assigned to a narrower time range and brings a complex of new features into relief.

The tomb of Ka-khent, which produced serving statuettes, offers a fairly firm date to the period of Niuserre since it occurs in a cluster of tombs thoroughly studied by Ann Macy Roth;[9] a shaft in the tomb of Ankh-haf, datable to the reign of Djedkare-Isesi or later, also yielded a relevant fragment.[10] Found in Ka-khent's tomb were a number of fragments of statuettes, including two millers, a double statuette of women pounding grain and sifting, brewers, a figure lifting a table, a partially nude male carrying jars, and a man cutting up a goose. A number of these pieces bore names, some seemingly of persons in the tomb or in adjacent tombs forming part of the analyzed complex. The heads and features appear proportional to slightly large, and the sizes of the figures are in the range of those previously discussed. Other, very fragmentary statuettes were associated with slightly later tombs in the same complex. The small (10-centimeters-high) limestone head from shaft 637 of Ankh-haf's tomb, while possibly somewhat larger than most of the examples already discussed, offers stylistic similarities to many of the heads of Ni-kau-inpu's and Djasha's serving statuettes (cat. nos. 137–143).

The foregoing data seem to indicate that the use of serving statuettes is first datable to a period ranging from the last third of the Fourth Dynasty to the very early Fifth Dynasty and that by the middle of the Fifth Dynasty there is a great expansion in their number and type. In chronological terms the groups may actually overlap considerably: for example, it is obvious that the statuettes of Medu-nefer in Group B are stylistically related to statuettes in Group C.

As for the serving statuettes in the exhibition, the Berkeley miller (cat. no. 136) does not closely parallel any of the pieces discussed here, but the groups of Ni-kau-inpu (cat. nos. 137–141) and Djasha (cat. nos. 142, 143) quite clearly have features of Group C: many statuettes showing diverse activities, possible groupings,[11] naming of family members (in the case of Ni-kau-inpu), and millers, all with one foot crossed over the other.[12]

Although the Saqqara style could well be independent in this type of object, serving statuettes at that site—from the tombs of Nen-khefet-ka, datable to Sahure, and Wer-irni, datable to Neferirkare or later—might support a slightly earlier date at Saqqara for the inception of some of the changes seen in Group C at Giza.[13] Nen-khefet-ka's tomb yielded headless fragments of three kneeling and crouching figures that bore the names of the owner. The mastaba of Wer-irni produced four statuettes (two female millers without crossed feet, a male brewer, and a man cleaning or lining a jar), three of which were inscribed with personal names. Of these three, two were further labeled as belonging to Wer-irni's mortuary estate. A kneeling statuette of Ka-em-ked, Ka Priest of Wer-irni, was also found. Wer-irni's figures indicate an interest in named statuettes and also in larger pieces than those seen at Giza (the brewer, for example, measures 42 centimeters in height). MH

1. The term is adopted from Roth (1997), who suggests it as being descriptive of the figures' function in the tomb but not determinative of their status while alive. (See entry for cat. no. 137.)
2. Most notable for this material are Cherpion 1989; Roth 1995; and Cherpion 1998.
3. For Mer-si-ankh, see Simpson 1974, pp. 7–8, 21–22; for figures, see ibid., p. 23, pl. 18. For

Kha-merer-nebti II, see most recently Callender
and Jánosi 1997, p. 6, n. 19, p. 10, nn. 33
(regarding the scattered fragments), 89 (referring
to a forthcoming contribution on the statuary).

4. Giza D 20; Porter and Moss 1974, p. 109;
   Cherpion 1989, p. 224. The miller is in the
   Roemer- und Pelizaeus-Museum, Hildesheim
   (19; Martin-Pardey 1977, pp. 53–59).

5. Porter and Moss 1974, p. 62; Cherpion 1998,
   p. 114. The statuette found in the serdab is
   mentioned in Abu Bakr 1953, p. 106, pl. 60.

6. Porter and Moss 1974, pp. 269–70; Cherpion
   1998, p. 114. The breweress found in the serdab is published in Hassan 1932, p. 115, pl. 71.

7. G 2415, Porter and Moss 1974, p. 93; Reisner
   (1942, p. 253) makes it clear the tomb predates the reign of Unis, and the hairstyle of the
   miller points to a probable earlier date in the
   Fifth Dynasty (Cherpion 1998, p. 116).

8. Hassan 1941, p. 111, pls. 34–36; Porter and
   Moss 1974, pp. 258–59; Cherpion 1989,
   criteria 17 and 24 are discernible in pl. 37.

9. Roth 1995, pp. 35–36 (dating), 57 (names),
   84ff. (statuette fragments found in serdabs and
   courts).

10. Porter and Moss 1974, pp. 257–58; Hassan
    1941, pl. 47 (2) shows the head; the name of
    Osiris in Ankh-haf's offering formula points
    to Isesi or later (ibid., pp. 115–16; on this dat-
    ing criterion, see recently Roth 1995, p. 35
    and note).

11. Groups carved as a single unit are known
    from the tombs of Ka-khent and Ni-kau-inpu.
    Thin bases known from the tombs of Medu-
    nefer and Ni-kau-inpu, inset in a second base
    in one instance in the latter group (see cat.
    no. 137, note 1), suggest the possibility of
    larger bases accommodating groupings.

12. Oriental Institute of the University of Chicago,
    OI 10622, 10638; Roemer- und Pelizaeus-
    Museum, Hildesheim, 20. Millers with this

foot position are found in relief in the tomb
of Ni-ankh-khnum and Khnum-hotep (Moussa
and Altenmüller 1977, pl. 23)—dated to the
reign of Niuserre—and on a false door in the
Egyptian Museum, Cairo, JE 56994 (Cherpion
1982, pl. 17).

13. For Nen-khefet-ka, D 47; Borchardt 1911,
    pp. 186–87; Porter and Moss 1979, p. 580;
    and Egyptian Museum, Cairo, CG 321–23.
    For Wer-irni, D 20; Borchardt 1911, pp. 86,
    88–91; Porter and Moss 1978, p. 478; and
    Egyptian Museum, Cairo, CG 110, 114,
    116, 118, 119.

136. MILLER

Fifth Dynasty?
Limestone with remains of paint
H. 18 cm (7⅛ in.); w. 11.9 cm (4¾ in.); d. 33 cm
(13 in.)
Phoebe Apperson Hearst Museum of Anthropology,
University of California at Berkeley 6–19766

Kneeling on knees and toes, the miller
applies the force of her weight to her hands
on the grindstone. Her head is raised to
look outward but slightly downward. Her
features are strong, and the nose, mouth,
and jaw protrude slightly. The eyes are well
proportioned in relation to the face, their
contours deeply incised and the eyeballs
somewhat rounded. She wears a dress whose

painted, V-shaped neckline is visible above
her breasts, although the line may be the
trace of a necklace (compare cat. no. 142).
Her hair and ears are completely covered by
a cloth that is gathered in a thick tail at the
back. The large grindstone slopes downward from each edge toward the center—
perhaps to hold the grain more efficiently or
because of erosion—and is painted red to
represent granite. The base was black.

The tomb from which the miller came
offers no good datable elements, and the
statuette's own features do not at this point
provide a compelling link to the groups discussed in the preceding note on dating. To
my knowledge, the headcloth tied so as to
cover the ears appears in Old Kingdom
statuary only on this piece and on two others—a miller and a baker from the tomb of
Ptah-shepses at Giza—which also bear at
least a general physiognomic resemblance
to this work.[1] Since Ptah-shepses' formal
statuary seems likely to date at the latest to
the reign of Niuserre or not much after, the
Fifth Dynasty may then serve as a provisional date for this statuette.[2]

Millers are perhaps the central type of
serving statuettes, being among the earliest
and the most frequently occurring. Serving
figures in general are closely connected with
food preparation, an activity with an obvious link to sustenance and rebirth for the
deceased, and millers surely embody this

function. Still, it is not clear why milling provided this focus rather than one of the other activities exhibited by such figures.

Another feature also suggests the special resonance of miller statuettes. This figure was found with two other serving statuettes, one of which was also a miller—but a miller whose head was raised to gaze directly forward and whose hair was close cropped and uncovered.[3] Tombs would occasionally have more than one example of a particular type of activity, but paired millers are found fairly regularly. Examination reveals that the head of one is often more upright and forward-looking while that of the other is bowed; moreover, the face of the figure with the bowed head may even show distinct signs of hardship or age.[4] Surely the millers are silent allusions to allegories or tales once current.   M H

1. Kunsthistorisches Museum, Vienna, ÄS 7500, and Roemer- und Pelizaeus-Museum, Hildesheim, 2140; Porter and Moss 1974, p. 151.
2. Cherpion 1998, pp. 120–21, 126–27; her reference to the tomb on p. 116 would seem to pertain to a statuette in the Egyptian Museum, Cairo (JE 43964), illustrated in Hornemann 1951–69, vol. 4, p. 833.
3. Berkeley 6–19812; Lutz 1930, pl. 42a.
4. For several pairs of millers, see the note on dating above. In addition to the Berkeley pair, those from the tombs of Ni-kau-inpu, Medu-nefer(?), and Wer-irni show different head positions. Wer-irni's miller with lowered head (Egyptian Museum, Cairo, CG 110) has a very lined face and pendulous breasts. Compare the young and the aged millers represented in a relief at the same museum (JE 56994; Cherpion 1982, pls. 17, 18), both of whom are named and who are thus clearly not the same figure at different stages of life and not identical with any of the other persons named on the false door, among whom is the tomb owner's wife. Single millers with hanging heads (Museum of Fine Arts, Boston, 12.1486) or lined faces (Louvre, Paris, E 7706) can also be noted.

PROVENANCE: Giza, Western Cemetery, mastaba G 1213 for University of California, Hearst Expedition, 1903–5

BIBLIOGRAPHY: Lutz 1930, p. 28, pl. 416; Smith 1946, p. 96; Breasted 1948, p. 20, no. 12; Porter and Moss 1974, p. 58

137. BUTCHER

Fifth Dynasty, probably reign of Niuserre
Limestone with remains of paint; knife restored
H. 37 cm (14⅝ in.); w 14.2 cm (5⅝ in.); d. 38 cm (15 in.)
Lent by the Oriental Institute of The University of Chicago 10626

The butcher leans far forward over a slaughtered ox, which is disproportionately small. Only the toes of his right foot rest on the thin, roughly cut base:[1] the heel, slightly raised to balance him, hangs over the edge. A whetstone attached to a strap is tucked into the waist of his kilt. Three of the ox's legs are bound together, but its right front leg is held by the butcher, who is preparing to cut it off with his knife. The head of the dead animal has fallen backward and over the edge of the base, its mouth hangs open slightly, and its spine projects painfully.

The butcher's head is large, with schematic ears and overlarge eyes, and his lower lip is noticeably fuller than the upper. As is common in these figures, the degree of cutting out of the stone, the complex postures, and the attention to the physical manifestations of the effort required by an activity—here demonstrated by details such as the raised heel and locked knees—are quite astonishing. Moreover, all these characteristics contrast with the composed, typically frontal presentation of the head and features, which recalls that of canonical Egyptian statuary meant to represent and house the spirit.

The butcher belongs to the Ni-kau-inpu group of serving statuettes, comprising twenty-six active figures or their appurtenances (cat. nos. 137–141). All but one (cat. no. 141) were purchased in 1920 with four statuettes of the official Ni-kau-inpu and his wife, Hemet-re, and are now in Chicago. The coherence of the group cannot be established archaeologically as the mastaba of their owner has never been located, and somewhat different styles can be recognized within the group. Yet other factors indicate that the association of the statuettes with one another and with Ni-kau-inpu is in large part reasonable: strong similarities exist among many of the serving figures, and even among them and those of the tomb owners; a number of the statuettes are identified as children of an unnamed person, apparently the deceased;[2] and the name of Ni-kau-inpu appears on the base slab for the model granary included in the group of statuettes.

This group has been assigned various dates. The statues of the owner and his wife offer no sure clues,[3] but as a whole the serving statuettes exhibit numerous affinities with those in Group C discussed in the note on dating above, and thus a date near the reign of Niuserre is suggested.

The term "servant statuette," long used for these Old Kingdom figures, derived from the context provided by relief depictions and by the wood groups and later estate models that succeeded the stone statuettes. Recent studies make it clear, however, that in Old Kingdom art relations and peers of the deceased can be represented as taking the roles of servants—which are after all an expression of the family's essential responsibility toward the deceased—presumably both to guarantee the deceased's sustenance and to permit themselves to accompany the deceased.[4] This is perhaps not so surprising; like the butcher, these occasionally rather large, carefully made stone figures with their benign expressions and busy domesticity have a strong, direct impact. Such figures are one manifestation of the Old Kingdom's broad interest in "action" or "role" statuary, which fulfilled purposes not entirely discrete from those of the seated and standing figures usually considered more basic and typical.[5]   M H

138

1. The statuette might have been set alone within a second base (as is Oriental Institute of the University of Chicago OI 10636, from the same group) or conceivably could have formed part of a larger grouping set into a single base.
2. The named models include the miller, "his daughter Nebet-em-pet" (Oriental Institute of the University of Chicago OI 10622); the sifting woman, "[his daughter? or estate] Semeret" (OI 10623); the loaf maker, "his son Min-khaef" (OI 10624); the cook, "his son Khenu" (OI 10629); the baker, "[   ]-Ima" (OI 10634); and a ladling or sieving woman, "daughter Mer[t?]" (OI 10635). Emily Teeter of the Oriental Institute of the University of Chicago kindly checked the inscriptions.
3. Hemet-re's long pleated dress occurs early and rarely (Staehelin 1966, p. 169, fig. 2), but at least one example (Metropolitan Museum,

62.201.2) can be added to the documentation. The fashion of the fringe on her forehead apparently extends not much past the reign of Niuserre (Cherpion 1998, p. 118).
4. Roth 1995, pp. 57, 84ff.; Roth 1997. The latter makes a strong case that such figures, placed in the serdab, are ka statuettes of the persons represented.
5. For example, scribe statuettes, kneeling offering kings, and prisoners were all role statues but also very potent figures in their different ways.

PROVENANCE: Said to be from Giza, Western Cemetery; purchased with a group of serving statuettes and statuettes of Ni-kau-inpu and his wife, Hemet-re, 1920

BIBLIOGRAPHY: Smith 1946, p. 100; Breasted 1948, pp. 35–36; Porter and Moss 1974, p. 300

138A,B. POTTER

Fifth Dynasty, probably reign of Niuserre
Limestone with remains of paint
a. Potter: h. 13.2 cm (5¼ in.); w. 6.7 cm (2⅝ in.);
d. 12.5 cm (4⅞ in.)
b. Vases: h. 1.8 cm (¾ in.); w. 4.8 cm (1⅞ in.)
Lent by the Oriental Institute of The University of
Chicago (a) 10628, (b) 10645

Knees drawn up before his chest, the potter
sits on a block. With his left hand he holds
the potting wheel, and with his right—
thumb on the inside and the other fingers
outside—he grasps the rim of the pot that
sits on the wheel. The final stage in shaping
a typical Meidum bowl (see cat. no. 159)
is depicted: as the potter's fingers form the
top part or rim of the fresh clay vessel, his
left hand pushes the wheel to rotate rapidly
on its base.[1] The three small separate vessels
should probably be associated with this figure; they are not wheel-made forms but
might hold the water or pigment needed by
the potter at various stages of the process.[2]

An emaciated man is represented: his flat,
long skull and his spine are sharply profiled;
the ribs are harshly defined on his back; his

cheeks are hollow beneath their bony ridges;
and his hands are huge on his thin arms.
His hairline recedes above each temple, its
contours emphasizing the heavy wrinkles
on his forehead.

This statuette is unusual in that it is
the only known depiction of a potter, as
well as one of the few of any craft occupation before wood models became popular. His pots were presumably needed in
the tomb to hold the food and provisions
prepared by the other serving statuettes in
the tomb. Moreover, while the millers
especially are occasionally haggard, realism
to the degree seen here—a reminder of
the sometimes harsh conditions of labor—
is otherwise unknown among the group.[3]

MH

1. The brown paint indicates the wheel is wood.
   The gray color of the base may be meant to
   represent stone or to signify that the base is
   smeared with clay. These features and others
   relating to pottery technology and the use of
   the simple, low wheel are discussed in Do.
   Arnold 1993a, pp. 49–51.
2. I owe these observations to Susan Allen.
3. For millers with seamed faces and one relief
   showing an emaciated or aged miller, see cat.
   no. 136, note 4. Emaciation is depicted most

usually among those at the fringes of society—
even literally, as in representations of dwellers
at the valley margins (see cat. no. 122).

PROVENANCE: Said to be from Giza, Western
Cemetery; purchased with a group of serving stat-
uettes and statuettes of Ni-kau-inpu and his wife,
Hemet-re, 1920

BIBLIOGRAPHY: Smith 1946, p. 100; Breasted
1948, pp. 49–50; Porter and Moss 1974, p. 300

139. Dwarf Musician

Fifth Dynasty, probably reign of Niuserre
Limestone with remains of paint
H. 12.5 cm (4⅞ in.); w. 7.2 cm (2⅞ in.); d. 9.6 cm
(3¾ in.)
Lent by the Oriental Institute of The University of
Chicago 10641

There are three harpists in the Ni-kau-inpu
group of serving statuettes (see entry for cat.
no. 137): a woman or girl (cat. no. 140),
this considerably smaller male dwarf, and a
similarly small female not in this exhibition.

With his overlarge head, long torso, short
legs, and small feet, this harpist is clearly a
dwarf. He sits with his bowed legs spread
straight out before him on either side of the
harp. The hem of his garment stretches over
his legs, but its upper edge is not visible. His
head is slightly raised, with the left ear—
behind which the harp rests—smaller and
more forward than the right. His arms jut
out realistically as he plays the instrument.
The harp itself, somewhat deteriorated and
broken at the top, shows three strings that
are wound at the top of the neck.

Dwarfs appear in the art of the Old
Kingdom in a range of social positions and
roles, the most eminent being men such as
Seneb and Per-ni-ankhu (cat. no. 88), who
were closely attached to the king, and
Khnum-hotep.[1] Most frequently they are
depicted among secondary figures in relief
scenes, where they are bearers of items of
personal attire (particularly those made
of cloth), tenders of animals, jewelers, and
entertainers, including dancers, singers,
and musicians.[2] Especially in the last roles
there may be associations with sexuality
and fertility, associations that become more
apparent in the Middle Kingdom, when
their connection with rebirth is also clear.[3]

Dwarfs carrying objects, as well as this
musician, are known among the serving
statuettes.[4]   MH

1. Porter and Moss 1974, pp. 101–3; Porter
   and Moss 1979, pp. 722–23; Hawass 1991c,
   pp. 157–62.
2. Dasen 1993, pp. 109–33.
3. Ibid., pp. 140–41; Bourriau 1988, pp. 121–22.
4. Breasted 1948, p. 58, nos. 2 (also from the
   Ni-kau-inpu group), 3.

PROVENANCE: Said to be from Giza, Western
Cemetery; purchased with a group of serving
statuettes and statuettes of Ni-kau-inpu and his
wife, Hemet-re, 1920

BIBLIOGRAPHY: Smith 1946, p. 101; Breasted
1948, p. 87; Porter and Moss 1974, p. 300

140. FEMALE HARPIST

Fifth Dynasty, probably reign of Niuserre
Limestone with remains of paint
H. 20.7 cm (8⅛ in.); w. 11 cm (4⅜ in.); d. 16.1 cm
(6⅜ in.)
Lent by the Oriental Institute of The University of
Chicago 10642

Sitting on the ground with her legs folded
to the right, the harpist wears a white dress
that appears to leave her breasts bare and
ends above the knees. While no strap is
apparent in the front, in the back the dress
seems to be supported over the left shoulder by a strap that is mostly covered beneath a larger, overlying piece of cloth.[1]

The figure's features, particularly the
mouth and chin, are rendered slightly differently from the majority of the Ni-kau-inpu
statuettes, including the two other harpists
(see cat. no. 139). She has a small, round
face with wideset eyes, a flat nose, a petite,
turned-down mouth, and a very short chin.

Her body curves forward and inward in the
act of playing her instrument, and her face
is tilted up slightly, perhaps to listen to the
tones the harp produces.

The shovel-shaped harp has five strings,
represented on a narrow ridge of stone.
The upper part of its neck may be slightly
broken off above the area where the strings
are wound and anchored by pegs, which
are depicted as a protruding area.[2]

Musicians are rare among serving statuettes.[3] However, harpists and flutists are
seen in reliefs, where they are usually juxtaposed with scenes of dancers and sometimes
have the names of the deceased's children.
Scraps of songs recorded in such scenes are
directed to the goddess Hathor or call the
deceased back to rejoin the family and enjoy
the offerings. It has been plausibly argued
that these scenes document beliefs or practices that are forerunners of the visits to the
tomb and the deceased that occur during
the New Kingdom Beautiful Festival of the
Valley, a great holiday overseen by Hathor

as the goddess of the West, the land of the
deceased.[4] Ni-kau-inpu's harpists may similarly play to summon him back to visit his
family in this world.   MH

1. This cloth could be the tie end of a knot or a
   shoulder pad on which to rest the instrument,
   although neither possibility can be substantiated.
   Cloths are sometimes slung over the shoulders
   of working figures in reliefs (Harpur 1987,
   pp. 170–71, nn. 121, 122). Longer scarves are
   occasionally worn by dancers and others associated with Hathor or by singers (Staehelin 1966,
   pp. 175–76; Hassan 1975a, fig. 7).
2. Manniche 1991, pp. 25–28.
3. In addition to those in the Ni-kau-inpu group,
   there is one in the Staatliche Sammlung Ägyptischer Kunst, Munich (Gl. 107; Porter and
   Moss 1979, p. 729; h. 40 cm), and possibly
   another, from Giza (field no. 39-4-1; Roth
   1995, pp. 156–57, pl. 130c).
4. Altenmüller 1978, pp. 1–24.

PROVENANCE: Said to be from Giza, Western
Cemetery; purchased with a group of serving stat-
uettes and statuettes of Ni-kau-inpu and his wife,
Hemet-re, 1920

BIBLIOGRAPHY: Smith 1946, p. 101; Breasted
1948, pp. 86–87; Porter and Moss 1974, p. 300

141. Nursing Woman

Fifth Dynasty, probably reign of Niuserre
Limestone with remains of paint
H. 10.5 cm (4⅛ in.); w. 5.7 cm (2¼ in.); d. 7 cm
(2¼ in.)
The Metropolitan Museum of Art, New York,
Purchase, Edward S. Harkness Gift, 1926
26.7.1405

The woman sitting on the ground here with one knee raised has a broad, flat face with wide, curvy lips and large eyes that seem to look directly outward. The top of her short, flaring wig or hair is covered by a white cloth. Against the taut hammock of cloth formed by the dress stretched between her legs, she holds a child, supporting its head with her left hand while pulling her breast toward its mouth with her right. The rather large child has yellow skin, indicating it is a girl, and wears a plain white garment ending below her knees. Her right hand is placed over the proffered nipple and her head is tilted back. Perhaps the little girl leans her head back to

gaze up at the woman as nursing babies do, or it may be that the woman is unaware the child's head is too far back, and the child grasps the breast in frustration. Squatting behind the woman's right hip is a nude child—a male, as indicated by the remains of red paint on his skin. He sits with legs folded beneath him and feet turned inward. His head is tilted far back. With both hands he stretches the woman's right breast as if it were rubber, pulling it between her arm and body to his mouth.

The inspired composition of this small piece and its exaggeration of physical capability belong to a Chaucerian world of folk vignettes and tales—a world occasionally glimpsed in milder form in Old Kingdom relief scenes recording the activities and speech of common people.[1]

Among Old Kingdom serving statuettes, women with children are an uncommon and nonstandardized subject.[2] This is the only known example depicting a nursing woman. Women with children are seen more frequently in reliefs, one of which, in

the tomb of Ni-ankh-khnum and Khnum-hotep, contains a strikingly comparable conjunction: in one register a woman speaks reassuringly to a male child standing at her back and clinging to her neck while she grinds grain; directly below, a woman tending a fire to cook bread nurses a child supported against her raised knees.[3]

The fact that this woman wears a small kerchief, as do so many of the female figures who perform food preparation tasks, may imply that she, too, works at another such task while she cares for her children.[4]

MH

1. Guglielmi 1984.
2. A headless figure in the Ägyptisches Museum, Universität Leipzig (2446), depicts a standing woman carrying a child, and a woman on a seat with a child on her lap is published in Roth 1995, pp. 140–41, pl. 101c.
3. Moussa and Altenmüller 1977, p. 68, pls. 23, 26. A small girl stands behind a miller in a relief in the Egyptian Museum, Cairo (JE 56994; Cherpion 1982, pl. 17). Other examples are noted in Fischer 1989a, pp. 5–6. See, generally, Roehrig 1996, pp. 16–19.
4. There is insufficient evidence, to be sure, but the seated woman with a child mentioned in note 2 above does not wear such a headcloth, nor do later representations of women nursing or otherwise solely occupied in child care.

PROVENANCE: Said to be from Giza, Western Cemetery

BIBLIOGRAPHY: Smith 1946, p. 101; Breasted 1948, p. 97 (2.1); Porter and Moss 1974, p. 300

142. WOMAN WITH A SIEVE

Mid-Fifth Dynasty
Limestone with remains of paint
H. 25 cm (9⅞ in.); w. 13.4 cm (5¼ in.); d. 23.2 cm (9⅛ in.)
Ägyptisches Museum, Universität Leipzig 2564

Sitting with her knees raised to her chest, the woman extends her forearms to grasp the sieve. Her slightly raised face displays wide eyes, a large nose, and a full, slightly asymmetrical mouth. Her short, flaring wig or hair is half covered by a kerchief. Traces of a necklace and of a bracelet on the right wrist can be seen. The sieve has a slightly flaring rim and is encircled by incised lines that may denote basketwork. It tilts slightly on the support stone beneath it; the stone is painted yellow, perhaps to represent both the mound of sifted material and the tray beneath it, although the material in the sieve is white.[1]

Sifting is required to separate either grain from impurities or meal from insufficiently ground grain; the round sieve shown here was used for the latter purpose. The grinding and sifting of grain are often directly linked in Old Kingdom representations, as, for example, in relief scenes from the tomb of Ni-ankh-khnum and Khnum-hotep. There the woman who is sifting prods the miller to hurry so that there will be meal to fill her sieve and jokingly calls her "Whitey," probably because the miller is covered in meal dust.[2] Indeed, almost every female serving statuette shown preparing food, including this one, wears some kind of tidy head covering.[3]

This figure is one of fifteen serving statuettes discovered in the serdab of the tomb of Djasha along with statues of Djasha himself, his wife, Hathor-weret, and a nude boy.[4] Djasha's serving statuettes have a considerably more unified appearance than those of Ni-kau-inpu (cat. nos. 137–141). As a group, they very frequently have overlarge heads and ears.[5] Although they display no names of owners or other individuals, they are closely comparable to the statuettes of the Ni-kau-inpu group in terms of richness, variety, and general appearance and should date to roughly the same period.

MH

1. Other figures engaged in sifting rest their round baskets on a basketwork tray or directly on the ground; see Breasted 1948, pp. 25–26.

2. Moussa and Altenmüller 1977, p. 68.

3. Some wear work caps bound with headbands, which may be painted red; others wear only the headbands. Regarding the caps, see Vogelsang-Eastwood 1993, pp. 171–78.

4. Most recently the statue of Djasha himself was dated to the Fifth Dynasty with some hesitancy, as features seeming to suggest an earlier date were noted (Krauspe 1997b, pp. 48–50).

5. These characteristics are especially marked in two other statuettes in the Ägyptisches Museum, Universität Leipzig (2566, 2570), and in one in the Egyptian Museum, Cairo (JE 37823).

PROVENANCE: Giza, serdab of Djasha, mastaba D 39/40, Steindorff excavation, 1905

BIBLIOGRAPHY: Breasted 1948, p. 25; Porter and Moss 1974, pp. 111–12; Krauspe 1997b, pp. 75–76

143. COOK

Mid-Fifth Dynasty
Limestone with remains of paint
H. 28.8 cm (11⅜ in.); w. 14.8 cm (5⅞ in.);
d. 19 cm (7½ in.)
Ägyptisches Museum, Universität Leipzig 2562

The cook sits with his knees drawn close against his chest and separated slightly. His rather round head rests on a thick neck. His large and sharply delineated features include a full mouth topped by a small, pencil-thin mustache, eyes that slant down slightly toward the outer corners, and quite large, very schematically indicated ears.

Before him on the base sits a kettle resting on a coal fire that is confined to a small, round platform. With his right hand the cook gingerly handles an object partially submerged in the cooking liquid—perhaps one of the foods being cooked,

which have been noted to resemble morsels of fish or meat.[1] The cook's left fist grasps the upper end of a triangular fan keeping the flames hot under the stew.

This statuette was found with the woman with a sieve (cat. no. 142) and thirteen others in the Fifth Dynasty tomb of Djasha at Giza.   MH

1. On the basis of the representations of cooks to which he had access, Breasted (1948, p. 45) suggested that such figures were preparing bread balls for fowl. However, fish is depicted being cooked along with fowl in marsh scenes from the Fourth Dynasty on; the cooking of fish and fowl along with meat is seen in kiosk and banquet scenes from the reign of Neferirkare onward (Harpur 1987, pp. 180, 189, 227).

PROVENANCE: Giza, serdab of Djasha, mastaba D 39/40, Steindorff excavation, 1905

BIBLIOGRAPHY: Smith 1946, p. 100; Breasted 1948, p. 45 (3.2); Porter and Moss 1974, pp. 111–12; Krauspe 1997b, p. 72

144. STELA OF RA-WER

Fourth Dynasty, reign of Shepseskaf, or Fifth
Dynasty, reign of Neferirkare
Egyptian alabaster with faint remains of paint
H. 85 cm (33½ in.)
Egyptian Museum, Cairo JE 6267

This magnificent stela, very original in its
concept, was discovered in a tomb located
southwest of the Great Sphinx at Giza. It is
distinguished by the quality of the carving
and by the precious material, Egyptian
alabaster, a translucent calcite that was
rarely used in nonroyal monuments. The
tomb belonged to Ra-wer, an intimate of
the king, and has yielded a great number
of statues (see entry for cat. no. 131). The
names of the deceased's estates include the
cartouches of several Fourth Dynasty kings,
the latest of them being Shepseskaf, but a
very interesting autobiographical inscription mentions Neferirkare, who reigned in
the Fifth Dynasty.[1] The date of the monument is thus controversial.[2] The tomb's
unusual layout included twenty-five serdabs
and at least twenty niches. At the back of
one of these niches archaeologists discovered this stela, still set into a brick wall. It
is well preserved, apart from chipping on
the sides.

Curiously, only the head of the figure was
rendered in sunk relief, with the body indicated solely by incised lines. The horizontal
inscription was also carved in sunk relief
and stands out clearly from the background.
The rest of the surface was polished with
great care.

Ra-wer is represented standing, dressed
in a simple kilt with triangular apron, knotted at the waist. The distinctive sash of the
cult priest is wrapped around his chest and
left shoulder. He is wearing a medium-length
wig, which falls over his shoulders and hides
his ears. At the ends of the carefully rendered locks, two oblique lines give an illusion of depth. On the tomb owner's chin is
a striated square beard. The thick eyebrow
follows the curve of the eye. A beautiful
broad collar adorns his neck: the alternating
rows of horizontal and vertical beads are
captured with the utmost precision. The
inscription gives only four of Ra-wer's many
titles: *sem* priest, ritualist, Initiate into the

Secret of Divine Words, and *khet* priest of
the god Min.

A similar relief on an alabaster altar
was discovered in the same tomb.[3] Sculpted
in sharp relief, it depicts Ra-wer standing,
dressed in a feline pelt and holding a scepter
and staff.   S-LT, CZ

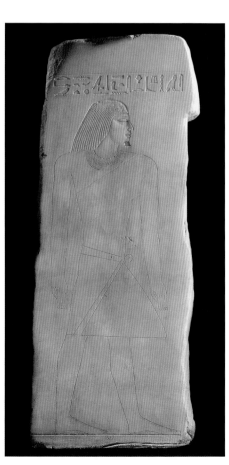

1. Roccati 1982, pp. 101–2.
2. The dating has given rise to many hypotheses.
   See Cherpion 1989, p. 227, n. 376; the cartouche of Shepseskaf appears in the tomb, and
   the inscription mentioning Neferirkare was
   probably added later.
3. Hassan 1932, p. 32, pl. 32.

PROVENANCE: Giza, Central Field, tomb of
Ra-wer, Hassan excavation, 1929–30

BIBLIOGRAPHY: Hassan 1932, pp. 24, 26,
pl. 28; Lange and Hirmer 1956, pl. 52; Donadoni
1969, p. 56, ill. on p. 58, cf. p. 56; Porter and
Moss 1974, p. 267; Corteggiani 1986, pp. 53–54,
no. 22; Cherpion 1989, p. 227 (for the tomb)

145. RELIEF OF ITUSH

Fifth Dynasty, reign of Djedkare-Isesi
Limestone
H. 42.6 cm (16⅞ in.); w. 74.4 cm (29⅛ in.);
d. 9.5 cm (3¾ in.)
Brooklyn Museum of Art, Charles Edwin
Wilbour Fund 37.25E

The subject of this relief fragment, Itush, is depicted in profile, a staff in his hand. Similar undamaged reliefs suggest he was standing, dressed in a long kilt. The large face, which belongs to a middle-aged man with a thick neck and fleshy chin, is remarkable for its expressive features. The slight concavity of the nose and the small, oblique eyes contribute to the illusion that this is a lifelike portrait. The figure and the inscriptions that accompany it stand out against the shallow, smoothed background. The modeling of the face is confined to large rounded curves on the surface, accompanied by a few precise notations, such as the arch of the eyebrow, the rimming of the upper eyelid, and the firm line of the mouth. The detail of the ear is particularly careful, and the outline

of the skull is unusually vigorous. A faint reworking is visible on the forehead, at the hairline. This is one of the masterpieces of Egyptian relief, true to the civilization's particular conventions for rendering the human body, such as the eye presented frontally on a face shown in profile.

The relief is also extremely important because it can be precisely dated. Itush, who bore the "great name" Semen-khu-ptah, was an important figure at the court of Djedkare-Isesi, according to the biographical inscriptions on his mastaba. (Other blocks from the mastaba are also housed in the Brooklyn Museum.) In particular, Itush performed the duties of secretary to the king, Director of the Dual Treasury, and Palace Metallurgist.[1]

The inscription accompanying this relief says the image is not a representation of the lofty personage himself but of another statue of him. What is left of the line of the shoulder suggests that, instead of showing the torso in its full breadth, the artist provided a profile view. This type of rendering, very unusual in ancient Egyptian art, was sometimes used to depict statues. The Egyptian formula that designates it, *seshep-er-ankh*,

is customarily translated as "statue from life"—that is, an imitation of reality—which has led scholars to reflect on the nature of portraiture in the pharaonic period. Current opinion holds that the phrase does not refer to the statue's appearance but to its function, which is that of all Egyptian funerary statues: to receive the offerings of food that will allow the deceased to live in the next world.[2] Perhaps this relief belonged to a scene in which such offerings were being made. But other hypotheses can be entertained: the relief may depict either the performance of rites in front of the statue or a sculptors' workshop.   CZ

1. Strudwick 1985, pp. 284–86.
2. Eaton-Krauss 1984, pp. 85–88, no. 103.

PROVENANCE: Saqqara, north of pyramid of Djoser, mastaba 14 (D 43); Henry Abbott collection, acquired after his death by The New-York Historical Society, New York; purchased 1948

BIBLIOGRAPHY: Mariette and Maspero 1889, pp. 296–97; Fazzini 1975, p. 32, no. 20a; Karig and Zauzich 1976, no. 15; Porter and Moss 1978, p. 452; Eaton-Krauss 1984, no. 134; Fazzini et al. 1989, no. 13

146A,B. The Hunt in the Desert from the Tomb of Pehen-wi-ka

Mid-Fifth Dynasty, probably reign of Neferirkare or two following reigns[1]
Limestone with remains of paint

a. H. 29 cm (11⅜ in.); w., top 46 cm (18⅛ in.), bottom 44.5 cm (17½ in.)
Ägyptisches Museum und Papyrussammlung, Staatliche Museen zu Berlin 1132

b. H. 28.5 cm (11¼ in.); w. 43 cm (16⅞ in.)
Brooklyn Museum of Art, Charles Edwin Wilbour Fund 64.147

The large mastaba designated D 70, which is north of the precinct of King Djoser at Saqqara, was for the most part constructed of sun-dried brick.[2] While a large courtyard and adjacent chapels and corridor-like serdabs in this tomb may have served the mortuary cults of other persons,[3] a group of stone-lined rooms in its west part was dedicated to Pehen-wi-ka, vizier, chief justice, and Overseer of Lay Priests at the nearby pyramid of King Userkaf. Most of the preserved relief decoration of the mastaba was located in the antechamber to Pehen-wi-ka's sanctuary, which was also decorated.[4] Two rooms to the west and north of the antechamber were undecorated. On the west wall of the antechamber the deceased was represented with his wife, Djefatsen,[5] and their son Iti. In three registers in front of the depictions of these family members,

scenes showed the netting of fish and fowl. At the bottom of the same wall, estate personifications bringing offerings were portrayed, while above the fowling scene men were shown leading desert animals toward the sanctuary. At the top of the wall a hunt in the desert was depicted in two main registers and one subregister. It is from this last scene that the present adjoining blocks are derived.[6]

The uppermost register of the Berlin block (a) preserves only the undulating desert ground with its remnants of red paint and, from left to right, the claw of a large bird, the four legs of a hoofed animal (some form of bovine or an antelope), and the legs of two ostriches. The most conspicuous creature in the middle register is a vividly depicted porcupine—the only known representation in pharaonic art of this animal,

a

which today is extinct in Egypt.[7] Without doubt intentionally, the artist juxtaposed the prickly rodent with a soft, furry feline of nondescript type. In the same register the hindquarters of a hoofed animal, probably a calf, is preserved at the right edge of the block. In the bottom register a leopard or cheetah observes with furtively lowered head the struggle to the death of a pair of canines —one a wild jackal, the other a domesticated dog with a collar around its neck. Before losses of relief surface around the muzzles of the canines occurred, presumably during World War II, it was possible to see that the dog had sunk its fangs into the jackal's neck, and the jackal's tongue protruded in agony.[8]

The Brooklyn block is dominated by the large and impressive figure of a male antelope mating with a female whose upper part alone remains. To the right of this pair we can make out the hindquarter of an animal —perhaps an antelope—giving birth. With great expressive effect, the male antelope breaks through the middle register, whose lower boundary ends at his left, under the front portion of a calf, and resumes, at a slightly higher level, at his right, under two figures of felines—one complete and the other partial. Visible in the uppermost register are the legs of another pair of mating antelopes as well as the front hoofs of a bovine that is confronting them. The animals in the middle and top registers, like those in the same registers of the Berlin block, walk on wavy forms that represent the hilly desert. This ground preserves its original red paint in places, the antelopes of the main mating group retain some reddish brown color on their bodies, and the female giving birth shows patches of red on its fur.

Pehen-wi-ka's desert hunt presents a much more peaceful picture than the royal hunting relief from Sahure's pyramid temple (cat. no. 112). It can be argued that this benign appearance is due to accidents of preservation that saved only a few of what may originally have been many depictions of kills such as the one in the jackal and dog group.[9] Yet even if there once were more scenes of violence, a striking number of animals in the Pehen-wi-ka reliefs roam the savanna undisturbed or mate and give birth, oblivious of any conflict that might be occurring. Clearly, then, these reliefs from the tomb of a vizier of the mid-Fifth Dynasty were influenced not only by such images as the great royal hunting reliefs from Sahure's early Fifth Dynasty temple but also by nature scenes in which the placid life of desert animals, with its mating, births,

b

and grazing, was represented without reference to violent human intervention. Such peaceful scenes are best known to us from the reliefs in the Room of the Seasons in the somewhat later sun temple of King Niuserre (cat. no. 120).

Stylistically, the Pehen-wi-ka reliefs are closer to the Sahure hunt sequence than to the Niuserre decorations.[10] The Pehen-wi-ka scenes are less crowded and complex than those of Niuserre. In the Pehen-wi-ka examples the animals and animal groups are clearly isolated from one another, each form is delicately sculpted, and the outlines of overlapping figures or parts of figures are not merely incised but are finely rounded. These characteristics strongly suggest that they date close to the time of Sahure, probably during the reign of his successor Neferirkare, or the two short reigns of Neferefre and Shepseskare that followed.[11] Any influences from peaceful nature scenes of the Room of the Seasons genre must derive from predecessors of Niuserre's sun temple reliefs.[13]

DOA

1. For a dating to the second half of the Fifth Dynasty, see Bothmer 1974, p. 69; and Harpur 1987, pp. 191, 192, 212 ("late Neuserre to mid-Izezi").
2. The descriptions of the mastaba structure are not entirely clear regarding which parts were built of brick and which of stone; Naville 1897–1913, vol. 1 (1897), p. 162, n. 6.
3. See Smith 1936, p. 405.
4. Lepsius 1849–58, vol. 2, pls. 45–47; Jacquet-Gordon 1962, pp. 366–70; Porter and Moss 1978, pp. 491–92. The false door from the sanctuary is in the Ägyptisches Museum und Papyrussammlung, Berlin, 1120. Lepsius 1849–58, vol. 2, pl. 48.
5. Harpur 1987, p. 15.
6. Bernard v. Bothmer (1974, pp. 67–69) discovered the connection between the two blocks. He also correctly pointed out that the place-

ment of the Berlin block as shown in Lepsius (1849–58, vol. 2, pl. 46) is wrong.
7. Störk 1984b, cols. 1232–33.
8. See the illustration of the block as it appeared in 1936 in Wreszinski (pl. 103), where the muzzle of the jackal and the teeth of the dog are still complete.
9. Another preserved scene of the kind is a group of a dog and a fallen antelope in the uppermost register of the Berlin block; see Lepsius 1849–58, vol. 2, pl. 46.
10. The close relationship of the boat scenes in the tomb of Pehen-wi-ka (ibid., pl. 45) to the Sahure reliefs has been pointed out by Harpur (1987, p. 56).
11. Grave doubts concerning Harpur's date of "late Neuserre to mid-Izezi" (1987, pp. 191, 192, 212; see note 1 above) for the Pehen-wi-ka decorations are also raised by a comparison with the Ra-em-kai reliefs (cat. no. 147), which are clearly close to those of the Niuserre sun temple in their crowding of figures, their complex compositions, and, above all, the style and execution of the relief work. While the Pehen-wi-ka figures have delicately rounded outlines and softly sculpted interior details, the Niuserre and Ra-em-kai forms are generally flat with a few boldly modeled details and much use of incised lines where figures or parts of figures overlap. For recent findings and observations on the reigns and building activities of Neferefre and Shepseskare, see Verner 1994a, pp. 76–79, 84–86, 131, 133–54.
12. On the sun temples of Sahure's successors, especially that of Neferirkare, see Verner 1994a, pp. 110–11; and Stadelmann 1984b, cols. 1094–99.

PROVENANCE: Saqqara, north of Djoser precinct, mastaba D 70*

BIBLIOGRAPHY: (a) Lepsius 1849–1858, vol. 2, pl. 46; Königliche Museen zu Berlin 1899, p. 55; Wreszinski 1936, pl. 103. (b) Romano in *Neferut net Kemit* 1983, no. 13; Romano in Fazzini et al. 1989, no. 11

*Porter and Moss 1978, pp. 491–92, pls. 46, 49. For a complete plan, see Mariette and Maspero 1889, pp. 370–72.

147. THE HUNT IN THE DESERT FROM THE TOMB OF RA-EM-KAI

Fifth Dynasty, probably reign of Djedkare-Isesi
Painted limestone
H. 92 cm (36¼ in.); w. 105 cm (41⅜ in.)
The Metropolitan Museum of Art, New York, Rogers Fund, 1908 08.201.1g

The chapel from which this relief comes was purchased by the Metropolitan Museum from the Egyptian government in 1907. It was part of a mastaba located north of the Djoser complex at Saqqara, in a section of the necropolis containing tombs of a number of individuals who were associated with Djedkare-Isesi, the eighth king of the Fifth Dynasty. The chapel was originally decorated for a man named Nefer-iretnes, but it was later appropriated for Prince Ra-em-kai, who was the "eldest son of the king." In a number of places in the tomb the inscriptions of the original owner have been erased and partially replaced by those of the prince. In one case, the figure of Nefer-iretnes as an older man has been recarved into the slender form of a young man, presumably to better reflect the age of the prince.[1]

This scene depicts a hunt in the desert. In the upper register a hunter (identified as such by the hieroglyphs in front of his head) watches as two hunting dogs attack a fox and a gazelle in the uneven terrain; two other dogs move off to the right. Above, a hare and another gazelle hide in the low vegetation. The gazelles and the dogs are identified by the hieroglyphs above them. In the register below, two hunters attempt to capture a group of ibex, which they will bring back to fatten in captivity before slaughtering them for meat. Above the hunter at the left a hedgehog is seen rooting around in the dry soil.[2] The text in front of the hunter at the right briefly describes his actions: "lassoing of an ibex by a hunter."

The violent energy of the desert hunting scene from the pyramid temple of Sahure (cat. no. 112), second king of the Fifth Dynasty, makes this version from the end of the dynasty seem almost benign. Clearly, this artist's vision of the theme is completely different. The delicacy of the wafer-thin relief makes this chapel a masterpiece of Fifth Dynasty carving. The graceful rendering of the animals demonstrates the artist's keen observation of the natural world. Always an integral part of any Egyptian work of

art, the hieroglyphic text has also been carefully carved and integrated into the composition. In general, more care has been taken with the modeling of the faces of the men and animals than with their bodies. However, the naked hunter at the lower right is a notable exception, with his well-muscled legs and extended right arm.

This scene is part of the narrow south wall of the offering chapel. Above it is an offering list, and below are two registers depicting boats. Only the seven blocks with the complete hunting scene have been included in this exhibition, but sections of the offering list and the upper register of the boating scenes above and below the hunt are visible in the photograph reproduced here.

CHR

1. The recarving is illustrated in Fischer 1959, fig. 10f.
2. A very similar hedgehog appears in the hunt scene from the Sahure pyramid temple (Borchardt 1913, pl. 17).

PROVENANCE: Saqqara, tomb of Prince Ra-em-kai, purchased from the Egyptian Government 1907

BIBLIOGRAPHY: Mariette and Maspero 1889, pp. 178–81 (D3); Duell 1938, vol. 2; Hayes 1946, pp. 170–78; Hayes 1953, pp. 94–102, esp. fig. 56; Porter and Moss 1978, pp. 487–88, with earlier bibliography; Do. Arnold 1995, p. 8, fig. 2

Late Fifth Dynasty
Limestone
H. 25 cm (9⅞ in.); w. 44 cm (17⅜ in.); d. 18 cm
(7⅛ in.)
Rijksmuseum van Oudheden, Leiden AM 102

Donkeys are seen here walking ankle-deep in stalks of grain on a threshing floor. They are driven by a man whose figure was depicted on an adjoining block. His stick is visible over the back of the donkey at the far right. In most scenes of this type a second man stands at the left to keep the animals moving in a circle. The drivers frequently call to one another—"Watch what you're doing!" and "Turn them around!"—their conversation written in hieroglyphs above the animals' heads. No trace of such a text is preserved at the top of this block, but there may have been an inscription on the block above.[1]

This herd conveys a sense of freedom, as do the threshing donkeys carved in the tomb chapels of Ra-em-kai,[2] Ka-em-rehu,[3] and Nefer-iretenef.[4] All of these chapels are originally from Saqqara, and all have been dated to about the reign of Djedkare-Isesi. Although not as chaotically arranged as the animals in these three tomb reliefs, the donkeys seen here are far more varied, both in individual poses and as a group, than the more regimented threshing donkeys seen in other tombs.[5] Two animals are bending down to eat. The one at the left, whose nose is missing, seems to have lowered its head far enough to nibble at the grain, while the one in the middle has its head only halfway to the floor. A third donkey is shown moving in the opposite direction, its head visible in the wide space between the last two donkeys in the main group. In a very unusual detail, the animal at the far left has been depicted with its ears pricked upward, as though its attention has been caught, perhaps by one of the drivers.

The animals have been well carved, with special attention paid to the contours of their necks and to their long muzzles. Judging by the different styles of carving seen in the outline of the eyes and the shape of the nostrils, it appears that at least two sculptors worked on the scene. One carved the four animals at the right and a second worked on the five animals at the left (including both of those with lowered heads). Partly because of the spacing of the animals at the right,

148. Two Young Dogs

Second half of Fifth Dynasty
Limestone with patina
H. 19 cm (7½ in.); w. 19 cm (7½ in.)
The Metropolitan Museum of Art, New York,
Rogers Fund, 1909 09.180.134

Two puppies stand side by side with slightly lowered heads, as if hesitating to approach some problem or adversary they cannot yet handle. Their young age is indicated by the round shape of their heads and their pendant ears.[1] The ground line on which the two animals stand ends in front of them. They must have been part of a subregister of a larger composition—perhaps a hunt in the desert.

The relief is of superb quality and its stylistic characteristics are typical for works of the Fifth Dynasty from the reign of Niuserre onward. Especially notable is the handling of the overlapping of parts of figures. In reliefs from the early Old Kingdom through the time of Sahure, figures are actually higher, if only by millimeters, than the areas they overlap. However, in reliefs of the later Fifth Dynasty all such areas are on the same level, and the impression of overlap is achieved solely by variations in the handling of the incisions that border the figures: the incision is sharp and almost perpendicular to the background where it borders the overlapping figures but slopes gently upward into the surface of the overlapped forms. For relief artists this technique was less time consuming than the older one and it enabled them to more easily compose all manner of intricate groupings. In the present work it is used prominently, while details of musculature and other body features are indicated by fine modeling. Early Sixth Dynasty relief work is, by contrast, higher and fuller, with only sparse modeling (cat. nos. 193, 194).   DOA

1. Fischer 1980a col. 77; Houlihan 1996, pp. 76–77, fig. 55.

PROVENANCE: Lisht North, pyramid of Amenemhat I, core, Metropolitan Museum of Art excavation, 1908–9

BIBLIOGRAPHY: Goedicke 1971, pp. 138–39

the sculptor of these donkeys has provided more hind legs (three sets on this block) and tails (two on this block) than are usually found in a group of animals facing the same direction.[6]

This block is identified as coming from Saqqara, although the tomb has not been located. The style of the carving and the freedom of the composition suggest that it dates to the end of the Fifth Dynasty.

CHR

1. Although such texts often almost touch the donkeys' ears, they are sometimes quite a distance above their heads, as in a relief from the tomb of Ra-em-kai in the Metropolitan Museum, New York (see note 2 below).
2. The Metropolitan Museum of Art, New York, 08.201.1; Hayes 1953, fig. 57.
3. Ny Carlsberg Glyptotek, Copenhagen; Mogensen 1921, p. 23, fig. 18.
4. Musées Royaux d'Art et d'Histoire, Brussels; Van de Walle 1930, pl. 4.
5. For example, in a relief in the tomb of Ti at Saqqara, dated to about the same period, the eleven threshing donkeys are shown in an unbroken line, except for an animal at the front, whose disembodied head is lowered over the grain on the floor. A single pair of hind legs and ten pairs of front legs are distributed among these donkeys; see Wild 1966, pl. 155.
6. One must assume that the hind legs and tail of the animal at the far right were carved on the adjoining block. As is quite common, the two donkeys leaning down to eat have no identifiable front legs (see the relief of threshing donkeys in the tomb of Mereruka at Saqqara for an exception; see Duell 1938, vol. 2, pl. 169), but the animal in the middle of this scene may belong to one of the pairs of hind legs. The donkey facing in the opposite direction is entirely without legs, as is also common in such scenes (however, in the relief in the tomb of Ra-em-kai seven donkeys are provided with a total of eighteen legs, some facing left and others right); see Hayes 1953, fig. 57.

PROVENANCE: Saqqara

BIBLIOGRAPHY: Porter and Moss 1979, p. 758, with earlier bibliography; Schneider 1997, p. 82, no. 111

150A–D. Market Scene from the Tomb of Tep-em-ankh

First half of Fifth Dynasty, reign of Sahure or later
Limestone with remains of paint
a. H. 35 cm (13¼ in.)
Musées Royaux d'Art et d'Histoire, Brussels
E 7297

b. W. 101 cm (39¼ in.)
Egyptian Museum, Cairo CG 1556

c. H. 30.5 cm (12 in.); w. 69 cm (27⅛ in.)
Petrie Museum of Egyptian Archaeology, University
College London UC 14309

d. H. 30.5 cm (12 in.); w. 67 cm (26⅜ in.)
Petrie Museum of Egyptian Archaeology, University
College London UC 14310

A fascinating glimpse into everyday life in ancient Egypt is provided by market scenes carved on tomb walls, frozen moments depicting the barter, purchase, and sale of food and manufactured products. These scenes of bustling human interaction must have been repeated up and down the Nile a thousand times every day, but within the repertoire of tomb decoration they are, paradoxically, quite rare. Only a handful of market scenes have survived from Old Kingdom chapels, most of them from the necropolis at Saqqara.[1] One of the most famous Saqqara examples comes from the tomb of Tep-em-ankh, a high official and mortuary priest who served the pyramid cults of a number of pharaohs of the Fourth and Fifth Dynasties.[2]

Situated to the north of Djoser's Step Pyramid complex, not far from the famous tomb of Ti, Tep-em-ankh's tomb was first excavated and briefly described by Auguste Mariette.[3] Although he did not systematically excavate the tomb, Mariette made a cursory plan that reveals a chapel facade and entrance to the north, a long north-south corridor containing false doors for Tep-em-ankh's wife, Nebu-hotep, and his son Hemmin and a smaller space, a chamber at the south end, with a third false door inscribed for Tep-em-ankh himself.[4]

Inscribed and decorated fragments from the tomb found their way into collections of Egyptian art throughout the world. In fact, the modern Egyptological discovery and reconstruction of far-flung portions of this ancient jigsaw puzzle has proven just as fascinating as the glimpse of the ancient Egyptian market provided by the reunited elements. The reconstruction shown (fig. 126) is the most complete that has yet appeared and

a

is published here for the first time. It displays the scene that once adorned the east wall of the long corridor and comprises the seven separate reliefs from five different collections on three continents that make up the ensemble as it is currently known; four of these reliefs have been gathered for the exhibition.

Portions of four separate registers, each treating different activities, are presented in this reconstruction. The register at the very top reveals merely the feet of some standing and kneeling figures, and a bound oval container at the far right (Egyptian Museum, Cairo CG 1541; not in exhibition). This object indicates that scribes, scribal equip-

ment, and the recording of accounts might well have been the subject here.[5]

The second register from the top is much better preserved. Recalcitrant taxpayers are ushered in under duress by the representatives of Tep-em-ankh's estate for bureaucratic (and/or physical?) retribution. The standing officials, all clothed in kilts and one or two even brandishing bastinadoes that end in carvings of human hands (Egyptian Museum, Cairo CG 1541),[6] clearly have the advantage over the hapless, naked tax evaders cowering in their grasp. The figure of the official on the Cairo block who holds his man by the hair may now be given fuller form by elements of a newly

b

identified adjoining relief in the Arthur M. Sackler Museum of Harvard University, Cambridge, Massachusetts.[7] The hieroglyphic captions between the figures list their names and titles.

The third and fourth registers from the top separate the market activities into two categories: transactions concerning foodstuffs and dealings that involve other products. The Brussels relief (a) at the left of the third register preserves a fishmonger peddling his catch with a fragmentary hieroglyphic phrase that may translate "I will select fish (for) him (while) they are healthy." In exchange for fish, the figure farthest to the left in the Cairo relief (b, CG 1556), identified as the "butler Iy-mery," offers a conical bread loaf, while the "butler Khenu" stands behind him with a basketful of bread on his shoulder. Occupying the right portion of the Cairo relief is the famous vignette of the "keeper of baboons, Hemu" holding yet another bastinado ending in a hand and escorting a male and female baboon on two leashes. The female clutches her young close to her chest,[8] while the male grabs the outstretched leg of a naked youth intent on plucking fruits or vegetables from a large basket. Hemu declares, "Go, look, there is your property," while the boy cries out, "Hey! Help! Strike in order to scare off this baboon!" Whether this boy is the keeper's assistant or a common thief is unclear, but

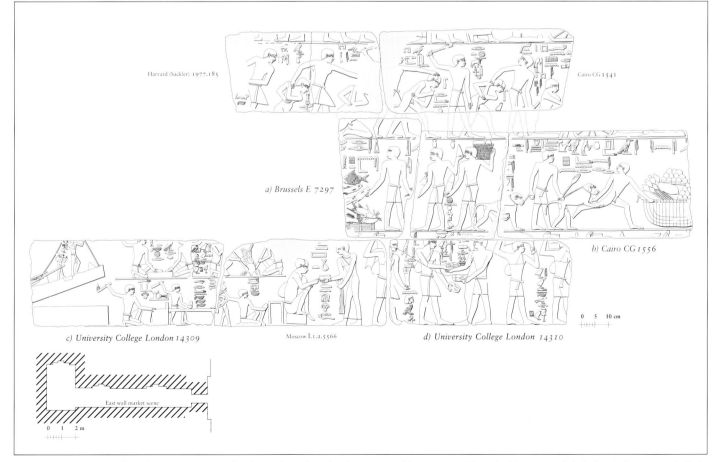

126. Reconstruction of market scene, east wall of corridor of tomb of Tep-em-ankh, Saqqara. The relief fragments labeled in italics are included in the exhibition. Uncollated drawing by Peter Der Manuelian

150c

Detail, cat. no. 150c

it is certain that the scene was intended to be humorous.

The fourth, or lowest, register preserves the largest number of figures, all engaged in the manufacture, purchase, or sale of various products. At the extreme left in the first London block (c, UC 14309) appears the prow of a ship with two individuals, one of whom is labeled "the Ka Priest Nefer-khui." To the right of the vessel the scene is split into two subregisters. The uppermost shows two kneeling men with upraised arms pounding metal upon a low platform; between them is the caption "Overseer of Metal Workers Ka-kher-ptah." To their right, starting in

150d

the London relief and spilling into the example in the Pushkin State Museum, Moscow (I.1.a.5566; not in the exhibition), two individuals stoke a fire whose flames lap upward. Between these two groups of men is a recitation invoking the appropriate deity, Sokar: "Sloth is unbearable to Sokar, O craftsman!" The lower subregister contains carpenters with adzes and mallets working on a bed, a bed leg, headrests, and a seat. The seated man in the center of the Moscow fragment offers a bowl to the standing woman to his right. While he exclaims, "Look, alabaster," the woman, who is ready to pay for the bowl with the onions in her left hand, tells him how to inscribe it: "Put 'for the Ka Priest' upon it."

The male figure to the right of the woman is preserved on three separate fragments (a, Brussels; Moscow; and d, London). The caption in front of him reads "Unguent has arrived for Tep-em-ankh," clearly indicating the import of the vessel in his outstretched hand. This brings us to the central vignette on the second London relief (d, UC 14310), in which sandals are exchanged for grain. The person on the left proffers his sandals, saying, "You will like (them); these (sandals) are good for you." To this the facing figure responds, "Take for yourself barley for these (sandals)." And farther to the right, in the final section of the scene, one of the two, hoisting a sack or full skin, exclaims, "I am heavily laden, O craftsman." These two men and others in the register have rounded baglike objects hanging from their backs that have been interpreted variously as purses or shopping containers.

The scenes spread over the four registers demonstrate the flurry of activity that transpired on or near Tep-em-ankh's estate and record as well the names of individuals the tomb owner deemed worthy of mention. The quality of the relief carving varies from block to block with the quality of the limestone. Some of the vignettes show an impressive attention to detail: for example, the modeling of the leg musculature is particularly well executed in the two figures on the left side of the Cairo relief (b, CG 1556) and the central figures of the second London relief (d, UC 14310). On the evidence of theme and style the relief can be dated to the first half of the Fifth Dynasty, an attribution supported by the fact that Sahure is the latest king mentioned on other reliefs found in the tomb.[9]   PDM

1. For a discussion of market scenes from the tombs of Ti, Ptah-shepses, Ankh-ma-hor, Ka-gemni, and others, see Hodjash and Berlev 1980, pp. 32, 49 (additional note); Lepsius 1849–58, vol. 2, pl. 96; Verner 1994b, esp. pp. 295–300; Moussa and Altenmüller 1977, pp. 79–86, pl. 24, fig. 10; and Kanawati and Hassan 1997, p. 33, pls. 5a, 38 (not a market, but a beer production scene). For an important recent study on women's activities within the market, see Eyre 1998, pp. 173–91.
2. Royal names inscribed in the tomb include Snefru, Khufu, Khafre, Menkaure, Userkaf, and Sahure; see note 4 below.
3. Mariette and Maspero 1885, pp. 196–201.
4. For the false doors, see Porter and Moss 1978, pp. 483 (2), 484 (4), (8); Egyptian Museum, Cairo, CG 1417 (Hemmin; Borchardt 1937, pp. 89–91, pl. 20); Cairo, CG 1415 (Nebu-hotep; ibid., pp. 84–87, pl. 19); and Cairo, CG 1564 (Tep-em-ankh; Borchardt 1964, pp. 28–30, pl. 64).
5. A fuller representation of wrapped containers of this kind and of kneeling figures that are clearly scribes occurs in the tomb of Ti at Saqqara; see Wild 1966, pls. 144b, 168; and Parkinson and Quirke 1995, p. 36, fig. 20.
6. For this relief, see Borchardt 1937, p. 244, pl. 52 (bottom).
7. I am indebted to David G. Mitten and Amy Brauer of the Harvard University Art Museums for allowing me to draw this fragment, for supplying photographs, and for providing the opportunity to collate it. The assignation of this relief to the tomb of Tep-em-ankh was first made by Edward Brovarski, whom I thank for bringing it to my attention.
8. Collation of the relief clearly reveals the face of the baby baboon, despite Hodjash and Berlev's insistence (1980, p. 41) that it is fruit in the female's hand.
9. Among the dates suggested by other scholars are "mid-Dynasty 5" (Baer 1960, p. 151 [559]); "Raneferef to Niuserre?" (Harpur 1987, p. 206); and "Sahure" (Cherpion 1989, p. 227).

PROVENANCE: Saqqara, mastaba 76 (Mariette mastaba D 11; often called "Tep-em-ankh II"), north of Djoser's Step Pyramid, east wall of corridor, Mariette excavation

BIBLIOGRAPHY: Mariette and Maspero 1885, pp. 196–201; Smith 1942, pp. 515–18, fig. 6; Porter and Moss 1978, pp. 483–84, esp. p. (5), with important bibliography; Hodjash and Berlev 1980, pp. 31–49; Hodjash and Berlev 1982, pp. 33, 35, 38–39, no. 3. (a) Bissing 1934b, pp. 5–6, no. 7, fig. 3. (b) Capart 1907, pl. 103 (top); Maspero 1907, vol. 2, pl. 11 (top); Klebs 1915, p. 33, fig. 20; Smith 1949, pp. 182 n. 1, 187, 342, fig. 225c; Borchardt 1964, pp. 17–18, pl. 61 (top); Butzer 1978, p. 59 (bottom). (c) Capart 1901, p. 12; Montet 1925, pp. 280 (12), 282; Stewart 1979, p. 7, no. 23, pl. 4. (d) Capart 1901, p. 13; Montet 1925, p. 325; Stewart 1979, p. 7, no. 24, pl. 5

THE TOMB OF METJETJI

The exact location of the tomb of Metjetji is not known, but this official's titles, in particular "honored by Unis, his master," suggest it was at Saqqara, near the pyramid of Unis; however, the area west of the Step Pyramid of Djoser once explored by Cecil Firth has sometimes been proposed.[1] Five statues and many sculpted fragments from this mastaba are in the collections of different museums; the Musée du Louvre has acquired from the same tomb a series of paintings whose original location—chapel or burial chamber—is unknown (cat. no.

157). All these decorations have been inventoried and commented upon in Kaplony's monograph.[2] Because Metjetji's titles mention King Unis, scholars have long believed that Metjetji lived during or slightly after that sovereign's reign. On the other hand, since the epithet "honored by Unis" seems to have been used for many years after the pharaoh's death, Metjetji's tomb may date to the end of the Old Kingdom or the beginning of the Middle Kingdom.[3] None of the arguments advanced so far has been decisive, however, and the existence of similar

paintings at Saqqara, discovered in the tomb of Nedjem-pet, mother of the vizier Mereruka,[4] is a persuasive reason for retaining the earliest date.

This exhibition offers a unique opportunity to compare the architectural fragments from Metjetji's tomb.   C Z

1. Bernard von Bothmer, conversation with the author, 1991.
2. Kaplony 1976.
3. This hypothesis has been proposed most recently by Munro (1994, pp. 245–77).
4. Kanawati and Hassan 1996, pp. 11–30, pls. 6, 7.

154

152

151. FRAGMENT FROM THE LEFT SIDE OF THE FACADE OF THE TOMB OF METJETJI

Fifth Dynasty, reign of Unis, or early Sixth
Dynasty
Painted limestone sculpted in sunk relief
H. 83 cm (32⅝ in.); w. 66 cm (26 in.)
Royal Ontario Museum, Toronto 953.116.1

Sunk relief, the technique used for the figures, is most often employed for sculpture
decorating the exterior of monuments; thus,
this fragment is probably from the facade
of Metjetji's mastaba. This fragment is
probably from the left side of the facade because Metjetji is looking toward the right.
The treatment is delicate, and the details
of the kilt and hair are elegant and precise.
Such facial features as the corners of the
lips are detailed.

The tomb owner is depicted in large scale
in the attitude of walking, his left leg forward. On his head, concealing his ears, is
a long wig with fine locks, and he wears a
short beard. He holds two emblems signifying his importance, a staff and a scepter
adorned with a papyrus umbel. His costume
is particularly refined: kilt with fully pleated
apron, bracelets, and a broad collar with
many rows. The shapes of the relief, firmly
outlined, are set deep in the stone and
painted in colors of red, yellow, and black.

A child is walking ahead, holding tightly
to Metjetji's staff. He is represented on a
smaller scale, to signify his lesser importance.
An inscription explains he is Metjetji's
"son whom he loves, Sabu-ptah."

Above the figures is a line of hieroglyphs
giving a shortened titulary for Metjetji:
"royal noble, Director of the Office of Tenants of the Palace, Metjetji."

The entire right half of the block is
occupied by an autobiographical inscription praising the tomb owner's merits as
a good son:

[I am an offering bearer whom his father
loved], an honored one whom his mother
blessed. Since I had them transported to
the beautiful West, they praise God for
me, for the daily offerings [I have brought]
to them. When I had them transported
to the beautiful West, I requested a coffin
from the Residence for them, as a royal
offering, [because I was] honored by the
king. I did not allow them to see any
unkindness, from their youth till they
joined the ground in the beautiful West. [I
was beloved of] everyone. I have done
nothing that could anger anyone since my
birth, for I am considerate when speaking
of all the king's works I have done.   CZ

PROVENANCE: Probably Saqqara, tomb of
Metjetji

BIBLIOGRAPHY: Kaplony 1976, pp. 31–32,
no. 7; Roccati 1982, pp. 145–46, § 123

152. Fragment from the Right Side of the Facade of the Tomb of Metjetji

Fifth Dynasty, reign of Unis, or early Sixth Dynasty
Painted limestone sculpted in sunk relief
H. 108 cm (42½ in.); w. 68 cm (26⅞ in.)
Ägyptisches Museum und Papyrussammlung, Staatliche Museen zu Berlin 32190

This block is decorated with a scene that is almost the mirror image of the one on the left side of the facade (cat. no. 151). A few differences can be noted in the details. The scepter decorated with a papyrus umbel passes behind Metjetji's body, following a convention of Egyptian relief that privileges orientation toward the left. The small figure holding tightly to the staff is not nude, but wears a kilt with a triangular apron. The text above him explains this is not the son of Metjetji shown on the previous block but is: "his son whom he loves, Ihy."

As on the left side of the facade, the scene is surmounted by a line of hieroglyphs giving an abridged titulary of the tomb's owner: "royal noble, Director of the Office of Tenants of the Palace, Metjetji."

The entire right half of the block is occupied by an inscription of a traditional type called Appeal to the Living, which invites passersby to celebrate the memory of the deceased:

You who live on the earth, thank the king so that you may live. Look after his works, protect his command, do what he likes. It will be more useful to the one who does this [than to the one for whom it is done]. He will be an honored one, whom his god loves. He will be safe because of it, and his conduct will be blessed throughout his whole life. It will be useful for him with the god, [in the beautiful necropolis of the West]. O you who shall come to this tomb, your heart will be pleasing to Osiris, lord of burial, if you say: Let the pure bread and beer be given to the Director of the Office of Tenants, Metjetji. [Your heart will be pleasing] to Anubis, lord of the West, if you offer everything that may be in your hands in the way of offerings that are presented to a spirit. I am a capable spirit, and I am a capable scribe who deserves to be acted for him. . . . As for any servant or any man of my funerary estate who will come to offer to me [and give me bread], I will let him see that he recognizes it is useful to offer to a spirit in the necropolis.   CZ

PROVENANCE: Probably Saqqara, tomb of Metjetji

BIBLIOGRAPHY: Kaplony 1976, pp. 33–44, no. 8; Roccati 1982, p. 146, § 124

153. Left Jamb of the Entry Door in the Facade of the Tomb of Metjetji

Fifth Dynasty, reign of Unis, or early Sixth Dynasty
Painted limestone sculpted in sunk relief
H. 142 cm (56 in.); w. 77.5 cm (30½ in.)
The Nelson-Atkins Museum of Art, Kansas City, Missouri, Purchase: Nelson Trust 52-7/1

The largest figure in the relief, Metjetji is shown striding forward, his left leg extended. He wears a long, plain wig that conceals his ears, and he has a short beard. He holds a long staff in his left hand, but the other emblem of his high status, a scepter decorated with a papyrus umbel, once held in his right hand, is not preserved (a transverse crack at the level of the figure's thighs has destroyed all the decoration and text in that area of the relief). Metjetji's plain kilt with apron, broad collar, and bracelets are similar to what he wears in the other reliefs in the tomb, but they are treated here with greater simplicity and less refinement. Here, too, the relief is cut deeply into the stone and the shapes are firmly outlined, as was customary for the sculpture decorating the exterior of monuments. This fragment was probably the left jamb of the entrance. The colors that remain on the relief are red, yellow, and black.

In contrast to the handling of his costume, the parts of Metjetji's body are carefully treated. In particular, the musculature of the arms and legs and the facial features —the corners of the mouth, the alae of the nose, the shape of the eye—are detailed.

A man is walking ahead of Metjetji. With his left hand he grasps Metjetji's staff, and with his right he holds a bird by its wings. He is depicted on a smaller scale, attesting to his lesser importance. An inscription explains that he is Metjetji's "eldest son [whom he loves], honored by his father, Ptah-hotep." Another son is depicted behind Metjetji, hugging his father's leg; an inscription indicates this is "his [son] whom he loves, Ihy."

The right side of the block is occupied by a large vertical inscription, its lower part now lost. It gave the names and titles of Metjetji: "royal noble, Director of the Office of Tenants of the Palace."

The scene is surmounted by four lines of hieroglyphs, remnants of an autobiographical text extolling the tomb owner's

popularity: "I was honored by men; I was beloved of the multitude. As for all who saw me anywhere ('A blessed soul and beloved man is coming,' they said of me in every place), Director of the Office of Tenants of the Palace, Metjetji." CZ

PROVENANCE: Probably Saqqara, tomb of Metjetji

BIBLIOGRAPHY: Kaplony 1976, pp. 26–31, no. 5; Roccati 1982, p. 145, § 121; Ward and Fidler 1993, p. 111

154. Right Jamb of the Entry Door in the Facade of the Tomb of Metjetji

Fifth Dynasty, reign of Unis, or early Sixth Dynasty
Painted limestone sculpted in sunk relief
H. 142.9 cm (56¼ in.); w. 76.2 cm (30 in.)
The Nelson-Atkins Museum of Art, Kansas City, Missouri, Purchase: Nelson Trust 52-7/2

The scene on this block is almost exactly like the one on the facing jamb (cat. no. 153), but in reverse. There are a few differences, however. Because this slab is undamaged, Metjetji's scepter decorated with a papyrus umbel is intact, and his kilt is well preserved. (The scepter here, unlike that in a similar relief from the same tomb, also oriented to the left [cat. no. 152], passes in front of the kilt.) Also a different son is represented walking in front of Metjetji and holding his staff. This small figure is "his eldest son whom he loves, Khuensobek." A young girl dressed in a long, clinging dress stands behind Metjetji, and the inscription gives her identity: "his daughter whom he loves, Iret-sobek."

In front of the tomb owner a large vertical inscription reads: "royal noble, Director of the Office of Tenants of the Palace, Metjetji, so called."

As on the facing jamb, the scene is surmounted by four lines of hieroglyphs, and the remnants of this autobiographical text attest that the deceased has properly paid the artisans who worked on his mastaba: "[As for all those who built me this tomb, I paid them], after they had performed the work here, with the copper that was an endowment from my personal property. I gave them clothes and provided their nourishment with the bread and beer from my personal property, and they praised God for me because of it. Director of the Office of Tenants of the Palace, Metjetji." cz

PROVENANCE: Probably Saqqara, tomb of Metjetji

BIBLIOGRAPHY: Kaplony 1976, pp. 26–31, no. 6; Roccati 1982, p. 145, § 122; Ward and Fidler 1993, p. 111

155. FALSE-DOOR STELA FROM THE TOMB OF METJETJI

Fifth Dynasty, reign of Unis, or early Sixth
Dynasty
Limestone
H. 140 cm (55⅛ in.); w. 70 cm (27½ in.)
The Metropolitan Museum of Art, New York,
Gift of Mr. and Mrs. J. J. Klejman, 1964 64.100

The false-door stela is a stone slab with a
niche representing a narrow doorway surmounted by a rolled mat. It was an essential element of Egyptian tombs. As the
principal site of the cult of the deceased person, it was the place where offerings were
brought and arranged on a stone table at
the base of the niche. The passageway
between the world of the dead and that of
the living, the false door can be considered
a miniature model of the tomb, with the
lower part representing the facade and the
upper part showing the interior.

Metjetji had himself depicted no fewer
than eight times on his false door. At the top
of the stela he is seated, holding a long staff
and a folded cloth. Three lines of inscription
promise him offerings, both during great
feasts and on a daily basis: bread, beer, meat,
fowl, green and black eye paint, and unguent.
In the offering scene just above the door he
is seated, extending his hand toward a table
laden with bread. All around him, hieroglyphs guarantee him offerings by the thousands, which are depicted at either side,
flanked by two images of Metjetji standing.
Similar representations appear at the bot-
toms of the doorjambs, with texts running
along them. They place the deceased under
the protection of the gods Anubis and
Osiris and express the wish that he may
"walk on the beautiful roads of the West
and enjoy a perfect burial in the necropolis."
Metjetji's many titles precede his name,
repeated ten times on the monument: "royal
noble, Director of the Office of Tenants of
the Palace, honored by the king, honored
by Unis." Except on the mat this name per-
petuating the memory of the deceased is
always placed in front of or above his portrait, which is shown in silhouette, in a
rudimentary style that contrasts with
the refinement of the scenes adorning the
facade (cat. nos. 151–154).   CZ

PROVENANCE: Probably Saqqara, tomb of
Metjetji

BIBLIOGRAPHY: Cooney 1953, pp. 19, 24,
fig. 14; *Gazette des Beaux-Arts* 49 (February 1967),
suppl., fig. 205; Kaplony 1976, pp. 48–49; Metropolitan Museum 1983, p. 93, fig. 14; Dorman,
Harper, and Pittman 1987, pp. 22–23; Fischer
1995, pp. 82 n. 15, 89

156. RELIEF OF DONKEYS FROM THE TOMB OF METJETJI

Fifth Dynasty, reign of Unis, or early Sixth
Dynasty
Painted limestone
H. 42 cm (16⅝ in.); w. 47 cm (18½ in.)
Royal Ontario Museum, Toronto 953.116.2

In this relief fragment five donkeys advance
in a line, sacks tied on their backs. Four
move obediently ahead, while the fifth bends
its head down to munch greedily on an ear
of grain. This delightful detail illustrates
the mastery Egyptian sculptors achieved in
the realm of animal art. It is admirable how

the artist, even while respecting such conventions of Egyptian design as the legs
shown in a staggered sequence and the single line of the donkeys' backs, was able to
capture convincingly the quivering of the
long ears and the facial expression of each
of the beasts. Though the relief was highlighted with red, yellow, and green paint,
the execution is rudimentary: for example,
the background is treated unevenly and
modeling is practically nonexistent. The
emphasis is placed on the incised outlines
of the figures.

The fragment was part of a harvest scene,
a theme often depicted in chapels. Arranged
along several registers, such agricultural

scenes showed the work cycle, from sowing to reaping. The wheat was destined for the table of the deceased, who was generously supplied with various breads and cakes.

The upper part of this block displays the feet of the peasants who were shown in the next register bringing in the sheaves. One sheaf is carefully depicted to the left of the donkeys. It has the barbs characteristic of the fat wheat (*Triticum turgidum*) grown in ancient Egypt. A hieroglyphic caption reads, "balance of sheaves: 1,300." Once they were placed in sacks, the sheaves were transported on the backs of donkeys. The inscription "herd of donkeys" above the animals defines their nature, supplementing the properties of the image with the precision of language.   CZ

PROVENANCE: Probably Saqqara, tomb of Metjetji

BIBLIOGRAPHY: Kaplony 1976, pp. 22–24, no. 3

157. WALL PAINTINGS FROM THE TOMB OF METJETJI

Fifth Dynasty, reign of Unis, or early Sixth Dynasty
Paint on *muna* over a smoothed coating
H., largest fragment 59 cm (23 ¼ in.); w., largest fragment 25 cm (9⅞ in.)
Musée du Louvre, Paris E 25512, 25513, 25521, 25522, 25524, 25535, 25537, 25538
Paris only

Metjetji's tomb was adorned with mural paintings as well as reliefs. The forty-two fragments in the Louvre collection are only a part of these decorations, and they come from different scenes. Thus, the aim of this display is not reconstitution but an evocation that takes into account the orientation of the figures and the themes illustrated: inspection of work in the fields and workshops, a harp concert, a game played on a checkerboard, the bringing of offerings, and funerary rites. As is usual in Egyptian tomb painting, the scenes are distributed along several registers—as many as five—interrupted by large images of the deceased or by vertical bands of colored rectangles. A series of horizontal bands, alternately red bordered by black, yellow, and solid black, make up the base of the decorated part.

This group belongs to a composition that represented Metjetji receiving the products of his estates. He appears at the far right

depicted in large scale, facing a procession of his servants. Standing and leaning on a staff, he wears a beaded broad collar, sandals,[1] and a feline pelt that partly covers his kilt and apron. A fragmentary inscription gives some of his titles: "Liege of the King of the Great Palace, Administrator of the Jackal, Director of the Office of the Khentiushes at the Great Palace, Chief Keeper of Fabrics, honored by Anubis who is on his mountain." At Metjetji's feet, one of his sons, named Ihy, holds in one hand a spotted greyhound on a leash; in the other he wields a whip. The young boy, dressed in a short loincloth and wearing a heart-shaped pendant, has his hair in a braid, called the "sidelock of youth," with a disk at the end.

A group of servants is advancing toward these two figures. Three of them are driving a herd of animals from the desert: an oryx with sharp horns and gazelles wearing collars. The colors are remarkably well preserved, as is the preparatory grid of the drawing. Particularly admirable is the shading around the forms of the animals and their delicately veined ears. At the top of the painting, a mutilated inscription captures snatches of a dialogue: "Bring him, companion!"; "young ibex." Other fragments belong to the same scene: a man, whose head is missing, holds an ox's hoof in his left hand; a handful of ducks with glistening plumage is escaping from his right. Above, traces of a representation of three scribes recording the offerings are visible. The scribe in the middle holds a rolled-up papyrus in his hand; an inscription designates him the "Scribe of the Divine Archives in the Great Palace, Iri." In front of him, in a damaged composition, priests are performing the rite of "reciting the glorifications for Metjetji." One of them is wearing the shoulder sash of a cult priest across his torso.   CZ

1. On sandals as a dating criterion, see Cherpion 1999.

PROVENANCE: Probably Saqqara, tomb of Metjetji; purchased 1964

BIBLIOGRAPHY: Porter and Moss 1979, pp. 646–47; Ziegler 1990b, pp. 123–51, no. 20

158. Chest

Fifth Dynasty
Wood, ivory, and Egyptian faience
H. 19 cm (7½ in.); w. 37.5 cm (14¼ in.); d. 23 cm
(9 in.)
Soprintendenza al Museo della Antichità Egizie,
Turin s.15709

Remains found in early tombs at Naga el-Deir and Saqqara show that wood chests, boxes, and caskets were already made in the Predynastic and Archaic Periods. In Old Kingdom tomb scenes they appear as standard household and tomb equipment, used for storage of linen, toiletries, cosmetics, jewels, and other items. Depictions of rectangular boxes with framework construction, similar to the present example, are common in Sixth Dynasty tombs, such as those of Ni-ankh-ba[1] and Mehu.[2] It has been suggested, however, that the Gebelein mastaba of Perim, where this box was found, dates to the Fourth Dynasty.[3]

The finely made chest has two parts: a rectangular inlaid box and a supporting frame of four legs joined by four crossrails. The wood side panels of the box are lined with vertically placed ivory rods, above which extends a frieze of alternating black and blue faience tiles. The top of the lid is decorated with two rows of four lotus flowers, made of blue and black faience, which are set against the white-yellow background of ivory plaques and interset with alternating vertical strips of ivory and faience. Long strips of ivory and faience form a rectangular border on the lid.   KG

1. Hassan 1975c, pl. 28A.
2. Altenmüller 1998, pl. 98.2.
3. Donadoni Roveri et al. 1993, p. 247.

PROVENANCE: Gebelein, mastaba of Perim, Schiaparelli excavation, 1914

BIBLIOGRAPHY: Scamuzzi 1965, pl. 11; Seipel 1975a, pp. 369–70, pl. 362a; Curto 1984a; Donadoni, Curto, and Donadoni Roveri 1990, p. 259; Donadoni Roveri et al. 1993, p. 247; Donadoni Roveri, D'Amicone, and Leospo 1994, p. 30, figs. 19, 20

159. BASIN AND EWER

Fifth Dynasty
Pottery
Basin: h. 10 cm (4 in.); d. 10 cm (4 in.)
Ewer: h. 18.2 cm (7⅛ in.); d. 13.5 cm (5⅜ in.)
Kunsthistorisches Museum, Ägyptisch-
Orientalische Sammlung, Vienna ÄS 7439

Basin and ewer sets such as this one constituted the equipment for hand washing during the Old Kingdom, both in everyday life
and in the next world. The Egyptian word
for this type of basin, *šʿwtj*, indicates that it
contained sand, which was used in hand
washing; the term for this sort of ewer,
ḥzmnı, implies that it was filled with a solution of water and natron.[1]

The basin is deep, with a flat base and
sharply flaring sides. The ewer has a broad
biconical body, a cylindrical neck with a
rolled rim, and a long cylindrical spout that
projects upward from the shoulder of the
vessel. Its slightly convex base clearly indicates that it was meant to be supported in
the basin. Both vessels have been thrown on
the wheel and covered with a polished red
coating. This polished red pottery of the Old
Kingdom is commonly called Meidum ware

because large numbers of bowls of this type
were found at the pyramid of Snefru at
Meidum.[2] This ware may be made of either
Nile or marl (desert) clay; the red-ocher coating is thick, even, and polished to a deep,
lustrous shine. Basin and ewer sets made of
metal were used by the living and included
in burials of the wealthy, while those in pottery were copied from the metal prototypes
and reserved for funerary use.[3] Whether in
pottery or metal, these sets were part of the
offering rites of the funerary meal, where
the need for hand washing before eating
was the same as in this world.

The form of this ewer, with its cylindrical
neck and straight tubular spout, is less common than the squat, biconical, neckless type
with rounded shoulder and beaklike, curved
spout. It is the latter type that is normally
represented in tomb scenes of the funerary
meal.[4] Model washing sets in metal or
stone could also be placed in the tomb.[5]

This set comes from the shaft of a
mastaba in the cemetery west of the pyramid of Khufu at Giza and is dated to the
Fifth Dynasty. The only grave offering
recovered from this subsidiary burial, it is
almost identical to a pottery set found in
a tomb at Armant, south of Thebes, and

dated by the excavators to the Fourth
Dynasty.[6] Parallels in metal have been found
at Giza in the Fourth Dynasty mastaba of
Prince Ba-baef and in a set purchased near
Qena and dated to the Sixth Dynasty.[7] SA

1. Balcz 1932, pp. 95–98, fig. 13; Hayes 1953,
   p. 119; Do. Arnold 1984, cols. 213–14.
2. Bourriau 1981, p. 18.
3. Do. Arnold 1984, col. 214.
4. Hayes 1953, p. 93, fig. 52; Junker 1953, p. 59,
   fig. 35.
5. See Hayes 1953, p. 119, fig. 72 (Metropolitan
   Museum, 11.150.2); and Radwan 1983, p. 52,
   no. 129A,B, pl. 24.
6. Mond and Myers 1937, vol. 1, pp. 21–22,
   vol. 2, pl. 30.4S_1,90S_1; Bourriau 1981, p. 52,
   nos. 84, 85. Other pottery examples come
   from an Old Kingdom tomb at El Kab, perhaps dated to the Fourth Dynasty (Quibell
   1898, p. 19, pl. 12.51,55), and from tomb
   5528 at Badari, dated to the Fourth Dynasty
   (Brunton 1927, p. 23; Brunton 1928,
   pls. 76.4T, 81.90J).
7. Radwan 1983, p. 46, no. 127A,B, pl. 23,
   p. 68, no. 185A,B, pl. 43.

PROVENANCE: Giza, Western Cemetery,
shaft 23, Junker excavation, 1912; gift of the
Wiener Akademie der Wissenschaften, 1913

BIBLIOGRAPHY: Junker 1943, pp. 160–61,
fig. 55; Seipel 1993, p. 116, no. 54; Seipel
1995, p. 44, fig. 5a, no. 1/5a

160. BOWL

Mid-Fourth to mid-Fifth Dynasty
Egyptian alabaster
H. 7 cm (2¾ in.); diam. 21.2 cm (8⅜ in.)
The Metropolitan Museum of Art, New York,
Rogers Fund, 1910 10.176.158

For this elegant round-bottomed vessel with flaring recurved rim the artist used a piece of veined Egyptian alabaster. Embedded in its semitranslucent white matrix is a band of irregularly spaced streaks of reddish brown that vary in intensity. In the finished work the veined band is positioned slightly off center, which lends an exciting, syncopated effect to the piece.

Bowls and basins with recurved rims were a standard vessel type in the Old Kingdom. They began to appear in the Third Dynasty and became ubiquitous from the beginning of the Fourth Dynasty.[1] The terracotta version, made of a hard fired clay and coated with a carefully burnished wash ranging from orange to reddish brown, was the typical tableware of the Pyramid Age. Representations in painting and relief show people drinking from such bowls and basins,[2] as well as using them at table for soups and stews[3] and preparing food in them.[4] In some pictures the vessels serve as flowerpots, and in one that shows net making a man soaks a rope through water in a pot with the distinctive recurved rim.[5] In a report on excavations around the pyramid at Meidum the great British archaeologist W. M. F. Petrie first described this ware in the most admiring terms.[6] The vessels have been called Meidum bowls ever since.

The stone Meidum bowl appeared at about the same time as the terracotta version. In reliefs in the early Fourth Dynasty tomb of Ra-hotep, a high official of King Snefru buried at Meidum, several vessels with the distinctive sickle-shaped rim are depicted and identified in inscriptions as made of granite and other stones.[7] And early examples of actual stone vessels of the type, most of which are alabaster, have been found in tombs of the Third Dynasty.[8] Because Egyptian alabaster is not a suitable material for holding liquids,[9] it must be assumed that these stone variants are imitations of the clay vessels made for use in burials. Stone was the material of eternity for the ancient Egyptians, and the terracotta bowl reproduced in stone and placed in a tomb clearly guaranteed unending sustenance for the deceased.

Since the stone vessels imitated their terracotta prototypes quite faithfully, it is possible to date the stone versions by comparing them to the clay prototypes, which have been excavated in great numbers and whose development archaeologists have been able to chart with fair accuracy. The features used for diagnosis are the height of the rim zone, the angularity of the edge below it, and the depth of the concave rim curve. This vessel's edge is less angular than those of the early Fourth Dynasty,[10] but it is more pronounced and has a broader rim zone than most examples from the late Fifth Dynasty.[11] Therefore a date in the late Fourth or early Fifth Dynasty appears to be indicated.[12]   DOA

1. The pottery of the Third Dynasty is still a largely unstudied field. A Third Dynasty date for early vessels with recurved rims is, however, indicated by shards from the tomb of Hesi-re; see Quibell 1913, p. 38, pl. 27.
2. Faltings 1998, p. 235 doc. 7.
3. Balcz 1933, pp. 21–26.
4. Faltings 1998, pp. 90 doc. 4, 233 doc. 3, 238–39 docs. 14, 16, 249–51 (bread making), 280–83 (basins with spout).
5. Balcz 1933, pp. 26–27 (flower vases), 29 (rope).
6. Petrie 1892, p. 35. The ware was described most recently by Kammerer-Grothaus (1998, vol. 2, pp. 79–82, with earlier bibliography).
7. Petrie 1892, pl. 13; Balcz 1933, p. 23, fig. 35.
8. Aston 1994, p. 132.
9. When modern vessels made of Egyptian alabaster are used as flower vases they shatter, since the water penetrates the hairline fissures in the stone and causes them to explode.
10. Quibell 1898, no. 2, pl. 3 (center); Reisner and Smith 1955, p. 65 (type 32), fig. 61.
11. Kaiser 1969, p. 81, fig. 10 (middle section).
12. For the closest parallels, see Reisner and Smith 1955, p. 69, fig. 79, no. 17t, and p. 81, fig. 110, no. 34-8-1 (G 4341B); also in Kaiser 1969, p. 81, fig. 10 (upper section); and Borchardt 1910, p. 117, fig. 155 (right center).

PROVENANCE: Unknown

BIBLIOGRAPHY: N. Scott 1944, fig. 18; Hayes 1953, p. 118

161. JAR

Mid-Fourth to mid-Fifth Dynasty
Egyptian alabaster
H. 33 cm (13 in.)
The Metropolitan Museum of Art, New York,
Rogers Fund, 1921 21.2.8

This imposing alabaster jar follows a prototype of a kind of metal vessel that was commonly used to pour water in libation rituals.[1]
The stone version seen here, surely made
for an upper-class burial, served to perpetu-
ate that ritual performance in eternity. Similar stone jars were found in tombs dating to
the Sixth Dynasty around Memphis and in
Middle and Upper Egypt (fig. 72).[2] But the
Metropolitan Museum's jar differs from
those examples in a number of significant
points: it has a broader body and a shorter
neck than the Sixth Dynasty vessels and
also displays a more pronounced separation
between body and neck because the widest
part of the broader shoulder is positioned
very close to the joint with the neck. Terracotta vessels that show similar features are
from the Fourth and Fifth Dynasties,[3] and a
similar date is indicated for the present vase.

The jar beautifully reveals how adeptly
ancient Egyptian artisans exploited the particular qualities of various stones. For this
vase the artist—surely intentionally—chose
a piece of alabaster whose characteristics
allowed him to form the neck and shoulder
from almost faultless semitranslucent creamy
white stone and produce a body covered
by a variety of undulating veins of orange,
light brown, and darker brown. Also contributing to the interesting effect is the presence overall of patches of a nontranslucent
chalk-white material whose irregular outlines seem to have been applied with a
painter's brush.   DOA

1. Balcz 1934, pp. 62–63. Milk pots of very similar shape (ibid., pp. 63–64, fig. 94) were made
from fired clay and are less likely to have been
imitated in stone. For metal examples of the
libation jar, see Radwan 1983, pp. 60, 62,
nos. 151, 160Q, pls. 28, 32 (both Sixth Dynasty),
pp. 81–82, nos. 194A, 195A, pl. 44 (First Intermediate Period).
2. Aston 1994, p. 132, no. 127. The groups
Aston assigns to the Fifth Dynasty (Mahasna

M 107: Garstang 1903, p. 30, pls. 37, 38, 43;
Mostagedda 689: Brunton 1937, p. 107, pl. 63;
and Mahasna M 70: Garstang 1903, p. 29,
pls. 34, 36, 43) surely date to the Sixth Dynasty,
as the presence of collared vases, as well as
other evidence, shows.
3. Brunton 1928, pl. 80, nos. 71A, 71B (Fourth
Dynasty); Reisner and Smith 1955, p. 69,
fig. 81, no. 14-1-16, G 4630A (Khafre to
Neferirkare). An interesting comparison can

be drawn between the Metropolitan Museum
vase and an elegant late Middle Kingdom
alabaster jar excavated at Kerma and now in
the Museum of Fine Arts, Boston, 21.2589
(Bonnet et al. 1990, p. 207, no. 243).

PROVENANCE: Unknown

BIBLIOGRAPHY: Hayes 1953, p. 118

BROAD COLLARS

Despite an abundance of artistic renderings, which attest that the broad collar (*wesekh*) (see "Jewelry in the Old Kingdom" in this catalogue, p. 304) was in general use, excavations have uncovered few complete examples. The plundering of necropolises provides one explanation for this, as the frequent presence of gold on mummies has been a strong lure for thieves since ancient times. Thieves often left behind only a few scattered elements of a precious hoard—a simple gold terminal in the tomb of Ka-gemni, a high official from the end of the Sixth Dynasty, or a few faience beads and a terminal in the tomb of Queen Iput, mother of King Pepi I.[1] Even when, by some chance, a tomb was not plundered, necklaces rarely survived intact because the natural deterioration of burials usually led to a dispersion of their beads. The broad collar of Henmu-baef from Giza,[2] on which the beads still occupied their original position, is a notable exception. The lack of precise data regarding the original arrangement of their beads often makes the reassembling of broad collars impossible. In a few cases, however, it has been possible to reconstruct them on the basis of information provided in excavation reports. PR

1. Firth and Gunn 1926: for Iput, see vol. 1, pp. 11–12, vol. 2, pl. 15B; for Ka-gemni, see vol. 1, pp. 20–23, vol. 2, pl. 15C.
2. Hassan 1953, pp. 9ff., pls. 13, 14.

162–164. FUNERARY ORNAMENTS FROM MASTABA OF NEFER-IHI AT GIZA

Mastaba D 208 at Giza, excavated by the von Sieglin expedition in 1903, possessed several shafts leading to various mortuary chambers. One of these chambers, accessible via shaft number 4, contained a sarcophagus sealed by five stone slabs. Inside, excavators found a large number of scattered beads that were later reassembled into a broad collar and two ankle bracelets (cat. nos. 162, 163). The chamber accessible via shaft number 9 yielded another, equally interesting set of funerary ornaments, composed primarily of a metal diadem[1] and a necklace (cat. no. 164).

1. Ägyptisches Museum, Universität Leipzig, 2500.

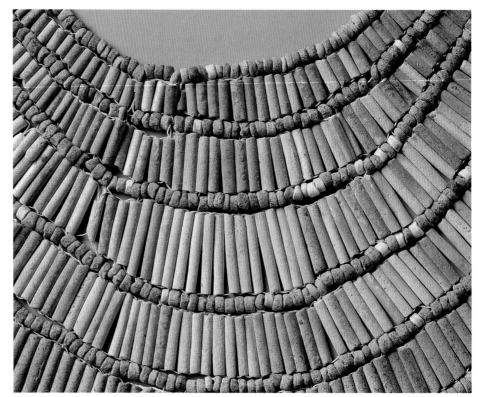

Detail, cat. no. 162

162. BROAD COLLAR

Fifth Dynasty
Egyptian faience
W. 30 cm (11⅞ in.)
Ägyptisches Museum, Universität Leipzig 3766

The broad collar found in mastaba D 208 at Giza is made up of five rows of cylindrical beads arranged vertically and framed by six rows of small disk-shaped beads. The beads, made of Egyptian faience, have lost most of their brilliant blue glaze and now have a matte brown hue, which produces a very different effect from that of the original. The curved shape of the necklace derives from the arrangement of the beads in decreasing order of size from the bottom to the top row and from the center toward the edges in each individual row. Semicircular elements called terminals were usually attached to the ends to join the strings of the necklace together, but they are missing in this case; the collar also does not seem to have had any pendants.

This kind of broad collar was very common, but there were also other types. One of these was smaller and composed of several rows of horizontally strung beads held together at regular intervals by small bead spacers, sometimes in the shape of a wave.[1] When both types of collars are depicted on statues that have retained their color, they are primarily green, blue, red, and yellow. PR

1. See, for example, Hassan 1932, pls. 42 (collar of Mereruka), 79 (collar found in the mastaba of Hesi and Ni-ankh-hathor).

PROVENANCE: Giza, mastaba of Nefer-ihi (D 208, shaft no. 4), von Sieglin expedition, 1903

BIBLIOGRAPHY: Steindorff and Hölscher 1991, pp. 100–104; Krauspe 1997a, p. 49

163. ANKLE BRACELET

Fifth Dynasty
Egyptian faience
L. 23.2 cm (9⅛ in.); w. 6.6 cm (2⅝ in.)
Ägyptisches Museum, Universität Leipzig 3767

This ankle bracelet, one of a pair discovered with the broad collar in mastaba D 208 (cat. no. 162), contains three rows of cylindrical beads that are strung vertically and framed by four rows of small disk-shaped beads. Since no bead spacer or clasp was apparently found in the sarcophagus, it is likely that the two bracelets were fastened simply by making a knot in the beading strings. As on the necklace, the beads have lost much of their original blue glaze and are now a relatively uniform brown.

In the Old Kingdom, ankle bracelets were worn almost exclusively by women; they appear on men's ankles in only a very few representations. In later periods, however, they are sometimes depicted adorning the gods. Known since the Predynastic Period but especially common from the beginning of the Fourth Dynasty through the end of the Old Kingdom, they were generally accompanied by a matching broad collar and wrist bracelets. It is sometimes difficult to distinguish the ankle and wrist bracelets from each other, and often only their location at the time of discovery makes such a determination possible. PR

PROVENANCE: Giza, mastaba of Nefer-ihi (D 208, shaft no. 4), von Sieglin expedition, 1903

BIBLIOGRAPHY: Steindorff and Hölscher 1991, pp. 100–104

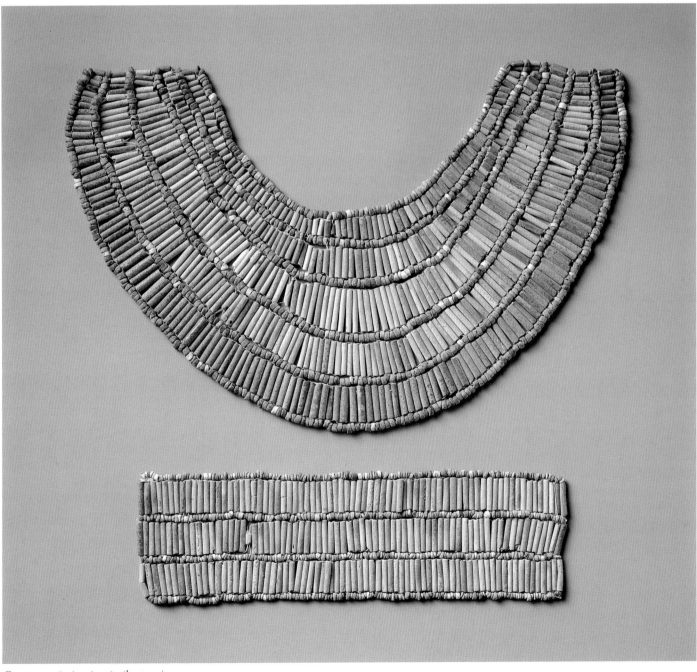

Cat. nos. 162 (top), 163 (bottom)

164. NECKLACE

Fifth Dynasty
Egyptian faience
L. 83 cm (32⅝ in.)
Ägyptisches Museum, Universität Leipzig 3770

Shaft number 9 of mastaba D 208 at Giza
led to a mortuary chamber containing the
sarcophagus of a woman buried with a diadem and this necklace, whose various elements were discovered scattered across the
bottom of the sarcophagus. Excavators
noted the presence of a metal wire, now lost,
on which the beads were originally strung.
As restored, the necklace comprises small
beetle-shaped amulets in blue faience inserted
between two rows of cylindrical and disk-
shaped beads, also in faience. Each insect
has two holes through it by which the two
rows of beads are interlocked.

   That the beetle motif appeared in the
Archaic Period (the First and Second
Dynasties) is attested by a piece of gold-
leaf jewelry found in a First Dynasty tomb
in Naga el-Deir.[1] The subject continued to
be popular in necklaces through the First
Intermediate Period. The finest examples
of these motifs are made of precious metal;
among them are fifty gold insects decorating
a necklace found in a tomb at Giza[2] and two
gold beetles, once inlaid with lapis lazuli,
from the tomb of Queen Iput at Saqqara.[3]
Most of the surviving examples are made
of faience, however, and they are either employed in necklaces such as this one[4] or form
a row of pendants in certain broad collars.[5]
The two species of beetles most commonly
represented are elaterids (*Agrypnus noto-
donta latr.*), which are widespread in Egypt,
and buprestids, which seem to be depicted
here.[6] In some instances, elaterids were
associated with the goddess Neith and were
supposed to bring her blessings upon the
person who wore their image.   PR

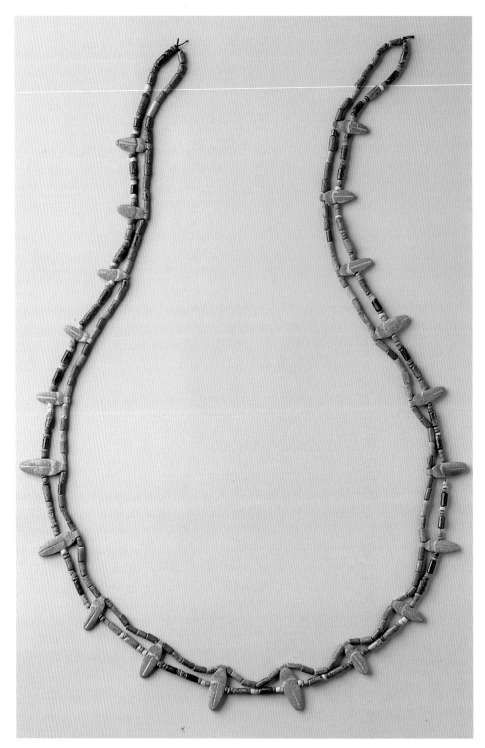

1. Reisner 1908, pls. 6, 9a.
2. Egyptian Museum, Cairo, JE 72334, necklace
   from tomb 294, Fifth Dynasty?; see Hassan
   1936.
3. See Firth and Gunn 1926, vol. 2.
4. See the necklace found in the tomb of
   Ni-hebsed-pepi, in Jéquier 1929, pp. 21–22.
5. Museum of Fine Arts, Boston, 13.3086,
   necklace of Impy from Giza, tomb G 2381A
   (Sixth Dynasty).

6. See Keimer 1931, pp. 159ff.

PROVENANCE: Giza, mastaba of Nefer-ihi
(D 208, shaft no. 9), von Sieglin expedition, 1903

BIBLIOGRAPHY: Steindorff and Hölscher 1991,
pp. 100–104; Krauspe 1997a, p. 50

165. Necklace

Fifth Dynasty
Carnelian, porphyry, steatite, and copper
L. 22 cm (8⅝ in.)
Trustees of the British Museum, London EA 62535

Extremely sober both in the shapes of its beads and in its materials, this necklace includes barrel-shaped and biconical carnelian beads; round, ridged beads in black-and-white porphyry; long biconical steatite beads; and a large biconical steatite bead, placed in the center and flanked on either side by a remnant of a disk-shaped copper bead. Its components were found around the neck of a deceased woman as part of a longer necklace, which also included large cylindrical green faience beads and four copper beads.[1]   PR

1. Currently British Museum, London, EA 62536; see Andrews 1981, vol. 1, p. 45, no. 244.

PROVENANCE: Mostagedda, tomb 1420, British Museum expedition, 1928–29

BIBLIOGRAPHY: Brunton 1937, p. 97, Tomb Register, pl. 45, Bead Register, pl. 49, Bead Corpus, pls. 58, 78 B3, 5, C7, M14, 79 B4–F8; Andrews 1981, p. 45, no. 243, pl. 20

166. BRACELET

Late Fifth or early Sixth Dynasty
Gold
L. 16.2 cm (6⅜ in.); w. 1.5 cm (⅝ in.)
Kunsthistorisches Museum, Ägyptisch-
Orientalische Sammlung, Vienna ÄS 7901

The jewelry found on the mummy of Ra-wer II—a simple necklace of small faience beads strung on a gold wire as well as this bracelet—was modest in design. The bracelet is made of thin gold leaf joined at the ends, which are round and perforated, probably so that a string fastener could be passed through them. One of the ends is slightly damaged.

It has been suggested that such bracelets originally covered plaster or copper cores[1] and had a purely funerary use. A similar technique was used in certain funerary diadems, composed of a copper or wood band covered with gold leaf perforated at either end.[2] Originating in the Fifth Dynasty, these bracelets have frequently been discovered in tombs dating from the end of the Old Kingdom to the beginning of the First Intermediate Period.[3] They are found in nonroyal as well as royal burials. A bracelet almost identical to this one adorned the wrist of Queen Iput at Saqqara.[4]   PR

1. Traces of copper have been found on some of these bracelets; Brunton 1928, p. 66.
2. For example, Ägyptisches Museum, Universität Leipzig, 2500.
3. For examples, see Hassan 1941, p. 142 (Ankh-haf, Sixth Dynasty); Junker 1944, p. 228 (Ptah-hotep, Sixth Dynasty); and Brunton 1927, pls. 45 (tomb 7334, Sixth Dynasty), 46 (tomb 7923, Seventh to Eighth Dynasty).
4. Egyptian Museum, Cairo, JE 47839; see Firth and Gunn 1926, vol. 1, pp. 11–12, vol. 2, pl. 15B.

PROVENANCE: Giza, mastaba of Ra-wer II, Junker excavation, 1913–14

BIBLIOGRAPHY: Junker 1938, pp. 223ff., fig. 45

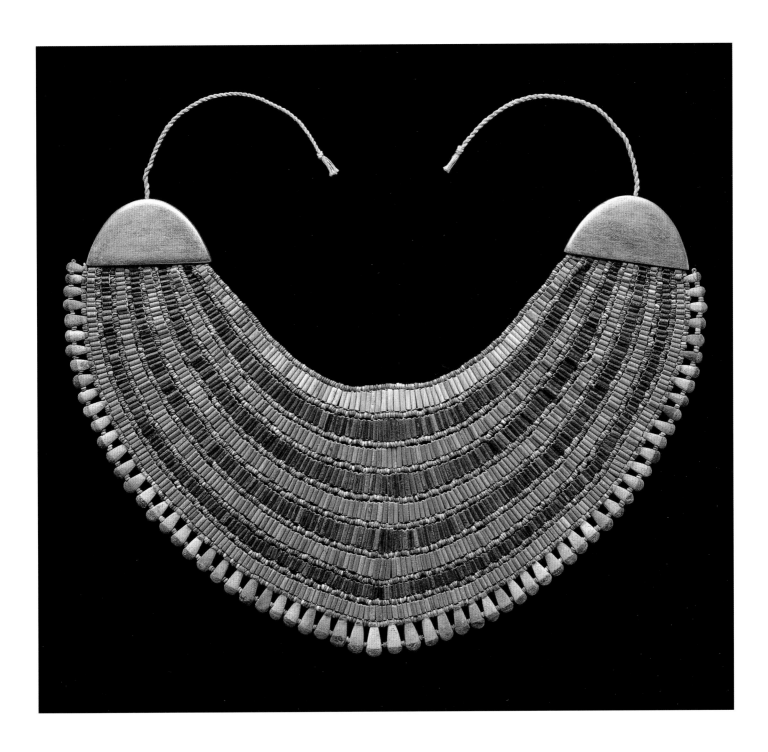

167. BROAD COLLAR

Fifth Dynasty?
Egyptian faience
H. 15 cm (5⅞ in.), w. 36 cm (14⅛ in.)
Museum of Fine Arts, Boston, Harvard University–
Museum of Fine Arts Expedition 13.4171

Nine rows of vertically arranged cylindrical beads separated by ten rows of small ring-shaped beads make up the body of this broad collar; its bottom row is composed of petal-shaped pendants with darkened tips. Here, as in other examples in the exhibition, the faience has lost much of its original color and displays light to dark brown tones, although certain beads have retained a light green hue. The collar was reconstructed from beads found in mastaba G 1360 at Giza and from pen-

dants that were also discovered there but apparently in a different, unidentified tomb. The gilded, semicircular terminals are a modern reconstruction, based on the usual shape of such elements.

Most likely dating to the Fifth Dynasty, G 1360 is one of the small tombs located among the large Fourth Dynasty mastabas in the Western Cemetery.   PR

PROVENANCE: Giza, Western Cemetery, mastaba G 1360, Reisner excavation, 1913

168, 169. FUNERARY ORNAMENTS FROM MASTABA S 309/316 AT GIZA

This set comes from mastaba S 309/316 at Giza, excavated by Hermann Junker in 1913. The tomb's owner, whose name is not known, is certainly the man who occupied the intact burial chamber accessible through shaft number 316, one of eight in the mastaba. Inside the sarcophagus, scattered around the skeleton, there were many remnants of a copper diadem covered in gold leaf, of a type illustrated in many Old Kingdom reliefs. Also found were elements of a broad collar and a faience bracelet (cat. nos. 168, 169). The excavation report indicates that the broad collar was covered with gold leaf at the time of discovery; some of this gold leaf is now in the collection of the Kunsthistorisches Museum in Vienna. The entire set has recently been restored and reconstructed.   PR

168. BROAD COLLAR WITH COUNTERPOISE

Late Fifth or early Sixth Dynasty
Egyptian faience and gold leaf
L. 26 cm (10¼ in.); w. 20 cm (7⅞ in.)
Kunsthistorisches Museum, Ägyptisch-Orientalische Sammlung, Vienna ÄS 9072

Few broad collars are as well preserved as this example, which is almost complete. It is composed of four rows of vertically arranged cylindrical beads, decreasing in size toward the edges and framed by five rows of small disk-shaped faience beads (their original blue, green, or yellow glaze has now faded to brown); the bottom row is made of teardrop pendants, yellow with a green dot at the lower end, separated by small beads. Pendants were often made in the shape of teardrops at the time this collar was made, but they could also assume the form of beetles or petals, especially during the Sixth Dynasty.

The front faces of the semicircular terminals are made of ocher-colored faience covered with gold leaf. Five holes bored through the terminals allow the strands to be joined into a single cord on either side. These cords, covered with small disk-shaped beads, are attached to a counterpoise made up of a small semicircular element, five rows of vertically strung cylindrical beads separated by smaller disk-shaped beads, and a row of teardrop pendants similar to that on the collar. The counterpoise, which hung at the wearer's back, was intended to hold the necklace in place by balancing its weight. Frequently shown in scenes depicting the fabrication of necklaces or award ceremonies, and later in object friezes from coffins, counterpoises are also often represented on the backs of statues. Few examples survive, and the presence of a counterpoise here may indicate that this collar was used during the owner's lifetime. Conversely, collars without a counterpoise are certain to have been merely funerary ornaments.   PR

PROVENANCE: Giza, mastaba S 316, Junker excavation, 1913–14

BIBLIOGRAPHY: Junker 1944, pp. 54ff.; Satzinger 1987, p. 83; Haslauer 1991, pp. 18–21

169. BRACELET

Late Fifth or early Sixth Dynasty
Egyptian faience
L. 16.5 cm (6½ in.); w. 3.5 cm (1⅜ in.)
Kunsthistorisches Museum, Ägyptisch-
Orientalische Sammlung, Vienna ÄS 9073

This bracelet from mastaba S 316 at Giza has ten strands of small, ring-shaped beads made of faience, which, like those of the matching collar (cat. no. 168), are now a relatively dark brown. Four bead spacers, placed at regular intervals, serve to strengthen the bracelet and to prevent the strands of beads from overlapping. The oldest known example of this type of bracelet, which was worn at least from the Third Dynasty on, was found in the tomb of Sekhemkhet, Djoser's successor, and includes nearly four hundred gold beads divided into ten rows, punctuated by five thin gold bead spacers.

During the Old Kingdom, such bead spacers, which also appear on some necklaces, could be either straight or wave-shaped.[1] Those of the present bracelet are straight, but three display a certain peculiarity: the front face contains a decoration in relief, composed of seven nearly round linked protuberances that end in a small appendage. Rather than the usual wave, this pattern resembles the pod of a plant. The pod might be from a carob, or perhaps a moringa, plant,[2] in which case the allusion would be either to the hieroglyph *nedjem*, suggesting the notion of sweetness, or to a sacred oil produced from carob. Nonetheless, this representation more closely resembles the acacia pod. Acacia seeds and pods are not unknown in Egyptian jewelry: many pieces from the Middle and New Kingdoms include beads in the shape of seeds, but only a very few reproduce the shape of the pod.[3] If the acacia plant is depicted on this bracelet, it would be one of the first appearances of the motif in Egyptian jewelry.　　　　PR

1. See, for example, Hassan 1932, pl. 79.
2. On the identification of the plant represented by the hieroglyph *nedjem*, see *Zeitschrift für ägyptische Sprache und Altertumskunde* 64 (1929), pp. 51ff.
3. Hayes 1953, pp. 232, 234, 236; Hayes 1959, pp. 13, 135; Wilkinson 1971, p. 81.

PROVENANCE: Giza, mastaba S 316, Junker excavation, 1913–14

BIBLIOGRAPHY: Haslauer 1991, pp. 18–21

SIXTH DYNASTY

170. Pepi I Kneeling

Sixth Dynasty, reign of Pepi I
Schist with inlaid eyes of alabaster and obsidian
mounted in copper cells
H. 15.2 cm (6 in.); w. 4.6 cm (1¾ in.); d. 9 cm
(3½ in.)
Brooklyn Museum of Art, Charles Edwin Wilbour
Fund 39.121

Pepi I kneels, leaning forward slightly from the hips, and offers small *nu* pots. The statuette rests on a small rectangular base. Across the front of the base an elongated cartouche naming Pepi the son of the goddess Hathor, Mistress of Dendara, is inscribed; at the king's right side another inscription gives his later prenomen, Meryre.[1]

The uraeus, now missing, was inset over the forehead at the lower edge of the sharply detailed *nemes*. The king's inlaid eyes and prominent mouth are bold and arresting in his face, with its smooth surfaces, broad cheeks, and rounded chin. The folds of flesh extending from the wings of the nose are subtly modeled. The rendering of the body is highly stylized. Strikingly long, pointed fingers and schematically rounded shoulder blades contrast with the suppressed modeling of the forms of the torso and arms. Stone has been removed between the arms and torso and between the legs and base.

A recent comprehensive stylistic study of Sixth Dynasty royal sculpture has demonstrated the existence during this period of a new attitude that privileged expressiveness and animation—a spirit perhaps best exemplified by the present work.[2] The animation of this sculpture is enhanced by the palpable tension of the kneeling pose, particularly as it is rendered here. The pose of the kneeling king expresses the idea of interaction with a god by a ruler who is both the son of the deity and the representative of the worldly realm. Although the pose can be traced back to the Fourth Dynasty, this statuette and a number of others plausibly ascribed to the Sixth Dynasty suggest that it may have been of particular interest at this time, perhaps as part of a general enrichment of royal iconography.[3]

Although the provenance of the piece is unknown, the inscription suggests Dendara as a possibility, and that location would accord with a known program of attention to Upper Egypt during the Sixth Dynasty.[4] The original placement of this statuette within the temple can only be conjectured: it might have been brought out to stand before the divine statue during certain rites or on festival days, or its shallow base might have been set into some more substantial piece of cult equipment, such as an offering table or model temple.[5]   MH

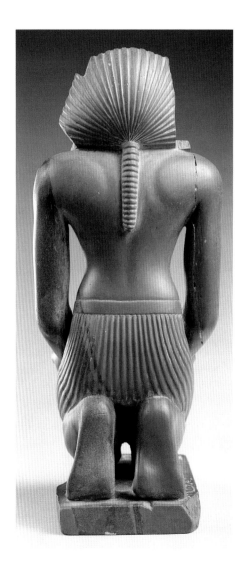

1. James 1974, p. 62.
2. Romano 1998, pp. 266–71 (formal elements and style). Romano (ibid., pp. 269–71) discusses the innovations in royal sculpture as an expression of the Second Style initially identified in private sculpture of the late Fifth and the Sixth Dynasty by Russmann (1995a), who also points out that there must have been religious impetus for the changes.
3. The pose is apparent on a fragment, probably from the Fourth Dynasty, showing a gneiss *nu* pot held by a cupped hand that rests on a thigh covered by the *shendyt* kilt, found in the valley temple or Harmakhis temple of Khafre (Roemer- und Pelizaeus-Museum, Hildesheim, 69; Martin-Pardey 1977, pp. 70–73); for possible additional examples from the Sixth Dynasty, see Romano 1998, pp. 272–73; and regarding iconographic enrichment, see ibid., pp. 263–65.
4. For general interest in Upper Egypt during the Sixth Dynasty, see Romano 1998, pp. 260–61; and for the relevant history of this particular statuette, see ibid., pp. 277–79.
5. See Aldred 1988a, pp. 46–47, for speculations about a sphinx of Merenre I (cat. no. 171).

PROVENANCE: Unknown

BIBLIOGRAPHY: Romano 1998, pp. 242–43 and passim, figs. 20–30

171. Sphinx of Merenre I

Sixth Dynasty, reign of Merenre I
Schist
L. 5.7 cm (2¼ in.); w. 1.8 cm (¾ in.); h. 3.2 cm
(1¼ in.)
Trustees of the National Museums of Scotland,
Edinburgh 1984.405

This tiny sphinx with the head of Merenre holds *nu* pots in cupped human hands. It reclines on a thin base that is inscribed between its extended forelegs with the king's prenomen, "Merenre," and again on the underside of the base with the further specification that he is "Beloved of the god who is lord of the Great Mansion," that is, Re of Heliopolis.[1]

The king wears a *nemes* with a low dome and has a broad face with large features; his long beard has the distinctive acute side profile frequently found in Old Kingdom representations. The lion's mane is cut in high, rounded relief, and the muscles of the forelegs in particular are modeled to a degree surprising in so small a piece. The forelegs and back of the hands lie flat against the base, unlike those found in New Kingdom offering sphinxes, whose forelegs are treated more like human forearms and raised above the base. The long, pointed fingers of the human hands are similar to those of the statue of Pepi I kneeling (cat. no. 170), although here the joints are articulated by folds and the nails are more clawlike. The long, tubular toes of the rear paws, and the fact that they are grasping some indeterminate object, indicate their assimilation to human hands, a phenomenon attested as early as the reign of Sahure.[2]

This is the earliest known example of an offering sphinx. Along with the statue of Pepi I—and indeed with the advent of the intense style discussed in relation to that piece—it suggests a modified emphasis in the role of the king with respect to the gods during the Sixth Dynasty.   M H

1. Aldred 1988a, p. 41, n. 4, pl. 10.
2. Fay (1995b, pp. 29–36) notes the same human appendages on a small sphinx of Merenre in Moscow.

PROVENANCE: Unknown

BIBLIOGRAPHY: Aldred 1988a, pp. 41–47; Romano 1998, pp. 46–47 and passim, figs. 39, 40

172. Pair Statue of Queen Ankh-nes-meryre II and Her Son Pepi II Seated

Sixth Dynasty, reign of Pepi II
Egyptian alabaster
H. 38.9 cm (15¼ in.); w. 17.8 cm (7 in.);
d. 25.2 cm (9⅞ in.)
Brooklyn Museum of Art, Charles Edwin Wilbour
Fund 39.119

Pepi II became king at about six years of age. In this representation, he is given the small stature of a child, but wears the *shendyt* kilt and the *nemes* headcloth of a ruler, suggesting that the statue was made early in his reign. In his right hand he clutches a piece of cloth, and his feet rest on a block inscribed with a text that reads, "King of Upper and Lower Egypt, Neferkare [Pepi II], beloved of Khnum, given all life like Re, forever."

Ankh-nes-meryre II is identified by the inscription in front of her feet as "Mother of the King of Upper and Lower Egypt, the god's daughter, the revered one, beloved of Khnum, Ankh-nes-meryre." Her tight sheath dress and tripartite wig were worn by nonroyal as well as royal women, but her royal status is signaled by the vulture headdress, an emblem of several goddesses and, by association, of queens.[1] In its smoothness, the bird's body contrasts with the textured wig. Its wings extend down behind Ankh-nes-meryre's ears. The body and legs, with their talons grasping the *shen* hieroglyph, form a wonderful decorative pattern across the back of her head; the tail feathers make an interesting transition into the similarly striated locks of hair. The now-missing vulture's head, made of stone or metal, was attached using the hole above the queen's forehead.

Pepi sits sideways on his mother's lap, and her left hand supports his back. Her right hand curves protectively over her son's knees and is covered by his extended left hand. This affectionate gesture, conveying a sense of interaction between the figures, is usually reserved for more informal, nonroyal group statuettes, such as the Fifth Dynasty representation of an anonymous woman suckling her children (cat. no. 141). There are no back pillars behind the upper bodies of the two royal figures, and the arms and legs of the queen have been separated almost entirely from the stone,[2] giving the statue a lightness and freedom unusual

172

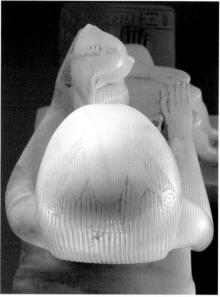

Detail, cat. no. 172

in Egyptian stone sculpture but more common in Old Kingdom works than in the art of later periods.[3]

Although not unprecedented in formal Egyptian art,[4] this pose is unusual because it presents two frontal views instead of one. It is unique in that it represents the king in a position subordinate to another human being. The ruler is the dominant figure in any group statue or relief, unless accompanied by a major god or goddess, who takes precedence. Consequently, more than one meaning has been attributed to this statue. On a ritual level, the queen may symbolize one of the great goddesses shown suckling the king in temple reliefs;[5] however, considering that Pepi was in reality a child king, a

more obvious allusion would be to the child god Horus with his mother and protector, the great goddess Isis.[6] This interpretation would parallel the secular one in which the dominance of the queen indicates the influential role she may have played during the minority of her son, but for which there is no written evidence.

The statue's provenance is unknown, but the epithet "beloved of Khnum" included in both inscriptions suggests that it was set up in a shrine at Elephantine (part of modern Aswan), a cult center for this god, who was Lord of the Cataract.   CHR

1. Originally associated with the vulture goddess Nekhbet in her human form, and then with

other goddesses, including Isis and Hathor, the headdress also became part of the iconography of queens. Sabbahy (1982, p. 317) has suggested that during the Old Kingdom wearing the headdress was the prerogative of the king's mother, but too few examples exist to warrant making this statement without caveats.

2. Her arms are actually still supported by small sections of stone running from the inner elbows to the hips, but they give the appearance of being separated completely from her body.

3. Dating from the Fourth Dynasty are a number of nonroyal statues that are more or less freed from their stone matrix. Examples include a graceful, though fragmentary, seated family group from Giza (G 1109) in the Phoebe Apperson Hearst Museum of Anthropology, University of California at Berkeley, 6-19785 (Lutz 1930, pl. 33b); the famous family group of the dwarf Seneb in the Egyptian Museum, Cairo, JE 51280 (Saleh and Sourouzian 1987, no. 39); and the pair statue of Iai-ib and Khuaut (cat. no. 83 in this publication). One of the few royal statues that exhibits this quality is the small, fragmentary Fifth Dynasty seated figure of King Neferefre from Abusir, now in the Egyptian Museum, Cairo, JE 98171 (Saleh and Sourouzian 1987, no. 38).

4. A small, very blocklike statuette of a woman with a child seated sideways on her lap was excavated in the Western Cemetery at Giza near a group of tombs dating to the late Fifth Dynasty, but no inscriptions accompanied the work. See Roth 1995, pl. 101c.

5. Because of the vulture crown, Cooney (1949a) has suggested Nekhbet as the goddess here, but see also Romano 1998, pp. 250–51.

6. In his brief abstract Cooney (1949a) dismisses this identification, but the obvious parallel between the child king Pepi and the child Horus was undoubtedly apparent to the ancient Egyptians and should be reconsidered by modern Egyptologists.

PROVENANCE: Unknown

BIBLIOGRAPHY: Romano 1998, pp. 248–52, figs. 41–53, with extensive earlier bibliography in n. 48

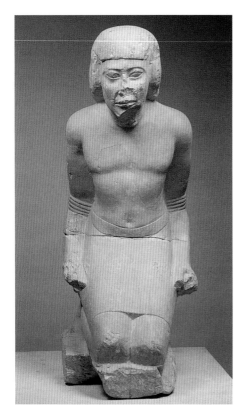

from the same find, were attributed to the reign of Djedkare-Isesi apparently for circumstantial reasons, which have, however, turned out to be mistaken.[4] In fact, the provenance of the pieces is not certain, but stylistic evaluation and archival information that has come to light strongly indicate that they should be assigned to the group from the pyramid temple of Pepi II.[5]

Although stereotypes of foreign physiognomies clearly existed during the Old Kingdom, they do not correspond well with those known and identified by ethnicity from the New Kingdom. The wide beard and jutting nose of this figure may indicate it depicts a northerner or an Asiatic.[6]

Statues of bound captives were placed in the pyramid complex, presumably along the causeway and in the *per-weru*, that is, where battle and triumph scenes occurred.[7] The consistency of the breaks at neck or shoulder and at midtorso argue strongly that the statues were ritually executed, presumably to mark some event in the history of the pyramid complex.[8] The remarkable expression of attitude and emotion on their faces—in this instance resignation and melancholy—is, then, not only a reflection of their general reaction to imprisonment but also the gaze they present at the moment of execution.[9]

MH

1. That this head and body actually join or, indeed, necessarily belong together cannot be determined without dismantling the statue. All the elements, however, belong to one stylistic group. See notes 4 and 5 below.
2. Relevant historical discussions are referenced, and a full analysis of the Neferirkare/Neferefre pieces is given, in Verner 1985a.

173. KNEELING CAPTIVE

Sixth Dynasty, reign of Pepi II
Limestone with remains of paint
H. 88.5 cm (34⅞ in.); w., at shoulders 33 cm
(13 in.); d. 49.5 cm (19½ in.)
The Metropolitan Museum of Art, New York,
Fletcher Fund, 1947 47.2

The captive kneels with his head slightly lowered. His chest and abdomen jut forward because his elbows are pinioned behind his back. A rope loops several times in horizontal strands around his upper arms above the elbow; the strands are gathered, secured, and tightened by repeated vertical lashings. The physically disfiguring effects of the binding are further expressed in the formless, pouchy modeling of the flesh on the chest and abdomen, where the skin is unnaturally stretched to the sides over the rib cage.

The captive is a non-Egyptian type. Beneath strong browridges his eyes are large and slightly slanted; the inner canthi have long extensions that run onto his nose. The nose is damaged, but its preserved root shows a pronounced jut. Very heavy furrows run from the wings of the nose to the corners of the wide, slightly crooked mouth, which protrudes in side view. The cheek-

bones are strong above sunken cheeks. The shape of the smooth hair is similar to that of the usual Egyptian short wig, except that a slight groove runs from the forehead to the top of the head and the profile from just about the level of the ears is diagonal to the shoulders. Although the captive's beard is broken away, preserved traces indicate that it was nearly as wide as the mouth.

The shoulders and much of the chest on the proper left side were broken off and restored at some time before the piece arrived at the Metropolitan Museum. A horizontal break (perhaps ancient) runs clean through the statue below the belt.[1]

The depiction of bound foreign captives in sculptural representations goes back at least to the earliest dynasties. Small votives aside, most of the early pieces—at least through the wood prisoner statuettes of Neferirkare or Neferefre[2]—were created as adjuncts to some other element. With the reign of Niuserre large sculptures of bound captives first appear; large, freestanding figures are known for most of the subsequent kings of the Fifth and Sixth Dynasties, including a great many such works for Pepi I and Pepi II.[3]

This sculpture and another of a kneeling captive (cat. no. 174), which is said to be

3. The large independent statues are: Niuserre (Borchardt 1907, p. 42); Djedkare-Isesi (Fakhry 1961a, pp. 180–81); Unis (Labrousse, Lauer, and Leclant 1977, p. 131); Teti (Lauer and Leclant 1972, pp. 84, 98–99); Pepi I (Lauer and Leclant 1970, pp. 55–62; Leclant 1979a, pp. 8–9); and Pepi II (Jéquier 1940, pp. 27–29). The Niuserre piece may be transitional: it is described as having a flat area on top, and stone is apparent behind the head in Borchardt's photograph.

4. The attribution to Djedkare-Isesi (Porter and Moss 1978, p. 424) was based on a similarity, noted by Ahmed Fakhry, to finds of Egyptian archaeologists at this king's complex in the 1940s and early 1950s. In fact, however, the heads of the Metropolitan Museum statues were already seen on the art market in 1916. Separate captives' bodies, apparently not fitting, and other heads appeared slightly later; all were rumored to have been found at Saqqara in the same place, that is, in a sort of triumphal hall (the *per-weru*?) along with a fragmentary inscription of Pepi II Neferkare.

5. Although few of these sculptures are well published, the strongly vertical facial furrows of this statue and the general physiognomy of the other captive (cat. no. 174) compare very closely with Jéquier 1940, pls. 2 (center right), 3 (center top), respectively (see note 3 above). The torsos show similarly splayed breasts and prominent lower rib cages; the bindings with smooth surfaces above the crook of the elbow parallel those of Pepi II's statues as seen in ibid., pl. 3, and differ from illustrated examples representing other kings.

6. Wildung 1973, pp. 108–16; Wildung 1980b, p. 260.

7. D. Arnold 1977, pp. 6–7; and D. Arnold 1997, pp. 73, 268, n. 128. He adds perhaps even the pillared court and transverse corridor. The actual archaeological context of these pieces is usually secondary and rarely offers very clear evidence. See also note 3 above regarding these particular statues.

8. See D. Arnold 1977, pp. 6–7; and D. Arnold 1997, pp. 73, 268, n. 128. Different circumstances have been suggested for the damage to particular groups, but consistency throughout the corpus is a powerful argument for a programmatic ancient intervention.

9. Bothmer 1982, pp. 27–39.

PROVENANCE: Unknown

BIBLIOGRAPHY: Hayes 1953, p. 114

174. KNEELING CAPTIVE

Sixth Dynasty, reign of Pepi II
Limestone with remains of paint
H. 86.7 cm (34⅛ in.); w., at shoulders, 31.5 cm (12⅜ in.); d. 40.5 cm (16 in.)
The Metropolitan Museum of Art, New York, Louis V. Bell Fund, 1964 64.260

The pose of this captive is quite similar to that of the preceding (cat. no. 173), but a different attitude is conveyed and a different nationality is represented. While the previous figure was subdued, this one has his head thrown back and his eyes are wide with terror. The jutting of his shoulder blades, the muscles in his upper arms, and the groove down his back are all exaggerated by the painfully contorted position of his arms. His torso is somewhat leaner than that of the first captive, but a similar physical stress is conveyed by his splayed breasts.

This captive's face is very broad at the cheeks and flat, even concave, in profile. There is a vertical indentation in his forehead over the nose, which is broken away. The browridges are quite rounded, and his eyes are very large, widely separated, and quite tilted; as on the other prisoner, the inner canthi are very long. The captive's hairstyle reveals the lower end of the ears. The original length of the distinctively wavy hair and of the narrow beard cannot be accurately estimated because missing stone was restored in the area of the left arm, breast, and neck before the piece was acquired by the Metropolitan Museum.[1]

The physiognomy of this captive, like that of the preceding, does not point clearly to any of the traditional enemies of Egypt, although the man does appear more likely to be from the contiguous deserts or the north than from the south.

The history and style of this piece and of prisoner statues in general are discussed in the previous entry.   MH

1. Without dismantling the statue, it is impossible to know if the head and body actually join (see cat. no. 173, notes 1, 4, and 5). The piece shows additional restoration where it was broken through the body horizontally just below the waistline, and then again vertically from front to back through the lower body and legs.

PROVENANCE: Unknown

BIBLIOGRAPHY: Unpublished

175. FRAGMENT WITH THE HEAD OF A GODDESS

Late Fifth or Sixth Dynasty
Limestone with remains of paint
H. 42 cm (16½ in.); w. 51 cm (20⅛ in.)
The Metropolitan Museum of Art, New York,
Rogers Fund, 1908 08.200.56

This large relief fragment preserves part of a colossal representation of a goddess. The piece was found in the early Twelfth Dynasty pyramid complex of Amenemhat I at Lisht, but it was not included in Hans Goedicke's catalogue of reused Old Kingdom blocks found at the site, presumably because the author believed that it dated to the Middle Kingdom.[1] However, the relief's scale, technique, and style strongly suggest that it should be assigned to the Old Kingdom.

Dominating the piece is a portion of an elaborate vulture headdress. Vultures symbolize Upper Egypt, and head coverings decorated with this bird belong to the regalia of goddesses and queens. Originally, the vulture's head must have protruded over the goddess's brow, while its tail feathers fanned out behind her head. Covering the top of the deity's head are the short, scalloped feathers of the vulture's body. The long feathers of the left wing fall behind the ear and once extended across the goddess's now-missing left shoulder. Deep and wide incised lines were used to define the feathers; thus, while each element of the headdress is distinctly rendered, the surface remains flat.

In contrast with the flatness of the feathers, both the eyebrow and the cosmetic line are raised in relief above the face. Artist's corrections are visible beneath the eyebrow and along the underside of the headdress. The eye was originally filled with inlays that must have given the face a startlingly lifelike appearance.[2] Only the area of the eye's outer canthus remains, with traces of the adhesive that once held the inlays in place. The goddess's completely preserved ear is narrow and elongated, with a wide, flat outer rim, or helix, that is slightly raised above the rest of the pinna. At the left, the helix curves sharply inward, bisecting the front of the pinna, which is carved down

to a lower level of the stone. The area just above the end of the helix is formed into an oval with pointed ends, while the area below is claw shaped. A swelling spike rises from the top of the long, wide lobe and joins the end of the rim. There are remains of yellow paint on the face and traces of blue on the eyebrow.

The large scale of the figure has parallels in Old Kingdom pyramid-temple decoration but not in extant early Twelfth Dynasty royal relief. Although large images of deities and kings have been found in temples of this period,[3] no figure as monumental as this is known. The Middle Kingdom relief figures discovered at the pyramid complex of Amenemhat I are often surprisingly small, even in key scenes where one would expect more sizable ones.[4] Also not attested in Middle Kingdom relief is the use of eye inlays,[5] an embellishment that occurs often in Old Kingdom temple decoration.[6]

Stylistic analysis indicates that the fragment should be assigned to the late Fifth Dynasty or Sixth Dynasty; an earlier date is ruled out by the flat surface treatment. On the evidence of inscriptions found thus far on other reused blocks from the pyramid complex of Amenemhat I, this dating can be refined to the reign of either Unis or Pepi II.[7] Furthermore, figures that once had inlaid eyes have been documented at the pyramid complexes of Unis[8] and Pepi II,[9] and the relief work from both sites is notable for the flatness of the interior detail.[10] A goddess from the pyramid temple of Unis has an elongated ear that is somewhat similar to the ear on the present fragment, although the forward sections above and below the inward-curving helix are considerably narrower in the former.[11] Elongated ears also appear on figures in the pyramid complex of Pepi II. They seem to have broader forward sections, but no detailed photographs are available for comparison.

In Old Kingdom royal reliefs, large-scale female figures are depicted in several types of scenes, where they participate in a variety of rituals. They may embrace the king, stand facing the king, suckle the young king, stand behind the king during various rites, present the king with the breath of life, or stand behind foreign prisoners as they are presented to the king.[12] Unfortunately, it is impossible to identify the ritual in which this figure took part because so little is preserved. However, the enormous size of the goddess indicates that it was an imposing and monumental representation.

A O

1. Goedicke 1971.
2. The Egyptians used several different types of materials to create eye inlays; see Lucas and Harris 1962, pp. 98–127. Unfortunately, the use of inlay in reliefs is only briefly discussed, in the introduction to the chapter.
3. For example, in Senwosret I's entrance chapel at Lisht (D. Arnold 1988, p. 80, pls. 49, 56); at Coptos (Bourriau 1988, pp. 22–24); and at Karnak (Saleh and Sourouzian 1987, no. 86; Aldred 1988b, p. 121).
4. For example, see Hayes 1953, pp. 172–74, figs. 103, 104. A scene of Amenemhat I embracing a goddess in which the figures are under lifesize was found in the king's pyramid complex; see Gautier and Jéquier 1902, pp. 95–97, fig. 109.
5. Inlaid eyes are, however, found in Middle Kingdom royal statuary; for examples, see Evers 1929, vol. 1, pls. 71–75, 113–16.
6. For eye inlays in Old Kingdom royal relief, see Smith 1946, p. 202. The author discusses a relief from the pyramid complex of King Teti, in which, most unusually, an eye inlay has been preserved.
7. Goedicke 1971, pp. 24–28. The possibility that blocks at Lisht come from the temples of kings whose cartouches have not been discovered cannot, however, be ruled out. For a recent addition to the kings named on reused blocks from Lisht, see the entry for cat. no. 103. For a relief from the pyramid temple of Pepi I that is very similar in scale, style, and subject and also includes artist's corrections, see Leclant 1979a, p. 23, n. 18, fig. 25.

8. See Labrousse, Lauer, and Leclant 1977, p. 85, doc. 29, pl. 31, pp. 97–99, doc. 50, pl. 35.

9. Jéquier 1938, p. 56, n. 1, pls. 11, 64.

10. For examples at the Unis complex, see Labrousse, Lauer, and Leclant 1977, pls. 28–38; and Forman and Quirke 1996, p. 53. For examples at the complex of Pepi II, see Jéquier 1938, passim.

11. Labrousse, Lauer, and Leclant 1977, p. 84, doc. 28, pl. 29. For a good photograph of this deity, see Forman and Quirke 1996, p. 53. The figure has carved eyes and striated hair.

12. Shown embracing the king: see Jéquier 1938, pls. 8, 12; and Labrousse, Lauer, and Leclant 1977, pp. 81–83, docs. 26, 27, pl. 30. Shown facing the king: see Jéquier 1938, pls. 12, 18. Shown suckling the young king: see Borchardt 1907, pp. 40–41, figs. 21, 23; Borchardt 1913, pl. 18; Jéquier 1938, pls. 30–33; and Labrousse, Lauer, and Leclant 1977, p. 84, doc. 28, pl. 29. Shown standing behind the king: see Borchardt 1907, p. 16, fig. 6, pl. 16; Borchardt 1913, pl. 18; Jéquier 1938, pls. 36, 41. Shown presenting the breath of life: see Jéquier 1938, pls. 36, 54. Shown presenting prisoners: see Borchardt 1913, pl. 1; and Labrousse, Lauer, and Leclant 1977, pp. 90–91, doc. 40, pl. 32.

PROVENANCE: Lisht North, pyramid complex of Amenemhat I, Metropolitan Museum of Art excavation, 1906–7

BIBLIOGRAPHY: Unpublished

176. RELIEF FRAGMENT FROM COPTOS

Sixth Dynasty, reign of Pepi II
Limestone
H. 58 cm (22⅞ in.); w. 61 cm (24 in.)
Petrie Museum of Egyptian Archaeology, University
College London UC 14281

Coptos was an ancient city forty kilometers north of Thebes in Upper Egypt. In antiquity the place was important because of its position at the mouth of a dry river valley, or wadi, known as Wadi Hammamat, through which access was gained to the coast of the Red Sea. The wadi, moreover, was home to some of the best of the hard stones of Egypt that were especially prized for use in fine statuary (cat. nos. 67, 68).[1] The principal deity of Coptos was the vegetation and fertility god Min, for whom the kings of the Old, Middle, and New Kingdom and finally King Ptolemy II built a succession of temples.[2] The present relief fragment, now in the Petrie Museum, and another relief found with it and now in the Manchester Museum were originally part of the decoration of the Old Kingdom temple of Min built at Coptos.[3]

On the left of a rather weathered block of local Coptite limestone we see part of the figure of King Pepi II, who is identified by a large cartouche with his birth name, "Pepi," and his throne name, "Neferkare." The king wears the royal kilt; in his right hand he carries a mace and in his left the long royal *mekes* scepter with its lotus-shaped element and crossbar in the lower section.[4] Above the cartouche are remains of the title "King of Upper and Lower Egypt," and on the right large hieroglyphs provide the name of the god Min with the remains of three ankh (life) signs above it and an *n* below it. It seems reasonable to suppose that a figure of the god confronted the king from the right. Most remarkable is the tightly spaced pattern of alternating symbols of stability and the goddess Bat that fills the area below the baseline on which the king stands. The Bat emblem—a frontal human face with cow ears and horns—also appears on the block showing Snefru's Heb Sed, where it is part of the insignia of the Controllers of the Palace, who accompanied the king at this festival (cat. no. 23).[5] Bat is a not very well understood deity with aspects of a sky goddess, whose characteristics and emblem were taken over largely by the goddess Hathor after the Old Kingdom.

Alternating symbols of the kind seen on the Petrie Museum relief usually appear on the daises of thrones or kiosks,[6] and Senwosret I, second king of the Twelfth Dynasty, is shown on a dais with such decorations, kneeling before the god Min in a relief at Karnak.[7] It is therefore possible that the alternating emblems on the present fragment were part of a cult installation peculiar to this god.[8]

This piece was certainly executed by local sculptors, for the flat and uneven figures and hieroglyphs differ considerably from the skillfully carved elements in the reliefs of Pepi II's Memphite funerary temple at Saqqara. Yet the general influence of Fourth Dynasty prototypes noticeable in the king's pyramid-temple reliefs (see "Royal Reliefs" by Dorothea Arnold in this catalogue, pp. 88–94) is also alive in the Coptos fragment. Thus, the large figures of the king and god(?) of the Coptos relief show parallels to the figures in the large compositions in Pepi II's pyramid temple, and even the detailed rope pattern of the Coptos cartouche reflects the inspiration of Fourth Dynasty examples.[9]   DOA

1. Fischer 1980b, cols. 737–41, with earlier bibliography.
2. Gundlach 1982, cols. 136–40. For the Old Kingdom, see McFarlane 1995, pp. 260–63.
3. McFarlane 1995, pp. 140–41, 256–57, 259. For the Manchester Museum piece, see also Petrie 1896, no. 8, pl. 5.

4. Fischer 1979a, pp. 24–25, especially the definition of the scepter on p. 24: "a symbol regularly wielded by the king in his priestly role as intermediary between mankind and the gods."

5. Fischer 1962a, pp. 11–15.

6. Borchardt 1913, pl. 44 (royal throne).

7. Lacau and Chevrier 1956, pl. 38.

8. Lacau (in ibid., pp. 128–29) refers to one such cult installation, the stairway used in the Min festival that is elaborately depicted at Medinet Habu. For this example and parallels, see Epigraphic Survey 1940, pls. 209–17. For a somewhat similar image from the Delta, see Jánosi 1998, pp. 56–58, pls. A, B.

9. Cherpion 1989, pp. 75–77.

PROVENANCE: Coptos, temple of Min, "face down to fill up some holes in the basal clay beneath the great sand bed of the Ptolemaic temple,"* Petrie excavation, 1893–94

BIBLIOGRAPHY: Petrie 1896, p. 4, no. 7, pl. 5; Stewart 1979, p. 7, no. 21, pl. 3, no. 2

*Petrie 1896, pp. 1, 4.

177A–D. PYRAMID TEXTS

Sixth Dynasty
Limestone with remains of paint
a. H. 24.5 cm (9⅝ in.); w. 25 cm (9⅞ in.)
Petrie Museum of Egyptian Archaeology, University College London UC 14540

Other fragments, not illustrated:
b. Musées Royaux d'Art et d'Histoire, Brussels E 2393 A-1

c. The Syndics of the Fitzwilliam Museum, Cambridge E 55.2, E 55.6, E 55.7, E 55.11, E 30.1935

d. Musée du Louvre, Paris E 32554, E 32556

The illustrated block of stone comes from the antechamber of the pyramid of Pepi I at Saqqara. The walls of the antechamber, like those of the other rooms of the pyramid's substructure, were inscribed with columns of Pyramid Texts designed to provide the spirit of the dead king with the means of daily rebirth. This fragment was part of columns 6 to 10 of the west end of the antechamber's north wall. Its hieroglyphs face left, toward the burial chamber, from which the spirit would emerge on its way out of the tomb at dawn. The north wall was one of the last the spirit would see before passing into the ascending corridor, which led outside.

The texts on this section of the wall deal with the king's ascension to the celestial realm—the home of the sun, the stars, and the other gods. Their five columns contain parts of three different spells typical of these texts:[1]

Col. 6: [This PEPI is on the way to the place of] the winepress; the food of this PEPI [is in the Field of Offerings] (PT 627B, Pyr. *1784a–b).

Col. 7: The house of this PEPI belonging to the sky [will not perish; the seat of this PEPI belonging to the earth] cannot be destroyed (PT 302, Pyr. 458b).

Col. 8: [The face of this PEPI is that of] falcons, the wings of this PEPI [are those of birds] (PT 302, Pyr. 461b–c).

Col. 9: [This PEPI has beat] his wings as a kite. [Someone] has flown, [people: this PEPI has flown away from you] (PT 302, Pyr. 463c–d).

Col. 10: [This PEPI is a boy] who came from Re; this PEPI has emerged from between the thighs [of the Ennead] (PT 655 = PT 704 = CT 364, Pyr. *1842a–b).

As in all such texts, a cartouche bearing the king's name ("this PEPI") and third-person references to the name have been substituted for the first-person pronoun.

The original use of the first person indicated that the texts were intended to be recited by the spirit itself; the change to the third person allowed the texts to be personalized for a particular pyramid.

Although first inscribed in the pyramid of Unis, the last king of the Fifth Dynasty, most of the Pyramid Texts are written in an archaic form of Egyptian that dates to perhaps the Fourth or early Fifth Dynasty. The celestial view of the king's afterlife found in many of the texts may, however, be even older.　　　　　　　JPA

1. The missing parts of the texts are supplied between square brackets. The abbreviations "PT" and "Pyr.," referring respectively to spells of the Pyramid Texts and sections of the spells, are based on the numbering system in Sethe 1922. The abbreviation "CT" refers to spells of the Coffin Texts, a later compilation of funerary texts.

PROVENANCE: (a) Saqqara, pyramid of Pepi I, north wall of antechamber

BIBLIOGRAPHY: (a) Sethe 1922, p. 136 (fragment D)

178A–C. Three Vases in the Shape of Mother Monkeys and Their Young

a. Sixth Dynasty, reign of Merenre I
Egyptian alabaster with traces of paint in left eye and traces of resin and pigment in inscription
H. 18.5 cm (7¼ in.)
Inscribed on right shoulder and upper arm of mother: "King of Upper and Lower Egypt Merenre living forever"
The Metropolitan Museum of Art, New York, Theodore M. Davis Collection, Bequest of Theodore M. Davis, 1915 30.8.134

b. Sixth Dynasty, reign of Pepi I
Egyptian alabaster with traces of paint in inscription on right arm of infant
H. 13.7 cm (5⅜ in.)
Inscribed on left arm of mother: "First occurrence of the Heb Sed (thirty-year jubilee); right arm of mother: "(female) tenant landholder (of the pyramid endowment of Pepi I called) 'The Perfection of (King) Meryre Endures'"; right arm of infant: "*Ny-khaswt*-Meryre (= King Meryre is a possessor of foreign lands)"
The Metropolitan Museum of Art, New York, Purchase, Joseph Pulitzer Bequest, Fletcher Fund, and Lila Acheson Wallace, Russell and Judy Carson, William Kelly Simpson, and Vaughn Foundation Gifts, in honor of Henry George Fischer, 1992 1992.338

c. Sixth Dynasty, reign of Pepi I
Egyptian alabaster
H. 14.4 cm (5⅝ in.)
Modern elements: black lid, dark fill in aperture, probably hole at bottom, and certainly dark fill in it
Inscribed on right shoulder and upper arm of mother: "King of Upper and Lower Egypt Meryre (Pepi I) living forever"
Kunsthistorisches Museum, Ägyptisch-Orientalische Sammlung, Vienna Äs 3886

These three vessels for precious oil were made in royal workshops of the Sixth Dynasty and are inscribed with the names of reigning kings of that era, Pepi I (b, c) or his son and heir, Merenre I (a).[1] One vessel (b) also carries the name of a nonroyal woman who held an office at the funerary establishment of Pepi I and a reference to the king's first Heb Sed, or thirty-year, jubilee. The implication is that the woman must have received the little oil flask from Pepi I on the occasion of that celebration (see "Stone Vessels" by Dorothea Arnold and Elena Pischikova in this catalogue, pp. 124–28). It is only logical to interpret the shorter inscriptions on the two other vases in the same way: these vessels must also have been gifts from reigning kings to favorite courtiers. Moreover, they too were probably given away at Sed festivals.

c

As gifts bestowed on these occasions, they may have contained oil used in the rituals performed at the celebration.

The form the vases take—that of mother monkeys embracing and being embraced by their young—is related to the material they contained: monkeys came to Egypt from countries to the south in the areas of modern Sudan and Ethiopia and along the Red Sea coast, places that supplied spices and other ingredients that Egyptians mixed with cosmetic oils and ointments. The maternal image was also a reminder that female forces could procure rebirth for kings and non-royals. As rebirth and renewal were achieved by means of the thirty-year festival, the connection with that occasion is appropriate, but the allusion also made the vessels suitable objects for the grave. Indeed most monkey vessels found in excavations come from burials. However, some of these show traces of wear, which indicates that they were used in life before they were buried with their tomb owners.[2] Other monkey flasks were dedicated to female deities and were excavated from the sanctuaries of these goddesses (see "Stone Vessels," pp. 128–29).

The monkeys of the present jars are shown wearing bracelets around their wrists to emphasize their tame nature. In certain pieces, moreover, the mother animal was further adorned with an actual necklace of faience beads, as excavated remains document.[3] Lids must have closed the apertures in the heads, and the astonishingly human-looking eyes (with eyebrows) of some figures, such as the monkey of the Davis Collection vase (a), were inlaid.

c

The student of Egyptian art will find remarkable how variously three individual stone-vessel sculptors, working almost at the same time, rendered the identical theme of the present works. The Davis Collection vase is the most statuelike of the three versions. The mother monkey sits upright, looking very dignified, with legs and arms and indeed all features described in a rather linear, abstract manner. The smallest variant, the honey-colored piece in the Metropolitan Museum (b), is the liveliest. The mother animal's legs are naturalistically rounded and spread outward; especially impressive is the portrayal of the decided hump in her back and of the way she bends over the infant that holds on to her breast. The vessel in the Kunsthistoriches Museum, Vienna (c), is the most clearly and sharply cut and beautifully conveys the expression of the benign, quite human-looking face with its wide-open eyes. All three pieces present a sensitively observed image of maternity that was seldom depicted with comparable emotion in Egyptian statues of human mothers.

DoA

a, b

1. For the family tree of these kings, see entry for cat. no. 184.
2. Fischer (1993, p. 4) observed traces of wear in the Vienna vase.
3. Valloggia 1980, pls. 13A, 14A.

PROVENANCE: (a) Unknown; (b) unknown; (c) said to be Elephantine

BIBLIOGRAPHY: (a) Dorman, Harper, and Pittman 1987, p. 20, no. 9; Do. Arnold 1993b, p. 6; Fischer 1993, p. 5, fig. 4; Do. Arnold 1995, p. 59, no. 80. (b) Do. Arnold 1993b, p. 6; Fischer 1993, pp. 1–9, fig. 1; Do. Arnold 1995, p. 59, no. 81; Minault-Gout 1997, p. 307, fig. 6a,b. (c) Satzinger 1994, p. 52, no. 34

179. JUBILEE JAR INSCRIBED WITH THE NAME OF PEPI I

Sixth Dynasty, reign of Pepi I
Egyptian alabaster with black fill in inscriptions
H. 7.2 cm (2⅞ in.)
Musée du Louvre, Paris, N 527

This unguent jar with a wide rim and flat foot has a disk-shaped lid with a circular protuberance on the inside. It is a type of receptacle that was common from the Fifth to the Eleventh Dynasty.[1] The wide opening makes it possible to draw liquid easily, and the flat lip accommodates a sealed lid.[2] The characteristic silhouette was perpetuated in hieroglyphic writing and was associated with unguents.[3]

Like most unguent jars, this example is carved in a translucent stone streaked with veins. Commonly called Egyptian alabaster, it is in fact not true alabaster, but calcite.[4] Beginning in the early dynasties, this was the stone of choice for unguent vessels, and the list of Egyptian alabaster jars inscribed with the names of Old Kingdom sovereigns is very long.[5] It is the most frequently used material, followed by diorite.[6] Although such royal vessels have been found throughout Egypt, they were probably all executed in workshops of the royal residence.[7] Workshop scenes and clues found on the objects themselves have given scholars an insight into the techniques used to make them, from the extraction of a block of stone at the quarry to the hollowing out of the vessel—generally done with a tubular copper drill—to the final buffing of the exterior.[8] The inside of this example and especially the bottom display very obvious grooves left by the drill.

On the belly of the jar two columns of incised hieroglyphs are highlighted with a black fill. From right to left they read: "the king of Upper and Lower Egypt Meryre [Pepi I], granted life eternal," and "first Heb Sed."

Many similar jars with inscriptions that mention the royal jubilee celebration (or Heb Sed; see cat. no. 180) have been found in Egypt and in neighboring countries, particularly in the ancient Phoenician city of Byblos, modern-day Jabayl. Most date to the Sixth Dynasty. Gifts from the king, these jars were valued more for their inscriptions than for the perfumed oils or unguents they contained, which were used in ceremonies. They reaffirmed the king's power, which, theoretically, was strengthened after thirty years of rule during the jubilee ceremony. Such a gift, even as it underscored the king's preeminence, particularly distinguished the person to whom it was presented.[9] CZ

1. Aston 1994, p. 104.
2. Bourriau 1984, col. 362.
3. Balcz 1932, p. 51, n. 3.
4. Most recently, De Putter and Karlshausen 1992, pp. 43–46; and Lilyquist 1995, p. 13, with earlier bibliography.
5. See the brief enumeration, with mention of origin, in Eichler 1993, pp. 299–307.
6. Ibid., p. 307 (2).
7. Ibid., pp. 307 (4), 308 (7).
8. For all these techniques, consult the bibliography in Spalinger 1982, pp. 126–27; El-Khouli 1978, pp. 789–801; and Lilyquist 1995, p. 13.
9. Minault-Gout 1997, pp. 305–14.

PROVENANCE: Unknown; brought to France from Egypt by Jean-François Champollion 1830

BIBLIOGRAPHY: Champollion 1835–45, vol. 2, pl. 188 (6); Pierret 1882, pp. 85–86, no. 352; Sethe 1903, p. 97; Gauthier 1907, p. 154; Vandier d'Abbadie 1972, pp. 128–29, no. 556, fig. 556; Ziegler 1993b, p. 201; Ziegler 1997b, p. 465, no. 4, fig. 6

180. JUBILEE JAR INSCRIBED WITH THE NAME OF PEPI II

Sixth Dynasty, reign of Pepi II
Egyptian alabaster
H. 15 cm (6 in.); diam., lid 19.9 cm (7⅞ in.)
Musée du Louvre, Paris N 648a,b

This unguent jar can be distinguished from a similar vessel dating from the reign of Pepi I (cat. no. 179) by its large size, its lid in the shape of a flat disk, and its inscription. On the body two columns of incised hieroglyphs appear inside a rectangular frame formed by the signs for "land" and "sky," supported by two *was* scepters. From right to left they read: "The King of Upper and Lower Egypt, Neferkare (Pepi II), alive like Re," and "Horus Netjeri-khau, alive like Re."

The text inscribed on the lid in a very elongated cartouche translates as: "Long live Horus Netjeri-khau, King of Upper and Lower Egypt, Neferkare, given life." CZ

PROVENANCE: Unknown; brought to France from Egypt by Jean-François Champollion 1830

BIBLIOGRAPHY: Pierret 1882, p. 84, no. 347; Gauthier 1907, p. 173; *Archeo*, no. 79 (1991), p. 63; Ziegler 1993b, p. 201; Ziegler 1997b, nos. 9, 10, figs. 11, 12

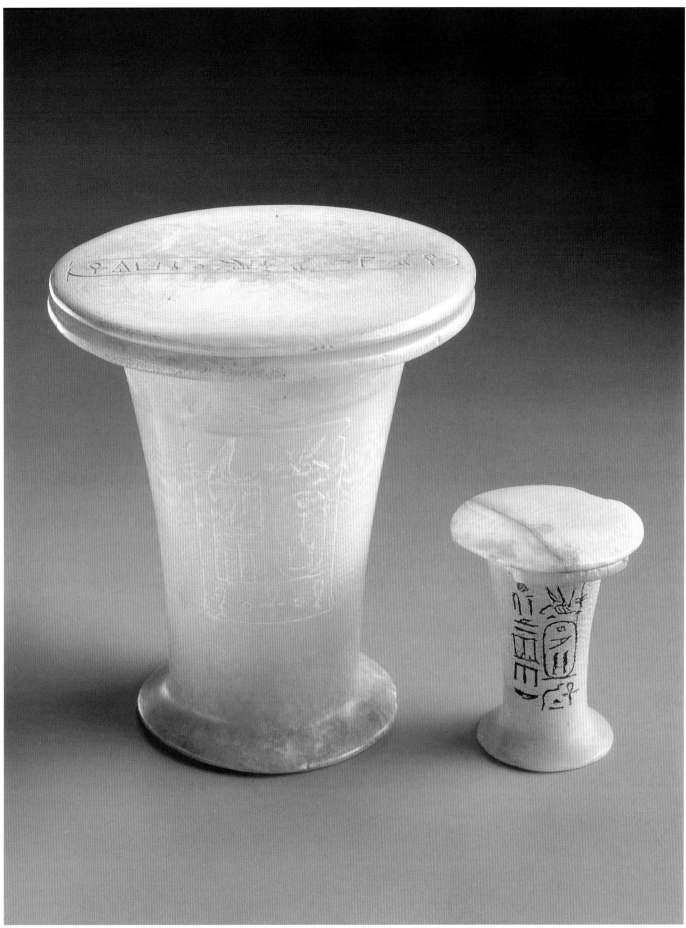

Cat. nos. 180, 179

182. SISTRUM INSCRIBED WITH THE NAME OF KING TETI

Sixth Dynasty, reign of Teti
Egyptian alabaster, remains of pigment in incised
decoration and resin in crevices; repairs in handle
and to falcon head; naos plate adhered with modern adhesive
H. 26.5 cm (10½ in.)
The Metropolitan Museum of Art, New York,
Purchase, Edward S. Harkness Gift, 1926
26.7.1450

The handle of this beautiful object appears
to be an elegant papyrus stalk crowned with
an umbel in bloom, into which the artist has
delicately incised the detail of the folioles
and beard of the plant. It supports a small
building, a chapel or naos, surmounted by
a cavetto cornice. A falcon stands proudly
at the top; in front of this bird of prey rears
a cobra with open hood. The delicate quality of the material, a translucent alabaster
with fine veining, is matched by the refinement of the style. This is a royal object, as
is shown by the inscriptions naming Teti,
first sovereign of the Sixth Dynasty. On the
preserved face of the naos, three of the
pharaoh's names appear framed by the sign
for "sky," supported by two *was* scepters:
from left to right, his Two Ladies name, his
Horus name, and his Son of Re name, Teti.
This titulary is accompanied by wishes for
eternal life and strength. A long vertical
inscription runs down the papyrus stalk:
"The King of Upper and Lower Egypt,
Son of Re, Teti, beloved of Hathor, Lady
of Dendara, may he live eternally."

This is not a decorative object, but a
musical instrument specific to pharaonic
Egypt and called by Egyptologists a naos
sistrum. It is one of the first examples
known of a type that persisted until the
Roman Period. A sort of musical rattle, the
sistrum was shaken in cadence, marking
the rhythm at religious ceremonies. Its
soothing music, evoking an ancient rite—
the "shaking of the papyrus"—warded off
the violence of dangerous deities, Hathor
in particular. According to myths, that
goddess could transform herself into a fear-
some lioness. She appears in the vertical inscription on the sistrum as a young woman
with two cow's horns, on which the sun
disk rests. Because this sistrum as a whole
can be read as a rebus, it is linked to late
texts that consider the instrument the incar-
nation of the goddess.[1] The papyrus stalk
refers to the rite of the same name; and the

181. BOX INSCRIBED WITH THE NAME OF KING MERENRE I

Sixth Dynasty, reign of Merenre I
Hippopotamus ivory
H. 3.6 cm (1½ in.); w. 14.6 cm (5¾ in.); d. 6.1 cm
(2½ in.)
Musée du Louvre, Paris N 794

This rectangular box belongs to a type well
documented for the late Archaic Period.[1]
The Old Kingdom has provided several
examples in wood, sometimes inlaid with
faience (cat. no. 158), and the form persisted
throughout pharaonic times, rendered in
various materials: alabaster,[2] copper,[3] or
precious wood. Because of the fragility of
the material, however, examples in ivory
are extremely rare.

The closing mechanism seems admirably
modern: the lid once slid on and off via a
system of slides. Significant traces of verdigris surrounding the hole inserted in the
center of one of the short sides suggest the
presence of a copper knob-fastener, now
lost. The lid and one of the sides bear an
incised inscription, highlighted with blue
pigment, which gives the titulary of King
Merenre I.

Various objects could be kept in this
sort of box: one in alabaster of similar size
contained cylindrical seals with the name of
Mentuhotep. Like headrests (cat. no. 183)
or jubilee jars (cat. nos. 179, 180) bearing
royal names, these were no doubt gifts
from the pharaoh that dignitaries treasured
and took to their graves.[4] If the Theban
provenance noted by Champollion is accurate, this artifact will prove extremely important for the history of Upper Egypt
during the Old Kingdom.   CZ

1. Killen 1994a, pp. 1–6.
2. With the name of King Mentuhotep of the Eleventh Dynasty, Louvre, Paris, E 25685.
3. With the name of Amenemhat II, Louvre, Paris,
   E 15128–29.
4. For example, objects with the name of Pepi I and
   Pepi II found in the tomb of the governors of
   Balat. See Minault-Gout 1997, pp. 305–14.

PROVENANCE: Thebes?;* brought to France
from Egypt by Jean-François Champollion 1830

BIBLIOGRAPHY: Champollion 1835–45, vol. 2,
pl. 188 (nos. 7, 7 bis); Pierret 1882, no. 613;
Gauthier 1907, p. 166; Tardy 1977, p. 62, fig. 3;
Ziegler 1993b, p. 204; Ziegler 1998, p. 408

*See the caption on a plate in Champollion (1835–45,
vol. 2, pl. 188), where the object appears as numbers
7 and 7 bis, among "objects from various sepulchres
in Qurna."

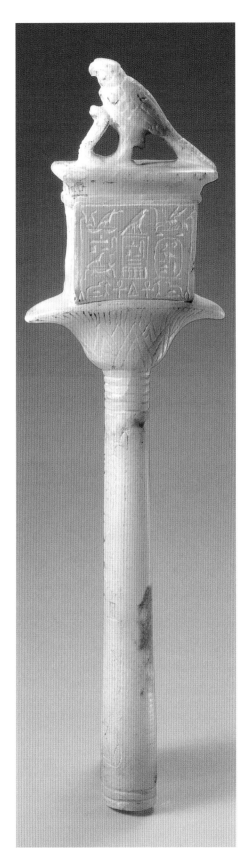

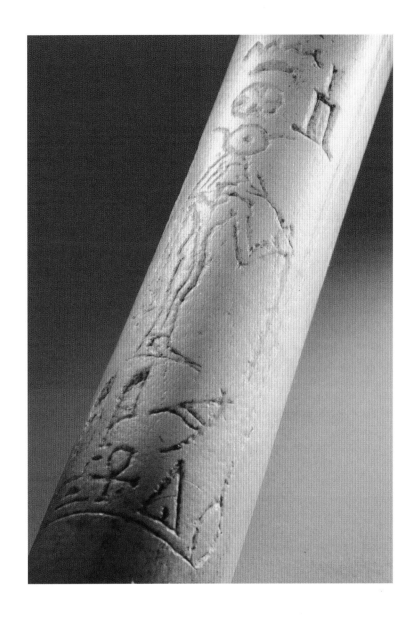

falcon and small building can be read as hieroglyphs composing the name of the goddess (Hat-Hor, meaning House of Horus), who is represented in her cobra form as the eye of Re. The inscription places King Teti under the protection of Hathor, Lady of Dendara, the great religious center of Upper Egypt, whose temple was considerably embellished by Sixth Dynasty sovereigns.[2]

In spite of its unusual material, this sistrum is not an ex-voto but may actually have been used. On the base of the naos are holes for small copper rods equipped with jangling disks; the rods, along with one of the walls forming a sound box, have disappeared, but their former presence is attested by traces of verdigris.   CZ

1. Daumas 1970a, p. 72.
2. For additions by Pepi I, see Romano 1998, pp. 236–37, n. 6.

PROVENANCE: Memphite region, "plateau of pyramids," according to vendor; Carnarvon collection

BIBLIOGRAPHY: Davies 1920, pp. 69–72, pl. 8; Burlington Fine Arts Club 1922, p. 90, no. 39; Schäfer and Andrae 1925, p. 260; Klebs 1931, pp. 60–63, fig. a; Schäfer and Andrae 1934, p. 270; Pijoán 1945, p. 163, fig. 214; Hayes 1953, pp. 125–26, fig. 76; Kayser 1969, fig. 65; Daumas 1970b, pp. 7–18; Ziegler 1979b, p. 32, n. 25; Ziegler 1984, col. 959, n. 17

183. HEADREST INSCRIBED WITH THE NAME OF PEPI II

Sixth Dynasty, reign of Pepi II
Ivory, probably from elephant, with faint remains
of blue paint in the inscriptions
H., headrest 21.8 cm (8⅝ in.); h., base 1.9 cm
(¾ in.); w. 19.1 cm (7½ in.); d. 7.8 cm (3⅛ in.)
Musée du Louvre, Paris N 646

Like the Japanese and certain peoples of
Africa today, in place of a pillow the ancient
Egyptians used a headrest, which looks
uncomfortable to Westerners.

   This rare and very precious example in
ivory has a head support that retains the
curve of the tusk from which it was sculpted;
the cavity is still quite visible. The support
rests on an abacus atop a fluted column
flared at the foot. This vertical stand is fixed
on a rectangular base, which bears the incised titulary of Pharaoh Pepi II, framed by
the sign for "sky"—that is, two *was* scepters and a horizontal line. A similar inscription, but written horizontally, runs along
one side of the base. This type of headrest,
inspired by architecture—for example,
the ribbed columns in the vestibule of
Djoser's funerary complex—was typical
in the Old Kingdom.[1] The materials most
frequently used were alabaster and wood;
these were sometimes covered with precious
metals, like one in the trousseau of Queen
Hetep-heres I, mother of King Khufu. Ivory
was very rarely used, no doubt because of
its fragility and rarity. Originating in the
heart of Africa, elephant ivory was an object of trade, as is recorded in inscriptions
from the Sixth Dynasty.[2] Like jubilee jars
(cat. nos. 179, 180) or boxes (cat. no. 181),
headrests inscribed with royal names were
probably prized gifts from the pharaoh that
were buried with their owners.[3]   CZ

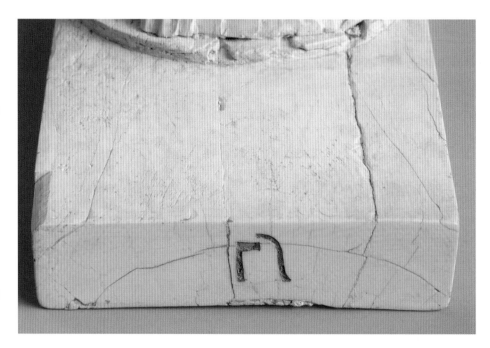

1. Examples include, for the Third Dynasty,
   from Kafr el-Ammar, Petrie Museum, London,
   UC 8585; for the Fourth Dynasty, Egyptian
   Museum, Cairo, JE 53262 (belonging to
   Queen Hetep-heres I); for the Fifth Dynasty,
   see Donadoni Roveri 1987, p. 131; for
   the Sixth Dynasty, see Valloggia 1986,
   pp. 73–74.
2. Roccati 1982, pp. 205 (Harkhuf), 218 (Sabni).
3. For example, objects with the name of Pepi I
   and Pepi II, found in the tomb of the governors of Balat; see Minault-Gout 1997,
   pp. 305–14.

PROVENANCE: Unknown; brought to France
from Egypt by Jean-François Champollion 1830

BIBLIOGRAPHY: Pierret 1882, no. 612; Michalowski 1968, fig. 806; Tardy 1977, p. 62, fig. 2;
Leclant et al. 1978, p. 233, fig. 224; Falgayrettes
1989, ill. p. 35; Ziegler 1993b, pp. 201, 207;
Ziegler 1998, p. 409

184. BREWER'S VAT OF QUEEN MOTHER ANKH-NES-PEPI (II)

Sixth Dynasty, reign of Pepi II
Egyptian alabaster, hieroglyphs filled with resin
H. 17.3 cm (6⅞ in.)
The Metropolitan Museum of Art, New York,
Gift of Mr. and Mrs. V. Everit Macy, 1923
23.10.10

This beautiful vase is made in two parts:
a deep basin with a round rim and small
spout and a flaring base decorated with
incised grooves that create the effect of a
reed construction. The two elements were
cemented together after the piece entered
the Metropolitan Museum's collection.
Below the rim on one side of the vessel
is a line of beautifully incised stylized
hieroglyphs. This inscription refers to the
queen mother Ankh-nes-pepi, here called
Ankh-nes-pepi (II), to distinguish her from
a half sister of the same name, for whom
the number (I) is used. The queen's name,
like that of her sister, can be written using
either of two names of King Pepi I, Pepi (as
here) or Meryre;[1] the name Ankh-nes-meryre
appears on the statuette in the Brooklyn
Museum that represents the queen with
her son Pepi II on her lap (cat. no. 172).
The relationship of the two women called
Ankh-nes-meryre/pepi, who were both
married to King Pepi I, and their positions
in the royal family of the Sixth Dynasty can
best be clarified in the family tree shown
above.[2] Ankh-nes-meryre/pepi (II) was
regent for Pepi II when he became king in
his infancy.

The inscription on the vase is usually
translated: "The king's mother [of?] the

Khui (of Abydos) = Nebet

Ankh-nes-meryre/pepi (I) = King Pepi I = Ankh-nes-meryre/pepi (II)

King Merenre I   Neith   King Pepi II

pyramid (of Pepi II) 'The Permanent Place
of Neferkare (Pepi II) Endures': Ankh-nes-
pepi."[3] The citation of the pyramid of Pepi II
(Neferkare) in Ankh-nes-pepi (II)'s title is a
peculiarity of Sixth Dynasty inscriptions that
has given rise to much speculation. Must
we consider the pyramid of a king to have
been identical with the pharaoh himself, so
that a queen or other royal woman could
be mother, wife, or daughter of a particular
pyramid?[4] Or does the linkage of the royal
woman with the pyramid imply only that
the lady in question received economic benefits from the funerary establishment attached
to a royal pyramid cult?[5] However the question is resolved—and scholars nowadays
seem to favor the second interpretation—
the controversy is an apt reminder that a
royal pyramid and its pyramid temple were
not only religious entities but also economic
institutions of great influence and power
because the cult of a dead king furnished
incomes to the numerous individuals who
served it.

This luxury stone vase, which may
have belonged to Queen Mother Ankh-nes-
pepi (II)'s funerary equipment or that of her
son King Pepi II, is also connected to practical realities through its prototype: the little vessel represents a miniature brewer's
vat on a reed stand. The actual vat would
have come up to about the hips of the

brewer, who might have been either a man
or a woman. The brewer set a sieve over
the vat's mouth and then worked soaked
pieces of lightly baked bread through it, for
the beer of ancient Egypt was bread juice
fermented with the help of date mash.[6]
After fermentation the brewer poured the
beer through the spout into jars, and the
drink was ready to be consumed. Beer was
a staple of the diet of the ancient people of
the Nile Valley, and with the stone version
of a vat in his or her burial outfit, the royal
tomb owner was guaranteed provision of
the beverage in eternity.   DoA

1. For the interchangeability of "Pepi" and "Meryre"
   in the name of this queen and her sister, see the
   references in Romano 1998, p. 248, n. 49.
2. See Seipel 1975, cols. 263–64.
3. James P. Allen (personal communication) proposes another translation for the inscription:
   "From the king's mother Ankh-nes-pepi [for]
   the pyramid [of Pepi II] 'The permanent place
   of the life of Neferkare [Pepi II].'" This wording
   would indicate that Ankh-nes-pepi (II) dedicated the vessel to her son's funerary cult.
4. Montet 1957, pp. 92–101.
5. See especially Málek 1970, pp. 238–40.
6. Helck 1975, cols. 789–92.

PROVENANCE: Unknown

BIBLIOGRAPHY: N. Scott 1944, fig. 18; Hayes
1953, pp. 129–30, fig. 79; Labrousse and Leclant
1998, pp. 95–100

185. ATJEMA STANDING

Sixth Dynasty
Painted limestone
H. 91 cm (35⅞ in.)
Egyptian Museum, Cairo CG 99

A man in one of the classic Old Kingdom poses is depicted in this large statue with well-preserved colors. Atjema is standing with his left foot forward, as if walking. His arms are held close to his sides, and, typically, he has a cylindrical object in his hands. The spaces between his torso and arms and separating his legs were painted black to give the illusion that the stone has been carved away. Atjema stands against a support that comes to the middle of his back. His narrow chest and slim waist form an elegant silhouette, but his musculature is not pronounced, with the exception of the pectorals, which are linear in design. The ridge of the tibia is fairly prominent.

Atjema's kilt, knotted at the waist and finely pleated in a herringbone pattern on the right side, is quite elaborate, and he wears a beautiful broad collar of seven rows of beads in alternating colors of blue and green and ending in a row of pendants. He wears a round wig that leaves the ears free in an altogether unusual manner, and his fine mustache is indicated with a stroke of black paint. On the pedestal, which is painted black, three columns of hieroglyphs inscribed in white in front of the right foot give the beginning and end of his proper name, a few common epithets, and his titles: "*Wab* Priest of the King and Priest of the Sun Temple of Sahure." These titles make it possible to establish a relatively precise date for the work. S-LT, CZ

PROVENANCE: Probably Saqqara

BIBLIOGRAPHY: Borchardt 1911, pp. 77–78, pl. 22; Vandier 1958, p. 62; Porter and Moss 1979, p. 722; Cherpion 1998, p. 112

This statue has been placed in the context of the Sixth Dynasty because it has many traits that appear to link it to works of that period. Most conspicuous are the narrow waist, disproportionately small hands,[1] and peculiar shape of the wig, which fits the head very closely and leaves the ears uncovered (see cat. no. 189).[2] Characteristics the piece owes to the artistic tradition of the Fifth Dynasty (and ultimately the Fourth), such as the prominent musculature of the forearm[3] and the strong delineation of the bottom of the breasts, are also found in a number of Sixth Dynasty works (cat. nos. 173, 174, 188, 190). Whether this representation of Atjema was created at the very end of the Fifth Dynasty or the beginning of the Sixth is impossible to say at present. DOA

1. Russmann 1995a, pp. 269–70.
2. The closest parallel is offered by the wood statue of Ni-ankh-pepi, Egyptian Museum, Cairo, CG 60; Borchardt 1911, pp. 52–53.
3. For the general lack of strong musculature in Second Style statuary, see Russmann 1995a, p. 240, and cat. nos. 170, 172 here.

186. Prince Tjau Seated on the Ground

Sixth Dynasty, reign of Merenre I or later
Graywacke
H. 34.5 cm (13⅝ in.)
Egyptian Museum, Cairo CG 120

This distinctive statuette depicts Prince
Tjau seated in an asymmetrical pose different from the usual cross-legged pose of a
scribe at work (cat. no. 134). His right leg
is pulled up in front of him and his left
folded beneath; each hand is placed on a
knee, indicating that he is at rest. He is
dressed in a plain kilt and wears a midlength, flaring wig that leaves his large ears
exposed. His extremely large, protruding
eyes and thick, rectangular mouth and the
very pronounced folds on either side of his
nose combine to produce a countenance
that is typical of the Sixth Dynasty style.
The eyebrows in sharp relief and the details
of the fingers and toes are rendered with a
stiffness and an austerity that are accentuated by the black stone—an unusual choice
for a nonroyal statue. Also unusual is the
placement of the short incised inscription—
"Prince Tjau"—so that it curves around
the left knee instead of running horizontally across the pedestal.

Statues that show a man seated in this
asymmetrical pose are characteristic of the
Sixth Dynasty.[1] For that reason the beautiful statue of Ni-ankh-re (Egyptian Museum,
Cairo, JE 53150) was long dated to this
period. Now, however, it is considered to be
an experimental work with no immediate
successor, executed in the Fourth Dynasty.
By contrast, this figure clearly dates to the
end of the Old Kingdom. Also found within
the tomb of Tjau, whose full name was
Tjau-merenre-nakht, was a headrest with
a longer inscription enumerating his titles:
"prince, Seal Bearer of the King of Lower
Egypt, Unique Associate, Director of
Khentiu-shes."[2] It may seem surprising that
such an important personage was represented by such a diminutive work, but during the Sixth Dynasty, statues, although
numerous, were often small.   SL-T, CZ

1. Cherpion 1998, p. 106.
2. Borchardt 1964, CG 1797.

PROVENANCE: Saqqara

BIBLIOGRAPHY: Borchardt 1911, p. 92, pl. 27;
Hornemann 1951–69, vol. 2 (1957), pl. 522;
Vandier 1958, pp. 68, 103, 138, pl. 21.3; *5000
ans* 1960, fig. 13, p. 23 (15); Buhl 1962, no. 66;
Porter and Moss 1979, p. 699; Cherpion 1998,
p. 106, fig. 34a

187. PSEUDOGROUP OF ITISEN

Sixth Dynasty
Painted grayish white limestone[1]
H. 53.3 cm (21 in.); w. 47.5 cm (18¾ in.);
d. 38 cm (15 in.)
Musée du Louvre, Paris N 44 (= A 43)

The term "pseudogroup" was coined by the Belgian Egyptologist Jean Capart. It designates a type of statue, specific to the Old Kingdom, composed of two or more representations of the same individual, which may be accompanied by other figures. Many hypotheses have been advanced about the function and meaning of such sculptures, which were deposited in tombs. Do they represent the same person at different stages of life? Should they be seen as an image of the tomb's owner accompanied by his ka, one of the components of the Egyptian spirit? Or, more simply, does this type of statue imitate the multifigure sculptures, such as those depicting Queen Mer-si-ankh and her family, carved in the tomb walls at Giza from the Fourth Dynasty on?

A recent study lists thirty-two pseudogroups.[2] This one, acquired by the Louvre in 1827, was among the earliest examples found. Itisen, Overseer of Mortuary Priests, is depicted twice, and a single inscription, placed on the base of the pedestal between the two figures, gives his identity. This Itisen is more than likely the same person as the subject of a pseudogroup in Copenhagen[3] who bears the same name and a similar title. If so, this sculpture must come from the nonroyal necropolis in Saqqara where the Copenhagen group was found.[4]

The two figures in the Louvre pseudogroup are identical in pose and costume; only the faces display significant differences. A minor variation in the size of the figures, their slightly off-center positions, a nearly imperceptible shift in the angle of the legs, and the irregularity at the top of the backrest do not alter the strong impression of the work's symmetry.

The two images of Itisen are seated side by side on a bench with a high back. The subject is dressed in a kilt rounded at the bottom edge and fastened by a belt that is diagonally striped at the end. The kilt is decorated on the right with rectilinear pleats. Only the outline and a few traces of color remain of the broad collar with blue and green bands. The legs are parallel. The arms are at his sides, the right hand grasps a folded cloth, and the left hand is flat on the knee. Itisen's silhouette hints at the block of stone from which the figure was carved. His face is framed by a flared wig, parted in the middle, that conceals a portion of his ears. The individual locks are indicated by grooves. The face is characterized by a relatively long nose and an unusually short chin. The drooping eyes, very large and not matched, are outlined with black paint. The upper eyelid is rimmed to the outer corner, and the lower eyelid has a flat edge. Remnants of black paint create the illusion that the man is cross-eyed. The drooping eyebrows, with tapered ends extending low on the temples, are indicated by a wide band in slight relief. The long nose has a very narrow base and prominent nostrils. The philtrum is well marked, and the straight, clearly outlined mouth with turned-down corners has a pronounced notch in the upper lip. The neck is short. The torso and belly, with semicircular navel, are thin and very flat, and the pectorals are tersely indicated by an incision. The narrowness of the waist is emphasized by the black paint that fills the negative space at the sides. The junction between the vertical plane of the torso and belly and the

horizontal plane of the knees is a sharp right angle. The face of the figure at the proper right seems younger, with very round cheeks and a pleasant expression. The figure on the proper left looks sullen; he has a higher forehead and seems to be lowering his head slightly. The bottom of his wig is more carefully carved and stands out cleanly from the back slab.

Traces of color are abundant on the figures and pedestal. Black was used for the wigs, eyes, and horizontal foot of the pedestal and to distinguish the arms from the waist and the legs from the seat and from each other. Red covered the bodies. A speckled pink imitating granite is evident on the middle of the seat between the two figures, and there are traces of blue and green on the broad collar and the right side of the neck of the figure at right.

Certain stylistic criteria, the most persuasive of which is the ridge of stone on the clenched right hand, suggest a date for the work; this detail appears only on statues of the Sixth Dynasty.[5] An example appears on the firmly dated statuette of King Pepi II seated on his mother's lap (cat. no. 172).

CZ

1. The quarry may have been at Tura or Minya.
2. Eaton-Krauss 1995, pp. 57–74.
3. Copenhagen NM A.A. b 27; Vandier 1958, pl. 34.2.
4. On the origin of this statue, see Eaton-Krauss 1995, p. 64.
5. Fischer 1962b, p. 65, n. 6.

PROVENANCE: Probably Saqqara; Brindeau collection; acquired 1827

BIBLIOGRAPHY: Champollion 1827, p. 67, no. 67; Rougé 1849, p. 28; *Encyclopédie photographique* 1935, pls. 38, 39; Boreux 1935–38, p. 806; Vandier 1958, pp. 89, 118, pl. 33.2; Hornemann 1951–69, vol. 4 (1966), p. 1115; Kanawaty 1985, p. 39; Eaton-Krauss 1995, pp. 63–66, no. 20; Ziegler 1997a, pp. 90–92, no. 25

188. MERYRE-HA-ISHETEF STANDING

Sixth Dynasty
Painted ebony
H. 51 cm (20⅛ in.)
Trustees of the British Museum, London EA 55722

Sedment is a vast necropolis located eight kilometers (five miles) northwest of Herakleopolis (present-day Ihnasya el-Medina), south of the oasis of Faiyum. As in most provincial cemeteries, the tombs were carved into the living rock. The tomb of Meryre-ha-ishetef, whom an inscription describes as "Unique Associate and lector-priest," was tucked away at the foot of a hill in this necropolis. It has been dated to the Sixth Dynasty, based on archaeological criteria and on the name of the deceased, a composite that begins with "Meryre," one of the names of Pharaoh Pepi I. A courtyard carved out of the rock allowed access to a room in which three women were laid to rest; the courtyard also communicated with a deep shaft leading to the burial chamber of the owner, who lay in a wood coffin. The funerary furnishings were few but of high quality. In addition to a headrest inscribed in his name, now also in the collection of the British Museum, archaeologists found three wood statues depicting Meryre-ha-ishetef, arranged in decreasing order of size, accompanied by a statue of a woman and models of servants.

The figures of the deceased, currently divided among the Egyptian Museum, Cairo (JE 46992),[1] the British Museum, and the Ny Carlsberg Glyptotek in Copenhagen (cat. no. 189), depict him nude at three different stages of life. They were obviously made by different sculptors.

This statue represents Meryre-ha-ishetef as an adolescent. He has a broad face, eyebrows indicated naturalistically, and full cheeks; the philtrum and the depressions on either side of the nose are discreetly suggested. With wide-open eyes, the figure advances with a certain naive brashness.

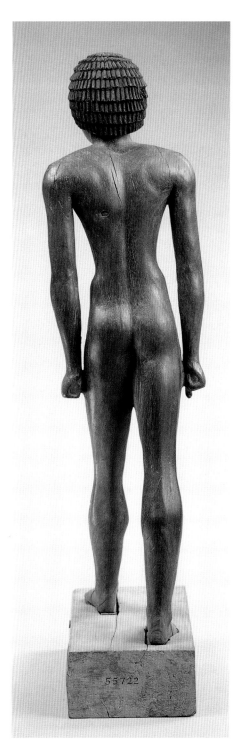

His arms are at his sides with fists clenched. As was the custom, the left foot is advanced, and the entire body is bent slightly forward in an attitude that has been interpreted as a sign of deference.[2] The arms are sculpted from the same block of wood as the body, a rare feat in a sculpture of this size, and the space separating them from the torso has been cut away. The nude body, thin and muscular, is admirably modeled.[3] It reflects the specific canon adopted in the Sixth Dynasty to depict the ideal of male beauty: disproportionately large head and a very slender form with nipped-in waist and slim hips.[4] Few Egyptian works display so much care in the treatment of such anatomical details as the musculature of the torso and back and the delicate bones of the clavicle, hips, and knees. Compare it with the older, extremely beautiful statue of Snefru-nefer nude (cat. no. 135) to see how, in the present work, the expression of well-being and physical strength is accompanied by a rarely equaled grace.   CZ

1. Saleh and Sourouzian 1987, no. 64.
2. Petrie and Brunton 1924, p. 3.
3. Compare it with the magnificent statue of Senedjem-ib Mehi, Overseer of All Construction Projects under King Unis, in the Museum of Fine Arts, Boston, 13.3466.
4. Russmann 1995a, pp. 269–70.

PROVENANCE: Sedment, Old Kingdom cemetery, tomb of Meryre-ha-ishetef, Petrie excavation, 1920–21; gift of the Egyptian Government as part of the division of finds

BIBLIOGRAPHY: Petrie and Brunton 1924, pp. 2–3, pls. 7, 8; Porter and Moss 1934, p. 115; Vandier 1958, p. 141, pl. 45.3; James and Davies 1984, p. 24, fig. 22; Limme 1984, cols. 790–91; Quirke and Spencer 1992, fig. 145

189. MERYRE-HA-ISHETEF WITH A STAFF

Sixth Dynasty
Painted cedar wood
H. 65.5 cm (25⅞ in.)
Ny Carlsberg Glyptotek, Copenhagen AEIN 1560

This statue of Meryre-ha-ishetef, "Unique Associate and lector-priest," was found in the same tomb with two others, also in wood and also nude. This example, which shows the subject as a mature man, is larger than the statue that depicts him as an adolescent (cat. no. 188). The pose is different, too. Here the tomb owner is standing, his right arm at his side and a staff in his left hand. A third and even larger figure (Egyptian Museum, Cairo, JE 46992) represents him in an identical attitude, equipped with a staff and scepter, and it is possible that the differences in size and accessories among the statues were intended to evoke all aspects

of the individual who, through the years and in the course of a successful career, gained in dignity. The nudity characteristic of many male statues from the Sixth Dynasty is not a mark of childhood but must be linked to changes in funerary beliefs.[1]

In this statue Meryre-ha-ishetef has reached middle age. His posture is more rigid and his stride less broad. The face has sagged; the eyes have large circles around them; the depressions around the nose are more pronounced; and two additional lines appear on either side of the philtrum. The stylized eyebrows accentuate the distinctive architecture of the face, in which the eyes, highlighted in black and white, occupy an inordinate amount of space. The neck is thinner, and the spindly body, treated with attention, has lost muscle tone. Curves have been replaced by angles, as the profile view eloquently shows. The hands and toes are nicely carved, particularly the long fingers of the right hand, with its nails painted

white. Because the statue is large, the arms were sculpted separately and fastened to the body with tenons, as were the feet from the heel forward.

In addition to its elegant silhouette, the statue is remarkable for its expressive face, which bears the marks of age and is rendered in the characteristic style of the Sixth Dynasty, with overlarge eyes, short nose framed by grooves, and a broad, strong mouth.   CZ

1. On this type of statue, see Schulz 1999.

PROVENANCE: Sedment, Old Kingdom cemetery, tomb of Meryre-ha-ishetef, Petrie excavation, 1920–21; acquired from the British School of Archaeology in Egypt 1921

BIBLIOGRAPHY: Petrie and Brunton 1924, pp. 2–3, pl. 9; Porter and Moss 1934, p. 115; Vandier 1958, p. 141, pl. 45.2; Limme 1984, cols. 790–91; Jørgensen 1996, pp. 94–95, no. 34 (with earlier bibliography)

190. Seal Bearer Tjetji as a Young Man

Sixth Dynasty, probably reign of Pepi I or
Merenre I
Painted wood with inlaid eyes of white limestone
and obsidian mounted in copper cells
H. 75.5 cm (29¾ in.)
Trustees of the British Museum, London EA 29594

The statue's pedestal gives the titles of its
owner and they are so distinguished—
"Seal Bearer of the King of Lower Egypt,
Unique Associate, lector-priest, Staff of
the Apis Bull, Controller of Bird Traps,
Director of Priests, initiate, honored by
the great god, Tjetji"—that they suggest a
man rich in years and experience. Yet the
subject is depicted as a young man, nude
and circumcised. The similarity of titles and
proper name invites us to identify this figure
with the Tjetji buried in tomb M 8 at the
necropolis of El-Hawawish at Akhmim.
An autobiographical inscription dates the
tomb to the reign of Pepi I or Merenre I
(see cat. no. 192).

Because this statue is large, the arms
and pedestal were sculpted separately; the
parts were assembled with a mortise-and-
tenon construction and then carefully polished. Abundant traces of color remain on
the wig's chiseled locks, on the pedestal,
and on the delicately incised nails highlighted in white.

Tjetji has his left leg forward. In his
bent left arm he holds a long staff (restored
in modern times), and his right arm is at
his side. The fingers of his right hand curl
around to form a hole, attesting that he
once held an accessory, probably a *sekhem*
scepter.[1] The full face is framed by a short
wig, whose wide, radiating crown of hair
falling over the forehead was very much in
vogue at the end of the Old Kingdom.[2] The
face is illuminated by enormous eyes, inlaid
in white limestone and obsidian mounted in
copper cells.[3] With its strong mouth and
short nose set off by deep lines in the cheeks,
Tjetji's physiognomy is characteristic of the
portrait style of the Sixth Dynasty. It can be
linked to a statue of Pepi I kneeling (cat.
no. 170) because of its brilliant, unusually
large eyes. The series of figures depicting
Meryre-ha-ishetef from Sedment, another
provincial necropolis (see cat. nos. 188, 189),
displays obvious affinities, in particular the
distinctive facial type and the elegant modeling of the slender nude body. Like the sub-

ject of the statues from Sedment, this distinguished personage apparently wanted to
record several aspects of his personality at
different stages in life, as well as to show
himself in what was probably a state of ritual nudity, for all eternity in his tomb.

Two other wood statues from Akhmim
are inscribed with the name of Tjetji.[4] They
display few affinities with each other or with
this piece. The first, housed in the Egyptian
Museum, Cairo (CG 221), bears titles too
common to allow us to link it to a specific
individual;[5] the second is in the Louvre
(cat. no. 191).   CZ

1. Like the statue of Meryre-ha-ishetef in the Egyptian Museum, Cairo, JE 46992, for example.

2. Ziegler 1997a, pp. 195–97, no. 55.
3. On this type of incrustation, which is different
from the technique used in earlier periods (the
Fourth and perhaps also the Fifth Dynasty),
see Lucas and Harris 1962, pp. 98–127.
4. Brovarski 1985, pp. 127–28; Kanawati
1980–92, vol. 7 (1987), pp. 57–58.
5. McFarlane 1987, pp. 63–73.

PROVENANCE: Not officially recorded,
but probably from Akhmim, cemetery of
El-Hawawish, tomb M 8

BIBLIOGRAPHY: Brovarski 1985, pp. 127
n. 69, 128, pl. 6; Kanawati 1980–92, vol. 7
(1987), p. 57, pl. 17; Potts 1990, p. 65; *Treasures
of the British Museum* 1990, p. 63, pl. 45;
Kanawati and McFarlane 1992, p. 10; Seipel
1992, pp. 142–43, no. 36; Blurton 1997, no. 2

191. SEAL BEARER TJETJI IN MIDDLE AGE

Sixth Dynasty, probably reign of Pepi I or
Merenre I
Acacia wood
H. 86 cm (33⅞ in.); w. 23.8 cm (9⅜ in.);
d. 51.3 cm (20¼ in.)
Musée du Louvre, Paris E 11566

Sculpted in carefully polished wood, Seal
Bearer Tjetji is depicted as a middle-aged
man, with massive head and fleshy body.
He is standing with his left foot forward,
his right arm at his side. The left arm is
extended and bent at a right angle. The
hands curve around a cylindrical hole
designed to house detachable elements,

probably a staff and scepter indicating the
subject's high rank.[1] The inscription on
the pedestal explains that Tjetji was "high
official, Seal Bearer of the King of Lower
Egypt, and Unique Associate."

He is dressed in a long kilt with apron,
held up by a plain belt that stands out in
sharp relief. The short, natural hair, once
painted black, is indicated by a slight ridge
along the hairline. The oval ears, flattened
against the brachycephalic skull, are extremely simplified.

The neck is thick, the face oval with
round cheeks and a pointed chin. The eyes
and adjoining areas have been gouged out;
there is no trace of eyebrows. The nose has
disappeared, except for the tip, which is very

thin with two lines indicating the wings of
the nostrils, a detail that is also found on
other statues from the Sixth Dynasty.[2] The
philtrum is etched in, and a slight furrow
borders each cheek. The thick, broad mouth
has a prominent lower lip; its contours are
completely outlined, even at the corners.

No clavicle is visible in the sunken and
fleshy chest; however, two wood pegs indicate the nipples, and a slight vertical groove
runs down to the teardrop-shaped navel,
which is pressed into a prominent belly. The
upper arms and forearms are treated as
round forms, with no musculature or bone
structure visible. The extended thumbs,
long and thin, have flat nails, with suggestions of outlines.

Detail, cat. no. 191

Below Tjetji's thick waist, the triangular apron hangs perfectly smooth. The long kilt clings to his thighs and posterior, which have been expressed as geometrical shapes. The legs are heavy, with thick ankles and prominent malleoli; their musculature is not visible. The back has been treated in a simplified manner, with a vertical indentation for the spinal column; each shoulder blade is indicated by a barely perceptible curve.

Although impressive in size, the figure has lost its past splendor. It was probably covered with a layer of painted stucco, as attested by a few patches of material still clinging to the kilt and by traces of white paint on this garment, red paint on the skin, and black paint on the hair. The viewer must

also mentally restore the brilliance of the once-inlaid eyes.

The titulary of this Tjetji suggests he belonged to the family of Akhmim nomarchs, and nothing prevents us from identifying him as the owner of tomb M 8, where the statue showing him as a young man (cat. no. 190) probably also originated. Stylistically, the work has much in common with a statue of Ni-ankh-pepi Kem excavated at Meir (Egyptian Museum, Cairo, CG 236), whose tomb is generally dated to the reign of Pepi I.[3] It, too, shows a stocky individual with short skull, sunken and fleshy chest, thick waist, and heavy legs. The tomb of Ni-ankh-pepi Kem has yielded another statue, very different but also in wood. The figure is nude, very long of body, and wears a small curly wig and a short kilt (Egyptian Museum, Cairo, CG 60). The presence of two figures in a single tomb, different in style but depicting the same person when young and when middle-aged, would therefore not be exceptional;[4] it would echo in statuary a theme that is commonplace in Sixth Dynasty reliefs.[5]   CZ

1. The appearance together of a long kilt and arms holding accessories is very rare (for two other examples, see Akhet-hotep [Zayed 1958, pl. 10], and the statue of a flutist found in Dahshur). Kilted figures generally have their arms hanging at their sides or hold a section of the garment in their fingers (for example, see Egyptian Museum, Cairo, CG 236).
2. Statue of Meryre-ha-ishetef from Sedment (Egyptian Museum, Cairo, JE 46992; Saleh and Sourouzian 1987, no. 64).
3. Blackman 1914, pp. 5, 9; Kessler 1982, col. 14.
4. For the coexistence of statues depicting the same figure in individualized and conventional aspects, see Bolshakov 1990, pp. 102–26.
5. For example, reliefs in the tomb of Ni-ankh-pepi Kem; see Blackman 1953, pl. 6.

PROVENANCE: Akhmim, probably necropolis of El-Hawawish, tomb M 8, 1890 excavation; purchased 1918

BIBLIOGRAPHY: Newberry 1912, pp. 101, 120; Porter and Moss 1937, pp. 19, 20; Vandier 1958, p. 90; Valloggia 1984, pp. 93–96; Brovarski 1985, p. 128; Kanawati 1980–92, vol. 7 (1987), pp. 57–58, pl. 20d; Ziegler 1990b, p. 272; Kanawati and McFarlane 1992, p. 10; Ziegler 1997a, pp. 152–54, no. 42

192. LEFT FRAGMENT OF A RELIEF OF SEAL BEARER TJETJI

Sixth Dynasty, reign of Merenre I
Painted limestone
H. 48 cm (19 in.); w. 48 cm (19 in.)
Musée du Louvre, Paris AF 9460

The necropolis of El-Hawawish houses tombs of governors who administered the ninth nome of Upper Egypt, located in a mountainous area northeast of the capital city, Akhmim. About halfway between Cairo and Aswan, Akhmim is the cult center of the ancient god of fertility Min. His sanctuary and a priesthood of both sexes—called, respectively, the stolists of Min and the watchwomen of Min—existed in Akhmim during the Old Kingdom. Briefly excavated in 1912 by the English archaeologist P. E. Newberry, the necropolis is currently the object of a systematic study conducted by the University of Sydney.[1] But the site, horribly plundered in the nineteenth century, was in a pitiful state in 1912, and it is now necessary to inventory works dispersed throughout the world to reconstitute the necropolis of the governors of Akhmim.

An important piece of the puzzle, the architrave to which this fragment belonged once adorned the facade of the rock-cut tomb of Prince Tjetji (or Tjetji Kai-hapi), the first Sixth Dynasty governor of Akhmim. The right fragment of the architrave (fig. 127) is now housed thousands of miles away, in the Field Museum of Natural History, Chicago. In the Chicago fragment Prince Tjetji, who bears the titles "Unique Associate" and "blessed," stands at the head of a group of five figures. He is depicted as walking, a long staff in his right hand, a *sekhem* scepter in his left. Dressed in a short kilt with triangular apron, he wears the shoulder sash of the cult priest, and a broad collar and bracelets complete his costume. "His wife, the royal ornament, Nefer-tjen-tet," stands respectfully behind him, arms at her sides; a sheath dress with pleated straps clings to her slender body. The lady is richly adorned with a necklace, arm bracelets, and anklets. Then come the children, arranged in descending order of size: first, "his eldest son, unique courtier, stolist of Min and Director of Priests, Khen-ankhu"; next, "his son, unique courtier, Shepsi-pu-min"; and finally, "his eldest daughter, whom he loves, Khemet-pu-netjeru." The scene, executed in sunk relief and highlighted with vivid colors—blue for the inscription, red and yellow for, respectively, the skin of men and women, and black for hair and eyes—has very pronounced stylistic peculiarities. All the figures are spindly, with angular profiles and conventional faces, and the women wear their curly hair off the ears. These details are of particular interest to art historians because the lintel can be very precisely dated to the reign of Merenre by its inscription.

The text occupying this fragment of Tjetji's architrave belongs to a classic literary genre, created in the Old Kingdom, called "autobiography." Inscriptions of this type were engraved in private tombs, and they present the life of the tomb's owner in narrative form. The dense columns of hieroglyphs seen here partly retrace the career of Tjetji, listing the sovereigns under whom he lived:

> Seal Bearer of the King of Lower Egypt, Unique Associate, lector-priest, stolist of Min, Director of Priests, the blessed Tjetji says: I was a young man who put on the headband under the reign of King Pepi [I]. I was Administrator of the Jackal. I was appointed Confidant to the King. I was appointed courtier and Director of Priests, every courtier who was in the [capital] city being placed under my supervision. I was appointed Unique Associate during the reign of Pepi [I]. When I was appointed Unique Associate, I was given access to the royal house, a wish that had not been granted to any other men. My wishes were granted in very great numbers by the Residence under the reign of Merenre [I]. I was appointed stolist of Min.

The decoration of Tjetji's tomb was certainly executed during or just after the reign of Merenre. The same date must also be assigned to the furnishings from his tomb and to two wood statues that very probably depict him (cat. nos. 190, 191).   CZ

1. Kanawati 1980–92.

PROVENANCE: Akhmim; consigned by the French Institute of Near Eastern Archaeology (IFAO) to the Musée du Louvre

BIBLIOGRAPHY: Grdseloff 1943b, p. 120; Roccati 1982, pp. 170–71; Brovarski 1985, pl. 8; McFarlane 1987, pp. 63–73; Kanawati 1980–92, vol. 8 (1988), p. 62, pl. 14a, fig. 35; Ziegler 1990b, pp. 270–73, no. 51; Fischer 1992, p. 145; Kanawati and McFarlane 1992, p. 11

127. Right fragment, Relief of Seal Bearer Tjetji. Field Museum, Chicago, 31700

193. FISHERMEN AND HERDSMEN WITH THEIR ANIMALS

Early Sixth Dynasty, reign of Teti or slightly later
Painted limestone
Left block: h. 47 cm (18½ in.); w. 66.5 cm (26⅛ in.)
Right block: h. 48.2 cm (19 in.); w. 78.7 cm (31 in.)
The Detroit Institute of Arts, City of Detroit
Purchase 30.371

The high official Ni-ankh-nesut must have lived at the end of the Fifth Dynasty and the beginning of the Sixth because his sons' names incorporated the names of King Unis and King Teti, who reigned during that time.[1] The reliefs of Ni-ankh-nesut's tomb— now scattered among many museums[2]— display workmanship of high quality and a rich variety of scenes. The present blocks depict herdsmen and their cattle crossing a branch of the Nile or a canal where fishermen have pulled in a net that is full of fish. The two groups, herdsmen with their cattle and fishermen, are linked by a common expanse of water that appears as a blue painted zone at the bottom of the relief. The legs of the cattle and herdsmen are represented in front of this blue zone, indicating that they are wading through the water,[3] while the fishermen appear on a narrow brown strip above the blue area, signifying that they are standing on the ground beside the water. Thus landscape and location are represented by a few emblematic props rather than by a naturalistically conceived image, a strategy that is typical for Egyptian art. In the case

of the Ni-ankh-nesut relief this representational approach allowed the artist to concentrate primarily on the composition.

The Ni-ankh-nesut composition relies on the juxtaposition of the rather dense group of bovines, stacked one behind the other with heads and foreparts forming a regular pattern, and the complex interplay of the fishermens' legs. The upright single figures—the herdsman with a stick on his shoulder who appears on the left and the man with a calf on his back in the center— stand out conspicuously from the other elements in the cattle group and draw attention to the way the men carefully coax the herd to cross the water. The man on the left uses his right hand to push and pat the back of the cow nearest him, and the man holding the calf uses the maternal instincts of the mother cow as a lure: where the calf goes, the mother will follow, and the rest of the herd will come after her. The mother, moreover, reassures her calf by touching its tongue with hers. Connections between the heads and bodies of the cattle are tenuous, and only eighteen legs are indicated for

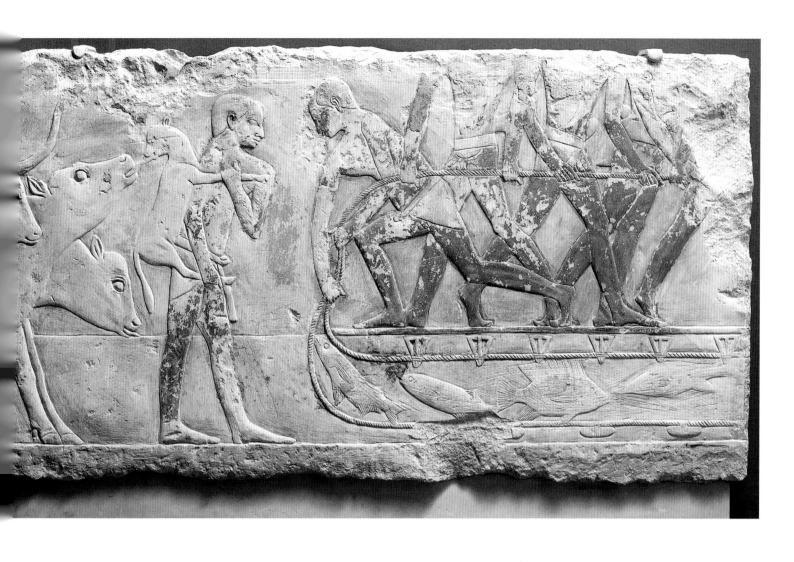

nine animals. Accuracy in such matters was less important to the artist than enriching his scene with little touches that reveal animal behavior—hence the beast taking a sip of the water through which the herd is moving.

That the fishermen are anticipating a good catch is expressed by their excited leg movements.[4] There are four big fish in the part of the net that is preserved, and these are depicted with so much attention to detail that their species can easily be identified. From left to right there are: a mullet (*Mugil* sp.),[5] an elephant-snout fish (*Gnathonemus cyprinoides*),[6] a tilapia or bolti fish (*Tilapia nilotica*),[7] and another type of elephant-snout fish (*Mormyrus kannume*), all species common in the Nile.[8] With similar attention to detail, the artist has also depicted oval stone sinkers along the bottom edge of the net and lightweight triangular swimmers that are probably made of wood along the top.[9] The net ends in two ropes that are gathered together in the hands of the first hauler. The fishermen behind him pull this rope toward the right of the scene, where at some point they would have met an additional group of men, now missing, who pulled the ropes attached to the other end of the net. Both fishermen and herdsmen are wearing very short kilts that do not cover the genitalia and reveal that the men have been circumcised.[10]

The style of the block is typical of works of the earlier Sixth Dynasty. The relief is higher than in Fifth Dynasty examples, and the edges are well rounded not only along the outlines of the figures but also where figures overlap. This gives the relief a fuller, more sculptural quality than is found in the comparatively tight and lean works of the Fifth Dynasty. Interior modeling, however, is more varied and subtle in Fifth Dynasty reliefs (cat. nos. 111–114).[11] The artist responsible for the Ni-ankh-nesut relief, for instance, has indicated details of musculature only sparingly, but he has emphasized the eyes and ears of the cattle and the hands and belts of the men with deep, strong carving, thus achieving an almost baroque expressiveness. The few traces of paint that remain suggest that the colors, such as the blue of the water and the deep reddish brown of the men's skin, were also strong and that the palette was rich in contrasts.   DOA

Detail, cat. no. 193

1. Smith 1946, p. 208, n. 1.
2. Porter and Moss 1979, pp. 694–96.
3. For the scenes of a herd wading through shallow water in contrast to other scenes where the water is deep, see Klebs 1915, pp. 60–61; Montet 1925, pp. 66–73; Vandier 1969, pp. 96–128; Harpur 1987, pp. 157, 348–50; and Altenmüller 1998, pp. 141–42.
4. For the iconography of dragnet fishing scenes, see Klebs 1915, pp. 74–75; Montet 1925, pp. 32–42; Vandier 1969, pp. 559–98; Moussa and Altenmüller 1977, pp. 96–97; Harpur 1987, pp. 145–48; and Altenmüller 1998, pp. 136–37.
5. Brewer and Friedman 1989, pp. 72–73.
6. Ibid., p. 50.
7. Ibid., pp. 77–79.

8. Ibid., pp. 51–52. For these fish species, see also Boessneck 1988, esp. fig. 213; and most recently, Sahrhage 1998.
9. Sahrhage 1998, p. 106.
10. Westendorf 1975, cols. 727–29; Kanawati and Hassan 1997, pp. 49–50.
11. For the relief style of the time, see also Smith 1946, p. 208.

PROVENANCE: Tomb of Ni-ankh-nesut, probably Saqqara

BIBLIOGRAPHY: Richardson 1931, pp. 33–36, ills.; Detroit Institute of Arts 1943, ill. p. 5; Detroit Institute of Arts 1949, pp. 1–3, ill.; Detroit Institute of Arts 1960, ill. p. 16

Detail, cat. no. 193

194. Still Life: Offerings for the Deceased

Early Sixth Dynasty
Painted limestone
H. 48 cm (18⅞ in.); w. 38.5 cm (15⅛ in.)
The Detroit Institute of Arts, Founders Society
Purchase, Hill Memorial Fund 76.5

In reliefs of the early Fourth Dynasty the provisions presented before a deceased individual seated at an offering table took the form of a few separate items set out side by side, more in the manner of hieroglyphs than as depictions of real objects (cat. nos. 51–53). During the Fifth Dynasty the number of objects shown increased considerably, until they appeared as great piles of food heaped in front of the tomb owner. By the time the present relief was carved, in the early Sixth Dynasty, the art of composing what we would today term a still life was at its height. Although the artist responsible for this image attempted to create the impression that objects were piled up randomly, he nevertheless ordered them in registers, as indicated by the straight line at the bottom of the block and another near the top.[1] In the very fragmentary upper register a large side of meat with curved ribs takes up most of the space, and beside it on the left are the bottom of an offering jar and the hoof from a joint of meat. At the bottom left of the more fully preserved register we see a large triangular loaf of bread painted yellow and a leg from another joint of meat. And arising from the baseline is a tumbled heap of ducks of various species crowned rather precariously by a plate on which figs have been arranged in an astonishingly orderly fashion, as well as various vegetables, including a huge lettuce, cucumbers, and squash. Some of the cucumbers and the lettuce still show green paint. Faint remnants of paint reveal the figs to have been light brown, the squash yellowish brown, the meat red, and the birds various colors with the feathering indicated by black lines. The intensity of the colors was enhanced by a dark blue background.

At the upper right edge of the relief we can discern the hand of an offering bearer presenting a duck, grasping its head with one hand and its wings with the other, now-missing, hand. These remains demonstrate that the fragment must originally have been part of a larger scene that represented the tomb owner seated at an offering table while attendants brought provisions for his eternal sustenance. Comparison with reliefs showing piles of offerings from dated tombs shows that the Detroit Institute piece is closest in composition and style to works from a number of tombs assigned to the reign of King Teti.[2] The height and roundness of the relief and the sparseness of the modeling within the figures combined with a few deeply carved details, such as the eyes and beaks of the birds, as well place it close to the large relief from Ni-ankh-nesut's tomb that is also in the Detroit Institute of Arts (cat. no. 193).   DOA

1. Peck (1980, p. 108) has furthermore demonstrated that the seemingly random heap of offerings was in fact rather carefully composed with the help of a grid whose basic unit was the ancient Egyptian digit equal to 1.87 centimeters. For the careful composition of another pile of offerings, see Altenmüller 1998, p. 185.
2. For the dates of tombs with still-life images, see Cherpion 1989, pp. 53, 176–77. Fifth Dynasty examples are in general much simpler than the Detroit piece. See, for instance, Steindorff 1913, pl. 126 (time of Niuserre). In terms of richness of objects displayed, works from the later Fifth Dynasty are closer to the Detroit Institute relief; see N. de G. Davies 1901, pls. 24, 34 (relevant to the offering bearer beside the heap); and Murray 1905, pl. 9 (reign of Djedkare-Isesi). Examples dated to the reign of Teti are Bissing 1905, pl. 17; Murray 1905, pl. 29; and Macramallah 1935, pl. 15. Later Sixth Dynasty decorations are less varied and complex in composition.

PROVENANCE: Probably Saqqara; ex collection Henry Nilsson, on loan to Medelhavsmuseet, Stockholm

BIBLIOGRAPHY: *Bulletin of the Detroit Institute of Arts* 55 (1976), p. 37, fig. 26; Peck 1980, pp. 102–8

195. RELIEF OF QAR SEATED

Sixth Dynasty, reign of Pepi I or later
Painted limestone
H. 62 cm (24⅜ in.); w. 118 cm (46½ in.)
Museum of Fine Arts, Boston, Harvard University–
Museum of Fine Arts Expedition 27.1134

196. RELIEF OF QAR HUNTING

Sixth Dynasty, reign of Pepi I or later
Painted limestone
H. 52.9 cm (20⅞ in.); w. 109.5 cm (43⅛ in.)
Museum of Fine Arts, Boston, Harvard University–
Museum of Fine Arts Expedition 27.1130

Mastaba G 7101, the tomb of Meryre-nefer, who was also called Qar, is just north of the large double mastaba of Kawab (G 7110–7120) in the cemetery east of Khufu's pyramid. Almost nothing is left of the superstructure, which was probably an enclosure rather than a traditional mastaba of nearly solid stone and rubble.[1] Cut into the bedrock of the plateau, the offering chapel was reached by means of a stairway, whose sides were lined with decorated slabs, which probably included these two blocks.

In the larger fragment (cat. no. 195), Qar is seated in an armchair before a table of offerings. In style, the chair, with its exceptionally high back and arms, is similar to a palanquin, as shown in another scene in this tomb.[2] However, more complete chairs of a similar style are preserved in two other scenes from Qar's tomb.[3] The figure of Qar has been executed in well-cut raised relief. The details of the face are particularly fine. The helix of the ear is indicated by a narrow relief line, and the large eye has been outlined in a similar fashion. The eyebrow has also been carved in relief. The mouth is well formed and sharply outlined. Substantial amounts of red paint are preserved on the surface, especially on Qar's body but also on some of the offerings, a number of which also retain traces of blue. Some black paint

is also preserved, and there are traces of gray paint in the area between the offerings and the inscription above.

In the smaller fragment (cat. no. 196), in which Qar is depicted hunting fowl with a throw stick, he is accompanied by a smaller man identified as Idu, who is probably the owner of an adjacent mastaba, G 7102. Texts in the two tombs indicate that Qar and Idu are probably father and son, but it is not absolutely clear which man belongs to which generation.[4]

The figures of Qar and Idu have been carefully modeled, and Qar's facial features have many of the same details as in the offering scene; however, the hunt has been executed in a different technique. Instead of working in low raised relief, the artist has created the illusion of relief by subtly low-ering the surface of the background down to the edge of the figures rather than removing it entirely.

Here, too, substantial amounts of red paint are preserved, and black paint is vis-ible on the wigs of the men and on some of the hieroglyphs. On both reliefs, the paint has been applied rather carelessly, especially on the human figures. This is most noticeable around the arms, where the red color spills over on the background. As in the relief of Qar seated, the back-ground of the hunt relief appears to have been painted gray.

The tomb of Qar has been dated to the reign of Pepi I or later in the Sixth Dynasty on the basis of the owner's title, "Tenant Farmer of the Pyramid of Meryre (Pepi I)." He was also Overseer of the Pyramid Towns of Khufu and Menkaure and Inspector of *Wab* Priests of the Pyramid of Khafre.

CHR

1. For a description of the complex, see Simpson 1976, pp. 1–2.
2. See ibid., fig. 27.
3. One of these may also belong to the stairwell decoration; the other is on a pillar farther inside the offering chapel; see ibid., figs. 16, 26b.
4. Reisner, who excavated the tomb, believed that Qar was Idu's son, but Simpson (1976) calls this into question.

PROVENANCE: (195 and 196) Giza, mastaba G 7101, Reisner excavation, 1924–25

BIBLIOGRAPHY: (195) Porter and Moss 1974, pp. 184–85; Simpson 1976, p. 2, frontis. (detail), pl. 4a, fig. 18a. (196) Porter and Moss 1974, pp. 184–85; Simpson 1976, pl. 4a, figs. 15, 18

197. Mummy Mask and Body Covering

Fifth or Sixth Dynasty
Plaster
Mask: h. 21 cm (8¼ in.)
Museum of Fine Arts, Boston, Harvard University–
Museum of Fine Arts Expedition 39.828

The practice of covering the head of a mummy with a layer of plaster that has been modeled to look like a human face seems to have begun during the Fifth Dynasty and continued into the Sixth Dynasty.[1] Twenty-nine examples of these plaster masks have been found, some in excellent condition, some very fragmentary. In execution the modeling of the features ranges from very crude to very careful. It appears that in most burials where plaster was used to enhance the mummy, only the head was coated, but in six instances large portions of the upper surface of the body were also covered.[2]

This plaster mask and mummy covering constitute the most complete example of the practice. Parts of the left shoulder, upper arms, torso, abdomen, and upper legs are preserved. The abdomen shows a well-defined navel, indicating that most of the body was represented without clothing; however, a loincloth covers the genitals. The mask is one of the most detailed, especially around the eyes, which are open, with both lids indicated.[3] As with most other well-executed masks, the browridges are clearly delineated, the nose is narrow and well defined, and the lips are sharply outlined. The face appears to be somewhat longer and narrower than in most other examples, but the photographs of these objects are taken from such a variety of angles and with such a range of lighting that comparison is difficult.[4]

This should not be thought of as a death mask, for the features were not cast from a mold made directly over the face of the deceased, a process that cannot be documented for the Old Kingdom, other opinions to the contrary.[5] The features appear to have been modeled by the hand of a confident artist in plaster that had been applied over the wrapped head of the mummy. Examples in the Museum of Fine Arts, Boston, that can be examined from the back show the impression of cloth over a curved surface, but no impression of the face of the deceased.[6] The plaster, which seems to have been applied in layers, is usually quite thick over the face, becoming much thinner toward the edges.

The majority of Old Kingdom plaster masks have been found at Giza, while Abusir and Saqqara have each yielded three. Although a few show the hairline, or perhaps a headcloth, across the forehead, most have no indication of hair.[7] Masks on which the sides of the head are preserved often have ears, but the most recently discovered example, which was found in an excellent state of preservation, has none.[8] These masks are not documented later than the Sixth Dynasty; they seem to be precursors of what would become the mummy mask, a piece of burial equipment that could be fashioned separately, before the burial, and then placed over the head and shoulders of the mummy, as a physical and probably amuletic protection of the deceased's head.

CHR

1. Reisner gives this range of dates for the examples in his unpublished manuscript in the Museum of Fine Arts, Boston (n.d., p. 702 and appendix L). This dating is supported by Roth (1995, p. 114).
2. For a catalogue of these and other related treatments of mummies in the Old Kingdom, see Tacke 1996.
3. The plaster mask found by Hawass (1992a, fig. 6) at Giza in 1987 also appears to have open eyes, although the lower lids are not so clearly indicated.
4. This face is certainly quite different from the other well-preserved example in the Museum of Fine Arts, Boston (37.644), from mastaba G 2092, published in Roth 1995, pl. 65.
5. The mold of a face, usually described as a death mask, was uncovered at Saqqara by Quibell during excavations in the pyramid temple of King Teti in 1908 (Quibell 1909, pp. 20, 112–13, pl. 55). It was identified by the excavator as dating to the Sixth Dynasty and is often

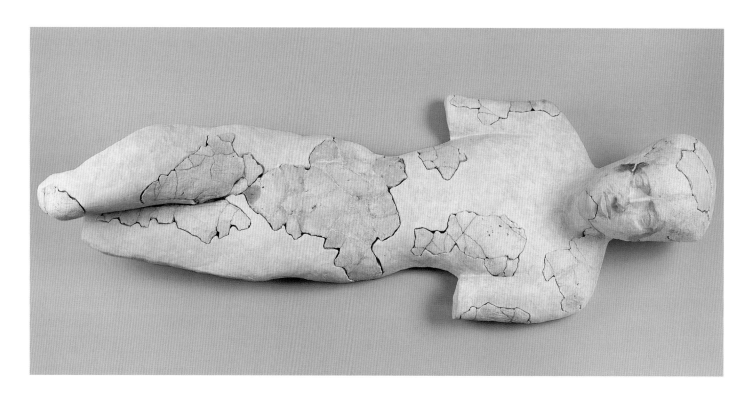

mentioned in discussions of both reserve heads and plaster mummy masks (Smith 1949, p. 27; Millet 1981, p. 130; Brovarski in D'Auria, Lacovara, and Roehrig 1988, p. 92; Tefnin 1991, p. 58, n. 3). However, the context in which the mold was found makes it impossible to date the object with any certainty. It was in the debris covering the ruined temple, about 70 centimeters (27 1/2 inches) above the floor level in an area that was dotted with intrusive New Kingdom tomb shafts. The area around Teti's pyramid complex produced material dating from the Old Kingdom to the Roman Period, and Saqqara was also the location of an early Christian monastery, although this is some distance to the south. Considering the long and intensive use of the site and the very disturbed nature of the context in which it was found, there appears to be no reason to date this mold to the Old Kingdom, and it could well come from a much later period.

6. I extend my thanks to Rita E. Freed for allowing me to examine these objects and to Peter Lacovara and Peter Der Manuelian for locating them as well as various unpublished references and excavation photographs.

7. On the head found at Giza by Hawass there was a copper headband covered with gold and faience beads. See Hawass 1992a, p. 333.

8. Ibid., pp. 331, 332, figs. 5, 6.

PROVENANCE: Giza, mastaba G 2037 B (shaft X), Reisner excavation, 1939

BIBLIOGRAPHY: Reisner n.d., p. 702 and appendix L; Smith 1949, p. 28; Porter and Moss 1974, p. 68; Brovarski in D'Auria, Lacovara, and Roehrig 1988, pp. 91–92; Tacke 1996, pp. 321–22, pl. 50a

198. HEADREST

Sixth Dynasty
Wood
H. 22.5 cm (8 7/8 in.); w. 22.2 cm (8 3/4 in.);
d. 8.6 cm (3 3/8 in.)
Kunsthistorisches Museum, Ägyptisch-Orientalische Sammlung, Vienna Äs 8445

Three jointed parts have been employed to make this skillfully carved headrest. A semicircular cradle, designed to support the head, is fixed to a grooved cylindrical shaft that flares at either end and rests on a finely detailed oval base. A cord delicately sculpted in relief encircles the foot of the base.

As a basic item of household equipment, the headrest was usually made of wood or stone; as a luxury item, it could be made of ivory. It might be gilded or upholstered with linen cushions, and texts or figures (sometimes human, sometimes divine) were occasionally inscribed or sculpted on its vertical shaft. Frequently included in funerary equipment (cat. no. 199), headrests are often represented on tomb reliefs, including those in the burial chambers of Hesi-re[1] and Mereruka[2] at Saqqara and Queen Mer-si-ankh III[3] at Giza.   JA

1. Quibell 1913, pls. 14, 21.
2. Duell 1938, pls. 92, 93.
3. Dunham and Simpson 1974, fig. 8.

PROVENANCE: Unknown

BIBLIOGRAPHY: Unpublished

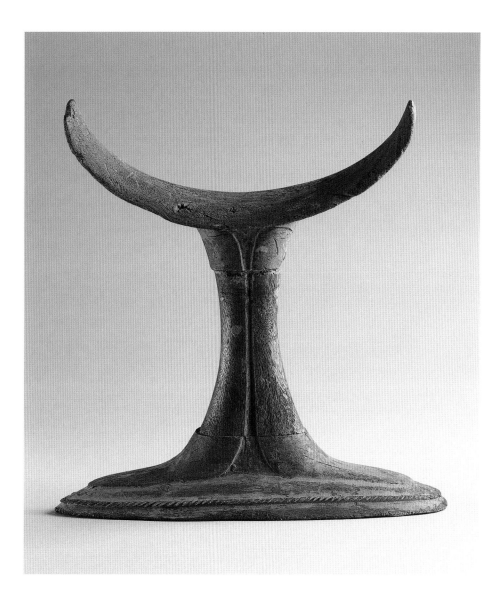

199. HEADREST

Old Kingdom
Ivory
H. 15.8 cm (6¼ in.); w. 14.4 cm (5⅝ in.);
d. 5.7 cm (2¼ in.)
Soprintendenza al Museo delle Antichità Egizie,
Turin s.14069

This elegant ivory headrest is composed of
a cradle resting on a flat piece that functions
as an abacus, two fluted colonnettes that
flare out at the bottom, and a quadrangular
base. Remnants of fabric, perhaps from the
cloth in which a mummy was wrapped, still
adhere to the surface of the cradle.

This headrest differs from most of the
others known (for example, cat. no. 198) in
that it has a double rather than a single support. It is not unique, however: an identical
headrest appears in paintings in the tomb of
Hesi-re at Saqqara, from the early Third
Dynasty,[1] and several tombs from Kafr el-
Ammar, dating to the early Old Kingdom,
have provided very similar pieces.[2] Moreover, the fluting of the supports is reminiscent of that found in a particular type of
column employed in Third Dynasty architecture. Such examples suggest that this work
dates to the early Old Kingdom, a period in
which the use of headrests was widespread.

Relatively common in tombs, these supports were generally placed either under or
near the head of the deceased. A large number of them, particularly those of wood or
alabaster, show signs of wear, which implies
that they were used in everyday life. Others,
of more fragile materials, such as the present
ivory example, were no doubt purely funerary objects. Headrests probably played an
important role in funerary beliefs during the
Old Kingdom; even afterward, they remained associated with the protection and
resurrection of the deceased. They appear
among the objects painted inside Middle
Kingdom coffins, and chapter 166 of the
Book of the Dead was subsequently devoted
to them. In the Late Dynastic Period they
became part of the mummy's equipment,
as small headrest-shaped amulets, often
made of hematite, were slipped between
the bandages.

1. Quibell 1913, pl. 14.

2. Petrie and Mackay 1915, pls. 11, 14, 17, 19.
One of these is in the collection of the Petrie
Museum, London, UC 8585.

PROVENANCE: Unknown; brought from Egypt
by Jean-François Champollion 1830

BIBLIOGRAPHY: Donadoni Roveri 1987, p. 131

200. NECKLACE

Sixth Dynasty
Egyptian faience
L. 30 cm (11⅞ in.)
The Syndics of the Fitzwilliam Museum,
Cambridge E 10-1907

Simple rows of beads in regular patterns
like those in the present necklace occur
in every period. This example was found
in a tomb in Rifeh in Middle Egypt, near
Asyut. It is characterized by an extremely
regular arrangement of ball beads made
of dark blue and green faience, alternating
with groups of small ring-shaped beads
in blue faience.   PR

PROVENANCE: Rifeh, Zarabey 72; gift of the
British School of Archaeology to the Fitzwilliam
Museum

BIBLIOGRAPHY: Unpublished

201. NECKLACE WITH AMULETS

Sixth to Eighth Dynasty
Gold and Egyptian faience
L. 25 cm (9⅞ in.)
The Syndics of the Fitzwilliam Museum,
Cambridge E 31-1930

Combined in this long necklace are minuscule ring-shaped gold beads, each less than .1 centimeter in length, small disk-shaped beads in blue and green faience, and six larger round beads made of gold leaf. As the necklace has been reassembled, the five gold amulets distributed among its beads may not be in their original positions. The center is currently occupied by an amulet measuring about 2.3 centimeters high that represents a cobra poised to strike and sitting on a basket. Made of thin gold leaf, the cobra has a rather rough outline, and no detail was incised or engraved on it. The two

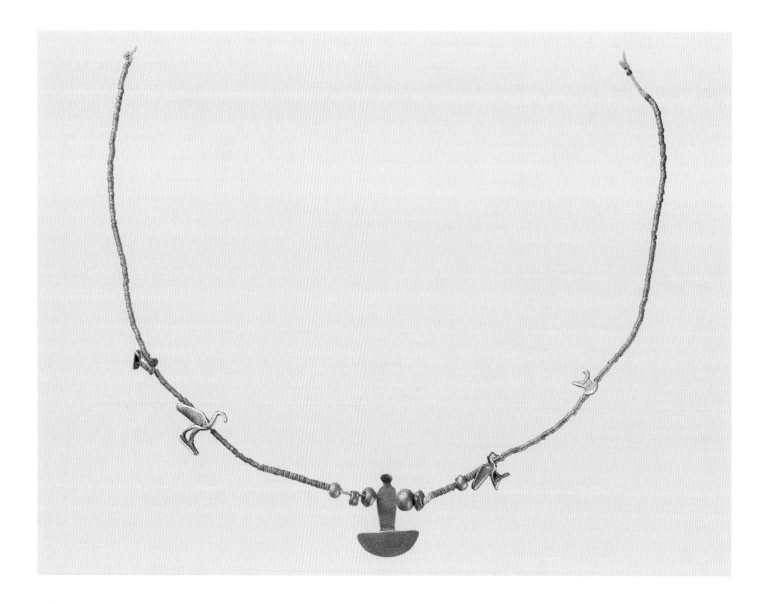

Cat. nos. 203, 202

ibis that frame it are also made of gold leaf that has been left smooth; the bird on the left is 1.3 centimeters high, the one on the right only .8 centimeter. The amulet on the far left, which is .8 centimeter high, is a tiny falcon balanced on the right by a small red crown set on a *neb* basket.

Ibis-shaped amulets in gold, electrum, or copper are relatively plentiful in tombs from the end of the Old Kingdom and the First Intermediate Period; they were probably linked to the god Thoth, with whom this bird is associated. The cobra poised to strike and the red crown set on a *neb* basket are insignia associated with pharaonic authority and power. Beginning in the First Intermediate Period, these symbols were appropriated by private individuals as part of a process that involved the extension of royal funerary prerogatives. Their presence among the equipment of the deceased was intended to allow the nonroyal dead to benefit in the hereafter from protection equivalent to that enjoyed by the king himself.   PR

PROVENANCE: Matmar, tomb 3025, British Museum expedition to Middle Egypt, 1929–31

BIBLIOGRAPHY: Brunton 1948, p. 47, nos. 70, 92, pl. 32

202. AMULET IN THE SHAPE OF A HARE

Sixth Dynasty
Gold
H. 1 cm (⅜ in.); w. 1.6 cm (⅝ in.)
Fondation Jacques-Edouard Berger, Lausanne

PROVENANCE: Unknown

203. AMULET IN THE SHAPE OF A STANDING DOG

Sixth Dynasty
Gold
H. 1.9 cm (¾ in.); w. 2.4 cm (1 in.)
Fondation Jacques-Edouard Berger, Lausanne

The body of each of these animals was formed from a single piece of gold; the ears were then added to the hare, the legs to the dog. Each has a ring for hanging, placed on the side of the hare and on the back of the dog. Although rather bulky, the two animals are not lacking in grace.

The subject, style, and technique of these amulets suggest a date at the end of the Old Kingdom. The oldest examples of gold amulets of this type, an oryx and a bull, were found at Naga el-Deir in the tomb of a woman from the First Dynasty.[1] A small number of similar examples, dating from the entire Old Kingdom period, can be found (cat. nos. 97, 209). A great many more of these gold amulets probably existed; to a large degree, plundering of tombs accounts for their disappearance. A beautiful set from the Sixth Dynasty tomb of Medu-nefer in Balat includes a walking human figure, an ibis, the god Heh, a walking dog, a *wedjat* eye, and an ankh.[2]

Amulets in both shapes seen here appeared at the end of the Old Kingdom. Representations of a walking dog might possibly be identified as the god Wepwawet, but the funerary god Anubis is a more likely association. From the Sixth Dynasty on, Anubis appeared either in that form or in the shape of a man with a dog's head—the two most characteristic representations of the god throughout pharaonic history.   PR

1. Egyptian Museum, Cairo, CG 53824-5; see Reisner 1908, pl. 9.
2. Valloggia 1986, vol. 1, p. 117, vol. 2, pl. 65.

PROVENANCE: Unknown

BIBLIOGRAPHY: Page-Gasser and Wiese 1997, p. 63, no. 36

204. NECKLACE WITH AMULETS

Sixth Dynasty
Gold, carnelian, steatite, and Egyptian faience
L. 40.5 cm (16 in.)
Trustees of the British Museum, London EA 62516

Clusters of many small, regular ring-shaped beads in gold, steatite, and faience are combined with a few barrel-shaped carnelian beads to make up this necklace. The gold beads were created simply by rolling up sheets of fine leaf. Several amulets are distributed along the length of the strand, including a small carnelian falcon at its center. This is flanked by two diminutive gold-leaf amulets, one depicting the front half of a lion and the other the god Heh. The latter displays almost no detail: only the face is indicated with an incision.

The regularity of the beads, the beauty of the materials, and the delicacy of the amulets make this necklace an extremely refined piece of jewelry. It was found with other jewelry of lesser value in the tomb of a young woman in Mostagedda.   PR

PROVENANCE: Mostagedda, tomb 785, British Museum expedition, 1928–29

BIBLIOGRAPHY: Brunton 1937, p. 99, Tomb Register, pl. 46, Bead Register, pl. 29, Bead Corpus, pl. 47, 45 K8; Andrews 1981, p. 44, no. 237, pls. 6, 19

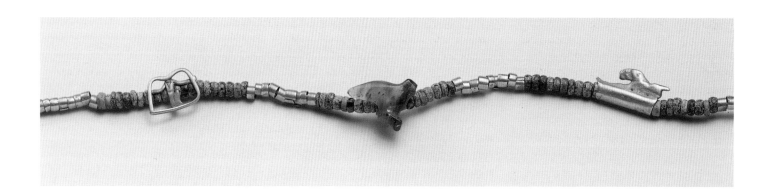

205. NECKLACE WITH AMULETS

Sixth Dynasty
Ivory, bone, and Egyptian faience
L. 37 cm (14⅝ in.)
Petrie Museum of Egyptian Archaeology, University
College London UC 18001

From the Sixth Dynasty on, and especially during the First Intermediate Period, amulets appeared much more frequently in tombs than in previous times—a development that no doubt reflects a corresponding increase in their use in everyday life. It is usual to find several dozen of them, sometimes minuscule, made of all sorts of materials, although faience was preferred.

This necklace employs the popular barrel-shaped or biconical beads, complemented by three large twisted cylinders. Among its most refined amulets are an ivory hare and two very simplified female figures in bone—the latter a fairly common motif but less so than male figures. Representations of children occur as well, as in the very schematic example here. The two female hippopotamuses on the necklace probably symbolize the goddess Taweret, who protected pregnant women and was undoubtedly associated with the idea of rebirth.[1] The scorpion, this one in ivory, appeared as a motif during the Old Kingdom and was later associated with the goddess Selket, protector of the deceased. Other amulets on this necklace depict a gazelle's head, the head of the goddess Hathor, a recumbent lion, a falcon, a scarab, and a *wedjat* eye (a representation of the god Horus's restored left eye).

Amulets in the shape of a scarab, one of the symbols most representative of Egyptian civilization, appeared in the Fifth Dynasty.[2] Nonetheless, tombs from the end of the Predynastic Period have been found to contain the hollowed-out bodies of these insects,[3] suggesting that they could be strung into necklaces as ornaments or as symbols. The motif was rapidly transposed into various materials, the earliest amulets being rather crudely executed in faience or glazed steatite. Later, inscriptions were placed on the flat side of scarab amulets, which served as seals. In tombs they replaced other kinds of seal amulets in use during the Old Kingdom.

Another important symbol in Egyptian civilization, the *wedjat* eye initially occurs in schematic representations in tombs dating from about the Fifth Dynasty. Many examples of this human eye decorated with a falcon's markings continued to be placed in tombs until the end of the pharaonic period.

Despite its somewhat coarse appearance—largely due to its brownish color, which results from the loss of glaze on the faience—this necklace must have originally been quite beautiful. Its value would have been enhanced by its supposed magical powers, since all sorts of benefits were ascribed to amulets. In particular, amulets in tombs were said to protect the deceased in the hereafter, aid in rebirth, and restore the full use of physical faculties.   PR

1. Amulets of Taweret appeared at the end of the Old Kingdom and remained in favor until the Roman Period. A very fine example in gold has been found in a tomb in Balat dating to the Sixth Dynasty (Valloggia 1978, pl. 36D, inv. no. 248).
2. Naga el-Deir, tomb N 954, for example. See Reisner 1932.
3. Tomb B 17 in Abadiya; tomb 120 in Tarkhan; tomb B 217 in Diospolis Parva. These bodies are carcasses of *Prionotheca coronata* (Olivier 1795); see Keimer 1931, p. 173; and Levinson and Levinson 1996, pp. 577–85.

PROVENANCE: Qaw el-Kebir, tomb 696

BIBLIOGRAPHY: Brunton 1927, pls. 44, 35, Amulet and Bead Corpus, pls. 93 2 H-6 and 3 L-12, 95 15 H-3, 96 21 M-6 and 12, 24 F-9, 28 C-3 and 32 G-4, 97 40 H-6, 42 C-6 and 45 M-9, 98 62 F-16, 99 74 B-4; Donadoni Roveri and Tiradritti 1998, p. 303, fig. 313

206. String of Beads

Sixth Dynasty
Egyptian faience, silver, and carnelian
L. 200 cm (78¾ in.)
Petrie Museum of Egyptian Archaeology, University
College London UC 20412

Discovered around the waist of a young woman buried in a small intact tomb, this very long string of beads was probably a type of belt. It is composed of small, regular ring-shaped beads made of green and black faience, along with a few silver and carnelian beads.

Near the center there is a small faience seal in the shape of a button. Several types of such seal amulets were found in the Old Kingdom: pyramid-shaped seals, small plaques adorned with an animal in relief, and these so-called button seals are the most numerous. Appearing during the Fifth Dynasty, and occurring most frequently in the Sixth, they are usually found around the burial sites of women and children.[1] Their use as seals seems to have been limited, for the incised motif on the bottom was probably intended to serve primarily as a protective device. Scarabs, which made their appearance during the same period, acquired inscriptions a short time later and gradually took their place. Unlike seal amulets, they were not reserved for use by women.   PR

1. Brunton 1927, p. 58; Brunton 1937, p. 108; Brunton 1948, p. 50.

PROVENANCE: Qaw el-Kebir, tomb 1023

BIBLIOGRAPHY: Brunton 1927, p. 27, no. 67, pl. 32

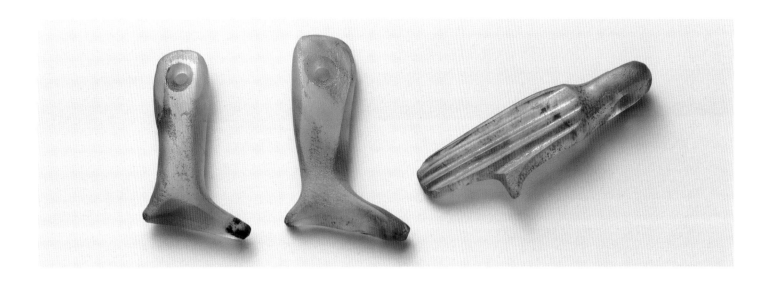

207. TWO AMULETS IN THE SHAPE OF A LEG

End of Old Kingdom
Carnelian
H. 2.1 cm, 2.4 cm (⅞ in., 1 in.)
The Visitors of the Ashmolean Museum, Oxford
1924.381

On these small carnelian amulets, the curve of the leg is well marked, and the sole and heel are clearly indicated. Each has a hole in its upper portion that allowed it to be suspended.

Although sometimes found at the neck level of the deceased, such amulets are usually located at ankle level. Often combined with shells, they generally belonged to anklets. The oldest examples, made of gold, seem to date to the end of the Third Dynasty.[1] Despite that early appearance and a few occurrences in the Fifth Dynasty, they seem to have become widespread only in the Sixth Dynasty.

The small tomb from which these amulets came was discovered intact and is notable for the beautiful set of jewelry it contained. Among its treasures were long strings of faience beads, a short string of gold beads, a gold amulet representing a *wedjat* eye, and five small gold amulets showing the god Heh (cat. no. 211).　　　　　　　PR

1. One is preserved in the Phoebe Apperson Hearst Museum of Anthropology, University of California at Berkeley; see Reisner 1932, pp. 198–99, pl. 39 (tomb N 524).

PROVENANCE: Hammamia, tomb 1981

BIBLIOGRAPHY: Brunton 1927, p. 34

208. AMULET IN THE SHAPE OF A HAND

Sixth Dynasty
Carnelian
H. 3 cm (1⅛ in.)
The Visitors of the Ashmolean Museum, Oxford
1914.662

This small amulet represents an extended hand with straight, elongated fingers. The furrows indicating the separations between the fingers extend fairly far onto the back of the hand. The wrist is well marked, the thumb long and slightly curved.

A great many amulets depicting parts of the human body have been retrieved from tombs that date from the end of the Old Kingdom (especially the Sixth Dynasty) and the First Intermediate Period. Acting as substitutes for the body part represented, in case it should happen to disappear, such pieces also guaranteed that that body part would function properly for the deceased. Amulets showing faces, extended hands, closed fists, and legs were most prevalent in the Old Kingdom; carnelian seems to have been the material of choice, with agate and faience also in evidence.

Hand-shaped amulets in particular were usually incorporated into necklaces and bracelets.　　　　　　　PR

PROVENANCE: Harageh, tomb 183

BIBLIOGRAPHY: Engelbach and Gunn 1923, p. 9, pl. 9.6

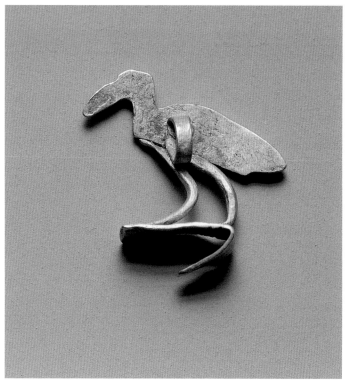

209. AMULET IN THE SHAPE OF AN IBIS

End of Old Kingdom
Gold
H. ca. 1.5 cm (⅝ in.)
Phoebe Apperson Hearst Museum of Anthropology,
University of California at Berkeley 6-22885

Ibis-shaped amulets have been found in tombs dating from as early as the end of the Old Kingdom[1] and are especially numerous in those from the very beginning of the First Intermediate Period. While a few examples in copper are known,[2] most are made of gold[3] or electrum.[4] Here, the bird's silhouette, cut from gold leaf that has been left smooth, is fairly precise although schematic; the beak in particular is poorly rendered. Depending on the design, the bird's perch may be more or less detailed, and here it is simply a curved metal rod.

As a depiction of a white ibis,[5] this amulet was undoubtedly linked to the god Thoth, to whom the bird is consecrated and whose name could even be written using the ibis hieroglyph. The same type of amulet, but in faience, has been retrieved from tombs of the Third Intermediate Period. PR

1. Valloggia 1986, vol. 2, pl. 65, inv. no. 921.
2. Mostagedda, tomb 1873; see Brunton 1937, pl. 57.
3. Matmar, tomb 415; see Brunton 1948, pl. 32. Mostagedda, tombs 542, 563, and 1913; see Brunton 1937, pl. 57.
4. Mostagedda, tomb 637; see Brunton 1937, pl. 57.
5. *Ibis religiosa aethiopica*; see Keimer 1930, p. 21.

PROVENANCE: Naga el-Deir

BIBLIOGRAPHY: Unpublished

210A,B. TWO BRACELETS

End of Old Kingdom or beginning of First Intermediate Period
Gold
a. Diam. 4.5 cm (1¾ in.)
b. Diam. 4.6 cm (1⅞ in.)
The Visitors of the Ashmolean Museum, Oxford
(a) 1924.370, (b) 1924.371

Discovered in a child's tomb, these two simple bands are made of thin, plain gold that has a reddish hue. Their round, non-perforated ends overlap, and their edges curve inward slightly. Such bracelets occur primarily between the end of the Old King-dom and the beginning of the First Inter-mediate Period.

Excavators considered these to be anklets because of their position in the tomb at the time they were discovered, but since the burial place had been plundered, they were probably not in their original location. In fact, anklets are generally quite different in form: several rows of beads joined together or, in modest tombs, simple strands of alter-nating beads and amulets, occasionally accompanied by shells.   PR

PROVENANCE: Qaw el-Kebir, tomb 7762

BIBLIOGRAPHY: Brunton 1928, p. 66, pl. 63

211. FIVE AMULETS DEPICTING THE GOD HEH

Beginning of First Intermediate Period
Gold
Average h. 1.2 cm (½ in.); average w. 1.5 cm
(⅝ in.)
The Visitors of the Ashmolean Museum, Oxford
1924.378

These five small gold amulets were found in the intact tomb of a woman in Hammamia, in the northern part of Upper Egypt. At the time of their discovery they were arranged on the skull of the deceased. At the center of each is a figure whose face and upper body, with extended arms, are presented frontally and whose lower body is in profile, with one knee to the ground and the other raised. A palm rib, the symbol for "year," is held in each hand, and its tips come together in a wave at the top. This is the typical depiction of the god Heh throughout the pharaonic era. The figures are rendered schematically here, with no attempt at naturalistic observation; the modeling is rudimentary and the long limbs are simplified. However, the details of the face, hair, and kilt are incised. A small ring affixed to the back of each amulet allowed it to be suspended.

Amulets in this shape are first known at the end of the Old Kingdom, during the Sixth Dynasty. Becoming more numerous during the First Intermediate Period and the Middle Kingdom, they were frequently made of openwork metal, either copper[1] or, more often, gold.[2] Some examples were produced in faience at the same time, but they are usually mediocre in quality and the subject is difficult to identify.

An amulet found in the mastaba of Medu-nefer in Balat is fairly similar stylistically to these;[3] it is also made of gold and dates to the end of the Sixth Dynasty. Given the site of their excavation, these amulets probably date a bit later, to the very beginning of the First Intermediate Period.

Since the name Heh means "million" and the god himself was a symbol of eternity, these amulets can be interpreted as wishes that the deceased will enjoy millions of years of life in the hereafter.   PR

1. See Brunton 1928, pl. 98, 61 B3, tomb 1991, Sixth Dynasty.
2. Ibid., pl. 98, 61 C3, 6, tombs 613 and 1055, Sixth Dynasty.
3. Valloggia 1986, vol. 2, pl. 65, inv. no. 920.

PROVENANCE: Hammamia, tomb 1981

BIBLIOGRAPHY: Brunton 1927, p. 34

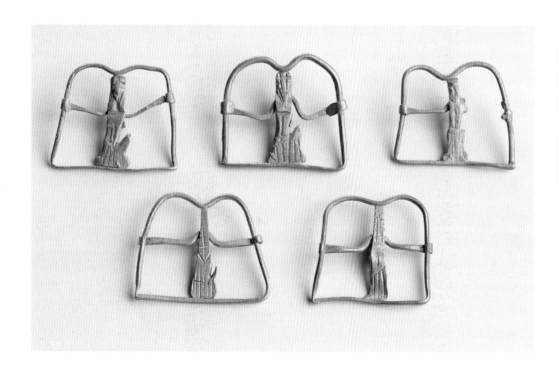

212. BASIN WITH HANDLE AND IMPLEMENT

Sixth Dynasty
Copper
Basin: h. 10.5 cm (4⅛ in.); d. 19.6 cm (7¾ in.)
Implement: l. 15 cm (5⅞ in.); w. .8 cm (⅜ in.)
Ägyptisches Museum, Universität Leipzig
2169 (basin), 2170 (implement)

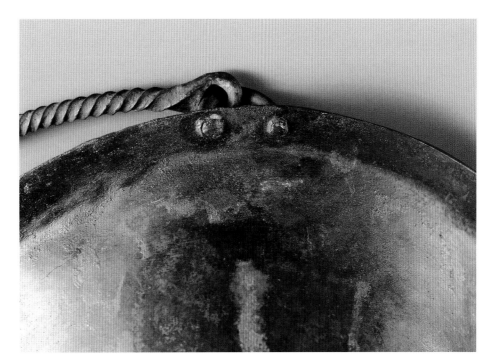

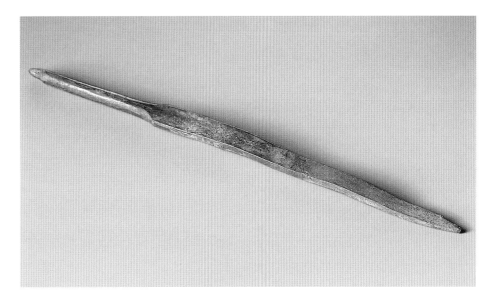

This copper basin with flat base, flaring sides, and twisted-bail handle was found with the copper implement resting in it. It is similar in shape and manufacture to the basins (*šꜤwtı*) that are part of the basin and ewer sets often found in Old Kingdom burials and represented in tomb reliefs and other ritual scenes through the New Kingdom (cat. no. 159).[1] It differs from the *šꜤwtı* type, however, in that the top of the vessel wall has been turned outward to form a flat, horizontal rim.[2] Bail handles on metal vessels were rare in the Archaic Period and the Old Kingdom: only one other example of a twisted-bail handle, from the tomb of Khasekhemui at Abydos, is known.[3] The two ends of the handle of this example were formed into rings and attached to the basin by loops made from copper rods that had been bent into a horseshoe shape, inserted through the flat rim, and hammered down on the underside. The implement, which may be a kind of spatula, has a rounded handle ending in a point. Its flat blade is still quite thick and uneven and has not been hammered down to form a thin edge.

The basin and implement were found in an undisturbed pit tomb in mastaba D 6 at Giza. This tomb was excavated in 1905 by Georg Steindorff, who stated in his excavation journal that the basin was found leaning against the head end of the sarcophagus and that it contained a gray-brown material.[4] Other tomb equipment included an alabaster headrest and a pottery jug with handle as well as an alabaster tablet and seven alabaster dishes for the seven sacred oils. Steindorff dated this burial to the Sixth Dynasty.[5]

While the contents of the basin were not analyzed, it is probable that the spatula-like tool was meant to be used to distribute or apply this substance, which may have been some sort of unguent. Together with the pottery jug and the set for the seven sacred oils, the basin and implement formed part of the ritual equipment of the burial.   S A

1. For a discussion of this form, see Balcz 1932, pp. 95–98, fig. 13; Do. Arnold 1977, cols. 483–86, fig. 1.9; and Do. Arnold 1984, cols. 213–14.
2. Basins such as this were formed by hammering a blank of metal over a series of inverted forms or anvils—a metalworking task depicted in tomb reliefs of the Old Kingdom. See Moussa and Altenmüller 1977, pl. 63.
3. A twisted handle is attached to a tall-shouldered jar found by Amélineau and now in the Musées Royaux d'Art et d'Histoire, Brussels (E 561; Amelineau 1902, p. 155, pl. 17.16). See also Radwan 1983, p. 15, no. 43, pls. A.43, 8.43.
4. The jar with twisted-bail handle found in a magazine in the tomb of Khasekhemui contained a fatty substance; see Amélineau 1902.
5. From the unpublished journal of Georg Steindorff (n.d., pp. 34–35), entry for Sunday, February 19, 1905.

PROVENANCE: Giza, mastaba D 6, Steindorff excavation, 1905

BIBLIOGRAPHY: Unpublished

213. Bowl with Spout

Sixth Dynasty
Copper
H. 6.1 cm (2⅜ in.); d. 12.1 cm (4¾ in.)
Kunsthistorisches Museum, Ägyptisch-
Orientalische Sammlung, Vienna ÄS 7441

This copper bowl, with a sharply carinated profile, slightly rounded base, and short, outward-flaring rim, has a tubular spout that projects upward at an angle from the shoulder. The separately cast spout was inserted through the vessel wall from the interior and then hammered in place.[1]

Very common beginning in the Archaic Period, spouted vessels in copper usually occur as part of basin and ewer sets, as spouted jars with necks, or as *heset* vases with spouts.[2] Spouted copper bowls, however, are unusual, and every other known example has a curved spout that is an extension of the rim.[3]

The forms that occur in metal are often paralleled in a type of polished red pottery called Meidum ware (see entry for cat. no. 159). This ware imitates the copper prototypes and, because of its more economical material, is often found as funerary equipment in Old Kingdom burials.[4] The form of a deep, sharply carinated bowl with an angular spout projecting from the shoulder, while exceptional in metal, is more common in pottery. It appears as early as the Fourth Dynasty, in the tomb of Queen Hetep-heres I at Giza.[5] Reisner states that this type of bowl, while prominent in the queen's funerary pottery and in other tombs of the Fourth Dynasty, had almost disappeared by the end of the dynasty.[6] This copper example, which is dated by the excavator to the Sixth Dynasty, was thus archaic by the time it was made—a metal replica of a pottery vessel shape no longer in use.

Representations of a similarly shaped bowl, being carried in procession in two offering scenes, exist in the Fifth Dynasty tomb of User-netjer at Saqqara. In the larger scene it is borne at the end of a group of priests performing the purification ritual before the tomb owner. In a smaller, fragmentary scene it is part of a procession that also includes a basin and ewer set and spouted *heset* vases.[7] This type of spouted bowl, when included in the funerary offerings of a tomb, would thus, like the basin and ewer set, play a part in the purification ritual. The small size of this bowl, as compared with those found in the tomb of Queen Hetep-heres and those depicted in private tomb reliefs, may indicate that it is a model made for funerary use.   S A

1. Radwan 1983, p. 62, no. 156, pl. 33.156.
2. Ibid., pls. 10.54A (basin and ewer set; tomb of Khasekhemui, Abydos), 23.127A (spouted jar; tomb of Ba-baef, Giza), 24.130A (*heset* vase; tomb of Ni-ankh-re, Giza).
3. Ibid., pls. 26.145A, 31.154F,G,I, 155C.
4. Bourriau 1981, p. 18.
5. Reisner and Smith 1955, figs. 73, 74. These spouted bowls belong to Reisner's Group D, type XXXVI, "flat-bottomed basin; recurved rim and long tubular spout" (ibid., p. 62).
6. Ibid.
7. Murray 1905, pp. 22–23, pls. 21, 25.

PROVENANCE: Giza, Western Cemetery, mastaba of Nefer-ihi (shaft 261), Junker excavation, 1912–14; gift of the Wiener Akademie der Wissenschaften

BIBLIOGRAPHY: Junker 1943, p. 162, fig. 55 (top); Radwan 1983, p. 62, no. 156, pl. 33.156

214. THIRTY-TWO MINIATURE VESSELS AND A TABLE

Fifth or Sixth Dynasty
Egyptian alabaster
Jars: h. 8504, 7.8 cm (3⅛ in.); 8505, 9.2 cm
(3⅝ in.); 8960, 6 cm (2⅜ in.); 8961, 6.3 cm
(2½ in.); 8962, 8 cm (3⅛ in.); 8963, 8 cm (3⅛ in.);
8964, 8.2 cm (3¼ in.); 8965, 5.6 cm (2¼ in.);
8966, 6.3 cm (2½ in.); 9031, 6.8 cm (2⅝ in.)
Jug: 8959, h. 8.8 cm (3½ in.)
Plates: diam. 8967, 5.7 cm (2¼ in.); 8968, 6.1 cm
(2⅜ in.); 8969, 5.2 cm (2 in.); 8970, 4.8 cm
(1⅞ in.); 8971, 5 cm (2 in.); 8972, 4.9 cm (1⅞ in.);
8973, 4.9 cm (1⅞ in.); 8974, 4.7 cm (1⅞ in.);
8975, 4.6 cm (1¾ in.); 9017, 4.2 cm (1⅝ in.);
9018, 4.1 cm (1⅝ in.); 9019, 4 cm (1⅝ in.);
9020, 4.2 cm (1⅝ in.); 9021, 4.2 cm (1⅝ in.);
9022, 4.4 cm (1¾ in.); 9023, 4.4 cm (1¾ in.);
9024, 4.5 cm (1¾ in.); 9025, 3.8 cm (1½ in.);
9026, 3.9 cm (1½ in.); 9027, 3.9 cm (1½ in.);
9028, 3.5 cm (1⅜ in.)
Table: 8958, top, h. 1.2 cm (½ in.); diam. 17.8 cm
(7 in.); foot, h. 5.6 cm (2¼ in.); max. w. 5.2 cm
(2⅛ in.)
Kunsthistorisches Museum, Ägyptisch-
Orientalische Sammlung, Vienna ÄS 8504, 8505,
8958–8975, 9017–9028, 9031

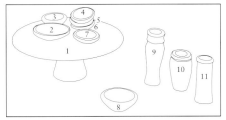

CAT. 215A

1: 8958	7: 9019
2: 8967	8: 8969
3: 9017	9: 8964
4: 9026	10: 8965
5: 9027	11: 8961
6: 9025	

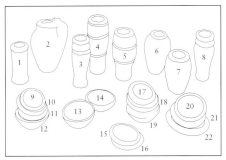

CAT. NO. 215B

1: 8960	12: 8970
2: 8959	13: 8972
3: 8504	14: 8975
4: 8505	15: 9020
5: 8962	16: 9023
6: 9031	17: 9018
7: 8966	18: 8974
8: 8963	19: 9873
9: 9028	20: 9024
10: 9022	21: 8971
11: 9021	22: 8968

Many stone containers made in ancient Egypt were imitations of clay or metal vessels used in everyday life (cat. nos. 160, 161), and their burial in tombs was believed to guarantee the deceased food and drink throughout eternity. Miniature stone vessels fulfilled the same function but were even further removed from the practicalities of daily life than their full-scale counterparts. These small, toylike objects imitated large utilitarian prototypes but were unusable not only by virtue of their size but also because they have solid bodies or only diminutive cavities. Indeed miniatures were essentially symbolic objects and thus ideally suited to accompany the dead into the afterlife.

Although it was found in a plundered burial chamber, the group of miniature vessels from which the present examples are drawn represents an almost complete set of the type Egyptians of the Old Kingdom deposited beside the sarcophagi of their relatives. When excavated this set still comprised seventy-seven objects: sixty-three cups and saucers (twenty-one of which are shown here), four shouldered jars and four slender bottles (three of each are here), two wine jars with the characteristic two grooves in the body, two cylindrical ointment jars, a juglet whose handle is not perforated to detach it from the body, and a low, disk-shaped tabletop and detached stand (all of which are included in the exhibition).

According to Hermann Junker, the great Austrian excavator of Giza mastabas, groups of about eighty miniature vessels were as a rule deposited beside a sarcophagus and these usually were made up of a basin and ewer for washing the hands and for libations (not present in the Vienna set; see cat. no. 159), seven vases for sacred oils (the juglet, the two cylindrical jars, and presumably the four shouldered jars of the Vienna group), eight beer and wine jars (there are only six in the Vienna set, the two wine jars and four slender bottles), and sixty small cups and saucers for solid food.[1]

In an intriguing argument Junker noted that the symbolic contents of the typical miniature vessels of these sets were remarkably similar to the items enumerated in the traditional offering lists of the Old Kingdom.[2] The offering list was depicted—often in a gridlike structure—on the stelae

and walls of the tomb's aboveground cult chamber, and in later times in the burial chamber as well,[3] to guarantee the symbolic performance of offering rites even if no relative was present to recite the spells and dedicate the offerings.[4] It has been shown that from the beginning of the Fifth Dynasty, if not earlier, such lists ideally consisted of about ninety-five items,[5] a number very close to the total of about eighty miniature vases in the characteristic set. Included in offering lists were water, incense, oils and ointments, beer, wine and other drinks, solid food such as bread, meat, fowl, vegetables, and various kinds of fruit, as well as an offering table.[6]

Junker suggested that the set of miniature vessels deposited in the subterranean burial chamber served as a kind of three-dimensional offering list to ensure that the offering ritual was performed for the deceased throughout eternity. The vessel set, according to this interpretation, would have represented not merely objects and provisions but also the performance of the ritual itself. The large numbers of vessels deposited—Junker reported finding no fewer than six hundred miniature containers in one tomb[7]—become understandable in connection with this hypothesis: repetition is a hallmark of ritual incantations.

DoA

1. Junker 1929, pp. 108–9.
2. Ibid., p. 108.
3. For the placement of offering lists, see Barta 1963, pp. 12, 26, 41–42, 51, 59–60, 72, 82–83.
4. It is beyond the scope of this text to discuss the details of the differences between offering lists that predominantly enumerate ideal tomb inventories, which Barta (ibid., pp. 7–10 and passim) maintains were the prevalent type in the earlier Old Kingdom, and the classic form, predominant from the Fifth Dynasty, which refers to the offering ritual.
5. Ibid., pp. 47–50, 73–75. See also Altenmüller (1972, pp. 79–83), who lists 116 items based on the Pyramid Texts.
6. Barta 1963, p. 48, no. 15.
7. Junker 1929, p. 108.

PROVENANCE: Giza, presumably mastaba of Ni-ankh-re (G IV S), at south side of Khufu's pyramid, burial chamber of south shaft, Junker excavation

BIBLIOGRAPHY: Junker 1951, p. 161, pl. 22d, and pp. 2, 91 (for the date)

GLOSSARY

akhet "inundation"; first season of the ancient Egyptian calendar year

ankh hieroglyphic sign and emblem for "life," originally the image of a three-looped bow

Anubis god of embalming, guardian of cemeteries

Atum creator god

ba manifestation of power of a deity; a person's afterlife form of existence, which has the ability to move

cartouche oval frame, representing a knotted rope, that encloses the nomen and prenomen of the king

double crown combination of the red crown and the white crown; symbolizes rule over a united Egypt

false door carved or painted representation of a niched doorway through which the deceased could communicate with the living and receive offerings

Heb Sed rejuvenation ceremony for the reigning king, theoretically celebrated after thirty years of rule; also called the Sed festival

Horus ancient sky god, often shown as a falcon or a man with a falcon's head; the embodiment of the powers of kingship

Horus name one of the five names of an Egyptian king; identifies him as the representative of the god Horus

ka the life force of a deity or person, which continues to exist after the latter's death

Maat goddess personifying order and justice in the world

mastaba rectangular superstructure of many Old Kingdom tombs; derived from the Arabic word meaning "bench"

nemes striped headcloth worn by Egyptian kings

nomarch local ruler of a nome

nomé term for each of the forty-two provinces or administrative units of Upper and Lower Egypt

nomen king's birth name; often accompanied by the epithet "Son of Re"

Nut goddess personifying the vault of the sky

peret "the coming forth (of the seeds)"; second season of the ancient Egyptian calendar year

prenomen name a king took upon his accession to the throne; also called the throne name; often accompanied by the title "King of Upper and Lower Egypt"

Re "sun," the most important name of the sun god, the creator and sustainer of the world, who travels in a bark through the sky by day and through the underworld by night

red crown the crown of Lower Egypt (the Delta)

Sed festival see Heb Sed

serdab closed statue chamber in an Old Kingdom mastaba; derived from the Arabic word meaning "cellar"

serekh simplified image of the royal residence surmounted by a falcon (symbol of Horus); encloses the Horus name of the king

shemu "harvest"; third season of the ancient Egyptian calendar year

shendyt tripartite kilt worn by the king

sistrum rattle used in religious ceremonies; consists of a handle attached to a soundbox in the shape of a shrine or to a loop to which loose rods that may hold metal disks are attached

Son of Re name see nomen

Thoth god of writing and counting; often shown as an ibis or a man with the head of an ibis

throne name see prenomen

Two Ladies name one of the five names of an Egyptian king; links him with the goddesses Nekhbet and Wadjet, protectors of Upper and Lower Egypt, respectively

titulary list of titles

uraeus sacred cobra, protector of the king; often attached to the front of the crown or *nemes*

white crown the crown of Upper Egypt (the Nile Valley south of the Delta)

BIBLIOGRAPHY

Abu Bakr, Abdel-Moneim

1937 *Untersuchungen über die ägyptischen Kronen*. Glückstadt, Hamburg, and New York.

1953 *Excavations at Giza, 1949–50; with a Chapter on "Brick Vaults and Domes in the Giza Necropolis by Dr. Al Badawy*. Cairo.

Abu Bakr, Abdel-Moneim, and A. Y. Mustafa

1971 "The Funerary Boat of Khufu." In *Aufsätze zum 70. Geburtstag von Herbert Ricke*, pp. 1–16. Wiesbaden.

Adam, J. P., and Christiane Ziegler

1999 *Les pyramides d'Égypte*. Forthcoming.

el-Aguizy, Ola

1987 "Dwarfs and Pygmies in Ancient Egypt." *Annales du Service des Antiquités de l'Égypte* 71, pp. 53–60.

Aldred, Cyril

1949 *Old Kingdom Art in Ancient Egypt*. London.

1954 "Fine Wood-Work." In *A History of Technology*, vol. 1, edited by Charles J. Singer et al., pp. 684–703. Oxford.

1965 *Egypt to the End of the Old Kingdom*. London.

1971 *Jewels of the Pharaohs: Egyptian Jewellery of the Dynastic Period*. London.

1978 "Statuaire." In *Le temps des pyramides: De la préhistoire aux Hyksos (1560 av. J.-C.)*, by Jean Leclant et al., pp. 171–225. Paris.

1980 *Egyptian Art in the Days of the Pharaohs, 3100–320 B.C.* London.

1982 *Egypt to the End of the Old Kingdom*. Reprint of the 1965 ed. London.

1988a "An Early Image-of-the-King." In *Pyramid Studies and Other Essays Presented to I. E. S. Edwards*, edited by J. Baines et al., pp. 41–47. London.

1988b *Egyptian Art in the Days of the Pharaohs, 3100–320 B.C.* London.

1992 *Egypt to the End of the Old Kingdom*. Reprint of 1965 ed. London.

1996 *Egyptian Art in the Days of the Pharaohs, 3100–320 B.C.* Reprint of 1980 ed. London.

Alexanian, Nicole

1993 "Mastabas II/1." *Mitteilungen des Deutschen Archäologischen Instituts, Abteilung Kairo* 49, pp. 278–83.

1995 "Die Mastaba II/1 in Dahschur-Mitte." In *Kunst des Alten Reiches: Symposium im Deutschen Archäologischen Institut Kairo am 29. und 30. Oktober 1991*, pp. 1–18. Sonderschrift, Deutsches Archäologisches Institut, Abteilung Kairo 28. Mainz.

1998 "Die Reliefdekoration des Chasechemui aus dem sogenannten *Fort* in Hierakonpolis." In *Les critères de datation stylistiques à l'Ancien Empire*, edited by Nicolas Grimal, pp. 1–29. Cairo.

1998a "Ritualrelikte an Mastabagräbern des Alten Reiches." In *Stationen: Beiträge zur Kulturgeschichte Ägyptens, Rainer Stadelmann Gewidmet*, edited by Heike Guksch and Daniel Polz, pp. 3–22. Mainz.

Allen, James P.

1992 "Re͑wer's Accident." In *Studies in Pharaonic Religion and Society in Honour of J. Gwyn Griffiths*, edited

by Alan B. Lloyd, pp. 14–20. London.

1994 "Reading a Pyramid." In *Hommages à Jean Leclant*, vol. 1, *Études Pharaoniques*, edited by Catherine Berger, Gisèle Clerc, and Nicolas Grimal, pp. 5–28. Institut Français d'Archéologie Orientale: Bibliothèque d'étude 106. Cairo.

Altenmüller, Hartwig

1972 *Die Texte zum Begräbnisritual in den Pyramiden des Alten Reiches*. Ägyptologische Abhandlungen 24. Wiesbaden.

1975 "Dramatischer Ramesseumpapyrus." In *Lexikon der Ägyptologie*, vol. 1, cols. 1132–40.

1977 "Grabausstattung und -beigaben." In *Lexikon der Ägyptologie*, vol. 2 , cols. 837–45.

1978 "Zur Bedeutung der Harfnerleider des Alten Reiches." *Studien zur altägyptischen Kultur* 6, pp. 1–24.

1980a "Jadgdarstellungen." In *Lexikon der Ägyptologie*, vol. 3, cols. 224–30.

1980b "Königsplastik." In *Lexikon der Ägyptologie*, vol. 3, cols. 557–610.

1998 *Die Wanddarstellungen im Grab des Mehu in Saqqara*. Archäologische Veröffentlichungen, 42. Mainz.

1998a "Daily Life in Eternity–The Mastabas and Rock-Cut Tombs of Officials." In *Egypt: The World of the Pharaohs*, edited by Regine Schulz and Matthias Seidel, pp. 78–93. Cologne.

Amélineau, Émile

1897 *Les nouvelles fouilles d'Abydos*. Vol. 2, *Seconde

campagne, 1896–1897*. Paris.

1902 *Les nouvelles fouilles d'Abydos, seconde campagne, 1896–1897: Compte rendu in extenso des fouilles; description des monuments et objets découverts*. Paris.

Amiet, Pierre, ed.

1967 *Vingt ans d'acquisitions au Musée du Louvre, 1947–1967*. Paris.

Amiran, Ruth

1969 *Ancient Pottery of the Holy Land: From Its Beginnings in the Neolithic Period to the End of the Iron Age*. With the assistance of Pirhiya Beck and Uzza Zevulun. [New Brunswick, New Jersey.]

Ancient Egypt 1966. *See* Elsasser and Fredrickson 1966.

Andreu, Guillemette

1997 "La fauss-porte de Ny-ka-Rê, Cleveland Museum of Art, no. 64.91." In *Études sur l'Ancien Empire et la nécropole de Saqqâra dédiées à Jean-Philippe Lauer*, edited by Catherine Berger and Bernard Mathieu, pp. 21–30. Orientalia Monspeliensia, 9. Montpellier: Université Paul Valéry.

Andreu, Guillemette, Marie-Hélène Rutschowscaya, and Christiane Ziegler

1997 *L'Égypte ancienne au Louvre*. Paris.

Andrews, Carol

1981 *Jewellery, I: From the Earliest Times to the Seventeenth Dynasty*. Catalogue of Egyptian Antiquities in the British Museum 6. London.

1990 *Ancient Egyptian Jewellery*. London: British Museum.

Anthes, Rudolf

1941 "Werkverfahren ägyptischer

Bildhauer." *Mitteilungen des Deutschen Instituts für Ägyptische Altertumskunde in Kairo* 10, pp. 79–121.

Arnold, Dieter

1977 "Rituale und Pyramidentempel." *Mitteilungen des Deutschen Archäologischen Instituts, Abteilung Kairo* 33, pp. 1–14.

1988 *The Pyramid of Senwosret I*. Vol. 1 of *The South Cemeteries of Lisht*. The Metropolitan Museum of Art Expedition, no. 22. New York.

1991 *Building in Egypt: Pharaonic Stone Masonry*. New York.

1994 *Lexikon der ägyptischen Baukunst*. Zurich.

1996 "Hypostyle Halls of the Old and Middle Kingdom?" In *Studies in Honor of William Kelly Simpson*, edited by Peter Der Manuelian, vol. 1, pp. 39–54. Boston.

1997 "Royal Cult Complexes of the Old and Middle Kingdoms." In *Temples of Ancient Egypt*, edited by Byron E. Shafer, pp. 31–85. Ithaca.

1998 "The Late Period Tombs of Hor-khebit, Wennefer, and Wereshnefer at Saqqâra." In *Les critères de datation stylistiques à l'Ancien Empire*, edited by Nicolas Grimal, pp. 31–54. Cairo.

Arnold, Dorothea

1977 "Gefäße, Gefäßformen (Gf.), Gefäßdekor." In *Lexikon der Ägyptologie*, vol. 2, cols. 483–501.

1984 "Reinigungsgefäße." In *Lexikon der Ägyptologie*, vol. 5, cols. 213–20.

1993a "Techniques and Traditions of Manufacture in the Pottery of Ancient Egypt." In *An Introduction to Ancient Egyptian Pottery*, edited by Dorothea Arnold and Janine Borriau, fasc. 1, pp. 5–141. Mainz.

1993b "Vase in the Shape of a Monkey with Its Young." In "Recent Acquisitions: A Selection." *Metropolitan Museum of Art Bulletin*, n.s., 51 (fall), p. 6.

1995 "An Egyptian Bestiary." *Metropolitan Museum of Art Bulletin*, n.s., 52, no. 4 (spring).

L'art de l'Ancien Empire

1999 *L'art de l'Ancien Empire égyptien: Actes du colloque, Musée du Louvre, 3–4 avril 1998*. Paris.

Assmann, Jan

1991 "Schrift, Tod, und Identität:

Das Grab als Vorschule der Literatur." In *Stein und Zeit: Mensch und Gesellschaft im alten Ägypten*, pp. 169–99. Munich.

1996 "Preservation and Presentation of Self in Ancient Egyptian Portraiture." In *Studies in Honor of William Kelly Simpson*, edited by Peter Der Manuelian, vol. 1, pp. 55–81. Boston.

Aston, Barbara G.

1994 *Ancient Egyptian Stone Vessels: Materials and Forms*. Studien zur Archäologie und Geschichte Altägyptens 5. Heidelberg.

Aufrère, Sydney, Nathalie Bossons, and Christian Landes

1992 *Catalogue de l'exposition Portes pour l'au-delà: L'Égypte, le Nil et le "Champ des offrandes."* Exh. cat. Lattes: Musée Archéologique de Lattes.

Badawy, Alexander

1978 *The Tomb of Nyhetep-Ptah at Giza and the Tomb of ʿAnkhmʿahor at Saqqara*. University of California Publications: Occasional Papers 11. Berkeley and Los Angeles.

Baer, Klaus

1960 *Rank and Title in the Old Kingdom*. Chicago.

Baines, John

1973 "The Destruction of the Pyramid Temple of Sahure." *Göttinger Miszellen* 4, pp. 9–14.

1985 *Fecundity Figures: Egyptian Personification and the Iconology of a Genre*. Warminster.

1995 "Kingship, Definition of Culture, and Legitimation." In *Ancient Egyptian Kingship*, edited by David O'Connor and David P. Silverman, pp. 3–47. Leiden and New York.

Baker, Hollis S.

1966 *Furniture in the Ancient World: Origins and Evolution, 3100–475 B.C.* London.

Balcz, Heinrich

1932 "Die Gefässdarstellungen des Alten Reiches." *Mitteilungen des Deutschen Instituts für Ägyptische Altertumskunde in Kairo* 3, pp. 50–87, 89–114.

1933 "Die Gefässdarstellungen des Alten Reiches." *Mitteilungen des Deutschen Instituts für Ägyptische Altertumskunde in Kairo* 4, pp. 18–36.

1934 "Die Gefässdarstellungen des Alten Reiches." *Mit-*

teilungen des Deutschen Instituts für Ägyptische Altertumskunde in Kairo* 5, pp. 45–94.

Bárta, Miroslav

1998 "Serdab and Statue Placement in the Private Tombs down to the Fourth Dynasty." *Mitteilungen des Deutschen Archäologischen Instituts, Abteilung Kairo* 54, pp. 65–75.

Barta, Winfried

1963 *Die altägyptische Opferliste von der Frühzeit bis zur griechisch-römischen Epoche*. Münchner ägyptologische Studien 3. Berlin.

1968 "Aufbau und Bedeutung der altägyptischen Opferformel." *Ägyptologische Forschungen* 24, pp. 3–11.

1980 "Kult." In *Lexikon der Ägyptologie*, vol. 3, cols. 840–44.

Baud, Michel

1998 "The Tombs of Khamerernebty I and II at Giza." *Göttinger Miszellen* 164, pp. 7–14.

Baud, Michel, and Vassil Dobrev

1995 "De nouvelles annales de l'Ancien Empire égyptien: Une 'Pierre de Palerme' pour la VIᵉ dynastie." *Bulletin de l'Institut Français d'Archéologie Orientale* 95, pp. 23–92.

El-Baz, Farouk

1988 "Finding a Pharaoh's Funeral Bark." *National Geographic* 173, no. 4 (April), pp. 513–33.

Beckerath, Jürgen von

1984 *Handbuch der ägyptischen Königsnamen*. Münchner Ägyptologische Studien 20. Munich.

Bénédite, G.

1908 "Un envoi de l'Institut Archéologique du Caire au Musée du Louvre." *Bulletin des Musées de France*, no. 2, p. 17.

1923 "La formation du Musée égyptien au Louvre." *Revue de l'art ancien et moderne* 43, pp. 161–72, 275–93.

Berlandini, Jocelyne

1982 "Meret." In *Lexikon der Ägyptologie*, vol. 4, cols. 80–88.

Berman, Lawrence Michael, and Bernadette Letellier

1996 *Pharaohs: Treasures of Egyptian Art from the Louvre*. Exh. cat. Cleveland.

Bernard, Marguerite

1966– "Les vases en pierre de
67 l'Ancien Empire (Vᵉ et VIᵉ dynasties)." Thesis, Univer-

sité Catholique de Louvain, Faculté de Philosophie et Lettres, Institut Supérieur d'Archéologie et d'Histoire de l'Art.

Bianchi, R. S.

1997 "An Elite Image." In *Chief of Seers: Egyptian Studies in Memory of Cyril Aldred*, pp. 34–48. London.

Bietak, Manfred

1988 Zur Marine des Alten Reiches." In *Pyramid Studies and Other Essays Presented to I. E. S. Edwards*, edited by John Baines et al., pp. 35–40. London.

1996 *Haus und Palast im Alten Ägypten*. Denkschriften der Gesamtakademie 14. International Symposium in Cairo, April 8–11, 1992. Vienna.

Bissing, Friedrich Wilhelm, Freiherr von

1905 *Die Mastaba des Gem-ni-kai*. Vol. 1. Berlin.

1911 *Die Mastaba des Gem-ni-kai*. Vol. 2. Berlin.

1914 *Denkmäler ägyptischer Skulptur*. Munich.

1934a *Ägyptische Kunstgeschichte von den ältesten Zeiten bis auf die Eroberung durch die Araber: Systematisches Handbuch*. Berlin.

1934b "Reliefs des Alten und Mittleren Reichs aus Sammlung von Bissing," part 2. *Bulletin van de Vereeniging tot Bevordering der Kennis van de Antieke Beschaving* 9, no. 2 (December), pp. 3–8.

Bissing, Friedrich Wilhelm, Freiherr von, and Hermann Kees

1922 *Untersuchungen zu den Reliefs aus dem Re-Heiligtum des Rathures*. Abhandlungen der Bayrischen Akademie der Wissenschaften, Philosophisch-philologische und Historische Klasse 32, part 1. Munich.

1923 *Die kleine Festdarstellung*. Vol. 2 of *Das Re-Heiligtum des Königs Ne-Woser-Re (Rathures)*, edited by Friedrich Wilhelm von Bissing. Leipzig.

1928 *Die grosse Festdarstellung*. Vol. 3 of *Das Re-Heiligtum des Königs Ne-Woser-Re (Rathures)*, edited by Friedrich Wilhelm von Bissing. Leipzig.

Bisson de la Roque, Fernand

1937 *Tôd (1934 à 1936)*. Fouilles de l'Institut Français du Caire 17. Cairo.

Blackman, Aylward M.

1914 *The Rock Tombs of Meir*. Vol. 1. Archaeological Survey of Egypt 22. London.

1953   *The Rock Tombs of Meir.* Vol. 5. Archaeological Survey of Egypt 28. London.

Blumenthal, Elke

1984   "Besprechungen: PM III², 1974–81." *Orientalistische Literaturzeitung* 79, cols. 547–51.

Blurton, T. Richard

1997   *The Enduring Image: Treasures from the British Museum.* Exh. cat. New Delhi and Mumbai, India. London.

Boeser, P. A. A., J. H. Holwerda, and A. E. J. Holwerda

1905   *Beschreibung der ägyptischen Sammlung des Niederländischen Reichsmuseums der Altertümer in Leiden.* Vol. 1, *Die Denkmäler des Alten Reiches.* 2 vols. Leiden.

Boessneck, Joachim

1988   *Die Tierwelt des Alten Ägypten: Untersucht anhand kunstgeschichtlicher und zoologischer Quellen.* Munich.

Boëthius, Axel

1978   *Etruscan and Early Roman Architecture.* 2d ed., revised by Roger Ling and Tom Rasmussen. New Haven.

Bolshakov, Andrey O.

1990   "The Ideology of the Old Kingdom Portrait." *Göttinger Miszellen* 117–18, pp. 89–142.

1991   "What Did the Bust of Ankhaf Originally Look Like?" *Journal of the Museum of Fine Arts* (Boston) 3, pp. 5–14.

1991a   "The Moment of the Establishment of the Tomb-Cult in Ancient Egypt." *Altorientalische Forschungen* 18, pp. 204–18.

1997   *Man and His Double in Egyptian Ideology of the Old Kingdom.* Ägypten und Altes Testament 37. Wiesbaden. Revised translation of the 1989 Russian ed.

Bonhême, M.-A., and Annie Forgeau

1988   *Pharaon: Les secrets du pouvoir.* Paris.

Bonnet, Charles, et al.

1990   *Kerma, royaume de Nubie: L'antiquité africaine au temps des pharaons.* Exh. cat. Geneva: Musée d'Art et d'Histoire.

Borchardt, Ludwig

1897   "Die Dienerstatuen aus den Gräbern des Alten Reiches." *Zeitschrift für ägyptische Sprache und Altertumskunde* 35, pp. 119–34.

1905   *Das Re-Heiligtum des Königs Ne-woser-Re (Rathures).* Vol. 1, *Der Bau.* Berlin.

1907   *Das Grabdenkmal des Königs Ne-user-Reˁ.* Ausgrabungen der Deutschen Orient-Gesellschaft in Abusir, 1902–1904, vol. 1. Leipzig.

1909   *Das Grabdenkmal des Königs Nefer-ir-ka-reˁ.* Ausgrabungen der Deutschen Orient-Gesellschaft in Abusir, 1902–1908, vol. 5; Wissenschaftliche Veröffentlichungen der Deutschen Orientgesellschaft, 11. Leipzig.

1910   *Das Grabdenkmal des Königs Sahu-Reˁ.* Vol. 1, Der Bau. Ausgrabungen der Deutschen Orientgesellschaft in Abusir, 1902–1908, vol. 6. Leipzig.

1911   *Die Pyramiden: Ihre Entstehung und Entwicklung. Als Erläuterung zum Modell des Grabdenkmals des Königs Sahu-Re bei Abusir.* Berlin.

1913   *Das Grabdenkmal des Königs Sahu-re.* Vol. 2: *Die Wandbilder.* With the collaboration of Kurt Sethe, Ernst Assmann, Max Hildesheimer, Oscar Heimrath. Ausgrabungen der Deutschen Orient-Gesellschaft in Abusir, 1902–1908, vol. 7. Leipzig.

1937   *Denkmäler des Alten Reiches (ausser den Statuen) im Museum von Kairo, Nr. 1295–1808.* Vol. 1, *Text und Tafeln zu Nr. 1295–1541.* Catalogue Général du Musée du Caire, 97. Cairo.

1964   *Denkmäler des Alten Reiches (ausser den Statuen) im Museum von Kairo, Nr. 1295–1808.* Vol. 2, *Text und Tafeln zu nr. 1542–1808.* Catalogue Général du Musée du Caire, 107. Cairo.

Borchardt, Ludwig, and Kurt Sethe

1892   "Zur Geschichte der Pyramiden." *Zeitschrift für ägyptische Sprache und Altertumskunde* 30, pp. 83–106.

Boreux, Charles

1925   *See* 1927.

1926   *L'art égyptien.* Paris.

1927   "Un bas-relief au nom d'une princesse royale de la IVᵉ dynastie." *Revue de l'Égypte Ancienne* 1, pp. 5–14.

1932   *Musée National du Louvre, Département des Antiquités Égyptiennes: Guide-catalogue sommaire.* 2 vols. Paris.

1935–   "Quelques remarques sur
38   les 'pseudo-groupes' égyp-

tiens." In *Mélanges Maspero*, pp. 805–15. Cairo.

1939a   *La sculpture égyptienne au Musée du Louvre.* Paris.

1939b   "Trois oeuvres égyptiennes de la donation Atherton Curtis (Musée du Louvre)." *Monuments Piot* 37, pp. 13–36.

Bothmer, Bernard von

1950   "Notes on the Mycerinus Triad." *Bulletin of the Museum of Fine Arts* (Boston) 48, pp. 10–17.

1960   *Egyptian Sculpture in the Late Period, 700 B.C. to A.D. 100.* Edited by Elizabeth Riefstahl. Exh. cat. Brooklyn Museum of Art.

1971   "A Bust of Ny-user-ra from Byblos in Beirut, Lebanon." *Kêmi* 21, pp. 11–16.

1974   "Pehenuka Reliefs in Brooklyn and Berlin." In *Festschrift zum 150 jährigen Bestehen des Berliner Ägyptischen Museums, Staatliche Museen zu Berlin. Mitteilungen aus der Ägyptischen Sammlung* 8. Berlin.

1974a   "The Karnak Statue of Ny-user-re." *Mitteilungen des Deutschen Archäologischen Instituts, Abteilung Kairo* 30, pp. 165–70.

1982   "On Realism in Egyptian Funerary Sculpture of the Old Kingdom." *Expedition* 24, no. 2, pp. 27–39.

Bourriau, Janine

1981   *Umm el Gaˁab: Pottery from the Nile Valley before the Arab Conquest.* Exh. cat. Cambridge: Fitzwilliam Museum.

1984   "Salbgefässe." In *Lexikon der Ägyptologie*, vol. 5, cols. 362–66.

1988   *Pharaohs and Mortals: Egyptian Art in the Middle Kingdom.* Exh. cat. Cambridge: Fitzwilliam Museum; and Liverpool.

Breasted, James Henry Jr.

1948   *Egyptian Servant Statues.* Bollingen Series, 13. New York.

Brewer, Douglas J., and Renée Friedman

1989   *Fish and Fishing in Ancient Egypt.* Natural History of Egypt 2. Warminster.

Brier, Bob

1994   *Egyptian Mummies: Unraveling the Secrets of an Ancient Art.* New York.

Brinks, Jürgen

1979   *Die Entwicklung der Königlichen Grabanlagen des Alten Reiches: Eine strukturelle und historische Analyse altägyptischer*

Architektur. Hildesheimer Ägyptologische Beiträge 10. Hildesheim.

British Museum

1964   *A General Introductory Guide to the Egyptian Collections in the British Museum* [by Thomas G. H. James and Arthur F. Shore]. London.

Brooklyn Museum

1952   *Egyptian Art in the Brooklyn Museum Collection.* Brooklyn.

Brovarski, Edward

1985   "Akhmim in the Old Kingdom and First Intermediate Period." In *Mélanges Gamal eddin Mokhtar*, edited by Paule Posener-Kriéger, pp. 117–53. Bibliothèque d'étude 97. Cairo.

1994a   "Abydos in the Old Kingdom and First Intermediate Period, Part I." In *Hommages à Jean Leclant*, vol. 1, *Études Pharaoniques*, edited by Catherine Berger, Gisèle Clerc and Nicolas Grimal, pp. 99–121. Bibliothèque d'étude 106. Cairo.

1994b   "Abydos in the Old Kingdom and First Intermediate Period, Part II." In *For His Ka: Essays Offered in Memory of Klaus Baer*, edited by David Silverman, pp. 15–44. Chicago.

Brunner, Hellmut

1936   *Die Anlagen der ägyptischen Felsgräber bis zum Mittleren Reich.* Ägyptologische Forschungen, no. 3. Gluckstadt and Hamburg.

1965   *Hieroglyphische Chrestomathie.* Wiesbaden.

Brunner-Traut, Emma

1977   "Geierhaube." In *Lexikon der Ägyptologie*, vol. 2, col. 515.

1995   *Die altägyptische Grabkammer Seschemnofers III. aus Gîsa: Eine Stiftung des Geheimen Hofrats Dr. H. C. Ernst von Sieglin an die Tübinger Universität.* Revised ed. Mainz.

Brunton, Guy

1920   *Lahun, I: The Treasure.* London.

1927   *Qau and Badari, I.* Publications of the Egyptian Research Account and British School of Archaeology in Egypt, 44. London.

1928   *Qau and Badari, II.* Publications of the Egyptian Research Account and British School of Archaeology in Egypt, 45. London.

1937   *British Museum Expedition to Middle Egypt, First and*

497

Second Years, 1928, 1929: Mostagedda and the Tasian Culture. London.

1948 *Matmar: British Museum Expedition to Middle Egypt, 1929–1931.* London.

Budge, E. A. Wallis

1909 *British Museum: A Guide to the Egyptian Galleries (Sculpture).* London.

1914 [as editor]. *Egyptian Sculptures in the British Museum.* London.

1920 *By Tigris and Nile: A Narrative of Journeys in Egypt and Mesopotamia on Behalf of the British Museum Between the Years 1886 and 1913.* 2 vols. London.

1922 *British Museum: A Guide to the Fourth, Fifth, and Sixth Egyptian Rooms, and the Coptic Room. . . .* London.

Buhl, Marie-Louise, ed.

1962 *5000 ars aegyptisk kunst.* Exh. cat. Humlebaek, Denmark: Louisiana Museum.

Bull, Ludlow

1935 "A Group of Egyptian Antiquities." *Metropolitan Museum of Art Bulletin* 30 (July), pp. 142–45.

Burlington Fine Arts Club

1922 *Burlington Fine Arts Club: Illustrated Catalogue of Ancient Egyptian Art.* Exh. cat. [by Percy E. Newberry and H. R. Hall]. London.

Butzer, Karl W.

1978 "The People of the River." In *Ancient Egypt: Discovering Its Splendors,* edited by William Kelly Simpson. Washington, D.C.

Byvanck, Alexander W.

1947 *De kunst der oudheid.* Vol. 1. 2d ed. Leiden.

Callender, Vivienne, and Peter Jánosi

1997 "The Tomb of Queen Khamerernebty II at Giza. A Reassessment." *Mitteilungen des Deutschen Archäologischen Instituts, Abteilung Kairo* 53, pp. 1–22.

Capart, Jean

1901 *Recueil de monuments égyptiens.* Brussels.

1902 *Recueil de monuments égyptiens.* Ser. 2. Brussels.

1904 *Les débuts de l'art en Égypte.* Brussels. Reprinted from the *Annales de la Société Royale d'Archéologie de Bruxelles* 17–18 (1903–4).

1907 *Une rue de tombeaux à Saqqarah.* 2 vols. Brussels.

1914a *Les monuments dits Hycsos.* Recherches d'art égyp-

tien, 1. Brussels. Reprinted from the *Annales de la Société Royale d'Archéologie de Bruxelles* 27 (1913), pp. 121–56.

1914b *Les origines de la civilisation égyptienne: Conférence faite à la Société d'Anthropologie de Bruxelles le 27-4-1914.* Brussels. Reprinted from *Bulletin de la Société d'Anthropologie de Bruxelles* 33.

1920 "Some Remarks on the Sheikh El-Beled." *Journal of Egyptian Archaeology* 6, pp. 225–33.

1921 "The Name of the Scribe of the Louvre." *Journal of Egyptian Archaeology* 7, pp. 186–90.

1924 *L'art égyptien: Études et histoire.* Vol. 1. Brussels.

1927 *Documents pour servir à l'étude de l'art égyptien.* Vol. 1. Paris.

1937 *L'art égyptien.* Vol. 3. Brussels.

1942 *L'art égyptien. Deuxième partie: Choix de documents accompagnés d'indications bibliographiques.* 4 vols. Brussels.

Capart, Jean, and Marcelle Werbrouck

1930 *Memphis à l'ombre des pyramides.* Brussels.

Capel, Anne K., and Glenn E. Markoe, eds.

1996 *Mistress of the House, Mistress of Heaven: Women in Ancient Egypt.* Exh. cat. Cincinnati Art Museum; Brooklyn Museum of Art. New York.

Carré, Jean-Marie

1956 *Voyageurs et écrivains français en Égypte.* 2d ed. 2 vols. Cairo.

Cenival, J.-L. de

1965 "Un nouveau fragment de la Pierre de Palerme." *Bulletin de la Société Française d'Égyptologie* 44, pp. 13–17.

1968 "Vingt ans d'acquisitions du Département des Antiquités Égyptiennes du Musée du Louvre." *Bulletin de la Société Française d'Égyptologie* 51, pp. 5–16.

Černý, Jaroslav

1943 "Philological and Etymological Notes." *Annales du Service des Antiquités de l'Égypte* 42, pp. 341–50.

Champollion, Jean-François

1827 *Notice descriptive des monuments égyptiens du Musée Charles X.* Paris.

1835– *Monuments de l'Égypte*
45   *et de la Nubie.* 4 vols. Paris.

Chappaz, Jean-Luc, and Sandra Poggia

1996 "Ressources égyptologiques informatisées, 2." *Bulletin de la Société d'Égyptologie de Genève* 20, pp. 95–113.

Chassinat, Émile

1901 "Note sur les fouilles d'Abou Roach." *Comptes rendus des séances de l'Académie des Inscriptions et Belles-Lettres,* pp. 616–19.

1920 *Sur deux panneaux de bois sculptés égyptiens de la VIᵉ dynastie.* Paris.

1921– "À propos d'une tête en
22   grès rouge du roi Didoufri conservée au Musée du Louvre." *Monuments Piot* 25, pp. 53–75.

Cherpion, Nadine

1980 "Le mastaba de Khabaousokar (MM A₂): Problèmes de chronologie." *Orientalia Lovaniensia Periodica* 11, pp. 79–90.

1982 "La fausse-porte d'Itefnen et Peretim au Musée du Caire." *Bulletin de l'Institut Français d'Archéologie Orientale* 82, pp. 127–43.

1984 "De quand date la tombe du nain Seneb?" *Bulletin de l'Institut Français d'Archéologie Orientale* 84, pp. 35–54.

1989 *Mastabas et hypogées d'Ancien Empire: Le problème de la datation.* Brussels.

1995 "Sentiment conjugal et figuration à l'Ancien Empire." In *Kunst des Alten Reiches: Symposium im Deutschen Archäologischen Institut Kairo am 29. und 30. Oktober 1991,* pp. 33–47. Sonderschrift, Deutsches Archäologisches Institut, Abteilung Kairo, 28. Mainz.

1998 "La statuaire privée d'Ancien Empire: Indices de datation." In *Les critères de datation stylistiques à l'Ancien Empire,* edited by Nicolas Grimal, pp. 97–142. Cairo.

1999 "Sandales et porte-sandales de l'Ancien Empire." In *L'art de l'Ancien Empire égyptien: Actes du Colloque, Musée du Louvre, 3–4 avril 1998.* Paris.

n.d. *Mastabas et hypogées d'Ancien Empire.* Vol. 2. Forthcoming.

Chevereau, Pierre-Marie

1987 "Contribution à la prosopographie des cadres militaires de l'Ancien Empire et de la Première Période Intermédiaire." *Revue d'égyptologie* 38, pp. 13–48.

Ching, Francis D. K.

1979 *Architecture: Form, Space & Order.* New York.

5000 ans

1960 *5000 ans d'art égyptien.* Exh. cat. Brussels: Palais des Beaux-Arts.

Clarac, Frédéric, comte de

1851 *Musée de sculpture antique et moderne; ou, Description historique et graphique du Louvre et de toutes ses parties. . . .* Vol. 5. Paris.

Clayton, Peter A.

1994 *Chronicle of the Pharaohs: The Reign-by-Reign Record of the Rulers and Dynasties of Ancient Egypt.* New York.

1995 *Chronique des pharaons: L'histoire règne par règne des souverains et des dynasties de l'Égypte ancienne.* Paris.

Cooney, John D.

1948 "A Colossal Head of the Early Old Kingdom." *Berliner Münzblätter* 9, no. 3, pp. 1–12.

1949a "Royal Sculptures of Dynasty VI." In *Actes du XXIᵉ Congrès International des Orientalistes (Paris, 23–31 juillet 1948),* pp. 74–76. Paris.

1949b "A Tentative Identification of Three Old Kingdom Sculptures." *Journal of Egyptian Archaeology* 31, pp. 54–56.

1952 "Three Egyptian Families of the Old Kingdom." *Berliner Münzblätter* 13, no. 3, pp. 1–18.

1953 "The Wooden Statues Made for an Official of King Unas." *Berliner Münzblätter* 15, no. 1, pp. 1–25.

1975 "Three Royal Sculptures." *Revue d'égyptologie* 27, pp. 78–85.

Corteggiani, Jean Pierre

1981 *Centenaire de l'Institute Français d'Archéologie Orientale.* Exh. cat. Cairo: Egyptian Museum.

1986 *L'Égypte des pharaons au Musée du Caire.* Rev. ed. Paris.

Curto, Silvio

1903 *Gli scavi italiani a el-Ghiza.* Rome. Reprinted 1963.

1984a *L'antico Egitto nel Museo Egizio di Torino.* Turin.

1984b "Standarte." In *Lexikon der Ägyptologie,* vol. 5, cols. 1255–56.

1988 "Les sites royaux héliopolis et Giza." In *Musée Égyptien de Turin: Civilisation des Égyptiens; les croyances religeuses.* Turin.

Dai Ejiputo ten
1988   *Dai Ejiputo ten: Doitsu Minshu Kyōwakoku, Berurin Kokuritsu Hakubutsukan (Bōde Hakubutsukan) zō. The Exhibition of Art Treasures of Ancient Egypt.* Tokyo National Museum; Kyoto National Museum; Hiroshima Prefectural Museum of Art; Fukuoka Art Museum; and Endo Chain, Sendai. Tokyo.

Daninos, A.
1886   "Lettre de M. Daninos-Bey à M. G. Maspero, directeur général des fouilles et musées d'Egypte, au sujet de la découverte des statues de Meidoum." *Recueil de travaux relatifs à la philologie et à l'archéologie égyptiennes et assyriennes* 8, pp. 69–73.

Daressy, G.
1910   "La tombe de la mère de Chéfren." *Annales du Service des Antiquités de l'Égypte* 10, pp. 41–49.

Dasen, Véronique
1993   *Dwarfs in Ancient Egypt and Greece.* Oxford and New York.

Daumas, François
1970a   "Les objets sacrés de la déesse Hathor à Dendara." *Revue d'égyptologie* 22, pp. 63–78.
1970b   "Les objets sacrés d'Hathor au temple de Dendara." *Bulletin de la Société Française d'Égyptologie* 57, pp. 7–18.

D'Auria, Sue, Peter Lacovara, and Catharine H. Roehrig
1988   *Mummies and Magic: The Funerary Arts of Ancient Egypt.* Exh. cat. Boston: Museum of Fine Arts.

Davies, Nina M.
1936   *Ancient Egyptian Paintings.* 3 vols. Chicago.

Davies, Norman de Garis
1901   *The Mastaba of Ptahhetep and Akhethetep at Saqqareh.* London.
1920   "An Alabaster Sistrum Dedicated by King Teta." *Journal of Egyptian Archaeology* 6, pp. 69–72.
1930   *The Tomb of Ken-Amun at Thebes.* 2 vols. The Metropolitan Museum of Art, Egyptian Expedition. New York.

Davis, Whitney
1989   *The Canonical Tradition in Ancient Egyptian Art.* Cambridge.

Dawson, Warren R., and Eric P. Uphill
1995   *Who Was Who in Egyptology.* 3d ed., revised by M. L. Bierbrier. London.

Delange, Elisabeth
1990   *Les bijoux de l'antiquité égyptienne.* Petits guides des grands musées. Paris.

Delange-Bazin, Elisabeth
1980   *Les bijoux de l'antiquité égyptienne.* Paris: Musée du Louvre.

Desroches Noblecourt, Christiane
1941   *L'art égyptien au Musée du Louvre.* Paris.
1963   *Tutankhamun: Life and Death of a Pharaoh.* London.
1986   *La femme au temps des pharaons.* Paris.
1991   "Les trois saisons du dieu et le débarcadère du ressucite." *Mitteilungen des Deutschen Archäologischen Instituts, Abteilung Kairo* 47, pp. 67–80.
1995   *Amours et fureurs de la lointaine: Clés pour la compréhension de symboles égyptiens.* Paris.

Desroches Noblecourt, Christiane, and Jean Vercoutter
1981   *Un siècle de fouilles françaises en Egypte, 1880–1980: À l'occasion du centenaire de l'École du Caire (IFAO).* Exh. cat. Tokyo: Palais de Tokyo.

Detroit Institute of Arts
1943   *The Detroit Institute of Arts, Paintings and Sculpture Illustrated.* Detroit.
1949   *Masterpieces of Painting and Sculpture from the Detroit Institute of Arts.* Detroit.
1960   *Treasures from the Detroit Institute of Arts.* Detroit.

Dobrev, Vassil
1992   "Recherches sur les rois de la IVième dynastie égyptienne." Vol. 1, "Des documents de Snefrou, Khoufou, Djededefrê." Dissertation, Paris.

Dominicus, Brigitte
1994   *Gesten und Gebärden in Darstellungen des Alten und Mittleren Reiches.* Studien zur Archäologie und Geschichte Altägyptens 10. Heidelberg.

Donadoni, Sergio
1955   *Arte egizia.* Turin.
1969   *Egyptian Museum: Cairo.*
1993   *L'art égyptien.* Paris.

Donadoni, Sergio, Silvio Curto, and Anna Maria Donadoni Roveri
1990   *Egypt from Myth to Egyptology.* Milan.

Donadoni Roveri, Anna Maria
1987   [as editor]. *Musée Égyptien de Turin. Civilisation des Égyptiens: La vie quotidienne.* Milan.

1988   [as editor]. *Egyptian Civilization.* Vol. 2, *Religious Beliefs.* Turin.
1989   [as editor]. *Civilisation des Égyptiens: Les arts de la célébration.* Turin: Musée Égyptien de Turin.
1990   "Gebelein." In *Beyond the Pyramids: Egyptian Regional Art from the Museo Egizio di Turino,* edited by G. Robins, pp. 23–29. Exh. cat. Atlanta.

Donadoni Roveri, Anna Maria, et al.
1993   *Il Museo Egizio di Torino: Guida alla lettura di una cililtà.* New ed. Novara.

Donadoni Roveri, Anna Maria, Elvira D'Amicone, and Enrica Leospo
1994   *Gebelein: Il villaggio e la necropoli.* Quaderni del Museo Egizio, serie collezioni, 1. Turin.

Donadoni Roveri, Anna Maria, and Francesco Tiradritti, eds.
1998   *Kemet: Alle Sorgenti del tempo.* Exh. cat. Ravenna: Museo Nazionale. Milan.

Dorman, Peter F., Prudence O. Harper, and Holly Pittman
1987   *Egypt and the Ancient Near East: The Metropolitan Museum of Art.* New York.

Dorner, Josef
1998   "Neue Messungen an der Roten Pyramide." In *Stationen: Beiträge zur Kulturgeschichte Ägyptens Gewidmet Rainer Stadelmann,* edited by Heike Guksch and Daniel Polz, pp. 23–30. Mainz.

Drenkhahn, Rosemarie
1975   "Bohrer." In *Lexikon der Ägyptologie,* vol. 1, cols. 845–46.
1976   *Die Handwerker und ihre Tätigkeiten im Alten Ägypten.* Ägyptologische Abhandlungen 31. Wiesbaden.

Dreyer, Günter
1986   *Der Tempel der Satet: Die Funde der Frühzeit und des Alten Reiches.* Elephantine, 8; Archäologische Veröffentlichungen, 39. Mainz.
1998   "Der erste König der 3. Dynastie." In *Stationen, Beiträge zur Kulturgeschichte Ägyptens Gewidmet Rainer Stadelmann,* edited by Heike Guksch and Daniel Polz, pp. 31–34. Mainz.

Drioton, E.
1943   "Une représentation de la famine sur un bas-relief égyptien de la Ve dynastie." *Bulletin de l'Institut d'Égypte* 25, pp. 45–63.

Dubis, Elzbieta
1992   "Some Remarks on Egyptian Reserve Heads." In *Studies in Ancient Art and Civilization* 4, pp. 19–25. Kraków.

Dubois, Jean Joseph
1837   *Description des antiquités égyptiennes, grecques et romaines, monuments cophtes et arabes, composant la collection de feu M. J. F. Mimaut.* Paris.

Du Bourguet, Pierre, and Étienne Drioton
1965   *Les pharaons à la conquête de l'art.* Paris.

Duell, Prentice
1938   *The Mastaba of Mereruka by the Sakkarah Expedition.* 2 vols. University of Chicago Oriental Institute Publications, 31, 32. Chicago.

Dunand, Françoise, and Roger Lichtenberg
1991   *Les momies: Un voyage dans l'éternité.* Paris.

Dunand, Maurice
1937   *Fouilles de Byblos: Atlas.* 2 vols. Paris.
1939   *Fouilles de Byblos.* Vol. 1, *1926–1932.* 2 vols. Paris.

Dunham, Dows
1936   "A Statuette of Two Egyptian Queens." *Bulletin of the Museum of Fine Arts* (Boston) 34 (February), pp. 3–5.
1938   "The Biographical Inscriptions of Nekhebu in Boston and Cairo." *Journal of Egyptian Archaeology* 24, pp. 1–8.
1939   "The Portrait Bust of Prince Ankh-haf." *Bulletin of the Museum of Fine Arts* (Boston) 37 (June), pp. 42–46.

Dunham, Dows, and William Kelly Simpson.
1974   *The Mastaba of Queen Mersyankh III: G 7530–7540.* Vol. 1 of *Giza Mastabas.* Boston.

Dürring, Norbert
1995   *Materialien zum Schiffsbau im Alten Ägypten.* Abhandlungen des Deutschen Archäologischen Instituts Kairo, ägyptologische Reihe 11. Mainz.

Eaton-Krauss, Marianne
1984   *The Representations of Statuary in Private Tombs of the Old Kingdom.* Ägyptologische Abhandlungen 39. Wiesbaden.
1995   "Pseudo-Groups." In *Kunst des Alten Reiches: Symposium im Deutschen Archäologischen Institut Kairo am 29. und 30. Oktober*

1991, pp. 57–74. Sonder-
schrift des Deutsches
Archäologisches Instituts,
Abteilung Kairo 28. Mainz.

1997 "Two Masterpieces of Early
Egyptian Statuary." *Oud-
heidkundige mededelingen
uit het Rijksmuseum van
Oudheden te Leiden 77*,
pp. 7–21.

1998 "Non-Royal Pre-Canonical
Statuary." *Bibliothèque
d'étude, Institut Français
d'Archéologie Orientale*
120, pp. 209–25.

Eaton-Krauss, Marianne, and
C. E. Loeben

1997 "Some Remarks on the
Louvre Statues of Sepa
(A36 and 37) and Nesames
(A38)." In *Chief of Seers:
Egyptian Studies in Mem-
ory of Cyril Aldred*, pp. 83–
87. London.

Edel, Elmar

1961 *Zu den Inschriften auf den
Jahreszeitenreliefs der
"Weltkammer" aus dem
Sonnenheiligtum des
Niuserre.* Nachrichten der
Akademie der Wissen-
schaften in Göttingen 1.
Philologisch-historische
Klasse, Jahrgang 1961, no.
8. Göttingen.

1964 *Zu den Inschriften auf den
Jahreszeitenreliefs der
"Weltkammer" aus dem
Sonnenheiligtum des
Niuserre.* Nachrichten der
Akademie der Wissen-
schaften in Göttingen, I.
Philologisch-historische
Klasse, Jahrgang 1963, no.
4–5. Göttingen.

1970a *Das Akazienhaus und seine
Rolle in den Begräbnisriten
des alten Ägyptens.* Mün-
chener ägyptologische Studien 24. Berlin.

1970b *Die Felsengräber der Qub-
bet el Hawa bei Assuan. II.
Abteilung: Die Althieratis-
chen Topfaufschriften.* Vol.
1, *Die Topfaufschriften aus
den Grabungsjahren 1960,
1961, 1962, 1963 und
1965. Part 2, Text (Fortset-
zung).* Wiesbaden.

1981 *Hieroglyphische Inschriften
des Alten Reiches.* Abhandlungen der Rheinisch-West-
fälischen Akademie der
Wissenschaften 67. Op-
laden.

1996 "Studien zu den Relieffrag-
menten aus dem Taltempel
des Königs Snofru." In
*Studies in Honor of William
Kelly Simpson*, edited by
Peter Der Manuelian, vol.
1, pp. 199–208. Boston.

Edel, Elmar, and Steffen Wenig

1974 *Die Jahreszeitenreliefs aus
dem Sonnenheiligtum des
Königs Ne-User-Re.* 2 vols.
Mitteilungen aus der Ägyptischen Sammlung 7. Berlin.

Edwards, I. E. S.

1961 *The Pyramids of Egypt.*
Revised ed. London.

1979 *The Pyramids of Egypt.*
Reprint of 1976 ed., with
revisions. Harmondsworth,
Middlesex.

1986 *The Pyramids of Egypt.*
New. ed. Harmondsworth,
Middlesex, and New York.

Eggebrecht, Arne, ed.

1986 *Das Alte Reich: Ägypten im
Zeitalter der Pyramiden.*
Roemer- und Pelizaeus
Museum, Hildesheim. Texts
by Bettina Schmitz, Regine
Schulz, and Matthias Seidel.
Hildesheim.

Égypte éternelle

1976 *Égypte éternelle: Chefs-
d'oeuvre du Brooklyn
Museum.* Exh. cat. Brussels:
Palais des Beaux-Arts.

Eichler, Eckhard

1993 *Untersuchungen zum Expe-
ditionswesen des ägyp-
tischen Alten Reiches.*
Göttinger Orientforschun-
gen, ser. 4, Ägypten 26.
Wiesbaden.

Elsasser, Albert B., and Vera Mae
Fredrickson

1966 *Ancient Egypt, an Exhibition at the Robert H. Lowie
Museum of Anthropology
of the University of California, Berkeley, March 25–
October 23, 1966.* Berkeley.

Emery, Walter B.

1938 *Excavations at Saqqara:
The Tomb of Hemaka.* Cairo.

1949 *Excavations at Saqqara:
Great Tombs of the First
Dynasty, I.* Cairo.

1954 *Excavations at Saqqara:
Great Tombs of the First
Dynasty, II.* Memoir of the
Egypt Exploration Society
46. Cairo.

1958 *Excavations at Saqqara:
Great Tombs of the First
Dynasty, III.* Memoir of the
Egypt Exploration Society
47. Cairo.

1961 *Archaic Egypt.* [Harmonds-
worth.]

Encyclopédie photographique

1935 *Encyclopédie photographique de l'art: Les antiquités
égyptiennes du Musée du
Louvre.* Vol. 1, *Le Musée du
Louvre: Égypte, Mésopo-
tamie.* Photographs chiefly
by André Vigneau. Paris.

Engelbach, Reginald

1915 *Riqqeh and Memphis, VI.*

Publications of the Egyptian
Research Account and
British School of Archaeol-
ogy in Egypt, 26. London.

1934 "A Foundation Scene of the
Second Dynasty." *Journal
of Egyptian Archaeology*
20, pp. 183–84.

Engelbach, Reginald, and Battiscombe George Gunn

1923 *Harageh.* British School of
Archaeology in Egypt and
Egyptian Research Account,
Twentieth Year, 1914, Pub-
lication 28. London.

Epigraphic Survey

1940 *Medinet Habu.* Vol. 4, *Festival Scenes of Ramses III.*
Chicago.

1980 *The Tomb of Kheruef: Theban Tomb 192.* Translation
of the texts by Edward
Wente. University of Chi-
cago, Oriental Institute
Publications 102. Chicago.

Evers, Hans Gerhard

1929 *Staat aus dem Stein: Denkmäler, Geschichte, und
Bedeutung der ägyptischen
Plastik während des Mitt-
leren Reichs.* 2 vols. Munich.

Eyre, Christopher J.

1987 "Work and the Organisation
of Work in the Old King-
dom." In *Labor in the
Ancient Near East*, edited by
Marvin A. Powell, pp. 5–47.
New Haven.

1998 "The Market Women of
Pharaonic Egypt." In *Le
commerce en Égypte anci-
enne*, edited by Nicolas
Grimal and Bernadette
Menu, pp. 173–91. Biblio-
thèque d'étude 121. Cairo.

Fairman, H. W.

1954 "Worship and Festivals in
an Egyptian Temple." *Bulletin of the John Rylands
Library 37*, pp. 165–203.

Fakhry, Ahmed

1935 *Sept tombeaux à l'est de la
grande pyramide de Guizeh.*
Cairo.

1942– *Recent Explorations in the
50 Oases of the Western
Desert. The Egyptian
Deserts: Bahria Oasis.* 2
vols. Cairo.

1959 *The Monuments of Sneferu
at Dahshur.* Vol. 1, *The
Bent Pyramid.* Cairo.

1961a *The Pyramids.* Chicago.

1961b *The Valley Temple.* Part 1,
The Temple Reliefs, part 2.
Vol. 2 of *The Monuments
of Sneferu at Dahshur.*
Cairo.

1993 *The Egyptian Deserts: Siwa
Oasis.* Cairo.

Falgayrettes, Christiane

1989 *Supports de rêves.* Exh. cat.

Paris: Musée Dapper. Fon-
dation Dapper, Catalogue,
no. 8. Paris.

Faltings, Dina

1998 *Die Keramik der Lebens-
mittelproduktion im Alten
Reich: Ikonographie und
Archäologie eines Gebrauchs-
artikels.* Studien zur Archäologie und Geschichte
Altägyptens 14. Heidelberg.

Fay, Biri

1995a "The Louvre Sphinx, A
23." In *Kunst des Alten
Reiches: Symposium im
Deutschen Archäologischen
Institut Kairo am 29. und 30.
Oktober 1991*, pp. 75–79.
Sonderschrift, Deutsches
Archäologisches Institut,
Abteilung Kairo, 28. Mainz.

1995b "More Old Kingdom
Sphinxes with Human
Hands." *Göttinger Miszel-
len 146*, pp. 29–36.

1995c "A Re-used Bust of Amenemhat II in the Hermitage."
Göttinger Miszellen 150,
pp. 51–64.

1996 *The Louvre Sphinx and the
Royal Sculpture from the
Reign of Amenemhat II.*
Mainz.

1998 "Royal Women as Represented in Sculpture during
the Old Kingdom." In *Les
critères de datation stylistiques à l'Ancien Empire*,
edited by Nicolas Grimal,
pp. 159–86. Cairo.

Fazzini, Richard A.

1975 *Images for Eternity: Egyp-
tian Art from Berkeley and
Brooklyn.* Exh. cat. San
Francisco: M. H. de Young
Memorial Museum.

Fazzini, Richard A., et al.

1989 *Ancient Egyptian Art in the
Brooklyn Museum.* Brook-
lyn and London.

Feucht, Erika

1967 *Die königlichen Pektorale:
Motive, Sinngehalt, und
Zweck.* Bamberg.

1986 *Vom Nil zum Neckar:
Kunstschätze Ägyptens aus
pharaonischer und kop-
tischer Zeit an der Universität Heidelberg.* Berlin.

1995 *Das Kind im alten Ägypten:
Die Stellung des Kindes in
Familie und Gesellschaft
nach altägyptischen Texten
und Darstellungen.* Frankfurt
am Main and New York.

Firth, Cecil M.

1929 "Excavations of the Department of Antiquities at Saqqara (October 1928 to
March 1929)." *Annales du
Service des Antiquités de
l'Égypte 29*, pp. 64–70.

Firth, Cecil M., and Battiscombe Gunn
1926 *Excavations at Saqqqara.* Vol. 7, *Teti Pyramid Cemeteries.* 2 vols. Cairo: Service des Antiquités de l'Égypte.

Firth, Cecil M., and James E. Quibell
1935 *Excavations at Saqqara: The Step Pyramid.* 2 vols. Cairo. Service des Antiquités de l'Égypte.

Fischer, Henry G.
1958 "Eleventh Dynasty Relief Fragments from Deir el Bahri." *Yale University Art Gallery Bulletin* 24 (October), pp. 29–38.
1959 "A Scribe of the Army in a Saqqara Mastaba of the Early Fifth Dynasty." *Journal of Near Eastern Studies* 18, pp. 233–72.
1962a "The Cult and Nome of the Goddess Bat." *Journal of the American Research Center in Egypt* 1, pp. 11–15.
1962b "A Provincial Statue of the Egyptian Sixth Dynasty." *American Journal of Archaeology* 66, pp. 65–69.
1963 "Varia Aegyptiaca." *Journal of the American Research Center in Egypt* 2, pp. 17–51.
1965 "Anatomy in Egyptian Art." *Apollo*, July, pp. 169–75.
1972a "Offerings for an Old Kingdom Granary Official." *Bulletin of the Detroit Institute of Arts* 51, pp. 69–80.
1972b "Some Emblematic Uses of Hieroglyphs with Particular Reference to an Archaic Ritual Vessel." *Metropolitan Museum Journal* 5, pp. 5–23.
1974 "Redundant Determinatives in the Old Kingdom." *Metropolitan Museum Journal* 8 (1973), pp. 7–25.
1976a "An Elusive Shape within the Fisted Hands of Egyptian Statues." *Metropolitan Museum Journal* 10 (1975), pp. 9–21.
1976b *Varia.* Egyptian Studies 1. New York: The Metropolitan Museum of Art.
1977a "Fächer und Wedel." *Lexikon der Ägyptologie*, vol. 2, col. 81.
1977b *The Orientation of Hieroglyphs.* Egyptian Studies 2. New York: The Metropolitan Museum of Art.
1978 "Quelques prétendues antiquités de l'Ancien Empire." *Revue d'égyptologie* 30, pp. 78–95.
1979 "Notes on Sticks and Staves in Ancient Egypt." *Metropolitan Museum Journal* 13 (1978), pp. 5–32.

1980a "Hunde." In *Lexikon der Ägyptologie*, vol. 3, col. 77.
1980b "Koptos." In *Lexikon der Ägyptologie*, vol. 3, cols. 737–41.
1984a "Rechts und Links." *Lexikon der Ägyptologie*, vol. 5, cols. 187–91.
1984b "Sonnenschirm." In *Lexikon der Ägyptologie*, vol. 5, col. 1104.
1986 *L'écriture et l'art de l'Égypte ancienne: Quatre leçons sur la paléographie et l'épigraphie pharaoniques.* Paris.
1987 "Encore des faux." *Chronique d'Égypte* 62, pp. 90–107.
1989a *Egyptian Women of the Old Kingdom and of the Heracleopolitan Period.* New York: The Metropolitan Museum of Art.
1989b "An Old Kingdom Expedient for Anchoring Inlaid Eyes." *Journal of Egyptian Archaeology* 75, pp. 213–14.
1992 Review of *Catalogue des stèles*, by Christiane Ziegler. *Orientalia* 61, no. 2, pp. 142–46.
1993 "Another Pithemorphic Vessel of the Sixth Dynasty." *Journal of the American Research Center in Egypt* 30, pp. 1–9.
1995 "The Protodynastic Period and Old Kingdom in The Metropolitan Museum of Art." In *Kunst des Alten Reiches: Symposium im Deutschen Archäologischen Institut Kairo am 29. und 30. Oktober 1991*, pp. 81–90. Sonderschrift, Deutsches Archäologisches Institut, Abteilung Kairo, 28. Mainz.

Fisher, Clarence S.
1924 *The Minor Cemetery at Giza.* Philadelphia: University Museum.

Forman, Werner, Bedrich Forman, and Milada Vilímková
1962 *Egyptian Art.* Translated by Till Gotteiner. London.

Forman, Werner, and Stephen Quirke
1996 *Hieroglyphs and the Afterlife in Ancient Egypt.* Norman, Oklahoma.

Franco, Isabelle
1993 *Rites et croyances d'éternité.* Paris.

Franke, Detlef, comp.
1992 *Photographs of Egyptian Art and of Egypt: The Hans Wolfgang Müller Archive.* 84 microfiches and guide. Leiden.

Frankfort, Henri
1948 *Kingship and the Gods: A Study of Ancient Near Eastern Religion as the Integration of Society and Nature.* Chicago.

Freed, Rita E.
1996 "An Addition to the Corpus of Old Kingdom Royal Statuary." In *Wege öffnen: Festschrift für Rolf Gundlach zum 65. Geburtstag*, edited by Mechthild Schade-Busch, pp. 49–52. Wiesbaden.

Freier, Elke, and Stefan Grunert
1984 *Eine Reise durch Ägypten: Nach den Zeichnungen der Lepsius-Expedition in den Jahren, 1842–1845.* Berlin.

Friedman, Florence Dunn
1995 "The Underground Relief Panels of King Djoser at the Step Pyramid Complex." *Journal of the American Research Center in Egypt* 32, pp. 1–42.
1996 "Notions of Cosmos in the Step Pyramid Complex." In *Studies in Honor of William Kelly Simpson*, edited by Peter Der Manuelian, vol. 1, pp. 337–51. Boston.
1998 [as editor]. *Gifts of the Nile: Ancient Egyptian Faience.* Exh. cat. Cleveland Museum of Art; Providence: Rhode Island School of Design, Museum of Art; Fort Worth: Kimbell Art Museum. London. Includes Friedman's essay, "Faience: The Brilliance of Eternity," pp. 15–21.

5000 *Jahre ägyptische Kunst*
1961 *5000 Jahre ägyptische Kunst.* Edited by Egon von Komorzynski. Exh. cat. Vienna: Künstlerhaus Wien.

Gaballa, Gaballa A.
1976 *Narrative in Egyptian Art.* Mainz.
1977 *The Memphite Tomb-Chapel of Mose.* Warminster.
1989 "Latest Excavation in Memphis: Progress Report." In *Fragments of a Shattered Visage: The Proceedings of the International Symposium of Ramesses the Great (Memphis State University, 1989)*, edited by E. Bleiberg and R. Freed, pp. 25–27. Memphis, 1991.

Gamer-Wallert, Ingrid
1998 *Von Giza bis Tübingen: Die bewegte Geschichte der Mastaba G 5170.* Tübingen.

Gardiner, Alan H.
1938 "The Mansion of Life and Master of King's Largess." *Journal of Egyptian Archaeology* 24, pp. 83–91.

Gardiner, Alan H., T. Eric Peet, and Jaroslav Černý
1952– *The Inscriptions of Sinai.* 2
55 vols. Vol. 1, 2d ed., revised and augmented by Jaroslav Černý; vol. 2, translation and commentary, edited by Jaroslav Černý. Memoirs of the Egypt Exploration Society, 45. London.

Garstang, John
1903 *Mahâsna and Bêt Khallâf.* Egyptian Research Account 7. London.

Gauthier, Henri
1907 *Le livre des rois d'Égypte.* Vol. 1, *Des origines à la fin de la XIIe dynastie.* Mémoires de l'Institut Français d'Archéologie Orientale 17. Cairo.

Gautier, Joseph E., and Gustave Jéquier
1902 *Mémoire sur les fouilles de Licht.* Memoires publiés par les membres de l'Institut Français d'Archéologie Orientale. Cairo.

Germond, P.
1989 "L'oryx, un mal-aimé du bestiaire égyptien." *Bulletin de la Société d'Égyptologie de Genève* 13, pp. 51–55.

Ghoneim, Zakaria
1956 *The Buried Pyramid.* London.
1957 *Horus Sekhem.Khet.: The Unfinished Step Pyramid at Saqqara.* Vol. 1. Cairo.

Gilbert, Pierre
1960 "L'exposition *5000 ans d'art égyptien*." *Chronique d'Égypte* 35, pp. 153–55.
1961 "Une tête de Mycérinus aux Musées Royaux d'Art et d'Histoire à Bruxelles." *Bulletin des Musées Royaux d'Art et d'Histoire* (Brussels) 33, pp. 48–52.

Ginter, Boleslaw, et al.
1998 *Frühe Keramik und Kleinfunde aus El-Tarif.* Vol. 1, *Vordynastische und archaische Funde.* Deutsches Archäologisches Institut Abteilung Kairo, Archäologische Veröffentlichungen, 40. Mainz.

Godron, Gérard
1964 "Une tête de Mycérinus du musée de Boston." *Bulletin de l'Institut Français d'Archéologie Orientale du Caire* 62, pp. 59–61.

Goedecken, Karin B.
1976 *Eine Betrachtung der Inschriften des Meten im Rahmen der sozialen und rechtlichen Stellung von Privatleuten im ägyptischen Alten Reich.* Ägyptologische

Abhandlungen 29. Wiesbaden.

Goedicke, Hans
1957 "Das Verhältnis zwischen königlichen und privaten Darstellungen im Alten Reich." *Mitteilungen des Deutschen Archäologischen Instituts, Abteilung Kairo* 15, pp. 57–67.
1960 *Die Stellung des Königs im Alten Reich.* Ägyptologische Abhandlungen 2. Wiesbaden.
1966 "Die Laufbahn des Mtn." *Mitteilungen des Deutschen Archäologischen Instituts, Abteilung Kairo* 21, pp. 1–71.
1971 *Re-used Blocks from the Pyramid of Amenemhet I at Lisht.* The Metropolitan Museum of Art Egyptian Expedition, no. 20. New York.

Goyon, Georges
1969 "Le cylindre de l'Ancien Empire du Musée d'Ismailia." *Bulletin de l'Institut Français d'Archéologie Orientale* 67, pp. 147–57.

Grdseloff, B.
1943a "Deux inscriptions juridiques de l'Ancien Empire." *Annales du Service des Antiquités de l'Égypte* 42, pp. 25–70.
1943b "Notes sur deux monuments inédits de l'Ancien Empire." *Annales du Service des Antiquités de l'Égypte* 42, pp. 107–25.

Great Sphinx Symposium
1992 *Book of Proceedings: The First International Symposium on the Great Sphinx.* Cairo.

Grimal, Nicolas
1996 "Travaux de l'Institut Français d'Archéologie Orientale en 1995–1996." *Bulletin de l'Institut Français d'Archèologie Orientale* 96, pp. 489–617.
1997 "Travaux de l'Institut Français d'Archéologie Orientale en 1996–1997" *Bulletin de l'Institut Français d'Archèologie Orientale* 97, pp. 313–429.
1998 [as editor]. *Les critères de datation stylistiques à l'Ancien Empire: Actes de la 2ᵉᵐᵉ rencontre internationale . . . tenue à l'Institut Français d'Archéologie Orientale du 10 au 13 novembre 1994.* Bibliothèque d'étude 120. Cairo.

Grimm, Alfred, Sylvia Schoske, and Dietrich Wildung
1997 *Pharao: Kunst und Herrschaft im Alten Ägypten.*

Exh. cat. Munich: Kunsthaus Kaufbeuren.

Groenewegen-Frankfort, Henriette A.
1951 *Arrest and Movement: An Essay on Space and Time in the Representational Art of the Ancient Near East.* London. Reprinted, Cambridge, Massachusetts, 1987.

Guglielmi, Waltraud
1975 "Ernte." In *Lexikon der Ägyptologie,* vol. 1, cols. 1271–72.
1984 "Reden und Rufe." In *Lexikon der Ägyptologie,* vol. 5, cols. 193–95.

Gundlach, Rolf
1982 "Min." In *Lexikon der Ägyptologie,* vol. 4, cols. 136–40.

Habachi, Labib
1963 "King Nebheptre Menthuhotp: His Monuments, Place in History, Deification, and Unusual Representations in the Form of Gods." *Mitteilungen des Deutschen Archäologischen Instituts, Abteilung Kairo* 19, pp. 16–52.

Haeny, Gerhard
1971 "Zu den Platten mit Opfertischszene aus Heluan und Giseh." In *Aufsätze zum 70. Geburtstag von Herbert Ricke,* pp. 153–59. Beiträge zur ägyptischen Bauforschung und Altertumskunde, no. 12. Wiesbaden.
1981 [as editor]. *Untersuchungen im Totentempel Amenophis' III.* Beiträge zur ägyptischen Bauforschung und Altertumskunde 11. Wiesbaden.

Haldane, Cheryl
1992 "The Lisht Timbers: A Report on Their Significance." In *The South Cemeteries of Lisht,* vol. 3: *The Pyramid Complex of Senwosret I,* by Dieter Arnold et al., pp. 102–12. Publications of The Metropolitan Museum of Art Egyptian Expedition 25. New York.

Hall, H. R.
1925 "An Alabaster Figure of the Fourth Dynasty in the British Museum." *Journal of Egyptian Archaeology* 11, p. 1.

Hall, R.
1981 "Fishing-Net Dresses in the Petrie Museum." *Göttinger Miszellen* 42, pp. 37–46.

Harpur, Yvonne M.
1980 "Zšš w3d Scenes of the Old Kingdom." *Göttinger Miszellen* 38, pp. 53–60.
1981 "Two Old Kingdom Tombs at Gîza." *Journal of Egyp-*

tian Archaeology 67, pp. 24–35.
1985 "The Identity and Positions of Relief Fragments in Museums and Private Collections: Miscellaneous Reliefs from Saqqâra and Gîza." *Journal of Egyptian Archaeology* 71, pp. 27–42.
1986a "The Identity and Positions of Relief Fragments in Museums and Private Collections: The Identity and Positions of Five Reliefs from Saqqara." *Mitteilungen des Deutschen Archäologischen Instituts, Abteilung Kairo* 42, pp. 59–66.
1986b "The Identity and Positions of Relief Fragments in Museums and Private Collections: Reliefs from a Dismantled Tomb in the Saqqara Necropolis." *Studien zur altägyptischen Kultur* 13, pp. 107–23.
1986c "The Identity and Positions of Relief Fragments in Museums and Private Collections: The Reliefs of R'-ḥtp and Nfrt from Meydum." *Journal of Egyptian Archaeology* 72, pp. 23–40.
1987 *Decoration in Egyptian Tombs of the Old Kingdom: Studies in Orientation and Scene Content.* London and New York.
1987a Brief Communications: Further Reliefs from the Chapel of R'-ḥtp at Meydum." *Journal of Egyptian Archaeology* 73, pp. 197–200.
1998 "Evolution of an Expedition." *Egyptian Archaeology,* no. 12, pp. 18–22.
n.d. Forthcoming book on tombs.

Harrell, J. A., and M. V. Brown
1994 "Chephren's Quarry in the Nubian Desert of Egypt." *Nubica* 3, no. 1, pp. 43–57.

Harris, J. R.
1955 "The Name of the Scribe in the Louvre—a Note." *Journal of Egyptian Archaeology* 41, pp. 122–23.

Hart, George
1991 *Pharaohs and Pyramids: A Guide through Old Kingdom Egypt.* London.

Harvey, Julia Carol
1994 "Typological Study of Egyptian Wooden Statues of the Old Kingdom." Ph.D. dissertation, London University.

Haslauer, Elfriede
1991 "Bestattungsschmuck aus Giza." *Jahrbuch der Kunsthistorischen Sammlungen in Wien* 87, pp. 9–21.

Hassan, Selim
1932 *Excavations at Giza.* Vol. 1, *1929–1930.* With the collaboration of Foad Boghdady. Oxford.
1936 *Excavations at Giza.* Vol. 2, *1930–1931.* With the collaboration of Abdelsalam Abdelsalam. Cairo.
1938 "Excavations at Saqqara, 1937–1938." *Annales du Service des Antiquités de l'Égypte* 38, pp. 503–21.
1941 *Excavations at Giza.* Vol. 3, *1931–1932.* With the collaboration of Banoub Habashi. Cairo.
1943 *Excavations at Giza.* Vol. 4, *1932–1933.* With the collaboration of Mahmoud Darwish. Cairo.
1944 *Excavations at Giza.* Vol. 5, *1933–1934, with Special Chapters on Methods of Excavation, the False-Door and Other Archaeological and Religious Subjects.* With the collaboration of Mahmoud Darwish. Cairo.
1946 *Excavations at Giza.* Vol. 6, *1934–1935.* Part 1, *The Solar Boats of Khafra, Their Origin and Development. . . .* Cairo.
1948 *Excavations at Giza.* Vol. 6, *1934–1935.* Part 2, *The Offering List in the Old Kingdom.* 2 vols. Cairo.
1949 *The Sphinx: Its History in the Light of Recent Excavations.* Cairo.
1951 *Excavations at Giza.* Vol. 6, *1934–1935.* Part 3, *The Mastabas of the Sixth Season and Their Description.* Cairo.
1953 *Excavations at Giza.* Vol. 7, *1935–1936. The Mastabas of the Seventh Season and Their Description.* Cairo.
1955 "The Causeway of Wnis at Saqqara." *Zeitschrift für ägyptische Sprache und Altertumskunde* 80, pt. 2, pp. 136–44.
1960a *Excavations at Giza, Season, 1936–37–38.* Vol. 9, *The Mastabas of the Eighth Season and Their Description.* Cairo.
1960b *Excavations at Giza, Season 1938–39.* Vol. 10, *The Great Pyramid of Khufu and Its Mortuary Chapel.* Cairo.
1975a *Excavations at Saqqara, 1937–1938.* Vol. 1, *The Mastaba of Neb-Kaw-Her.* Re-edited by Zaky Iskander. Cairo.
1975b *Excavations at Saqqara, 1937–1938.* Vol. 2, *Mas-*

tabas of Ny-ʿankh-Pepy and Others. Re-edited by Zaky Iskander. Cairo.

1975c *Excavations at Saqqara, 1937–1938*. Vol. 3, *Mastabas of Princess Hemet-Rʿ and Others*. Re-edited by Zaky Iskander. Cairo.

Hawass, Zahi

1980 "Archaic Graves at Abou-Rawash." *Mitteilungen des Deutschen Archäologischen Instituts, Abteilung Kairo* 38, pp. 229–40.

1985 "The Khufu Statuette: Is It an Old Kingdom Sculpture?" In *Mélanges Gamal eddin Mokhtar*, edited by Paule Posener-Kriéger, vol. 1, pp. 379–94. Bibliothèque d'étude 97. Cairo.

1987 "The Funerary Establishments of Khufu, Khafre, and Menkaure during the Old Kingdom." Ph.D. dissertation, University of Pennsylvania, Philadelphia.

1990 *The Pyramids of Ancient Egypt*. Pittsburgh: Carnegie Museum of Natural History.

1991a "A Group of Unique Statues Discovered at Giza, I: Statues of the Overseers of the Pyramid Builders." Paper delivered at the symposium *Kunst des Alten Reiches*; published 1995.

1991b "A Group of Unique Statues Discovered at Giza, II: An Unfinished Reserve Head and a Statuette of an Overseer." Paper delivered at the symposium *Kunst des Alten Reiches*; published 1995.

1991c "The Statue of the Dwarf Pr-n(j)-ʿnh(w), Recently Discovered at Giza." *Mitteilungen des Deutschen Archäologischen Instituts, Abteilung Kairo* 47, pp. 157–62.

1992a "A Burial with an Unusual Plaster Mask in the Western Cemetery of Khufu's Pyramid." In *The Followers of Horus: Studies Dedicated to Michael Allen Hoffman, 1944–1990*, edited by Renée Friedman and Barbara Adams, pp. 327–36. Egyptian Studies Association Publication, no. 2; Oxbow Monograph 20. Oxford.

1992b "History of the Sphinx Conservation." In *Book of Proceedings: The First International Symposium on the Great Sphinx*. Cairo.

1994 "A Fragmentary Monument of Djoser from Saqqara."

1995 "A Group of Unique Statues Discovered at Giza," parts 1, 2. In *Kunst des Alten Reiches: Symposium im Deutschen Archäologischen Institut Kairo am 29. und 30. Oktober 1991*, pp. 91–95, 97–101. Sonderschrift, Deutsches Archäologisches Institut, Abteilung Kairo, 28. Mainz.

1995a "The Programs of the Royal Funerary Complexes of the Fourth Dynasty." In *Ancient Egyptian Kingship*, edited by David O'Connor and David P. Silverman, pp. 221–62. Leiden.

1996a "The Discovery of the Satellite Pyramid of Khufu (GI-d)." In *Studies in Honor of William Kelly Simpson*, edited by Peter Der Manuelian, vol. 1, pp. 379–98. Boston.

1996b "The Workmen's Community at Giza." In *Haus und Palast im alten Ägypten*, pp. 53–67. International Symposium, Cairo, April 8–11, 1992. Denkschriften der Gesamtakademie 14. Vienna.

1996c *See* Hawass and Verner 1996.

1997a "The Discovery of a Pair-Statue near the Pyramid of Menkaure at Giza." *Mitteilungen des Deutschen Archäologischen Instituts, Abteilung Kairo* 53, pp. 289–93.

1997b "The Discovery of the Harbors of Khufu and Khafre at Giza." In *Études sur l'Ancien Empire et la nécropole de Saqqâra dédiées à Jean-Philippe Lauer*, edited by Catherine Berger and Bernard Mathieu, pp. 245–56. Orientalia Monspeliensia, 9. Montpellier: Université Paul Valéry.

1997c "The Pyramids." In *Ancient Egypt*, edited by D. Silverman, pp. 168–91. London.

1997d "Zahi Hawass Talks to KMT about Matters on the Giza Plateau." *KMT* 8, no. 2 (summer), pp. 16–25.

1998 "A Group of Unique Statues Discovered at Giza, III: The Statues of Jnty-šdw, Tomb GSE 1915." In *Les critères de datation stylistiques à l'ancien empire*, edited by Nicolas Grimal, pp. 187–208. Cairo.

1998a "Pyramid Construction: New Evidence Discovered in Giza." In *Stationen, Beiträge*

zur Kulturgeschichte Ägyptens Gewidmet Rainer Stadelmann*, edited by Heike Guksch and Daniel Polz, pp. 53–62. Mainz.

1999 "A Unique Old Kingdom Headrest and Offering Tablet of Seven Sacred Oils Found at Saqqara." *Memnonia* 9 (1998), forthcoming.

Hawass, Zahi, and Mark Lehner

1994 "The Sphinx: Who Built It, and Why?" *Archaeology*, September–October, pp. 30–41.

1997 "Builders of the Pyramids." *Archaeology*, January–February, pp. 30–43.

Hawass, Zahi, and Miroslav Verner

1996 "Newly Discovered Blocks from the Causeway of Sahure (Archaeological Report)." *Mitteilungen des Deutschen Archäologischen Instituts, Abteilung Kairo* 52, pp. 177–86.

Hayes, William C.

1946 "Egyptian Tomb Reliefs of the Old Kingdom." *Metropolitan Museum of Art Bulletin*, n.s., 4 (March), pp. 170–78.

1948 "Recent Additions to the Egyptian Collection." *Metropolitan Museum of Art Bulletin*, n.s., 7 (October), pp. 60–63.

1953 *The Scepter of Egypt*. Pt. 1: *From the Earliest Times to the End of the Middle Kingdom*. New York: The Metropolitan Museum of Art.

1959 *The Scepter of Egypt*. Pt. 2: *The Hyksos Period and the New Kingdom (1675–1080)*. New York: The Metropolitan Museum of Art.

1962 *Guide to the Collections: Egyptian Art*. New York: The Metropolitan Museum of Art.

1963 "Reports of the Departments: Egyptian Art." *Metropolitan Museum of Art Bulletin*, n.s., 22 (October), pp. 65–66.

Heinrich, Ernst

1936 *Kleinfunde aus den archaischen Tempelschichten in Uruk*. Ausgrabungen Deutschen Forschungsgemeinschaft in Uruk-Warka 1. Berlin and Leipzig.

Helck, Wolfgang

1956 "Wirtschaftliche Bemerkungen zum Privat Grabbesitz im Alten Reich." *Mitteilungen des Deutschen Archäologischen Instituts, Abteilung Kairo*, 14, pp. 63–75.

1966 "Zum Kult an Königsstatuen." *Journal of Near

Eastern Studies* 25, pp. 32–41.

1968 *Geschichte des alten Ägypten*. Handbuch der Orientalistik, ser. 1, Der Nahe und der Mittlere Osten 1, Ägyptologie, section 3. Leiden.

1975 "Bier." In *Lexikon der Ägyptologie*, vol. 1, cols. 789–92.

1977 "Gauzeichen." In *Lexikon der Ägyptologie*, vol. 2, cols. 422–26.

1979 "Die Datierung der Gefässaufschriften der Djoserpyramide." *Zeitschrift für ägyptische Sprache und Altertumskunde* 106, pp. 120–32.

1980 "Maße und Gewichte (Pharaonische Zeit)." In *Lexikon der Ägyptologie*, vol. 3, cols. 1199–1209.

1981 *Geschichte des Alten Ägypten*. [2d ed.] Handbuch der Orientalistik, ser. 1, Der Nahe und der Mittlere Osten, vol. 1, Ägyptologie, section 3. Leiden.

1982 "Palermostein." *Lexikon der Ägyptologie*, vol. 4, cols. 652–54.

1984 "Schesemu." In *Lexikon der Ägyptologie*, vol. 5, cols. 590–91.

1986 *Politische Gegensätze im alten Ägypten: Ein Versuch*. Hildesheimer ägyptologische Beiträge 23. Hildesheim.

1987 *Untersuchungen zur Thinitenzeit*. Ägyptologische Abhandlungen 45. Wiesbaden.

Herodotus

1998 *The Histories*. Translated by Robin Waterfield; introduction and notes by Carolyn Dewald. New York.

Hibbard, Howard

1980 *The Metropolitan Museum of Art*. New York.

Hickmann, H.

1952 "Le métier de musicien au temps des Pharaons." *Cahiers d'histoire égyptienne* 4, no. 2, pp. 79–101.

Hittah, Muhammad Abd al-Tawwab, and Hishmat Misihah

1979 *Mallawi Antiquities Museum: A Brief Description*, by Hishmat Messiha and Mohamed A. Elhitta. Cairo. Translation of *Dalil Mathaf Athar Mallawi*.

Hodjash, Svetlana I., and Oleg D. Berlev

1980 "A Market-Scene in the Mastaba of Dꜣḏꜣ-m-ʿnḫ (Tp-m-ʿnḫ?)." *Altorientalische Forschungen* 7, pp. 31–49. Berlin.

503

1982 *The Egyptian Reliefs and Stelae in the Pushkin Museum of Fine Arts, Moscow.* Translated by Oleg Berlev. Leningrad.

Holden, Lynn
1981 "An Anubis Figure in the Boston Museum of Fine Arts." In *Studies in Ancient Egypt, the Aegean, and the Sudan: Essays in Honor of Dows Dunham on the Occasion of His 90th Birthday, June 1, 1980,* edited by William Kelly Simpson and Whitney M. Davis, pp. 99–103. Boston.

Holliday, Peter J., ed.
1993 *Narrative and Event in Ancient Art.* Cambridge.

Hölscher, Uvo
1912 *Das Grabdenkmal des Königs Chephren.* Vol. 1 of *Veröffentlichungen der Ernst von Sieglin Expedition in Ägypten,* edited by Georg Steindorff. Leipzig.

Hornemann, Bodil
1951– *Types of Ancient Egyptian*
69 *Statuary.* 7 vols. Copenhagen.

Hornung, Erik
1975 "Aker." In *Lexikon der Ägyptologie,* vol. 1, cols. 114–15.

Houlihan, Patrick F.
1986 *The Birds of Ancient Egypt.* Warminster.
1996 *The Animal World of the Pharaohs.* London and Cairo.

Huntington, Susan L.
1985 *The Art of Ancient India: Buddhist, Hindu, Jain.* New York.

Ikram, Salima
1999 "Hyenas: Hunters or Hunted? The Iconography of the Hyena in the Old Kingdom." In *Iubilate Conlegae: Studies in Memory of Abdel Aziz Sadek,* part 3, edited by Charles Van Siclen, III. San Antonio. Forthcoming.

Ikuinen
1973 *Ikuinen Egypti; Aegyptus Aeterna: Staatlichen Museen zu Berlin im Atenemin Taidemuseo.* Helsinki.

Iversen, Erik
1987 "Some Remarks on the ḥꜣw-nbw.t." *Zeitschrift für ägyptische Sprache und Altertumskunde* 114, pp. 54–59.

Jacquet-Gordon, Helen K.
1962 *Les noms des domaines funéraires sous l'Ancien Empire.* Institut Français d'Archéologie Orientale. Bibliothèque d'étude 34. Cairo.

1977 "Güterprozession." In *Lexikon der Ägyptologie,* vol. 2, cols. 919–20.

Jaksch, Heiner
1985 "Farbpigmente aus Wandmalereien Altägyptischer Gräber und Tempel: Technologien der Herstellung und mögliche Herkunftsbeziehungen." Ph.D. dissertation, University of Heidelberg.

James, T. G. H. (Thomas Garnet Henry)
1953 *The Mastaba of Khentika called Ikhekhi.* With the collaboration of M. R. Apted. Archaeological Survey of Egypt, Memoir 30. London.
1961 *Hieroglyphic Texts from Egyptian Stelae, etc., in the British Museum.* Vol. 1. 2d ed. London.
1963 "The Northampton Statue of Sekhemka." *Journal of Egyptian Archaeology* 49, pp. 5–12.
1974 *Corpus of Hieroglyphic Inscriptions in the Brooklyn Museum.* Vol. 1, *From Dynasty I to the End of Dynasty XVIII.* Wilbour Monographs 6. Brooklyn.

James, T. G. H. (Thomas Garnet Henry), and W. V. Davies
1984 *British Museum: Egyptian Sculpture.* London.

Jánosi, Peter
1994 "Die Entwicklung und Deutung des Totenopferraumes in den Pyramidentempeln des Alten Reiches." In *Ägyptische Tempel—Struktur, Funktion, und Programm: Akten der Ägyptologischen Tempeltagungen in Gosen 1990 und in Mainz 1992,* edited by Rolf Gundlach and Matthias Rochholz, pp. 143–63. Hildesheimer Ägyptologische Beiträge, 37. Hildesheim.
1996 *Die Pyramidenanlagen der Königinnen: Untersuchungen zu einem Grabtyp des Alten und Mittleren Reiches.* Untersuchungen der Zweigstelle Kairo des Österreichischen Archäologischen Institutes 13. Vienna.
1997 *Österreich vor den Pyramiden: Die Grabungen Hermann Junkers im Auftrag der Österreichischen Akademie der Wissenschaften in Wien bei der grossen Pyramide in Giza.* Vienna.
1998 "Reliefierte Kalksteinblöcke aus dem Tempel der 12. Dynastie bei 'Ezbet Rushdi el-Saghira (Tell el-Dabᶜa).'"

Ägypten und Levante 8, pp. 51–81.

Jaroš-Deckert, Brigitte
1984a *Das Grab des Jnj-jtj.f, Die Wandmalereien der XI. Dynastie. Grabung im Asasif, 1963–1970, 5; Deutsches Archäologisches Institut, Abteilung Kairo, Archäologische Veröffentlichungen 12.* Mainz.
1984b "Steingefässe." In *Lexikon der Ägyptologie,* vol. 5, cols. 1283–87.

Jaroš-Deckert, Brigitte, and Eva Rogge
1993 *Statuen des Alten Reiches.* Corpus Antiquitatum Aegyptiacarum: Kunsthistorisches Museum Wien: Ägyptisch-Orientalische Sammlung, fasc. 15. Mainz.

Jelinkova, E.
1950 "Recherches sur le titre *Hrp Hwwt Nt* 'Administrateur des domaines de la couronne rouge.'" *Annales du Service des Antiquités de l'Égypte* 50, pp. 321–62.

Jenkins, Nancy
1980 *The Boat beneath the Pyramid: King Cheops' Royal Ship.* London and New York.

Jéquier, Gustave
1913 *Histoire de la civilisation égyptienne des origines à la conquête d'Alexandre.* Paris.
1929 *Fouilles à Saqqarah: Tombeaux de particuliers contemporains de Pepi II.* Service des Antiquités de l'Égypte. Cairo.
1933 *Fouilles à Saqqarah: Les pyramides des reines Neit et Apouit.* Service des Antiquités de l'Égypte. Cairo.
1934 "Vases de pierre de la VIᵉ dynastie." *Annales du Service des Antiquités de l'Égypte* 34, pp. 97–113.
1935 "Vases de pierre de la VIᵉ dynastie: Note additionelle." *Annales du Service des Antiquités de l'Égypte* 35, p. 160.
1936 *Fouilles à Saqqarah: Le tombeau royal.* Vol. 1 of *Le monument funéraire de Pepi II.* Service des Antiquités de l'Égypte. Cairo.
1938 *Fouilles à Saqqarah: Le temple.* Vol. 2 of *Le monument funéraire de Pepi II.* Service des Antiquités de l'Égypte. Cairo.
1940 *Fouilles à Saqqarah: Les approches du temple.* Vol. 3 of *Le monument funéraire de Pepi II.* Service des Antiquités de l'Égypte. Cairo.

Jick, Millicent
1996 "G 7440Z and Boston's Bead-Net Dress." *KMT* 7, no. 2 (summer), pp. 73–74.

Johnson, Sally B.
1990 *The Cobra Goddess of Ancient Egypt: Predynastic, Early Dynastic, and Old Kingdom Periods.* London and New York.

Jones, Dilwyn
1988 *A Glossary of Ancient Egyptian Nautical Titles and Terms.* London.
1995 *Boats.* Austin.

Jørgensen, Mogens
1996 *Catalogue Egypt I (3000–1550 B.C.): Catalogue.* Copenhagen: Ny Carlsberg Glyptotek.

Journey to the West
1979 *Journey to the West: Death and Afterlife in Ancient Egypt.* Exh. cat. Berkeley: Robert H. Lowie Museum of Anthropology.

Junge, Friedrich
1995 "Hem-iunu, Anch-ha-ef und die sog. <Ersatzköpfe>." In *Kunst des Alten Reiches: Symposium im Deutschen Archäologischen Institut Kairo am 29. und 30. Oktober 1991,* pp. 103–9. Sonderschrift, Deutsches Archäologisches Institut, Abteilung Kairo, 28. Mainz.

Junker, Hermann
1914 "The Austrian Excavations, 1914." *Journal of Egyptian Archaeology* 1, pp. 249–53.
1928 "Von der ägyptischen Baukunst des Alten Reiches." *Zeitschrift für ägyptische Sprache und Altertumskunde* 63, pp. 1–14.
1929 *Giza I . . . : Die Mastabas der IV. Dynastie auf dem Westfriedhof.* Denkschrift der Kaiserlichen Akademie der Wissenschaften in Wien 69. Vienna.
1931 *The Offering Room of Prince Kaninisut.* Vienna.
1934 *Giza II . . . : Die Mastabas der beginnenden V. Dynastie auf dem Westfriedhof.* Vienna.
1938 *Giza III . . . : Die Mastabas der vorgeschrittenen V. Dynastie auf dem Westfriedhof.* Vienna.
1940 *Giza IV . . . : Die Mastaba des em Kꜣꜣmanh (Kai-em-anch).* Vienna.
1941 *Giza V . . . : Die Mastaba des Snb (Seneb) und die umliegenden Gräber.* Vienna.
1943 *Giza VI . . . : Die Mastabas des Nfr (Nefer), Φdf.jj (Kedfi), Kꜣ.hjf (Kaꜥjef)*

und die westlich anschliess-enden Grabanlagen. Vienna.

1944 *Giza VII . . . : Der Grabschnitt des Westfriedhofs, I.* Vienna.

1947 *Giza VIII . . . : Der Grabschnitt des Westfriedhofs, II.* Vienna.

1950 *Giza IX . . . : Das Mittelfeld des Westfriedhofs.* Vienna.

1951 *Giza X . . . : Der Friedhof südlich der Cheopspyramide Westteil.* Vienna.

1953 *Giza XI . . . : Der Friedhof südlich der Cheopspyramide.* Vienna.

1955 *Giza XII . . . : Schlußband mit Zusammenfassungen und Gesamt-Verzeichnissen von Band I–XII.* Vienna.

1963 *Leben und Werk in Selbstdarstellung.* Sitzungsberichte der Österreichischen Akademie der Wissenschaften, 242.5. Vienna.

Kahl, Jochem, Nicole Kloth, and Ursula Zimmermann

1995 *Die Inschriften der 3. Dynastie: Eine Bestandsaufnahme.* Ägyptologische Abhandlungen 56. Wiesbaden.

Kaiser, Werner

1956 "*Zu den Sonnenheiligtümern der 5. Dynastie.*" Mitteilungen des Deutschen Archäologischen Instituts, Abteilung Kairo 14, pp. 104–15.

1967 *Ägyptisches Museum Berlin.* Berlin.

1969 "Die Tongefässe." In *Das Sonnenheiligtum des Königs Userkaf,* vol. 2: *Die Funde,* edited by Elmar Edel. Cairo.

1971 "Die kleine Hebseddarstellung im Sonnenheiligtum des Neuserre." In *Aufsätze zum 70. Geburtstag von Herbert Ricke,* edited by Schweizerischen Institut für Ägyptische Bauforschung und Altertumskunde in Kairo, pp. 87–105. Beiträge zur ägyptischen Bauforschung und Altertumskunde 12. Wiesbaden.

1982 "Zur Entwicklung des abydenischen Königsgrabes." In *Umm el-Qaab: Nachuntersuchungen in frühzeitlichen Königsfriedhof—2. Vorbericht, Mitteilungen des Deutschen Archäologischen Instituts, Abteilung Kairo* 38, pp. 241–60.

1985 "Zur Entwicklung und Vorformen der frühzeitlichen Gräber mit reich gegliederter Oberbaufassade." In *Mélanges Gamal eddin Mokhtar,* edited by Paule Posener-Kriéger, vol. 2,

pp. 25–38. Bibliothèque d'étude 97. Cairo.

1998 "Zur Entstehung der Mastaba des Alten Reiches." In *Stationen, Beiträge zur Kulturgeschichte Ägyptens Gewidmet Rainer Stadelmann,* edited by Heike Guksch and Daniel Polz, pp. 73–86. Mainz.

Kammerer-Grothaus, Helke

1998 *Frühe Keramik und Kleinfunde aus El-Tarîf.* Vol. 2, *Keramik aus den Mastabas des alten Reiches.* Deutsches Archäologisches Institut Abteilung Kairo, Archäologische Veröffentlichungen, 40. Mainz.

Kanawati, Naguib

1980– *The Rock Tombs of el-*
92 *Hawawish: The Cemetery of Akhmim.* Vols. 1–9. Sydney.

1981 "The Living and the Dead in Old Kingdom Tomb Scenes." *Studien zur altägyptischen Kultur* 9, pp. 213–24.

1993 *The Tombs of el-Hagarsa.* With contributions by E. S. Bailey et al. Australian Center for Egyptology, Reports, 4, 6. Sydney.

Kanawati, Naguib, and Ali Hassan

1996 *The Teti Cemetery at Saqqara.* Vol. 1, *The Tombs of Nedjet-em-pet, Sa-aper and Others.* Australian Center for Egyptology, Reports, 8. Warminster.

1997 *The Teti Cemetery at Saqqara.* Vol. 2, *The Tomb of Ankhmahor.* Australian Center for Egyptology, Reports, 9. Warminster.

Kanawati, Naguib, and Ann McFarlane

1992 *Akhmim in the Old Kingdom.* Part 1, *Chronology and Administration.* Australian Center for Egyptology, Studies, 2. Sydney.

1993 *Deshasha, the Tombs of Inti, Shedu and Others.* With contributions by Nabil Charoubim, Naguib Victor, and Atef Salama. Australian Center for Egyptology, Reports, 5. Sydney.

Kanawaty, M.

1985 "Les acquisitions du Musée Charles X." *Bulletin de la Société Française d'Égyptologie* 104, pp. 31–54.

1990 "Vers une politique d'acquisitions: Drovetti, Durand, Salt et encore Drovetti." *Revue du Louvre,* no. 4, pp. 267–71.

Kantor, Helen

1957 "Narration in Egyptian

Art." *American Journal of Archaeology* 61, pp. 44–54.

Kaplony, Peter

1963 *Die Inschriften der ägyptischen Frühzeit.* 3 vols. Ägyptologische Abhandlungen 8. Wiesbaden.

1964 *Die Inschriften der ägyptischen Frühzeit: Supplement.* Ägyptologische Abhandlungen 9. Wiesbaden.

1968 "Eine neue Weisheitslehre aus dem Alten Reich (die Lehre des Mttj in der altägyptischen Weisheitsliteratur)," parts 1, 2. *Orientalia,* n.s., 37, pp. 1–62, 339–45.

1973 *Beschriftete Kleinfunde in der Sammlung Georges Michailidis: Ergebnisse einer Bestandsaufnahme im Sommer 1968.* Istanbul.

1976 *Studien zum Grab des Methethi.* Monographien der Abegg-Stiftung Bern 8. [Riggisberg.]

1986 "Zepter." In *Lexikon der Ägyptologie,* vol. 6, cols. 1373–89.

Karig, Joachim Selim, and Karl-Theodor Zauzich

1976 *Ägyptische Kunst aus dem Brooklyn Museum.* Exh. cat. Berlin: Ägyptisches Museum Berlin.

Kayser, Hans

1964 *Die Mastaba des Uhemka: Ein Grab in der Wüste.* Hannover.

1969 *Ägyptisches Kunsthandwerk: Ein Handbuch für Sammler und Liebhaber.* Bibliothek für Kunst- und Antiquitätenfreund 26. Braunschweig.

Keimer, Ludwig

1930 "Quelques hiéroglyphes représentant des oiseaux." *Annales du Service des Antiquités de l'Égypte* 30, pp. 1–26.

1931 "Pendeloques en forme d'insectes faisant partie de colliers égyptiens," part 1. *Annales du Service des Antiquités de l'Égypte* 31, pp. 145–86.

1934 "Pendeloques en forme d'insectes faisant partie de colliers égyptiens," part 2. *Annales du Service des Antiquités de l'Égypte* 34, pp. 177–213.

1957 "Notes de lecture (suite)." *Bulletin de l'Institut Français d'Archéologie Orientale* 56, pp. 97–120.

Kelley, A. L.

1974 "Reserve Heads: A Review of the Evidence for Their Placement and Function in

Old Kingdom Tombs." *Journal of the Society of the Studies of Egyptian Antiquities* 5, no. 1, pp. 6–12.

Kemp, Barry J.

1989 *Ancient Egypt: Anatomy of a Civilization.* London.

Kendall, T.

1981 An Unusual Rock-Cut Tomb at Giza." In *Studies in Ancient Egypt, the Aegean, and the Sudan: Essays in Honor of Dows Dunham on the Occasion of His 90th Birthday, June 1, 1980,* edited by William Kelly Simpson and Whitney M. Davis, pp. 104–14. Boston.

Kessler, Dieter

1982 "Meir." *Lexikon der Ägyptologie,* vol. 4, cols. 14–19.

el-Khouli, Ali

1978 *Egyptian Stone Vessels, Predynastic Period to Dynasty III: Typology and Analysis.* 3 vols. Mainz.

1991 *Meidum.* Australian Center for Egyptology, Reports, 3. Sydney.

el-Khouli, Ali, and Naguib Kanawati

1989 *Quseir el-Amarna: The Tombs of Pepy-ankh and Khewen-wekh.* Australian Center for Egyptology, Reports, 1. Sydney.

1990 *The Old Kingdom Tombs of el-Hammamiya.* Australian Center for Egyptology, Reports, 2. Sydney.

Killen, Geoffrey P.

1980 *Ancient Egyptian Furniture.* Vol. 1, *4000–1300 B.C.* Warminster.

1994a *Ancient Egyptian Furniture.* Vol. 2, *Boxes, Chests, and Footstools.* Warminster.

1994b *Egyptian Woodworking and Furniture.* Buckinghamshire.

Klebs, Luise S.

1915 *Die Reliefs des Alten Reiches (2980–2475 v. Chr.): Material zur ägyptischen Kulturgeschichte.* Heidelberger Akademie der Wissenschaften, Philosophisch-historische Klasse, Abhandlungen 3. Heidelberg.

1931 "Die verschiedenen Formen des Sistrums." *Zeitschrift für ägyptische Sprache und Altertumskunde* 67, pp. 60–63.

Klemm, Dietrich D.

1991 "Calcit-Alabaster oder Travertin? Bemerkungen zu Sinn und Unsinn petrographischer Bezeichnungen in der Ägyptologie." *Göttinger Miszellen* 122, pp. 57–70.

Klemm, Rosemarie, and Dietrich Klemm
1981 *Die Steine der Pharaonen.* Exh. cat. Munich: Staatliche Sammlung Ägyptischer Kunst München.
1993 *Steine und Steinbrüche im Alten Ägypten.* Berlin, Heidelberg, and New York.

Komorzinsky, Egon R. von
1965 *Das Erbe des Alten Ägypten.* Vienna.

Königliche Museen zu Berlin
1899 *Ausführliches Verzeichnis der aegyptischen Altertümer und Gipsabgüsse.* 2d ed. Berlin.

Korecky, M.
1983 *Objevy pod pyramidami.* Prague.

Kozloff, Arielle P.
[1970] *An Introduction to the Art of Egypt in the Cleveland Museum of Art.* Cleveland.
1982 "Weserkaf, Boy King of Dynasty V." *Bulletin of the Cleveland Museum of Art* 69, no. 7 (September), pp. 211–23.

Kozloff, Arielle P., and Betsy M. Bryan
1992 *Egypt's Dazzling Sun: Amenhotep III and His World.* Exh. cat. Cleveland: Cleveland Museum of Art; Fort Worth: Kimbell Art Museum; Paris: Galeries Nationales du Grand Palais.

Krauspe, Renate
1986 *Altägyptische Gotterfiguren.* Leipzig.
1987 *Ägyptisches Museum der Karl-Marx-Universität Leipzig: Führer durch die Ausstellung.* Leipzig.
1997a [as editor]. *Das Ägyptische Museum der Universität Leipzig.* Mainz.
1997b [as editor]. *Statuen und Statuetten.* Vol. 1 of *Katalog ägyptischer Sammlungen in Leipzig.* Mainz.

Kroeper, Karla, and Lech Krzyzaniak
1992 "Two Ivory Boxes from Early Dynastic Graves in Minshat Abu Omar." In *The Followers of Horus: Studies Dedicated to Michael Allen Hoffman, 1944–1990,* edited by Renée Friedman and Barbara Adams, pp. 207–214. Egyptian Studies Association Publication 2, Oxbow Monograph 20. Oxford.

Kromer, Karl
1978 *Siedlungsfunde aus dem frühen Alten Reich in Giseh: Österreichische Ausgrabungen, 1971–75.* Vienna.
1991 *Nezlet Batran: Eine Mastaba aus dem Alten Reich bei Giseh (Ägypten). Österreichische Ausgrabungen, 1981–1983.* Vienna.

Kuény, G.
1950 "Scènes apicoles dans l'ancienne Egypte." *Journal of Near Eastern Studies* 9, pp. 84–95.

Kunsthistorisches Museum Wien
1988 *Führer durch die Sammlungen.* Vienna.

Labrousse, Audran
1994 "Les reines de Teti, Khouit et Ipout Ire: Recherches architecturales." *Bibliothèque d'étude* 106, pp. 231–43.
1996 *L'architecture des pyramides à textes, I: Saqqara Nord.* 2 vols. Mission Archéologique de Saqqara 3; Bibliothèque d'étude 114. Cairo.

Labrousse, Audran, Jean-Philippe Lauer, and Jean Leclant
1977 *Le temple haut du complexe funéraire du roi Ounas.* Mission Archéologique de Saqqarah 2; Bibliothèque d'étude 73. Cairo.

Labrousse, Audran, and Jean Leclant
1998 "Nouveaux documents sur la reine Ankhenespépy II, mère de Pépy II." In *Stationen, Beiträge zur Kulturgeschichte Ägyptens Gewidmet Rainer Stadelmann,* edited by Heike Guksch and Daniel Polz, pp. 95–100. Mainz.

Labrousse, Audran, and Ahmed M. Moussa
1996 *Le temple d'accueil du complexe funéraire du roi Ounas.* Bibliothèque d'étude 111. Cairo.

Lacau, Pierre, and Henri Chevrier
1956 *Une chapelle de Sésostris Ier à Karnak.* Service des Antiquités de l'Égypte. Cairo.

Lacau, Pierre, and Jean-Philippe Lauer
1959– *La pyramide à degrés.* Vol. 61 4: *Inscriptions gravées sur les vases.* Cairo.
1965 *La pyramide à degrés.* Vol. 5: *Inscriptions à l'encre sur les vases.* Cairo.

Laclotte, J.
1989 "Les donateurs du Louvre." *Revue du Louvre,* no. 2, pp. 74–78.

Lacovara, Peter
1995 "The American Discovery of Ancient Egypt." In *The American Discovery of Ancient Egypt,* edited by Nancy Thomas. Exh. cat. Los Angeles County Museum of Art.
1996a "A Faience Tile of the Old Kingdom." In *Studies in Honor of William Kelly Simpson,* edited by Peter Der Manuelian, vol. 2, pp. 487–91. Boston.
1996b "A New Look at Ankhhaf." *Egyptian Archaeology* 9, pp. 6–7.
1997 "The Riddle of the Reserve Heads." *KMT* 8, no. 4 (winter 1997–98), pp. 28–36.

Lacovara, Peter, and C. Nicholas Reeves
1987 "The Colossal Statue of Mycerinus Reconsidered." *Revue d'égyptologie* 38, pp. 111–15.

Landström, Björn
1970 *Ships of the Pharaohs: 4000 Years of Egyptian Shipbuilding.* Garden City, 1970. Translation of *Egyptiska skepp, 4000–600 f. Kr.* Stockholm.

Lange, Kurt, and Max Hirmer
1956 *Egypt: Architecture, Sculpture, Painting in Three Thousand Years.* Translated from the first German edition by R. H. Boothroyd. London.
1957 *Ägypten: Architektur, Plastik, Malerei in drei Jahrtausenden.* 2d ed. Munich.
1961 *Egypt: Architecture, Sculpture, Painting in Three Thousand Years.* 3d ed. Translated from German by R. H. Boothroyd. London.

Lapp, Günther
1993 *Typologie der Särge und Särgkammern von der 6. bis 13 Dynastie.* Studien zur Archäologie und Geschichte Altägyptens, 7. Heidelberg.

Lauer, Jean-Philippe
1934 "Fouilles du Service des Antiquités à Saqqarah (Secteur Nord) (novembre 1933—mai 1934)." *Annales du Service des Antiquités de l'Égypte* 34, pp. 54–69.
1936– *La pyramide à degrés:* 39 *L'architecture.* 3 vols. Cairo.
1938 "Restauration et transfert au Musée Égyptien d'un panneau orné de faïences bleues extrait de la pyramide à degrés à Saqqarah." *Annales du Service des Antiquités de l'Égypte* 38, pp. 551–65.
1949 "Note complémentaire sur le temple funéraire de Khéops." *Annales du Service des Antiquités de l'Égypte* 49, pp. 111–23.
1955 "Le temple haut de la pyramide du roi Ouserkaf à Saqqarah." *Annales du Service des Antiquités de l'Égypte* 53, pp. 119–33.
1962 *Histoire monumentale des pyramides d'Égypte.* Vol. 1: *Les pyramides à degrés (IIIe dynastie).* Cairo.
1976 *Saqqara: The Royal Cemetery of Memphis. Excavations and Discoveries since 1850.* London.
1988 *Le mystère des pyramides.* New ed. Paris.
1996 "Remarques concernant l'inscription d'Imhotep gravée sur le socle de statue de l'Horus Neteri-khet (roi Djoser)." In *Studies in Honor of William Kelly Simpson,* edited by Peter Der Manuelian, vol. 2, pp. 493–98. Boston.

Lauer, Jean-Philippe, and Jean Leclant
1969 "Découverte de statues de prisonniers au temple de la pyramide de Pepi I." *Revue d'égyptologie* 21, pp. 55–62.
1972 *Le temple haut du complexe funéraire du roi Téti.* Mission Archéologique de Saqqarah 1. Bibliothèque d'étude 51. Cairo.

Lawrence, A. W. (Arnold Walter)
1996 *Greek Architecture.* 5th ed., revised by R. A. Tomlinson. New Haven.

Leclant, Jean
1951 "Le rôle du lait et de l'allaitement d'après les textes des pyramides." *Journal of Near Eastern Studies* 10, pp. 123–27.
1961 "Sur un contrepoids de Menat au nom de Taharqa, allaitement et 'apparition' royale." In *Mélanges Mariette,* Bibliothèque d'étude 32. Cairo: Institut Français d'Archéologie Orientale.
1975 "Biene." In *Lexikon der Ägyptologie,* vol. 1, cols. 786–89.
1979a *Recherches dans la pyramide et au temple haut du Pharaon Pepi Ier, à Saqqarah.* Scholae Adriani de Buck memoriae dicatae 6. Leiden.
1979b "Fouilles et travaux en Égypte et au Soudan, 1977–1978." *Orientalia* 48, pp. 340–412.

Leclant, Jean, and Gisèle Clerc
1993 "Fouilles et travaux en Égypte et au Soudan, 1991–1992." *Orientalia,* n.s., 62, fasc. 3, pp. 175–295.

Leclant, Jean, et al.
1978 *Le temps des pyramides.* Univers des formes. Paris.

Leemans, C.
1840 *Description raisonée des monumens égyptiens.* Lei-

den: Rijks-museum van Oudheden.

Lefebvre, Gustave, ed. and trans.
1982 *Romans et contes égyptiens.* Paris.

Lehner, Mark
1985 *The Pyramid Tomb of Queen Hetep-heres and the Satellite Pyramid of Khufu.* Sonderschrift der Deutsches Archäologisches Institut, Abteilung Kairo 19. Mainz.
1985a "The Development of the Giza Necropolis: The Khufu Project." *Mitteilungen des Deutschen Archäologischen Instituts, Abteilung Kairo* 41, pp. 109–43.
1991 "Computer Rebuilds the Ancient Sphinx." *National Geographic* 179, no. 4 (April), pp. 32–39.
1992 "Reconstructing the Sphinx." *Cambridge Archaeological Journal* 2, no. 1, pp. 3–26.
1997 *The Complete Pyramids: Solving the Ancient Mysteries.* London and New York.
1998 "Niches, Slots, Grooves, and Stains: Internal Frameworks in the Khufu Pyramid?" In *Stationen, Beiträge zur Kulturgeschichte Ägyptens Gewidmet Rainer Stadelmann,* edited by Heike Guksch and Daniel Polz, pp. 101–13. Mainz.

Leospo, Enrichetta
1988 "Woodworking: Furniture and Cabinetry." In *Egyptian Civilization: Daily Life,* edited by Anna Maria Donadoni Roveri, pp. 120–59. Turin.
1989 "Lastre di decorazione parietale dalla capella di Sepedhotep." In *Dal museo al museo: Passato e futuro del Museo Egizio di Torino,* edited by Anna Maria Donadoni Roveri. Turin.

Lepsius, Richard
1849– *Denkmaeler aus Aegypten*
58 *und Aethiopien.* 13 vols. Berlin.

Lesko, Barbara S.
1998 "Queen Khamerernebty II and Her Sculpture." In *Ancient Egyptian and Mediterranean Studies in Memory of William A. Ward,* edited by Leonard Lesko, pp. 149–62. Providence, R.I.

Levinson, H., and A. Levinson
1996 "Prionotheca Coronata Olivier (Primelinae, Tenebrionidae) Recognized as a New Species of Venerated Beetles in the Funerary Cult of Pre-dynastic and Archaic Egypt." *Journal of Applied Entomology* 120, no. 10, pp. 577–85.

Lexikon der Ägyptologie
1975– *Lexikon der Ägyptologie.*
92 Edited by Wolfgang Helck, Eberhard Otto, and Wolfhart Westendorf. 7 vols. Wiesbaden.

Lilyquist, Christine
1995 *Egyptian Stone Vessels: Khian through Tuthmosis IV.* Appendix by Edward W. Castle. New York.

Limme, Luc
1984 "Sedment." In *Lexikon der Ägyptologie,* vol. 5, cols. 790–91.

Loret, V.
1899 "Fouilles dans la nécropole memphite (1897–1899)." *Bulletin de l'Institut Égyptien,* ser. 3, no. 10, pp. 85–86.

Lucas, Alfred, and John R. Harris
1962 *Ancient Egyptian Materials and Industries,* by Alfred Lucas. 4th ed., revised and enlarged by John R. Harris. London.

Lutz, Henry Frederick
1927 *Egyptian Tomb Steles and Offering Stones of the Museum of Anthropology and Ethnology of the University of California.* Egyptian Archaeology 4. Leipzig.
1930 *Egyptian Statues and Statuettes in the Museum of Anthropology of the University of California.* Egyptian Archaeology 5. Leipzig.

Mace, Arthur C.
1922 "Excavations at Lisht." *Metropolitan Museum of Art Bulletin* 17 (December), pp. 4–18.

MacGregor sale
1922 *Catalogue of the MacGregor Collection of Egyptian Antiquities.* Sale cat., Sotheby, Wilkinson and Hodge, London, June 26–30, July 3–6.

Macramallah, Rizkallah
1935 *Fouilles à Saqqarah: Le mastaba d'Idout.* Service des Antiquités de l'Égypte. Cairo.

Málek, Jaromír
1970 "Princess Inti, the Companion of Horus." *Journal of the Society for the Study of Egyptian Antiquities* 10, pp. 238–40.
1986 *In the Shadow of the Pyramids: Egypt during the Old Kingdom.* London.
1988 "The 'Altar' in the Pillared Court of Teti's Pyramid-Temple at Saqqara." In *Pyramid Studies and Other Essays Presented to I. E. S. Edwards,* pp. 23–34. London.

Manniche, Lise
1991 *Music and Musicians in Ancient Egypt.* London.
1994 *L'art égyptien.* Paris.

Der Manuelian, Peter
1982 "Furniture." In *Egypt's Golden Age: The Art of Living in the New Kingdom, 1558–1085 B.C.,* pp. 63–64. Exh. cat. Boston: Museum of Fine Arts.
1996 "March 1912: A Month in the Life of American Egyptologist George A. Reisner." *KMT* 7, no. 2 (summer), pp. 60–75.
1997 "Tombs and Temples." In *Ancient Egypt,* edited by D. P. Silverman, pp. 192–211. London.
1998a "The Problem of the Giza Slab Stelae." In *Stationen: Beiträge zur Kulturgeschichte Ägyptens, Rainer Stadelmann Gewidmet,* edited by Heike Guksch and Daniel Polz, pp. 115–34. Mainz.
1998b "Digital Epigraphy: An Approach to Streamlining Egyptological Epigraphic Method." *Journal of the American Research Center in Egypt* 35, pp. 97–113.

Maragioglio, Vito, and Celeste Ambrogio Rinaldi
1963 *L'architettura delle piramidi menfite.* Vol. 2, *La piramide di Sechemkhet, la layer pyramid di Zaulet-el-Aryan e le minori piramidi attribuiti alla III dinastia.* Rapallo.
1966 *L'architettura delle piramidi menfite.* Vol. 5, *Le piramidi di Zedefrâ e di Chefren.* Rome.
1970 *L'architettura delle piramidi menfite.* Vol. 7, *Le piramidi di Userkaf, Sahura, Neferirkara; la piramide incompiuta e le piramidi minori di Abu Sir.* Rapallo.

Mariette, Auguste, and Gaston Maspero
1885 *Les mastabas de l'Ancien Empire: Fragment du dernier ouvrage de A. Mariette publié d'après le manuscript de l'auteur par G. Maspero.* Paris.
1889 *Les mastabas de l'Ancien Empire: Fragment du dernier ouvrage de A. Mariette, publié d'après le manuscrit de l'auteur, par G. Maspero.* Paris.

Martin, Karl
1978 *Reliefs des Alten Reiches.* Part 1. Corpus Antiquitatum Aegyptiacarum, Lose-Blatt-Katalog ägyptischer Altertümer: Pelizaeus Museum, Hildesheim, fasc. 3. Mainz.
1984 "Sedfest." In *Lexikon der Ägyptologie,* vol. 5, cols. 782–90.
1986 "Vogelfang, -jagd, -netz, -steller." In *Lexikon der Ägyptologie,* vol. 6, cols. 1051–54.

Martin-Pardey, Eva
1976 *Untersuchungen zur ägyptischen Provinzialverwaltung bis zum Ende des Alten Reiches.* Hildesheimer ägyptologische Beitrag 1. Hildesheim.
1977 *Plastik des Alten Reiches I.* Corpus Antiquitatum Aegyptiacarum, Pelizaeus-Museum, Hildesheim. Mainz.
1984a "Rahotep." In *Lexikon der Ägyptologie,* vol. 5, cols. 86–87.
1984b "Salbung." In *Lexikon der Ägyptologie,* vol. 5, cols. 367–69.

Maruéjol, Florence
1991 *L'art égyptien au Louvre: Oeuvres choisies.* Paris.

Maruéjol, Florence, and T. Julien
1987 *L'art du monde au Musée du Louvre: L'Orient ancien et L'Égypte.* Paris.

Maspero, Gaston
1891– "Notes au jour le jour–V."
92 *Proceedings of the Society of Biblical Archaeology* (London) 14, pp. 305–27.
1907 *Le Musée Égyptien.* Cairo.
1912a *Égypte.* Ars-una species-mille; Histoire générale de l'art. Paris.
1912b *Essais sur l'art égyptien.* Paris.
1915a *Guide du visiteur au musée du Caire.* 4th ed. Cairo.
1915b *Le Musée Égyptien: Recueil de monuments et de notices sur les fouilles d'Égypte.* Vol. 3. Cairo.

Masterpieces of Fifty Centuries
1970 *Masterpieces of Fifty Centuries.* Exh. cat. New York: The Metropolitan Museum of Art.

McFarlane, Ann
1987 "The First Nomarch at Akhmim: The Identification of a Sixth Dynasty Biographical Inscription." *Göttinger Miszellen* 100, pp. 63–72.
1995 *The God Min to the End of the Old Kingdom.* Australian Centre for Egyptology, Studies 3. Sydney.

McLeod, Wallace
1982 *Self Bows and Other Archery Tackle from the Tomb of Tutʿankhamūn.* Tutʿankhamūn's Tomb Series, edited by John R. Harris, 4. Oxford.

Meinertzhagen, Richard
1930 *Nicoll's Birds of Egypt.* 2 vols. London.

Merveilles du Louvre
1958 *Merveilles du Louvre.* Vol. 1, *Du IVe millénaire avant J. C. à l'aube de la renaissance.* Paris.
1970 *Merveilles du Louvre.* New ed. Paris.

Metropolitan Museum
1962 *Egyptian Art: Guide to the Collections.* The Metropolitan Museum of Art, Guide to the Collections 3. New York.
1983 *The Metropolitan Museum of Art Guide.* New York.

el-Metwally, Emad
1992 *Entwicklung der Grabdekoration in den altägyptischen Privatgräbern: Ikonographische Analyse der Totenkultdarstellungen von der Vorgeschichte bis zum Ende der 4. Dynastie.* Göttinger Orientforschungen, 4 Reihe: Ägypten 24. Wiesbaden.

Michalowski, Kazimierz
1968 *L'art de l'ancienne Égypte.* 2d ed. Paris.
1969 *Art of Ancient Egypt.* Translated and adapted from the Polish and French by Norbert Guterman. New York.

Midant-Reynes, Béatrix
1992 *Préhistoire de l'Égypte: Des premiers hommes aux premiers pharaons.* Paris.

Millet, Nicholas B.
1981 "The Reserve Heads of the Old Kingdom." In *Studies in Ancient Egypt, the Aegean, and the Sudan: Essays in Honor of Dows Dunham on the Occasion of His 90th Birthday, June 1, 1980,* edited by William Kelly Simpson and Whitney M. Davis, pp. 129–31. Boston.

Minault-Gout, Anne
1992 *Le mastaba d'Ima-Pepi (Mastaba II).* Fouilles de l'Institut Français d'Archéologie Orientale du Caire, 33. Cairo.
1997 "Sur les vases jubilaires et leur diffusion." In *Études sur l'Ancien Empire et la nécropole de Saqqâra dédiées à Jean-Philippe Lauer,* edited by Catherine Berger and Bernard Mathieu, pp. 305–14. Orientalia Monspeliensia, 9. Montpellier: Université Paul Valéry.

Mogensen, Maria
1921 *Le mastaba égyptien de la Glyptothèque Ny Carlsberg.* Copenhagen.
1930 *La Glyptothèque Ny Carlsberg: La collection égyptienne.* Copenhagen.

Mond, Robert, and Oliver H. Myers
1937 *Cemeteries of Armant, I.* 2 vols. London.

Montet, Pierre
1925 *Les scènes de la vie privée dans les tombeaux égyptiens de l'Ancien Empire.* Publications de la Faculté des Lettres de l'Université de Strasbourg 24. Strasbourg.
1928 *Byblos et l'Égypte: Quatre campagnes de fouilles à Gebeil, 1921–1922–1923–1924.* 2 vols. Bibliothèque archéologique et historique 11. Paris.
1956 *Isis; ou, À la recherche de l'Égypte ensevelie.* Paris.
1957 "Reines et pyramides." *KÊMI, Revue de philologie et d'archéologie égyptiennes et coptes* 14, pp. 92–101.

Moret, Alexandre.
1902 *Le rituel du culte divin journalier en Égypte, d'après les papyrus de Berlin et les textes du temple de Séti Ier à Abydos.* Annales du Musée Guimet, Bibliothèque d'étude 14. Paris.

Morgan, Jacques de
1895 *Fouilles à Dahchour, mars–juin 1894.* With the collaboration of M. Berthelot, G. Legrain, and G. Jéquier. Vienna.
1903 *Fouilles à Dahchour en 1894–1895.* With the collaboration of G. Legrain and G. Jéquier. Vienna.

Moussa, Ahmed M.
1981 "Excavations in the Valley Temple of King Unas at Saqqara." *Annales du Service des Antiquités de l'Egypte* 64, pp. 75–77.
1985 "Excavations in the Valley Temple of King Unas at Saqqara." *Annales du Service des Antiquités de l'Egypte* 70, pp. 33–34.

Moussa, Ahmed M., and Hartwig Altenmüller
1971 *The Tomb of Nefer and Ka-hay.* Old Kingdom Tombs at the Causeway of King Unas at Saqqara, Archäologische Veröffentlichungen 5. Mainz.
1977 *Das Grab des Nianchchnum und Chnumhotep.* Old Kingdom Tombs at the Causeway of King Unas at Saqqara Excavated by the Department of Antiquities, Archäologische Veröffentlichungen 21. Mainz.

Müller, Christa
1984 "Schminken." In *Lexikon der Ägyptologie,* vol. 5, col. 666.

Müller, Hans W.
1964 "Der gute Gott Radjedef, Sohn des Rê." *Zeitschrift für ägyptische Sprache und Altertumskunde* 91, pp. 129–33.
1972 *Staatliche Sammlung Ägyptischer Kunst.* Edited by Beatrix Gressler-Löhr and Hans Wolfgang Müller. Munich.
1992 Müller Archive. *See* Franke 1992.

Müller, Hugo
1938 *Die Formale Entwicklung der Titulatur der ägyptischen Könige.* Ägyptologische Forschungen 7. Glückstadt.

Munro, Peter
1993 *Der Unas-Friedhof Nord-West: Topographisch-historische Einleitung.* Vol. 1, *Das Doppelgrab der Königinnen Nebet und Khenut.* Mainz.
1994 "Bemerkungen zur Datierung Mttj's: Zu seinen Statuen Brooklyn 51.1 / Kansas City 51-1 und zu verwandten Rundbildern." In *Hommages à Jean Leclant,* vol. 1, *Études Pharaoniques,* edited by Catherine Berger, Gisèle Clerc and Nicolas Grimal, pp. 245–77. Institut Français d'Archéologie Orientale: Bibliothèque d'étude 106. Cairo.

Murray, Margaret A.
1905 *Saqqara Mastabas.* Part 1. London.
1930 "A Pharaoh of the Old Kingdom." *Ancient Egypt,* 1930, pp. 8–10.

Myers, P., and L. van Zelst
1977 "Neutron Activation Analysis of Limestone Objects: A Pilot Study." *Radiochimica Acta* 24, pp. 197–204.

Naissance de l'écriture
1982 *Naissance de l'écriture: Cuneiformes et hiéroglyphes.* Exh. cat. Paris: Galeries Nationales du Grand Palais.

Naville, Edouard
1891 *Bubastis (1887–1889).* Memoir of the Egypt Exploration Fund 8. London.
1897– [as editor]. *Denkmäler aus*
1913 *Aegypten und Aethiopien: Text.* 5 vols. Vol. 1, *Unteraegypten und Memphis.* With the collaboration of Ludwig Borchardt; revised by Kurt Sethe. Leipzig.
1898 *The Temple of Deir el Bahari.* Part 3, *End of Northern Half and Southern Half of the Middle Platform.* Memoir of the Egypt Exploration Fund 14. London.
1909 "Têtes de pierre déposées dans les tombeaux égyptiens." In *Mémoires publiés à l'occasion de Jubilé de l'Université de Genève 1559–1909.* vol. 2. pp. 5–11. Geneva.

Needler, Winifred
1959 "Three Relief-Sculptures of the Early Pyramid Age from Lisht." *Annual, Art and Archaeology Division, Royal Ontario Museum, Toronto,* pp. 32–39.

Neferut net Kemit
1983 *Neferut net Kemit: Egyptian Art from the Brooklyn Museum.* Organized by the Yomiuri Shimbun; edited by Teisuke Yakata. Exh. cat. Tokyo: Isetan Museum; Osaka: Hanshin Department Store; Saga Prefecture Art Museum; Kagoshima Prefectural Museum of Culture. Tokyo.

Newberry, Percy E.
1912 "The Inscribed Tombs of Ekhmin." *Annals of Archaeology and Anthropology,* pp. 99–120.

Nour, Mohammad Zaki, Zaki Iskander, Mohammad Saleh Osman, and Ahmad Youssof Moustafa
1960 *The Cheops Boats.* Part 1. Cairo: Antiquities Department of Egypt, Ministry of Culture and National Orientation.

O'Connor, David
1992 "The Status of Early Egyptian Temples: An Alternative Theory." In *The Followers of Horus: Studies Dedicated to Michael Allen Hoffman, 1944–1990,* edited by Renée Friedman and Barbara Adams, pp. 83–98. Egyptian Studies Association Publication 2, Oxbow Monograph 20. Oxford.
1995 "Introductory Paper for Seminar on Narrative in the New Kingdom." Typescript, fall seminar, Institute of Fine Arts, New York University.
1996 "Sexuality, Statuary, and the Afterlife: Scenes in the Tomb-Chapel of Pepyankh (Heny the Black)." In *Studies in Honor of William Kelly Simpson,* edited by Peter Der Manuelian, vol. 2, pp. 621–33. Boston.
1998 "The Interpretation of the Old Kingdom Pyramid Complex." In *Stationen: Beiträge zur Kulturge-*

schichte Ägyptens; Rainer
Stadelmann Gewidmet,
edited by Heike Guksch and
Daniel Polz, pp. 135–44.
Mainz.

Olivier, Guillaume A.
1795 Entomologie; ou, Histoire
naturelle des insectes. Cole-
opteres 3. Paris.

O'Mara, Patrick F.
1979 The Palermo Stone and the
Archaic Kings of Egypt. La
Canada.

Osing, Jürgen
1977 "Gottesland." In Lexikon
der Ägyptologie, vol. 2,
cols. 815–16.

Otto, Eberhard
1960 Das ägyptische Mundöff-
nungsritual. 2 vols. Ägyptologische Abhandlungen 3.
Wiesbaden.

Page, Anthea
1976 Egyptian Sculpture, Archaic
to Saite, from the Petrie
Collection. Warminster.

Page-Gasser, Madeleine, and
André B. Wiese
1997 Ägypten: Augenblicke der
Ewigkeit. Unbekannte
Schätze aus Schweizer Pri-
vatbesitz. With contribu-
tions by Thomas Schneider
and Silvia Winterhalter.
Exh. cat. Basel: Antikenmu-
seum Basel und Sammlung
Ludwig; Geneva: Musée
Rath. Mainz.

Paget, R. F. E., and A. A. Pirie
1898 The Tomb of Ptah-hetep.
Publications of the Egyptian
Research Account and
British School of Archaeol-
ogy in Egypt 2. London.
Published with The Rames-
seum, by James E. Quibell.

Parkinson, Richard B., and
Stephen Quirke
1995 Papyrus. With contributions by Ute Wartenberg
and Bridget Leach. London:
British Museum; and Austin.

Patch, D. Craig
1995 "A 'Lower Egyptian' Costume: Its Origin, Development, and Meaning." Journal
of the American Research
Center in Egypt 32, pp.
93–116.

Patočková, Barbora
1998 "Fragments de statues
découverts dans le mastaba
de Ptahchepses à Abousir."
In Les critères de datation
stylistiques à l'Ancien Empire, edited by Nicolas Grimal, pp. 227–33. Cairo.

Peck, William H.
1980 "Offerings for the Deceased."
Bulletin of the Detroit
Institute of Arts 58, pp.
102–8.

Perrot, Georges, and Charles
Chipiez
1882 Histoire de l'art dans
l'antiquité. Vol. 1, L'Égypte.
Paris.

Petrie, Hilda Urlin, and Margaret
Alice Murray
1952 Seven Memphite Tomb
Chapels. British School of
Egyptian Archaeology, Pub-
lications 65. London.

Petrie, W. M. F. (William
Matthews Flinders)
1883 The Pyramids and Temples
of Gizeh. London.
1892 Medum. London.
1894 A History of Egypt. Vol. 1,
From the Earliest Times to
the XVIth Dynasty. London.
1896 Koptos. London.
1898 Deshasheh 1897. Egypt
Exploration Fund Memoir
15. London.
1901 The Royal Tombs of the
Earliest Dynasties. Part II.
Excavation Memoirs 21.
London.
1901a Diospolis Parva: The Cemeteries of Abadiyeh and Hu,
1898–9. With chapters by
Arthur C. Mace. Memoir of
the Egypt Exploration Fund
20. London.
1903 Abydos Part II, 1903.
Memoir of the Egypt Exploration Fund 24. London.
1906 Researches in Sinaï. London
and New York.
1916 "New Portions of the
Annals." Ancient Egypt,
1916, pp. 114–20.
1917 Tools and Weapons Illustrated by the Egyptian
Collection in University College, London, and 2,000
Outlines from Other Sources.
British School of Archaeology in Egypt and Egyptian
Research Account, Publication 30. London.
1939 The Making of Egypt. London.
1990 The Pyramids and Temples
of Gizeh. New and revised
edition, updated by Zahi
Hawass. London.
1994 Amulets, Illustrated by the
Egyptian Collection in University College, London.
Reprint ed. London. First
published 1914.

Petrie, W. M. F., and Guy Brunton
1924 Sedment. Vol. 1. Publications of the Egyptian
Research Account and
British School of Archaeology in Egypt 34. London.

Petrie, W. M. F., and Ernest Mackay
1915 Heliopolis, Kafr Ammar,
and Shurafa. With chapters
by G. A. Wainwright, R.
Engelbach, D. E. Derry, and

W. W. Midgley. Publications
of the Egyptian Research
Account and British School
of Archaeology in Egypt 24.
London.

Petrie, W. M. F., Ernest Mackay,
and Gerald Wainwright
1910 Meydum and Memphis, III.
London.

Petrie, W. M. F., Gerald A. Wainwright, and Alan H.
Gardiner
1913 Tarkhan I and Memphis V.
British School of Archaeology in Egypt and Egyptian
Research Account, Publication 33. London.

Petrie, W. M. F., Gerald Wainwright, and Ernest Mackay
1912 The Labyrinth Gerzeh and
Mazghuneh. London.

Pfirsch, L.
1990 "Les bâtisseurs des pyramides de Saqqara." In
Saqqara: Aux origines de
l'Égypte pharaonique, Les
dossiers d'archéologie,
March–April, pp. 32–35.

Piehl, Karl
1886 Inscriptions hiéroglyphiques
recueillies en Europe et en
Égypte. Vol. 1. Leipzig.

Pierret, Paul
1873– Description sommaire des
95 salles du Musée égyptien, by
Emmanuel de Rougé. New
ed. revised by Pierret. Paris.
1882 Musée du Louvre: Catalogue de la Salle Historique.
2d ed. Paris.

Pijoán, José
1945 Summa Artis: Historia general del arte. Vol. 3, El arte
egipcio hasta la conquista
romana. Madrid.
1950 Summa Artis: Historia general del arte. Vol. 3, El arte
egipcio hasta la conquista
romana. 3d ed. Madrid.

Pirenne, Jacques
1961 Histoire de la civilisation de
l'Égypte ancienne. Vol. 1,
Premier cycle: Des origines
à la fin de l'Ancien Empire
(±2200 av. J.-C.). Neuchâtel
and Paris.

Porter, Bertha, and Rosalind L. B.
Moss
1934 Topographical Bibliography
of Ancient Egyptian Hieroglyphic Texts, Reliefs, and
Paintings. Vol. 4, Lower
and Middle Egypt. Oxford.
1937 Topographical Bibliography
of Ancient Egyptian Hieroglyphic Texts, Reliefs, and
Paintings. Vol. 5, Upper
Egypt: Sites. Oxford.
1951 Topographical Bibliography
of Ancient Egyptian Hieroglyphic Texts, Reliefs, and
Paintings. Vol. 7, Nubia,

Deserts, and Outside Egypt.
Oxford.
1974 Topographical Bibliography
of Ancient Egyptian Hieroglyphic Texts, Reliefs, and
Paintings. Vol. 3, Memphis,
part 1, Abu Rawash to
Abusir. 2d ed., revised by
Jaromír Málek. Oxford.
1978 Topographical Bibliography
of Ancient Egyptian Hieroglyphic Texts, Reliefs, and
Paintings. Vol. 3², Saqqâra
to Dahshûr, fasc. 1. Oxford.
1979 Topographical Bibliography
of Ancient Egyptian Hieroglyphic Texts, Reliefs, and
Paintings. Vol. 3², Memphis,
part 2, Saqqâra to Dahshûr,
fasc. 2. 2d ed., revised by
Jaromír Málek. Oxford.
1981 Topographical Bibliography
of Ancient Egyptian Hieroglyphic Texts, Reliefs, and
Paintings. Vol. 3², Memphis,
part 2, Saqqâra to Dahshûr,
fasc. 3. Second edition,
revised by Jaromír Málek.
Oxford.

Posener, Georges
1960 De la divinité du pharaon.
Paris.

Posener-Kriéger, Paule
1976 Les archives du temple
funéraire de Néferirkarê-
Kakaï (Les papyrus
d'Abousir): Traduction et
commentaire. 2 vols. Bibliothèque d'étude 65, nos.
1–2. Cairo.

Posener-Kriéger, Paule, and Jean
Louis de Cenival
1968 Hieratic Papyri in the Brit-
ish Museum. Fifth Series:
The Abu Sir Papyri.
London.

Potočková, B.
1998 "Fragments de statues
découverts dans le mastaba
de Ptahchepses à Abousir."
Paper given at the conference "Criteria for the Dating of Iconography and
Style of the Old Kingdom,
IFAO, Cairo, 10–13
November." Bibliothèque
d'étude 120, pp. 227–33.

Potts, Timothy
1990 Civilization: Ancient Treasures from the British
Museum. Exh. cat. Can-
berra: Australian National
Gallery; Melbourne:
Museum of Victoria.

Poulsen, Vagn
1968 Ägyptische Kunst: Altes und
Mittleres Reich. Königstein.

Preliminary Report
1976 Preliminary Report on
Czechoslovak Excavations
in the Mastaba of Ptahshepses at Abusir, by Z. Zába,

Miroslav Verner, et al. Prague: Universita Karlova.

Priese, Karl-Heinz

1984 *Die Opferkammer des Merib.* Berlin.

1991 [as editor]. *Ägyptisches Museum.* Exh. cat. Berlin: Museumsinsel Berlin, Staatliche Museen zu Berlin, Stiftung Preussischer Kulturbesitz. Mainz.

Profil du Metropolitan Museum

1981 *Profil du Metropolitan Museum of Art de New York: De Ramses à Picasso.* Exh. cat. Bordeaux: Galerie des Beaux-Arts. [Paris.]

de Putter, Thierry, and Christina Karlshausen

1992 *Les pierres utilisées dans la sculpture et l'architecture de l'Égypte pharaonique: Guide pratique illustré.* Brussels.

Quibell, James E.

1898 *El Kab.* Egyptian Research Account Memoir 3. London.

1900 *Hierakonpolis I.* Egyptian Research Account Memoir 4. London.

1902 *Hierakonpolis II.* Egyptian Research Account Memoir 5. London.

1909 *Excavations at Saqqara.* Vol. 3, *(1907–1908).* Cairo.

1913 *Excavations at Saqqara.* Vol. 5, *(1911–1912): The Tomb of Hesy.* Cairo.

1923 *Excavations at Saqqara.* Vol. 6, *(1912–1914): Archaic Mastabas.* Cairo.

1934 "Stone Vessels from the Step Pyramid." *Annales du Service des Antiquités de l'Égypte* 34, pp. 70–75.

Quibell, James E., and Angelo G. K. Hayter

1927 *Excavations at Saqqara.* Vol. 8, *Teti Pyramid, North Side.* Cairo.

Quirke, Stephen

1997 "Gods in the Temple of the King: Anubis at Lahun." In *The Temple in Ancient Egypt: New Discoveries and Recent Research,* edited by Stephen Quirke, pp. 24–48. London.

Quirke, Stephen, and A. Jeffrey Spencer, eds.

1992 *The British Museum Book of Ancient Egypt.* London.

Radwan, Ali

1983 *Die Kupfer- und Bronzegefäße Ägyptens: Von den Anfängen bis zum Beginn der Spätzeit.* Prähistorische Bronzefunde, ser. 2, 2. Munich.

1991 "Recent Excavations of Cairo University at Abusir." In International Congress of Egyptology (6th; Turin),

Sesto Congresso Internazionale di Egittologia . . . [Abstracts of Papers]. [Turin.]

1995 "A Cemetery of the 1st Dynasty." In *Gedenkschrift für Winfried Barta: Htp dj n hzj,* pp. 311–14. Frankfurt am Main.

Ranke, Hermann

1935 *Die ägyptischen Personennamen.* Vol. 1, *Verzeichnis der Namen.* Glückstadt.

1936 *The Art of Ancient Egypt: Architecture, Sculpture, Painting, Applied Art.* Vienna and London.

Redford, Donald B.

1992 *Egypt, Canaan, and Israel in Ancient Times.* Princeton.

Reeves, Nicholas

1990 *The Complete Tutankhamun: The King, The Tomb, The Royal Treasure.* London.

Reisner, George Andrew

n.d. "A History of the Giza Necropolis I.2." Typescript, Department of Egyptian, Nubian, and Ancient Near Eastern Art, Museum of Fine Arts, Boston.

1908 *The Early Dynastic Cemeteries of Naga-ed-Dêr.* Vol. 2, part 1. Leipzig.

1915 "Accessions to the Egyptian Department during 1914." *Bulletin of the Museum of Fine Arts* (Boston), 13, pp. 29–36.

1931 *Mycerinus: The Temples of the Third Pyramid at Giza.* Cambridge, Massachusetts. Reprinted 1995.

1932 *A Provincial Cemetery of the Pyramid Age, Naga-ed-Dêr.* University of California, Berkeley, University of California Publications: Egyptian Archaeology 6, part 3. Berkeley.

1934 "The Servants of the Ka." *Bulletin of the Museum of Fine Arts* (Boston) 32, no. 189 (February), pp. 2–12.

1936 *The Development of the Egyptian Tomb down to the Accession of Cheops.* Cambridge, Massachusetts.

1942 *A History of the Giza Necropolis, Volume I.* Cambridge, Massachusetts.

Reisner, George Andrew, and C. S. Fisher

1914 "Preliminary Report on the Work of the Harvard-Boston Expedition in 1911–13." *Annales du Service des Antiquités de l'Égypte* 13, pp. 227–52.

Reisner, George Andrew, and William Stevenson Smith

1955 *A History of the Giza*

Necropolis. Vol. 2, *The Tomb of Hetep-Heres the Mother of Cheops: A Study of Egyptian Civilization in the Old Kingdom.* Cambridge, Massachusetts.

Reuterswärd, Patrik

1958 *Studien zur Polychromie der Plastik.* Vol. 1, *Ägypten.* Stockholm.

Richardson, E. P.

1931 "An Egyptian Old Kingdom Relief." *Bulletin of the Detroit Institute of Arts* 12, pp. 33–36.

Richer, Paul Marie L. P.

1925 *Le nu dans l'art.* Vol. 1, *Les arts de l'Orient classique, Égypte-Chaldée-Assyrie.* Paris.

Ricke, Herbert

1944 *Bemerkungen zur ägyptischen Baukunst des Alten Reiches.* Vol. 1. Beiträge zur ägyptischen Bauforschung und Altertumskunde 4. Zürich.

1950 *Bemerkungen zur ägyptischen Baukunst des Alten Reiches.* Vol. 2. Beiträge zur ägyptischen Bauforschung und Altertumskunde 5. Cairo.

1965 *Das Sonnenheiligtum des Königs Userkaf.* Vol. 1, *Der Bau.* Wiesbaden.

1970 *Der Harmachistempel des Chefren in Giseh.* Beiträge zur ägyptischen Bauforschung und Altertumskunde 10. Wiesbaden.

1981 "Der Totentempel Amenophis' III: Baureste und Ergänzung." In *Untersuchungen im Totentempel Amenophis' III,* edited by Gerhard Haeny. Wiesbaden.

Rites de l'éternité

1982 *Les rites de l'éternité dans l'Égypte ancienne.* Exh. cat. Bayonne: Musée Bonnat.

Roberts, David

1995 "Age of Pyramids: Egypt's Old Kingdom." *National Geographic* 187 (January), pp. 2–43.

Robins, Gay

1994 *Proportion and Style in Ancient Egyptian Art.* Austin.

Roccati, Alessandro

1982 *La littérature historique sous l'Ancien Empire égyptien.* Paris.

1987 "Art et technique de l'écriture." In *Musée Égyptien de Turin, Civilisation des Égyptiens: La vie quotidienne,* edited by Anna Maria Donadoni Roveri, pp. 20–45. Milan.

Rochholz, Matthias

1994a "Sedfest, Sonnenheiligtum, und Pyramidenbezirk: Zur Deutung der Grabanlagen der Könige der 5. und 6. Dynastie." In *Ägyptische Tempel: Struktur, Funktion und Programm. Akten der Ägyptologischen Tempeltagungen in Gosen 1990 und in Mainz 1992,* edited by Rolf Gundlach and Matthias Rochholz, pp. 255–80. Hildesheimer ägyptologische Beiträge 37. Hildesheim.

1994b "Statuen und Statuendarstellungen im Grab des Pth-špss." *Studien zur altägyptischen Kultur* 21, pp. 259–73.

Roehrig, Catharine H.

1996 "Woman's Work: Some Occupations of Nonroyal Women as Depicted in Ancient Egyptian Art." In *Mistress of the House, Mistress of Heaven: Women in Ancient Egypt,* edited by Anne K. Capel and Glenn E. Markoe, pp. 13–24. Exh. cat. New York.

Romano, James F.

1979 *The Luxor Museum of Ancient Egyptian Art: Catalogue.* Cairo.

1985 "Comptes rendus: 'A Royal Statue Reattributed,' by W. V. Davies." *Journal of Egyptian Archaeology* 71, reviews supplement, pp. 38–41.

1990 *Daily Life of the Ancient Egyptians.* Pittsburgh.

1998 "Sixth Dynasty Royal Sculpture." In *Les critères de datation stylistiques à l'Ancien Empire,* edited by Nicolas Grimal, pp. 235–303. Cairo.

Rössler-Köhler, Ursula

1980 "Löwe, L.—Köpfe, L.—Statuen." In *Lexikon der Ägyptologie,* vol. 3, cols. 1080–90.

1989 "Die rundplastische Gruppe der Frau Pepi und des Mannes Ra-Schepses." *Mitteilungen des Deutschen Archäologischen Instituts, Abteilung Kairo* 45, pp. 261–74.

Roth, Ann Macy

1988 "The Organization of Royal Cemeteries at Saqqara in the Old Kingdom." *Journal of the American Research Center in Egypt* 25, pp. 201–14.

1991 *Egyptian Phyles in the Old Kingdom: The Evolution of a System of Social Organization.* Studies in Ancient

Oriental Civilization 48. Chicago.

1993 "Social Change in the Fourth Dynasty: The Spatial Organization of Pyramids, Tombs, and Cemeteries." *Journal of the American Research Center in Egypt* 30, pp. 33–55.

1994 "The Practical Economics of Tomb-Building in the Old Kingdom: A Visit to the Necropolis in a Carrying Chair." In *For His Ka: Essays Offered in Memory of Klaus Baer,* edited by David P. Silverman, pp. 227–40. Chicago.

1995 *A Cemetery of Palace Attendants: Including G 2084–2099, G 2230 + 2231, and G 2440.* Vol. 6 of *Giza Mastabas.* Boston.

1997 "Were Serdab Statues Cult Statues?" Paper adapted from a talk presented at the Glanville Seminar at Cambridge University, May 1997, pp. 1–14.

Rougé, Emmanuel, Vicomte de
1849 *Notice des monuments exposés dans la Galerie d'Antiquités Égyptiennes au Musée du Louvre.* Paris.

1852 *Notice des monuments exposés dans la Galerie d'Antiquités Égyptiennes au Musée du Louvre.* Paris.

1855 *Notice sommaire des monuments égyptiennes exposés dans les galeries du Musée du Louvre.* Paris.

1883 *Notice des monuments exposés dans la Galerie d'Antiquités Égyptiennes au Musée du Louvre.* 7th ed. Paris.

Rowe, Alan
1931 "The Eckley B. Coxe, Jr., Expedition Excavations at Meydûm, 1929–30." *Museum Journal* 22, pp. 5–84.

Russmann, Edna R.
1989 *Egyptian Sculpture: Cairo and Luxor.* Austin.

1995a "A Second Style in Egyptian Art of the Old Kingdom." *Mitteilungen des Deutschen Archäologischen Instituts, Abteilung Kairo* 51, pp. 269–79.

1995b "Two Heads of the Early Fourth Dynasty." In *Kunst des Alten Reiches: Symposium im Deutschen Archäologischen Institut Kairo am 29. und 30. Oktober 1991,* pp. 111–18. Sonderschrift, Deutsches Archäologisches Institut, Abteilung Kairo 28. Mainz.

Rzepka, Slawomir
1995 "Some Remarks on the Rock-Cut Group-Statues in the Old Kingdom." *Studien zur altägyptischen Kultur* 22, pp. 227–36.

1996 "The Pseudo-Groups of the Old Kingdom—a New Interpretation." *Studien zur altägyptischen Kultur* 23, pp. 335–47.

1998 "Some Remarks on Two Mycerinus Group Statues." *Göttinger Miszellen* 166, pp. 77–90.

Saad, Zaki Yusef
1947 *Royal Excavations at Saqqara and Helwan (1941–1945).* Cahier: Supplément aux Annales du Service des Antiquités de l'Égypte 3. Cairo.

1951 *Royal Excavations at Helwan (1945–1947).* Cahier: Supplément aux Annales du Service des Antiquités de l'Égypte 14. Cairo.

1957 *Ceiling Stelae in Second Dynasty Tombs from the Excavations at Helwan.* Cahier: Supplément aux Annales du Service des Antiquités de l'Égypte 21. Cairo.

1969 *The Excavations at Helwan: Art and Civilization in the First and Second Egyptian Dynasties.* Norman, Oklahoma.

Sabbahy, Lisa Kuchman
1982 "The Development of the Titulary and Iconography of the Ancient Egyptian Queen from Dynasty One to Early Dynasty Eighteen." Ph.D. dissertation, University of Toronto.

Sahrhage, Dietrich
1998 *Fischfang und Fischkult im Alten Ägypten.* Mainz.

Sainte Fare Garnot, Jean
1950 *L'Égypte.* Histoire générale de l'art. Paris.

Saleh, Abdel-Aziz
1974 "Excavations around Mycerinus Pyramid Complex." *Mitteilungen des Deutschen Archäologischen Instituts, Abteilung Kairo* 30, pp. 131–54.

Saleh, Mohammed
1977 *Three Old-Kingdom Tombs at Thebes: I. The Tomb of Unas-Ankh, no. 413; II. The Tomb of Khenty, no. 405; III. The Tomb of Ihy, no. 186.* Archäologische Veröffentlichungen 14. Mainz.

Saleh, Mohammed, and Hourig Sourouzian
1986 *Offizieller Katalog die Haupt-*

werke im Ägyptischen Museum Kairo. Mainz.

1987 *The Egyptian Museum Cairo: Official Catalogue.* Mainz.

Satzinger, Helmut
1987 *Ägyptisch-Orientalische Sammlung des Kunsthistorisches Museum Wien.* Exh. cat. Munich.

1994 *Das Kunsthistorische Museum in Wien: Die Ägyptisch-Orientalische Sammlung.* Zaberns Bildbände zur Archäologie 14. Mainz.

1998 "Living Images–The Private Statue." In *Egypt: The World of the Pharaohs,* edited by Regine Schulz and Matthias Seidel, pp. 94–103. Cologne.

Sauneron, Serge, and Henri Stierlin
1975 *Edfou et Philae: Derniers temples d'Égypte.* Paris.

Scamuzzi, Ernesto
1965 *Egyptian Art in the Egyptian Museum of Turin: Paintings, Sculpture, Furniture, Textiles, Ceramics, Papyri.* New York.

Schäfer, Heinrich
1908 *Priestergräber.* Leipzig.

1919 *Von ägyptischer Kunst, besonders der Zeichenkunst. Eine Einfuhrung in die Betrachtung ägyptischer Kunstwerke.* 2 vols. Leipzig.

1963 *Von ägyptischer Kunst: Eine Grundlage.* 4th ed., edited by Emma Brunner-Traut. Wiesbaden.

1974 *Principles of Egyptian Art.* Revised, edited, and translated from the 4th ed. of *Von ägyptischer Kunst,* with an introduction by John Baines; epilogue by Emma Brunner-Traut. Oxford.

1986 *Principles of Egyptian Art.* Reprint, with revisions by Emma Brunner-Traut, translated and edited by John Baines. Oxford.

Schäfer, Heinrich, and Walter Andrae
1925 *Die Kunst des Alten Orients.* Propyläen Kunstgeschichte 2. Berlin.

1934 *Die Kunst des Alten Orients.* [2d ed.] Berlin.

Scharff, Alexander
1940 "On the Statuary of the Old Kingdom." *Journal of Egyptian Archaeology* 26, pp. 41–50.

1947 *Das Grab als Wohnhaus in der ägyptischen Frühzeit.* Sitzungsberichte der Bayerischen Akademie der Wissenschaften, Philosophisch-historische Klasse,

Jahrgang 1944/46, vol. 6. Munich.

Scheel, Bernd
1989 *Egyptian Metalworking and Tools.* Shire Egyptology 13. Aylesbury.

Schmidt, Heike
1991 "Zur Determination und Ikonographie der sogenannten Ersatzköpfe 'm῾k nfr sḏm n rmṯ.'" *Studien zur altägyptischen Kultur* 18, pp. 331–48.

Schmitz, Bettina
1976 *Untersuchungen zum Titel sꜣ-njśwt "Königssohn."* Habelts Dissertationsdrucke: Reihe Ägyptologie, no. 2. Bonn.

1984 "Schesemtet." In *Lexikon der Ägyptologie,* vol. 5, cols. 587–90.

1986 "Sitzbild des Wesirs Hemiunu." In *Das Alte Reich: Ägypten im Zeitalter der Pyramiden; Roemer- und Pelizaeus-Museum,* edited by Arne Eggebrecht, pp. 36–39. Hildesheim.

1996 In *Pelizaeus-Museum Hildesheim: The Egyptian Collection.* Mainz.

Schneider, Hans
1997 *Life and Death under the Pharaohs: Egyptian Art from the National Museum of Antiquities in Leiden, The Netherlands.* Exh. cat. Perth: Western Australian Museum.

Schorsch, D.
1992 "Copper Ewers of Early Dynastic and Old Kingdom Egypt—an Investigation of the Art of Smithing in Antiquity." *Mitteilungen des Deutschen Archäologischen Instituts, Abteilung Kairo* 48, pp. 145–59.

Schoske, Sylvia
1986 "Staatliche Sammlung Ägyptischer Kunst." *Münchner Jahrbuch der bildenden Kunst,* pp. 213–22.

1990 *Schönheit, Abganz der Göttlichkeit, Kosmetik im Alten Ägypten.* With Alfred Grimm and Barbara Kreissl. Schriften aus der ägyptischen Sammlung 5. Munich.

Schoske, Sylvia, and Alfred Grimm
1995 *Staatliche Sammlung Ägyptischer Kunst München.* Zaberns Bildmande zur Archäologie 31. Mainz.

Schott, Erika
1972 "Die heilige Vase des Amon." *Zeitschrift für ägyptische Sprache und Altertumskunde* 98, pp. 34–50.

Schott, Siegfried
1950 "Bemerkungen zum ägyp-

tischen Pyramidenkult." In *Bemerkungen zur ägyptischen Baukunst des Alten Reiches,* edited by Herbert Ricke, vol. 2, pp. 133–224. Cairo.

1965 "Aufnahmen vom Hungersnotrelief aus dem Aufweg der Unaspyramide." *Revue d'égyptologie* 17, pp. 7–13.

1970 "Ägyptische Quellen zum Plan des Sphinxtempels." In *Der Harmachistempel des Chefren in Giseh,* edited by Herbert Ricke, pp. 47–79. Wiesbaden.

Schulz, Regine
1995 "Überlegungen zu einigen Kunstwerken des Alten Reiches im Pelizaeus-Museum, Hildesheim." In *Kunst des Alten Reiches: Symposium im Deutschen Archäologischen Institut Kairo am 29. und 30. Oktober 1991,* pp. 119–31. Sonderschrift, Deutsches Archäologisches Institut, Abteilung Kairo 28. Mainz.

1999 "Figures masculines nues de l'Ancien Empire." In *L'art de l'Ancien Empire égyptien: Actes du Colloque, Musée du Louvre, 3–4 avril 1998.* Paris.

Schulz, Regine, and Matthias Seidel, eds.
1998 *Ägypten: Die Welt der Pharaonen.* Cologne.

Schürmann, Wolfgang
1983 *Die Reliefs aus dem Grab des Pyramidenvorstehers Ii-nefret.* Karlsruhe.

Scott, Gerry D., III
1986 *Ancient Egyptian Art at Yale.* New Haven: Yale University Art Gallery.

1989 "The History and Development of the Ancient Egyptian Scribe Statue." 4 vols. Ph.D. dissertation, Yale University, New Haven.

Scott, Nora E.
1944 *The Home Life of the Ancient Egyptians.* Metropolitan Museum Picture Book. New York.

1948 "Memy-Sabu and His Wife." *Metropolitan Museum of Art Bulletin,* n.s., 7 (November), pp. 95–100.

1952 "Two Statue Groups of the V Dynasty." *Metropolitan Museum of Art Bulletin,* n.s., 11 (December), pp. 116–22.

1973 "The Daily Life of the Ancient Egyptians." *Metropolitan Museum of Art Bulletin,* n.s., 31 (spring), pp. 123–72.

Scott-Moncrieff, Philip D.
1911 *Hieroglyphic Texts from*

Egyptian Stelae, &c., in the British Museum. London.

Seidel, Matthias
1996 *Die königlichen Statuengruppen.* Vol. 1, *Die Denkmaler vom Alten Reich bis zum Ende der 18. Dynastie.* Hildesheimer Ägyptologische Beiträge 42. Hildesheim.

Seidelmayer, Stephan
1998 "Ägyptens Weg zur Hochkultur." In *Ägypten: Die Welt der Pharaonen,* edited by Regine Schulz and Matthias Seidel. Cologne.

Seipel, Wilfried
1975 "Anchnesmerire I. u. II." In *Lexikon der Ägyptologie,* vol. 1, cols. 263–64.

1975a "Kleinkunst und Grabmobiliar." In *Das Alte Ägypten,* by Claude Vandersleyen, pp. 359–83. Berlin.

1980 *Untersuchungen zu den ägyptischen Königinnen der Frühzeit und des Alten Reiches: Quellen und historische Einordnung.* Vienna.

1992 *Gott, Mensch, Pharao: Viertausend Jahre Menschenbild in der Skulptur des Alten Ägypten.* Exh. cat. Vienna: Kunsthistorisches Museum Wien.

1993 *Götter, Menschen, Pharaonen: 3500 Jahre ägyptische Kultur, Meisterwerke aus der ägyptisch-orientalischen Sammlung des Kunsthistorisches Museums Wien.* Stuttgart.

1995 "Wasser und Wein im pharaonischen Ägypten." In *Wasser und Wein,* edited by Werner Hofmann, pp. 43–54. Vienna.

Sethe, Kurt
1903 *Urkunden des Alten Reiches.* Vol. 1. Leipzig.

1922 *Die altägyptischen Pyramidentexte.* Vol. 3. Leipzig.

1933 *Urkunden des Alten Reiches.* Vol. 2. Leipzig.

Sharawi, G., and Yvonne M. Harpur
1988 "The Identity and Positions of Relief Fragments in Museums and Private Collections: Reliefs from Various Tombs at Saqqâra." *Journal of Egyptian Archaeology* 74, pp. 57–67.

Shoukry, Muhammad Anwar
1951 *Die Privatgrabstatue im Alten Reich.* Cahier: Supplément aux Annales du Service des Antiquités de l'Egypte 15. Cairo.

Siècle de fouilles
1981 *Un siècle de fouilles françaises en Égypte, 1880–*

1980: À l'occasion du centenaire de l'École du Caire (IFAO). Exh. cat. Paris: Musée d'Art et d'Essai; Tokyo: Palais de Tokyo. Cairo.

Simpson, William Kelly
1949 "A IV Dynasty Portrait Head." *Metropolitan Museum of Art Bulletin,* n.s., 7 (June), pp. 286–92.

1976 *The Mastabas of Qar and Idu, G 7101 and 7102.* Vol. 2 of *Giza Mastabas.* Boston.

1978 *The Mastabas of Kawab, Khafkhufu I and II: G 7110-20, 7130-40, and 7150, and Subsidiary Mastabas of Street G7100.* Vol. 3 of *Giza Mastabas.* Boston.

1980 *Mastabas of the Western Cemetery, I.* Vol. 4 of *Giza Mastabas.* Boston.

1982 "Nefermaat." In *Lexikon der Ägyptologie,* vol. 4, cols. 376–77.

Smith, William Stevenson
1936 "Appendix C: Topography of the Old Kingdom Cemetery at Saqqarah." In George A. Reisner, *The Development of the Egyptian Tomb Down to the Accession of Cheops.* Cambridge, Massachusetts.

1937 "The Paintings of the Chapel of Atet at Mêdûm." *Journal of Egyptian Archaeology* 23, pp. 17–26.

1942 "The Origin of Some Unidentified Old Kingdom Reliefs." *American Journal of Archaeology* 46, pp. 509–31.

1946 *A History of Egyptian Sculpture and Painting in the Old Kingdom.* Boston and London. Reprinted, Oxford, 1978.

1949 *A History of Egyptian Sculpture and Painting in the Old Kingdom.* 2d ed. Boston and London. Reprinted, New York, 1978.

1952 *Ancient Egypt as Represented in the Museum of Fine Arts.* 3d ed. Boston.

1952a "Inscriptional Evidence for the History Dynasty." *Journal of Near Eastern Studies* 11, no. 2 (April), pp. 113–28.

1958 *The Art and Architecture of Ancient Egypt.* Harmondsworth and Baltimore.

1960 *Ancient Egypt as Represented in the Museum of Fine Arts.* 4th ed. Boston.

1965 *Interconnections in the Ancient Near East: A Study of Relationships between*

the Arts of Egypt, the Aegean, and Western Asia. New Haven.

1971 "The Old Kingdom in Egypt and the Beginning of the First Intermediate Period." In *The Cambridge Ancient History,* vol. 1, part 2, *Early History of the Middle East,* chap. 14, pp. 145–207. 3d ed. Cambridge.

1981 *The Art and Architecture of Ancient Egypt.* 2d ed., revised by William Kelly Simpson. London. Reprinted 1990.

Smyth, Charles Piazzi
1880 *Our Inheritance in the Great Pyramid.* 4th ed. London. First published London, 1864.

Sourouzian, Hourig
1995 "L'iconographie du roi dans la statuaire des trois premières dynasties." In *Kunst des Alten Reiches Symposium im Deutschen Archäologischen Institut Kairo am 29. und 30. Oktober 1991,* pp. 133–54. Sonderschrift des Deutsches Archäologisches Instituts, Abteilung Kairo 28. Mainz.

1998 "Concordances et écarts entre statuaire et représentations à deux dimensions des particuliers de l'époque archaïque." In *Les critères de datation stylistiques à l'Ancien Empire,* edited by Nicolas Grimal, pp. 305–52. Cairo.

Spalinger, Gretchen L.
1982 "Stone Vessels." In *Egypt's Golden Age: The Art of Living in the New Kingdom, 1558–1085 B.C.,* pp. 126–27. Exh. cat. Boston: Museum of Fine Arts.

Spanel, Donald
1988 *Through Ancient Eyes: Egyptian Portraiture.* Exh. cat. Birmingham, Alabama: Birmingham Museum of Art.

Spencer, A. Jeffrey
1979 *Brick Architecture in Ancient Egypt.* Warminster.

1980 *Early Dynastic Objects: Catalogue of Egyptian Antiquities in the British Museum.* Vol. 5. London.

1993 *Early Egypt: The Rise of Civilisation in the Nile Valley.* London: British Museum.

1996 [as editor]. *Aspects of Early Egypt.* London: British Museum.

Spiegel, Joachim
1938 *Kurze Führer durch das Ägyptische Museum der Universität Leipzig.* Leipzig.

1953 *Das Werden der altägyptischen Hochkultur.* Heidelberg.

Spiegelberg, Wilhelm
1918 "Der ägyptische Possessivartikel." *Zeitschrift für ägyptische Sprache und Altertumskunde* 54, pp. 104–10.

Stadelmann, Rainer
1981a "Die ḫntjw-š, der Königsbezirk š n pr-ꜥꜣ und die Namen der Grabanlagen der Frühzeit." *Bulletin du centenaire* (IFAO, Cairo), 1981, pp. 153–64.
1981b "La ville de pyramide à l'Ancien Empire." *Revue d'égyptologie* 33, pp. 67–77.
1982 "Die Pyramiden des Snofru in Dahschur: Erste Bericht über die Ausgrabungen an der nördlichen Steinpyramide." *Mitteilungen des Deutschen Archäologischen Instituts, Abteilung Kairo* 38, pp. 380–93. Includes "Marques et graffiti à Dahchour Nord," by Hourig Sourouzian.
1983 "Die Pyramiden des Snofru in Dahschur: Zweiter Bericht über die Ausgrabungen and der nördlichen Steinpyramide mit einem Exkurs über Scheintür oder Stelen im Totentempel des AR." *Mitteilungen des Deutschen Archäologischen Instituts, Abteilung Kairo* 39, pp. 225–41.
1984a "Khaefkhufu = Chephren: Beiträge zur Geschichte der 4. Dynastie." *Studien zur altägyptischen Kultur* 11, pp. 165–72.
1984b "Sonnenheiligtum." In *Lexikon der Ägyptologie,* vol. 5, cols. 1094–99.
1985a *Die ägyptischen Pyramiden: Vom Ziegelbau zum Weltwunder.* Darmstadt.
1985b "Taltempel." In *Lexikon der Ägyptologie,* vol. 6 (1986), cols. 189–93.
1985c "Die Oberbauten der Königsgräber der 2. Dynastie in Saqqara." In *Mélanges Gamal eddin Mokhtar,* edited by Paule Posener-Kriéger, vol. 2, pp. 295–307. Bibliothèque d'étude 97. Cairo.
1987 "Königinnengrab und Pyramidenbezirk im Alten Reich." *Annales du Service des Antiquités de l'Égypte* 71, pp. 251–60.
1990 *Die grossen Pyramiden von Giza.* Graz.
1991 *Die ägyptischen Pyramiden: Vom Ziegelbau zum Welt-*

wunder. Kulturgeschichte der Antiken Welt 30. 2d ed., revised. Mainz.
1993 "Pyramiden und Nekropole des Snofru in Dahschur: Dritter Vorbericht über die Grabungen des Deutschen Archäologischen Instituts in Dahschur." *Mitteilungen des Deutschen Archäologischen Instituts, Abteilung Kairo* 49, pp. 259–94.
1994 "Die sogenannten Luftkanäle der Cheopspyramide: Modellkorridore für den Aufstieg des Königs zum Himmel." *Mitteilungen des Deutschen Archäologischen Instituts, Abteilung Kairo* 50, pp. 285–94.
1994a "König Teti und der Beginn der 6. Dynastie." In *Hommages à Jean Leclant,* vol. 1, *Études pharaoniques,* edited by Catherine Berger, Gisèle Clerc, and Nicolas Grimal, pp. 327–35. Bibliothèque d'étude 106. Cairo.
1995a "Builders of the Pyramids." In *Civilizations of the Ancient Near East,* edited by Jack M. Sasson, vol. 2, pp. 719–34. New York.
1995b "Der Strenge Stil der frühen Vierten Dynastie." In *Kunst des Alten Reiches: Symposium im Deutschen Archäologischen Institut Kairo am 29. und 30. Oktober 1991,* pp. 154–66. Sonderschrift, Deutsches Archäologisches Institut, Abteilung Kairo, 28. Mainz.
1996 "Origins and Development of the Funerary Complex of Djoser." In *Studies in Honor of William Kelly Simpson,* edited by Peter Der Manuelian, vol. 1, pp. 787–800. Boston.
1997a *Die ägyptischen Pyramiden: Vom Ziegelbau zum Weltwunder.* Kulturgeschichte der Antiken Welt 30. 3d ed., revised. Mainz.
1997b "The Development of the Pyramid Temple in the Fourth Dynasty." In *The Temple in Ancient Egypt: New Discoveries and Recent Research,* edited by Stephen Quirke, pp. 1–16. London.
1998a "Formale Kriterien zur Datierung der königlichen Plastik der 4. Dynastie." In *Les critères de datation stylistiques à l'Ancien Empire,* edited by Nicolas Grimal, pp. 353–87. Cairo.
1998b "La tombe royale au temps des pyramides." In *Egypt:*

The World of the Pharaohs, edited by Regine Schulz and Matthias Seidel, pp. 47–77. Cologne.

Stadelmann, Rainer, Nicole Alexanian, Herbert Ernst, Günter Heindl, and Dietrich Raue
1993 "Pyramiden und Nekropole des Snofru in Dahschur: Dritter Vorbericht über die Grabungen des Deutschen Archäologischen Instituts in Dahschur." *Mitteilungen des Deutschen Archäologischen Instituts, Abteilung Kairo* 49, pp. 259–94.

Staehelin, Elisabeth
1966 *Untersuchungen zur ägyptischen Tracht im Alten Reich.* Münchner ägyptologische Studien 8. Berlin.

Steckeweh, Hans
1936 *Die Fürstengräber von Qaw.* Veröffentlichung der Ernst von Sieglin Expedition 6. Leipzig.

Steindorff, Georg
n.d. "Giza." Unpublished journal in the archives of the Ägyptisches Museum der Universität Leipzig.
1910 "Der Ka und die Grabstatuen." *Zeitschrift für ägyptische Sprache und Altertumskunde* 48, pp. 152–59.
1913 *Das Grab des Ti.* Veröffentlichungen der Ernst von Sieglin Expedition in Ägypten 2. Leipzig.
1923 *Die Kunst der Ägypter.* Leipzig.
1937 "Ein Reliefbildnis des Prinzen Hemiun." *Zeitschrift für ägyptische Sprache und Altertumskunde* 73, pp. 120–21.
1951 *A Royal Head from Ancient Egypt.* Translation by Richard Ettinghausen. Freer Gallery of Art Occasional Papers 1, no. 5. Washington, D.C.

Steindorff, Georg, and Uvo Hölscher
1991 *Die Mastabas westlich der Cheopspyramide: Nach des Ergebnissen der in den Jahren 1903–1907 im Auftrag der Universität Leipzig und des Hildesheimer Pelizaeus-Museums unternommenen Grabungen in Giza.* Edited by Alfred Grimm. 2 vols. Münchener ägyptologische Untersuchungen 2. Frankfurt am Main.

Steinmann, Frank
1991 "Untersuchungen zu den in der handwerklich-künst-

lerischen Produktion beschäftigten Personen und Berufsgruppen des Neuen Reiches." *Zeitschrift für ägyptische Sprache und Altertumskunde* 118, pp. 149–61.

Stewart, H. M.
1979 *Egyptian Stelae, Reliefs, and Paintings from the Petrie Collection,* Part 2: *Archaic Period to Second Intermediate Period.* London.

Stocks, Denys
1986 "Egyptian Technology II: Stone Vessel Manufacture." *Popular Archaeology,* May, pp. 14–18.

Störk, Lothar
1984a "Rind." In *Lexikon der Ägyptologie,* vol. 5, cols. 257–63.
1984b "Stachelschwein." In *Lexikon der Ägyptologie,* vol. 5, cols. 1232–33.
1986 "Ziege." In *Lexikon der Ägyptologie,* vol. 6, cols. 1400–1401.

Strudwick, Nigel
1985 *The Administration of Egypt in the Old Kingdom: The Highest Titles and Their Holders.* London and Boston.

Tacke, Nikolaus
1996 "Die Entwicklung der Mumienmaske im Alten Reich." *Mitteilungen des Deutschen Archäologischen Instituts, Abteilung Kairo* 52, pp. 307–36.

Tardy
1977 *Les ivoires.* Vol. 2. Paris.

Tawfik, Sayed
1991 "Recently Excavated Ramesside Tombs at Saqqara, I: Architecture." *Mitteilungen des Deutschen Archäologischen Instituts, Abteilung Kairo* 47, pp. 403–9.

Tefnin, Roland
1987 "Le roi, la belle, et la mort: Modes d'expression du corps en Égypte pharaonique." *Revue de l'Université de Bruxelles,* no. 3–4, pp. 165–66.
1988 *Statues et statuettes de l'Ancienne Égypte.* Brussels.
1991 *Art et magie au temps des pyramides: L'énigme des têtes dites de "remplacement."* Monumenta Aegyptiaca 5. Brussels.
1991a "Les têtes magiques de Gizeh." *Bulletin de la Société Française d'Égyptologie,* no. 120 (March), pp. 25–37.

Terrace, Edward L. B.
1961 "A Fragmentary Triad of

King Mycerinus." *Bulletin
of the Museum of Fine
Arts* (Boston) 59, no. 316,
pp. 40–49.
1967 *Egyptian Paintings of the
Middle Kingdom: The
Tomb of Djehuty-Nekht.*
New York.
Terrace, Edward L. B., and Henry
G. Fischer
1970 *Treasures of Egyptian Art
from the Cairo Museum:
A Centennial Exhibition,
1970–1971.* Exh. cat.
Boston: Museum of Fine
Arts.
Thomas, Nancy
1995 *The American Discovery of
Ancient Egypt.* With essays
by Gerry D. Scott, III, and
Bruce G. Trigger. Exh. cat.
Los Angeles County Museum
of Art; Saint Louis Art
Museum; and Indianapolis
Museum of Art.
1996 [as editor]. *The American
Discovery of Ancient Egypt:
Essays.* With essays by
James P. Allen, Dorothea
Arnold et al. Los Angeles.
Treasures of the British Museum
1990 *Daiei Hakubutsukan gei-
jutsu to ningen ten / The
Treasures of the British
Museum: Art and Man.*
Exh. cat. Setagaya Art
Museum; Yamaguchi Pre-
fectural Museum of Art;
Osaka: National Museum
of Art. N.p.
Troy, Lana
1986 *Patterns of Queenship in
Ancient Egyptian Myth and
History.* Uppsala.
Vachala, Břetislav
1992 "Fragment einer Töpfers-
zene aus der Ptahschepses-
Mastaba." *Göttinger
Miszellen* 130, pp. 109–11.
1995 "Eine Darstellung des
Senet-Brettspiels aus der
Ptahschepses-Mastaba in
Abusir." *Göttinger Mis-
zellen* 148, pp. 105–8.
Vachala, Břetislav, and Dina Faltings
1995 "Töpferei und Brauerei im
AR—einige Relieffragmente
aus der Mastaba des Ptah-
schepses in Abusir." *Mit-
teilungen des Deutschen
Archäologischen Instituts,
Abteilung Kairo* 51,
pp. 281–86.
Valbelle, Dominique
1998 *Histoire de l'état pharao-
nique.* Paris.
Valbelle, Dominique, and Charles
Bonnet
1996 *Le sanctuaire d'Hathor,
maîtresse de la turquoise:
Sérabit el-Khadim au
Moyen Empire.* Paris.

Valloggia, Michel
1978 "Rapport préliminaire sur
la première campagne de
fouilles à Balat (Oasis de
Dakhleh)." *Bulletin de
l'Institut Français d'Archéologie Orientale* 78, pp.
65–80.
1980 "Deux objets thériomorphes
découverts dans le mastaba
V de Balat." In *Livre du
centenaire, 1880–1980,*
edited by Jean Vercoutter,
pp. 143–51. Mémoires pub-
liés par les Membres de
l'Institut Français d'Archéologie Orientale du Caire
104. Cairo.
1984 "Égypte pharaonique:
Livres." *Chronique
d'Égypte* 59, pp. 93–96.
1986 *Le Mastaba de Medou-
Nefer.* With the collaboration of Nessim H. Henein.
2 vols. Fouilles de l'Institut
Français d'Archéologie Orientale 31, nos. 1–2. Balat 1.
Cairo.
1989 "Un groupe statuaire
découvert dans le mastaba
de Pepui-jma à Balat." *Bulletin de l'Institut Français
d'Archéologie Orientale* 89,
pp. 271–82.
1994 "Le complexe funéraire de
Radjedef à Abou-Roasch:
État de la question et per-
spectives de recherches."
*Bulletin de la Société Fran-
çaise d'Égyptologie* 130,
pp. 5–17.
1995 "Fouilles archéologiques à
Abu Rawash (Égypte): Rap-
port préliminaire de la campagne 1995." *Genava* 43,
pp. 65–72.
1997 "La descenderie de la pyramide de Radjedef à Abu
Rawash." In *Études sur
l'Ancien Empire et la nécropole de Saqqâra dédiées à
Jean-Philippe Lauer,* edited
by Catherine Berger and
Bernard Mathieu, pp. 417–
28. Orientalia Monspeliensia, 9. Montpellier: Université Paul Valéry.
Vandersleyen, Claude
1973 "Les proportions relatives
des personnages dans les
statues-groupes." *Chro-
nique d'Égypte* 48, pp.
13–25.
1975a *Das Alte Ägypten.* With
contributions by Hartwig
Altenmüller, Dieter Arnold,
et al. Propyläen Kunst-
geschichte 15. Berlin.
1975b "Objectivité des portraits
égyptiens." *Bulletin de la
Société Française d'Égyp-
tologie* 73, pp. 5–27.

1977 "Ersatzkopf." In *Lexikon
der Ägyptologie,* vol. 2,
cols. 11–14.
1980 "La statue d'Amenophis I
(Turin 1372)." *Orients
Antiquus* 19, pp. 133–37.
1982 "Porträt." In *Lexikon der
Ägyptologie,* vol. 4, cols.
1074–80.
1983 "La date du Cheikh el-Beled
(Caire CG 34)." *Journal of
Egyptian Archaeology* 69,
pp. 61–65.
1987 "Une tête de Chéphren en
granit rose." *Revue d'égyptologie* 38, pp. 194–97.
1997 "Ramsès II admirait
Sésostris Iᵉʳ." In *Chief of
Seers: Egyptian Studies in
Memory of Cyril Aldred,*
pp. 285–90. London.
Vandier, Jacques
1948 *Musée du Louvre, Le
Départment des Antiquités
Égyptiennes: Guide som-
maire.* Paris.
1949 "Portraits de rois." *L'amour
de l'art* 18, no. 3, pp. 217–
22.
1950 "Acquisitions du Département des Antiquités Égyp-
tiennes." *Bulletin des
Musées de France,* no. 2,
pp. 25–30.
1951 *La sculpture égyptienne.*
Paris.
1952a *Manuel d'archéologie égyptienne.* Vol. 1, *Les époques
de formation,* part 1, *La
préhistoire.* Paris.
1952b *Manuel d'archéologie égyptienne.* Vol. 1, *Les époques
de formation,* part 2, *Les
trois premières dynasties.*
Paris.
1952c *Musée du Louvre, Le
Départment des Antiquités
Égyptiennes: Guide som-
maire.* Paris.
1954 *Manuel d'archéologie égyptienne.* Vol. 2, *Les grandes
époques,* part 2, *L'architecture funéraire.* Paris.
1958 *Manuel d'archéologie égyptienne.* Vol. 3, *Les grandes
époques: La statuaire.* Paris.
1964 *Manuel d'archéologie égyptienne.* Vol. 4, *Bas relief et
peintures, scènes des la vie
quotidienne.* Paris.
1968a "Nouvelles acquisitions,
Musée du Louvre, Départe-
ment des Antiquités Égyptiennes." *Revue du Louvre,*
no. 2, p. 108.
1968b "Une stèle égyptienne portant un nouveau nom royal
de la troisième dynastie."
*Comptes rendus des séances
de l'Académie des Inscriptions et Belles-Lettres,* July,
pp. 16–22.

1969 *Manuel d'archéologie égyptienne.* Vol. 5, *Bas reliefs et
peintures, scènes de la vie
quotidienne.* Paris.
1970 *Musée du Louvre, Le
Département des Antiquités
égyptiennes: Guide som-
maire.* Paris.
1974 "La publication des textes
du Musée du Louvre." In
*Textes et langages de l'Égypte
pharaonique, cent cinquante
années de recherches, 1822–
1972: Hommage à Jean-
François Champollion,*
pp. 159–67. Bibliothèque
d'étude 64, no. 3. Cairo.
Vandier, Jacques, and Emmanuel
Sougez
n.d. *Le Louvre.* Vol. 1, *Sculpture
égyptienne.* Babigny [1950?].
Vandier d'Abbadie, Jeanne
1972 *Catalogue des objets de toi-
lette égyptiens.* Paris: Musée
du Louvre.
Varille, Alexandre
1938 *La tombe de Ni-ankh-Pepi
à Zàouyet el-Maytîn.* Mémoires de l'Institut Français
du Caire 70. Cairo.
Vercoutter, Jean
1980a *L'école du Caire, 1880–
1980.* Cairo.
1980b [as editor]. *Livre du Centenaire, 1880–1980.* Mém-
oires publiés par les Membres
de l'Institut Français d'Archéologie Orientale du Caire
104. Cairo.
1985 "Les 'affamés' d'Ounas et le
changement climatique de
la fin de l'Ancien Empire."
In *Mélanges Gamal eddin
Mokhtar,* edited by Paule
Posener-Kriéger, vol. 2,
pp. 327–37. Bibliothèque
d'étude 97. Cairo.
1986 *À la recherche de l'Égypte
oubliée.* Paris.
1992 *L'Egypte et la vallée du Nil.*
Vol. 1, *Des origines à la fin
de l'Ancien Empire, 12,000–
2000 av. J.-C.* Paris.
1993 "Le rôle des artisans dans la
civilisation égyptienne."
Chronique d'Égypte 68,
pp. 70–83.
1998 *À la recherche de l'Égypte
oubliée.* New ed. Revised by
Anne Gout. Paris.
Verhoeven, Ursula
1984 "Semat-weret." In *Lexikon
der Ägyptologie,* vol. 5,
cols. 836–37.
Verner, Miroslav
1979 "Neue Papyrusfunde in
Abusir." *Revue d'égyptologie* 31, pp. 98–100.
1984 "Excavations at Abusir:
Season 1982—Preliminary
Report." *Zeitschrift für
ägyptische Sprache und*

Altertumskunde 111, pp. 70–78.

1985a "Les sculptures de Rênef-eref decouvertes à Abousir." *Bulletin de l'Institut Français d'Archéologie Orientale* 85, pp. 267–80.

1985b "Les statuettes de prisonniers en bois d'Abousir." *Revue d'égyptologie* 36, pp. 145–52.

1986a *Abusir I. The Mastaba of Ptahshepses: Reliefs.* Vol. 1. Prague.

1986b "Excavations at Abusir: Season 1984/1985—Preliminary Report." *Zeitschrift für ägyptische Sprache und Altertumskunde* 113, pp. 154–60.

1986c "Supplément aux sculptures de Rêneferef découvertes à Abousir." *Bulletin de l'Institut Français d'Archéologie Orientale* 86, pp. 361–66.

1992a *Abusir* II: *Baugraffiti der Ptahschepses-Mastaba.* Prague.

1992b "Funerary Boats of Neferirkare and Raneferef." In *The Intellectual Heritage of Egypt: Studies Presented to László Kákosy by Friends and Colleagues on the Occasion of His 60th Birthday,* pp. 599f. Studia Aegyptiaca 14. Budapest.

1994a *Forgotten Pharaohs, Lost Pyramids: Abusir.* Prague.

1994b "The Tomb of Fetekta and a Late Dyn. 5–Early Dyn. 6 Cemetery in South Abusir." *Mitteilungen des Deutschen Archäologischen Instituts, Abteilung Kairo* 50, pp. 295–305.

1995 *Abusir III: The Pyramid Complex of Khentkaus.* With contributions by Paule Posener-Kriéger and Peter Jánosi. Prague.

Verner, Miroslav, et al.
1990 *Unearthing Ancient Egypt, 1958–1988.* Prague.

Vogelsang-Eastwood, Gillian
1993 *Pharaonic Egyptian Clothing.* Leiden and New York.

van de Walle, Baudouin
1930 *Le mastaba de Neferirtenef aux Musées Royaux d'Art et d'Histoire à Bruxelles.* Brussels.

1957 "Remarques sur l'origine et le sens des défilés de domaines dans les mastabas de l'Ancien Empire." *Mitteilungen des Deutschen Archäologischen Instituts, Abteilung Kairo* 15, pp. 288–96.

1978 *La chapelle funéraire de Neferirtenef.* Brussels.

Ward, Roger B., and Patricia J. Fidler, comps. and eds.
1993 *The Nelson-Atkins Museum of Art: A Handbook of the Collection.* New York.

Warren, Peter
1969 *Minoan Stone Vases.* Cambridge.

Weeks, Kent R.
1994 *Mastabas of Cemetery G 6000: Including G 6010 (Neferbauptah); G 6020 (Iymery); G 6030 (Ity); G 6040 (Shepseskafankh).* Vol. 5 of *Giza Mastabas.* Boston.

Weigall, Arthur E. P. B.
1924 *Ancient Egyptian Works of Art.* London.

Weill, Raymond
1908 *Les origines de l'Égypte pharaonique, première partie: La IIᵉ et IIIᵉ dynasties.* Annales du Musée Guimet; Bibliothèque d'étude 25. Paris. Also issued as the author's thesis under title, *Des monuments et de l'histoire des IIᵉ et IIIᵉ dynasties égyptiennes.*

1911– "Monuments nouveaux
12   des premières dynasties." *Sphinx* 15, pp. 1–35.

1938 "Notes sur les monuments de la pyramide à degrés de Saqqarah d'après les publications d'ensemble." *Revue d'égyptologie* 3, pp. 115–27.

Wenig, Steffen
1966 *Die Jahreszeitenreliefs aus dem Sonnenheiligtum des Königs Ne-user-re.* Kleine Schriften 11. Berlin: Staatliche Museen zu Berlin.

Westendorf, Wolfhart
1975 "Beschneidung." In *Lexikon der Ägyptologie,* vol. 1, cols. 727–29.

1991 "Die 'Löwenmöbelfolge' und die Himmels-Hieroglyphe." *Mitteilungen des Deutschen Archäologischen Instituts Abteilung Kairo* 47, pp. 427–34.

Wiebach, Silvia
1981 *Die ägyptische Scheintür: Morphologische Studien zur Entwicklung und Bedeutung der Hauptkultstelle in den Privat-Gräbern des Alten Reiches.* Hamburg. Doctoral thesis, Universität Hamburg.

Wiedemann, A.
1898 "Zwei ägyptische Statuen des Museums zu Leiden." *Orientalische Literaturzeitung* 15, pp. 269–73.

Wild, Henri
1953 *Le tombeau de Ti. Vol. 2, La chapelle* [part 1]. Mémoires publiés par les membres de

l'Institut Français d'Archéologie Orientale du Caire, 65, fasc. 2. Cairo.

1966 *Le tombeau de Ti. Vol. 3, La chapelle* [part 2]. Mémoires publiés par les membres de l'Institut Français d'Archéologie Orientale du Caire 65, fasc. 3. Cairo.

Wildung, Dietrich
1969 *Die Rolle ägyptischer Könige im Bewusstsein ihrer Nachwelt. Vol. 1, Posthume Quellen über die Könige der ersten vier Dynastien.* Münchener ägyptologische Studien 17. Berlin.

1972 "Two Representations of Gods from Early Old Kingdom." *Miscellanea Wilbouriana* 1, pp. 145–60.

1973 "Der König Ägyptens als Herr der Welt?" *Archiv für Orientforschung* 24, pp. 108–16.

1980a *Fünf Jahre: Neuerwerbungen der Staatlichen Sammlung Ägyptischer Kunst München, 1976–1980.* Mainz.

1980b "Berichte der Staatlichen Kunstsammlungen (Neuerwerbungen): Staatliche Sammlung Ägyptischer Kunst." *Münchner Jahrbuch der bildenden Kunst* 31, pp. 259–64.

1980c "Königskult." In *Lexikon der Ägyptologie,* vol. 3, cols. 533–34.

1982a "Berichte der Staatlichen Kunstsammlungen (Neuerwerbungen): Staatliche Sammlung Ägyptischer Kunst." *Münchner Jahrbuch der bildenden Kunst* 33, pp. 187–202.

1982b "Zur Einführung." In *Das Menschenbild im Alten Ägypten: Porträts aus vier Jahrtausenden.* Exh. cat. Hamburg: Interversa.

1982c "Pastenfüllung." In *Lexikon der Ägyptologie,* vol. 4, col. 913.

1982d "Privatplastik." In *Lexikon der Ägyptologie,* vol. 4, cols. 1112–19.

1990 "Bilanz eines Defizits, Problemstellungen und Methoden in der ägyptischen Kunstwissenschaft." In *Studien zur ägyptologischen Kunstgeschichte,* pp. 57–80. Hildesheimer ägyptologische Beiträge 29. Hildesheim.

1996 *Sudan: Antike Königreiche am Nil.* Exh. cat. Munich, Paris, Amsterdam, Tou-

louse, Mannheim, 1996–1998. Munich.

1998 "Technologische Bemerkungen zur Kunst des Alten Reiches: Neuen Fakten zu den Ersatzköpfen." In *Les critères de datation stylistiques à l'Ancien Empire,* edited by Nicolas Grimal, pp. 399–406. Cairo.

1999 "La Haute-Égypte: Un style particulier de la statuaire de l'Ancien Empire." In *L'art de l'Ancien Empire égyptien: Actes du Colloque, 3–4 avril 1998.* Paris.

Wilkinson, Alix
1971 *Ancient Egyptian Jewellery.* London.

Williams, Caroline Ransom
1932 *The Decoration of the Tomb of Per-Neb: The Technique and Color Conventions.* The Metropolitan Museum of Art, Department of Egyptian Art, Publications 3. New York.

Winlock, Herbert E.
1934 *The Treasure of El Lahun.* The Metropolitan Museum of Art, Department of Egyptian Art, Publications 4. New York.

de Wit, C.
1956 "Enquête sur le titre de *smr pr.*" *Chronique d'Égypte* 31, no. 61, pp. 89–104.

1972 "La circoncision chez les anciens Égyptiens." *Zeitschrift für ägyptische Sprache und Altertumskunde* 99, pp. 41–48.

Wittkower, Rudolf
1995 *Qu'est-ce que la sculpture?: Principes et procédures.* Paris.

Wolf, Walther
1957 *Die Kunst Aegyptens, Gestalt und Geschichte.* Stuttgart.

Wood, Wendy
1974 "A Reconstruction of the Triads of King Mycerinus." *Journal of Egyptian Archaeology* 60, pp. 82–93.

1977 "Early Wooden Tomb Sculpture in Ancient Egypt." Ph.D. dissertation, Case Western Reserve University, Cleveland.

1978 "A Reconstruction of the Reliefs of Hesy-Re." *Journal of the American Research Center in Egypt* 15, pp. 8–24.

1987 "The Archaic Stone Tombs at Helwan." *Journal of Egyptian Archaeology* 73, pp. 59–77.

Worsham, C. E.
1979 "A Reinterpretation of the So-called Bread Loaves in Egyptian Offering Scenes."

Journal of the American Research Center in Egypt 16, pp. 7–10.

Wörterbuch der aegyptischen Sprache

1926– *Wörterbuch der aegyptis-*
63 *chen Sprache.* Edited by Adolf Erman and Hermann Grapow. 7 vols. Leipzig and Berlin.

Wreszinski, Walter

1936 *Atlas zur altaegyptischen Kulturgeschichte.* Part 3, fasc. 10. Leipzig.

Yoyotte, Jean

1968 *Treasures of the Pharaohs: The Early Period the New Kingdom, the Late Period.* Geneva.

Zayed, Abd el-Hamid

1958 "Le tombeau d'Akhti-Hotep à Saqqara." *Annales du Service des Antiquités de l'Égypte* 55, no. 1, pp. 127–37.

Ziegler, Christiane

1979a "La fausse-porte du Prince Kanefer 'fils de Snéfrou.'" *Revue d'égyptologie* 31, pp. 120–34.

1979b *Catalogue des instruments de musique égyptiens.* Paris.

1984 "Sistrum." *Lexikon der Ägyptologie,* vol. 5, cols. 959–63.

1986 "Une stèle de la collection Saint-Ferriol." *Revue du Louvre,* no. 1, pp. 39–44.

1990a *Le Louvre: Les antiquités égyptiennes.* Paris.

1990b *Catalogue des stèles, peintures et reliefs égyptiens de l'Ancien Empire et de la Première Période Intermédiaire, vers 2686–2040 avant J.-C.* Paris: Musée du Louvre, Département des Antiquités Égyptiennes.

1993a *Le Mastaba d'Akhethetep: Une chapelle funéraire de l'Ancien Empire.* Paris.

1993b "Champollion en Égypte: Inventaire des antiquités rapportées au Musée du Louvre." In *Aegyptus museis rediviva: Misc. De Meulenaere,* pp. 197–213. Brussels.

1994 "Notes sur la reine Tiy." In *Hommages à Jean Leclant,* vol. 1, *Études pharaoniques,* edited by Catherine Berger, Gisèle Clerc, and Nicolas Grimal, pp. 531–48. Bibliothèque d'étude 106. Cairo.

1995a "Acquisitions: Cannes Musée de la Castre." *Revue du Louvre,* no. 1, p. 76.

1995b "L'Ancien Empire au Musée du Louvre: Jalons pour une histoire de l'art." In *Kunst des Alten Reiches: Symposium im Deutschen Archäologischen Institut Kairo am 29. und 30. Oktober 1991,* pp. 167–73. Sonderschrift, Deutsches Archäologisches Institut, Abteilung Kairo, 28. Mainz.

1996 "Acquisitions." *Revue du Louvre,* no. 3, p. 88.

1997a *Musée du Louvre, Département des Antiquités Égyptiennes: Les statues égyptiennes de L'Ancien Empire.* Paris.

1997b "Sur quelques vases inscrits de l'Ancient Empire." In *Études sur l'Ancien Empire et la nécropole de Saqqâra dédiées à Jean-Philippe Lauer,* edited by Catherine Berger and Bernard Mathieu, pp. 461–89. Orientalia Monspeliensia, 9. Montpellier: Université Paul Valéry.

1997c "Les statues d'Akhethetep, propriétaire de la chapelle du Louvre." *Revue d'égyptologie* 48, pp. 227–45.

1998 "À propos de quelques ivoires de l'Ancien Empire conservés au Louvre." *Bibliothèque d'étude* 120, pp. 407–19.

Ziegler, Christiane, et al.

1997 "La mission archéologique du Musée du Louvre à Saqqara: Résultats de quatre campagnes de fouilles de 1993 à 1996." *Bulletin de l'Institut Français d'Archéologie Orientale* 97, pp. 269–92.

Zivie, Christiane M.

1974 "Giza, Saqqara ou Memphis?" *Göttinger Miszellen* 11, pp. 53–58.

1976 *Giza au deuxième millénaire.* Bibliothèque d'étude 70. Cairo.

1984 "Sphinx." In *Lexikon der Ägyptologie,* vol. 5, cols. 1139–47.

Zivie-Coche, Christiane M.

1991 *Giza au deuxième millénaire: Autour du temple d'Isis Dame des Pyramides.* Boston.

1997 *Sphinx!: Le père, la terreur.* Paris.

Zuber, A.

1956 "Techniques de travail des pierres dures dans l'Ancienne Égypte." *Techniques et civilisation* 5, no. 5, pp. 161–80, 195–215.

INDEXES

INDEX OF OWNERS

INDEX OF SITES

This index gives place names and burial sites mentioned in the catalogue. Under each site, burial places are listed first by number, then alphabetically by type, for example, mastaba, pyramid complex, or tomb; see the General Index for listings by tomb owners' names. **Boldface** page references indicate principal discussions; *italic* page references indicate illustrations.

GENERAL INDEX

Inti-shedu
  statues, seated, Giza, GSE 1915, 163, 300–303, *300, 301, 302*; cat. nos. 89, 90, 92
  statue, standing, Giza, GSE 1915, 163, 300, *300, 302, 302*; cat. no. 91
  tomb, Giza, GSE 1915, 163, 300–303, *300, 301, 302*; cat. nos. 89, 90, 91, 92; fig. 120
Iput, 135, 164, 171, 422, 426
Iput II, 11
Ipy, relief, *110, 112*, 115n.; fig. 69
Irery, 107, 108, 114n., 305n.
Iret-sobek, 413
Iru-ka-ptah, tomb, Saqqara, 48, *48*, 369; fig. 27
Isis, goddess, 139, 439
Iskander, Zaki, 158
Itet and Nefer-maat, Meidum, mastaba 16, 29, 38, 134–35, **199–201**, *199, 200, 201*, 202–204, *202, 203*, 212, 222, 225; cat. nos. 24a,b,c, 25 a,b,c; figs. 103, 104
Iteti, tomb, 48
Itisen, pseudogroup, probably Saqqara, 63, **459–60**, *459*; cat. no. 187
Itju, mastaba, Giza, 58, 236n., 244, 292, **293–94**, *293, 294*, 381, 439n.; cat. no. 83; fig. 119
Itush, relief, Saqqara, mastaba 14 (D 43), **397**, *397*; cat. no. 145
Iunu, mastaba, Giza, G 4150, 248n.
Iy-ka, wife of, relief, 113n.
Iy-nefer, relief, 107
Izi, 112, 115n., 361
Izi of Edfu, statue, 70

jar
  Giza, tomb of Ba-baef, 491n.
  inscribed with name of King Unis (Louvre, Paris), 127, **361–62**, *361*; cat. no. 123
  Kerma (Museum of Fine Arts, Boston), 421n.
  Mahasna, 421n.
  Mostagedda, 689, 421n.
  ointment, 123–25
  of unknown provenance (Metropolitan Museum, New York), 124, **421**, *421*, 493; cat. no. 161
  See also jubilee jar
Jéquier, Gustave, 11, 92, 135
jewelry, 127, 304–5, 422–31
Jones, Michael, 151
Josephus, Flavius, 221
jubilee jar
  inscribed with name of Pepi I (Louvre, Paris), 10, 123, 125, 127, **448**, *449*, 452; cat. no. 179
  inscribed with name of Pepi II (Louvre, Paris), 123,

124, 125, 126, **448**, *449*, 452; cat. no. 180
Junker, Hermann, 77, 140, *142*, 146, 150, 157, 233, 246, 493; fig. 82

ka, 41, 44, 459
Ka-apar, reliefs, 114n.
Ka-em-ah, Giza, G 1223, mastaba, 37n., 38n.
Ka-em-heset, 114n., 367n.
Ka-em-ked, statue, 63, *63*, 71n., 386; fig. 35
Ka-em-nefret, relief, 108, *110*, 114n.; fig. 67
Ka-em-rehu, 114n., 402
Ka-gemni, 9, 36, 115n., 135, 422
Kai, 150, 362
  statue, Saqqara, 57, 260, 297, **362**, *363, 364*; cat. no. 124
Kai-em-ankh, 146
Kaiser, Jutta, *159*, 160; fig. 98
Kaiser, Werner, *159*, 160; fig. 98
Ka-khent, tomb, Giza, 386
Ka-nefer, tomb, Giza, G 2150, 114n., 235
Ka-ni-nisut I, mastaba, Giza, G 2155, 30, *31, 31*, 146, 229, 325; fig. 15d
Ka-pu-ptah and Ipep, pair statue, Giza, G 4461, *380*, **381**, *381*; cat. no. 133
Katep and Hetep-heres, pair statue, probably Giza, **290–91**, *290, 291*; cat. no. 82
Kawab, mastaba, Giza, G 7110/20, 6, 38, 61, 251n., 305
Kenamun, tomb, 204n.
Ketisen, Lady, 296, 297
Khaba, 155
Kha-bau-sokar, mastaba, Saqqara, A2 (FS 3073), 38, 38n., 104, 106, 107, 194
Khaemwase, 133
Khafre (Chephren), 6, 139, 157, 194, 253, 255, 257n., 260, 329
  faces, said to be from Giza, 255, **256**, *256, 257, 257, 258*, 262, 289n.; cat. nos. 59, 60
  heads, 53, 54, 233n., **255**, *255, 257, 259*, 259, **260**, *260*, **261–62**, *261*, 289n.; cat. nos. 58, 61, 62, 63
  pyramid complex, Giza, 146–47, 155
  pyramid, 6, 20, 214, 265
  pyramid temple, 41, 42, *43*, 54, 100n., 133, 233n., **259**, *259*, **262–63**, *262, 264*, 289n.; cat. nos. 61, 64; fig. 20
  valley temple, 41, 42, *42, 43*, 53, 54, 164, 215, **253**, *253*, **260**, *260*, **261–62**, *261, 265*, 289n., 435; cat. nos. 56, 62, 63; fig. 19

statues of, 7, *52*, 53, 54, 133, 134, 152n., 164, 238, 239, 252, **253**, *253*, 254, 255, 259, 269, 276, 281, 316, 330n.; cat. no. 56; figs. 28, 112
Khafre's queen, statue, 70n.
Kha-merer-nebti, 7, 263
Kha-merer-nebti II, 269, 278, 386
Khasekhemui, 4, 13, 54, 59, 89–90, 489, 491n.
Khendjer, pyramids, 136
Khentet-ka, statue, Giza, G 4970, 62, 244, **286–88**, *287, 288*, 384; cat. no. 80
Khenti-amentiu, god, 19, 347n.
Khentika-Ikhekhi, tomb, 36
Khenti-kauef, 286
Khent-kawes, 7, 157, 282
Khent-kawes II, 151
Khenut, tomb, 36
Khepri, god, 354
Kheruef, 127
Khnum, god, 4, 277n.
Khnum-hotep, 108, 164, 391
Khouli, Ali el-, 156
Khuaut, 293
Khuen-khnum, relief, 115n.
Khuen-nebti, 375
Khuen-nub, 370
Khuen-re, 386
  statue, Giza, Menkaure cemetery, MQ 1, 61, 251n., **278**, *279*; cat. no. 72
Khuen-sobek, 413
Khufu (Cheops), 5–6, 21, 54–55, 113n., 114n., 139, 151, 155, 194, 244
  colossal head, possibly of, 54, **194**, *194*, 219; cat. no. 21
  funerary boat, 146, 150, 157–58
  pyramid complex, Giza, 22, 29, 142, 147, 155, 164, 215, 225, 228
  Great Pyramid, 6, *6*, 98, 123, *138*, 214, 220, **221**, *221, 222, 222*; cat. nos. 35, 36, 37; figs. 2, 108
  pyramid temple, 98, 150, 196
  wives, tombs of, 29
  small head, possibly of, 54, **219**, *219*; cat. no. 34
  statuette, 5–6, 54, 194, 219, 260
Khufu-ankh, 384
Khufu-khaf, mastaba, Giza, G 7140, 107, *109*, 113n., 233n., 265; fig. 65
Khui (of Abydos), 10, 454
Khui-wer, cult chamber, Giza, 48
king (pharaoh)
  as god king, 5
  cult of, 160, 215
  depiction of, in temple complexes, 94–98
  dress and symbols of power of, 53
  estates of, 195
  function of, in Egyptian society, 51

gifts from, 448, 450, 452
kings' lists, 3
names and titles of, 8
postures of, in statuary, 53
strengthened by rituals, 358
suckled by goddess, 352–53
Kromer, Karl, 149

Labrousse, Audran, 136
Lacovara, Peter, 79
Lauer, Jean-Philippe, 135, 136
Leclant, Jean, 136
Lehner, Mark, 147, 151, 214
Lepsius, Karl Richard, 3, 139–40
Lesseps, Ferdinand-Marie de, 133
Loret, Victor, 135
Lower Egypt. *See* Egypt

Maat, goddess, 5, 337
mace head, of Scorpion (Ashmolean Museum, Oxford), rubbing, 89, *89*, 90; fig. 53
MacGregor, Reverend William, 257
Makra-Malla, Rizkall, 156
Mallakh, Kamal el-, 156, 157–58, *158*; fig. 95
Mamun, Caliph al-, 152n.
Ma-nefer, mastaba, Saqqara, H 2, 63, 109, 110, 114n., 115n.
Manetho, chronology of, 3
Mariette, Auguste, 6, 118, 133–35, 139, 188
market scene, tomb of Tep-em-ankh, Saqqara, 404, *405*; cat. no. 150a–d; fig. 126
masks, 255, 476
Maspero, Gaston, 11, 135, 142
mastabas
  derivation of word, 37
  plunder of, 74–75
  structure of, 21, 27–39, 142; figs. 14, 15
Medu-nefer, mastaba, Balat, 481, 488
Medu-nefer, tomb, Giza, 386
Mehaa, 10
Mehi, tomb texts of, 149
Mehu, 11, 115n., 418
Meidum ware, 390, 419, 420, 491
Memi, 283, 294
  and Sabu, pair statue, probably Giza, 62, **294–96**, *295*, 365, 381; cat. no. 84
  statue, Giza, D 32A, mastaba chapel, 57, 283, **283**, *283*; cat. no. 77
Meni, tomb, 250
Menkare-Nitocris, 11
Menkauhor, 8, 55
Menkaure (Mycerinus), 7, 139, 151, 194, 278, 316, 329
  colossus, 315
  heads, Giza, 7, 54, 55, 271, **273–76**, *273, 275, 276*, 317n.; cat. nos. 69, 70
  pair statue, 7, 41, *50*, 53, 54, 62, 145, **268–71**, *269, 270, 271, 274*, 294n., 444; cat. no. 67
  pyramid complex, Giza, 145, 155, 271

PHOTOGRAPH CREDITS